AFRICAN PRINT CULTURES

AFRICAN PERSPECTIVES
Kelly Askew and Anne Pitcher
Series Editors

African Print Cultures: Newspapers and Their Publics in the Twentieth Century, edited by Derek R. Peterson, Emma Hunter, and Stephanie Newell

Unsettled History: Making South African Public Pasts, by Leslie Witz, Gary Minkley, and Ciraj Rasool

African Print Cultures

*Newspapers and Their Publics
in the Twentieth Century*

EDITED BY
Derek R. Peterson,
Emma Hunter,
and Stephanie Newell

University of Michigan Press
Ann Arbor

Copyright © 2016 by Derek R. Peterson, Emma Hunter, and Stephanie Newell
All rights reserved

This book may not be reproduced, in whole or in part, including illustrations, in any form (beyond that copying permitted by Sections 107 and 108 of the U.S. Copyright Law and except by reviewers for the public press), without written permission from the publisher.

Published in the United States of America by the
University of Michigan Press
Manufactured in the United States of America
♾ Printed on acid-free paper

2010 2018 2017 2016   4 3 2 1

A CIP catalog record for this book is available from the British Library.

ISBN 978-0-472-07317-7 (hardcover : alk. paper)
ISBN: 978-0-472-05317-9 (paper : alk. paper)
ISBN 978-0-472-12213-4 (e-book)

CONTENTS

Acknowledgments ix
A Note on Orthography xi

CHAPTER 1
Print Culture in Colonial Africa
DEREK R. PETERSON AND EMMA HUNTER 1

PART I: AFRICAN NEWSPAPER NETWORKS

CHAPTER 2
Transatlantic Passages: Black Identity Construction in West African and West Indian Newspapers, 1935–1950
LESLIE JAMES 49

CHAPTER 3
Creole Pioneers in the Nigerian Provincial Press
DAVID PRATTEN 75

CHAPTER 4
The Sociability of Print: 1920s and 1930s Lagos Newspaper Travel Writing
REBECCA JONES 102

CHAPTER 5
Colonial Modernity and Tradition: Herbert Macaulay, the Newspaper Press, and the (Re)Production of Engaged Publics in Colonial Lagos
WALE ADEBANWI 125

PART II: EXPERIMENTS WITH GENRE

CHAPTER 6
Experiments with Genre in Yoruba Newspapers of the 1920s
KARIN BARBER   151

CHAPTER 7
Everyday Poetry from Tanzania: Microcosm of the Newspaper Genre
KELLY ASKEW   179

CHAPTER 8
Private Entertainment Magazines and Popular Literature Production in Socialist Tanzania
UTA REUSTER-JAHN   224

CHAPTER 9
"True to Life": Illuminating the Processes and Modes of Yoruba Photoplays
OLUBUKOLA A. GBADEGESIN   251

PART III: NEWSPAPERS AND THEIR PUBLICS

CHAPTER 10
Komkya and the Convening of a Chagga Public, 1953–1961
EMMA HUNTER   283

CHAPTER 11
Making Constituency in the Province: The *Osumare Egba* (1935–1937) and the Agenda of Abẹokuta Modernization
OLUWATOYIN BABATUNDE ODUNTAN   306

CHAPTER 12
"I will decide who will speak": Street Parliaments and the Newspaper Ecology in Eldoret's *Kamukunji*
DUNCAN OMANGA   335

PART IV: AFTERLIVES

CHAPTER 13
The Afterlife of Words: Magema Fuze, Bilingual Print Journalism, and the Making of a Self-Archive
HLONIPHA MOKOENA   361

CHAPTER 14
   From Corpse to Corpus: The Printing of Death in
   Colonial West Africa
   STEPHANIE NEWELL   389
CHAPTER 15
   Afterword
   STEPHANIE NEWELL   425

Contributors   435
Index   439

ACKNOWLEDGEMENTS

African Print Cultures is the fruit of a network joining scholars who have been engaged in a long conversation about the history of newspapers in Africa. We are drawn together by two axiomatic presumptions: first, that newspapers were created out of a network of textual exchanges; and second, that the study of newspapers must therefore be multisited. Scholarship on African journalism cannot be defined by the embankments of area studies. More than any other textual matter, newspapers were in circulation. Editors culled material from other publications without regard to copyright. They argued with each other and commented on each other's work. African newspapers constituted a field through which stories, sermons, reports, obituaries, and other genres traveled from one place to another. The study of this compositional work requires a scholarship that is attentive to the different places where news was made.

The beginnings of what we call the "African Print Cultures Network" lie in 2007, when David Pratten, Karin Barber, and Stephanie Newell first met to map out the textual and editorial connections joining West African newspapers of the early twentieth century. In 2011 they invited the East Africa scholars Kelly Askew and Derek Peterson to join them. Meetings were thereafter held in Oxford and in Ann Arbor. In these workshops we worked to trace the movements of texts between West and East Africa. We were trying to reconstruct the genealogy of newspapers, focusing on the editorial strategies—citation, plagiarism, clipping—by which editors and contributors made connections between one locale and another. In July 2013 the members of the network—now much enlarged—met at the University of Birmingham. There most of the chapters included in the present volume were presented and discussed.

We gratefully thank the several organizations that funded and supported the work leading up to the production of this book. Funding for the 2011 and 2012 meetings in Oxford came from the University of Michigan's Mellon-Sawyer seminar on "Ethnicity in Africa" and from Oxford University's John Fell Fund. We thank Rouven Kunstmann and the staff at Oxford's African Studies Centre, which organized these occasions, and Kate Skinner and Francesca Orsini, whose lively comments greatly enriched our conversations. The December 2012 meeting in Ann Arbor was organized by the African Studies Center, whose administrative staff, Devon Keen and Sandra Schulze, we gratefully thank. Funding came from the African Heritage Initiative of the African Studies Center, the Institute for the Humanities, the Office of the Vice President for Research, the College of Literature, Science and the Arts, the International Institute, and the Rackham Graduate School of the University of Michigan. We thank the participants at that occasion, and especially Brandi Hughes, Hilina Seife, Sara Katz, and Paul Hebért, whose work on the circulation of African American and Afro-Caribbean newspapers inspired us to think about African newspapers in a wider frame.

The 2013 meeting in Birmingham was hosted by the Department of African Studies and Anthropology and funded largely by the Cadbury Foundation. At Birmingham we had the good fortune to learn from a number of scholars working in the field. We particularly thank Modestus Fosu, Adebayo Mosobalaje, Nozomi Sawada, Katharine Oke, Diana Jeater, Harri Englund, Rotimi Fasan, Carli Coetzee, Anastasia Lyakhovich, Bodil Frederiksen, Grace Musila, Emelinda Liberato, Oluwule Coker, Paulo Fernandes, Michel Doortmont, and Holly Ellis, whose insightful papers helped to sharpen and broaden our thinking about newspapers and their circulation in Africa. The Birmingham conference was organized by David Kerr, whom we gratefully thank.

The production of this book has been an entirely pleasant undertaking, made more pleasant by the good humor and competence of the editorial staff at the University of Michigan Press. We particularly thank Ellen Bauerle and Susan Cronin. The manuscript as a whole received a review from Isabel Hofmeyr and from an anonymous reader on behalf of the University of Michigan Press. We thank them both for the care and attention they lavished upon the book.

Ann Arbor, Edinburgh, and New Haven
July 2015

A NOTE ON ORTHOGRAPHY

The orthographies of African languages have changed over time. In this book we reproduce quoted text as it was originally written, reflecting the authors' own usage. Where African-language words appear in the course of exposition in the essay—for example, place-names, personal names, titles, etc.—we have adopted the conventional orthography for that language.

CHAPTER 1

Print Culture in Colonial Africa

DEREK R. PETERSON AND EMMA HUNTER

This book claims African newspapers as subjects of historical study.[1] Scholars conventionally treat newspapers as conveyances for data, a means of assessing a public's view of current affairs. By reading newspapers in this way, scholars make it hard to see the creative work that editors did to organize and produce the news. They also make it hard to see what African readers gained in their engagements with media. African editors had to create interest groups. They used the techniques of their trade—cutting-and-pasting, summarization, citation, excision, juxtaposition—to make connections and draw linkages. Newspapers were therefore the forcing-houses for new political solidarities: they launched campaigns and gave a tempo to things. Newspapers were also the hosts for new forms of address. They were the incubators for the creation of literary genres and the genesis of new African voices.

The press in colonial Africa was never free. Newspapers were partisan, involved in the politics and passions of their time. Editors were in no position to stand back and offer a dispassionate account of events. Until the mid-twentieth century, the infrastructure of newspaper publishing was precarious and insecure. Newspapers were often the fruit of editors' individual perseverance and commitment. Sol Plaatje, editor of the South African newspaper *Tsala ea Batho*, was obliged to do the job of several men: one of his contemporaries remembered that he

> collected the post, opened and read letters ... and kept records. ... He read papers of other publishers and editors; Government gazettes and papers and translated all from English into Tswana and Xhosa. Using a typewriter he arranged all ideas and news, proof-read various communications and letters and after correcting [and] editing them sent everything to the printing press.[2]

Eridadi Mulira launched his newspaper *Uganda Empya* (New Uganda) early in March 1953.³ He arranged a bank loan with which he bought a secondhand Ford to use in distributing the paper. The newspaper was initially printed on three different presses. After some time Mulira found the funds to purchase a secondhand press, and thereafter he printed four pages, while the Uganda Bookshop Press printed the other four pages. He had to rise as early as 2:00 a.m. on Thursday—the day the newspaper was produced—in order to collate the paper in time for the newspaper's delivery deadline at 6:00 a.m. During the whole life of the newspaper, as he wrote in his autobiography, he labored twenty hours a day, working "as editor, manager, circulation manager and parcels boy, reporter, subeditor, proof reader and cash collector. It was a terrific job."

Men like Plaatje and Mulira had to work so hard because their newspapers were undercapitalized. There were no endowments. Editors had to incite people's passions, demand their attention, and make readers out of them. The journalist I. B. Thomas, about whom Rebecca Jones writes in the present volume, made long trips through upcountry Nigeria, identifying new readers and expanding the distribution network for his newspaper. The Tanzanian journalist Faraji Katalambulla habitually identified himself to readers of his magazine as "the one who loves you" (Reuster-Jahn, this volume). Other editors made larger claims on readers' loyalties. They argued that buying a newspaper was an act of public service. When the Tanganyikan newspaper *Bukya na Gandi*, aimed at a Haya readership, appealed for funds to avoid closure in 1952, a reader wrote about the shame that the Haya people would feel if they lost their newspaper. "Other tribes are going to judge us as men of weak character" if the newspaper was closed, he warned.⁴ Sol Plaatje's paper *Tsala ea Batho* was printed in several languages, "Serolong" (now a dialect of seTswana), Sepedi, isiXhosa, and others. He hoped that readers from different communities would compete to outdo each other in their support of the newspaper. "The Barolong people must not lag behind," he wrote to a chief of the Barolong, "because if they don't involve themselves and make an effort unity will be founded on the terms of the [Pedi people]."⁵ The work of editing overlapped with the work of the booster. Both entailed the promotion of shared identities.

Very little of what these editors published was news. For the longest time, there were no bylines, and neither were dated reports that pertained to specific events. There was poetry (Askew, this volume). There were historical essays (Mokoena, this volume). There was travel writing (Jones, this volume). There were quotations from Holy Scripture, proverbs, and excerpts from secular philosophy. In her study of Mahatma Gandhi's South African newspaper Isabel Hofmeyr has argued that the publication of this decidedly uncontemporary material was animated by a political philosophy that slowed things down, encouraging readers to practice careful, disciplined, reflective reading.[6] That may well have been true for Gandhi's printing press. But for most editors the guiding concern was to fill space, meet deadlines, attract advertisers, and sell newspapers. They were businessmen, not philosophers. Most newspapers did not have a staff with which to practice investigative reporting. Busy editors populated their newspapers with editorials, letters from correspondents, and articles clipped from other places. It was only later that news—dated reports, engaged with contemporary events, pertinent to the affairs of the locality, skeptical of the official account of things—became a constant presence in most African newspapers. The genesis of news reporting seems to have been contemporary with the campaign, the rally, and the rise of celebrities. The great men of the mid-twentieth century—Jomo Kenyatta, Nnamdi Azikiwe, Kwame Nkrumah, Ọbafẹmi Awolọwọ, Herbert Macaulay, and others—were, among other things, journalists. Their public personalities were formed through the mediation of print. Their bylines were trademarks. Thus Azikiwe was "Zik," Awolọwọ was "Awo," Francis Nwia-Kofi Nkrumah was "Kwame Nkrumah," and Johnstone Kamau was "Jomo Kenyatta." In the newspaper their complicated and winding biographies could—like their names—be compressed and made into a label, a slogan. Men like these found, in the newspaper, a means to take a position and launch campaigns. It was in this environment that news reporting surfaced. The exposé, the investigative report, these and other "hard news" genres were produced by people who saw themselves as empowered to contest the official version of things. The fourth estate was a platform from which to comment on public affairs.

In most scholarly work newspapers are used as barometers of changing political opinion. One of the earliest studies of the West African press, written in 1951, concluded that "nationalism formed the very *raison d'etre* of the press in British West Africa."[7] For the eminent political scientist James Smoot Coleman, "The most potent instrument used in the propagation of nationalist ideas and racial consciousness has been the African-owned nationalist press."[8] In his 1968 study *Origins of Modern African Thought*, Robert July devoted a full chapter to the figure of the journalist, and relied heavily on the press as a source through which to trace Africa's intellectual history from the nineteenth century up to the mid-twentieth century.⁹ More recently the media scholar Les Switzer has edited two important books about African-run newspapers in South Africa.¹⁰ For Switzer, the black press was a showcase for "voices of protest and resistance" (as the title of one of the volumes puts it). He organizes the study of newspaper history around the chronology of black nationalism: from mission beginnings to the "early resistance press" to the "later resistance press" and, finally, to "alternative voices in the last generation of apartheid."¹¹ There are other typologies: Joseph Campbell, for example, classifies African newspapers as "vanguard," "subservient," "reinforcing," or "clandestine."¹²

The presumption that newspapers were, or should have been, venues for "voices of protest and resistance" is derived from an axiom: that—as the Zambian scholar Francis Kasoma put it—there is "a causal linkage between a free press and democracy."¹³ This presumption guides both scholarship and policymaking. Many governments in postcolonial Africa viewed the free press as a dangerous threat to their rule.¹⁴ Whereas in colonial times newspapers had been weapons in the hands of African nationalists, postcolonial newspapers were often brought under the control of ruling parties. In 1962, the United Nations adopted a resolution regretting the high proportion of the world's population that was "denied effective enjoyment of the right to information" and drawing attention to the role of the press and other media in "education and in economic and social progress generally."¹⁵ By the 1990s, as the old one-party regimes were challenged by pressures for democratization, policymakers were preoccupied with newspapers' role in driving and sustaining political transformation. A UNESCO seminar in Windhoek in 1991 insisted that "the establishment, maintenance and fostering of an independent, pluralistic and free press is essential to the development and maintenance of democracy in a nation, and for economic development."¹⁶

Here we show that African newspapers were more than vehicles for protest against autocratic rule. Some editors claimed to eschew politics altogether, aiming to remake readers' moral and religious lives by publishing instructive and edifying texts. Even the most politically engaged newspapers published jokes and poems alongside their sharp-edged editorials. Newspapers' content often had little to do with a particular time and place in which they were published. The South African writer Magema Fuze published a biography of his mentor, Bishop Colenso, thirty-seven years after Colenso's death (Mokoena, this volume). West African editors similarly printed obituaries of long-deceased people, offering exemplary models for the benefit of the living. These life stories were sometimes collected and bound as books, making them available as material objects for preservation in readers' private libraries (Newell, this volume). The dead were a vital constituency for African editors to represent. They helped bring larger themes into view. The poetry that today fills the pages of Tanzania's newspapers is engaged with "everyday" concerns, but it speaks to broader issues, lifting current events onto a plane that exceeds the contemporary preoccupations of journalism (Askew, this volume). Editors' concerns were not always au courant.

Neither were African newspapers always framed within the geographic space of the nation. Some editors saw the whole black world as an arena for newsgathering. George Padmore composed hundreds of articles about events in the West Indies, and African editors put them on the front pages of their newspapers (James, this volume). Padmore wrote in English, the language of West Indian politics, and many of the leading Pan-Africanist newspapers were published in English. But vernacular-language newspapers could also work within a Pan-African frame. The Ganda intellectual Abubakar Mayanja read George Padmore's books as a student, and in 1952 he published a Luganda-language article in the Anglican newspaper *Ebifa*, arguing that "the meaning of Christian civilization is to place an African in his position ... to serve superior races, to draw water and split firewood for him."[17] Mayanja's phraseology mirrored Padmore's 1931 book *The Life and Struggles of Negro Toilers*.[18] Vernacular-language newspapers did not work within narrow horizons. Men like Mayanja shuttled between languages and political scales, borrowing texts, making connections between one frame and another, and engaging vernacular readerships in global discourses.

African newspapers were composed of materials that were authored elsewhere and subsequently clipped, translated, and reprinted. They were part of what Antoinette Burton and Isabel Hofmeyr have called an "imperial commons," composed of "cuttings from elsewhere, each page convening its own miniature empire."[19] African editors had little regard for copyright. Neither did their contemporaries elsewhere in the world. The editorialist "A Banker" composed dozens of high-flown essays for the *Gold Coast Leader*, an English-language newspaper published in Accra. His subject matter was vast: he wrote about geology, astronomy, the Atonement, and other human universals. Several of his editorials were reprinted, without attribution, in Australian newspapers: "A Shrouded World," originally printed in the *Gold Coast Leader* on 15 October 1904, was reprinted in the *Northern Territory Times and Gazette* on 9 February 1906; "A Venerable Stronghold," published in the *Leader* on 21

September 1907, was reprinted in the *Otago Witness* on 6 November and in the *Age*, in New South Wales, on 5 November 1907.[20] It is impossible to study this material according to the logic of area studies—as the product of a particular people's historical experience, as pertinent primarily to a locality. African newspapers took shape within an economy of textual circulation through which material and stories moved laterally, without respect for geography.

But even as we acknowledge that African newspapers were produced within a deterritorialized textual commons, we also argue that Africa's newspaper history was distinctive. In no other part of the world was population history more fluid; and in no other part of the world were newspapers more essential in the constitution of political communities. It is not that writing, or books, were foreign to Africa: the trans-Saharan commerce in Islamic manuscripts dates back to medieval times; the world's oldest surviving Christian manuscript was composed in Ethiopia sixteen hundred years ago.[21] What was new about newspapers was their power to convene people in new ways. Until recent times Africa has been a place of open frontiers, and human populations were mobile and multilingual. Only occasionally were political authorities able to settle people in place, limit their movements, and impose a monoculture upon them.[22] The dynamism of Africa's population history made the work of the political organizer—and the newspaper editor—more vexed, more demanding, and more exciting. Print technology offered African political organizers and culture brokers a powerful tool for self-constitution, opening up channels of communication that had not previously existed. As we discuss below, the historical convergence of language standardization and print technology allowed for the fast expansion of print vernaculars and the cultivation of readerships that recognized a particular language as their own cultural property. That is why newspapers were so exciting to their readers. They had the revolutionary power to create solidarities and convene communities.

In content this book is weighted toward the Nigerian newspaper industry—the subject of six chapters—and the newspapers of eastern Africa—the subject of four chapters. As we shall see below, East and West Africa were out of sync in a great number of ways, and in South Africa there was again a different chronology. Yet here we show that it is both possible and productive to compare. *African Print Cultures* focuses on the mechanics of news-making: on the selective and idiosyncratic choices that editors made as they engaged with their audiences; on the itineraries that editors embarked upon as they recruited readers; on the literary experiments that newspapermen sponsored as they looked for new voices with which to speak. These chapters also show how newspapers took on lives of their own. Readers intervened in their pages and created new publics in ways that editors could not fully control. Texts had afterlives. They formed part of what the historian Tony Ballantyne has termed a "world of paper."[23] They traveled and were read and interpreted in diverse contexts far from that in which they were originally produced. They provided readers with a discursive repertoire, and served to compose and script political arguments. Later, they entered libraries and became authoritative sources for public memory. Newspapers were an infrastructure for public culture.

THE BIRTH OF THE NEWSPAPER

In most of Africa the origins of the newspaper lie in the Christian missionary endeavor. For missionaries, newspapers were vehicles by which to manage the enlargement of scale in their work, a means also to shape converts' reading habits.[24] "Having taken the step of teaching them to read, it is of vital importance that we keep them supplied with good Christian reading matter so that they may be grounded firmly in Christian teaching," wrote a missionary in Tanganyika.[25] The first newspaper in Yorubaland was *Iwe Irohin*, launched by Anglican missionaries in 1859 (Oduntan, this volume). In the German colony of Togo the first newspaper was entitled *Mia Hôlô*, or "Our Friend," published by Catholic missionaries in German and Ewe from the 1890s.[26] The earliest newspaper in southern Africa was *Umshumayeli Wendaba*, the "Publisher of News," brought out by Wesleyan Methodist missionaries between 1837 and 1841. It was printed in Xhosa and English, and contained Christian homilies and devotional texts.[27] In southeastern Africa, missionaries founded *Inkanyiso yase Natal*, the "Enlightener of Natal," in 1889 (Mokoena, this volume). East Africa's first newspaper was *Msimulizi*, published by the Universities' Mission to Central Africa at Kiungani College in Zanzibar.

Colonial governments were quick to adopt the technology of print in order to disseminate information to their subjects.[28] The first newspaper in French West Africa was an official publication, *Le Moniteur du Sénégal et Dépendances*, established in 1856.[29] When Cameroun passed from German colonial rule to become a League of Nations Mandate under the French, the new government launched *La Gazette du Cameroun*, which imparted official information while also providing a forum for an emerging francophone elite.[30] The sultan of Zanzibar, Sayyid Barghash b. Saïd, was sufficiently impressed by his encounter with the world of publishing during his 1875 visit to Egypt that he returned to Zanzibar with a printing press in his possession. His successors subscribed to newspapers from across the Arab world.[31] In 1915, the British Protectorate government in Zanzibar launched a weekly newspaper written in Arabic and Arabic-script Swahili, whose mission was to help the inhabitants of the island "find a means to quench the severe thirst that befalls them, by which we mean the thirst of coming upon the spring of the correct news."[32]

The monopolies that missionaries and government held did not last long.[33] In eastern and southern Africa missionary-run newspapers became the training grounds for the earliest African journalists. The first African-run newspaper in Uganda, *Sekanyolya*, was edited by Sefanio Sentongo, who had learned his trade while working on the missionary newspaper *Ebifa*.[34] Kenya's first Africa-run newspaper, *Mwigwithania*, was edited by Johnstone (later Jomo) Kenyatta, who had learned the business during his apprenticeship at the Presbyterian mission station in Thogoto.[35] South Africa's first African-run newspaper, *Imvo Zabantsundu*, was published from 1884 by John Tengo Jabavu. He had begun his career as editor for the Presbyterian missionary newspaper *Isigidimi sama Xosa*.[36] In West Africa it was the anglophone elite—many of them creoles, descended from repatriated slaves—who established a vibrant English-language newspaper industry. As Stephanie Newell has argued, the editors and proprietors of the *Gold Coast Leader*, the *Lagos Standard*, and other newspapers thought themselves as custodians of a civilizational trust: it was their task to superintend and protect a nascent English-language public sphere. They wrote in English in order to engage colonial authorities in argument and articulate public opinion. In the absence of "parliaments and other assemblies wherein the people give effective voice to their wants and have the means of securing them," wrote an editor in 1905, newspapers constituted "Our Fourth and Only Estate."[37] In the French colony of Senegal, where there were regular elections in the long-established four communes and where there were relatively liberal laws governing press freedom, there was a lively newspaper business by the 1880s.[38] In the rest of francophone West Africa the newspaper business expanded during the interwar years. These newspapers couched their critical commentary on French colonial rule within an overarching discourse of loyalism.[39]

In West Africa a vibrant English- and French-language newspaper industry engaged Africans in the affairs of the metropole. In East Africa, by contrast, English-language newspapers like the *East African Standard* or the

Uganda Argus were, until the mid-twentieth century, addressed to the small community of white settlers and officials. African newspapers in East Africa were generally published in vernacular languages or, alternately, in Swahili, which was a lingua franca on the Indian Ocean coast and in parts of upland East Africa. In West Africa the industry was transformed by Nnamdi Azikiwe, the American-educated journalist who, in 1937, launched the *West African Pilot*, an English-language newspaper with mass circulation. His aim, as he recounted in his autobiography, was to "revolutionize journalism as it had been practiced in Nigeria . . . and demonstrate that journalism can be a successful business enterprise."[40] By 1949 Azikiwe, taking advantage of credit facilities he enjoyed as a shareholder in the African Continental Bank, had moved the *Pilot* to a mechanical press.[41] There were no East African analogues to Azikiwe's newspapers. The Luo Thrift and Trading Corporation was the first African organization to own a printing press in East Africa. The press printed as many as four vernacular-language newspapers. It ran at a steady loss, as none of the editors could pay their bills on time. In 1949—the same year that Azikiwe expanded the *Pilot*'s print run—the corporation had to relocate its press from Nairobi to the provincial town of Kisumu, in Kenya's west, where it printed letterheads and receipt books.[42] Newspaper circulation in East Africa was comparatively small. In 1950 the five leading African-run newspapers in Kenya had a combined circulation of thirteen thousand copies a week.[43] Azikiwe's *Pilot* sold seventeen thousand copies a day.[44]

The historical chronology of the newspaper business was offset in West and East Africa. These differences illuminate the differing ways in which the public sphere was organized on the two sides of the continent. In West Africa the anglicized elite, many of them descended from liberated slaves, used newspapers to defend their membership within an English-speaking *civitas*.[45] That is why the editorials of "A Banker," published in the Gold Coast, could circulate widely in the English-speaking world (above). They were produced by an author who claimed membership within a universal civilization. Much the same was true of the francophone press, for the African writers who published in French newspapers claimed to be members of a wider francophone world. In East Africa, by contrast, there was no African elite to whom colonial powers owed a civilizational debt. Christian missionaries had established freed slave settlements in Bagamoyo and elsewhere on the East African coast in the mid-nineteenth century, but these small settlements did not approach the scale of the grand experiment of Sierra Leone. Where in West Africa the anglicized elite could claim to be defending Britain's historic commitment to civilizational uplift, East Africans were colonial subjects. They were not endued with the moral capital to demand membership in the metropolitan public sphere.[46]

Editors in East Africa wrote for different audiences, and for different ends, than their West African colleagues. Readerships were segmented along linguistic lines; publishers' finances were more precarious; and editors had more reason to cultivate a close relationship with their readers. They had to speak as defenders of public morality, to espouse conservative values, to speak on behalf of a people. It is not that East African writers and newspaper editors were less creative, less adventurous, or less inclined toward political activism than their West African contemporaries. It is that the relationship between newspapers and their publics was differently structured in different parts of the continent. In West Africa the vernacular language newspapers of the 1920s and 1930s—like, for example, the Yoruba-language press—were full of literary novelties. This experimentation was occasioned by elite Lagosians' effort to expand their constituencies, reach out to new readers, and make commoners actors in the political field (Barber, this volume). In interwar East Africa the only newspaper industry that similarly sought to engage the urban masses was in Buganda, where *Sekanyolya*, *Munyonyozi*, and other journals campaigned against the corruptions of the kingdom's elite.[47] Here, as in Lagos, editors' effort to reach out to a popular constituency was the occasion for experimentation. The same men who sponsored the newspapers of the 1920s were also behind a new religious movement, the Malakites, whose members refused to accept the authority of Buganda's aristocracy. They used the press that printed their newspapers to produce lengthy epistles condemning Buganda's Protestant ruling elite for their un-Christian, unfaithful failure to depend on God.[48] In Buganda as in Yorubaland the effort to engage new constituencies encouraged editors to adopt novel authorial positions and try out new voices.

In Kenya, by contrast, there was a close fit between newspapermen and their readers. Readers and editors had attended the same schools; contributors to the first Gikuyu-language newspaper, *Mwigwithania*, usually listed the mission stations they were associated with alongside their signatures. There was a relatively constrained literary canon. The New Testament was the primary text with which writers could work. In Gikuyu, Dholuo, and other Kenyan languages, readers and editors were occupied with the work of cultural exegesis, expanding the Christian canon by collecting proverbs and folktales and by composing unifying mythology.[49] It was not until the 1940s, when primary school enrollments expanded and the number of vernacular-language readers rose, that newspaper editors sought to reach out to the teeming thousands in Nairobi. African editors launched some forty new newspapers between 1947 and 1952. Many of these newspapers were edited by people who had hitherto been marginal to Kenya's literary culture, among them a carpenter, a shoemaker, a driver, a sign writer, and a bookbinder.[50]

It was here, in the differing newspaper histories of West and East Africa, that the two regions' public cultures were differently ordered. In French West Africa, where the publishing industry had long linked metropole and colony, the idea of *Francophonie* was to hold an enduring significance, and up to the time of independence African workers were organizing around the interests they shared with workers in metropolitan France.[51] After independence new states gave the French language pride of place in public life, and activists who sought to advance the vernacular found it hard to claim space.[52] In British West Africa, where an anglophone elite had used newspapers to promote their membership in the English-speaking world, it was to be in English that national identity was conceived. Ghana's president, Kwame Nkrumah, was formerly a newspaperman. He outlawed parties that were based on ethnic loyalties. "There should be no reference to Fantis, Ashantis, Ewes, Gas, Dagombas, strangers and so forth, but that we should call ourselves Ghanaians—all brothers and sisters, members of the same community—the state of Ghana," he argued.[53] In Kenya, Uganda, and Tanzania, by contrast, the languages of political discourse were vernaculars. There were, surely, nationalist parties that campaigned in English. But the languages of deep politics were Gikuyu, Dholuo, Luganda, and Swahili. It was in these languages that the most vexed, most divisive, and most meaningful debates about political community were conducted.[54]

NEWSPAPERS AND MORAL REFORM

As Isabel Hofmeyr has noted, a didactic tone suffuses much African print culture.[55] Regardless of whether their newspapers were pro-establishment or populist in orientation, editors saw themselves as reformers, duty-bound to curb corruption and uphold standards.

African editors inherited from their missionary teachers a desire for uniformity in grammar and orthography. Missionaries' evangelical theology inclined them to regard vernacular language as an essential expression of a people's identity, a vehicle, therefore, for Christian revelation.[56] In most parts of Africa they made the first formal studies of African languages, compiled the first word lists, authored the grammar books, and composed the dictionaries.[57] Like missionaries, newspapermen sought uniformity and consistency in typefaces, spelling, and grammar. Sol Plaatje, the most widely read black journalist in southern Africa, was also an advocate for language reform. In 1916, while resident in England, he coauthored a reading book in seTswana, set in the International Phonetic Alphabet.[58] In the following decades he published a series of newspaper editorials advocating for consistency and regularity in the spelling of African languages.[59] The Ganda intellectual Eridadi Mulira became interested in language reform when, in the late 1930s, he wrote several articles for publication in the Protestant church newspaper *Ebifa* and the Catholic-owned *Matalisi*.[60] He soon discovered, he wrote, that "if I was to write in Luganda, I must first do something about the language itself." There were at that time several different spelling systems for Luganda: the Protestants used diacritical marks to identify long consonants and bars to mark vowels, while the Catholics doubled long consonants and marked vowels with a circumflex. In 1940 Mulira, together with a cohort of schoolteachers and newspaper editors, formed the "Luganda Society," which over the course of four years met to discuss orthography and compose a report. In 1949 he went to the School of Oriental and African Studies, where he worked with the linguist Edith O. Ashton to produce a Luganda-English dictionary.[61]

Newspapers were engines for the standardization of African languages. Newspapermen thought it was their vocation to extend the reach of their vernaculars. When the Kenyan schoolmaster Benaiah Ohanga visited Kampala, he read through an assortment of newspapers and was surprised to discover that his own language, Dholuo, shared vocabulary and grammar with the Lango language of eastern Uganda.[62] In his report he recommended that an interterritorial Luo language committee should be established. Ohanga foresaw a future in which Luo would rank with Swahili and Hausa as one of the preeminent lingua francas of Africa. Upon his return to Kenya he encouraged the leadership of the Luo Union—an ethnic welfare association—to establish an "authentic, rural centered, cheap selling Luo organ to meet the needs and requirements of the semi-illiterate village folk."[63] As the secretary for the government's Luo Language Committee, Ohanga brought out a primer titled "How to Spell Luo" and launched a Dholuo essay competition, in which secondary school students were encouraged to write biographies of eminent Africans in the vernacular.[64]

Their editorship of newspapers endowed African journalists with the proprietorship of their people's culture. Editors saw themselves as being responsible for cleaning up a people's way of life. A great many newspapermen were also moral reformers: the Yoruba journalist I. B. Thomas created the fictional character Ṣẹgilọla in order to articulate axiomatic warnings against urban decadence (Barber, this volume); the publishers of the Tanzanian magazine *Sani* created comic characters who warned readers against the dangers of drunkenness (Reuster-Jahn, this volume); the Yoruba composers of photoplays offered readers lessons for good living (Gbadegesin, this volume). What was it about editorship that inclined African journalists toward cultural reformism? Editors were already at work straightening out the language. Cultural life, too, seemed to need editing. In 1944 the newspaperman Eridadi Mulira had an early-morning dream about the reorganization of Buganda's government. The ideas, he said, "came as if someone was dictating from an unseen source."[65] Shortly thereafter Mulira formed the "African Cultural Society." The aim, he said, was to "take all culture by the horn and in the end try to produce a synthesis of culture which would be our own." For Mulira as for other editors, cultural reform involved the scripting of social relations. That is why the newspaper was essential. It was the venue wherein a particular people could, all at once, be remonstrated with. The linguist Benaiah Ohanga thought *Ramogi*, the newspaper of the Luo Union, ought to encourage the "elimination of the conditions which make for the persistence of superstitious and diabolic beliefs, particularly witchcraft in all its forms."[66] On *Ramogi's* pages contributors chronicled a range of social ills and debated techniques by which to bring about reform. In September 1949, for instance, a contributor asked Luo people to "abolish the shameful habits of Luo women: smoking the burning side of cigarettes; wearing short dresses; putting too many pins in their hair; buying fish bones in foreign hotels and being employed as *ayahs* [nursemaids]." He also complained over men who played guitars in brothels and talked to each other in the Gikuyu language, instead of Luo.[67]

But if newspapers were vehicles for editors' agendas, readers could set the agenda, too, by sending letters, asking questions of editors, and contributing their poems and stories. And if they were unhappy with the direction an editor took, they lost no time in making their voices heard. When J. V. Clinton, the editor of the *Nigerian Eastern Mail*, expressed support for the firms that were underpaying Nigerian producers for their crops, the newspaper's readers chided him for his credulity and advised him not to "rush his views into print," but first to understand the "feeling and views of the people" (Pratten, this volume). In East Africa, the government committee charged with standardizing the Swahili language hoped to use the pages of the Tanganyika periodical *Mambo Leo* to promote a new orthography of the Swahili language.[68] The new spellings were trialed for several months before *Mambo Leo*'s editor, faced with complaints from his readers, admitted defeat and agreed to return to the earlier orthography.[69] Yoruba newspapers regularly tried out literary experiments and invited readers to respond with their criticisms and comments, which they duly did. Those experiments that proved unpopular were abandoned (Barber, this volume).

As newspapers traveled further afield, editors struggled to grasp, measure, and evaluate the identities of their readers. In her chapter Rebecca Jones describes how editors sought to domesticate their readers, inserting real or imagined names of readers they had met or whose villages they had visited into the text. In doing so they created a distinctive "sociability of print" (Jones, this volume). Readers seem to have enjoyed the sociable interactions that newspapers enabled. Contributors to *Mwigwithania*—Kenya's first African-run newspaper—hymned the praises of the journal. "There is no joy equal to this of having a little book in Kikuyu," wrote one reader. In the newspaper "the Kikuyu will be able to give advice to each other, so that the people of our country may agree together."[70] In early twentieth-century South Africa, readers would assemble around a newspaper and treat it as an object for discussion and debate (Mokoena, this volume). When the Yoruba photoplay magazine *Atọka* began to invite letters from readers in 1971, correspondents appealed for the establishment of clubs across the country where readers could gather to discuss and respond to the photoplays (Gbadegesin, this volume). In the Kenyan town of Eldoret, the focus of Duncan Omanga's chapter, newspapers provided a focus for a kind of street parliament. The headlines set the subjects for discussion, but it was Kegode, self-proclaimed "Kofi Annan" of the group that convened around his newspaper stall, who established the rules of engagement. In the streets of Eldoret we can see, in microcosm, the kinds of communities that must have developed around newspapers in other times and places.

THE PRESS AND THE CAMPAIGN

More than any other kind of author, newspapermen know themselves to be addressing an audience. No other printed media is so immediately available to its readers. It was the evidence of their readers' attention—available in circulation figures and other measurements—that seems to have emboldened newsmen to see themselves as spokesmen for a people. The present volume is full of newsmen—Herbert Macaulay, Isaac Theophilus Wallace-Johnson, and others—who found themselves on the wrong side of the law. They were, all of them, editors who felt empowered to trim, delete, re-form, and reorganize received wisdom. They thought of themselves as new men, unbeholden to old proprieties and establishment interests, spokesmen for a newly empowered majority. That was the political theory underlying the formation of the newspaper *Osumare Egba*, launched in 1935 in Abẹokuta in Nigeria. "The old order changeth yielding place to the new," wrote the newspaper's founders in one of their editorials (Oduntan, this volume). The newspaper's editors campaigned against the town's chiefs, claiming that literate men ought to be given positions of authority in local government.

Many editors presented themselves as the voice of the people, a crucial instrument by which readers' views could be made known to the authorities. The editor of the *Nigerian Eastern Mail*, J. V. Clinton, made a yearly tour reporting on progress in government business. Clinton's journalists likewise toured their districts, inspecting canteens, commenting on the availability of police services, and evaluating civic facilities (Pratten, this volume). In Buganda, the newspaper *Ddoboozi lya Buganda* (the "Voice of Buganda") published a regular flow of advice for government officials: one correspondent suggested that bicycle thieves should upon conviction have one arm amputated and an ear cut off; another asked government to tighten traffic laws and punish lorry drivers who drove dangerously.[71] When in 1952 *Ddoboozi* was enlarged to eight pages, its editor noted that "all the officers in the administration of the Protectorate buy *Ddoboozi*, and we send a copy to the Colonial Office in England."[72] The newspaper was essential reading, incumbent on any thinking person, an aspect of their civic duty. It claimed to mediate the relationship between rulers and ruled.

The work of newspaper writing was thereby linked with the work of political advocacy. Editors were very often activists. The actor and the reporter were not separate, and neither was the event always distinct from the report. Newspapermen moved in and out of the frame, sometimes reporting on events, other times creating occasions for reportage. The *Uganda Post*, for example, was avidly involved in the 1953–55 campaign to secure the return of the Kabaka, the ruler of Buganda, who had been deposed and exiled by an autocratic British governor. The British thought the *Post*'s editor, Joseph Kiwanuka, to be a "violent malcontent."[73] Kiwanuka was on several occasions present when angry crowds confronted government chiefs thought to be disloyal to the exiled Kabaka.[74] Early in 1956 he helped to organize a mock funeral for the county chief of Kyaddondo county. Four thousand people gathered on the day of the chief's supposed funeral. There was a mannequin attired in bark cloth, as if it were a corpse; it was raised aloft, stabbed three times, then burned and beaten.[75] All of this was reported in Kiwanuka's newspapers. He must have taken courage from his readers' support. When British officials obliged him to furnish a bond of two thousand shillings as a disincentive toward the publication of incendiary material, it was the newspaper's readers who raised the money and paid the bond.[76]

Newspapermen had to be partisans. There was no secluded office to retreat to. Most of Buganda's newspapermen were based in Katwe, in urban Kampala. They shared space, paper, typewriters, and staff with the political organizations on which they reported. News happened on their doorsteps. In March 1954, the assistant commissioner of police called Eridadi Mulira and several other newspaper editors for a meeting in his office.[77] There he upbraided them for the inaccuracies of their reporting, and asked the editors to check with the government's director of information before going to press. Mulira, in reply, told the policeman that "they are all too busy and had no time to get around." There were no telephones with which to ring up government officials and check information. There in Katwe, newspapers editors were close to the event. It was hard to get away.

From an early date chiefs—the legatees of colonial "indirect rule"—thought newspapers to be subversive to their authority. In 1930 the Kabaka of Buganda, Daudi Cwa, bristled at an article published in the newspaper *Munyonyozi*. He thought it was "my duty to keep a strict watch over these newspaper articles which deal in politics," and averred that it was "highly undesirable and most inadvisable to allow ignorant natives to maliciously attack high officials of my government on political questions on which such writers have no right to speak."[78] Buganda's chiefs expected deference from their people. Commoners addressed their chiefs from the knees, using obsequious language to cloak their requests.[79] Newspapermen addressed chiefs without guile. They knew themselves to be engaged in a controversial task. The masthead for *Munyonyozi*, one of Buganda's first newspapers, depicted a man, standing proudly erect, with his hand raised aloft, making a declarative statement. Another man, positioned to the speaker's side, recoils, as if in shock. Newspapermen expected to surprise and antagonize their readers.

Newspapers like *Munyonyozi* were new media, opening up spaces where people hitherto marginal to the practice of politics could make their voices

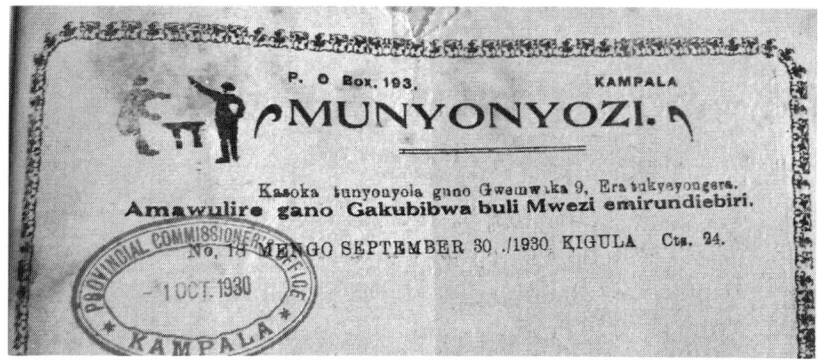

Fig. 1. The Bataka Party newspaper *Munyonyozi* ("The Explainer").

heard, unencumbered by the etiquette and decorum that chiefs expected of their subjects. When in 1956 the anthropologist Lloyd Fallers attended a branch meeting of the Uganda National Congress in rural Buganda, he found hundreds of men assembled outdoors in a hollow square, with the leader at the center, seated at a table. Laid on the table were two books: *The Complete Self-Educator* and *Rovering to Success*.[80] The former title was a compendium of useful facts and information; the latter book was a collection of aphorisms authored by Baden-Powell, the founder of the Boy Scouts. Here there was a novel information economy. Here commoners could access data, statistics, historical examples, and sources of self-motivation, outside the circuitry of chiefly patronage. Over the course of the meeting the leader read out the contents of several vernacular newspapers, then led a discussion of the issues of the day.[81] The topics of discussion ranged widely: one part concerned the unfairness of the kingdom's traffic rules; another part took up the distribution of 154 square miles of freehold land, recently given by the British government to the kingdom's authorities. Newspapers made commoners actors in the theater of politics. They invited people to comment on contemporary affairs.

Newspapers thereby played a critical role in the demographic enlargement of politics, in the enlisting of popular support, in the composition of African nationalism. The constituencies who politicians addressed often overlapped with the audiences that newsmen were also addressing. There was an organizational and infrastructural overlay between the newspaper and the nationalist party. The politician Herbert Macaulay founded Nigeria's first political party, the Nigerian National Democratic Party, in 1923; two years later he launched Nigeria's first daily newspaper, the *Lagos Daily News* (Adebanwi, this volume). Macaulay led the campaign for the restoration of the Eleko, the ruler of Lagos, who had been deposed by the British in 1920 and sent into exile in 1925. In his newspaper he chronicled the abuses meted out to the Eleko's supporters, who were "prosecuted, persecuted, jailed and hounded down" by a dictatorial British governor. When in 1931 the Eleko was restored, it came as a victory for narrative, the summative event in an eleven-year work of political and discursive organization.

Newspapers propel political movements by putting disparate events together, on the page, and making it seem as though everyone were acting in unison. They make disconnected people feel themselves to be co-travelers. That is why Pixley ka Isaka Seme, one of the founders of the newly established South African Native National Congress, thought it imperative that the new party should have its own newspaper. In 1912 he traveled to Swaziland to collect a printing press donated by the Swazi queen regent; and thereafter he set about organizing *Abantu-Batho*, "The People."[82] Newspapers made disparate persons into a singular people, with a definite article. The press played a critically important role in the definition of patriotic behavior. When in 1959 the Uganda National Movement launched a boycott against the Indian traders who dominated Kampala's business, it was the vernacular press that made the boycott effective. *Uganda Empya* reported in May 1959 that children at Aggrey School had refused to buy groundnuts from an African woman who had come to sell them. She had purchased the nuts from an Indian wholesaler. "Even the Young are Nationalists," read the headline.[83] Newspapers created categories with which readers could classify individuals' conduct. They made even the most inconspicuous transactions into public events.

The campaigning newsmen of Buganda and South Africa erected a narrative architecture around the field of real life and invited people to act in conformity with the typecast characters they defined. That is what a campaign is: an ideational structure that links up disconnected dispositions, events, and activities and makes them seem to be choreographed. Newspapers transform actions with cloudy and complicated motivations into momentum.

PRESS CONTROLS

Colonial officials looked with suspicion upon the campaigning journalists of the mid-twentieth century. In Buganda the populist press was said to be "wild, irresponsible, frequently near-seditious, and more serious still, it tends to stir up enmity and distrust."[84] As consumers of media, Africans were thought to be credulous, easily swayed, uncritical of press reports, and susceptible therefore to demagoguery. In Uganda the director of education, the commissioner of police, and the provincial commissioner were responsible for vetting films to be screened in Kampala's cinemas. The grounds on which films could be censored were extensive: the committee forbade films that "upset the susceptibilities of any section of the people before whom it is to be exhibited," films that were "likely to bring white women into disrepute," and "crook films, and those portraying drunkenness, so called European high life and scenes of violent industrial unrest."[85] Radio was likewise carefully supervised. When in the early 1940s British officials first contemplated the introduction of wireless radio broadcasting in eastern Africa, they worried that radio programs were liable to be misunderstood. "The African can discount a bazaar [sic] rumor," wrote an official, "but it may be some time before he can discredit an inaccurate or alarmist account of a broadcast which will be regarded at first as authoritative."[86] When the first large consignment of wireless sets was delivered to Uganda, they were distributed exclusively to government chiefs and to headmasters of missionary schools.[87]

Colonial authorities sought to exert a similar level of oversight over the production and distribution of print media. In francophone Africa, colonial regimes sought to restrict the circulation of anticolonial newspapers published in Paris, fearing their power to radicalize colonized populations.[88] In Sierra Leone, an agitated colonial governor was given the power in 1939 to impose a two-year prison term on "any person who imports, publishes, sells, offers for sale, distributes, or reproduces any publication the importation of which has been prohibited" (Newell, this volume). In Uganda a 1954 ordinance empowered government to suppress any newspaper that was said to be "dangerous to peace and good order."[89] In other territories more subtle measures were employed. The governor of Dahomey responded to the growth of a critical African press in the 1930s by funneling funding and news material to a newspaper, *Le Coeur du Dahomey*, that was sympathetic to government.[90]

But whether subtle or more blatant, colonial press controls were often ineffective in the face of editors' ingenuity.[91] Colonial governors might attempt to close borders and place certain kinds of texts out of bounds, but men like Isaac Theophilus Wallace-Johnson skirted around the edges of the law, finding means to circumvent the apparatus of government oversight (Newell, this volume). And after the Second World War African editors increasingly found allies in

Europe. A series of international agreements made the free press fundamentally part of the architecture of human rights law. At the same time the Empire Press Union, an association of journalists, took an active interest in colonial legislation, campaigning against ordinances that violated press freedom.[92]

The connections that African newsmen made were often out of alignment with the containments of colonial government.[93] African American and Afro-Caribbean newspapers played an increasingly important role in provisioning African newspapers with material by which to enlarge local politics. The editor of eastern Africa's first African-run newspaper, Z. K. Sentongo, was an avid reader of W. E. B. DuBois's magazine *Crisis*.[94] He told DuBois that *Crisis* had taught him about "Negro movements going on in certain places in America, about the progress and improvement of the black people in the world." The news had "brought me a burning heart which resulted in publishing a newspaper ... with a view of trying to help those movements even here."[95] So too did the Garveyite paper *Negro World* attract African readers. In the mid-1920s a group of Ganda teachers and soldiers met regularly to discuss the paper.[96] They opened up a correspondence with Harry Thuku, the exiled leader of the Kenya-based East African Association, about the shared destiny and struggles of Africa's people.[97] "I am striving, struggling, trying day and night to have something done for my beloved race," wrote Reuben Spartas in a 1925 letter to Thuku.[98] "I shall not end till the whole Black Race, the whole of Africa has been thoroughly redeemed." A few years later, Spartas was to found the African Orthodox Church in Uganda and undergo ordination as priest at the hands of a Garveyite bishop.[99]

Newspapers furnished the informational and discursive infrastructure for Pan-Africanism. The most extensive network centered around George Padmore, who from a base in London published hundreds of articles in newspapers in Africa and the Caribbean: 182 articles in the *Ashanti Pioneer* between 1947 and 1950; 508 articles for the *West African Pilot*. Padmore's newspaper industry was meant to convey a sense of anticolonial momentum: by juxtaposing events in Africa with events elsewhere in the colonial world, he sought to draw together the struggles of West Indians with West Africans (James, this volume). East Africans were likewise drawn into Padmore's publishing industry. When in 1946 the News Film Company released its documentary of the Victory Parade in London, the editor of the Kenyan newspaper *Habari* published an article complaining that none of the East African soldiers on parade had been pictured in the film.[100] The text for *Habari*'s article came from George Padmore's "African Press Agency." Padmore was reminding British and African readers about soldiers' self-sacrifice on behalf of the British Empire. His writing helped to lay the groundwork for postwar claim-making in anglophone Africa.

British and French officials sought to segment colonized people from the flow of media and discourse that was shaping the mid-twentieth-century world. Their efforts to constrain Africans' reading habits reached their fullest expression in the detention camps of Kenya, where tens of thousands of Gikuyu men and women suspected of loyalty to the Mau Mau movement were rounded up, incarcerated, and subjected to a coercive program of reeducation. British officials kept careful control over the printed material that came into detainees' hands. Warders were encouraged to clip readers' letters from the *East African Standard* and explain to cooperative detainees "how irresponsible some of these readers' letters are."[101] British government supplied Kenya's people with a flood of anodyne and inoffensive publications. A Department of Information was established in 1954, with branches in each of Kenya's provinces.[102] Within a year the department was publishing seventeen million pages of news and information in fifteen different languages.[103]

One of the newspapers launched during this time was *Atīrīrī*, a newspaper produced at Athi River detention camp and circulated mainly among ex-detainees. Typed and duplicated on a Roneo machine, one thousand copies of *Atīrīrī* appeared in Gikuyu language each week. British officers thought that *Atīrīrī* could help to "re-educate these Africans and . . . convince them that our plans are better and hold promise of a brighter future than those of the Mau Mau."[104] African readers seem to have had rather different interests than that. The most popular part of the newspaper was the fiction. Over the course of several editions *Atīrīrī*'s editor, the detainee Gakaara wa Wanjau, published a novel entitled *She Must Quit This Home*. Its subject was the difficulty of managing kin relations from afar. It featured a young man, recently married to a woman of whom his mother did not approve. While the young man labored in a faraway place, his bride, residing with his parents, was subjected to nighttime visitations from a threatening, ghostly voice. Overcome with fear, the young woman sank into an incoherent stupor. It was only when the young man returned to his home that the truth came out: the ghostly voice had been the man's mother, who had hoped to intimidate the young woman into separating from her son. Gakaara's message was clear: household management required men's constant attention and parents' goodwill. His readers thought the story to be of great importance. "We are in full agreement . . . that a young man has a right to choose a girl to marry him," wrote two detainees from Kamiti prison. "This story has not only given advice to young people but also to the parents."[105]

Gakaara's story was composed in constrained circumstances, under the watchful eye of the camp commandant, in a journal that served the propagandistic purposes of government. Gakaara wrote it because he needed a voice with which to speak to larger issues. It is not that the story contains the secretive seeds of rebellion. It is, rather, that it says things that could not be expressed in prose. Gakaara was dramatizing the circumstances in which he and many of his fellows found themselves: separated from their families, subject to other people's malevolence and whims, unable to supervise their households. Fiction was a recourse. It opened up a space by which to advance the politically and socially controversial argument that young men had the right to make their own decisions.[106]

EXPERIMENTS WITH VOICE

It is not too much to say that the newspaper was the forcing house for the production of African literature. A great many authors who later published fictional books first tried out the fictional voice in the space of the newspaper. The first English-language novel written by an African, *Marita: Or the Folly of Love*, was published as a newspaper serial over two years between 1886 and 1888.[107] In francophone Africa, most African literature published between 1913 and 1960 appeared in the periodical press.[108] Isaac Babalọla Thomas's novel about the dying prostitute Sẹgilọla—the first novel in the Yoruba language—was published in serial form in the newspaper *Akede Eko* between 1929 and 1930 (Barber, this volume). The famed Sesotho writer Thomas Mofolo was a reporter and a proofreader for the Paris Evangelical Mission Society newspaper *Leselinyana la Lesotho*; he published his novel, *Moeti oa Bochabela* ("Traveler to the East"), in installments on the newspaper's pages.[109] The Kenyan novelist Ngugi wa Thiong'o began his literary career as a newspaperman: he published several short stories and some eighty essays in the Nairobi press between May 1961 and August 1964.[110] The Tanzanian writer Faraji Katalambulla published *Picha ya Pacha* as a story in a 1980 number of *Film Tanzania*, then as a photo essay in the same journal, and in 2007 as a play, bound between two covers (Reuster-Jahn, this volume).

Publishing their work in newspapers gave African authors a ready-made income, brought them into contact with their readerships, and allowed them to try out new things, gauge reactions, and claim credit for their work. The isiZulu writer Magema Fuze published a series of articles concerning his mentor, the missionary bishop John W. Colenso, in the newspaper *Ilanga lase Natal* in 1920. The articles drew from an earlier set of articles he had published in 1901 in the newspaper *Ipepa lo Hlanga*. As Hlonipha Mokoena argues in the present volume, Fuze thought of an individual's life history as an ongoing plot, a subject to be returned to. Publication was not the end point. Fuze pled for feedback from his readers, asking for both financial and textual contributions in support of the writing of his great work on the history of the Zulu people. The Swahili newspaper poets of whom Kelly Askew writes are displaced from the interactive oral performance contexts in which their art first developed. But in the newspaper they can find new audiences. In everything they solicit responses, inviting other poets to try out a turn of phrase or respond to enigmas. The newspaper gives the poet an engaged audience.

But there is more to it than that. The fictional voice was, for some African writers, a means of escaping from the confinements of political discourse, a strategy for evading colonial censorship, a way of reaching for a different register, of claiming high ground. By writing fiction, African authors could lift their text out of the mundane intricacies of their time and inhabit another plane. Swahili newspaper poets distill an essence from the mundane events of their contemporary time. Profundity is an affect generated by a felicitous organization of words and phrases. Profundity is also an artifice of the printer. The obituary notices of which Stephanie Newell writes were often arranged as acrostic poems, with the dead person's name providing the first letter for a line. Acrostics moved individuals' names from the horizontal plane to the vertical, lifted the name out of the passing flow of type and made it obligatory for the reader to notice it. Arranged as an acrostic, the name became an icon, an occasion for remembrance. It was destined to be clipped and preserved. And indeed, many West Africans did save obituary notices: they were republished in the press in the years and decades following the individual's death. The authors of obituary notices in the West African press and the Swahili poets that populate Tanzania's newspapers were animated by the same concerns. They sought to move outside the horizontal flow of type that led toward a final punctuation. They sought to cheat time of its spoils.

The same impulse drives the production of fiction. Fiction was a way by which authors already engaged in political argument could find another register in which to write. In 1914 the newspaperman Sol Plaatje went to London on behalf of the South African Natives National Congress, of which he was elected general secretary. It was there that he published his famous *Native Life in South Africa*.[111] In expository prose it laid out Plaatje's case against the 1913 Native Land Act, which had dispossessed tens of thousands of African landholders. The book was based on the investigative reports that Plaatje had earlier published in the South African press. It was full of third-person descriptions of the people whom Plaatje called the "fugitives," refugees in their own homelands. During the same year he published *Native Life* Plaatje also brought out *Sechuana Proverbs with Literal Translations and Their European Equivalents*.[112] The work is a statement about cultural equivalence. Its pages are laid out in columns, with English on the left and Tswana on the right. Some 732 Tswana proverbs are printed up, with a direct translation and a "European Equivalent." Plaatje was showing that Tswana people possessed a cultural and literary system that mirrored English literature. It was a mark of civilizational attainment, a liberal assertion of Tswana people's capacities, and a rebuke, therefore, to the dehumanizing policies of South Africa's government.

But neither *Native Life* nor the book of proverbs could make the victims of the 1913 Natives Land Act into human beings. *Native Life* was written as a third-person exposé; the "fugitives" are largely nameless, dramatic only in their dispossession. There are no private agonies, no inward life at all. Their travails are the trials of the generality of black South Africans. It is the flatness of the journalistic analytic that seems to have led a dissatisfied Plaatje toward fictional writing. His novel *Mhudi*, published in 1930, was composed in the late 1910s in the same notebook in which he drafted a pamphlet condensing the argument of *Native Life in South Africa*.[113] In any given day he seems to have moved between exposition of fact and the imaginative work of fiction. He seems to have gloried in the freedoms of fiction: he told his mentor, Silas Molema, that *Mhudi* had "plenty of love, superstitions and imaginations."[114] In the novel, Plaatje shows the highveld to be home to complex, culturally variegated, and politically sophisticated African societies prior to the arrival of Afrikaner *trekboers*. He contrasts this picture of reason and decorum with the abuses meted out on the African servants of the Afrikaners, who are, before the reader's eyes, chastised with whips and burned with pokers. But he also dramatizes other forms of engagement. The *trekboers* may flog their servants, but one of their number, Phil Jay, is both humane and human. He forms a close friendship with the novel's male protagonist, Ra Thaga; they teach each other their vernacular languages and live in each other's homes. Here, evoked in fiction, was the kind of social interaction that the liberal Plaatje wished to sponsor in fact.

The novel *Mhudi* carried forward, in fictional voice, the argument that Plaatje was making more generally. In his journalism, he sought to highlight the injustice of the Native Land Act. In his fiction, he made African communities sympathetic. He personified the "fugitives" of whom he had written in *Native Life*, giving them ambitions, loves, personalities, and interior lives. In *Mhudi* Plaatje vacated the journalistic voice of narrative exposition and occupied a different position in relation to his subject.

PRÉCIS

This book is divided into four thematic parts. The first part is about the work that newspaper editors and contributors did to relate events within their locality to happenings in far-off places. Atlantic studies scholars' focus on African diasporas too often ignores the infrastructures that enabled networks to emerge. Newspapers helped to constitute the Black Atlantic as an arena of discourse and as a platform of action.[115] Within the space of the newspaper editors could juxtapose texts composed elsewhere with the local news, making it possible for readers to imagine themselves as confreres of people with whom they had no direct relationship. In attenuating space newspapers mediated the relationship between people, making new solidarities thinkable.

Leslie James's chapter illuminates the newspaper business of the Trinidadian Pan-Africanist George Padmore. Between 1936 and 1957 he was based in London, and during that time he published an astonishingly large number of articles in African, Afro-Caribbean, and African American newspapers. Many of his publications were actually clippings lifted out of one newspaper and sent to another, sometimes with an introductory comment from Padmore himself. By the operation of his scissors Padmore brought different colonial contexts into dialogue with each other. His incredible industry, James shows, was a mechanism by which the circuitry of the pan-African world was formed. There was a radical politics involved in the editorial work of selection and clipping. Conservatives, too, could clip, plagiarize, and republish. David Pratten's chapter focuses on the *Nigerian Eastern Mail*, a provincial newspaper headquartered in Nigeria's hinterland. Its editor, J. V. Clinton, was a scion of the anglophone elite of colonial Nigeria. He had subscriptions to a range of African American newspapers, and he regularly printed up articles from the black press in his own newspaper. He looked for strange stories about people who changed race, whose skin was suddenly turned from black to white.

Pratten argues that Clinton's clippings were an expression of his ambivalence about race-based politics. At a time when racial identities were being mobilized as a basis for anticolonial action, Clinton argued that the British Empire remained the most trustworthy custodian of black people's political future. Clinton's line of argument was decidedly out of time in 1930s Nigeria. Pratten argues that the foreclosure of Clinton's newspaper helps us see precisely how the liberal politics of West Africa's creole elite gave way to new kinds of activism.

Rebecca Jones's essay is, like Leslie James's, about the networks that newspapermen created. I. B. Thomas, editor of the Lagos-based Yoruba-language newspaper *Akede Eko*, worked on a smaller scale than George Padmore. But like Padmore, he used the newspaper to make comparisons and liken local events to things happening at a distance. Thomas printed up several travelogues in the course of the 1920s and 1930s describing his journeys to the far distant hinterlands of Yorubaland. His narratives were exuberantly social, full of details about the personalities and communities with which he interacted. Jones argues that Thomas's travel narratives were a textual record of the newspaper's circulation. They helped Lagos readers to feel themselves as sharing a set of interests with people whom they had never met. The constitution of a Yoruba public, argues Jones, was animated in part through the social work of editors like Thomas. Herbert Macaulay—the subject of Wale Adebanwi's chapter—was a contemporary of I. B. Thomas. Like Thomas, he was a man of Lagos; and like many of the town's people, he was deeply troubled when, in 1920, the British government of Nigeria summarily unseated the ruler of Lagos, the Eleko. Thomas and Macaulay inhabited the same world, but the networks in which they moved were organized on different lines. Thomas traveled along the railroad and addressed himself to his public mainly in Yoruba. Macaulay wrote in English, and on several occasions he traveled by steamship to London to pursue legal arguments before the Privy Council. Thomas very often wrote under a pseudonym. Macaulay was a celebrity. His newspaper, the *Lagos Daily News*, was a vehicle for his arguments against colonial rulers. On its pages Macaulay enlisted liberal political theory to support a campaign for the restoration of the Eleko's authority. Like George Padmore, his celebrity was produced through the press: his byline was also a trademark, a sales device, and a persona. Taken together, these two chapters help us glimpse the infrastructures through which different colonial public spheres were called into being.

News was never composed ex nihilo. It was assembled by editors who made strategic choices about the communities that they wished to address and about the historical destiny that they were bound to meet. The second part—titled "Experiments with Genre"—shows how editors sought to hail the audiences that they hoped to instruct. The chapters in this part are about writing strategy. For poets, as for writers of narrative fiction, newspapers were spaces where plotlines, images, and vocabulary could be experimented with. By publishing in newspapers, authors could find a prefabricated readership to engage with and try out techniques that could, later, get recycled and make their way into the pages of a book. In this way, newspapers helped to incubate the development of new literary genres.

Karin Barber's chapter is a study of literary entrepreneurship in the Yoruba-language press of the 1920s. Barber argues that the Lagos elite, shaken by the deposition of the town's ruler, felt obliged to broaden the base of heir political support by engaging commoners and cultivating constituencies. The impulse toward populism in turn fertilized innovations in the Yoruba press, whose editors sought to broaden their newspapers' circulation and excite a wider readership. It was during this time that a whole range of literary experiments appeared in newspapers: advice columns, travelogues, and novelistic fiction, composed in the first person. These experimental literary forms, Barber suggests, manifested editors' search for new modes of address, new ways of hailing and engaging readers. Populism was an engine for literary and cultural creativity. Kelly Askew's chapter surveys the Swahili-language poetry that populates the pages of Tanzania's press. Swahili newspapers are—like the Yoruba newspapers of the 1920s—full of narrative reportage, but they are also home to literary experiments: encomiums to important men, personal advertisements, obituary poems, acrostics. Askew argues that this creativity is animated by the broader, historically formed interest among Swahili people in poetic expression. These poets were very much engaged in the mundane news of the day, and they comment on it in verse. But poetic verse also reaches beyond reportage: as poets, writers address themselves to God, profess their love for another person, and extol an editor's generosity. The poetic voice speaks from outside the chronological confinements of the newspaper and engages with bigger things.

The two essays that conclude this second part chronicle the editorial work by which new styles are created. *Drum* magazine, published in Sophiatown in South Africa, brought a whole new aesthetic to African journalism more generally. At its height in the late 1950s *Drum* had a larger circulation than any other publication in Africa, regardless of language.[116]

Its embrace of the trappings of urbanity gave editors in Nigeria, Tanzania, and elsewhere a new aesthetic. Uta Reuster-Jahn's chapter is focused on the entertainment magazines that flourished in socialist Tanzania. Their subject matter was strictly constrained by government, which did not allow them to comment on political affairs. Editors therefore found their material in domestic life: in family conflicts, inheritance disputes, and other generational conflicts. In all of these arenas editors propounded the moral virtues—discipline, hard work, sexual constancy—that were essential elements in socialist discourse more generally. These editors were creating stereotypes that represented dispositions, proclivities, and sentiments that socialist discourse sought to engage. Entertainment magazines were a visual dramatization of the moral agenda of Tanzanian socialism. The Yoruba photoplays that are the subject of Olubukola Gbadegesin's chapter were, like the Swahili entertainment magazines, created by editors who were reading *Drum*. Yoruba theatrical troupes had long been purveyors of drama, comedy, and tragedy. In the 1960s and 1970s a cohort of editors placed this performance art on the printed page. The magazines that they produced were—like their Swahili counterparts—didactic in character. And yet, as Gbadegesin shows, Yoruba editors engaged in creative work: they manipulated photos to impute movement and action to otherwise static scenes; they developed techniques to incorporate drawing with photography; they populated photographic imagery with onomatopoeic text, making the written page an analogue for a sonic landscape. Reuster-Jahn and Gbadegesin help us see how editorial creativity can fashion new things even while working on stock themes.

The book's third part, which we call "Newspapers and Their Publics," is about the ways in which African newspapers cajoled new kinds of communities into being. The focus here is on the infrastructure of addressivity. Like newspapers everywhere, African newspapers necessarily had limited circulation. But editors were always working to expand their readerships, sending copies through the post, or on the railway line, to far distant communities of prospective readers. On the pages of the newspaper they addressed themselves to a community that had shared interests, that needed to know of events that concerned them. In this way newspapers helped to constitute and populate a public sphere.

Emma Hunter's chapter focuses on the Swahili-language newspaper *Komkya*, published by the Kilimanjaro local government, in northern Tanzania, during the 1950s and 1960s. The Chagga politicians who backed

Komkya were—like the Yoruba elites of whom Barber writes—seeking to expand the base of their political support. *Komkya* was an aspect of a larger effort to consolidate Chagga political identity and to unify disparate people. But the newspaper was more than an instrument for constituency-building. The newspaper's layout—one section allocated to women's issues, another appropriated by young men—gave readers an occasion to define and defend their particular sectional identities. By constituting a Chagga readership as segmentary, with discrete interests, the newspaper helped to develop a model of community that was founded not on consensus but on argument and debate. The Yoruba newspaper *Osumare Egba*—the subject of Toyin Oduntan's chapter—was, like *Komkya*, meant to define and defend the local interests of a particular cultural community. Its editors thought of themselves as protectors of Abẹokuta's distinctive historical inheritance, which was endangered by the expansive irredentism of nearby Lagos. But while they spoke as civic patriots, *Osumare Egba*'s editors also found themselves at odds with the town's leadership, which was dominated by chiefs. Editors and other literate men felt themselves excluded from positions of authority and beholden to a leadership that was antiquated and out of touch with a changing world. Their newspaper, Oduntan shows, was an effort to broadcast their particular voice in local affairs. Here was a platform for a form of authority grounded not on patronage or on ancestry but on technical know-how.

Duncan Omanga's chapter is a sociology of the *kamukunji*, an assembly of newspaper readers in Eldoret, in western Kenya. In contemporary Kenya—as, we must imagine, in Chagga territory and in provincial Nigeria—newspapers are prompts for oral discourse. The headlines, visible from the street corners where the men of the *kamukunji* stand, set an itinerary for a debate over the matters of the day. Vendors, too, help set an agenda: as Omanga shows, the vendor Kegode structures debate in the Eldoret *kamukunji* by asking provocative questions, inviting replies from specific individuals. There is, in other words, a social architecture around news readership, a set of authorities who organize and channel Eldoret people's engagements with the news. The work of editorship does not stop at the newsman's desk: the flow of information is everywhere composed, organized, canalized.

The book's final part, "Afterlives," is about the *longue durée* of history. Newspapers are, of course, periodicals: they publish material that pertains to a specific period of time. But for many readers—and for many editors—they are also objects that are worthy of retention. Newspapers are collectors' items. They can be squirreled away in files or tin trunks, clipped and pasted into scrapbooks, or bound and placed in university libraries. In their apparent permanence newspapers allow contributors to imagine themselves writing for posterity, to address themselves to generations yet unborn. It is this proleptic quality that invites contemporary authors to see newspapers as a suitable forum for memorials.

Hlonipha Mokoena's chapter focuses on the Zulu writer Magema Fuze, the author of the celebrated book *The Black People and Whence They Came*, the first Zulu-language book to be written by a Zulu person.[117] Fuze was an avid writer of newspaper articles, contributing in particular to John Dube's important *Ilanga lase Natal*. For Fuze, newspaper writing was not a distraction from work on the book. Fuze saw the newspaper as a dialogic medium, a platform where the cooperative labor of historical reconstruction could take place. On its pages the triumphs of his people's past, and the story of his own coming of age, could be composed and revised. Fuze and other Zulu literates found in the newspaper a way of making themselves historical figures, whose experiences and knowledge could, they thought, be exemplary for the future. Stephanie Newell's chapter is likewise about the afterlives that published material can enjoy. In the West African press of the late nineteenth and early twentieth centuries, memorials were printed up, saved, and republished decades after the death of an honored man or woman. In this way the dead were given a continued role to play in the contemporary world: as archetypes whose experiences and convictions could be made to inform present-day heroes. Editors' aim, argues Newell, was to generate an archive of African heroes in order to relativize colonial authorities' pretensions toward cultural superiority. Even tricksters like I. T. A. Wallace-Johnson, who published a satirical memorial marking the supposed death of a political antagonist, found space within the form. Memorials were a genre in which editors could transform complicated life histories into sources of instruction and vehicles for political commentary.

The space for the free press was substantially foreclosed after African colonies became independent states. African leaders thought themselves at the head of a people who were, or ought to be, politically and culturally sovereign. Seen in this light there was little space for criticism or dissent. In Ghanaian president Kwame Nkrumah's memorable formulation, the "true African journalist" now worked "for the organ of the political party to which he himself belongs and in whose purpose he believes."[118] Kenyan president Jomo Kenyatta told the International Press Institute that the media's role was to act as a "stronghold of ethics," and urged journalists to "positively promote national development and growing self-respect."[119] All over Africa independent newspapers were closed and state-run media took their place. In Uganda, Joseph Kiwanuka's newspapers, which had been at the heart of the 1958–60 campaign against Indian business (above), were shuttered in the early 1960s.[120] In 1968 Ugandan president Milton Obote had the editor of the magazine *Transition* arrested and imprisoned. In a televised debate one of Obote's cabinet ministers called *Transition* "dirty, subversive and emotional."[121] When Idi Amin came to power he reorganized the newspaper industry by fiat, and from 1972 the *Voice of Uganda* was made the official vehicle for government communication and the sole English-language newspaper in the country.[122] Government officials were thereafter barred from giving interviews with foreign journalists.[123] That same year Tanzania's government consolidated the country's newspapers into a small number of state-owned publications.[124] In Ghana the *Ashanti Pioneer*, the newspaper wherein George Padmore had published hundreds of articles, was brought under the control of the Nkrumah government in 1962. The editor spent four and a half years in prison for "destructive criticism of the government."[125]

Independence involved political consolidation. It severed networks.[126] In a former time radical newspapermen had seen themselves as the voice of a people whose interests were at odds with colonial government. In the 1960s this form of spokesmanship was labeled unpatriotic, and newspapers were closely aligned with the interests of state-building. And yet, even in these changed circumstances, newspapermen continued to pursue a vocation as arbiters of culture and as representatives of a people. Faraji H. Katalambulla's *Film Tanzania*, launched in 1969, was legally barred from commenting on political affairs, but over the course of several years his photojournal was a space where the dynamics of Tanzanian socialism could be defined and debated (Reuster-Jahn, this volume). The newspaper *Ngurumo*, Tanzania's most widely read daily, was an engine for the development of Swahili orthography and grammar. In 1965 the newspaper announced that an association of Swahili poets had set up a special committee to monitor the way that the Swahili language was being used in the media.[127] The newspaper hosted a wide-ranging discussion over the spelling of particular words, with contributors debating whether words of Arabic derivation ought to be built into the official dictionary of an African-run state.[128] In Kenya the writer Gakaara wa Wanjau, imprisoned by colonial authorities for eight long years, was released in 1960. He used the material he had composed while in detention as the starting point for his publishing career. Over the course of three decades he brought out dozens of books: there was a clutch of reading primers for students of Gikuyu, Dholuo, Kalenjin, and Kikamba; a series of moralistic novelettes; hymnbooks, ethnographic texts, and historical studies. The name of his first book series—*Atīrīrī* (I Say to You)—was borrowed from the title of the detention camp newspaper that he had edited.

By giving authors a concrete, enumerable, and apparently attentive audience, newspapers can transform the report into the manifesto and make writing into a political and moral vocation. No other form of writing—not the novel, nor the history book, nor the play—can be so immediately pertinent. Newspapers emerge on a daily (or weekly) basis. They are always current. They are consumed in public spaces and discussed on street corners. Their distribution networks are visible, as are their buyers. The newspaper makes it possible for the writer—who must otherwise wonder over the efficacy of her words—to think herself addressing attentive and biddable readers. It is the compression of newspaper writing—the proximity of author to audience, the punctuality of the publication, the immediacy of the content—that makes authors into arbiters of culture and political life. Some newspapermen, like George Padmore, Herbert Macaulay, or Wallace-Johnson, became celebrities. Others disguised themselves behind pseudonyms. All of them felt themselves to be in close, intimate touch with their audiences. That is why I. B. Thomas spent so much time getting to know his readers. That is why Swahili poets take such pleasure in their competitive compositions. That is why Yoruba photojournalists invited their readers to "come along with us" (Gbadegesin, this volume). In the newspaper authors found it possible to address a people who they named as their own. There they could establish a connection, outside the official circuitry of government, with a community. It is from this place that the vocation of the reformer, and of the campaigner, spring. Even when governments close down channels for political criticism, it is this vocation that endures.

BIBLIOGRAPHY

Ashton, E. O., E. M. K. Mulira, E. G. M. Ndawula, and A. A. Tucker. *A Luganda Grammar*. London: Longmans, Green, 1954.

Askwith, Tom. *From Mau Mau to Harambee*. Edited by Joanna Lewis. Cambridge: Cambridge African Studies Centre, 1995.

Azikiwe, Nnamdi. *My Odyssey: An Autobiography*. New York: Praeger, 1970.

Baden-Powell, Robert. *Rovering to Success: A Book of Life Sport for Young Men*. London: Herbert Jenkins, 1922.

Ballantyne, Tony. "Paper, Pen and Print: The Transformation of the Kai Tahu Knowledge Order." *Comparative Studies in Society and History* 53 (2011): 232–60.

Barber, Karin. *Print Culture and the First Yoruba Novel: I.B. Thomas's "The Life Story of Me, Sẹgilọla" and Other Texts*. Leiden: Brill, 2013.

Bjornson, Richard. *The African Quest for Freedom and Identity: Cameroonian Writing and the National Experience*. Bloomington: Indiana University Press, 1991.

Breckenridge, James. *Forty Years in Kenya*. Bridport: Creeds, [2005].

Brennan, James. "Communications and Media in African History." In *Oxford Handbook of Modern African History*, edited by John Parker and Richard Reid, 492–509. Oxford: Oxford University Press, 2013.

Burton, Antoinette, and Isabel Hofmeyr, eds. *Ten Books That Shaped the British Empire: Creating an Imperial Commons*. Durham, NC: Duke University Press, 2014.

Campbell, W. Joseph. "African Cultures and Newspapers." In *The Function of Newspapers in Society: A Global Perspective*, edited by Shannon Martin and David Copeland, 31–46. Westport, CT: Praeger, 2003.

Coleman, James S. "Nationalism in Tropical Africa." *American Political Science Review* 48 (1954): 404–26.

Condon, John C. "Nation Building and Image Building in the Tanzanian Press." *Journal of Modern African Studies* 5, no. 3 (1967): 335–54.

Cooper, Frederick. *Citizenship between Empire and Nation: Remaking France and French Africa, 1945–1960*. Princeton, NJ: Princeton University Press, 2014.

Cooper, Frederick. *Decolonization and African Society: The Labor Question in British and French Africa*. Cambridge: Cambridge University Press, 1996.

Couzens, Tim, and Stephen Gray. "Printers' and Other Devils: The Texts of Sol T. Plaatje's 'Mhudi.'" *Research in African Literatures* 9, no. 2 (1978): 198–215.

Cryle, Denis. "A British Legacy? The Empire Press Union and Freedom of the Press, 1940–1950." *History of Intellectual Culture* 4, no. 1 (2004): 1–13.

Edmonds, W. D. "The Newspaper Press in British West Africa 1918 to 1939." MA thesis, Bristol University, 1951.

Englebert, Pierre. "Compliance and Defiance to National Integration in Barotseland and Casamance." *Africa Spectrum* 40, no. 1 (2005): 29–59.

Feierman, Steven. *Peasant Intellectuals: Anthropology and History in Tanzania*. Madison: University of Wisconsin Press, 1990.

Gadsden, Fay. "The African Press in Kenya." *Journal of African History* 21, no. 4 (1980): 515–35.

Hachten, William A. *Muffled Drums: The News Media in Africa*. Ames: Iowa State University Press, 1971.

Hanson, Holly. *Landed Obligation: The Practice of Power in Buganda*. Portsmouth, NH: Heinemann, 2003.

Hofmeyr, Isabel. *Gandhi's Printing Press: Experiments in Slow Reading*. Cambridge, MA: Harvard University Press, 2013.

Hofmeyr, Isabel. *The Portable Bunyan: A Transnational History of "The Pilgrim's Progress"*. Princeton, NJ: Princeton University Press, 2003.

Hofmeyr, Isabel. "Towards a History of the Book and Literary Culture in Africa." In *Literary Cultures and the Material Book*, edited by Simon Eliot, Andrew Nash, and Ian Willison. London: British Library Publishing, 2007.

Hunter, Emma. "'Our Common Humanity': Print, Power and the Colonial Press in Interwar Tanganyika and French Cameroun," *Journal of Global History* 7, no. 2 (2012): 279–301.

Hunter, Emma. *Political Thought and the Public Sphere in East Africa: Freedom, Democracy and Citizenship in the Era of Decolonization*. Cambridge: Cambridge University Press, 2015.

Ivaska, Andrew. *Cultured States: Youth, Gender, and Modern Style in 1960s Dar es Salaam*. Durham, NC: Duke University Press, 2011.

Jeppie, Shamil. "Writing, Books, and Africa." *History and Theory* 53 (2014): 94–104.

Jones, D. J., and S. T. Plaatje. *A Sechuana Reader in International Phonetic Orthography*. London: University of London Press, 1916.

July, Robert W. *The Origins of Modern African Thought: Its Development in West Africa during the Nineteenth and Twentieth Centuries*. London: Faber and Faber, 1968.

Kasoma, Francis P. "The Role of the Independent Media in Africa's Change to Democracy." *Media, Culture and Society* 17, no. 4 (1995): 537–55.

Kenyatta, Jomo. "An Address to the International Press Institute Conference in Nairobi in 1968." *Africa Today* 16, no. 3 (1969): 5–6.

Kitching, A. L., G. R. Blackledge, and E. M. K. Mulira. *A Luganda-English and English-Luganda Dictionary*. London: Society for Promoting Christian Knowledge, 1952.

Kodesh, Neil. *Beyond the Royal Gaze: Clanship and Public Healing in Buganda*. Charlottesville: University of Virginia Press, 2010.

Krätli, Graziano, and Ghislaine Lydon. *The Trans-Saharan Book Trade: Manuscript Culture, Arabic Literacy and Intellectual History in Muslim Africa*. Leiden: Brill, 2011.

Lambert, Michael C. "Violence and the War of Words: Ethnicity vs. Nationalism in the Casamance." *Africa* 68, no. 4 (1998): 585–602.

Landau, Paul. *Popular Politics in the History of South Africa, 1400–1948*. Cambridge: Cambridge University Press, 2010.

Langley, J. Ayodele. *Pan-Africanism and Nationalism in West Africa, 1900–1945: A Study in Ideology and Social Classes*. Oxford: Clarendon Press, 1973.

Lawrance, Benjamin N. *Locality, Mobility, and Nation: Periurban Colonialism in Togo's Eweland, 1900–1960*. Rochester, NY: University of Rochester Press, 2007.

le Roux, Elizabeth. "Book History in the African world: The State of the Discipline." *Book History* 15 (2012): 248–300.

Limb, Peter, ed. *The People's Paper: A Centenary History and Anthology of* Abantu-Batho. Johannesburg: Wits University Press, 2012.

Lindfors, Bernth. *Early East African Writers and Publishers*. Trenton, NJ: Africa World Press, 2011.

Lonsdale, John. "'Listen While I Read': Patriotic Christianity among the Young Kikuyu." In *Christianity and Social Change in Africa: Essays in Honor of J.D.Y. Peel*, edited by Toyin Falola, 563–94. Durham, NC: Carolina Academic Press, 2005.

Lonsdale, John. "The Moral Economy of Mau Mau: Wealth, Poverty, and Civic Virtue in Kikuyu Political Thought." In *Unhappy Valley: Conflict in Kenya and Africa*, by John Lonsdale and Bruce Berman, 315–504. London: James Currey, 1992.

Lüsebrink, Hans-Jürgen. *La conquête de l'espace public colonial*. Frankfurt am Main: IKO Verlag für Interkulturelle Kommunikation, 2003.

Maake, Nhlanhla P. "A Survey of Trends in the Development of African Literatures in South Africa: With Specific Reference to Written Southern Sotho Literature, c. 1900–1970s." *African Languages and Cultures* 5 (1992): 157–88.

McNee, Lisa. "Togo." In *Censorship: A World Encyclopedia*, vol. 4, ed. Derek Jones. London: Fitzroy Dearborn, 2001.

Mokoena, Hlonipha. *Magema Fuze: The Making of a* Kholwa *Intellectual*. Pietermaritzburg: University of KwaZulu-Natal Press, 2011.

Nelson, Daniel. "Newspapers in Uganda." *Transition* 35 (1968): 29–33.

Newell, Stephanie. *Marita; or, The Folly of Love: A Novel by A. Native*. Leiden: Brill, 2002.

Newell, Stephanie. *The Power to Name: A History of Anonymity in Colonial West Africa*. Athens: Ohio University Press, 2013.

Padmore, George. *The Life and Struggles of Negro Toilers*. London: Red International of Labour Unions, 1931.

Peterson, Derek R. *Creative Writing: Translation, Bookkeeping, and the Work of Imagination in Colonial Kenya*. Portsmouth, NH: Heinemann, 2004.

Peterson, Derek R. *Ethnic Patriotism and the East African Revival: A History of Dissent*. Cambridge: Cambridge University Press, 2012.

Peterson, Derek R. "Ethnography and Cultural Innovation in Mau Mau Detention Camps: Gakaara wa Wanjau's *Mīhīrīga ya Agīkūyū*." In *Ten Books That Shaped the British Empire: Creating an Imperial Commons*, edited by Antoinette Burton and Isabel Hofmeyr, 216–37. Durham, NC: Duke University Press, 2014.

Peterson, Derek R. "The Politics of Transcendence in Colonial Uganda." *Past and Present* 230, no. 1 (2016): 197–225.

Peterson, Derek R., and Edgar Taylor. "Rethinking the State in Idi Amin's Uganda: The Politics of Exhortation." *Journal of Eastern African Studies* 7, no. 1 (2013): 58–82.

Pettegree, Andrew. *The Invention of News: How the World Came to Know about Itself*. New Haven: Yale University Press, 2014.

Plaatje, Sol. *Native Life in South Africa, before and since the European War and the Boer Rebellion*. London: P.S. King, 1916.

Plaatje, Sol. *Sechuana Proverbs with Literal Translations and Their European Equivalents*. London: Kegan Paul, 1916.

Plaatje, Sol. "Uniform Spelling." *English in Africa* 3, no. 2 (1976): 45–50.

Richards, Audrey. "Authority Patterns in Traditional Buganda." In *The King's Men: Leadership and Status in Buganda on the Eve of Independence*, edited by L. Fallers, 256–93. London: Oxford University Press, 1964.

Sadgrove, Philip C., ed. *History of Printing and Publishing in the Languages and Countries of the Middle East*. Oxford: Oxford University Press, 2005.

Sanneh, Lamin. *Translating the Message: The Missionary Impact on Culture*. Maryknoll, NY: Orbis, 1989.

Schramm, Wilbur. *Mass Media and National Development: The Role of Information in the Developing Countries*. Stanford, CA: Stanford University Press, 1964.

Scotton, James F. "The First African Press in East Africa: Protest and Nationalism in Uganda in the 1920s." *International Journal of African Historical Studies* 6, no. 2 (1973): 211–28.

Switzer, Les, ed. *South Africa's Alternative Press: Voices of Protest and Resistance, 1880–1960*. Cambridge: Cambridge University Press, 1997.

Switzer, Les, and Mohamed Adhikari, eds. *South Africa's Resistance Press: Alternative Voices in the Last Generation under Apartheid*. Athens: Ohio University Press, 2000.

Thuku, Harry. *Harry Thuku: An Autobiography*. Nairobi: Oxford University Press, 1970.

Von Eschen, Penny. *Race against Empire: Black Americans and Anti-colonialism, 1937–1957*. Ithaca, NY: Cornell University Press, 1997.

Welbourn, F. B. *East African Rebels: A Study of Some Independent Churches.* London: SCM Press, 1961.

Yates, Barbara A. "Knowledge Brokers: Books and Publishers in Early Colonial Zaire." *History in Africa* 14 (1987): 311–40.

Zachernuk, Philip S. Colonial Subjects: An African Intelligentsia and Atlantic Ideas. Charlottesville: University Press of Virginia, 2000.

NOTES TO CHAPTER ONE

1. Archives are referenced as follows: KNA: Kenya National Archives, Nairobi; UNA: Uganda National Archives, Entebbe; BNA: British National Archives, Kew; AS: Archives du Sénégal, Dakar; TNA: Tanzania National Archives; AOM: Archives d'Outre Mer, Aix-en-Provence; USNA: United States National Archives, College Park.

2. From Molema's unpublished autobiography. Quoted in Peter Limb, ed., *The People's Paper: A Centenary History and Anthology of* Abantu-Batho (Johannesburg: Wits University Press, 2012), 25–26.

3. The material that follows is from Mulira's autobiography, in Cambridge University, Centre of African Studies, Mulira papers, Gen. 1/2.

4. Letter from Wilfrid Mutahyabarwa, "On one man's shoulders!," *Bukya na Gandi*, 4 October 1952, 2.

5. University of the Witwatersrand Historical Papers, collection A979: Sol Plaatje to "Sir," 14 August 1912.

6. Isabel Hofmeyr, *Gandhi's Printing Press: Experiments in Slow Reading* (Cambridge, MA: Harvard University Press, 2013).

7. W. D. Edmonds, "The Newspaper Press in British West Africa 1918 to 1939," MA thesis, Bristol University, 1951, 76–77; cited in J. Ayodele Langley, *Pan-Africanism and Nationalism in West Africa, 1900–1945: A Study in Ideology and Social Classes* (Oxford: Clarendon Press, 1973), 120.

8. James S. Coleman, "Nationalism in Tropical Africa," *American Political Science Review* 48, no. 2 (1954): 404–26, 418.

9. Robert W. July, *The Origins of Modern African Thought: Its Development in West Africa during the Nineteenth and Twentieth Centuries* (London: Faber and Faber, 1968).

10. Les Switzer, ed., *South Africa's Alternative Press: Voices of Protest and Resistance, 1880–1960* (Cambridge: Cambridge University Press, 1997); Les Switzer and Mohamed Adhikari, eds., *South Africa's Resistance Press: Alternative Voices in the Last Generation under Apartheid* (Athens: Ohio University Press, 2000).

11. Les Switzer, "Introduction: South Africa's Alternative Press in Perspective," in Switzer, *South Africa's Alternative Press*, 3.

12. W. Joseph Campbell, "African Cultures and Newspapers," in *The Function of Newspapers in Society: A Global Perspective*, ed. Shannon Martin and David Copeland (Westport, CT: Praeger, 2003), 31–46.

13. Francis P. Kasoma, "The Role of the Independent Media in Africa's Change to Democracy," *Media, Culture and Society* 17, no. 4 (1995): 537–55, 539.

14. See, for example, John C. Condon, "Nation Building and Image Building in the Tanzanian Press," *Journal of Modern African Studies* 5, no. 3 (1967): 335–54.

15. Foreword in Wilbur Schramm, *Mass Media and National Development: The Role of Information in the Developing Countries* (Stanford, CA: Stanford University Press, 1964), vii.

16. "Declaration of Windhoek," 3 May 1991, http://www.unesco.org/webworld/fed/temp/communication_democracy/windhoek.htm (accessed online 4 August 2014).

17. BNA FCO 141/18246: Abubakar Mayanja, "Christian Civilization," *Ebifa*, 2 December 1952. Padmore's influence on Mayanja is described in BNA FCO 141/18246: Principal, Makerere College, to Acting Governor, 6 April 1953.

18. George Padmore, *The Life and Struggles of Negro Toilers* (London: Red International of Labour Unions, 1931).

19. Antoinette Burton and Isabel Hofmeyr, "Introduction: The Spine of Empire? Books and the Making of an Imperial Commons," in *Ten Books That Shaped the British Empire: Creating an Imperial Commons*, ed. Antoinette Burton and Isabel Hofmeyr (Durham, NC: Duke University Press, 2014), 5.

20. The editorials of "A Banker" are mentioned in Stephanie Newell, *The Power to Name: A History of Anonymity in Colonial West Africa* (Athens: Ohio University Press, 2013). The reprints are in *Northern Territory Times and Gazette* 1769 (9 February 1906): 4; *Otago Witness* 2799 (6 November 1907): 88; and *New Age* 48 (5 November 1907): 8.

21. See Graziano Krätli and Ghislaine Lydon, *The Trans-Saharan Book Trade: Manuscript Culture, Arabic Literacy and Intellectual History in Muslim Africa* (Leiden: Brill, 2011) and Shamil Jeppie, "Writing, Books, and Africa," *History and Theory* 53 (2014): 94–104. For a useful summary see Elizabeth le Roux, "Book History in the African World: The State of the Discipline," *Book History* 15 (2012): 248–300.

22. John Iliffe, *Africans: The History of a Continent* (Cambridge: Cambridge University Press, 1995); Paul Landau, *Popular Politics in the History of South Africa, 1400 to 1948* (Cambridge: Cambridge University Press, 2010).

23. Tony Ballantyne, "Paper, Pen and Print: The Transformation of the Kai Tahu Knowledge Order," *Comparative Studies in Society and History* 53, no. 2 (2011): 232–60.

24. Isabel Hofmeyr, *The Portable Bunyan: A Transnational History of "The Pilgrim's Progress"* (Princeton, NJ: Princeton University Press, 2003).

25. Diocese of Central Tanganyika archives, "Missionaries' Annual Letters" file: Dennis Cordell, circular letter, 19 July 1955.

26. Benjamin N. Lawrance, *Locality, Mobility, and Nation: Periurban Colonialism in Togo's Eweland, 1900–1960* (Rochester, NY: University of Rochester Press, 2007), 160.

27. Switzer, "Introduction," 23.

28. As in early modern Europe. Andrew Pettegree, *The Invention of News: How the World Came to Know about Itself* (New Haven: Yale University Press, 2014), 6–7.

29. Hans-Jürgen Lüsebrink, *La conquête de l'espace public colonial* (Frankfurt am Main: IKO Verlag für Interkulturelle Kommunikation, 2003), 29.

30. Richard Bjornson, *The African Quest for Freedom and Identity: Cameroonian Writing and the National Experience* (Bloomington: Indiana University Press, 1991), 23; Emma Hunter "'Our Common Humanity': Print, Power and the Colonial Press in Interwar Tanganyika and French Cameroun," *Journal of Global History* 7, no. 2 (2012): 283.

31. Philip C. Sadgrove, "The Press, Engine of a Mini-renaissance in Zanzibar (1860–1920)," in *History of Printing and Publishing in the Languages and Countries of the Middle East*, ed. Philip Sadgrove (Oxford: Oxford University Press, 2005), 153 and 156–57.

32. Sadgrove, "The Press," 173.

33. See Barbara A. Yates, "Knowledge Brokers: Books and Publishers in Early Colonial Zaire," *History in Africa* 14 (1987), 328, on attempts by missionaries in the Congo to keep a monopoly of print.

34. James F. Scotton, "The First African Press in East Africa: Protest and Nationalism in Uganda in the 1920s," *International Journal of African Historical Studies* 6, no. 2 (1973): 211–28.

35. John Lonsdale, "'Listen While I Read': Patriotic Christianity among the Young Kikuyu," in *Christianity and Social Change in Africa: Essays in Honor of J.D.Y. Peel*, ed. Toyin Falola (Durham, NC: Carolina Academic Press, 2005), 563–94.

36. Switzer, "Introduction," 26.

37. Newell, *Power to Name*, 31.

38. July, *Modern African Thought*, 345, 367.

39. Lüsebrink, *La conquête de l'espace*, 30.

40. Nnamdi Azikiwe, *My Odyssey: An Autobiography* (New York: Praeger, 1970), 291.

41. Azikiwe, *My Odyssey*, 310–11.

42. Fay Gadsden, "The African Press in Kenya," *Journal of African History* 21, no. 4 (1980): 515–35, 527.

43. Gadsden, "African Press in Kenya," 526.

44. Azikiwe, *My Odyssey*, 303; Fred Omu, *Press and Politics in Nigeria, 1880–1937* (London: Longman, 1978), 239.

45. Newell, *Power to Name*; Philip Zachernuk, *Colonial Subjects: An African Intelligentsia and Atlantic Ideas* (Charlottesville: University Press of Virginia, 2000).

46. Even so, abolitionist rhetoric had purchase in East Africa's politics. See Derek R. Peterson, ed., *Abolitionism and Imperialism in Britain, Africa and the Atlantic* (Athens: Ohio University Press, 2011).

47. Scotton, "First African Press."

48. Derek R. Peterson, "The Politics of Transcendence in Colonial Uganda," in *Past and Present* 230, no. 1 (2016): 197–225.

49. Lonsdale, "Listen While I Read."

50. Gadsden, "African Press in Kenya."

51. Frederick Cooper, *Citizenship between Empire and Nation: Remaking France and French Africa, 1945–1960* (Princeton, NJ: Princeton University Press, 2014).

52. Michael C. Lambert, "Violence and the War of Words: Ethnicity vs. Nationalism in the Casamance," *Africa* 68, no. 4 (1998): 585–602; Pierre Englebert, "Compliance and Defiance to National Integration in Barotseland and Casamance," *Africa Spectrum* 40, no. 1 (2005): 29–59.

53. Kwame Nkrumah, *I Speak of Freedom: A Statement of African Ideology* (Westport, CT: Greenwood Press, 1976), 168.

54. Argued most influentially in John Lonsdale, "The Moral Economy of Mau Mau: Wealth, Poverty, and Civic Virtue in Kikuyu Political Thought," in John Lonsdale and Bruce Berman, *Unhappy Valley: Conflict in Kenya and Africa* (London: James Currey, 1992); and Steven Feierman, *Peasant Intellectuals: Anthropology and History in Tanzania* (Madison: University of Wisconsin Press, 1990). Latterly, see Holly Hanson, *Landed Obligation: The Practice of Power in Buganda* (Portsmouth, NH: Heinemann, 2003); Derek R. Peterson, *Ethnic Patriotism and the East African Revival: A History of Dissent* (Cambridge: Cambridge University Press, 2012); Neil Kodesh, *Beyond the Royal Gaze: Clanship and Public Healing in Buganda* (Charlottesville: University of Virginia Press, 2010); and Emma Hunter, *Political Thought and the Public Sphere in East Africa: Freedom, Democracy and Citizenship in the Era of Decolonization* (Cambridge: Cambridge University Press, 2015).

55. Isabel Hofmeyr, "Towards a History of the Book and Literary Culture in Africa," in *Literary Cultures and the Material Book*, ed. Simon Eliot, Andrew Nash, and Ian Willison (London: British Library Publishing, 2007), 128.

56. Lamin Sanneh, *Translating the Message: The Missionary Impact on Culture* (Maryknoll, NY: Orbis, 1989).

57. Derek R. Peterson, *Creative Writing: Translation, Bookkeeping, and the Work of Imagination in Colonial Kenya* (Portsmouth: Heinemann, 2004); Landau, *Popular Politics*, chap. 3.

58. D. J. Jones and S. T. Plaatje, *A Sechuana Reader in International Phonetic Orthography* (London: University of London Press, 1916).

59. Collected in Solomon Plaatje, "Uniform Spelling," *English in Africa* 3, no. 2 (1976): 45–50.

60. Cambridge University, Centre of African Studies, Mulira papers, Gen. 1/2: Eridadi Mulira's autobiography (typescript, n.d.).

61. E. O. Ashton, E. M. K. Mulira, E. G. M. Ndawula, and A. A. Tucker, *A Luganda Grammar* (London: Longmans, Green, 1954); A. L. Kitching, G. R. Blackledge, and E. M. K. Mulira, *A Luganda-English and English-Luganda Dictionary* (London: Society for Promoting Christian Knowledge, 1952).

62. KNA PC Nyanza 3/6/129: Benaiah Ohanga, "The Nilotic Peoples of Central Africa," 1 May 1946.

63. KNA DC Kisumu 1/28/8: Ohanga to General Secretary, Luo Union, 22 October 1946.

64. KNA PC Nyanza 3/6/129: Luo Language Committee to all Heads of Department, 18 July 1947.

65. Cambridge University, Centre of African Studies, Mulira papers, Gen. 1/2: Eridadi Mulira's autobiography (typescript, n.d.).

66. KNA DC Kisumu 1/28/8: Ohanga to General Secretary, Luo Union, 22 October 1946.

67. *Ramogi*, 1 September 1949, reported in KNA DC Kisumu 1/28/56: Kenya Information Office, "Summary of Opinion on African Affairs Expressed in the Kenya Press," 1 to 15 September 1949.

68. TNA AB/1269: "Report of the Committee for the Standardization of the Swahili Language," 10 October 1925.

69. TNA AB/1269: Editor, *Mambo Leo* to Director of Education, "Report of the Committee for the Standardisation of the Swahili Language," 15 March 1926, f. 128.

70. KNA DC/Machakos 10B/13/1: "One from Karura" to the editor, *Mwigwithania* 1, no. 4 (1929).

71. Z. Munaba, "Bicycle Registration," *Ddobozi*, 10 July 1952; "Lorries Are

Dangerously Driven," *Ddobozi*, 15 October 1952; "Theft by Government Servant," *Ddobozi*, 1 May 1953, all in UNA Office of the President, Confidential papers, box 24, file S.5190.

72. *Ddobozi* (7 November 1952), in UNA Office of the President, Confidential papers, box 24, file S.5190.

73. BNA FCO 141/18264: Commissioner of Police to Chief Secretary, 8 December 1955.

74. BNA FCO 141/18264: Special Branch to Chief Secretary, 16 November 1955.

75. Described in BNA FCO 141/18265: Special Branch to Chief Secretary, 6 January 1956.

76. BNA FCO 141/18264: Commissioner of Police to Chief Secretary, 8 December 1955.

77. BNA FCO 141/18136: Assistant Commissioner of Police, Report, 30 March 1954.

78. UNA "C series," box 15, file C.1329: Daudi Cwa to P. C. Buganda, 1 October 1930.

79. A. I. Richards, "Authority Patterns in Traditional Buganda," in *The King's Men: Leadership and Status in Buganda on the Eve of Independence*, ed. L. Fallers (London: Oxford University Press, 1964), 256–93.

80. *The Complete Self-Educator* (London: Odhams Press, 1939); Robert Baden-Powell, *Rovering to Success: A Book of Life Sport for Young Men* (London: Herbert Jenkins, 1922).

81. USNA RG 84, Consulate General, Kampala, General Records, 1956–61, box 1, file 350.1: L. Fallers, "The Uganda National Congress," n.d. (but 1956).

82. Peter Limb, ed., *The People's Paper: A Centenary History and Anthology of Abantu-Batho* (Johannesburg: Wits University Press, 2012).

83. "Even the Young Are Nationalists," *Uganda Empya*, 19 May 1959.

84. UNA Office of the President Confidential papers, box 4, file S.3190: Governor to W. Gorell Barnes, 8 May 1954.

85. Jinja District Archives file M/16/3: E. Twining, Stage Plays and Cinematograph Exhibitions Licensing Board, to all members, 20 April 1933.

86. UNA Chief Secretary's Office papers, box 62, file 11,507: Information Officer, Kampala, to Chief Secretary Entebbe, 12 July 1941.

87. UNA Chief Secretary's Office papers, box 62, file 11,507: Information Officer, Kampala to Commissioner on Special Duty, n.d. (but 1945).

88. Lisa McNee, "Togo," in *Censorship: A World Encyclopedia*, ed. Derek Jones (London: Fitzroy Dearborn Publishers, 2001) vol. 4, 2433. See, for example, AOM FM/1AFFPOL/979: "Journaux Interdits," *La Gazette du Cameroun*, 15 February 1934.

89. UNA Office of the President Confidential papers, box 4, file S.3190: Governor to W. Goreel Barnes, 8 May 1954.

90. Lüsebrink, *La conquête de l'espace*, 36

91. Newell, *Power to Name*, chap. 3.

92. Denis Cryle, "A British Legacy? The Empire Press Union and Freedom of the Press, 1940–1950," *History of Intellectual Culture* 4, no. 1 (2004): 1–13.

93. Penny Von Eschen, *Race against Empire: Black Americans and Anticolonialism, 1937–1957* (Ithaca: Cornell University Press, 1997).

94. UNA "C Series," box 10, file C.671: W. E. Owen to Chief Secretary, Entebbe, 24 October 1922.

95. University of Massachusetts Amherst, W. E. B. DuBois Papers: Z. K. Sentongo to DuBois, 12 April 1922.

96. UNA "C series," box 13, file C.1002: Commissioner of Police to Chief Secretary, Entebbe, 18 January 1927.

97. See Harry Thuku, *Harry Thuku: An Autobiography* (Nairobi: Oxford University Press, 1970).

98. UNA "C series," box 13, file C.1002: Spartas to Thuku, 20 June 1925.

99. Described in F. B. Welbourn, *East African Rebels: A Study of Some Independent Churches* (London: SCM Press, 1961), chap. 5.

100. "Serekali ya Kiingereza Imekataza Watu Waona Cinema ya Askari Kiafrika," *Habari*, 25 July 1946. Referred to in KNA CS 2/8/125: Acting Information Office to Chief Secretary, 12 August 1946. Thanks to Emma Park for this reference.

101. KNA AB 11/59: Jos Dames, "Distribution of Periodicals," 1 July to 30 September 1957.

102. Government of Kenya, *Department of Information Annual Report, 1955* (Nairobi: Government Printer, 1956), 1. See Myles Osborne, "'The Rooting Out of Mau Mau from the Minds of the Kikuyu Is a Formidable Task': Propaganda and the Mau Mau War," *Journal of African History* 56, no. 1 (2015): 77–97.

103. KNA AB 11/59: Officer in charge of Community Development, Nyeri District, to Secretary, Ministry of Community Development, 2 July 1957.

104. Tom Askwith, *From Mau Mau to Harambee*, ed. Joanna Lewis (Cambridge: Cambridge African Studies Centre, 1995), 101.

105. Imperial and Commonwealth Museum, James Breckenridge Papers, file with no cover: Letter from J. Maruga and David Kimenyithia, in *Atīrīrī* 2, no. 3 (19 October 1957).

106. Gakaara also practiced ethnography. See Derek R. Peterson, "Ethnography and Cultural Innovation in Mau Mau Detention Camps: Gakaara wa Wanjau's *Mīhīrīga ya Agīkūyū*," in Burton and Hofmeyr, *Ten Books That Shaped the British Empire*, 216–37.

107. Stephanie Newell, *Marita: Or the Folly of Love: A Novel by A. Native* (Leiden: Brill, 2002).

108. Lüsebrink puts the figure at 95 percent. *La conquête de l'espace*, 12; Bjornson, *African Quest*, 23–30.

109. Nhlanhla P. Maake, "A Survey of Trends in the Development of African Literatures in South Africa: With Specific Reference to Written Southern Sotho Literature, c. 1900–1970s," *African Languages and Cultures* 5 (1992): 157–88.

110. Bernth Lindfors, *Early East African Writers and Publishers* (Trenton, NJ: Africa World Press, 2011), chap. 1.

111. Sol Plaatje, *Native Life in South Africa, Before and Since the European War and the Boer Rebellion* (London: P.S. King, 1916).

112. Sol Plaatje, *Sechuana Proverbs with Literal Translations and Their European Equivalents* (London: Kegan Paul, 1916).

113. The notebook is kept in the library of the School of Oriental and African Studies, entitled "Notebook containing miscellaneous notes, press cuttings and part of an early draft of Mhudi," n.d.

114. Quoted in Tim Couzens and Stephen Gray, "Printers' and Other Devils: The Texts of Sol T. Plaatje's 'Mhudi,'" *Research in African Literatures* 9, no. 2 (1978): 198–215.

115. Von Eschen, *Race against Empire*.

116. Switzer, "Introduction," 42; see R. Neville Choonoo, "The Sophiatown Generation: Black Literary Journalism during the 1950s," in Switzer, *South Africa's Alternative Press*, 252–65.

117. The subject of Mokoena's *Magema Fuze: The Making of a* Kholwa *Intellectual* (Pietermaritzburg: University of KwaZulu-Natal Press, 2011).

118. Quoted in James Brennan, "Communications and Media in African History," in *Oxford Handbook of Modern African History*, ed. John Parker and Richard Reid (Oxford: Oxford University Press, 2013), 492–509, 497.

119. Jomo Kenyatta, "An Address to the International Press Institute Conference in Nairobi in 1968," *Africa Today* 16, no. 3 (1969): 5–6.

120. Daniel Nelson, "Newspapers in Uganda," *Transition* 35 (1968), 29–33.

121. USNA RG 59, Central Foreign Policy Files, 1967–69, box 2558, file POL Uganda: Kampala Embassy to State Department, 21 January 1968.

122. Derek R. Peterson and Edgar Taylor, "Rethinking the State in Idi Amin's Uganda: The Politics of Exhortation," *Journal of Eastern African Studies* 7, no. 1 (2013): 58–82.

123. Kabale District Archives NW/CM Box 11, "Newspaper and Press Relations" file: Henry Kyemba to all District Commissioners, 24 May 1971.

124. Andrew Ivaska, *Cultured States: Youth, Gender, and Modern Style in 1960s Dar es Salaam* (Durham, NC: Duke University Press, 2011), 28–34.

125. William A. Hachten, *Muffled Drums: The News Media in Africa* (Ames: Iowa State University Press, 1971), 169.

126. An argument made first in Fred Cooper, *Decolonization and African Society: The Labor Question in British and French Africa* (Cambridge: Cambridge University Press, 1996).

127. No author, "Kamati ya Kusahihisha Kiswahili," *Ngurumo*, 7 January 1965.

128. See, for example, letter from J. S. Sitebo, "Fadhaa na Fazaa," *Ngurumo*, 2 January 1965; letter from Mubarak A. D. Mafazi, "Fadhaa na Fazaa"; letter from Mathias E. Mnyampala, "Fadhaa na Fazaa," *Ngurumo*, 8 January 1965.

PART I

African Newspaper Networks

CHAPTER 2

Transatlantic Passages

Black Identity Construction in West African and West Indian Newspapers, 1935–1950

LESLIE JAMES

Take up the Black Man's Burden
Ye cannot stoop to less.
Will not your fraud of "freedom"
Still cloak your greediness?
But, by the gods ye worship,
And by the deeds ye do,
These silent, sullen peoples,
Shall weigh your gods and you.[1]

In August 1949, in the bottom corner of the fifth page and adjacent to a question-and-answer section called "Cocoa Farmers' Corner," readers of the Gold Coast's *Ashanti Pioneer* discovered the defiant words of West Indian activist and intellectual Hubert H. Harrison's poem, "The Black Man's Burden." Of the many replies to Rudyard Kipling's infamous entreaty for American empire, "The White Man's Burden" (1899), Harrison's poem was originally published in New York in 1920 as an epilogue to *When Africa Awakes*, a book that announced the new militancy of the Harlem Renaissance's New Negro.

The seemingly inconsequential appearance of this poem at the back of a Gold Coast newspaper almost three decades after its original publication, however, belies its multiplex significance. Harrison's rejoinder embodied a resolute call to solidarity among the millions of black people oppressed across the globe. The poem appeared in the *Ashanti Pioneer* one year after major rioting in Accra and less than two months after future prime minister Kwame Nkrumah announced the formation of his Convention People's Party, which would lead the British colony's Positive Action campaign for independence. And, importantly, these lyrics arrived on the pages of the *Ashanti Pioneer* via its London correspondent, the Trinidadian Pan-Africanist George Padmore. Beyond the impassioned beauty of the poem itself, then, it is the tool of borrowing, the medium through which it was conveyed, and the routes and individuals through which it traveled to arrive on the printed page across the Atlantic, that augmented the poem's meaning. Written by a West Indian in New York City, published in a book that called up the diasporic homeland in its title, and sent back to Africa through the English metropole by another West Indian activist, the printing of this poem exemplified the operative use of daily newspapers as an expression of what Brent Hayes Edwards has termed a "black international."[2]

The *Ashanti Pioneer* began its daily print run in the late 1930s, as one instance of a corps of English-language newspapers that surfaced at the same moment across West Africa. These newspapers benefited not only from the established resources and journalism of the burgeoning black American press, but also from papers emerging out of a militant labor movement in the Caribbean. Indeed, these newspapers were sometimes in dialogue. How this dialogue was facilitated, and what its implications for the forging of political community were, is the subject of this chapter. As the example of Harrison's reprinted poem suggests, the logistical and material ways that African newspapers were compiled bears as much weight as the content itself. The international networks and the conceptual parameters that operated in the background to facilitate the development of local newspapers moves to the foreground when we consider the transnational groupings that newspapers helped to articulate. The techniques of placement on the page, of textual borrowing, and the nodes through which information moved imbued the newspaper's content with multiple meanings. One of the results of these techniques, this chapter argues, was to offer readers the possibility of viewing themselves not only as part of a local or national community, but as part of a wider collective based on similar racial and colonial experiences. However, by emphasizing the methods and tools that were harnessed—often against the divergent and fractious messages produced in a press that included authors with various political aims and perspectives—the chapter accents the contingent or, rather, dependent aspects of these collectives. Against the vagaries of colonial censorship and in the context of the scant financial resources these newspaper proprietors could employ, these papers relied on personal connections between editors and journalists, and the creative application of clipping and borrowing, in order to present readers with deterritorialized affinities.

THE PRESS AND THE FORGING OF AN INTERNATIONAL PUBLIC SPHERE

The parallel development, in the first decades of the twentieth century, of newspapers owned and operated by people of color in Africa, the Americas, the Caribbean, and Europe has generated a wealth of evidence and interest supporting both Benedict Anderson's arguments about the solidification of national identities through print, and Edwards's argument that print media allowed "transnational groupings" to articulate themselves into "collectives and collaborations in a manner that was otherwise impossible."[3] Penny Von Eschen has shown that the creative use of new technologies by the black American press, particularly after the Second World War, unified intellectuals and activists in Africa, Britain, and the United States and drew black American struggles into a wider anticolonial discourse.[4] Indeed, there is now a substantial body of work that shows how black politics in the United States was conceived not only in solidarity with anticolonial struggles but, rather, as a component part—where black Americans also lived under a form of colonial subjugation.[5] Anticolonialism and antiracism, therefore, existed on a similar plane; and newspapers are now recognized as a prime vehicle through which these "deterritorialized" forms of affinity were forged.[6] Race-specific discourses that fed predominantly upon identification as a racially oppressed class of "blacks" or "Asians," or adhered to a more diffuse color-conscious cosmopolitanism, often existed in the print public sphere alongside imagined communities unified through colonialism as common denominator.[7] These newspapers simultaneously articulated both more restrictive, anticolonial nationalist identities and more diffuse, conceptual forms of identification; as Lara Putnam argues, they "fed new internationalisms as well as new nationalisms."[8]

The newspapers that are the subject of this chapter, which appeared across the British Atlantic in the 1930s—from the *African Morning Post* (1935) and the *Ashanti Pioneer* (1939) in the Gold Coast, to Nnamdi Azikiwe's Nigerian serials, including Lagos's *West African Pilot* (1937), to Jamaica's *Public Opinion* (1937), and to Trinidad's *The People* (1933)—were one constitutive part of this "burgeoning, multi-sited black press."[9] The fact that each of these papers is regarded by historians as having played a prominent role in articulating its colony's nationalist demands during the era that led to political independence, means that how they also cultivated an international scope of vision is of particular interest. These newspapers built upon a number of common practices and traditions passed down by earlier generations of editors and journalists across the black world, but also faced new challenges wrought by a worldwide depression, interwar restrictions on migration, and the further narrowing of colonial press laws and censorship that emerged in the context of the Second World War, which all served to narrow the field in which newspapers operated.

By the early twentieth century, educated leaders in Africa, the Caribbean, and the United States were adeptly employing newspapers and periodicals as a discursive space from which they could comment on their political and social position. In the United States, the writers and activists of the Harlem Renaissance who harnessed the newspaper as a political tool, built upon the nineteenth-century legacy of Frederick Douglass's abolitionist journalism, W. E. B. DuBois's application of periodicals and newspapers to his political endeavors, and the investigative journalism of antilynching campaigner Ida B. Wells, to name a few.[10] When Marcus Garvey's *Negro World* appeared not only on the streets of New York, from which it was printed, but also across pool halls in the American South, the fruit plantation barracks in Central America, and the mines of Kimberley in South Africa, it did so as the most well known and internationalist of a number of newspapers spawned from the radical political organizations emerging in the 1920s United States.[11] These newspapers with a worldwide reach furnished an additional arm to a scaffold of popular local newspapers in each specific locale. Several of these American newspapers were the work of Caribbean migrants who did not completely settle in the United States but retained ties and moved between their communities in America and the West Indies. These included students, political activists, and migrant workers who set up and contributed their letters, opinion pieces, and news items to papers throughout the circum-Caribbean.[12]

Newspapers in the British Caribbean had served, since at least the latter nineteenth century, as the means for the educated population of color to enter the public sphere, absent access to official political arenas.[13] During the interwar period, Caribbean newspapers began to take on the issues of workers and to shift from a largely middle class constituency. Before *The People* became a prominent voice of Trinidad's labor movement and a site for the expression of revolt during the riots and rebellion that swelled across the Caribbean in the second half of the 1930s, literary magazines like the *Beacon*, which printed some of the work of those who would also write for *The People*, delved into the island's political debates.[14] *The People* was edited at various times by political figures like Ralph Mentor and Tubal Uriah Butler, both union leaders with contentious and fluctuating affiliations within Trinidad's political scene between the 1930s and the 1950s. In its earliest days, before Jamaica's *Public Opinion* became an organ for Norman Manley and the People's National Party, Ralph Dalleo argues, this Jamaican newspaper most closely resembled Trinidad's *Beacon*.[15] Launched in 1937 by O. T. Fairclough, Frank Hill, and H. P. Jacobs, *Public Opinion* featured a regular column after 1943 by Wilfrid A. Domingo, a political firebrand who served as one of the earliest editors of Garvey's *Negro World* from New York but also floated back and forth to his native Jamaica.[16]

Further back, in the first two decades of the twentieth century, English-language newspapers were set up in places like Panama and Costa Rica thanks to the relatively high literacy rates of British West Indian migrant workers. These connected workers and their families to the Caribbean islands and to migrant communities in the United States. Those who read these English-language newspapers in Central America also corresponded with—and sometimes held subscriptions for—black American newspapers like the *Chicago Defender* and the *Pittsburgh Courier*. The latter held large circulation figures in the United States but also some international subscriptions, and their pages included regular and relatively prominent international news coverage.

While these newspapers from the United States are the most well known and recognized on the print circuit with an international edge, we know that Africa was not divorced from these developments. In South Africa in the first decades of the twentieth century, both Sol Plaatje and Clements Kadalie founded and edited several newspapers during their lifetime as a platform for their activism. These efforts could also involve reprinting articles from black American newspapers.[17] In early twentieth-century West Africa, African newspaper editors encouraged new readerships and young writers from the newly educated constituents of the colonies. They also began to access services such as Reuters that allowed editors to print international news and thus cultivate connections between geographically dispersed imperial subjects.[18] But it was in the 1930s that the West African press truly blossomed.[19] This was caused by access to new technologies of mass production, combined with the significant boon to circulation figures produced by the Italo-Abyssinian crisis. Indeed, it has been estimated that between 1934 and 1936, as the crisis in Ethiopia developed, some Gold Coast and Nigerian newspapers doubled their circulation.[20] And it was during these same years that a young Nnamdi Azikiwe, future inaugural president of Nigeria, served as editor of the *African Morning Post* in Accra and increased sales of the daily from two thousand in 1934 to ten thousand by 1936.[21]

Yet at the same time as African and Caribbean newspapers found new audiences and forged a more vocally radical anticolonial politics, they faced new restrictions that hindered their capacity to connect their readers to a wider political community. In May 1936 Azikiwe was charged with sedition on four counts and briefly jailed. Following his discharge after a successful appeal, Azikiwe returned to his native Nigeria to start the *West African Pilot* in 1937 and form Zik's Press Limited. Seditious Publications Ordinances—passed in London in the early 1920s—plagued the editors of newspapers in British colonies. Wartime censorship between 1939 and 1945 did not help matters. When Wilfrid A. Domingo attempted to return to Jamaica in 1942, he was arrested before he even disembarked, and found himself imprisoned by the governor for, among other things, promoting "feelings of color prejudice and racial animosity."[22] In 1944 Roger Mais, one of Jamaica's most distinguished poets and a regular contributor of prose and poetry to *Public Opinion*, also found himself imprisoned for six months (he served four months before release) for endangering "the efficient prosecution of the war" for his article "Now We Know."[23] In 1941 Kay Donnellan, editor of Trinidad's labor newspaper, the *Vanguard*, was detained by the governor under Colonial Defence Regulations, with tragic consequences. Although the circumstances are not entirely clear, it seems that after two months of internment Donnellan attempted an escape: her body was found the next morning, drowned in the Gulf of Paria.[24]

Many of the newspapers founded by Africans and those of African descent in the colonies operated on a shoestring budget and could be crippled by legal charges. Meager finances also meant that, unlike some of the newspapers of the early twentieth century in the Gold Coast, Sierra Leone, and Nigeria tracked by Newell, many of the English-language papers forged in the 1930s could not afford subscriptions to Reuters. Only in October 1944 was the *West African Pilot* able to acquire a license, after which the paper announced that, as the agent for British West Africa, it would be happy to facilitate access to Reuters for other newspapers.[25] However, even this access was limited by the whims of the colonial administration. Renewal of the license was refused in 1946 under the colonial administration's powers exercised through the

Wireless Telegraphy Ordinance. The license was only renewed again at the end of 1947.[26] In that same year and with the Colonial Office's encouragement, the Mirror Group of London acquired a paper in Nigeria, subsequently extending operations to the Gold Coast and Sierra Leone with the explicit intention of challenging the growth of African-owned newspapers.[27] Finally, it was not just the production of the printed word and its movement that was hindered by the mid-1930s, when these newspapers came of age, but also the movement of people. Racially based immigration laws in the United States and later in Central and South America slowly plugged much of the migration between the Caribbean and the Americas that had fostered newspaper networks in the 1910s and 1920s.[28] The newspapers in West Africa and the West Indies that would articulate the demand for self-determination in the decade before independence thus emerged in a particular era that was ripe for internationalist connections, but also limited in how these collaborations could be facilitated.

A LINCHPIN FOR TRANSATLANTIC PRINT NETWORKS: THE JOURNALISM OF GEORGE PADMORE

How, then, did newspapers actually present information that made it possible for colonial and racial fraternities to be imagined? While certainly not the only device, one of the most useful tools at their disposal emerged in the form of one metropolitan journalist: George Padmore. Padmore's network spanned all the corners of the anglophone Atlantic. Based in London between 1935 and 1957, Padmore produced articles that appeared in various organs of the British Left throughout the 1930s and 1940s. He was a war correspondent for the *Chicago Defender* and the *Pittsburgh Courier*. After meeting Azikiwe in the United States briefly when they both studied there, and after cultivating a relationship with several West African editors when he worked for the Communist International between 1930 and 1933, he produced articles for the *African Morning Post* during and after Azikiwe's editorship.[29] Despite never returning to his native Trinidad after he left in 1924 at the age of twenty-one, he retained political connections with activists and intellectuals in the West Indies, becoming the "London Correspondent" who informed West Indian workers of the reaction in London to their strikes and protests in the second half of the 1930s.[30] Not only were his articles some of the first to consistently report on international events in these young newspapers, but by the late

1940s his celebrity became a marketable commodity with which newspapers could sell front-page headlines that drew local struggles into the global arena.

The total number of articles Padmore produced for African American newspapers between 1934 and 1949 in the pages of the *Amsterdam News*, the *Baltimore Afro-American*, the *Pittsburgh Courier*, but overwhelmingly the *Chicago Defender*, reached over a thousand. The high number of articles in black American newspapers is largely a result of his job with the *Chicago Defender* during the war and the large number of short reporter-style articles (as opposed to editorial analysis and comment) in these years. Tailoring his articles to his audience, many of these articles during the war reported on the activities of black American and colonial troops. During and after the war, any form of the color bar in Europe, the colonies, or especially South Africa figured prominently in Padmore's writing.

From 1935 to 1939 Padmore wrote 86 articles for the *African Morning Post*. By the late 1940s his name became the headlining draw in several West African newspapers, resulting in 182 articles for the *Ashanti Pioneer* in the three years from 1947 and 1950 and a remarkable 508 articles between 1937 and 1950 for the *West African Pilot*. Across the Atlantic, Padmore's articles appeared on occasion in the *Barbados Advocate* and the *Bermuda Recorder*. Between 1943 and 1952 he wrote 73 articles for Jamaica's *Public Opinion*. And from 1936 to 1954 he produced a combined total of 207 articles for Trinidad labor newspapers *The People*, the *Vanguard*, and the *Clarion*.

In almost all these newspapers, Padmore was identified at one time or another as the paper's "London Correspondent." This was more than just a moniker: Padmore's journalism embodied the principle behind it. One of the primary roles he assumed for himself was to provide regular updates to those living in British colonies in Africa and the West Indies about how colonial affairs were being interpreted and debated in Britain. Many of these "articles" were either summaries of colonial questions in the House of Commons (as told from his regular "perch" in the gallery during question time), or reviews of "what's happening" in the British press. With titles like "British Politics Today: Review of Political Parties," "Colonial Questions in Parliament," "British Press Spotlight on Colonies," or "Large Amount of Space Devoted to Problems in Colonies by British Press," Padmore often organized the spectrum of the latest British political opinion, from the far right to the far left, for his readers.[31] Many of his articles went so far as to be near-verbatim reports from Hansard's parliamentary proceedings or clippings of British newspaper articles with a paragraph introduction by Padmore himself. However, as we shall see in the last section of this chapter, the cumulative impact of this clipping and plagiarism, when read against the context of their new readership in the colonies, was to inscribe new meaning and new life into these texts.

For Padmore, journalism served as a political tool in two respects: as a news bulletin that could keep people in the colonies aware of activities elsewhere, and as a conduit for his own intellectual arguments. The political activities of Padmore and the various organizations he affiliated with in London often featured in his journalism. This was Padmore's way of making people in the colonies aware of the efforts of Africans and those of African descent in Great Britain on their behalf—it was a way of fostering unity. As his friend Peter Abrahams described it, his journalism was an incredible "industry" Padmore created in order to "inform the whole colonial world" from London.[32] In the late 1930s, this often stemmed from the Italo-Abyssinian crisis and, more generally, from the debates raging in Europe about the rise of fascism. In September 1937, Padmore's Trinidadian readers learned of a rally organized by Padmore's International African Service Bureau, and read verbatim the resolutions produced from the meeting. Barbadian seaman Chris Jones spoke about those killed and injured in a strike against starvation conditions in Bridgetown; and Sierra Leonean I. T. A. Wallace-Johnson described the laws against sedition in British Africa that resulted in the deportation of Africans who criticized Government rule.[33] "When the British people talk of Fascism," Wallace-Johnson declared, "they should look not to Germany and Italy, but within their own Empire, where their ruling classes have filched the lands from the natives whom they have forced to work for them in wretched conditions and for less than starvation wages; where they have turned the whole land into one large concentration camp."[34] This article thus routed information about the conditions in Africa and the West Indies through London, but it also echoed one of the main arguments Padmore himself was articulating at the time about colonial fascism. Indeed, Padmore's books and journalism often worked in tandem to articulate his ideological challenge against the colonial state. In his book *How Britain Rules Africa* (1936) but also in articles like "Colonial Fascism in the West Indies" that appeared in *The People*, Padmore vociferously argued that colonial rule, in Africa and the West Indies alike, was itself fascist.

And his arguments did not fall on deaf ears. His efforts translated, already by the late 1930s, into Padmore's presence in these newspapers not just as a journalist himself, but also by way of responses to his intellectual arguments. In May 1938 Trinidad's *The People* reprinted an article by Ann Headford, from

Wallace-Johnson's *African Sentinel*. Headford used Padmore's Comintern-published book, *The Life and Struggles of Negro Toilers* (1931), to highlight starvation in the West Indies, concluding that "the conditions of the Trinidad women are characteristic of conditions of working-class women all the world over."[35] In a 1938 review of Padmore's twelve-page pamphlet "Hands Off the Protectorates," the literary editor of *The People* described Padmore's work as "an exposure of the shocking conditions to which our brothers in South Africa are subjected." The reviewer made the link between Padmore's description of southern Africa and prior articles in *The People* about discrimination in the Rhodesias, observing that the horrible conditions readers were hearing about "exist in an Empire whose rulers are always boasting what a great privilege it is to the colored man to be a member of it." This editor concluded: "Well might Mr. Padmore describe [the British Empire] as 'fascist aggression within the Empire.'"[36] Padmore's journalism thus served to affect the identification of a community connected through imperial rule, and drawn closer through a consciousness not only of imperial oppression but of a singular intellectual argument *against* that rule.

WHAT'S IN A NAME? CONNECTING THE CONTENT OF NEWS ACROSS THE ANGLOPHONE ATLANTIC

The global war between 1939 and 1945 certainly disrupted the transatlantic connections as well as the forceful colonial critiques attempted in newspapers in the late 1930s. Censorship meant that newspapers in these years largely reported on the progress of the war and the colonial contribution to the war effort. However, by the end of 1944 and early 1945 articles began to emerge again, particularly in West African newspapers, which compelled readers to connect their daily news to events in other British colonies. By the end of the war, Padmore was a well-known and respected correspondent, judging by the articles and comments that mention his work. His headshot in Trinidad's *Vanguard* was accompanied by a designation of Padmore as the "Greatest Negro in London."[37] In 1946 a reader named J. A. Abidemi informed the *West African Pilot* that he always prioritized Padmore's articles, which he declared had "helped to translate the more the popular motto" of the newspaper—"Show the Light and the People Will Find the Way"—in "the real sense of it."[38] For this reader, then, Padmore's journalism provided not only information, but agency to discern and discover his own political awakening. Drawing on

Padmore's name, in the 1940s editors increasingly placed his articles as the front-page headline and often juxtaposed news items on the printed page in a manner that effected multiple meanings read across individual stories. When stories were read side by side, colonial development was redefined as colonial exploitation; messages of constitutional reform, freedom, and democracy earned new connotations as stymied and insubstantial political progress.

What, then, could readers discover in Padmore's signature? One key intention of his journalism was to convey a sense of anticolonial momentum. Although not always successful, Padmore's articles were intended to counter what Newell has rightly identified as a tendency toward "colonial competition" in African newspapers: in this case, the inclination of some to stack advances in one colony begrudgingly against their own.[39] In this respect, for example, the *Pilot*'s articles tended toward resentment of the establishment of the University of the West Indies, and of funds announced under the Colonial Development and Welfare Act for West Indian schools and teachers.[40] Countering this, Padmore made the case that advances in one colony set a precedent for others and, conversely, that decline could be brought to bear elsewhere. And resistance to colonial rule could be infectious. Thus any advance toward, or demand for, constitutional change in the West Indies was reported in West Africa, and vice versa. News of the constitutional reforms enacted in Trinidad and Jamaica in 1941 appeared on the front page of several issues of the *West African Pilot* in 1941. One article in the *Pilot* quoted *The People*'s argument that the supposed "blessing" of the recent constitutional change, which increased electoral representation on the Legislative Council, was "neither progress nor reform."[41] Straddling all these months of news coverage in 1941 about West Indian constitutional change in the *Pilot* was the reprinting of a speech by Azikiwe in forty-five sequential instalments entitled "The Legislative Council of Nigeria." The *Pilot*'s audience thus read debates about constitutional change in their own colony alongside those across the Atlantic in Jamaica and Trinidad, and Padmore's article connected the *Pilot* to *The People*. Similarly, in 1944 Jamaican readers learned of the demands for self-government and read the manifesto of West African editors who made their case during a tour of Britain under the auspices of the British Council.[42] And in 1949 Padmore provided his Nigerian and Gold Coast readers with comparisons of constitutions in the Gold Coast and in Trinidad.[43]

If similar demands for constitutional change were one protest, then the swelling wave of strikes and protests in the latter half of the 1940s was another. In July 1945, readers of *Public Opinion* in Jamaica learned of the general strike in Nigeria and the brief closure of the Zik Press; and in 1946 readers of the *Pilot* took home a lesson about the need for unity from the strike of Jamaica's railway workers.[44] "Sparks of revolt and unrest," Padmore declared in the *Chicago Defender*, were "lighting up the 'Dark Continent'" as thousands of railway workers staged a general strike in Rhodesia and workers in Dakar went on strike, affecting all essential services.[45] Even workers in the Belgian Congo were striking for better wages and working conditions.[46]

But one of the most consistent issues Padmore reported upon, and perhaps the best example of how his articles targeted the context of specific audiences, was in articles about resource extraction and industry in the colonies. Articles related to the economy of colonial resources provide some of the clearest examples of how the reading of text outside the margin of each column itself, and across the printed page, instilled alternative meanings beyond the content of a specific article. Articles primarily based upon direct quotation and containing no argument or opinion acquired polemic when juxtaposed with other articles on the page. In July 1938, *The People* presented two articles sent by "Our London Correspondent" side by side. The first was the direct quotation of a speech made in Oxford by the colonial secretary, Malcolm MacDonald, in which he insisted that "the main purpose of the British Empire is the gradual spread of freedom" even "among the most backward race of Africa." Next to this speech ran the summary of another address, this time given in London by Nii Amaa Ollennu, who was visiting London from the Gold Coast. Ollennu first described the extreme poverty of his community that hindered development, including lack of educational access and promotion to professional careers. This poverty, he argued, contrasted with the fact that the colony produced two-thirds of the world's supply of cocoa and also held deposits of gold, diamonds, and manganese. "From the earliest penetration of West Africa by Europeans," Ollennu reportedly concluded, the chief "motive had been trade." Aligning these articles on the printed page served as a critique of European imperialism, minus any direct authorial comment.[47]

The correlation between the cocoa industry in West Africa and the sugar industry in the West Indies became the most prevalent way Padmore linked different experiences of resource extraction. In November 1944, he reported for his Jamaican readers the findings of a government white paper that announced a wartime profit of over £3 million from West African cocoa.[48] In August 1949, as debates raged about how to tackle the swollen shoot disease debilitating the production of West African cocoa and impacting the price of this primary export commodity, Padmore reported in the *Ashanti Pioneer*—a newspaper located in a particularly prominent region for Gold Coast cocoa farming—that a delegation of the British West Indies Sugar Association was in London to negotiate a better price for the colony's sugar. Padmore's front-page headline, the "West Indian Sugar Battle Continues," contained an official statement by "His Majesty's Government." Recognizing that "the prosperity of the sugar industry is vital to the maintenance of an adequate standard of living in sugar producing colonies such as the British West Indies," the Government assured the delegation that it would "make long-term arrangements which will give to the efficient producer of sugar . . . firm assurances of markets for agreed tonnages of sugar at reasonably remunerative prices to be negotiated by the producers."[49] In the adjacent column to this statement on the calculation of the price of West Indian sugar, the *Ashanti Pioneer* ran the announcement that the Gold Coast Cocoa Marketing Board was adjusting the price of cocoa from sixty-five shillings a load to forty-five shillings, based upon "the demand for cocoa in relation to estimated supplies and the probable price trends."[50]

While the *Ashanti Pioneer* came out in favor of the price reduction, noting that the quality of the cocoa needed to be improved, the price drop was, unsurprisingly, not without controversy. Padmore's article concluded by summarizing for his Gold Coast readers the argument being made in London's *Evening Standard* that, in order to ensure Britain's sugar supply, it needed to maintain the prices guaranteed through "imperial preference" rather than bulk purchasing. "If British goods are to compete in the world's markets," Padmore quoted the press baron Lord Beaverbrook as saying, then "the foodstuffs and raw materials which this country imports must be purchased more cheaply."[51] In other words, the British public sphere in Padmore's eyes was rife with arguments that the price of colonial commodities needed to be kept as low as possible in the interest of the British people first.

Padmore was, in almost all cases for these newspapers, not only their earliest "foreign correspondent"; he also consciously reported news that would draw together the struggles of West Indians and West Africans. West Indians understood how "imperial preference" had destroyed their economic diversity and made them reliant upon sugar. Readers of the *Ashanti Pioneer* understood these same problems in terms of the cocoa industry. By reporting in each region on developments in the latter, Padmore worked to build up consciousness around the similar struggles of peoples in each region. And it was not simply the content of the articles themselves that encouraged the reader to draw parallels to peoples and regions outside her or his own locale, to imagine him- or herself as part of a theoretical rather than a territorial community such as one based on race or colonial status. It was also the surrounding text on the printed page and the historical context of the readership as a whole. Read in isolation, Padmore's articles can appear unremarkable. Read within the container of these papers as a whole, the ways in which deterritorialized identities were facilitated by editors and by the daily imprint of the news becomes clearer.

TOOLS OF THE TRADE: THE MOVING WORD AND THE FORGING OF COLLECTIVE IDENTITIES

George Padmore's journalism and his relationship to these newspapers exemplified but did not entirely comprise the practices of quotation, reprinting, the harnessing of celebrity, and the routing of information through the metropole that are evident in the British West African and West Indian press. This final section will examine in more detail how various forms of reprinting could serve to effect collective transnational identities based upon both racial and colonial identifiers.

When *The People* began publication in Trinidad in 1933, it was primarily a local weekly newspaper committed to a pan-Africanist outlook, which it expressed primarily by reprinting longer articles from newspapers in England or the Gold Coast like the *Gold Coast Spectator* or the *Gold Coast Independent*. On 4 August 1934, the paper reprinted an exposition entitled "The Colour Bar," originally published in England in the *Daily Herald* and then reprinted in the *Gold Coast Spectator* after a correspondent sent it to the editors as justification for debates under way in the Gold Coast about racial discrimination exhibited there. The correspondent intended the article as evidence against the "ignorance" of some who denied the racialist attitudes of British officials.[52] The "first coloured President of the Oxford Union," D. F. Karaka, wrote the article. Karaka related instances of racial discrimination—closed doors to colored undergraduates in Oxford; the denial of tickets and accommodation by tourist agencies when attempting vacation outside Oxford—experienced by himself but mainly by "Indians and other coloured men in England[,] who will substantiate" both his broad and specific claims. Offenses were, Karaka noted, based "not on the personality of the individual" but "his colour" applied "equally to all coloured people." "The causes of this colour prejudice," Karaka concluded, could be traced to the "opportunity the white races have had for exploiting coloured people" through centuries past.⁵³ Printed originally in the metropole and routed through Africa and then to the West Indies, this article located racial discrimination of all colored peoples in imperial forms of domination. The multiple routes and layers of clipping, extracting, and reimprinting at work here, made their way to readers who would then read the international folds of the text in their own locale.

The discussion of discrimination experienced by both Asian and African peoples was not inconsequential to readers of *The People*. Although this would change in the second half of the 1930s, at this time the paper was largely hostile to the claims of formerly indentured Indian plantation sugar workers who made up a substantial proportion of the island's population.⁵⁴ Racial divisions in Trinidad at this time were sharp; and so the description of discrimination by Asian groups that would have held less meaning for the Gold Coast readers with which *The People* allied, could be read differently when reprinted for the third time, in the Caribbean. Thus in addition to the multiplex and adverse meanings—of the structure of colonial economies, the use of its resources, and the meaning of freedom—the tool of reprinting in different racial contexts meant that texts could take on ancillary layers of racial connotation.

The significance of the network of papers and editors described in this chapter becomes evident especially in the latter 1940s, when, now often with some access to Reuters and international news services, these papers continued to reprint articles from their respective newspapers—sometimes next to columns with wireless dispatches—and to comment on these articles and on the importance of the existence of their sister newspapers. Articles from the Zik Press were frequently reprinted across the Atlantic in West Indian newspapers. Starting in 1945, *Public Opinion* announced that it would frequently be reprinting the "punchful writings" of Azikiwe.⁵⁵ Here, the transcolonial celebrity of Azikiwe and Padmore bears some resemblance to that of Herbert Macaulay, discussed by Adebanwi in this volume. And just as Macaulay's victory in the Eleko case in the 1920s prompted messages of solidarity from other West African newspapers, the forced closure of the *West African Pilot* during the Nigerian general strike in July 1945 stimulated *Public Opinion*'s increased interest in the Zik Press. From 1948 to 1950 the *Ashanti Pioneer* culled many of its articles from *Public Opinion* and the *West African Pilot*, as well as the *Gold Coast Observer* and the *African Worker*. It also took advantage of Padmore's celebrity by running, often as the front-page headline, articles "sent by George Padmore," with an accompanying fine print identifying the actual author by name.⁵⁶ By 1949, Padmore's name held the headlining spot almost every day. Many of these articles tapped into the continued debates about colonial trade unionism in Africa and the West Indies at the time. In January 1948, next to a local notice of the tragic drowning of a young shore worker at a port in Accra, the *Ashanti Pioneer* ran Padmore's headlining story about criticism of "colonial agitators" like Azikiwe of Nigeria, Alexander Bustamente of Jamaica, and T. Uriah Butler of Trinidad. Culling most of the information for his article from the *Economist*, Padmore outlined the antagonism toward these men expressed by British Trade Unionist F. W. Dalley to colonial trade unionism.⁵⁷ Padmore's continued practice of clipping and reprinting was thus accompanied by local news stories that connected the Ashanti reader to workers in other parts of Africa and the West Indies.

As a way of understanding how practices like clipping and reprinting became a tool that infused new meaning into the flatness that can be read within these routines, we can return to where we began—to "The Black Man's Burden." For the front-page article of the issue in which "The Black Man's Burden" appeared was another piece sent "From George Padmore." This article was a printing of the closing remarks of Undersecretary of State for the Colonies David Rees-Williams, given during the latest House of Commons debate on colonial affairs. Repeating a practice long held in colonial newspapers of printing official statements and speeches by colonial governors or those in Whitehall, the article was a verbatim reprinting of Rees-Williams's speech with no editorial comment. Instead, "The Black Man's Burden" provided the comment. Rees-Williams's speech waxed upon the duty of colonial administrators to now work to restore some of the "colour" to people's lives that had been lost through colonial rule. Whereas in the precolonial days, "people lived a life which was undoubtedly brutal," each person "had a certain status in the community." The primary problem colonial administrators were now faced with was how to "restore to these people the colour which has been taken out of their lives" and "give back to them the feeling that they are persons and that each of them is not merely one of a large number of quite indistinguishable units."⁵⁸ Read against "The Black Man's Burden," which powerfully hailed the collective identity of color, Rees-Williams's patronizing call for Britain to benevolently restore "color" to the individual becomes representative of an attitude Rees-Williams likely had not intended to convey. Like the Tanzanian newspapers discussed by Askew in this volume, poetry could address topics found in other sections of a single issue of a paper. Here, however, the comment is neither direct nor actually intended in the original poetry. Yet I argue that "The Black Man's Burden" provided a particularly poignant commentary to the prose speech of Undersecretary of State for the Colonies David Rees-Williams.

CONCLUSION

In her examination of the practices of reprinting in circum-Caribbean newspapers, Putnam describes how these papers drew heavily not only on the U.S. black press but also on articles written by white progressive activists or professional experts, a practice she calls "glossing" for its clipping of expert statements followed by regular riffs that transformed "imperial apologia" into "a brief against imperial rule."[59] The juxtaposition of "The Black Man's Burden" and Rees-Williams's speech was nothing else if not this. Indeed, the newspapers covered in this chapter also contained editorials, letters to the editor, and journalistic comment that did respond directly to official speeches and articles by metropolitan "colonial experts." But what these newspapers could get away with under colonial regimes was also always precarious. Accusations of sedition, followed with imprisonment or fines, were always on the horizon. News juxtaposition offered another, more subtle option. The reprinting of "The Black Man's Burden" in the same issue as Rees Williams's imperial aggrandizement called out the hypocrisy of the speech, but it was also something slightly different from Putnam's adept description of "glossing." What we see in the examples covered in this chapter is the printing of announcements, colonial officials' speeches, or BBC broadcasts common in the established colonial newspapers of the day but without direct riffs or introductions against the content. Padmore himself rarely commented on the clippings and quotations he sent in—his reputation and the opinions he boldly stated in other articles often imbued the pieces "sent by George Padmore" with enough critical attention from the reader. These were not glossing, but actually stamping, imprinting, and hardening the authoritative words of politicians and colonial officials, made ridiculous when printed in an alternate context.

If, as Emma Hunter's chapter in this volume reminds us, publics are diverse and in flux, it is also true that the kinds of deterritorialized publics that expressed shared racial and colonial affinities were also dependent: they relied on networks of editors and journalists who read and shared their material, and who creatively marshaled the printed page to offer readers new ways of interpreting the text. Further research is required in order to determine exactly how substantial this technique was in proportion to the entire newspaper content over time. But what this chapter draws attention to is another practice that could substitute for the explicit comment that told a reader how to interpret global and local events. As Karin Barber argues in this volume, newspapers mobilized "overlapping formats" to express their "co-participation" in the shared field of print. In her Yoruba-language papers of the 1920s, Barber shows how newspapers used multiple forms of address, blurring the lines between audience and addressee in a style where "indirection finds direction out." In the West African and West Indian newspapers studied here the reprinting of news, poetry, and speeches, as well as the routes and personalities that facilitated the travel of text, allowed readers to ask the crucial question: where is this text speaking from?

The practice of clipping, reprinting, and quotation could be dismissed as the product of impoverished, inexperienced newspapers that were not, truly, engaged in the journalistic profession. These practices were, undoubtedly, mainly the result of necessity. Yet they also presented a kind of opportunity contained within the genre itself. Through repetition, contrast, and combination, new amalgams and hybrid newspaper genres were also possible. And this, in turn, fostered the kinds of collective and collaborative communities that connected Africa and the African diaspora. If we are to search for expressions of collective consciousness within Africa and the African diaspora, it is to the method as much as the content of newspapers that we may now turn.

BIBLIOGRAPHY

Anderson, Benedict. *Imagined Communities: Reflections on the Origin and Spread of Nationalism*. London: Verso, 1983.

Asante, S. K. B. *Pan-African Protest: West Africa and the Italo-Ethiopian Crisis, 1934–1941*. London: Longman, 1977.

Blight, David W. *Frederick Douglass' Civil War: Keeping Faith in Jubilee*. Baton Rouge: Louisiana State University Press, 1989.

Bogues, Anthony. *Black Heretics, Black Prophets: Radical Political Intellectuals*. New York: Routledge, 2003.

Bolland, O. Nigel. *The Politics of Labour in the British Caribbean: The Social Origins of Authoritarianism and Democracy*. Kingston: Ian Randle Publishers, 2001.

Campbell, Susan. "Kay Donnellan, Irishwoman, and Radicalism in Trinidad, 1938–1941." *Journal of Caribbean History* 44, no. 1 (2010): 75–104.

Chick, John. "Cecil King, the Press, and Politics in West Africa." *Journal of Modern African Studies* 34, no. 3 (1996): 375–93.

Dalleo, Raphael. "The Public Sphere and Jamaican Anticolonial Politics: Public Opinion, Focus, and the Place of the Literary." *Small Axe* 14, no. 2 (2010): 56–82.

Edwards, Brent Hayes. *The Practice of Diaspora: Literature, Translation, and the Rise of Black Internationalism*. Cambridge, MA: Harvard University Press, 2003.

Flint, John E. "'Managing Nationalism': The Colonial Office and Nnamdi Azikiwe, 1932–1943." *Journal of Imperial and Commonwealth History* 27, no. 2 (1999): 143–58.

Fraser, Cary. "The Twilight of Colonial Rule in the British West Indies: Nationalist Assertion vs Imperial Hubris in the 1930s." *Journal of Caribbean History* 30, nos. 1–2 (1996): 1–27.

Harold, Claudrena N. *The Rise and Fall of the Garvey Movement in the Urban South, 1918–1942*. New York: Routledge, 2007.

Hart, Richard. "Origin and Development of the Working Class in the English-Speaking Caribbean Area, 1897–1937." In *Labour in the Caribbean*, edited by Malcolm Cross and Gad J. Heuman, 43–79. London: Macmillan, 1988.

Hart, Richard. *Towards Decolonization: Political, Labour, and Economic Development in Jamaica, 1938–1945*. Kingston: Canoe Press, 1999.

Hill, Robert A. *Africa for the Africans*. The Marcus Garvey and UNIA Papers, vol. 10. Berkeley: University of California Press, 2006.

Hogsbjerg, Christian. *Mariner, Renegade and Castaway: Chris Braithwaite*. London: Redwords, 2013.

Horne, Gerald. *The End of Empires: African Americans and India*. Philadelphia: Temple University Press, 2008.

Idemili, Sam O. "What the 'West African Pilot' Did in the Movement for Nigerian Nationalism between 1937–1957." *Black American Literature Forum* 12, no. 3 (1978): 84–91.

James, Leslie. *George Padmore and Decolonization from Below: Pan-Africanism, the Cold War, and the End of Empire*. Basingstoke: Palgrave, 2015.

James, Leslie. "'Playing the Russian Game': Black Radicalism, the Press, and Colonial Office Attempts to Control Anti-colonialism in the Early Cold War, 1946–1950." *Journal of Imperial and Commonwealth History* 43, no. 3 (2015): 509–34.

James, Winston. *Holding Aloft the Banner of Ethiopia: Caribbean Radicalism in Early Twentieth-Century America*. London: Verso, 1998.

Makalani, Minkah. *In the Cause of Freedom: Radical Black Internationalism from Harlem to London, 1917–1939*. Chapel Hill: University of North Carolina Press, 2011.

McKeown, Adam. *Melancholy Order: Asian Migration and the Globalization of Borders*. New York: Columbia University Press, 2008.

Munro, John. "The Anticolonial Front: Cold War Imperialism and the Struggle against Global White Supremacy, 1945–1960." PhD dissertation, University of California, Santa Barbara, 2009.

Murapa, Rukudzo. "George Padmore's Role in the African Liberation Movement." PhD dissertation, Northern Illinois University, 1974.

Neptune, Harvey R. *Caliban and the Yankees: Trinidad and the United States Occupation*. Chapel Hill: University of North Carolina Press, 2007.

Newell, Stephanie. "Articulating Empire: Newspaper Readerships in Colonial West Africa." *New Formations* 73 (2011): 26–42.

Newell, Stephanie. *The Power to Name: A History of Anonymity in Colonial West Africa*. New African Histories. Athens: Ohio University Press, 2013.

Omu, Fred I. A. "The Dilemma of Press Freedom in Colonial Africa: The West African Example." *Journal of African History* 9, no. 2 (1968): 279–98.

Omu, Fred I. A. *Press and Politics in Nigeria, 1880–1960*. Atlantic Highlands, NJ: Humanities Press, 1978.

Plummer, Brenda Gayle. *In Search of Power: African Americans in the Era of Decolonization, 1956–1974*. Cambridge: Cambridge University Press, 2012.

Post, Ken. *Arise Ye Starvelings: The Jamaican Labour Rebellion of 1938 and Its Aftermath*. The Hague: Nijhoff, 1978.

Post, Ken. *Strike the Iron. A Colony at War: Jamaica, 1939–1945*. 2 vols. Atlantic Highlands, NJ: Humanities Press, 1981.

Putnam, Lara. "Circum-Atlantic Print Circuits and Internationalism from the Peripheries in the Interwar Era." Forthcoming in *Print Culture Histories Beyond the Metropolis*, edited by James J. Connolly, Patrick Collier, Frank Felsenstein, Kenneth R. Hall, and Robert G. Hall. Toronto: University of Toronto Press, 2016.

Putnam, Lara. *Radical Moves: Caribbean Migrants and the Politics of Race in the Jazz Age*. Chapel Hill: University of North Carolina Press, 2013.

Putnam, Lara. "Provincializing Harlem: The 'Negro Metropolis' as Northern Frontier of an Interconnected Greater Caribbean." *Modernism/Modernity* 20, no. 3 (2013): 469–84.

Quartey, K. A. B. Jones. *A Summary History of the Ghana Press, 1822–1960*. Accra-Tema: Ghana Publishing, 1974.

Shaloff, Stanley. "Press Controls and Sedition in the Gold Coast, 1933–1939." *International Journal of African Historical Studies* 6, no. 2 (1973): 211–28.

Singh, Kelvin. *Race and Class Struggles in a Colonial State: Trinidad, 1917–1945*. Calgary: University of Calgary Press, 1994.

Slate, Nico. *Colored Cosmopolitanism: The Shared Struggle for Freedom in the United States and India*. Cambridge, MA: Harvard University Press, 2012.

Smith, Faith. *Creole Recitations: John Jacob Thomas and Colonial Formation in the Late Nineteenth-Century Caribbean*. Charlottesville: University of Virginia Press, 2002.

Solomon, Mark I. *The Cry Was Unity: Communists and African Americans, 1917-36*. Jackson: University Press of Mississippi, 1998.

Spitzer, Leo, and La Ray Denzer. "I.T.A. Wallace-Johnson and the West African Youth League: Part 1 & 2." *International Journal of African Historical Studies* 6, nos. 3-4 (1973): 413-52, 565-601.

Stevens, Margaret. "The Early Political History of Wilfred A. Domingo, 1919-1939." In *Caribbean Political Activism: Essays in Honour of Richard Hart*, edited by Rupert Lewis, 118-41. Kingston: Ian Randle, 2012.

Turner, Joyce Moore. "Richard B. Moore and the Caribbean 'Awaymen' Network." *Journal of Caribbean History* 46, no. 1 (2012): 60-94.

Turner, Joyce Moore, and W. Burghardt Turner. *Caribbean Crusaders and the Harlem Renaissance*. Urbana: University of Illinois Press 2005.

Twumasi, Yaw. "Press Freedom and Nationalism under Colonial Rule in the Gold Coast (Ghana)." *Journal of the Historical Society of Nigeria* 7, no. 3 (1974): 499-520.

Vinson, Robert. "Providential Design: American Negroes and Garveyism in South Africa." In *From Toussaint to Tupac: The Black International since the Age of Revolution*, edited by Michael O. West, William G. Martin, and Fanon Che Wilkins, 130-54. Chapel Hill: University of North Carolina Press, 2009.

Von Eschen, Penny M. *Race against Empire: Black Americans and Anticolonialism, 1937-1957*. Ithaca, NY: Cornell University Press, 1997.

Watson, Roxanne. "'Now We Know': The Trial of Roger Mais and Public Opinion in Jamaica, 1944." *Journal of Caribbean History* 46, no. 2 (2012): 183-211.

NOTES TO CHAPTER TWO

1. Hubert H. Harrison, "The Black Man's Burden: A Reply to Rudyard Kipling," reprinted in *Ashanti Pioneer*, 8 August 1949, 5. Originally published in Harrison, *When Africa Awakes* (Baltimore, MD: Black Classic Press, 1997), 145.

2. Brent Hayes Edwards, *The Practice of Diaspora: Literature, Translation, and the Rise of Black Internationalism* (Cambridge, MA: Harvard University Press, 2003).

3. Edwards, *Practice of Diaspora*; Benedict Anderson, *Imagined Communities* (London: Verso, 1983).

4. Penny Von Eschen, *Race against Empire: Black Americans and Anticolonialism, 1937–1957* (Ithaca, NY: Cornell University Press, 1997).

5. Brenda Gayle Plummer, *In Search of Power: African Americans in the Era of Decolonization, 1956–1974* (Cambridge: Cambridge University Press, 2012); Gerald Horne, *The End of Empires: African Americans and India* (Philadelphia: Temple University Press, 2008); Von Eschen, *Race against Empire*; John Munro, "The Anticolonial Front: Cold War Imperialism and the Struggle against Global White Supremacy, 1945–1960," PhD dissertation, University of California, Santa Barbara, 2009.

6. Stephanie Newell, "Articulating Empire: Newspaper Readerships in Colonial West Africa," *New Formations* 73 (2011), 26–42, 29.

7. Nico Slate, *Colored Cosmopolitanism: The Shared Struggle for Freedom in the United States and India* (Cambridge, MA: Harvard University Press, 2012).

8. Lara Putnam, "Circum-Atlantic Print Circuits and Internationalism from the Peripheries in the Interwar Era," forthcoming in *Print Culture Histories: Beyond the Metropolis*, ed. James Connolly (Toronto: University of Toronto Press, 2015).

9. Lara Putnam, "Provincializing Harlem: The 'Negro Metropolis' as Northern Frontier of an Interconnected Greater Caribbean," *Modernism/modernity* 20, no. 3 (2013): 469–84.

10. For the radical praxis of Wells-Barnett and Du Bois, see Anthony Bogues, *Black Heretics, Black Prophets: Radical Political Intellectuals* (London: Routledge, 2003). For Douglass see David Blight, *Frederick Douglass' Civil War: Keeping Faith in Jubilee* (Baton Rouge: Louisiana State University Press, 1989).

11. For the circulation of the *Negro World* in Africa see Robert Hill, ed., *The Marcus Garvey and UNIA Papers: Africa for the Africans*, vol. 10 (Berkeley: University of California Press, 2006). See also Robert Vinson, "Providential Design: American Negroes and Garveyism in South Africa," in *From Toussaint to Tupac: The Black International since the Age of Revolution* ed. Michael O. West, William G. Martin, and Fanon Che Wilkins (Chapel Hill: University of North Carolina Press, 2009), 130–54. For the circulation of the *Negro World* in the US South see Claudrena Harold, *The Rise and Fall of the Garvey Movement in the Urban South, 1918–1942* (London: Routledge, 2007). For radical black journalism in the 1920s and 1930s United States, see Minkah Makalani, *In the Cause of Freedom: Radical Black Internationalism from Harlem to London, 1917–1939* (Chapel Hill: University of North Carolina Press, 2011); Joyce Turner Moore with W. Burghardt Turner, *Caribbean Crusaders and the Harlem Renaissance* (Urbana: University of Illinois Press, 2005); Mark Solomon, *The Cry Was Unity: Communists and African-Americans, 1917–1936* (Jackson: University of Mississippi Press, 1998); Winston James, *Holding Aloft the Banner of Ethiopia: Caribbean Radicalism in Early Twentieth Century America* (New York: Verso, 1998).

12. Margaret Stevens, "The Early Political History of Wilfred A. Domingo, 1919–1939," in *Caribbean Political Activism: Essays in Honour of Richard Hart*, ed. Rupert Lewis (Kingston: Ian Randle Publishers, 2012), 118–41; Lara Putnam, *Radical Moves: Caribbean Migrants and the Politics of Race in the Jazz Age* (Chapel Hill: University of North Carolina Press, 2013). For the Caribbean-American network see also Joyce Moore Turner, "Richard B. Moore and the Caribbean 'Awaymen' Network," *Journal of Caribbean History* 46, no. 1 (2012): 60–94.

13. Faith Smith, *Creole Recitations* (Charlottesville: University of Virginia Press, 2002), 27.

14. Harvey Neptune, *Caliban and the Yankees: Trinidad and the Yankees* (Chapel Hill: University of North Carolina Press, 2007), esp. 19–50. For more on *The People* see Kelvin Singh, *Race and Class Struggles in a Colonial State: Trinidad, 1917–1945* (Jamaica: University of the West Indies Press, 1994). For the rebellions in the West Indies in the second half of the 1930s see O. Nigel Bolland, *The Politics of Labour in the British Caribbean: The Social Origins of Authoritarianism and Democracy in the Labour Movement* (Kingston: Ian Randle, 2001); Cary Fraser, "The Twilight of Colonial Rule in the British West Indies: Nationalist Assertion vs. Imperial Hubris in the 1930s," *Journal of Caribbean History* 30 (1996): 1–27; Ken Post, *Arise Ye Starvelings: The Jamaican Labour Rebellion of 1938 and Its Aftermath* (The Hague: Martinus Nijhoff, 1978); Richard Hart, "Origin and Development of the Working Class in the English-Speaking Caribbean Area, 1897–1937," in *Labour in the Caribbean*, ed. Malcolm Cross and Gad Heuman (London: Macmillan, 1988), 43–79.

15. Raphael Dalleo, "The Public Sphere and Jamaican Anticolonial Politics: Public Opinion, Focus, and the Place of the Literary," *Small Axe* 32 (June 2010): 56–82.

16. For detail on the editors and journalists of *Public Opinion*, see Richard Hart, *Towards Decolonization: Political, Labour, and Economic Development in Jamaica, 1938–1945* (Kingston: Canoe Press, 1999).

17. Putnam, "Circum-Atlantic Print Circuits."

18. Newell, "Articulating Empire," 28–29.

19. For the press in the Gold Coast see K. A. B. Jones-Quartey, *A Summary History of the Ghana Press, 1822–1960* (Accra-Tema: Ghana Publishing, 1974); Y. Twumasi, "Press Freedom and Nationalism under Colonial Rule in the Gold Coast (Ghana)," *Journal of the Historical Society of Nigeria* 7, no. 3 (1974): 499–520; Stanley Shaloff, "Press Controls and Sedition in the Gold Coast, 1933–1939," *International Journal of African Historical Studies* 6, no. 2 (1973): 211–28. For the press in Nigeria see Fred Omu, *Press and Politics in Nigeria, 1880–1960* (Atlantic Highlands, NJ: Humanities Press, 1978); Sam O. Idemili, "What the 'West African Pilot' Did in the Movement for Nigerian Nationalism between 1937–1957," *Black American Literature Forum* 12, no. 3 (1978): 84–91. For the most lucid critical anal-

ysis of the West African press in recent scholarship see Stephanie Newell, *The Power to Name: A History of Anonymity in Colonial West Africa* (Athens: Ohio University Press, 2013). It is worth noting that despite burgeoning scholarship on the West African press, the 1940s and 1950s remain underresearched and that, in general, scholars have experienced repeated difficulty identifying definitive circulation figures and readership of West African newspapers. My current research hopes to unearth more information on audience, circulation, and policy changes over time in West African newspapers during the 1940s and 1950s.

20. S. K. B. Asante, *Pan-African Protest: West Africa and the Italo-Ethiopian Crisis, 1934–1941* (London: Longman, 1977), 69.

21. John E. Flint, "'Managing Nationalism': The Colonial Office and Nnamdi Azikiwe, 1932–1943," *Journal of Imperial and Commonwealth History* 27, no. 2 (1999): 143–58.

22. For details of Domingo's arrest as well as the relationship between the People's National Party and *Public Opinion*, see Ken Post, *Strike the Iron: A Colony at War. Jamaica, 1939–1945* 2 vols. (Atlantic Highlands, NJ: Humanities Press, 1981).

23. Roxanne Watson, "'Now We Know': The Trial of Roger Mais and *Public Opinion* in Jamaica, 1944," *Journal of Caribbean History* 46, no. 2 (2012): 183–211.

24. Susan Campbell, "Kay Donnellan, Irishwoman, and Radicalism in Trinidad, 1938–1941," *Journal of Caribbean History* 44, no. 1 (2010): 75–104.

25. "Reuters News Service in West Africa," *West African Pilot*, 13 October 1944.

26. "Ban on Zik's Press Wireless Lifted: It Can Be Renewed," *West African Pilot*, 9 October 1947.

27. John Chick, "Cecil King, the Press, and Politics in West Africa," *Journal of Modern African Studies* 34, no. 3 (1996): 375–93; Leslie James, "'Playing the Russian Game': Black Radicalism, the Press, and Colonial Office Attempts to Control Anti-colonialism in the Early Cold War, 1946–1950," *Journal of Imperial and Commonwealth History*, doi:10.1080/03086534.2014.974892.

28. Putnam, *Radical Moves*, 145–52. For border construction and in particular the racial elements of border control in the United States, see Adam McKeown, *Melancholy Order: Asian Migration and the Globalization of Borders* (New York: Columbia University Press, 2008).

29. For the connections with West African press figures during his Comintern years, see Twumasi, "Press Freedom and Nationalism," 501–4.

30. For more on George Padmore's political development and his journalism see Leslie James, *George Padmore and Decolonization from Below: Pan-Africanism, the Cold War, and the End of Empire* (Basingstoke: Palgrave, 2015).

31. George Padmore, "British Politics Today: Review of Political Parties," *The*

People 20 March 1937, 4; "Colonial Questions in Parliament," *The People*, 12 March 1938, 9; "British Press Spotlight on Colonies," *Ashanti Pioneer*, 24 December 1949, 1; "Large Amount of Space Devoted to Problems in Colonies by British Press," *African Morning Post*, 20 January 1939, 1.

32. Quoted in Rukudzo Murapa, "George Padmore's Role in the African Liberation Movement," PhD dissertation, Northern Illinois University, 1974, 80.

33. Wallace-Johnson's previous and subsequent brilliant encounters with seditious legislation are expertly detailed in Newell, *Power to Name*, 74–101.

34. Our London Correspondent, "Africans Hold Mass Meeting in London," *The People*, 4 September 1937, 3. For information on Chris Jones see Christian Hogsbjerg, *Mariner, Renegade and Castaway: Chris Braithwaite* (London: Redwords, 2013). For I. T. A. Wallace-Johnson see Leo Spitzer and LaRay Denzer, "I.T.A. Wallace-Johnson and the West African Youth League: Part 1 & 2," *International Journal of African Historical Studies* 6, nos. 3–4 (1973): 413–52, 565–601.

35. Ann Headford, "If You Were the Wife of a Trinidad Worker?" *The People*, 7 May 1938.

36. "Hands Off the Protectorates: Review by the Literary Editor," *The People*, 10 September 1938, 2.

37. *The Vanguard*, 18 March 1944.

38. J. A. Abidemi, "Tribute to George Padmore," *West African Pilot*, 4 September 1946. See also "Thank You, Mr. George Padmore!" *West African Pilot*, 28 June 1946.

39. Newell, "Articulating Empire," 28.

40. Editorial, "The Challenge of the West Indies," *West African Pilot*, 14 February 1948, 2. For debates on education in Nigeria and the West Indies see also "The Future of Our Education," *West African Pilot*, 8 January 1945, 2; "Colonial Office Gives Grants of 700,000 for Education Need in the West Indies," *West African Pilot*, 9 January 1945, 1; "Royal Commission on Higher Education Recommends University for West Indies," *West African Pilot*, 20 May 1944, 1.

41. "West Indians Criticise Reform and Demand Dominion Status," *West African Pilot*, 21 May 1941, 1. Although Padmore is not identified by name here, as was true of most articles by "Our London Correspondent" during the war, the content of the article (including the quotation from *The People*, which we know Padmore was also writing for) and the stamp that these articles arrived by air mail and were "Censored by the Ministry of Information" means that they were, in all likelihood, written by Padmore. Padmore worked daily from the Ministry of Information during the war as correspondent for the *Chicago Defender*, and his articles for this paper were marked in a similar fashion. See James, *George Padmore*, 69–95.

42. George Padmore, "Shock for Imperialists," *Public Opinion*, 5 February 1944, 4.

43. George Padmore, "Gold Coast Constitution Compared with Trinidad," *West African Pilot*, 22 February 1949, 2–3.

44. George Padmore, "Africans Appeal to World's Workers for Nigerian Strikers," *Public Opinion*, 27 July 1945, 2; Editorial, "Jamaica's Lesson to Nigerian Workers," *West African Pilot*, 8 March 1946, 2.

45. Padmore, "African Rail Strike, Farm Revolt Plague British," *Chicago Defender*, 22 December 1945, 8; Padmore, "South Rhodesian Railwaymen Now Strike and Sympathising African Miners Join," *West African Pilot*, 30 November 1945, 1; Padmore, "Excellent Discipline of the Rhodesian Strikers Defeats Aim of Government," *West African Pilot*, 1 December 1945, 1.

46. Padmore, "Africans in Belgian Congo Strike for Higher Wages and Better Conditions," *West African Pilot*, 28 December 1945, 1.

47. "Mr. McDonald on Empire's Aims: Claims Freedom for All King's Subjects," and "Shocking Conditions in West Africa: Poverty and Exploitation," *The People* 23 July 1938, 9.

48. Our London Correspondent, "UK Declare Over £3,000,000 Profit from West African Cocoa," *Public Opinion*, 24 November 1944, 2.

49. George Padmore, "West Indian Sugar Battle Continues," *Ashanti Pioneer*, 25 August 1949, 1.

50. "New Cocoa Price is 45s.," *Ashanti Pioneer*, 25 August 1949, 1.

51. George Padmore, "West Indian Sugar Battle Continues," *Ashanti Pioneer*, 25 August 1949, 1.

52. "The Colour Bar," *The People*, 4 August 1934, 3.

53. "The Colour Bar," *The People*, 4 August 1934, 3.

54. Singh, *Race and Class Struggles*, 118–119.

55. "Azikiwe Hits Out," *Public Opinion*, 2 August 1945, 3–4.

56. Select examples include J. Halcro Ferguson, "Election Clouds over Jamaica," *Ashanti Pioneer*, 20 September 1949, 1, Sent by George Padmore from *The Observer*; "Hostel for African Students," *Ashanti Pioneer*, 17 November 1949, 1, Sent by George Padmore from *The London Times*; "War on Colonialism Very Alive: New UN Measure Defeats Tricks of Colonial Powers," *Ashanti Pioneer*, 15 December 1949, 1, Sent by George Padmore from *The National Guardian*, New York; Lord Milverton, "Race Relations in Africa," *Ashanti Pioneer*, 29 March 1950, 1, Sent by George Padmore from *The Sunday Times*.

57. George Padmore, "All Eyes on Colonial Agitators," *Ashanti Pioneer*, 22 January 1948, 1.

58. "Rees-Williams Winds Up Debate," *Ashanti Pioneer*, 8 August 1949, 1.

59. Putnam, "Circum-Atlantic Print Circuits."

CHAPTER 3

Creole Pioneers in the Nigerian Provincial Press

DAVID PRATTEN

This is the story of the life and career of a provincial creole printman, James Vivian Clinton, who edited the *Nigerian Eastern Mail*, in Calabar, South Eastern Nigeria, from 1935 to 1951.[1] It investigates his position in the politics of race, nation, and empire in the lead-up to the Second World War, taking one year, 1937 as its focus. The episode intersects with the central historical lens on the relationship between print and nation by addressing the significance of race and identity, both local and transcontinental, in the imaginings of African nationalism.

In conceiving the form of emerging "national" communities Benedict Anderson argued that "pilgrim Creole functionaries and provincial Creole printmen played the decisive historic role."[2] It is a point that often seems overlooked and therefore merits reiteration. Anderson did not just argue that the circulation and shared consumption of print served to forge national identities, a thesis that has become well established. As he famously said, the newspaper quite naturally, and even apolitically, created an imagined community among a specific assemblage of fellow readers who read the same commercial, administrative, and society news in the early gazettes. He also argued that broad contextual factors such as shared economic interest or political ideology did not create in themselves the shape of these new national communities. Rather, Anderson showed how "Creole states" were formed and led by people who shared a common language and common descent with those against whom they fought.[3] And in accomplishing *this* specific task, he said, pilgrim creole functionaries and provincial creole printmen played the decisive historic role.

This creole elite, who constituted simultaneously a colonial community and an upper class, bridged a political paradox: they were economically and politically subjected, but also essential to the stability of the empire.[4] For Anderson it was this bridge, the collective historical experience, that connected creole pioneers with the "modular" American and European forms of national society. This has proved a contentious point in the comparative analysis of anticolonialism and nationalism. As Patterjee observed, it was not modular European forms of national society that were propagated within anticolonial nationalism but a whole range of regional and racial forms that were imagined.[5] Indeed in developing this critique Newell has shown how Anderson's definition of print nationalism is anachronistic in the context of the heterogeneous "national" identities that appeared in the West African press in the early twentieth century.[6] A single newspaper issue, for instance, could contain ideas of the "nation" that would include "local ethno-regional 'nations' like the Fante or the Igbo, and/or the colonial British West African 'nation' stretching from Nigeria up to the Gambia, and/or the global pan-African 'nation,' reaching from West Africa to the Caribbean, London and North America, and/or loyalty to the British Crown."[7] The press embraced this eclectic array of identities, and as a result was less politically coherent than the standard theories of nationalism assume. As the following story illustrates, however, while papers could contain these apparently contradictory views of the nation, they did not do so without consequences and casualties.

This chapter, then, concerns the very specific role of creole pioneers and printmen in the politics of nationalism in Nigeria and assesses how their role might be seen to be decisive. For Anderson creole in Mexico meant someone of European descent born in the Americas, while in the West African context these creole pioneers were the descendants of freed African American, West Indian, and liberated African slaves who settled in Sierra Leone and Liberia from the 1780s to the 1880s. Anderson's theory would suggest that the creole printmen were critical in shaping popular consciousness of West African nationalism. And indeed the foundations of this political ideology were laid out by a series of prominent early West African newspaper proprietor-editors, Edward Blyden, J. E. Casely Hayford, Herbert Macaulay, and Isaac Theophilus Wallace-Johnson, who were all creole printmen.

What this story narrates, however, is the moment at which and the reasons why their critical vantage point is lost; the point at which the coastal creole intelligentsia's model of nationalism was superseded. Clinton's story illustrates the significance of this moment precisely because he is a provincial and largely peripheral figure. What this analysis of his newspaper in 1937 shows is an editor's attempt to make sense of this fast-moving cultural and political dynamic being played simultaneously across local and international terrain. The news in 1937 was of the rise of fascism, the politics of appeasement, U.S. race politics, anticolonial economic protest, and provincial political representation. These "stories" were interrelated. How one was reported determined the editorial stance on another. And the reporting of these stories shaped the nationalist project. During this period the transatlantic interconnections between coastal West African journalists and their African American counterparts intensified to bring race and identity into focus as a key interpretative lens on imperialism. Views on race and empire were worked out in relation to events near and far that connected global circuits of print media. The political ground shifted quickly in the lead-up to the Second World War, and at this moment a creole coastal intelligentsia's vision of national politics collides with a Nigerian one. For some this "news" was not just reported, but became their political agenda. For others, like Clinton, this was a moment when momentum was lost, when they were excluded from new networks, and when they became the foil, not the forefront, of nationalist politics.

To focus largely on a single year, 1937, is to disrupt the typical linear narrative of press culture and nationalism. The year 1937 enables us to examine not a progression but proximate, contingent factors. In this respect we avoid both Jameson's synchronic problems of historical analysis (of identifying a uniform period) as well as the diachronic problem of historical construction (as a succession of stages).[8] In terms of nationalism this selective approach enables us to avoid a teleology that would equate the "progressives" of the 1930s to the postwar "political class," since as Peel reminds us, "There was . . . a certain disjunction as well as a linkage between 'nationalism,' *qua* the national anticolonial movement, and the local political tendencies related to it."[9]

To analyze these disjunctions, disconnections, and disarticulations we need to examine the very provinciality of these creole newspapers. The historian of the Lagos-based newspapers Fred Omu wrote that provincial newspapers were of little importance in the political evolution of Nigeria. He argued that they contributed to inculcating the habit of reading and "general enlightenment" but "did not make any noteworthy contributions to the advancement of political ideas or to the resolution of political controversies."[10] Yet, by focusing on the provincial press, as this case attests, enables us to enhance our understanding of the contingent entanglements of class, capital, and colonialism. This perspective illustrates not only that news media structure relationships between journalists and officials, and between colonial state and society, but that the nature of these relationships produces a set of strategic texts for imagining the nation. Looking at the social history of colonial-era press from this provincial perspective signals the importance of the West African coastal intelligentsia and their intellectual values to the formation of print cultures, but alerts us to the ways in which anticolonial critique shifted contingently and historically.

CREOLE PIONEERS

As with many West African newspapers published from the 1850s onward, the *Nigerian Eastern Mail*'s origins lay in the wanderings of a cosmopolitan coastal intelligentsia and the professional acumen of a Sierra Leonean diaspora in law and journalism. J. V. Clinton, editor of the *Nigerian Eastern Mail*, was the product of two extraordinary creole families—the Clintons and the M'Carthys. His grandfathers, on his maternal and paternal sides, were friends, and had married sisters, daughters of the one of the most famous figures in Sierra Leoneon history. The interconnection of these families is best illustrated in the society wedding held in St George's Cathedral, Freetown on 16 March 1892. The marriage was of Miss Emma Charlotte Davies, eldest daughter of Surgeon-Major William Broughton Davies[11] to Mr. James Clinton of Axim, Gold Coast. The best man was Hon. James A. M'Carthy, and the bridesmaids included the bride's sister Alice Maud Davies, whom M'Carthy would marry in the same cathedral two years later.

The bridegroom in 1892, Mr. James C. Clinton, was from Sierra Leone but had settled in Axim, Gold Coast, where he had established the mahogany trade and had founded the firm of J. & C. Clinton & Co, which he ran with his brother Charles.[12] Axim was a major port for the export of timber products at this time, and the firm was reported to have traded on as large a scale as any European firm.[13] James invested the profits of his trade in the education of his son Charles Warner Clinton in the law. C. W. Clinton was called to the bar at Lincoln's Inn in 1905 and spent his early career practicing law in Accra and Sekondi.[14] During the 1910s he practiced in southern Nigeria, and from 1919 settled in Calabar, where he would become leader of the Eastern Bar and the Legislative Council member for the city.

Like the Clintons, the M'Carthys also invested their commercial dividends into their children's legal training, and also traversed Sierra Leone and

Fig. 1. The proprietor, editor and staff of the Nigerian Eastern Mail, 1937. CW Clinton is front row 3rd from left, and JV Clinton is front row 4th from left.

the Gold Coast. James A. M'Carthy's father was a wealthy shopkeeper on Wilberforce Street in Freetown and was regarded as "one of the most prominent and active citizens in the country and participated largely in the affairs of the country."[15] James was sent to England, where he won a scholarship at the Inner Temple and was called to the bar in 1879. Fyfe reports that he was shortly afterward married at a fashionable London church to "Lillie" Vivian, daughter of a Hull town councillor, who returned with him to Freetown but who died in 1889.[16] The following year James A. M'Carthy was appointed queen's advocate, the senior Crown law officer at that period and a post that carried with it a seat on the Executive and Legislative Councils. He became the first mayor of Freetown Municipality in 1894, but was sent to the Gold Coast later that year, where he would serve as the solicitor general and at times as the acting attorney general based in Accra.

Hon. J. A. M'Carthy's eldest son, Leslie Ernest Vivian M'Carthy, was born in Freetown in 1885 and was educated at Clapham School, before reading law at Keble College, Oxford. In 1918 L. E. V. M'Carthy was selected as a Sierra Leonean representative to the British West African Conference,[17] and in 1920 became joint secretary for Sierra Leone of Casely Hayford's National Congress of British West Africa (NCBWA). He was appointed a Crown counsel in 1928 and was promoted to the position his father had filled, attorney general, in 1933. The circumstances of the promotion reflected changes. In part it was to shore up political relations at a moment in the early 1930s when Africans, who had been perceived as important partners in the spread of mission education and colonial administration, were being relegated to more junior positions.[18]

James M'Carthy also had a daughter from his first marriage, Muriel Eunice, and in 1901 she married James Clinton's son, Charles Warner, in Sekondi, Gold Coast. The following year Charles and Muriel had a son, James Vivian, who was born in Axim. J. V. Clinton was educated at Taunton School and Downing College, Cambridge. He was called to the bar at Lincoln's Inn in 1924. Originally intending to qualify for a government surveyor's license, he subsequently entered the family profession and established his own legal practice in Port Harcourt, Nigeria, where in 1927 an undiagnosed illness robbed him of his hearing. Despite five years of treatment in England and on the continent, he became completely deaf, and though he lip-read well, his career in law was cut short and he turned to journalism. J. V. Clinton worked on the *Sierra Leone Weekly News* from December 1932 to April 1935, then left for Nigeria, where he edited the *Nigerian Eastern Mail*, which was owned by his father, from August 1935 to October 1951.[19]

These biographies serve to confirm the image of successful creole families and their careers straddling commerce, law, administration, and journalism along the West African coast during the early twentieth century. Their cosmopolitan circuits also produced an intellectual tradition, a political stand on issues of race, empire, and nation. Clinton's family history was intimately tied to a progressive, Pan-African intellectual tradition. By 1937, however, this established, transnational elite's grip on these positions and traditions began to loosen. As Zachernuck has outlined in his analysis of the Nigerian elite under colonial rule:

> The intelligentsia of the interwar years had shifted their centre of gravity from the Atlantic toward the Nigerian interior. . . . The lines of division among the elite became increasingly complex, shaped by personality, political choices, and ethnicity.[20]

By focusing on Clinton's editorial record in 1937 we may begin to identify these lines of personality, politics, and identity in their historical complexity.

THE POLITICS OF IMPROVEMENT

Clinton's editorial stance in the *Nigerian Eastern Mail*—the self-styled "voice of the East"—set a progressive and patriotic public tone. It was practical, conservative, and reformist and reflected its editors' concern with the "politics of improvement" that was strongly inflected with the intellectual tradition suggested by his family's biography. In his preface to a collection of speeches by Casely Hayford published in 1949, L. E. V. M'Carthy summed up the National Congress's approach to reform in education, local government, and social welfare as "constructive and practical" while not always advancing as rapidly to suit all tastes.[21] His nephew, J. V. Clinton, positioned himself firmly within this tradition. The pillars of this philosophy stretched back via Casely Hayford to Blyden. African development in this framing rested with "cultured" West Africans familiar with local politics. It was elite-driven, concerned with maintaining good relations with Britain and was based on a regional loyalty rather than an ethnic notion of West African nationality.

At the heart of this reformist agenda was agitation for elective representation. Lord Hailey's observations of West African nationalism in 1937 confirmed the point. The local political class, he wrote, "has not proceeded beyond the ideals of early Victorian radicalism; its ambition is a larger representation in the legislature, and a greater share in government employ; it seems to make little appeal to the uneducated or rural element."[22] The political tradition of the creole coastal intelligentsia to whom Clinton was related therefore sought reforms of the colonial system rather than its overthrow, and was premised on an ethos of self-improvement, not self-determination.

The progressive reputation of the *Mail* and its editor was a widely acknowledged. In the second-anniversary issue of 28 August 1937 the U.S.-trained politician and founder of the Nigerian Youth Movement, Eyo Ita, wrote:

> The Nigerian Eastern Mail stands for a deep principle. It has been animated by the "Service of the People." ... It serves alike the European and the African. Its news and messages are for all-Ibo, Yoruba, Efik, Ibibio, Hausa, British, French, Spaniard, all! But best of all it seeks to raise in the heart of the African negro people a racial and national self-respect. By teaching and by examples it has sought diligently to point the way and pave the way for the race up-climbing and national self-respect. Think of the supreme and practical interest which it has taken in our economic and political problems, in our great

educational enterprise, the National Institute Project, in our League Movement and the Women's Congress, in the National Congress and in other matters which affect the entire West Africa and its aspiration to nationhood. The Eastern Mail has done well in the very difficult art of achieving an identity and yet remaining quite cosmopolitan. It is not easy to stand for something and still be friendly to all.[23]

Just as it was lauded by key political figures like Ita, the *Mail*'s conservative but independent editorial stance was also highly regarded in colonial circles. The resident of Calabar Province commented, for instance, that it was "remarkable for its tone of moderation and intelligent criticism."[24] Yet Ita's observations were both precise and prescient—it was not easy to retain an identity and keep one's friends. Clinton and the *Mail* sought to bridge local and cosmopolitan identities, but in so doing its political position was precarious.

The paper was produced by and for an educated literate class—self-defined as the "reading public," and in common with Nigerian newspapers of this interwar period the *Mail*'s identity was inextricably linked to the concerns of these "progressive" products of the mission schools. These were the "A-Lights" (a play on "elites") of their generation—the lawyers, teachers, educated merchants, clerks of the expanding colonial and mercantile bureaucracy. Most were also members of the local associations that had grown up in the expanding towns and cities—these were the so-called improvement or patriotic unions. The relationship between the *Nigerian Eastern Mail* and the various improvement unions like the Ibibio Union and the Calabar Youth League Movement in Calabar Province was close. Local agents, press representatives upon whom the papers were heavily dependent both to collect news and to sell copies, were leading members of the Ibibio Union. S. E. Hezekiah was the *Mail*'s representative in Uyo and then Port Harcourt before taking up an appointment with the Ibibio Union's National Secretariat as a field secretary.[25] News about improvement unions dominated the pages of the mail. Letter writers bemoaned the fact that there were too many. Accounts of their meetings were published routinely along with news of send-offs and marriages of union members.

During the interwar years these unions and newspapers like the *Nigerian Eastern Mail* cultivated a "civic" ethos, tempering critique of the colonial state with constructive engagement in a "politics of petitioning."[26] Editorials and columns set out criticisms of chiefs abusing their privileges, of European companies making profits at the expense of local producers, and of traditional customs, brideprice for instance, which young men struggled to raise in order to marry. Yet within the same edition the pages of the *Mail* were also brimming with the civic engagement typical of the 1930s politics of improvement. Each year, for instance, Clinton went on tour around the province to report on progress and to review developments. His journalists also toured their respective districts, where they inspected institutions and facilities—canteen cleanliness, the size of staff accommodation, the availability of police services, and the inconvenience of ferry services—in each instance calling on district officers to intervene. In the context of an initiative to clear "slum markets" in Calabar in October 1937, Clinton's editorial neatly captures this ethos of social progress premised on cooperation and loyalty:

> We must especially congratulate His Honour the Resident on the willing ear he has always lent to the voice of responsible public opinion as expressed through the press and through representative bodies such as the Calabar Youth League Movement. We look forward to a new era of social progress in which the public will cooperate loyally and intelligently with the authorities, and the authorities with a true democratic spirit, will lend a willing and considerate ear to the views and aspirations of the people.[27]

Clinton's conception of these popular aspirations focused on education projects. Fund-raising subscriptions for schools was a prominent feature of society life in Calabar and appeared prominently in the pages of the *Mail*. In January 1937, for instance, the paper reported on a football match held for the West African Students Union Day Celebration and the donation of over £6 for WASU's African Hostel in London. Inspired by the fund-raising success of a public subscription for the coronation celebrations for King George VI in May, Clinton also sought to apply this "lesson" to more local plans for the Calabar National School. In July he took the "practical" ethos further and reported that "the editor and the entire staff of the Nigerian Eastern Mail put down their pens and helped clear the site for the Calabar National Institute."[28] In these endeavors he was warmly spurred on by his readers. In "Our Mail bag" letters arrived encouraging Clinton's mass education initiatives and commended him: "You have a destiny and an important part to play in the fight against superstition and ignorance."[29]

In terms of educational developments newspapers like the *Mail* mapped the "rising aspirations of the educated west African 'scholar,' their clubs and societies and the 'para-colonial networks' they formed."[30] The Opobo Literary

Society, for instance, celebrated its fifth anniversary in 1937 and was seeking affiliation with the "Great Thoughts Literary Circle in London." These self-styled "ambitious youths" reviewed a year of debates, speeches, and "general reading." Their lectures had been on diverse topics including religion, bribery, civic pride, and African marriage, and a debate had been held titled "Africans are not yet fit for self-government."[31]

Clinton's nationalism and his own views on the self-government debates of the time were inherited from his coastal creole family, and inflected by a Pan-African "progressive" politics. In the anniversary edition of 28 August 1937 Clinton's comments highlight a deep ambivalence toward the political trends that were engulfing him in that moment: "The words national and nationalism assault the ear on all sides. These are words that we hold in some fear and suspicion, yet we note with joy and gladness the very evident spirit of social cohesion and community mindedness that is moving through the land."[32] While he persists with his progressive civic-minded politics—it is evident that the very class of educated scholars that Clinton sought to promote was now beginning to contest the political space he occupied.

Whereas Ayandele presents the coastal creole elite as "victims" of their acculturation caught "betwixt and between" the European and African worlds,[33] Zachernuk casts this intelligentsia's medial position as caught in a malaise of the 1930s, when it was hard to maintain the initiative. Their position was not easy to hold, he argues, since increasing access to education brought an indigenous elite to assume the legacy of a largely foreign one: "If they were victims in the sense of being colonial subjects, they were also part of an established colonial middle class with vested interests to defend.... they were actively building their own world, struggling to meet their needs in a location surrounded by diverse African societies and awash in Atlantic currents."[34] The events of 1937 would being these currents into focus.

1937

The *Nigerian Eastern Mail* celebrated its second anniversary in 1937, and the scale of its business belied its provincial profile. The *Mail* claimed to have the largest circulation for any weekly paper in Nigeria; the paper claimed that its "estimated reader circulation" was over fifteen thousand (based on a print run of 3,150).[35] At the end of January a new press with brass rather than iron rollers was installed and page size increased. "Even though the increase in size of sheet has added over 50 per cent column space to the Nigerian Eastern Mail," Clinton noted, "we still find a superfluity of documents on our hands and still gravely deliberate on what to print and what to leave out.[36] More than one hundred agents distributed the paper across the region. In the 27 February edition Clinton reported, "Owing to pressure of space we are no longer able to publish regularly the list of towns and villages in which our agents sell the Nigerian Eastern Mail."[37]

Circulation was up, distribution was expanding, copy was flowing in, and advertising revenue, reflecting a revitalized local economy, was healthy. The front page of each issue contained the usual shipping news, listing arriving and departing first-class passengers, and the all-important palm produce prices—oil on its way to English soap factories and kernels for margarine. Market prices overall were improving in 1936–37, but the returns to farmers were not, a discrepancy blamed on the "combine," the price-fixing monopoly of British trading firms who were allocated 60 percent of the available capacity on Elder Dempster ships. Clinton's editorials chastised the monopoly, while an undercurrent of discontent brewed in the letters pages about the source of the *Mail*'s advertising revenue. Adverts for the United Africa Company in the combine, for example, appeared alongside those for firms from Liverpool like Herschell & Co., who announced that they supplied all classes of goods direct to traders and individuals all over West Africa and were, in capital letters—"in no combine."

The international news throughout 1937 focused on the rise of fascism and on the events of interrelated global conflicts: the Spanish Civil War, the Abyssinian war, and the Sino-Japanese War. In Ethiopia during February there were fatal reprisals for an attempted assassination of the Italian viceroy. In Spain Guernica was bombed in April, and by August Japan had occupied Beijing. The conflicts would be fused in November when Italy joined the Nazi-led Anti-Comintern Pact that had been established between Germany and Japan the previous year. The headline of the *Mail*'s 2 January edition captured the insecurities wrought by these global developments. The "Word from the Father of Indirect Rule" reproduced Lord Lugard's speech on "Colonial Problems" made at the Royal Empire Society in London, which was copied or "culled" from the *Gold Coast Independent*. Referring to Germany's demand to reacquire control of former colonies, Lugard sought to reassure readers in the colonies: "To hand over on demand, as though they were slaves or cattle, peoples to whom we have pledged our protection, is neither consistent with our national honour nor, in the long run would such a surrender make for peace."[38]

Writing from the perspective of the United States, Von Eschen has shown that the global dynamics generated by the Second World War brought a common history of all peoples of African descent to the forefront of black American politics. From the watershed of the Italian invasion in 1935, she argued that "African American political discourse was keenly informed by and deeply responsive to events in Africa ... and throughout the colonized world."[39] As a result, a cast of activists, journalists, and editors clustered in black American newspapers—the *Chicago Defender*, the *Pittsburgh Courier*, the *Crisis*, and the *New York Amsterdam News*—formed a dense nexus, with journalists and publishers from London to Lagos and Johannesburg marshalling the resources of important middle-class and entrepreneurial institutions to create an international anticolonial discourse. Print journalism therefore provided the vehicle for the creation of this imagined diaspora and unified intellectuals, activists, and agendas across the globe. And while the U.S. black press began to see racial politics through anticolonial eyes, the reverse was also true, and the West African press saw its anticolonial politics through more explicitly racial lenses.

During 1937 the tensions concerning race and empire increased as the restoration of German colonies appeared to become a very real alternative to appeasement. With the former German colony of Cameroon as an immediate neighbor, and the Spanish island of Fernando Po just off the coast, the geopolitical implications for observers in Calabar were acutely felt:

> For ourselves we have not the least doubt that the natives of British mandated territories would regard the return of their German masters as nothing less than unmitigated tragedy. The German Colonials (in South Africa, East Africa and elsewhere) are quite frank in their opinion that the Black Man is a lower order of creation and that any attempts at racial equality are not to be tolerated.[40]

Indeed, the international news of military assaults became fused with important discourses of race and antifascism. Clinton wrote of a fear that Germany would draw a color line across West Africa, rendering a complete separation of black and white peoples:

> When German pilots ... can bomb defenceless Spanish towns ... the variety of non-intervention that satisfies the British and French Governments is a source of wonder and indignant astonishment.... If Franco wins, ... we may

have Hitler as our next door neighbour in Fernando Po, and more Africans will be victims of the Fascist ideas of the subject races' place in the scheme of things.[41]

By October fears circulated that Britain and France would accept Italian sovereignty of Abyssinia in return for Italy withdrawing "volunteers" from Spain, and in December Hitler had told a party of foreign journalists in Nuremberg that "Europe will never be able to settle down and have peace until the former German colonies in Africa now under British and French control are returned to Germany."[42] "Colonial appeasement," as it was termed, was indeed discussed extensively by Chamberlain's government, though it was never approved either as direct cession or as a revision of League of Nation mandates. Opposition from African populations was significant in the debates, which questioned Hitler's assertion of a "moral right" to repartition, though it was his apparently overblown claims of raw material starvation that decided the matter, since oil, iron, and coal were not found in great quantities in the former German territories.[43] What was seen in London as Germany's economic and political expansion was seen in Calabar in predominantly racial terms.

Clinton's main concern, nevertheless, was to hold the European powers to the promises set out by Lugard, and to provide the protection given Calabar's precarious provincial setting. His tone was of pleading and resignation. In a December editorial he wrote of Germany's colonial demands, "Bad as are the signs of the times we can only persevere in the hope that Britain and France will resist the temptation to commit this last treachery."[44] But black nationalists elsewhere were not so resigned and had viewed the 1935 invasion of Ethiopia on a broader scale entirely, and as a major watershed in a race war of European colonial expansion.[45] There was tension then between interpretations of the Ethiopian conflict, between antifascist and anticolonial views and those who perceived the fascist attack in primarily racial rather than geopolitical terms. The international reporting on the rise of fascism and on U.S. racial politics is elided, and as Von Eschen notes, the architects of the African nationalist diaspora would successfully "bridge and transform these two world views by arguing that anticolonialism and antiracism were necessary pre-conditions for democracy everywhere."[46]

This bridging and the deft slippage of political and geographical registers—from the provincial to the international, and from the antifascist to the anticolonial—was never quite achieved in the pages of the *Mail*. Clinton's editorial voice on the anticolonial continued to echo the familiar logic of paternal protection of Lugard's speech. And while his editorials against German racism were explicit, his stance toward questions of race itself was curiously more muted. In his reporting on race in the *Nigerian Eastern Mail* of 1937 it is striking to note a series of articles and reports "culled" from the *Chicago Defender* and the *Afro-American* that report on extraordinary incidents of skin color transformation. In the 23 January issue of the *Mail* a headline appeared that "Lew Leslie wants his actors black." The American vaudeville producer Lew Leslie had brought his "Blackbirds" dance troupe on tour to London during 1936, and it was reported that the showman claimed that the artists he brought from America had changed several shades lighter after being in London for a few months: "But Leslie wants them good and coloured. When his performers start bleaching out or making up lighter they are inclined to forsake their 'native' style in entertainment also and model themselves on white stars, he declared."[47]

The February issues of the paper also recounted sensational stories of skin color transformations from across the Atlantic. On 13 February 1937 under the headline "It's an Act of God" the strange case of William Pickens White was culled from the *Afro-American*. Having woken up to discover that his skin had turned white, he was reported as saying, "Now that I'm white I'd rather stay that way." The report continued that some of his "white inquisitors have suggested that he pass as white and enjoy the privilege of the white man."[48] Two weeks later, the 27 February 1937 issue contained a similar headline: "Pastor Once Negro turns White." While holding a revival the reverend minister A. H. Madison from Whitesberg, Kentucky, claimed that this "freak of nature" was due to his "fervent prayers asking God to make him white so he could preach to members of the race and the Whites also."[49] And in May the case of Pauline Cockburn, wife of a Harlem real estate dealer, was reported in which her eviction from an exclusive white housing estate was heard at the New York State Supreme Court, a case for which the anthropologist Franz Boas, teaching at Columbia University, provided a technical definition of a "negro." She was so light skinned, it was reported, that for three years she had attracted no attention.[50]

These stories were culled from the U.S. press and reprinted for the readers of provincial Calabar without commentary or interpretation. Perhaps they should be read simply as part of the reporting on U.S. race politics that they appear alongside: accounts of discrimination and lynchings in Mississippi, and of pen-profiles celebrating "heroes of the race" such as Booker T. Washington and accounts of Paul Robeson's latest movies. But perhaps Clinton's own silence on these stories, in that they were "culled" without making capital from them, should also be read in relation to Clinton's own creole identity and to the ambivalence he expressed toward the ways in which race and antifascism were being articulated with a more radical domestic political agenda of anticolonialism.

It is telling to note that the articles in the *Mail* that most directly address the racial dimensions of the expanding global conflict were not in Clinton's own words then, but in his reprinting of speeches by famous international commentators. In reproducing speeches by Nehru and Langston Hughes, for instance, Clinton was able to connect, to "articulate" in Newell's terms, to supplement local perspectives from those from further afield. Much of this news came from the *Chicago Defender*, which had become the most influential black weekly newspaper in the United States by the beginning of the First World War, and from the left-leaning *Daily Herald*, which had the largest international daily circulation of any newspaper in the 1930s.[51] But while editorial "culling" from across the Atlantic enabled some editors to "ventriloquise challenges to existing hierarchies,"[52] this was not the case for Clinton.

Various speeches concerning the Ethiopian crisis were reprinted from other publications in the *Mail*. The speech "Too Much of Race" by the poet Langston Hughes was reprinted in a special exclusive:

> I come from a land whose democracy from the very beginning has been tainted with race prejudice born of slavery ... we see in the tragedy of Spain how far the world oppressors will go to retain their power. Those who have already practised bombing the little villages of Ethiopia now bomb Guernica and Madrid. The same Fascist beasts who forced Italian peasants to fight in Africa now force African moors to fight in Europe. They do not care about colour when they can use you for profits or for war.[53]

Hughes's internationalist poetry, as Dawahare observes, aimed to transcend the categories of "race" and "nation" in order to overcome the fragmentation of global working-class struggles.[54] "Race means nothing when it can be turned to Fascist use," Hughes concluded. While the editor and the poet shared an abhorrence of fascist intervention in Ethiopia, Hughes's championing of authentic African aesthetics and working-class interests sits uneasily with Clinton's own political tradition. The act of "culling," or "ventriloquism," was effective where the editor's perspectives were delivered by proxy, but the clippings from radical figures like Hughes in the *Mail* did not convey Clinton's voice and did not reflect his own identity and historical experience.

There is an absence of comment articulating or bridging between these debates over appeasement, class, race, imperialism, and democracy in the *Mail*. For Clinton these debates are focused through his provincial and progressive editorial stance—his hopes for "social cohesion and community mindedness," not nationalism, his fears of a West African color bar, and his pleadings to the imperial powers to protect African peoples. The Ethiopian crisis could not form part of a class-based or anti-imperial political platform for him. Clinton's perspective seems not only provincial but increasingly peripheral to the emergence of an Afro-American public sphere. And to cite Hughes is indicative and especially incongruous in the context of emerging rivalries since Hughes shared a "pan-African brotherhood"[55] with Nnamdi Azikiwe.

THE REPUTE OF A RURAL PAPER

In January 1937 Nnamdi Azikiwe had been sentenced to six months' imprisonment as a result of the famous Gold Coast sedition trial with I. T. A. Wallace-Johnson. It is not clear whether the connection ever spurred their personal rivalry, but as acting attorney general, Clinton's uncle, L. E. V. M'Carthy, had initially led the prosecution team in the sedition case.[56] By October "Professor" Azikiwe was traveling widely in Nigeria and in Kano gave a five-hour lecture to a four-thousand-strong audience on the subject of the "Crucifixion of Ethiopia." The message that European aggression on the African continent was the result of imperialist ambitions was being popularized across Nigeria in person and in print. Azikiwe's *Renascent Africa*, published that year and distributed free with subscriptions at the launch of the *West African Pilot*, spoke openly about the "grip of imperialism," again bridging the international and the nationalist anticolonial agendas. The 8 January 1938 edition of the *Mail* reported that Zik's *Pilot* was selling well and that there were very few copies left for the provinces.

In his history of the Nigerian press Omu observed that "by the mid-1930s no newspaper existed to crystallize and canalise the growing nationalist influences of the inter-war years."[57] The *West African Pilot*, launched in November 1937, became the central outlet of a nationalist consciousness that had been awaiting this stimulus. The *Pilot*, like the *African Morning Post* Azikiwe had edited in the Gold Coast, set out to address a mass audience with simple, hard-hitting, and often scurrilous language, designed to be read aloud by literates to illiterates. Circulation was the key to its financial as well as political success, and while the *Mail*'s circulation had increased to 3,150 in 1937, the *Pilot*'s initial circulation was 9,200.[58] Historically, then, this moment also represented a vital stage in the transformation of elite nationalism from an agenda of political representation into a political movement.[59]

Within a few months, questions over the *Mail*'s political credentials began to appear in the *Pilot*. It was not the war or race, however, that would be pivotal as the register of political discourse shifted. It was the economy, and specifically the imperial grip on price controls. Criticism focused on the fact that Clinton and the *Mail* accepted advertising revenue from "combine" firms at a time when these firms were withholding better producer prices even though wholesale prices were soaring.[60] A reader wrote in to say that one of the *Mail*'s own correspondents was quoted in the *Pilot* as having said, "If the Mail were to champion the people's cause [on the combine question] and oppose the United Africa Company they might loose [sic] their advertisements."[61] Clinton was clearly taken aback by this development. He had been writing against the combine in his editorials throughout 1937, but the accusation of complicity by taking advertising money from UAC struck at the heart of Clinton's progressive position. He was incredulous in his editorial, and wrote: "We cannot seriously suppose that an editor of Zik's calibre would deliberately stoop to such a stunt in an attempt to advertise his own paper and damage the repute of a rural paper."[62]

In this moment Clinton's political legitimacy ebbs. He is increasingly disconnected from the African American public sphere and out of touch with local public opinion. Commentators had warned him of this trend. "Once or twice," Asuquo Nyong, a teacher at Duke Town School and general secretary of the Calabar Youth League Movement, wrote in August, "conclusions have been reached and comments made which were not the result of mature consideration of all issues involved, with the result that there was a deadly clash with public opinion. My advice is that the Editor should not rush his views to print, particularly in vital matters affecting the welfare of the masses, before he has the opportunity of understanding the feelings and views of the people."[63] Working within the enclave of the educated elite "reading public," Clinton was not adept at gleaning the opinions of this "new" public, conceived as mass and popular.

Not only were his views out of touch with populist sentiment, but emerging identity politics in Calabar also shifted the basis of his political legitimacy. The progressive unions that had been so closely aligned to the "improvement politics" Clinton championed were beginning to be accused of fomenting interethnic tension.[64] The particular target for agitation among the progressive union membership in Calabar was the domination of access to political positions by the Atlantic intelligentsia, and in this case the Clintons. A decade earlier, in 1928, J. V. Clinton's father, C. W. Clinton, was returned unopposed as Calabar's representative to the Legislative Council (though two Efik barristers also had their names in the election list). The question of whether he should continue to represent Calabar came to a head in May 1938. Clinton's editorial of 7 May, "Last Week's Election Meeting in Calabar," bemoaned an emerging sentiment of 'tribal' prejudice around the Legislative Council seat, especially with slogans of "No Foreign Representative for Calabar." Almost imperceptibly the Clintons, pillars of local Calabar society, had become "outsiders." It was at this moment, then, that "concern with racial—and even West African—uplift became specifically Nigerian."[65] And of course Nigerian was precisely what Clinton could not claim to be.

Within a few years it became impossible for the creole elite to stand for political office in Calabar Province. In March 1944 the nomination of Gage O'Dwyer, as the representative of Ibibio Division to the Legislative Council, was met with stinging opposition on the grounds that he was a Sierra Leonean and as such was "ignorant of the life and thought of the Ibibio people."[66] Despite these developments Clinton's own political ambitions were far-reaching and undiminished. He launched his political manifesto for the People's Party of South-Eastern Nigeria just a few months later.[67] It was a radical agenda and included proposals to abolish chiefs, codify customary law, fund mass education, encourage stronger consumer cooperative societies, establish women's representative bodies, and defend freedom of speech. A month after its launch, however, Clinton reported that nobody had signed up for his party. He did not recruit a single member, "nobody but ourselves."[68] In cosmopolitan Lagos it mattered less that political careers were launched by newspaper owners who were Sierra Leonean descendants. In the provinces it had begun to matter a great deal.

By 1944 the scope of debates concerning political representation had moved on, and the identity of Legislative Council members was quickly supplanted by questions over an agenda focused on Nigeria's future. The former National Congress agenda of legislative representation that had remained contentious through the 1930s was rejected as political demands leaped ahead on the road to self-government.[69] The Nigerian Youth Movement's political charter, adopted in 1937, was for "complete autonomy,"[70] an agenda championed and defended by its political successor, the National Council of Nigeria and the Cameroons (NCNC). Azikiwe's comments on the initial stages of this debate are illustrative of how his relationship with Clinton had developed since 1937:

> In the early years of the N.C.N.C., Mr J. V. Clinton, O.B.E., then Editor of the now defunct Nigerian Eastern Mail, used to gun for nationalists who demanded self-government. He claimed that Nigeria was too backward either to appreciate it or to be worthy of this political honour.[71]

Matters came to a head in light of the stand for self-government adopted by the West African Students Union in London. As a result, Reginald Sorensen, MP, advocated that Britain should indicate a time limit of ten to fifteen years to enable British West Africa to be self-governing. Zik reported that Sorensen's plea was played down by the British press and suppressed by the Public Relations Department of Nigeria. It was left, he argued, to the *West African Pilot* and the *Daily Service* to publicize and support Sorensen's statement, and local reaction, he said, was "electrifying." A public debate was held in Calabar, chaired by C. W. Clinton, the *Mail*'s proprietor and J. V. Clinton's father. Those proposing self-government, Dr. Ma Majekodunmi and Mr. Asuquo Nyong, won the debate by acclamation. Zik would later write, "This did not satisfy Mr J.V. Clinton, who did not hesitate to use the columns of his newspaper to mis-educate and confuse the public on this issue. There was widespread opposition to the effort of his press to stultify the aspirations of Nigerians and subsequently his newspaper became defunct."[72]

The basis of political legitimacy had changed. Education was now privileged above wealth, family background, or affiliation with the 'civilizing mission', and membership of the intelligentsia was increasingly Nigerian as opposed to "native foreigner."[73] Most important of all, perhaps, was that the content of the political agenda had shifted. Clinton's brand of pan–West Africanism, like the National Congress his uncle helped found, had proved to have only a temporary currency as Africans were forced "to turn inwards"[74] to narrower, ethnic definitions of nationality during the Depression. And in the unfolding political rivalries beyond the editorials and headlines, personality counted and the contrasts were stark. Clinton was educated at Cambridge, Zik at Howard; Clinton lip-read and was conservative, Zik was charismatic and addressed crowds of thousands; Zik had been imprisoned for sedition, Clinton was awarded the Order of the British Empire for "services to the field of journalism" in 1949.

CONCLUSION

The year 1937 was an important watershed. It marked divergent and complex trajectories among a transatlantic diaspora in which a shared racial discourse became embedded in print culture because of both events in the United States and the territorial expansions of Germany, Italy, and Japan. The interconnections between coastal West African journalists and their African American counterparts were significant, but not so simple that race politics in the United States was cast in an anticolonial light in Africa while African anticolonialism was framed in a racial light. These new political dynamics were modulated through existing editorial frameworks, and Clinton's *Nigerian Eastern Mail*, remaining steadfast in its progressive heritage, retained a discourse of loyalty to the Crown. Clinton's curious silence on the U.S. press, his defensiveness in relation to the combine, and his trust in the British protection meant he was unable to make political capital from the rapidly unfolding trends of 1937.

What had been lauded as an editorial stance that appealed to Africans and Europeans alike became hard to balance during 1937, losing momentum in the more radical, racialized discourse that was inflected in anticolonial protest. The *Mail* reflected but did not project this trend. Its pages document the shifting coordinates of this network, and the changing tone of this discourse. But Clinton could not direct it. As a creole pioneer, Clinton played a role pivotal in imagining the self-governing nation of Nigeria—not because it was his vision, but precisely because it was not. Clinton's position had become a foil to the nationalists. The new nationalist project was played out simultaneously across different terrains—anticolonialism was about the combine's control of palm oil prices in Calabar Province, just as much as it was about imperial designs across the continent in Ethiopia as well as racial discrimination across the Atlantic in the United States. Clinton's attempts to internationalize and articulate with these debates was constrained by his own politics of loyalism and progress, and by his own identity.

Indeed, when the government faced increasingly robust populist attacks from the overtly nationalist "Zik Press" during the Second World War itself, it had even more reason to welcome Clinton's conservative editorial policy. The resident wrote:

> The comparatively healthy tone of public opinion in the Province is due in no small degree to the influence of Mr JV Clinton, Editor of the "Nigeri-

an Eastern Mail." In refusing to be coerced into the parrot-like repetition of empty slogans, and in attempting always balanced, reasoned and progressive comment on matters of public interest, Mr Clinton has continued to render most valuable public service.[75]

Just after the war an unofficial survey was conducted among the reading public of the southeast that showed that the government papers, the *Gazette* and the *Nigeria Review*, were popular among civil servants and because of their coverage of Nigerian troops serving overseas. Among the newspaper-reading public, 15 percent took the *Nigerian Eastern Mail*, and did so for the accuracy of its reporting and the balance of its views expressed in Clinton's editorials. But significantly, almost 30 percent of the sample read Nnamdi Azikiwe's *Nigerian Eastern Guardian*, readers for whom the charismatic editor's syndicated column "Inside Stuff" was a particular attraction. In 1949 Azikiwe's publishing enterprise sought to launch a direct competitor to Clinton's provincial paper.[76]

The eclectically plural nationalisms that appeared in the Nigerian press had consequences and casualties. Room for maneuver for intermediary figures like Clinton could run out, and having entered into a consortium to move the *Nigerian Eastern Mail* to the regional hub of Enugu and increase circulation in 1951, Clinton watched the paper fold.[77] After several government positions through the 1950s and early 1960s (including in the Ministry of Information) Clinton fell back upon his writing, specifically fiction writing. He was engaged in a correspondence college course and sought to place with popular magazines short story manuscripts deriving from his exercises. Indeed, in his later years Clinton wrote for many women's magazines, sometimes using a woman's pseudonym in an effort to make a living during what appeared to have been increasingly hard times. In 1971 he published *The Rescue of Charlie Kalu* with the Heinemann Secondary Readers series for schoolchildren.[78]

Models of local and global articulation and networks are clearly significant to this story; as Lester illustrates, "Colonial and metropolitan sites articulated materially, but also discursively . . . and produced the communicative circuits of empire."[79] But it is equally important to recall the disarticulations and dislocations that these dynamics generated. Each different site within these imperial networks had "its own possibilities and conditions of knowledge."[80] Widening local participation in politics and economic tensions created by the Depression combined to nudge the coastal intelligentsia, the creole elite, out of their dominant position in provincial centers like Calabar along the West African coast. And in this context the intellectual histories of those provincial printmen meant that sometimes the very people able to bridge coastal cultures were not able to bridge transcontinental ones.

REFERENCES

Anderson, Benedict. *Imagined Communities: Reflections on the Origin and Spread of Nationalism.* New York: Verso, 1983.

Asante, Samuel. K. B. *Pan-African Protest: West Africa and the Italo-Ethiopian Crisis, 1934–1941.* London: Longman, 1977.

Ayandele, Emmanuel A. *The Educated Elite in the Nigerian Society.* Ibadan: Ibadan University Press, 1974.

Azikiwe, Nnamdi. *The Development of Political Parties in Nigeria: An Address Delivered on June 11th, at Rhodes House, Oxford.* London, 1957.

Casely Hayford, J. E. *West African Leadership . . . Public Speeches Delivered by the Honourable J. E. Casely Hayford.* Ilfracombe: Arthur H. Stockwell, 1951.

Chatterjee, Partha. "Whose Imagined Community?" *Millennium: Journal of International Studies* 20, no. 3 (1991): 521–25.

Dawahare, Anthony. "Langston Hughes's Radical Poetry and the 'End of Race.'" *MELUS* 23, no. 3 (1998): 21–41.

Dixon-Fyle, Mac. "The Saro in the Political Life of Early Port Harcourt, 1913–49." *Journal of African History* 30, no. 1 (1989): 125–38.

Flint, John E. "'Managing Nationalism': The Colonial Office and Nnamdi Azikiwe, 1932–43." *Journal of Imperial and Commonwealth History* 27, no. 2 (1999): 143–58.

Fyfe, Christopher. *A History of Sierra Leone.* London: Oxford University Press, 1962.

Jameson, Fredric. "Periodizing the 60s." *Social Text* 9–10 (1984): 178–209.

Lester, Alan. *Imperial Networks: Creating Identities in Nineteenth-Century South Africa and Britain.* New York: Routledge, 2001.

Martin, Guy. *African Political Thought.* New York: Palgrave Macmillan, 2012.

Newell, Stephanie. "Articulating Empire: Newspaper Readerships in Colonial West Africa." *New Formations* 73 (2011): 26–42.

Newell, Stephanie. "'Paracolonial' Networks: Some Speculations on Local Readerships in Colonial West Africa." *Interventions: International Journal of Postcolonial Studies* 3, no. 3 (2001): 336–54.

OBIWU. "The Pan-African Brotherhood of Langston Hughes and Nnamdi Azikiwe." *Dialectical Anthropology* 31 (2007): 143–65.

Omu, Fred I. A. *Press and Politics in Nigeria, 1880–1937.* London: Longman, 1978.
Peel, J. D. Y. *Ijeshas and Nigerians: The Incorporation of a Yoruba Kingdom, 1880s–1970s.* Cambridge: Cambridge University Press, 1983.
Said, Edward W. *Culture and Imperialism.* New York: Knopf, 1993.
Shaloff, Stanley. "Press Controls and Sedition Proceedings in the Gold Coast, 1933–39." *African Affairs* 71 (284) (1972): 241–63.
Stedman, Andrew D. *Alternatives to Appeasement: Neville Chamberlain and Hitler's Germany.* London: Tauris Academic Studies, 2011.
Von Eschen, Peggy M. *Race against Empire: Black Americans and Anticolonialism, 1937–1957.* Ithaca, NY: Cornell University Press, 1997.
Wyse, A. J. G. "The Sierra Leone Branch of the National Congress of British West Africa, 1918–1946." *International Journal of African Historical Studies* 18, no. 4 (1985): 675–98.
Zachernuk, Philip S. *Colonial Subjects: An African Intelligentsia and Atlantic Ideas.* Charlottesville: University Press of Virginia, 2000.

NOTES

1. My thanks to Stephanie Newell for her encouragement with this research, and to Andrea Grant for her archival research assistance in 2011.

2. Benedict Anderson, *Imagined Communities: Reflections on the Origin and Spread of Nationalism* (New York: Verso, 1983), 65.

3. Anderson, *Imagined Communities*, 47.

4. Anderson, *Imagined Communities*, 58.

5. Partha Chatterjee, "Whose Imagined Community?," *Millennium: Journal of International Studies* 20, no. 3 (1991): 521–25.

6. Stephanie Newell, "Articulating Empire: Newspaper Readerships in Colonial West Africa," *New Formations* 73 (2011): 26–42.

7. Newell, "Articulating Empire," 26.

8. Fredric Jameson, "Periodizing the 60s," *Social Text* 9–10 (1984): 178–209.

9. J. D. Y. Peel, *Ijeshas and Nigerians: The Incorporation of a Yoruba Kingdom, 1880s-1970s* (Cambridge: Cambridge University Press, 1983), 179.

10. F. I. A. Omu, *Press and Politics in Nigeria, 1880–1937* (London: Longman, 1978), 27.

11. William Broughton Davies was selected, along with James Africanus Beale Horton and Samuel Campbell, to train as a doctor in London and Edinburgh before taking up a commission in the army; see Christopher Fyfe, *A History of Sierra Leone* (London: Oxford University Press, 1962), 294.

12. *Gold Coast Nation*, 19 December 1912.

13. *Gold Coast Leader*, 16 November 1918.

14. Lincoln's Inn, *Black Books*, V, 1905: 434.

15. *Sierra Leone Weekly News*, 25 June 1910. See also Fyfe, *History of Sierra Leone*, 451, 469, 493.

16. Fyfe, *History of Sierra Leone*, 424. He remarried, to Alice Maud Davies, in 1894.

17. *Lagos Weekly Record*, 15 and 22 June 1918.

18. Stanley Shaloff, "The Africanization Controversy in the Gold Coast, 1926–1946," *African Studies Review* 17, no. 3 (1974): 493–504. M'Carthy went on to write the laws of the Gold Coast and was knighted in 1949.

19. The *Sierra Leone Weekly News* was established by Reverend Joseph May with assistance from Joseph Blyden in 1884.

20. Philip S. Zachernuk, *Colonial Subjects: An African Intelligentsia and Atlantic Ideas* (Charlottesville: University Press of Virginia, 2000), 94.

21. Joseph Ephraim Casely Hayford, *West African Leadership . . . Public Speeches Delivered by the Honourable J. E. Casely Hayford, Etc.* (Ilfracombe: Arthur H. Stockwell, 1951).

22. Lord Hailey, "Nationalism in Africa," *Journal of the African Society* 36 (1937): 140–41.

23. *Nigerian Eastern Mail*, 28 August 1937.

24. MSS Afr. S. 1505.1, Annual Report, Calabar Province (1946).

25. During 1948–49 the newspaper had a regular "Ibibio Union" column.

26. Mac Dixon-Fyle, "The Saro in the Political Life of Early Port Harcourt, 1913–49," *Journal of African History* 30, no. 1 (1989): 127.

27. *Nigerian Eastern Mail*, 2 October 1937.

28. *Nigerian Eastern Mail*, 3 July 1937.

29. *Nigerian Eastern Mail*, 19 January 1937.

30. Stephanie Newell, "'Paracolonial' Networks: Some Speculations on Local Readerships in Colonial West Africa," *Interventions: International Journal of Postcolonial studies* 3, no. 3 (2001): 336–54.

31. *Nigerian Eastern Mail*, 6 February 1937.

32. *Nigerian Eastern Mail*, 28 August 1937.

33. Emmanuel A. Ayandele, *The Educated Elite in the Nigerian Society* (Ibadan: Ibadan University Press, 1974).

34. Zachernuk, *Colonial Subjects*, 71.

35. *Nigerian Eastern Mail*, 16 January 1937.

36. *Nigerian Eastern Mail*, 30 January 1937.

37. *Nigerian Eastern Mail*, 27 February 1937.

38. *Nigerian Eastern Mail*, 2 January 1937.

39. Penny M. Von Eschen, *Race against Empire: Black Americans and Anticolonialism, 1937–1957* (Ithaca, NY: Cornell University Press, 1997), 8.
40. *Nigerian Eastern Mail*, 5 June 1937.
41. *Nigerian Eastern Mail*, 19 June 1937.
42. *Nigerian Eastern Mail*, 4 December 1937.
43. Andrew D. Stedman, *Alternatives to Appeasement: Neville Chamberlain and Hitler's Germany* (London: Tauris Academic Studies, 2011), 72–73.
44. *Nigerian Eastern Mail*, 4 December 1937.
45. Von Eschen, *Race against Empire*, 11.
46. Von Eschen, *Race against Empire*, 11.
47. *Nigerian Eastern Mail*, 23 January 1937.
48. *Nigerian Eastern Mail*, 13 February 1937. Pickens White suffered from vitiligo, a skin-depigmentation condition.
49. *Nigerian Eastern Mail*, 27 February 1937.
50. *Nigerian Eastern Mail*, 1 May 1937.
51. One source of these reports was a new mail order service established during 1937 by Nyomibidi Bros and Co., importers of newspapers, periodicals, magazines, books, and stationery.
52. Newell, "Articulating Empire," 35.
53. *Nigerian Eastern Mail*, 2 October 1937, originally published in *Crisis Magazine*, September 1937.
54. Anthony Dawahare, "Langston Hughes's Radical Poetry and the 'End of Race,'" *MELUS* 23, no. 3 (1998): 21–41.
55. OBIWU, "The Pan-African Brotherhood of Langston Hughes and Nnamdi Azikiwe," *Dialectical Anthropology* 31 (2007): 143–65. Both were alumni of Lincoln, protégés of Alain Locke at Howard, and wrote poetry for and of one another.
56. Stanley Shaloff, "Press Controls and Sedition Proceedings in the Gold Coast, 1933–39," *African Affairs* 71, no. 284 (1972): 241–63.
57. Omu, *Press and Politics*, 68.
58. Omu, *Press and Politics*, 264.
59. John E. Flint, "'Managing Nationalism': The Colonial Office and Nnamdi Azikiwe, 1932–43," *Journal of Imperial and Commonwealth History* 27, no. 2 (1999): 146.
60. Criticism of the *Mail* had begun in July and coincided with a "mass meeting" of the Calabar Youth League Movement, which protested against the "soaring prices."
61. An article in the 16 April 1938 issue of the *Mail*, "A Libel on the Eastern Mail. Letter from A. Reader from Zaria," recounted a piece in the Owerri news

section of the *West African Pilot* of 29 March in which Mr. Abbey, the *Mail*'s own touring correspondent, alleged the *Mail* had been silent on "pool" (combine) issues until the *Pilot* had raised the alarm.

62. *Nigerian Eastern Mail*, 16 April 1938. The protests about low producer and high wholesale prices was widespread, and in early 1938 the National Youth Movement in Lagos, which Azikiwe had joined on his return to Nigeria, also protested (successfully) against the price-fixing monopoly of the European cocoa pool.

63. *Nigerian Eastern Mail*, 28 August 1937.

64. In a commentary defending the organizations, Asuquo Nyong captured this tension: "It is in the nature of things that there should be such more or less tribal organisations as the Ibo Tribe Union, Ibibio Welfare Union, Calabar Youth League.... The mere existences of these organisations is not necessarily an evidence of tribal prejudice as some people appear to think. It is their modus operandi that will intensify or diminish tribal prejudice" (*Nigerian Eastern Mail*, 30 April 1938).

65. Zachernuk, *Colonial Subjects*, 112. Agitation over nominations for a legislative seat in Lagos during 1941 also split the NYM into factions along ethnic lines (Flint, "Managing Nationalism," 150 n. 25).

66. *Nigerian Eastern Mail*, 11 March 1944.

67. *Nigerian Eastern Mail*, 9 December 1944.

68. *Nigerian Eastern Mail*, 23 December 1944.

69. Zachernuk, *Colonial Subjects*, 112.

70. Nnamdi Azikiwe, *The Development of Political Parties in Nigeria: An Address Delivered on June 11th, at Rhodes House, Oxford* (London, 1957).

71. Azikiwe, *Development of Political Parties*, 12. Azikiwe was scornful of a series of political ideas emanating from Calabar. While acknowledging the foundational role of the Nigerian Youth League Movement, he would later recall Eyo Ita's ideas as "partly utopian and partly parochial."

72. Azikiwe, *Development of Political Parties*, 12.

73. Zachernuk, *Colonial Subjects*, 112.

74. Samuel K. B. Asante, *Pan-African Protest: West Africa and the Italo-Ethiopian Crisis, 1934–1941* (London: Longman, 1977), 22.

75. Annual Report, Calabar Province (1947), Rhodes House, Oxford: MSS Afr. S. 1505.2.

76. Nnamdi Azikiwe to The Secretary, Native Authority, Calabar, 8 July 1948, National Archive Calabar: CADIST 3.3.133.

77. As the epilogue to Omu's *Press and Politics* indicates, the early 1950s were

a heady time of newspaper buyouts and mergers, including with international print consortia.

78. "Correspondence relating to the publication of Rescue of Charlie Kalu by J.V. Clinton," 1968–1972, University of Reading Archives, Special Collections (HEB 67/02).

79. Alan Lester, *Imperial Networks: Creating Identities in Nineteenth-Century South Africa and Britain* (New York: Routledge, 2001), 6.

80. Edward W Said, *Culture and Imperialism* (New York: Knopf, 1993), 60.

CHAPTER 4

The Sociability of Print

1920s and 1930s Lagos Newspaper Travel Writing

REBECCA JONES

> Mo ki gbogbo ẹnyin oluka iwe irohin mi yi yika gbogbo aiye, inu mi dun pupọ lati ni itankalẹ iwe irohin "Akede Eko" yi kakiri gbogbo agbegbe ilu ti mo de wọnyi; gẹgẹbi ọba ni awọn enia ti nwọn ka "Akede Eko" nyọ fẹrẹ mọ mi, Inu gbogbo wọn dun pupọ lati fi oju wọn kan mi.[1]
>
> I greet all you readers of my newspaper all around the world. I was very happy to spread this newspaper *Akede Eko* around all these towns that I came to; the people who read *Akede Eko* were as pleased to know me as to see an *Ọba*.[2] They were all very happy to lay their eyes on me.
> —I. B. Thomas, "Ero L'Ọna," *Akede Eko*, 21 February 1931

In February 1931, Isaac Babalọla Thomas, editor-proprietor of the Yoruba-language Lagos newspaper *Akede Eko*, set out on a monthlong journey from Lagos across southern Nigeria.[3] Thomas's journey took him by train from Lagos to Ibadan, and then on to Ọyọ, Awẹ, Ogbomọṣọ, Oṣogbo, Ilọrin, Ileṣa, Ile-Ifẹ, Akurẹ, and Ondo in the Yoruba region, before reaching Benin City, Warri, Onitsha, Asaba, Enugu, and Aba on the southern coast. Over the following three months, he published nine travelogues, each in the form of a first-person letter to readers written in the midst of the journey. With each travelogue spanning up to two pages of the newspaper, they tell in humorous and idiosyncratic detail Thomas's experiences of traveling by steamer, train, and lorry, his encounters with friends old and new, and his impressions of the towns and people he visits.

Throughout the 1920s, the editors of the Lagos newspapers embarked on "publicity tours" of Nigeria during which they "establish[ed] agents and generally ma[de] themselves known to as many people as possible."[4] And indeed, Thomas explained to his readers that he was traveling in order to "ni itankalẹ iwe irohin 'Akede Eko' yi kakiri gbogbo agbegbe ilu" ("to spread my newspaper *Akede Eko* around all the towns").[5] Since establishing *Akede Eko* in 1928, Thomas had regularly set out on such promotional journeys, and these became the basis for some of his travel accounts.

But Thomas had begun publishing travel narratives at least two years earlier, beginning with his series "Ero L'Ọna" ("The Traveler"), published in 1926 in the Yoruba newspaper *Eleti-Ọfẹ*, for which he was then a writer. The series describes a three-month journey, for work-related reasons that are not specified in detail, from Lagos to the port town of Sapele (in present-day Delta State) and home again. When Thomas left *Eleti-Ọfẹ* to found *Akede Eko* in 1928, he took the "Ero L'Ọna" format with him, and published at least three further "Ero L'Ọna" series in *Akede Eko* between 1929 and 1931, two of which detail journeys across Nigeria's southern coast, while the third describes his travels to the nearby Yoruba town of Ijẹbu-Ode. Thomas claimed to have received a favorable response to previous travelogues, which had encouraged him to publish more:

> Lati igbati a ti ṣe ikede fun irin ajo mi lọ si ọna ilu awọn Ijẹbu ti di titẹ sinu iwe irohin *Akede Eko* yi ni pupọ awọn ọmọ Ijẹbu, yala l'ode Eko, tabi lati ọna idalẹ ni nwọn ti wa ri mi, tabi ti nwọn kọ iwe *letters* si mi wipe inu awon dun lọpọlọpọ fun pe emi fẹ rin irin ajo lọ si igboro ilu won, nwọn si sọ fun mi pe inu awọn yio dun pupọ bi emi ba le ṣe gbogbo awọn irohin nipa irin ajo mi na fun gbogbo aiye ka gẹgẹbi iṣe mi l'abẹ *Ero L'Ọna*.[6]

> From the time that my journey to the Ijẹbu towns was announced in print in this *Akede Eko*, many Ijẹbu people, whether from around Lagos, or who had seen me elsewhere, or who had written letters to me saying they were very pleased that I wanted to travel to their town, said they would be very happy if I would write the news of my journey for all the world to see as part of my series *Ero L'Ọna*.

As this chapter will describe, there were a number of other writers of travel narratives in the Yoruba press in the 1920s and 1930s. But Thomas's were some of the most inventive, full of stories, jokes, songs, and detailed descriptions of life on the road. As was commonly the style in the Yoruba-language newspapers of the 1920s, they are bombastic, emotional, and often full of hyperbole (see Barber, this volume). Thomas's rhetorical set-pieces include proverbs, quotations from the Bible, panoramas, melodramatic depictions of sorrow at leaving his family, effusive declarations of the wonders of travel, praise of his hosts, greeting readers with Itsekiri and Igbo words he had encountered on his travels, and onomatopoeic descriptions of the sights and sounds of travel: "Fo o o o o!!!"[7] cries a ship's horn, while a train makes the sound "Fakafiki-fakafiki!"[8] and cockerels crow "Cockadoodledo!" "Omije anu" ("tears of sorrow")[9] roll down Thomas's face as he leaves home, and he often reports crying out in amazement at the wonders he encounters: "Emi kẹ! Emi kẹ! Emi kẹ!" ("Me! Me! Me!"),[10] he exclaims on being picked up by a dazzling car.

Thomas justified the publication of travel narratives by suggesting that from them his readers would gain ẹ̀kọ́ (lessons, an education) and ọgbọ́n (wisdom).[11] Before the 1929 series of "Ero L'Ọna," Thomas published an article titled "Irin-Ajo" ("Journeys" or "Traveling") in which he encourages "enia wa" ("our people") to travel more "kakiri-aiye gẹgẹbi ẹkọ" ("all around the world as an education"). As well as traveling, he suggests, one should narrate the experience of travel to others: it is a pity that many Lagosians who have traveled "ko sọ gbogbo ohun ti oju wọn ba pade ninu irin ajo na fun awọn ọmọ ẹlẹgbẹ wọn gbọ" ("do not talk about all the things they laid eyes on during the journey, for their acquaintances to hear"), and he advises the reader: "Ẹ mura lati ri ọgbọn kọ ninu awọn arẹwa irin-ajo gbajumọ Editor na" ("Be prepared to learn wisdom from the beautiful journeys of the respected editor").[12]

However, while increased knowledge for both traveler and reader may have been an explicit justification for the travel narratives (and is one they share with travel narratives the world over),[13] one of the most striking features of these travelogues is their exuberant sociability, centered on the writer, his hosts, and his readers. As this chapter will describe, Thomas's travel narratives frequently pause to name, thank, and describe his hosts, friends, acquaintances, and colleagues, to the extent that some of the most volubly sociable travelogues are almost overwhelmed by the author's namedropping. Although Thomas does describe panoramas, urban landscapes, and the sights of traveling, the narratives are principally informed not by the travel writer's gaze or the visuality of the travel narrative—as was often the case in colonial European travel narratives[14]—but by social relationships and a whirlwind of people Thomas visits.

Thomas's travel narratives are often addressed directly to readers, as was the custom of the newspapers of the 1920s (see also Peterson and Hunter; Reuster-Jahn, this volume, on the intimacy of many newspapers' addresses to their readers).[15] There is, furthermore, sometimes overlap claimed or implied between addressed readers and named "travellees," as many of Thomas's hosts are imagined or named as readers of his newspapers. This chapter explores how this figure of the named, real-life intradiegetic reader (the reader *within* the text), encountered through travel and travel writing, both reflects and produces the growing readerships of the Yoruba-language Lagos newspapers as they spread across Nigeria. I argue that by textualizing the newspapers' and their writers' movement across space, and their encounters with newspaper readers and patrons throughout Nigeria, the travel narratives play out the writers' growing influence in front of readers' eyes.

TRAVEL NARRATIVES FORGED IN THE PUBLIC SPACE OF THE NEWSPAPERS

Thomas was not the only newspaper travel writer. Five Yoruba newspapers were founded in Lagos in the 1920s, marking a particularly inventive phase in Yoruba-language newspaper publishing, and firmly establishing the role of local editors and writers.[16] Nigerian travel narratives had been published in these Yoruba newspapers since almost their earliest days; one of the first was the five-part serial "Irin-Ajo Lati Eko Lọ Si Kamerun" ("A Journey from Lagos to Cameroon"), published under the pseudonym Ajeji (a Yoruba word meaning "stranger" or "foreigner") in *Eko Akete* in 1923. This was the beginning of a small but enduring trend, with at least fifteen travel narratives published in the Yoruba newspapers *Akede Eko*, *Eleti-Ọfẹ*, and *Eko Akete* between 1923 and 1931. These travel narratives describe their writers' journeys to nearby Ikorodu, Ijẹbu Ode, and Badagry, to the hinterland towns of Ibadan, Ijẹbu Ode, and Ileṣa, and farther afield to Port Harcourt, Onitsha, and other non-Yoruba towns across the southern coast of Nigeria.[17]

The writers of these travel narratives were sometimes other newspaper editors, as in the case of E. A. Akintan, the editor of the Yoruba newspaper *Eleti-Ọfẹ*. But they also included other local intellectuals, such as prominent local historian A. K. Ajiṣafẹ, and pseudonymous writers such "Gay," who was a regular contributor to *Eleti-Ọfẹ* and who wrote two travel narratives in English.[18] After Thomas's 1931 series "Ero L'Ọna Ijẹbu-Ode" ("The Traveler to Ijẹbu-Ode"), this intense publication of travel narratives in the Yoruba newspapers died down. But occasional Nigerian travel series continued to be published into the 1940s and 1950s (see Pratten, this volume, on newspaper editors' tours of Nigeria), and international travel accounts also emerged in greater numbers.

While the style of the travel narratives varied from writer to writer, Akintan, Ajiṣafẹ, and Thomas published the longest and most inventive travel narratives. Despite differences of content, their narratives coalesced into a fairly standardized form. Thomas and Akintan describe meetings with newspaper distributors, readers, and patrons alongside church services and visits to local schools, while in some of his shorter narratives Akintan also describes visits to several Yoruba ọbas. A. K. Ajiṣafẹ, meanwhile, was traveling "lati tubọ wadi aṣa ati ofin ati awọn ọgbọn aṣiri ilẹ Yoruba daradara . . . fun ṣiṣe iwe ọgbọn ati iṣeṣi ilu wa fun aiye lati mọ" ("to research thoroughly the customs, laws, and ancient wisdom of Yorubaland . . . in order to write a book about the wisdom and characteristics of our town for the world to know").[19] His narrative not only describes people and towns, but also gives accounts of Ajiṣafẹ's audiences with Yoruba ọbas, who shared their knowledge of the history of their towns with him.

A comparison with existing forms of locally circulating travel writing emphasizes both the subjective and the public nature of the Lagos newspaper travel narratives. Some of the earliest written travel narratives by Yoruba speakers were the nineteenth-century journals and travel accounts of Yoruba ex-slaves and missionaries such as Samuel Ajayi Crowther, who traveled extensively throughout the Yoruba region in the service of the Church Missionary Society. Crowther's journals were published and read principally in Britain,[20] and were written "in the tradition of early nineteenth-century travellers"[21]—that is, the tradition of European exploration and colonial travel writing. Accordingly, Claudia Gualtieri surmises that Crowther's "discourse is clearly addressed to his British audience and the Church Missionary Society, and in doing so he distances himself from local non-westernized people who are said not to understand him."[22] However, by the early twentieth century, the "explosion of writing and print"[23] in Nigeria and elsewhere in Africa meant that diary-keeping was no longer the preserve of missionaries nor designed to be read overseas, but had also been adopted by other literate Yoruba-speakers including clergy, politicians, clerks, artisans, teachers, and intellectuals.[24]

We can certainly locate the newspaper travelogues as a product of this growing culture of literate self-documentation.[25] But the personal journals kept by missionaries and other literate Nigerians are often full of details of bodily hardship, repetitive church visits, drudgery and hard work, household arrangements and bills paid, and times of arrival and departure: the "day of small things," as J. D. Y. Peel puts it, quoting the missionaries quoting the Bible.[26] The newspaper travel writers, by contrast, already present their traveling as extraordinary, and so their texts document not everyday lived experience, but the most unusual moments of their experience, written explicitly as literary texts, designed to be published.

Indeed, travel narratives written specifically for publication had also been a feature of Lagos print culture since its earliest days. As Karin Barber describes, many of the early diaries and letters written by literate Yoruba speakers were "largely, though perhaps not exclusively, modeled on European prototypes."[27] Similarly, the Lagos newspapers occasionally printed foreign-authored travel writing about West Africa, suggesting that the Lagos travel writers are likely to have been familiar with the conventions of European travel writing.

Moreover, adventure novels such as H. Rider Haggard's *King Solomon's Mines* were also circulating in early twentieth-century West Africa,[28] and Thomas's wilder descriptions of his perilous adventures may owe something to these stories. Bunyan's *Pilgrim's Progress* was also available in Lagos in both Yoruba and English at this time, having been translated into Yoruba as far back as 1866,[29] and thus "indigenized" as part of Yoruba print culture.[30] While there is no direct evidence of influence in the travel narratives, the familiarity of *The Pilgrim's Progress* for Yoruba-language readers means that it could certainly have alerted the travel writers to the possibilities of episodic writing, the journey as a structuring device, and the use of set pieces and dialogue.

However, the Yoruba newspaper travel narratives were swiftly put to local uses, and also developed out of Lagos's particular historical and cultural circumstances.[31] The anglophone Lagos newspapers of the late nineteenth and early twentieth centuries, like newspapers across the West African coast, sometimes printed pieces describing West Africans' travels overseas.[32] They also frequently printed short, factual accounts of individuals' travels within Nigeria: often colonial officers' tours, leisure or work trips by colonial officers or elite Lagosians to regions just outside Lagos, or hometown visits by Lagosian hometown associations.[33] These seemed to appeal to their writers owing to the prestige of having one's social and political life and networks broadcast in print.

A number of more extensive and discursive intra-Nigerian travel narratives were published in the anglophone press of the 1910s. Such travel narratives were expressive of a growing desire among Lagos intellectuals to use their personal experiences of the Yoruba hinterland to (re)claim an affiliation with the Yoruba-speaking region. Their narratives document and valorize Yoruba culture, history and current affairs, often in terms that express their own "civilization" while simultaneously claiming their distinctiveness from European culture.[34] For instance, in the ethnographic-style series "A Tour to the Hinterland," published in the *Lagos Weekly Record* in 1912, "Our Special Correspondent" travels to the Yoruba-speaking towns of Ibadan, Abẹokuta, Ọyọ, Oṣogbo, Ẹdẹ, Ileṣa, and Ifẹ, where he comments on political institutions, rulers, roads, and industry.[35] "Our Special Correspondent" also ventured beyond the Yoruba-speaking region, reflecting growing press interest in the incipient nation of Nigeria: his 1913 series "A Trip to Northern Nigeria and Back" details travels in Zaria, Kano, Katsina, and beyond.[36]

Some of the travel narratives published in the Yoruba-language newspapers in the 1920s and 1930s shared a similar interest in autoethnography[37] and in the documentation of Yoruba or Nigerian culture and society. Those writers who traveled in the nearby Yoruba hinterland often report on local life for their readers, many of whom, as Saros[38] or long-standing Lagosians, claimed ancestry in the Yoruba hinterland but may not have had much firsthand knowledge of it. "Gay," meanwhile, published an English-language travel narrative in *Eleti-Ọfẹ* about his journeys to Ibadan and Badagry, in which he describes Badagry in a tone barely distinguishable from colonial travel writing:

> Houses are built in large compound of about 50 by 200 feet of lands, they are generally more or less family houses, each compound is surrounded by fence made of bamboo, most of the houses are built of thatch. The people who inhabited this country are called "Egun" they lived a simple life, and though they appear to be poor yet they seem to be happy. Majority of them speak in the Yoruba dialect, that simply shows that their descendants must have migrated many years ago from the Yoruba hinterland.[39]

However, many of the Yoruba travel narratives were distinctive in their simultaneous interest in writing the author's self. In this regard, a useful comparison lies not so much in the Lagos press as in a travel account published in the *Gold Coast Leader* by J. G. Mullen, ostensibly a Gold Coast clerk who had traveled to Cameroon and who was subsequently stranded there when the First World War broke out. Mullen's lively account of his journey from present-day Buea into central Cameroon was serialized between 1916 and

1918.⁴⁰ Mullen's circumstances were different; the Lagos travel writers were established local intellectuals and newspapermen, while Mullen claimed to be a clerk. Moreover, Thomas's and Akintan's travel accounts were firmly attached to their public personae, while "Mullen" appears possibly to have been a pseudonym, someone unknown in the press, or even partly fictional.[41] However, like Mullen's narratives, Thomas's newspaper travelogues especially are playful, carefully crafted, and idiosyncratic, distinct from the more impersonal travel reports common in the anglophone press in the 1910s. They are confident in the writer's subjectivity and personal experience as a tool for interpreting the world, much as Stephanie Newell suggests that Mullen "continuously asserts his rationality, his personality, and his ability to reflect on the human condition."[42]

Mullen's narrative was, Newell argues, "without precedent" in colonial Ghana,[43] an early attempt at "writing the self" made possible by the "open, experimental space of the Gold Coast newspapers."[44] The Yoruba travel narratives, too, developed in a period characterized by experiments with literary form and genre.[45] As Karin Barber (this volume) demonstrates, alongside local news, the Yoruba newspapers printed literary texts ranging from *oríkì*[46] to biography, history, poetry, and plays. The first Yoruba novels or novellas—*Ìtàn Èmi Ọmọ-Orùkàn* by E. A. Akintan, and I. B. Thomas's *Ìtàn Ìgbésí-Aiyé Èmi Sẹ̀gilọlá Ẹlẹ́yinjú Ẹgẹ́ Ẹlẹ̀gbẹ̀rùn Ọkọ Láiyé*[47]—were serialized in the newspapers in 1928 and 1929 respectively.[48] Barber's description of Thomas's *Ìtàn Ìgbésí-Aiyé Èmi Sẹ̀gilọlá* could equally be applied to Thomas's travelogues: "They overflowed with emotion, mixing pious exhortations with knowing and nostalgic allusions to the shared popular culture of Lagos, past and present."[49] In fact, Thomas's 1929 "Ero L'Ọna" stops abruptly midjourney and is followed six weeks later by *Ìtàn Ìgbésí-Aiyé Èmi Sẹ̀gilọlá*, as if the travel narrative and the serialized novel were competing for space with one another (and indeed *Ìtàn Ìgbésí-Aiyé Èmi Sẹ̀gilọlá* appears to have been more popular, provoking numerous appreciative letters from readers).[50] The travel narratives thus also form part of this story of the early days of Yoruba print culture, providing space for experiments with genre, form, and audience that subsequently gave birth to the serialized newspaper novel in Yoruba.[51]

TRAVEL NARRATIVES AS DISPLAYS OF SOCIAL CONNECTEDNESS

In her account of Mullen's travelogue, Stephanie Newell describes how Mullen's "relish for plot, action, the exotic and the production of a page-turner seem to override the rules of autobiography."[52] However, in the Yoruba newspaper travelogues, it is not literariness that disrupts the narratives, but their namedropping, the creation and display of complex networks of contacts, and of a sociability that is characteristic of the print culture of early twentieth-century Lagos.

The travel writers used their writing to depict their personal and professional networks spreading across Nigerian space. I. B. Thomas's accounts of his adventures are striking for Thomas's representation of himself as well connected despite southern Nigeria's physical and cultural distance from Lagos. Facing limited infrastructure for traveling as a stranger in this era, Thomas usually depicts himself staying with friends or readers of his newspaper, often migrant Lagosians. His 1931 "Ero L'Ọna" series, at a length of over ten thousand words in nine installments, encompasses a cast of over seventy named characters, mostly friends, business contacts, and important local figures, alongside many unnamed "friends and acquaintances" and townspeople. Thomas's hosts and contacts were from educated and professional circles, broadly similar to Thomas himself: the 1931 series mentions encounters with clerks, traders, teachers, shop owners, pastors, postmasters, a produce buyer, and a medical officer. Thomas also describes encounters with readers, distributors, and representatives of his newspaper, and with political figures such as the exiled Eleko of Lagos and other Yoruba *ọbas*. Although most of his encounters are with people bearing Yoruba or Saro names, he also narrates meetings with named Gold Coasters and Europeans. Those people whose religion he mentions are almost entirely Christians, and many are described as having migrated from Lagos or having family connections there. Even though he often traveled to southern and southeastern Nigeria, where he encountered Igbo-, Ijaw- and Itsekiri-speakers, he rarely represents dialogue or substantial encounters with speakers of these languages, instead offering limited representations of them as "uncivilized" or awaiting the benefits of missionary contact. His personal encounters, therefore, tended to be limited to Yoruba or Lagosian migrants.

I. B. Thomas's frenetic representation of his sociability even encompasses mentions of deceased family and acquaintances, so that he represents his networks spreading across time as well as space. Thus in his 1929 "Ero L'Ọna," for instance, he describes a meeting with Archdeacon D. C. Crowther, in which Crowther was delighted to discover that Thomas was "okan ninu awọn ọmọ-ọmọ Daddy-Ẹlẹkun ni igboro ita-Balogun" ("one of the grandchildren of Daddy-Elekun in the town of Ita-Balogun").[53] Thomas adds: "Tani le sọ bi ori mi ti wule to nigbati alagba-ẹnire-Ojiṣẹ-Ọlọrun yi pi'tan diẹ fun mi nipa igbesi-aiye baba to bi baba mi" ("Who can say how much my head swelled up when this elder pastor recounted a little for me the life history of my grandfather").[54]

Akintan and Ajiṣafẹ, too, depict the Yoruba towns to which they travel as permeated with friends, colleagues, and acquaintances, encompassing editors, priests, writers, schoolteachers, and readers of Akintan's newspaper, *Eleti-Ọfẹ*. Akintan describes some differences of status and education; non-elite acquaintances such as "ọkunrin alagba dudu ara Ibadan kan" ("an elderly black Ibadan man"),[55] who carries his bags, remain nameless. However, the majority of people he meets are named and depicted as being much like him: literate and "civilized." Ajiṣafẹ's account, meanwhile, centers on meetings with *Ọba*s and other rulers for his historical research, as well as colonial officials who help arrange his visits. But he also reports visits to over twenty relatives and friends, clerks, pastors, church congregations, and the Ẹgba Association of Ifẹ, alongside unnamed acquaintances.

As well as these arranged visits and hospitality, Thomas's, Akintan's, and Ajiṣafẹ's texts describe *alabápàdé* (chance meetings) with friends and acquaintances on the streets of the towns they visit: Thomas, for instance, narrates a chance encounter with former pupils from Lagos in a small town in southeastern Nigeria.[56] Such encounters allow the writers to represent their circles of influence as being so extensive and mobile that they could unexpectedly meet acquaintances anywhere. Thus while the Gold Coast travel writer J. G. Mullen emphasizes his isolation, as neither a Cameroonian "native" nor a German,[57] the Lagos travelogue writers represent precisely the opposite: their social connectedness within Nigeria.

The writers' display of their sociability and networks was accompanied by ritualized representations of their hosts' hospitality, to the extent that sometimes the travel narratives read as a vehicle for the writer's display of gratitude and connectedness. The writers nearly always describe being met by a friend, showered with delicious food and drink, shown around the town, and introduced to their hosts' friends. Their descriptions of this hospitality become predictable, reproduced sometimes with identical phrasing from one series to another. They praise qualities of their hosts, especially their hospitality—hosts welcome Thomas "tọwọ tẹsẹ" ("with open arms")[58] or "gẹgẹbi ọba ti nṣe enia l'alejo" ("in just the way an *ọba* treats a visitor")[59]—as if the narratives are *oríkì* (praise poetry) transformed into writing.[60]

It is likely that Thomas was aware of libel cases increasingly landing at the feet of newspaper editors, and was thus careful to avoid anything but bland assertions of his hosts' good character.⁶¹ But moreover, in a short piece called "Irin-Ajo" ("Traveling") that prefaces his 1929 travel narrative, Thomas describes the importance of what he sees as a distinctively Yoruba traveling sociability based on *iwà* (behavior or character): "Bi o ti le wun ki awọn Yoruba tabi ọmọ Eko meji ma rẹ pọ to ni ile, ṣugbọn nigba nwọn ba f'oju ganni arawọn ni idalẹ, bi ọmọ iya ni nwọn mba arawọn lo pọ; iwa yi dara pupọ, o si yẹ fun wa gẹgẹbi ọmọ Yoruba lati ṣ'ogo le iwa rere na l'ori; ẹ jẹ ki gbogbo wa papa awọn enia wa ti nwọn mbẹ ni idalẹ tubọ ma tẹ siwaju nipa titẹle iwa rere na"⁶² ("Whatever terms two Yorubas or Lagosians are on at home, when they run into each other on a journey, they get on like children of the same mother. This behavior is very good, and it is befitting for us as Yorubas to boast about this good character. Let all of us, especially our people abroad, increasingly continue to display this good behavior"). The travel narratives can thus be read as an opportunity for Thomas to portray both himself and his hosts as *ọmọlúwàbí*—people of good character—amid webs of reciprocated welcome and hospitality.

The travel writers did not depict all of Nigeria as a known place, full of friends and acquaintances. The sociability of the travel narratives occurs against a backdrop of unnamed Nigerians, whether the Yoruba-speaking "ara ilu oke" ("hinterland people") or the Itsekiri and Igbo peoples, whom Thomas describes variously as friendly and welcoming, benign but ignorant heathens or even former cannibals.⁶³ But nonetheless, despite these moments of defamiliarization, the travel narratives imply that wherever the writer travels, a Yoruba Christian or Lagosian awaits him with familiar rituals of hospitality.

CO-OPTING READERS THROUGH TRAVEL

While travelogues may have had some literary appeal for the Lagos travel writers, the traveling newspaper editors were first and foremost taking advantage of new travel infrastructure in order to expand their readerships. Accordingly, the sociability of the travel narratives demonstrates the demands print culture made upon editors, authors, and readers, and in particular how Thomas's networking enabled him to imagine and convene changing newspaper readerships.

In the opening installment of his 1929 "Ero L'Ọna," Thomas informs his readers that he is traveling "fun ire ati ilọsiwaju iwe irohin mi yi" ("for the benefit and the progress of this, my newspaper"), and he reminisces about a previous journey to Minna, Jos, Kaduna, and Kano that "ṣe iwe irohin mi yi li ore pupọ" ("made this my newspaper many friends").⁶⁴ The spread of the newspapers reflected the growth of communities of educated Africans across Nigeria.⁶⁵ In the 1920s, *Akede Eko*, *Eko Akete*, and *Eleti-Ọfẹ* printed news from and about the Yoruba region and the rest of Nigeria, often tracing the routes of the growing Nigerian rail network. News was printed from Bauchi, Kaduna, Maiduguri, Zaria, Port Harcourt, Kano, Gusau, Ekiti, Ọffa, Abẹokuta, Warri, Ẹdẹ, Enugu, Ileṣa, Ibadan, Ọyọ, Ilọrin, Ogbomọṣọ, Ikalẹ, Oṣogbo, Ondo, Ijẹbu Rẹmọ, Ọwọ, and Minna, as well as foreign cities such as Freetown, London, and Medina. *Akede Eko* sometimes published articles about towns that I. B. Thomas had recently visited on his travels.

Thomas represented himself as especially successful in establishing his newspaper throughout Nigeria. In 1929, *Akede Eko* boasted (in English), "There is hardly any town in the Province where the *Akede Eko* cannot now be bought. The ambition and energy of this enterprising Editor is well known to many in this community."⁶⁶ In 1931, Thomas elaborated on his newspaper's growing reach, again emphasizing his personal work:

> Emi ko le rohin tan bo ti jẹ pe iwe irohin "Akede Eko" yi ti fi ẹsẹ mu'lẹ to ni igboro ilu Ilesha, okiki iwe irohin "Akede Eko" yi ko ni ẹgbẹ ni igboro ilu Ilesha; ẹnu ya emi papa . . . mo ti tun gbiyanju lati fi ẹsẹ iwe irohin mi "Akede Eko" na mu'lẹ ninu awọn ilu titun wọnyi bi:—Ọyọ, Awẹ, Ogbomọshọ, Akurẹ, Ondo, Ọwọ, Benin City, Onitsha, Ẹnugu, Aba, laisọ ti ilu Port Harcourt to jẹ pe iwe irohin "Akede Eko" ti di onile ati ọlọna ni igboro ilu na.⁶⁷

> Since the newspaper *Akede Eko* has become established in Ileṣa, the fame of this newspaper *Akede Eko* has no competitor in Ileṣa; even I was surprised. . . . I also tried to establish my newspaper *Akede Eko* among these new towns: Ọyọ, Awẹ, Ogbomọṣọ, Akurẹ, Ondo, Ọwọ, Benin City, Onitsha, Enugu, Aba, without mentioning Port Harcourt, where the *Akede Eko* newspaper has become local in that town.

With Thomas establishing this connection between his own travels and the spread of *Akede Eko*, his travelogues' representations of sociability were not just an attempt to demonstrate his personal social connections. Many of the people Thomas encounters during his travels are described as readers, or newly co-opted readers, of his newspaper. Just as Thomas depicts his network of acquaintances stretching throughout Nigeria, so too he imagines readers of the *Akede Eko* permeating the towns to which he travels. In 1929, for instance, Thomas reports an encounter with a prominent newspaper reader in Port Harcourt: "inu mi si dun pupọ lati gbọ wipe ẹni're Lọya Lucas jẹ ọkan pataki ni ilu Pọta yi to nka iwe irohin (Akede Eko) nigbagbogbo; ẹnu kekere kọ lo si ya mi nigbati Lọya Lucas bo 'Kudi' (owo) lu mi wipe on fi ṣe iranl'ọwọ fun mi ninu iṣẹ iwe irohin na" ("I was very pleased to hear as well how the good Lawyer Lucas was one of the important people of this town, Port Harcourt, who reads the newspaper (*Akede Eko*) all the time; I was not a little surprised when Lawyer Lucas gave me 'Kudi' (money) to help me in my enterprise of the newspaper").[68]

Thomas also used the travelogues to bolster the reputation of the newspaper in the eyes of its existing and potential readership, by representing its both eminent and growing readership, gained through Thomas's travels. While in Muṣin, for example, he notes that he has met "Oloye Fatayọ ni ilu Muṣhin yi ati awọn enia pataki diẹ ni ilu na, gbogbo wọn ni nwọn si ṣe ileri wipe awọn yio ma ra iwe irohin 'Akede Eko' ka lọsọsẹ lati isisiyi lọ titi lailai—Bẹni ko ri, Amin!" ("Chief Fatayọ in Muṣin, and a few other important people of the town. All of them promised they would buy *Akede Eko* to read every week, from now and forever more—may it be so, amen!").[69] Thomas's descriptions of the work of spreading the reach of his newspapers remind us that, as Karin Barber points out, Yoruba print culture "did not follow automatically from the availability of printing technology. It was a creation, an innovation that participants consciously worked on."[70]

Throughout his travel narratives, Thomas often rhetorically greets and addresses his readers directly, summoning them with a degree of intimacy. His farewell letter in 1929, for instance, sends greetings to "ẹnyin ẹbi on ara mi olufẹ, si ẹnyin ọkawe mi, si ẹnyin ọrẹ mi olufẹ, si ẹnyin alabaṣiṣẹ mi ọwọn, ati si olukuluku ẹnyin enia ti ẹ o da mi l'ọla lati ka iwe idagbere mi yi" ("you my beloved family and people, to you my readers, to you my dear friends, to you my dear colleagues, and to each of you people who will do me the honor of reading this my farewell letter").[71] He rhetorically commands readers to respond to him and even pray for him: "Alafia ni emi ero l'ọna mbẹ l'oni, mo si ni ero wipe alafia ni gbogbo ẹnyin ọkawe mi na mbẹ bakanna, ẹ maṣe gbagbe mi ninu adura nyin" ("I, the traveler, am in good health today, and I think you, my readers, are too. Don't forget me in your prayers").[72]

But Thomas's textual representations of traveling encounters with readers and patrons meant that Thomas could claim that the readers he addressed were not just these "implied" or "imagined" audiences, but also actual readers, named and co-opted into the text. The newspapers' circulations were indeed small enough for Thomas to know many of his readers personally, although also growing, as Thomas claimed; *Akede Eko*'s circulation increased from eight hundred readers weekly to a thousand readers weekly from 1929 to 1930, while *Eleti-Ofẹ* averaged around seven hundred readers per week from 1925 to 1930.[73]

Thus in the middle of his 1931 "Ero L'Ọna" series, Thomas printed a separate article in which he addresses particular readers, explaining that he had now returned home and wanted to greet friends, readers, and "awọn aimọye enia rere" ("countless good people") who had welcomed him on his journeys. He lists seventeen individually named men whom he thanks for hosting him on his journey (and adds that he also thanks their wives for the delicious food they provided).[74] It is not clear whether these hosts were readers of the newspaper; the list of names can be read as a rhetorical gesture designed to advertise Thomas's connectedness. Nonetheless, the text implies or even conscripts these hosts as individual readers—in Garrett Stewart's sense of the reader "conscripted" or "deliberately drafted"[75] by the text to play particular roles, as "part of the script"[76]—by addressing them directly, and in doing so it marshals them as evidence of the newspaper's pan-Nigerian readership.

What is so important about the hospitality Thomas encounters from the friends he meets as he travels is therefore that it is recorded *in print*, for readers to see. There is a power play of reciprocity enacted through the printed text; his hosts' hospitality puts Thomas in their debt, so in return he offers display and archiving in print of his hosts' generosity and status. When Thomas encounters a car belonging to his hosts in Aba, he stresses the spectacle his hosts have put on for him: the car is "alarabara" ("resplendent"), while its driver "fa ọṣọ yọ nipataki" (is decked out "in splendid style"). This is so, Thomas jokes, because the driver had been told he was driving the editor of the *Akede Eko*, and that if he didn't impress him, the newspaper "yio kede rẹ fun araiye gbọ" ("would proclaim it for the world to hear").[77] Thomas represents his own power as generating the owner's lighthearted but calculated display of spectacular hospitality; that power is produced by Thomas's ability to broadcast the printed word to a wider readership. Thomas thus generates a form of authorship centered on his ability to write about others. He uses his travel narratives to maneuver or script his readers, asking them to accept the power of print to broadcast social relations to "araiye" (the "people of the world"). His praising of his hosts is performative and generative; by holding out the possibility of naming someone publicly as a generous host, it *makes* future hosts generous, reminiscent of the way *oríkì* are imagined to actualize the performance of the latent qualities of a person whom they name.[78]

But as Stephen Colclough reminds us, readers may "rebel against, comply with or simply ignore" textual instructions, conventions, or attempts to control reader responses.[79] In the Lagos travelogues we read not the readers' responses, but the authors' attempts to make audiences and to suggest how readers should respond to a growing print sphere. The travel narratives' apparent openness to the representation of figures beyond the writer is filtered through the writer's power to choose whom to represent; opposing or subversive voices never appear. The sociability of the travel narratives is thus not necessarily a polyvocality; the writers are staging dialogues, rather than allowing the hosts' own voices to permeate the texts. Non-Yoruba speakers, such as Igbo- and Itsekiri-speakers, furthermore, occupy an ambiguous position in the travel narratives, often unnamed and not the subjects of the sociability of the travel narratives, sometimes even objectified as naked bodies or former cannibals. However, Thomas also teaches his readers a small number of Igbo and Itsekiri words by printing them in his travel narratives, as if imagining how (limited) dialogue with speakers of these languages could be opened up within the expanding scope of Nigerian print culture.[80]

The desire to name one's readers has been present in many kinds of texts. Jon Klancher, in his study of readerships in early nineteenth-century Britain, attributes writers' increasingly conscious *creation* of readerships to the uncertainty of the eighteenth century, when "no single, unified 'reading public' could be addressed" and thus writers "carved out new readerships and transformed old ones."[81] We see a similar uncertainty about readerships in the Lagos travelogues, as the newspapers' readerships were no longer necessarily primarily Lagosians—as was imagined by the newspapers to have been the case in the late nineteenth century[82]—but could potentially be convened all over Nigeria, as the travel narratives themselves suggest.

We could therefore also read in the travel narratives what Patrick Brantlinger describes as "the nervousness of authors about how their stories may be *mis*interpreted by readers whom they have no way of knowing, much less controlling."[83] Thomas depicts himself *knowing* his readers, meeting them and controlling their responses to his presence—but at the same time his travel narratives also represent the expanding scope of the newspapers, to the point at which the newspaper editor or writer could no longer know *all* his readers. By encountering and naming his readers and potential readers, Thomas develops a particular sociability of print based on displaying and addressing friends and readers in an apparently intimate tone—while also reaching toward ever greater audiences.

CONCLUSION

It is because of the importance of representations of the author's personal sociability that the Lagos newspapers travel writers often used their own names rather than the pseudonyms that otherwise permeated the early colonial-era newspapers in West Africa. This use of their own names was not simply the default option; I. B. Thomas demonstrated his mastery of the playful pseudonym as he ventriloquized the fictional Lagos prostitute Sẹgilọla in his novel *Ìtàn Ìgbésí-Aiyé Èmi Sẹ̀gilọlá*,[84] suggesting that he could easily have adopted a pseudonym for his travel narratives had he wished. This is not to say that Thomas the sociable traveler was not also a persona; but nonetheless it was, as Stephanie Newell puts it, an "authorial body"[85] to which Thomas found it useful to assign his real name. As Newell has shown, particularly from the 1940s, journalists such as Azikiwe and Wallace-Johnson often chose to use their own names; "they generally *wanted* readers to attribute the content of their columns to a physically present, politically active person."[86] The 1920s travel narratives were less politically oriented, but they nonetheless express similar ideas about real names as a marker of the "physically present" writer.

Thus in their travel narratives, I. B. Thomas and E. A Akintan textualize not only their own importance as social actors, but also the newspapers' growing and increasingly translocal and transnational readerships. The Lagos travel narratives' emphasis on dialogue and sociability, rather than the traveler's gaze, is a function not only of the writers' relationship with their Lagosian migrant "travellees"—as partners in civilization, rather than subjects in relation to the colonizer more typical of contemporaneous European travel writing—but also of their addressive print culture that enabled and expected the incorporation of readers, patrons, and "travellees."

BIBLIOGRAPHY

Adams, Percy. *Travel Literature and the Evolution of the Novel*. Lexington: University Press of Kentucky, 1983.

Adler, Judith. "Travel as Performed Art." *American Journal of Sociology* 94, no. 6 (1989): 1366–91.

Barber, Karin. *I Could Speak until Tomorrow*. Edinburgh: Edinburgh University Press, 1991.

Barber, Karin. "I.B. Akinyẹle and Early Yoruba Print Culture." In *Recasting the Past: History Writing and Political Work in Modern Africa*, edited by Derek Peterson and Giacomo Macola, 31–49. Athens: Ohio University Press, 2009.

Barber, Karin. "Introduction: Hidden Innovators in Africa." In *Africa's Hidden Histories: Everyday Literacy and Making the Self*, edited by Karin Barber, 1–24. Bloomington: Indiana University Press, 2006.

Barber, Karin. *Print Culture and the First Yoruba Novel: I. B. Thomas's "Life Story of Me, Sẹgilọla" and Other Texts*. Leiden: Brill, 2012.

Barber, Karin. "Translation, Publics, and the Vernacular Press in 1920s Lagos." In *Christianity and Social Change in Africa: Essays in Honour of J. D. Y. Peel*, edited by Toyin Falola, 187–208. Durham, NC: Carolina Academic Press, 2005.

Brantlinger, Patrick. *The Reading Lesson: The Threat of Mass Literacy in Nineteenth-Century British Fiction*. Bloomington: Indiana University Press, 1998.

Colclough, Stephen. *Consuming Texts: Readers and Reading Communities, 1695–1870*. Basingstoke: Palgrave Macmillan, 2007.

Doortmont, Michel. "Recapturing the Past: Samuel Johnson and the Construction of the History of the Yoruba." PhD dissertation, Erasmus Universiteit Rotterdam, 1994.

Echeruo, Michael. *Victorian Lagos: Aspects of Nineteenth Century Lagos Life*. London: Macmillan, 1977.

Falola, Toyin. *Yoruba Gurus: Indigenous Production of Knowledge in Africa*. Trenton, NJ: Africa World Press, 1999.

Gualtieri, Claudia. *Representations of West Africa as Exotic in British Colonial Travel Writing*. Lewiston: Edwin Mellen Press, 2002.

Hofmeyr, Isabel. *The Portable Bunyan: A Transnational History of "The Pilgrim's Progress"*. Princeton, NJ: Princeton University Press, 2004.

Jones, Rebecca. "The Benefits of Travel: Travel Writing in the Lagos Newspapers 1912–1931." *Journal of History and Cultures* 2 (2013): 39–56.

Jones, Rebecca. "Journeys to the Hinterland: Early Twentieth Century Nigerian Domestic Travel Writing and Local Heterogeneity." *Postcolonial Text* 9, no. 4 (2014): 1–19.

Klancher, Jon P. *The Making of English Reading Audiences, 1790–1832*. Madison: University of Wisconsin Press, 1987.

Newell, Stephanie. "An Introduction to the Writings of J.G. Mullen, An African Clerk, in the Gold Coast Leader, 1916–19." *Africa* 78, no. 3 (2008): 384–400.

Newell, Stephanie. "Newspapers, New Spaces, New Writers: The First World War and Print Culture in Colonial Ghana." *Research in African Literatures* 40, no. 2 (2009): 1–15.

Newell, Stephanie. *The Power to Name: A History of Anonymity in Colonial West Africa*. Athens: Ohio University Press, 2013.

Ní Loingsigh, Aedín, *Postcolonial Eyes: Intercontinental Travel in Francophone African Literature*. Liverpool: Liverpool University Press, 2009.

Olukotun, Ayo. "At the Barricades: Resurgent Media in Colonial Nigeria, 1900–1960." In *The Foundations of Nigeria: Essays in Honour of Toyin Falola*, edited by Adebayo Oyebade, 229–46. Trenton, NJ: Africa World Press, 2003.

Omu, Fred I. A. *Press and Politics in Nigeria, 1880–1937*. London: Longman, 1978.

Peel, J. D. Y. "For Who Hath Despised the Day of Small Things? Missionary Narratives and Historical Anthropology." *Comparative Studies in History and Society* 37, no. 3 (1995): 581–607.

Pratt, Mary Louise. *Imperial Eyes: Travel Writing and Transculturation*. 2nd ed. London: Routledge, 2008.

Rubery, Matthew. *The Novelty of Newspapers: Victorian Fiction after the Invention of News*. Oxford: Oxford University Press, 2009.

Sawada, Nozomi. "The Educated Elite and Associational Life in Early Lagos Newspapers: In Search of Unity for the Progress of Society." PhD dissertation, University of Birmingham, 2011.

Spurr, David. *The Rhetoric of Empire: Colonial Discourse in Journalism, Travel Writing and Imperial Administration*. Durham, NC: Duke University Press, 1993.

Stewart, Garrett. *Dear Reader: The Conscripted Audience in Nineteenth-Century British Fiction*. Baltimore: John Hopkins University Press, 1996.

Trager, Lillian. *Yoruba Hometowns: Community, Identity and Development in Nigeria*. Boulder, CO: Lynne Rienner, 2001.

Urry, John. *The Tourist Gaze*. 2nd ed. London: Sage, 2002.

Zachernuk, Philip S. *Colonial Subjects: An African Intelligentsia and Atlantic Ideas*. Charlottesville: University Press of Virginia, 2000.

NOTES TO CHAPTER FOUR

1. I. B. Thomas, "Ero L'Ọna," *Akede Eko*, 21 February 1931, 7.

2. A traditional ruler of a town.

3. I gratefully acknowledge an Arts and Humanities Research Council Doctoral Studentship that enabled me to carry out the research for this chapter, and the European Research Council–funded project "Knowing Each Other: Everyday Religious Encounters, Social Identities and Tolerance in Southwest Nigeria" (grant agreement no. 283466), which enabled me to revise the chapter.

Note on orthography: I have used full diacritics for the Yoruba words that I have used in the main text of this chapter, except for personal names and places, for which I have used only sub-dots. However, many Yoruba texts themselves use diacritics inconsistently. For quotations from Yoruba texts, I have preserved their original diacritics, and I have also faithfully reproduced all spelling and orthographical mistakes in the original Yoruba texts.

4. Fred I. A. Omu, *Press and Politics in Nigeria, 1880–1937* (London: Longman, 1978), 84.

5. I. B. Thomas, "Ero L'Ọna," *Akede Eko*, 21 February 1931, 7.

6. I. B. Thomas, "Ero L'Ọna" Ijẹbu Ode," *Akede Eko*, 26 September 1931, 8.

7. I. B. Thomas, "Ero L'Ọna," *Akede Eko*, 18 April 1929, 7.

8. I. B. Thomas, "Ero L'Ọna," *Akede Eko*, 2 February 1931, 6.

9. I. B. Thomas, "Ero L'Ọna," *Akede Eko*, 18 April 1929, 6.

10. I. B. Thomas, "Ero L'Ọna," *Akede Eko*, 16 May 1929, 7.

11. For more on the travel writers' notions of the benefits of travel, see Rebecca Jones, "The Benefits of Travel: Travel Writing in the Lagos Newspapers 1912–1931," *Journal of History and Cultures* 2 (2013): 39–56.

12. "Irin-Ajo," *Akede Eko*, 11 April 1929, 6.

13. Judith Adler, "Travel as Performed Art," *American Journal of Sociology* 94, no. 6 (1989): 1382.

14. See, for instance, the "imperial I/eye" and commanding gaze of the imperial travel writer, "surveillance" as a trope of imperial rhetoric, and the "tourist gaze" in Mary Louise Pratt, *Imperial Eyes: Travel Writing and Transculturation*, 2nd ed. (London: Routledge, 2008); David Spurr, *The Rhetoric of Empire: Colonial Discourse in Journalism, Travel Writing and Imperial Administration* (Durham, NC: Duke University Press, 1993); John Urry, *The Tourist Gaze*, 2nd ed. (London: Sage, 2002).

As Aedín Ní Loingsigh has shown, African travel writers make use of the gaze too—and indeed, at times, so do the 1920s Lagos newspaper travel writers—but nonetheless the Lagos newspaper travel writers' focus on sociability is distinctive. Aedín Ní Loingsigh, *Postcolonial Eyes: Intercontinental travel in Francophone African literature* (Liverpool: Liverpool University Press, 2009).

15. Karin Barber, *Print Culture and the First Yoruba Novel: I. B. Thomas's "Life Story of Me, Segilọla" and Other Texts* (Leiden: Brill, 2012), 42–48; Karin Barber, "Translation, Publics, and the Vernacular Press in 1920s Lagos," in *Christianity and Social Change in Africa: Essays in Honour of J. D. Y. Peel*, ed. Toyin Falọla (Durham, NC: Carolina Academic Press, 2005), 188.

16. Barber, *Print Culture*, 27–34.

17. See Jones, "The Benefits of Travel" for a more detailed history of the development of Yoruba-language travelogues in the 1920s.

18. Although usually referred to as Yoruba-language newspapers, these newspapers also regularly published some columns in English.

19. A. K. Ajiṣafẹ, "Irin-Ajo Kakiri Ilu Oke," *Akede Eko*, 28 June 1930, 5.

20. Michel Doortmont, "Recapturing the Past: Samuel Johnson and the Construction of the History of the Yoruba," PhD dissertation, Erasmus Universiteit Rotterdam, 1994, 43.

21. Doortmont, "Recapturing the Past," 39.

22. Claudia Gualtieri, *Representations of West Africa as Exotic in British Colonial Travel Writing* (Lewiston, NY: Edwin Mellen Press, 2002), 229–30.

23. Karin Barber, "Introduction: Hidden Innovators in Africa," in *Africa's Hidden Histories: Everyday Literacy and Making the Self*, ed. Karin Barber (Bloomington: Indiana University Press, 2006), 1.

24. Barber, "Introduction," 1–21.

25. It is certainly possible that the Lagos travel writers could have read the CMS and other missionaries' travel journals. Thomas and the other travel writers may have had access to missionary reports via the CMS Bookshop, which was by the 1920s well established in Lagos (Doortmont, "Recapturing the Past," 41–47). Thomas in particular may have known Samuel Ajayi Crowther's work, being acquainted with Crowther's son (Archdeacon D. C. Crowther, whom Thomas reports meeting on one of his journeys) and grandson, Herbert Macaulay, whose biography Thomas wrote.

26. J. D. Y. Peel, "For Who Hath Despised the Day of Small Things? Missionary Narratives and Historical Anthropology," *Comparative Studies in History and Society* 37, no. 3 (1995): 581–607.

27. Barber, "Introduction," 7.

28. Stephanie Newell, "An Introduction to the Writings of J.G. Mullen, an African Clerk, in the Gold Coast Leader, 1916–19," *Africa* 78, no. 3 (2008): 390.

29. Isabel Hofmeyr, *The Portable Bunyan: A Transnational History of "The Pilgrim's Progress"* (Princeton, NJ: Princeton University Press, 2004), 242.

30. Hofmeyr, *The Portable Bunyan*, 192.

31. At the same time, it is worth noting that the Lagos travel narratives were not unique in West Africa; for instance, travel narratives were also published in the francophone Cameroonian press in the early twentieth century (Emma Hunter, personal communication, 23 March 2014), and in the colonial Gold Coast press.

32. For instance, see J. A. Payne's accounts of his trip to England via Sierra Leone, Senegal, and South America for the Colonial and Indian Exhibition of 1886, published in several Lagos newspapers, as described in Nozomi Sawada, "The Educated Elite and Associational Life in Early Lagos Newspapers: In Search of Unity for the Progress of Society," PhD dissertation, University of Birmingham, 2011, 222–35. Sawada suggests that Payne used his experience of travel, broadcast through the press, to "confirm his elite position and respectability" in Lagos society.

33. Hometown associations were organizations established by Yoruba migrants and their descendants in Lagos and other large towns. See Lillian Trager, *Yoruba Hometowns: Community, Identity and Development in Nigeria* (Boulder, CO: Lynne Rienner, 2001).

34. See Philip S. Zachernuk, *Colonial Subjects: An African Intelligentsia and Atlantic Ideas* (Charlottesville: University Press of Virginia, 2000), 119–24; Karin Barber, "I.B. Akinyẹle and Early Yoruba Print Culture," in *Recasting the Past: History Writing and Political Work in Modern Africa*, ed. Derek Peterson and Giacomo Macola (Athens: Ohio University Press, 2009), 32–34.

35. Our Special Correspondent, "A Tour to the Hinterland," *Lagos Weekly Record*, 19 October 1912; 26 October 1912; 9 November 1912.

36. Our Special Correspondent, "A Trip to Northern Nigeria and Back," *Lagos Weekly Record*, 2 August 1913; 9 August 1913, 16 August 1913. Although Our Special Correspondent did not refer to his or her gender, female writers were so few among the Lagos newspaper writers at the time that I have deliberately used the masculine pronoun.

37. Mary Louise Pratt defines autoethnography as "instances in which colonized subjects undertake to represent themselves in ways that *engage with* the colonizer's terms . . . in response to or in dialogue with . . . metropolitan representations": Pratt, *Imperial Eyes*, 9.

38. Saros were ex-slave Sierra Leoneans or their descendants who had settled in Lagos and the hinterland, many of whom were of Yoruba descent. In the nineteenth century they had formed Lagos's elite, and though by the 1920s that elite was more diverse, they maintained a distinctive culture based on Christianity and literacy.

39. Gay, "A Travellers' Obsevations [sic]," *Eleti-Ọfẹ*, 1 September 1926, 10.

40. Newell, "Writings of J.G. Mullen," 384–400; Stephanie Newell, "Newspapers, New Spaces, New Writers: The First World War and Print Culture in Colonial Ghana," *Research in African Literatures* 40, no. 2 (2009): 1–15.

41. Newell, "Writings of J.G. Mullen," 389–90.

42. Newell, "Newspapers, New Spaces," 9.

43. Newell, "Newspapers, New Spaces," 5.

44. Newell, "Newspapers, New Spaces," 11.

45. Barber, *Print Culture*, 48–65.

46. Yoruba oral praise poetry or attributive poetry.

47. "The life story of me, Segilola of the fascinating eyes, she who had a thousand lovers in her life" in Karin Barber's translation: Barber, *Print Culture*, 34–65.

48. Barber, *Print Culture*, 34–65.

49. Barber, *Print Culture*, 5.

50. Barber, *Print Culture*, 6.

51. There was a similarly close and symbiotic relationship between travel writing, newspapers, and the novel in Europe; see Percy Adams, *Travel Literature and the Evolution of the Novel* (Lexington: University Press of Kentucky, 1983).

52. Newell, "Writings of J.G. Mullen," 393.

53. I. B. Thomas, "Ero L'Ọna," *Akede Eko*, 9 May 1929, 4.

54. I. B. Thomas, "Ero L'Ọna," *Akede Eko*, 9 May 1929, 4.

55. E. A. Akintan, "Irin Ajo Lati Eko Lọ Si Ilẹsa," *Eleti-Ọfẹ*, 24 November 1926, 9.

56. I. B. Thomas, "Ero L'Ọna!," *Eleti-Ọfẹ*, 30 June 1926, 8. Before becoming a newspaper editor, Thomas had worked as a schoolteacher in Lagos.

57. Newell, "Newspapers, New Spaces," 4.

58. I. B. Thomas, "Ero L'Ọna," *Akede Eko*, 9 May 1929, 7.

59. I. B. Thomas, "Ero L'Ọna," *Akede Eko*, 9 May 1929, 7.

60. Thanks to Kelly Askew (personal communication, 23 April 2012) for this observation.

61. Libel was an ever-present threat for colonial West African newspapers; see Ayo Olukotun, "At the Barricades: Resurgent Media in Colonial Nigeria, 1900–1960," in *The Foundations of Nigeria: Essays in Honour of Toyin Falola*, ed. Adebayo Oyebade (Trenton, NJ: Africa World Press, 2003), 237–39.

62. I. B. Thomas, "Irin-Ajo," *Akede Eko*, 11 April 1929, 6.

63. See Jones, "The Benefits of Travel" for more on the travel writers' depictions of Nigerian space and of non-Yoruba societies.

64. I. B. Thomas, "Idagbere 'Ero L'Ọna,'" *Akede Eko*, 11 April 1929, 7. The issues of the newspapers possibly containing the narrative describing this trip to northern Nigeria were not available during my research in the National Archives of Nigeria.

65. See Zachernuk, *Colonial Subjects*, 91.

66. "News and Notes," *Akede Eko*, 9 May 1929, 8.

67. I. B. Thomas, "Ero L'Ọna," *Akede Eko*, 14 March 1931, 6.

68. I. B. Thomas, "Ero L'Ọna," *Akede Eko*, 9 May 1929, 6.

69. I. B. Thomas, "'Ero L'Ọna' Ijẹbu Ode," *Akede Eko*, 3 October 1931, 4.

70. Barber, "I. B. Akinyẹle," 47.

71. I. B. Thomas, "Idagbere "Ero L'Ọna," *Akede Eko*, 11 April 1929, 7.

72. I. B. Thomas, "Ero L'Ọna," *Akede Eko*, 14 February 1931, 7.

73. Omu, *Press and Politics*, 261–62.

74. I. B. Thomas, "A Lọ Were! A Bọ Were!! Oju T'Ẹni Ti Ko Lọ!!!" *Akede Eko*, 21 March 1931, 8.

75. Garrett Stewart, *Dear Reader: The Conscripted Audience in Nineteenth-Century British Fiction* (Baltimore: John Hopkins University Press, 1996), 8.

76. Stewart, *Dear Reader*, 6.

77. I. B. Thomas, "Ero L'Ọna," *Akede Eko*, 16 May 1929, 7.

78. Karin Barber, *I Could Speak until Tomorrow* (Edinburgh: Edinburgh University Press, 1991), 75–78.

79. Stephen Colclough, *Consuming Texts: Readers and Reading Communities, 1695–1870* (Basingstoke: Palgrave Macmillan, 2007), 15.

80. For more on the travel writers' varying representations of Nigerian spaces and peoples, see Rebecca Jones, "Journeys to the Hinterland: Early Twentieth Century Nigerian Domestic Travel Writing and Local Heterogeneity," *Postcolonial Text* 9, no. 4 (2014): 6–9.

81. Jon P. Klancher, *The Making of English Reading Audiences, 1790–1832* (Madison: University of Wisconsin Press, 1987), 3.

82. Michael Echeruo, *Victorian Lagos: Aspects of Nineteenth Century Lagos Life* (London: Macmillan, 1977), 6.

83. Patrick Brantlinger, *The Reading Lesson: The Threat of Mass Literacy in Nineteenth-Century British Fiction* (Bloomington: Indiana University Press, 1998), 19, cited in Colclough, *Consuming Texts*, 21.

84. Barber, *Print Culture*; Stephanie Newell, *The Power to Name: A History of Anonymity in Colonial West Africa* (Athens: Ohio University Press, 2013), 139–58.

85. Newell, *Power to Name*, 149.

86. Newell, *Power to Name*, 17.

CHAPTER 5

Colonial Modernity and Tradition

Herbert Macaulay, the Newspaper Press, and the (Re)Production of Engaged Publics in Colonial Lagos

WALE ADEBANWI

An extraordinary incident[1] happened in the Colony of Lagos in 1920. A White Cap Chief, Chief Oluwo (Amọdu Tijani), challenged the British colonial government's claim over land that was supposed to have been "ceded" to the British by Dosunmu, the former Eleko (king of Lagos), in the Treaty of Cession (1861). The British proclamation of the Colony of Lagos was based on this treaty. This was, therefore, a fundamental challenge to British suzerainty in Lagos. In 1919, the Court of Nigeria decided that the chief could only exercise administrative rights of a "seigneurial kind"[2] over the land. Dissatisfied, the chief appealed to the Judicial Committee of the Privy Council (JCPC) in England. In 1921, the Privy Council, in *Amodu Tijani v. Secretary, Southern Provinces*,[3] decided in favor of the chief by ruling that the treaty of 1861 did not affect the "undisputed right of the Community."[4] The JCPC added that King Dosunmu, when he entered into a treaty with the British in 1861, did not have "feudal authority" or "seigniorial rights" over his chiefs and the land held in trust by them.[5]

In the case involving the "adjudication of colonial difference,"[6] Chief Oluwo, who traveled to England to represent his community, was supported universally by the people of Lagos. He was specifically encouraged and accompanied by Herbert Macaulay, a journalist, surveyor, and the grandson of the first African bishop, Bishop Ajayi Crowther, and one of the key members of the emergent local elite in Lagos. Macaulay was described in the *Lagos Weekly Record* as one who could "speak the white man's language with poise and authority."[7] He served as the secretary and interpreter to Oluwa during the appellant's journey to London.[8] Macaulay was more significant than that, however. He was a thorn in the side of the colonial government[9] as well as the conservative elite of the island who supported the colonial government. He was also one of the best-educated elite supporters of the ruling house, called the House of Dosunmu (or House of Docemo, by the British). Given the crucial nature of "landed interests" in a "traditional African community," as Richard Sklar puts it,[10] Macaulay's image soared further with the victory over the government of Nigeria at the Privy Council. He gloried in his assumed status as "Minister Plenipotentiary of the House of Docemo."

Being a journalist back in the colony, Macaulay knew the power of the press in Britain. He granted an interview to the *Daily Mail* in London stating that seventeen million natives recognized the Eleko's claim to be the "King of Lagos," while characterizing the treatment of the Eleko by the colonial government in Nigeria as "Empire breaking rather than Empire making."[11] Condemned by the colonial governor, Hugh Clifford, as a "master of mischief making"[12] for his activities in London, Macaulay responded in the *Lagos Weekly Record* that the governor was "glaringly pervert[ing] a simple statement,"[13] with "infamous libel" and "personal attacks."[14] He also lamented Clifford's "manifestation of a vigorous partisanship comparable only with a character of an overzealous orator in Hyde Park." Macaulay published an essay in England entitled "Justitia Fiat: The Moral Obligation of the British Government to the House of King Docemo of Lagos,"[15] in which he documented the case for the recognition of the rights of the House of Dosunmu. Macaulay had been entrusted with the silver staff of office presented to the late King Akintoye by Queen Victoria in 1852. He carried this around in England as if it were equal to the mace of Parliament. Subsequently, Macaulay, alongside Chief Oluwa, returned triumphantly to Lagos.

Bonny Ibhawoh, in his important book on imperial jurisprudence in the colonial era, argues that the Privy Council and the other imperial courts of appeal "were key sites where colonial legal modernity was fashioned."[16] Here I argue that the foundations of the discourses and conditions that encouraged the imperial subjects in Nigeria to turn "colonial modernity against the colonizer"[17] by seeking the intervention of the imperial courts in resolving the tension between colonial modernity and tradition were laid in the newspaper articulations and contestations of what constituted the rational basis for resolving this tension. This chapter illustrates the agency of the newspaper proprietors, journalists, and the newspaper press in a colonial context and the politically constituted claims made on behalf of their readers, and the public in general, on the relationship between "modernity" and "tradition."

Macaulay generated newspaper content from specific historical experiences, both modern and traditional, and deployed them in articulating the place of tradition in the modern context of late nineteenth-century and early twentieth-century Lagos. I argue here that Macaulay's location at the interstices of modernity and tradition in colonial Lagos and his interpretation, through his activities and his journalism, of the proper relationship between "old" and "new" practices and the engaged public that he (re)produced through them, constituted a problem for the colonialists, not just in terms of the domination of the colonial space, but also in relation to the question of (colonial) *rule*, which was fundamentally predicated not only on violent, but also nonforcible (discursive), hegemony. Even while affirming the suzerainty of the British Crown and embracing modernity in many ways, Macaulay subverted colonial governmentality and challenged colonial modernity. Yet the public that he convened, spoke to, and spoke for, in and through the newspapers, including his *Lagos Daily News*, which constituted one of his main sources of strength, became a threat to one of the most important means by which colonial governmentality established and preserved itself: hegemonic consensus.

Using archival materials and historical sociology, the chapter examines how Macaulay leveraged the newspaper press in making politically constitutive claims on the readership, and through this avenue, on the emergent colonial public and the colonial government, particularly on the question of the proper relationship between (emergent) modernity and (extant) tradition in early twentieth-century Nigeria.

HERBERT MACAULAY: COLONIAL MODERNITY AND THE NEWSPAPERS PRESS

Even though *local* "modern" intellectual activities in nineteenth-century West Africa originated in and developed around missionary Christianity and, thus, were often led by clergymen who had benefited from mission education.[18] Intellectual leadership was soon taken up by newspapermen who became the most critical section of the emergent elite and the intellectual class in the subregion. From Liberia and Sierra Leone to Ghana and Nigeria in British West Africa, these newspapermen were not only shaped by the reality and the challenges of emergent colonial modernity, they also worked hard to shape various publics' perception of, attitude toward, and reactions to this reality and challenges, publics that were imagined and also produced through newspapers.

The famous Apapa land case that took Herbert Macaulay to the Privy Council in company of Oluwo, *Amodu Tijani v. Secretary, Southern Nigeria* (1921), became the basis of a another political crisis regarding the House of Docemo, headed by Eṣugbayi Eleko, and legal challenge, *Eshugbayi Eleko v. Government of Nigeria* (1928), in which Macaulay was again central.[19] Both cases and controversies were used by Macaulay to contest the colonial order and negotiate his take on colonial modernity. I suggest that we read Macaulay's discursive negotiation of colonial modernity against the backdrop of Frederick Cooper's challenge to students of colonial studies to transcend the scholarly tradition of "treating colonialism abstractly, generically, as something to be juxtaposed with an equally flat vision of European 'modernity.'"[20] This is important, among other reasons, because coupling colonialism and modernity without examining the dialectics of the relationship of the two ignores "native agency as it was conditioned in its encounter with modernity"[21] and colonialism. Indeed, what a critical account of the discursive hegemony of colonialism alerts us to is the fact that the attempts to represent colonialism *as* modernity in Africa not only produced the imposition of concepts and practices (by the colonialists), but also encouraged the emergence of rival motifs among the colonized that engaged with (colonial) modernity and contested a hegemonic and singular understanding of this modernity[22]—as well as the proper and acceptable way of approaching and practicing *modernity* in the African context. Colonialism, particularly in Africa, opened up the space for both discursive and material contestations by the "natives" regarding how to understand and relate to colonial modernity.

Olayinka Herbert Samuel Heelas Macaulay is a good example of what Cooper describes as a "colonized intellectual," one who contested colonial modernity and articulated alternative visions of modernity.[23] However, while he explicitly and practically engaged the claims of colonial agents to represent modernity and the ideals of the Enlightenment, he accepted and adopted some aspects of the representations of modernity by the colonial agents, but he also defended aspects of existing cultural repertoires that were not mere replications of Western practices. He articulated and defended local ideas of order and progress, which he was convinced were not incompatible with Western ideas of progress, freedom, and justice. In this articulation of, engagement with, or rejection of specific aspects of colonial modernity, for Macaulay, the newspaper press—in itself an instrument of modernity—was central. He used this instrument of modernity to articulate, preserve, and protect neotraditionalism as a way of promoting human liberty, the freedom of colonial people, and their rights in relation to traditional practices. Thus, Macaulay became the "epicenter of indigenous opposition to the British."[24]

As evident in his activities and his writings in the newspapers, Macaulay did not have a teleological view of modernity. For him, there was no trajectory leading from "tradition" to "modernity" in the Africa of his age. He approached both as existing concurrently. While he identified and embraced the opportunities for personal, social, and political advancement within colonial modernity, he denied a view of every existing indigenous (African) process or institution as backward or oppressive. Thus, he was as enthusiastic about the opportunities offered by colonial modernity as he was opposed to aspects of this modernity that attempted to tame or sterilize what he once described in an editorial in the *Lagos Daily News* as the "immemorial customs" of his people.[25] He was often eager to construct continuity, if not similarity, between some practices in the *modern* metropole (England) and *traditional* Lagos of the early twentieth century.[26]

While he accepted the legitimacy of colonial rule, he never accepted the "logical extinction" of tradition that was intrinsic to colonial understanding of modernity. In fact, he believed that his people, the Yoruba, particularly Lagosians, by the late nineteenth and early twentieth centuries, possessed many of the values and virtues of modernity, just like Europeans. In one editorial, Macaulay quoted, approvingly, a 1909 report by some European experts that stated that "politeness and patriotism are the two great qualities most prominent in the [Yoruba] race. Taken as a body, the chiefs of Yorubaland might serve as a model of politeness to any people in Europe."[27]

As a social and political agent in colonial Nigeria, Macaulay enjoyed the absolute confidence of an important segment of traditional groups in Lagos,[28] whom he defended throughout his life in the newspaper press. There was no respected newspaper of his period from the late nineteenth century to the first half of twentieth century that didn't publish at least one of Macaulay's articles, even before he started his own *Lagos Daily News* (*LDN*). However, by the time he founded the *LDN* in November 1925, Macaulay had quarreled with almost all the newspaper proprietors in Lagos, because he couldn't stand any newspaper refusing to publish his articles. When they refused, he would promptly arrange to print the article privately and publish it as a pamphlet.[29]

Macaulay's *LDN* declared him "a dominant factor in Nigerian politics."[30] His many agitations against the colonial government and eventful career won him the popular title of "father of Nigerian nationalism."[31]

However, he embodied the larger web of contradictions in which the emerging Lagos elite and intelligentsia were caught. Macaulay's attitude to traditional rulers, particularly the House of Dosunmu, reflected the tensions of the marriage of modernity and tradition.[32] The intelligentsia and the local elite were opposed to the indirect rule system through which the British ensured that "natural (traditional) rulers" *ruled* the natives on behalf of the British colonial officers. They saw this as anachronistic and undemocratic. Yet, in their struggles for racial validation and cultural authenticity, a section of the intelligentsia and elite also protected or supported some aspects of existing institutions or practices that they insisted were part of their tradition, and thus should be respected and sustained by the colonialists. Macaulay was one of the strongest voices among this class of Lagosians. Factional politics in Lagos was the context of the rise of Macaulay to city, regional, and consequently, national prominence. However, his accession to popular leadership in Lagos "aroused bitter divisions and dissensions which conditioned political activity for a long time."[33]

The Apapa land case and *Eshugbayi v Officer Administering the Government of Nigeria*, otherwise called the "Eleko Question," are major examples of how Macaulay engaged in the process of producing specific publics, directly or indirectly, publics that were also the targets of his newspaper activism. Through the engagement of these publics with specific social, political, and legal crises in Lagos, newspaper readers also helped in generating newspaper materials. The politically constitutive assertions that Macaulay claimed to make on behalf of his publics also involved the (re)producing and (re)defining of these publics and their interests in late nineteenth-century and particularly early twentieth-century Lagos.

CONTESTING COLONIAL MODERNITY: MACAULAY, THE COLONIAL PRESS, AND THE (RE)PRODUCTION OF ENGAGED PUBLICS IN COLONIAL LAGOS

> Of all Liberties, freedom to know, to speak and to criticize stands first: this freedom is the bugbear of Tyrants.... A press that is not free cannot achieve a higher standing as an institution than that of a gramophone industry.
> —HERBERT MACAULAY[34]

With the victory in the Apapa land case at the Privy Council in England and his deft use of the English press to propagate his cause, Macaulay competently displayed to the colonial government in Nigeria and the Lagos public that he knew well how to use the resources and institutions of modernity—the courts (both in the colony and in the metropole), the press, publicity, the mobilization of public opinion, ideas of liberty, justice, equity, rights to property, and so on—to defend the cause of tradition and the rights of the indigenous people of Lagos. In this way, Macaulay, despite the strong opposition from some members of the modern elite in Lagos, was engaged in the (re)production of engaged publics in Lagos, and eventually the rest of Nigeria, particularly in regard of what constituted the proper relationship between colonial modernity and tradition. He also helped (re)define how modernity could be domesticated in the context of a transforming traditional society and how the emerging modern public in Lagos was to relate to this modernity while respecting and preserving existing practices.

How did he do this? First, in colonial Nigeria, the newspaper press was at the center of the sociocultural and political process as interpreter, critic, defender, elaborator, and guarantor of the local people's rights, culture, and worldview. Even though Macaulay's publics were composed of both literate (including the local modern and traditional elite and the colonialists) and illiterate (traditional elites and the masses) people, what he wrote and published, his mix of journalism with activism, achieved a salience that was difficult, if not impossible, to ignore. This constituted the basis of his power and legitimacy in colonial Lagos. By writing constantly in the press, he helped to consolidate and elaborate the role of debate and dissent in a transforming society such as late nineteenth- and early twentieth-century Lagos. Also, by founding the *Lagos Daily News*, the first daily newspaper in Nigeria, Macaulay sought to fully demonstrate that it was possible in the Lagos of the era to create the conditions for a "daily plebiscite," to use Ernest Renan's famous phrase. The attempt to convoke this daily plebiscite in addition to his activism and defense of tradition attracted to Macaulay as much of a following as it attracted powerful adversaries among the traditional and modern elites. By denying the colonial government and the colluding modern elite the exclusive power to define modernity for the Lagos public, Macaulay helped in determining the validity of existing (neotraditional) practices and values in a "modernizing" metropolis in the first half of the twentieth century.

The "Eleko Question," a cultural, social, and political controversy that lasted from 1920 to 1931, was a direct result of Macaulay's actions and statements in England, during and after the Apapa land case. More specifically, it resulted from what Macaulay was reported to have stated in the London tabloid the *Daily Mail*. One of the critical pillars of colonial modernity that the land case and Macaulay's writings and statements in the press (both in Nigeria and in England) challenged was the attempt by the colonial government to reform or transform the criteria on which land claims were based. This was also related to the transformation in (1) the existing kin-based stratification system displaced by colonial stratification, which was based on different criteria informed by "modernity," and (2) the link of this kin-based stratification to the major institutions of Lagos indigenous society and the "overriding ideology that articulates" these relationships.[35] While some supported the structural changes that colonial modernity sought to impose on the existing system and the overriding ideology that informed it in the name of "modernity" and "progress," people like Macaulay opposed these structural changes, while insisting that progress and modernity, particularly as related to justice, equity, and freedom, were not incompatible with existing, indeed, neotraditional institutions and practices. It was against this backdrop that his opinion published in the *Daily Mail* in London constituted the basis for a crisis. It provoked a reaction from the colonial government that, in turn, became a template for a struggle on how to reconcile colonial modernity with (neo) traditional logic and practices.

The attempt to *domesticate* modernity by the likes of Macaulay was organized not merely on the basis of opposition to alien rule. It was mobilized in opposition to any form of *rule* that was subversive of the *traditional*, and also *popular*, practices of the people of Lagos. Therefore, in straddling both modern and traditional elites and representing the tensions between the two in particular ways in the newspaper press, as well as through other public contexts, Macaulay's basic premise was that (colonial) modernity had to reconcile itself with tradition (or neotradition) rather than vice versa. The colonial government and its supporters among the modern elite argued either that tradition had to reconcile itself with (colonial) modernity or that tradition had to give way completely in the context of (colonial) modernity. Therefore, the victory of "tradition" before the ultimate symbol of (colonial) modernity in London, the Privy Council, was a fundamental challenge to the legitimacy of the position of the colonial government and its supporters, such as Kitoyi Ajasa, the publisher of the *Nigerian Pioneer*.

In the *Daily Mail* interview, Macaulay allegedly stated that the Eleko, Eṣugbayi, was recognized by the seventeen million people of Nigeria as their king. He reportedly added that the total revenue of the colony, that is, about five million pounds sterling, rightly belonged to the Eleko. Hugh Clifford, the governor-general of Nigeria, stated in his address to the Nigerian Council on 29 December 1920 that Macaulay's "preposterous claims" would have been ignored but for the fact that the Eleko had entrusted his staff of office to Chief Oluwa and Macaulay, who took it everywhere they visited in England. Added Clifford, "Mr. Macaulay's irresponsible vapourings were thus transformed from worthless and wilful distortions of historical fact into statements of claims and alleged grievances made in the British Press, on the authority of the accredited linguist of the House of Docemo."[36]

However, Clifford's reaction—and the subsequent government's action—was based on the interpretation of the *Daily Mail* interview as published in the *African World* edition of 10 July 1920. What Macaulay actually told the *Daily Mail* was that the Eleko was "acclaimed by seventeen million Nigerians as the titular king of Lagos," and not that he was acknowledged as the king of Nigeria. He added that the grandfather of the Eleko ceded the port and island of Lagos to the British government in 1861, but that the Eleko now earned less than the lowest-paid European gardener and that his palace had been allowed to fall into decay, even though the British had promised King Dosunmu a pension equal to that of the net revenue of the colony. He described the king of Lagos as "the chief negro" in *a* dominion (notably not described as *his* dominion) that was three times the size of Great Britain.[37]

Clifford's condemnation of Macaulay in his address to the Nigerian Council forced Macaulay to respond in a pamphlet published in London.[38] This matter could not have led to a controversy if only the government decided to read the original interview in the *Daily Mail*. Even so, asks Patrick Cole in his important book, *Modern and Traditional Elites in the Politics of Lagos*, why should a claim that seventeen million Nigerians recognized the Eleko as the king of Lagos and that the government had not been fair to the Eleko and his grandfather invite such strong reactions from the colonial government?[39] But Cole fails to offer a direct answer to this critical question. The answer, I suggest, lies in the point articulated earlier. Whether in what he actually said or in what he was taken to have said, Macaulay's direct challenge to the legitimacy and authority of the colonial government through his writings in the newspapers and his social and political activities, particularly his use of both the newspaper press and traditional institutions/processes to challenge the colonial government and expose its duplicity, constituted the background to the response of the government to what Macaulay (might have) told the *Daily Mail*. Indeed, that Macaulay was able to communicate with publics both in

Nigeria and in England that accepted his alternative reading of the reality in the colony helped in no small measure in contesting the colonial government's attempt to impose a monolithic and hegemonic understanding of that reality.

In the context of the existing polarity in Lagos among pro- and antigovernment traditional and modern elites, the government and its supporters decided to use the statement credited to Macaulay to discredit the man and embarrass the Eleko. Even though the Eleko responded that he had given his staff to Chief Oluwa and not Macaulay and dissociated himself from what Macaulay said in London, the colonial government insisted on what it considered the *proper* way in which the Eleko must denounce Macaulay. The Eleko insisted that since he had given his staff to Chief Oluwa, who had yet to return from London with Macaulay, the government ought to wait until Chief Oluwa's return. However, since all these points were not sufficient to satisfy the colonial government, on 22 November 1920, Eleko Eṣugbayi issued a statement to all the newspapers in Lagos denouncing Macaulay's alleged statement in London. He assumed that that would be the end of the controversy.

The reaction of the colonial government to the Eleko's offers and public denunciation of Macaulay's alleged statement was very interesting. While a member of the traditional elite made claims that were based on rationality and the best principles of British jurisprudence—in which (1) a man cannot be made to suffer for the statement of another whom he had not authorized to speak on his behalf, and, (2) a man cannot be accused without being given an opportunity to defend himself—it is interesting that the colonial government, which claimed to have been founded on these principles, rejected the argument of the king. Apart from this, it was also interesting that while the Eleko was willing to use one of the modern instruments of mass communication introduced to Africa by Europeans, that is, the newspaper press, to communicate with his publics, the colonial government rejected the newspaper press as the appropriate means of mass communication for a *traditional* king in *modern* Lagos to communicate with his people.

However, the colonial government's attitude, and the decision of the Eleko, can be understood against the backdrop of the reality of the relationship between modernity and tradition in early twentieth-century Lagos. The Eleko knew that his denunciation of Macaulay in the newspaper press would only be read by the modern (educated) elite, a small minority. However, the colonial government also realized as much. Insisting that the Eleko must denounce Macaulay by asking his bellman and town crier to go round the town, as was the tradition, reading a denunciation of Macaulay's statement by the Eleko to the masses of Lagos, the government wanted the message to reach the primary public of the Eleko and Macaulay, and to shame the latter among them. However, the Eleko rejected the means of communication preferred by the colonialists. Subsequently, the government suspended the Eleko and withdrew its recognition of his position and stopped his stipend.

The withdrawal of recognition from the Eleko, according to the government, meant that he would be regarded as a "private citizen." Macaulay's response was to show the absurdity of the government's position that the Eleko had had "no political significance" and "no official position" prior to the controversy over his *Daily Mail* interview.[40] He asked, "From what function was the prince, who has no political significance, suspended?" He asked further, why did the government instruct the Eleko to ask Chief Oluwa to return his staff, if the Eleko had "no official position"? Why did the government ask the Eleko to denounce him, if the king had "no political significance"?[41] The *West Africa* newspaper described Macaulay's attack on the government's position, entitled "The Incorrigibility of Sir Hugh Clifford," as "an intellectual treat . . . [conducted] with . . . Socratic thoroughness."[42]

However, despite the withdrawal of recognition, the Eleko continued to live in his palace and to receive guests. He had the support of his subjects, as well as the support of important sections of the traditional and modern elite led by Macaulay and key newspapers. In addition to writing in the existing newspapers in defense of the Eleko, he later founded his own newspaper, the *LDN*, where Macaulay continued the battle over the House of Dosunmu, constantly narrating the background of the crisis. For instance, the paper insisted that in the period between the withdrawal of recognition and the exile of the Eleko (1920–25), the Eleko's supporters were "prosecuted, persecuted, jailed and hounded down."[43] Indeed, in those five years, the anti-Eleko elements, including the major newspaper that represented them, Kitoyi Ajasa's *Nigerian Pioneer*, triumphed over the pro-Eleko elements. This was due principally to the attitude of the colonial officers ruling Lagos in these years, including the acting governor, F. M. Baddeley, and the resident, Major Birrell-Gray,[44] both of whom the *LDN* dismissed as colonial officers who mistook ruthlessness for efficiency and violated the principles of enlightened governance, contrary to "the British tradition," by acting as if the government had no duty to justify its activities to the governed.[45] Such was the effect of the *LDN*'s attacks on the colonial officials that Baddeley stated that Birrell-Gray's "firmness, dignity and tact," which "earned the highest commendation of the Government and of all right thinking citizens," did not "spare him from *a torrent of scurri-*

lous vituperations and abuse from certain sections of the press"[46]—which many understood to be a reference to Macaulay's *LDN*.

The general (legal, social, and political) struggle to reverse the decision on the Eleko, and, specifically, the petition by members of the House of Dosunmu, received full coverage by the *LDN* and its rival newspapers, particularly the *Nigerian Pioneer*. While the *LDN* praised the petition, the *Pioneer* excoriated the writers while commending the "firm policy" of Birrell-Gray. The *Pioneer* also rejoiced at the rejection of the petition.[47] Moreover, the *Pioneer* wondered why it took the government so long to end "a useless mischievous official friendship" with the Eleko, who had inherited his father's character as a "rogue and fool."[48] Even though the anti-Eleko, progovernment traditional and modern elite, as represented by the *Pioneer*, were happy with the withdrawal of recognition, they insisted that the government should depose the king and send him into exile. They wanted to have someone who was supportive of the government, and opposed to Macaulay, installed as the Eleko.

Taking the contrary position, the *LWR* and *Times of Nigeria* criticized Clifford. However, the *Record*, even though it condemned the action of the governor, claimed that its intervention was "from the standpoint of the impartial investigator."[49] The *Record*'s editorial stated clearly that the paper's proprietor, Thomas Horatio Johnson, had earlier been contacted by Governor Clifford and asked to pass on the threat of the government to the Eleko.[50] Jackson stated that he advised the governor against his planned action. However, after the governor carried out this threat, in the controversy that ensued it was evident that Jackson was uncomfortable with the role of Macaulay as the Eleko's principal adviser. Also, Jackson felt the Eleko, in embracing Macaulay, had been ungrateful to people like himself. The editorial regretted that the Eleko was "blessed with very short memories forgetting even the *meritorious services of those who have spent the best part of their time, brains and money in extricating him from any particular or specific danger* or from any political morass into which he may have rashly plunged himself."[51]

However, after five years, it was evident to the government that the suspension of the recognition of the Eleko, which had raised tension in the town between the two groups, would have to be revisited. The government did not have a go-between to relay its messages to the masses of Lagos because of the absence of a king. The government wished to depose and deport the king, but the existing law did not empower it to do so. Governor Clifford maintained publicly that the deposition was a matter for the members of the ruling house. A petition organized by Macaulay and Thomas Jackson of the

Record and signed by seventeen thousand people in Lagos, asking for the restoration of the recognition of the Eleko, was dismissed by Governor Clifford as "barren of result and . . . therefore not worth a moment's effort or a single penny-piece."[52] When Clifford added that the petition was signed by "the native of the best intellect and highest character," Macaulay responded that "such incorrigibility passes one's understanding" and that Clifford's "idea of intelligence [is] limited to a disposition to say 'yes, *sha, massa*' ["yes, sir, master"]."[53] Macaulay later wrote that given the kind of "mentality" displayed by Clifford in his relationship with the people of Lagos, it was no surprise that he "refused to listen to the many importunations on behalf of Prince Eleko, emanating from all sources both from Europeans and natives even from the prince's . . . enemies."[54] The pro-Eleko newspapers attacked Governor Clifford incessantly over the Eleko matter, to the extent that he lost his popularity, even among the educated elite. In May 1925, when he left Nigeria, the unpopular, progovernment newspapers such as the *Pioneer* eulogized him,[55] but the Macaulay press dismissed him as one with "autocratic spirit," adding that Clifford "has rudely violated . . . the common rule of courtesy and decency with a signal disregard for that very high and dignified position in which it hath pleased Almighty God to place him as representative of His Most Gracious Majesty, the King, in this Great Dependency of the British Empire."[56]

In the middle of this battle, Macaulay realized that he needed his own organ, so that he didn't have to rely on publishing articles in friendly newspapers. He therefore set up his *Lagos Daily News* in 1925. The newspaper was "a stormy mouthpiece" of the man who designated himself "Controlling Editor and Joint Proprietor" and was reputed to have "wielded the most deadly pen in Nigeria's press history."[57]

Clifford's successor, Governor Graeme Thompson, was worse than Macaulay and Jackson and their newspapers, *LDN* and *LWR*, respectively, could have imagined. When twenty-two members of the ruling family wrote to the Eleko in June 1925 asking him to vacate his palace, the Iga, within fourteen days and appointing Ibikunle Akintoye in his place, the government's wish was complied with. Under Thompson, the colonial government affirmed the decision of the members of the ruling house and served the Eleko with a deportation order to be obeyed within twenty-four hours. Ajasa's *Pioneer*[58] celebrated the deposition.

For the next six years, Eleko Eṣugbayi was banished to Ọyọ, in the interior. Macaulay, advertised by the *LDN*[59] as one with "genuine affection" for Eṣugbayi, however, did not give up. His campaign in support of Eṣugbayi was driven by Macaulay's firm belief in defending the integrity of traditional institutions, which were honored by the best practices of British jurisprudence, in opposition to the arbitrariness and injustice perpetrated by the colonial officials against the Eleko, a British citizen, as the *LDN* reported and editorialized.[60]

Macaulay's argument, again, emphasized the reconciliation of tradition and modernity in the peculiar way in which he and the *LDN* imagined and practiced this reconciliation. The Eleko was being defended on the basis of "tradition," yet Macaulay and the *LDN* appealed to the public to see the issue as one about the violation of the rights of a "British *citizen*."[61] Indeed, in the bizarre way in which colonialism unfolded in Nigeria, those who lived in the colony of Lagos were quasi-British citizens, while those who lived in the rest of the country, "the Protectorate," were "protected subjects." While Macaulay and the *Lagos Daily News* and other pro-Eleko newspapers defended the rights of Nigerians in general, they were also very eager to appropriate the unique status of Lagosians as British citizens in the pursuit of justice and equity. Also, because of the way in which the narration of the victory over the colonial government at the Privy Council was constructed by Macaulay, the Privy Council had come to be regarded by the Lagos public, particularly the pro-Eleko public, as the "custodian of the people's liberty."[62]

Within twenty-four hours of the deposition of the Eleko, Macaulay and others secured the services of lawyers to contest the decision in court. Suffering several setbacks in the courts in Nigeria, the Eleko's lawyers appealed again to the Privy Council in London. The new onslaught against the colonial government gained vigor as the Ilu (Town) Committee, composed of representatives of the indigenous elite who owed allegiance to the House of Dosunmu, was formed. It was an alliance between traditional and modern elites of Lagos. This committee was eventually co-opted into the Nigerian National Democratic Party (NNDP) formed by Macaulay and others.

Such was the centrality of the newspaper reporting and commentary on the Eleko case that when the Supreme Court of Nigeria on 13 August 1925 refused the motion of the Eleko's lawyers for a writ of habeas corpus to be served on the police officer who executed the deportation order, T. H. Jackson, the editor of the *LWR*, published a three-part piece in which he dismissed the whole process as a "legal charade" and expressed doubts on the impartiality of the Supreme Court judges.[63] For this, Jackson was jailed for two months and fined twenty-five pounds.[64]

In June 1928, the Privy Council decided that the Eleko could apply for a writ of habeas corpus. There was great excitement in Lagos. Consequently, Macaulay's newspaper, the *LDN*, published a rumor stating that because of the Privy Council's decision, the Eleko would return from exile to Lagos. The paper added that the colonial government was planning to assassinate the Eleko upon his return to Lagos. For this report in his newspaper, Macaulay was sentenced to six months imprisonment with hard labor, which only increased his popularity in Lagos.[65] When he was released in February 1929, Macaulay described in his newspaper how the people of Lagos were "mad with joy" over his return.[66]

After a long and tortuous process between the courts in Nigeria and the Privy Council in London, the Privy Council decided on 24 March 1931 that the Eleko case be returned to Nigeria and heard all over again. But because the Supreme Court in Nigeria had erred, when the Privy Council returned the case there earlier, the Privy Council spelled out clearly how the Nigerian courts should proceed and on what matters of law their decision would be based.[67] Effectively, the Privy Council's decision was a slap in the face of the colonial government in Nigeria and the Nigerian judiciary.[68] It was clear that the government's case against the Eleko had collapsed. Macaulay had won, again, against the colonial government. The *LDN* reprinted the full judgment of the Privy Council on 10 April 1931. One part that was particularly instructive was where the Council held that

> in accordance with British jurisprudence, no member of the Executive can interfere with the liberty and property of the subject except on condition that he can support the legality of his action before a court of justice . . . it is the tradition of British Justice that Judges should not shrink from deciding such issues in the face of the Executive.[69]

The government was still in a quandary when a new governor, Sir Donald Cameron, arrived in Lagos on 17 June 1931. A few days later, he announced that the government was no longer interested in pursuing the Eleko case. Consequently, the Eleko was allowed to return to his palace in Lagos. The whole of Lagos erupted in joy as the Eleko returned. An unofficial holiday was declared. Macaulay's hero status was reconfirmed and even enlarged. Folk songs were composed and sung in Lagos in praise of the Eleko and Macaulay. The Eleko himself, when he reached his palace, broke out in a song "Eki Makoli o" ("Hail Macaulay!").[70]

Messages of congratulations to Macaulay and the Eleko were received from all over Nigeria and the West Coast of Africa, including from Liberia, Gold Coast (later Ghana), and Sierra Leone. Newspapers in these countries, such as the *Sierra Leone Weekly News* and the *Gold Coast Leader*, welcomed the decision as a vindication of the rights of British subjects in Africa. Macaulay's *Lagos Weekly News* devoted many editions in 1931 to reprinting the most important documents relating to the Eleko case.[71] In a major editorial celebrating the victory of the Eleko, the *LDN* described Eṣugbayi as one whose "heroic stand had stayed the hand of autocratic government."[72] The paper expressed gratitude to the Eleko for the "herculean struggles for the sacred cause of Truth and Justice," for regaining "that precious liberty of the subject which was, by a strong arm, being wrenched from us."[73] The *LDN* added, on behalf of a public for which it had defended "truth and justice," that "we are grateful to think that in these days when prejudice seems to be getting [the] upper hand over justice and good government, you [Eṣugbayi] have been the means of rousing that spirit of truth, justice and fair play."[74] With his triumphant return from exile, the *LDN* concluded that the Eleko "has allayed our suspicions as to the soundness of the system of government, it has subdued our excitement and alarm, which had reached their utmost tension and has grounded and re-established the faith of the wavering."[75]

Five years after the matter was resolved, Macaulay's paper still felt the need to restate the entire course of the controversy, if only to emphasize what Frederick Cooper would describe as "the efforts of colonized people to [simultaneously] deflect and appropriate elements of colonizing policies."[76] After recalling how Eṣugbayi Eleko was removed and deported for "no reasonable cause" and replaced by his first cousin, Prince Ibikunle Akintoye—who died barely three years after his installation—the *LDN* editorialized on the front page that the Lagos public was opposed to the emergence of the now late king (Akintoye), who was supported by the colonial government:

> More than four-fifth of the Native Community were not in favour of his having usurped the position of the Head of the House of Docemo with the support of Chief Obanikoro, *an unpopular chief, and a handful of the descendants of former Rulers of Lagos . . . who managed to secure the recommendation of the Resident of the Colony, and the approval of the Officer Administering the Government of Nigeria*, on the 8th of August, 1925. . . . *And so long as that unconstitutional act continued to receive British official support in Lagos, that inglorious minority party as long continued to widen the breach* and use every

possible opportunity to persecute and prosecute as many members of the majority party in this community almost to the point of rebellion.[77]

The paper then noted that matters had worsened until the British officers were replaced. Here *LDN* contrasted the "unconstitutional act" of "British official support" given to Akintoye by British colonial officers, such as Sir Frank M. Baddeley, with the "statesmanship" of Baddeley's successor, Sir Cameron:

> Things went, however, from bad to worse, upon [Akintoye's] death, until the arrival of His Excellency, Sir Donald Cameron . . . who with the *very strong British Arm of Justice, righted the wrong*, and in doing so, that *might statesman* condemned the Boomerang.[78]

The Oluwa and the Eleko cases and the controversies they generated, partly because of the way they were covered, reported, and commented upon in the newspapers, particularly the pro-Eleko newspapers, clearly reflected the centrality of Macaulay and his conception of the relationship between modernity and tradition. Given the fact that he needed widespread support for his position, it is no surprise that Macaulay used the newspapers in the (re)production of his public and in ensuring that this public could become engaged in the critical issues that he canvassed and promoted. As one of the most critical interpreters of colonial modernity in relation to tradition in Africa, in general, and colonial Nigeria, in particular, and specifically late nineteenth-century and early twentieth-century Lagos, Macaulay's journalism represented one of the strongest challenges to the hegemonic consensus that the colonialists sought to impose on Lagos and the rest of Nigeria. It wasn't just his activities as a social agitator, organizer, and politician that challenged the colonial government; I suggest that his writings, particularly through the newspaper press, which convened a public and articulated and shared ideas that the colonialists considered subversive to their nonforcible domination, were most threatening to the hegemony of the colonialist and their *unilateral* and self-serving interpretation of modernity. They were, therefore, eager to gag colonized intellectuals such as Macaulay and Jackson, who insisted on a *bilateral*, if not multiple, interpretation of modernity in the African context, while providing the rival motifs that challenged the narrow interpretations by the colonialists.

When Eleko Eşugbayi died on 24 October 1932, barely a year after he returned to the throne, there was disagreement in the press on his legacy. Kitoyi Ajasa of the *Pioneer* dismissed him as a "rogue and fool," one whose "acts of omission and commission . . . were those of his advisers, of men who traded [on] his weakness, of political adventurers who live buy their wits through him."[79] In an obvious reference to Macaulay, the *Pioneer* added that Eṣugbayi "had not the sufficient character to denounce [the 'political adventurers']" and concluded that the late Eleko's attempt "to idolize and apotheosize the most astute of them" was "a tragedy to Lagos which even the Prince's death has not removed."[80] The *LDN* countered this in an eulogy in which Eṣugbayi was praised as a symbol of liberty and justice.[81]

CONCLUSION

Some scholars have argued that colonial modernity should be approached as "colonial governmentality," because this modernity involved the creation of a certain kind of subject.[82] As a "distinctive political rationality," colonial modernity, argues David Scott, was not only geared toward producing "governing effects on colonial conduct"; it was also concerned with "*disabling old forms of life* by systematically breaking down their conditions, and with constructing in their place new conditions."[83] Herbert Macaulay, using the newspaper press that convened, mobilized, and deployed a specific kind of public in colonial Nigeria, struggled to contest the attempt by the colonial government to disable "traditional" forms of life and institutions in Lagos. His articulation of rival versions of modernity exemplified the fact that, like many in the public that he convened and galvanized, Macaulay was not the desired kind of colonial subject. While he envisioned the construction of new conditions in the colony of Lagos, he challenged the colonial government regarding what constituted the elements and dimensions of these new conditions—and, thus, the kind of subjects it could create and subsequently govern. Despite the colonial state's attempt at the "marginalization of resistance," Macaulay used the newspaper press and the specific kinds of public that this institution helped to produce and nurture as critical forms of counterhegemonic discourse and force, respectively. Given that Lagos was the "center of power in [colonial] Nigeria," Macaulay and other educated elites of Lagos were regarded by both the educated and the illiterate masses in the city and in the rest of Nigeria as their champions,[84] as the *LDN* repeatedly asserted.[85] There was, therefore, a certain assumption of manifest destiny reflected in Macaulay's writings in the newspapers. As Karin Barber (this volume) points out, Macaulay's attitude was confirmed, as his activism on the Eleko affair helped him secure a following partly responsible for the victory of his political party, the Nigerian National Democratic Party (NNDP), in every election to the Legislative Council from 1922 up to the late 1930s.

For Macaulay and the pro-Eleko newspaper press, given that modernity is a fundamental expression of the belief in the natural and inalienable freedom of human beings and the human capacity for reason,[86] the colonized people were capable of mobilizing this freedom and capacity for reason in making a choice in regard to what to protect and nurture in their existing traditions. The freedom to do this and the reason mobilized in the process were not, and did not need to be, antithetical to modernity as assumed by the colonial officials in Lagos. The reconciliation of existing institutions and practices such as the *ọbaship* (kingship) in Lagos, for Macaulay and the wider pro-Eleko press, did not represent a regression into a fossilized past; it was reconcilable with an open embrace of the ideals of the Enlightenment in colonial Africa. In fact, from the perspective of Macaulay, it can be concluded that "colonial modernity represented a compromise both with metropolitan modernity as well as indigenous traditions," to use the words of Dulip M. Menon.[87] Even though Macaulay and the pro-Eleko newspaper press in Lagos, particularly the *LDN*, did not attempt to transform European modernity into a "New African modernity," as Ntongela Masilela argues in the case of Xhosa intellectuals in South Africa,[88] by becoming "*modern agents* [themselves] through political praxis" grounded in the newspaper press, media actors like Macaulay represented the interests of the indigenous people ("natives") through the reconciliation of tradition and modernity. Thus, it is evident that the newspaper press played a critical role in domesticating modernity and reconciling it with existing institutions and practices.

By challenging the hegemonic consensus on the modernity-tradition interface that the colonial project was attempting to impose on Lagos, and the rest of Nigeria and Africa, Macaulay helped in defending tradition and redefining and rearticulating modernity to their publics. The assumption—and argument—that educated persons in Africa ought to lose "their regard for native institutions" that contained "retrograde customs" that were capable of keeping native society "static and unprogressive"[89] was strongly contested by Macaulay's journalism as "contumelious" and rife with "shameless misrepresentations and insulting references"[90] to the cultures of the people. A succinct tribute to Macaulay, noting his approach to the interface of colonial modernity and tradition, was rendered by the editor of the *Daily Service*: "One could doubt whether Macaulay's brand of nationalism was impersonal, selfless or disinterested, but one could never doubt that he succeeded to a remarkable degree to inspire in his people some sense of pride in their own indigenous institutions."[91] There could be no better validation of Macaulay's success in (re)producing an engaged public in Lagos that defended its own understanding of modernity in relation to tradition.

REFERENCES

Adegboyega, Obadia. *Notes and Comments on the Life of Mr. H. Macaulay*. Lagos: n.p, n.d.

Clifford, Hugh. "Address to the Nigerian Council." Lagos, December 29, 1920.

Cole, Patrick. *Modern and Traditional Elites in the Politics of Lagos*. Cambridge: Cambridge University Press, 1975.

Coleman, James S. *Nigeria: Background to Nationalism*. Berkeley: University of California Press, 1958.

Cooper, Frederick. *Colonialism in Question: Theory, Knowledge, History*. Berkeley: University of California Press, 2005.

Goscha, Christopher. "Writing Decolonization: Turning Technology against the Colonizer during the Indochina War, 1945–1954." *Comparative Studies in Society and History* 54, no. 4 (2012): 798–831.

Ibhawoh, Bonny. *Imperial Justice: Africans in Empire's Court*. Oxford: Oxford University Press, 2013.

July, Robert W. *The Origins of Modern African Thought: Its Development in West Africa during the Nineteenth and Twentieth Centuries*. New York: Praeger, 1967.

Lawal, Olakunle A., and Oluwasegun M. Jimoh. "Missiles from 'Kirsten Hall': Herbert Macaulay versus Hugh Clifford, 1922–1931." *Lagos Historical Review* 12 (2012): 41–63.

Macaulay, Herbert. "The Incorrigibility of Sir Hugh Clifford." *West Africa*, n.d.

Macaulay, Herbert. *"Justitia Fiat": The Moral Obligations of the British Government to the House of King Docemo in Lagos*. Pamphlet No. 133. London: West Africa, 1921.

Masilela, Ntongela. "African Intellectual and Literary Responses to Colonial Modernity in South Africa." In *Grappling with the Beast: Indigenous Southern African Responses to Colonialism, 1840–1930*, edited by Peter Limb, Norman Etherington, and Peter Midley, 245–75. Leiden: Brill, 2010.

Menon, Dilip M. "Religion and Colonial Modernity: Rethinking Belief and Identity." *Economic and Political Weekly* 37, no. 17 (2002): 1662–67.
Omu, Fred. *Press and Politics in Nigeria, 1880–1937.* Atlantic Highlands, NJ: Humanities Press, 1978.
Peel, J. D. Y. *Religious Encounter and the Making of the Yoruba.* Bloomington: Indiana University Press, 2000.
Perham, Margery. *Native Administration in Nigeria.* London: Oxford University Press, 1937.
Scott, David. *Refashioning Futures: Criticism after Postcoloniality.* Princeton, NJ: Princeton University Press, 1999.
Sklar, Richard L. *Nigerian Political Parties: Power in an Emergent African Nation.* Princeton, NJ: Princeton University Press, 1963.
Táíwo, Olúfémi. *How Colonialism Preempted Modernity in Africa.* Bloomington: Indiana University Press, 2010.
Thomas, Isaac B. *Life History of Herbert Macaulay.* Lagos: Printed at Tika-To[r]e Press, 1948.
Wagner, Peter. *Modernity: Understanding the Present.* Cambridge: Polity Press, 2012.

NEWSPAPERS/PERIODICALS

West Africa, London.
Lagos Daily News, Lagos.
Lagos Weekly Record, Lagos.
Nigerian Pioneer, Lagos.

NOTES TO CHAPTER FIVE

1. It was so described by Margery Perham, *Native Administration in Nigeria* (London: Oxford University Press, 1937), 265.
2. Perham, *Native Administration in Nigeria*, 265.
3. Otherwise known as the "Apapa Land Case."
4. Perham, *Native Administration in Nigeria*, 265.
5. Bonny Ibhawoh, *Imperial Justice* (Oxford: Oxford University Press, 2013), 1.
6. Ibhawoh, *Imperial Justice*, 4.
7. 10 September 1921, 8.
8. Richard Sklar, *Nigerian Political Parties* (Princeton, NJ: Princeton University Press, 1963), 44; Ibhawoh, *Imperial Justice*, 134.

9. Olakunle A. Lawal and Oluwasegun M. Jimoh, "Missiles from 'Kirsten Hall': Herbert Macaulay versus Hugh Clifford, 1922–1931," *Lagos Historical Review* 12 (2012): 50.

10. Sklar, *Nigerian Political Parties*, 44.

11. Sklar, *Nigerian Political Parties*, 266.

12. *Lagos Weekly Record*, 2 May 1925.

13. *Lagos Weekly Record*, 2 May 1925.

14. *Lagos Weekly Record*, 2 May 1925.

15. Herbert Macaulay, *"Justitia Fiat": The Moral Obligations of the British Government to the House of King Docemo in Lagos*, Pamphlet No. 133 (London: West Africa, 1921).

16. Ibhawoh, *Imperial Justice*, 4.

17. Christopher Goscha, "Writing Decolonization: Turning Technology against the Colonizer during the Indochina War, 1945–1954," *Comparative Studies in Society and History* 54, no. 4 (2012): 801.

18. Robert W. July, *The Origins of Modern African Thought: Its Development in West Africa during the Nineteenth and Twentieth Centuries* (New York: Praeger, 1967); J. D. Y. Peel, *Religious Encounter and the Making of the Yoruba* (Bloomington: Indiana University Press, 2000).

19. For Macaulay's earlier clashes with the colonial government, see Lawal and Jimoh, "Missiles from Kirsten Hall."

20. Frederick Cooper, *Colonialism in Question* (Berkeley: University of California Press, 2005), 3–4.

21. Olúfémi Táíwo, *How Colonialism Preempted Modernity* (Bloomington: Indiana University Press, 2010), 16.

22. Cooper, *Colonialism in Question*, 4; Táíwo, *How Colonialism Preempted Modernity*, 3–17.

23. Táíwo, *How Colonialism Preempted Modernity*, 113–14.

24. Lawal and Jimoh, "Missiles from Kirsten Hall," 42.

25. *Lagos Daily News*, 18 July 1936, 5; henceforth *LDN*.

26. See *LDN*, 18 July 1936, 5.

27. *LDN*, 21 July 1936, 5.

28. See Sklar, *Nigerian Political Parties*, 47.

29. Omu, *Press and Politics*, 65.

30. 14 November 1936, 5.

31. For more on the biography of Herbert Macaulay, see I. B. Thomas, *Life History of Herbert Macaulay* (Lagos: Printed at Tika-To[r]e Press, 1948), and Obadia Adegboyega, *Notes and Comments on the Life of Mr. H. Macaulay* (Lagos: n.p., n.d.).

32. See Omu, *Press and Politics*, 222.
33. Omu, *Press and Politics*, 22.
34. Quoted in Patrick Cole, *Modern and Traditional Elites in the Politics of Lagos* (Cambridge: Cambridge University Press, 1975), 120.
35. Cole, *Modern and Traditional Elites*, 120.
36. Hugh Clifford, "Address to the Nigerian Council" (Lagos, 29 December, 1920) in Cole, *Modern and Traditional Elites*, 48. Clifford obviously used a pedantic phrase in describing Macaulay as the spokesman of the House of Docemo.
37. Cole, *Modern and Traditional Elites*, 126, emphasis added.
38. Macaulay, *Justitia Fiat*, 9.
39. Cole, *Modern and Traditional Elites*, 126–127.
40. Herbert Macaulay, "The Incorrigibility of Sir Hugh Clifford," *West Africa*, n.d.
41. Macaulay, "The Incorrigibility."
42. *West Africa*, 11 July 1931.
43. *LDN*, 16 July 1931.
44. Cole, *Modern and Traditional Elites*, 134–35.
45. *LDN*, 25 August 1931.
46. Cole, *Modern and Traditional Elites*, 252.
47. See *Nigerian Pioneer*, 28 August 1925, 20 November 1925, 4 December 1925; *LDN* 11 April 1931.
48. Omu, *Press and Politics*, 225.
49. *Lagos Weekly Record*, 23–30 April 1921, 6, henceforth *LWR*.
50. *LWR*, 26 February–26 March 1921, 6.
51. *LWR*, 23–30 April 1921, 5, emphasis added.
52. *LWR*, 20 January 1923.
53. *LWR*, 2 May 1925.
54. *LWR*, 2 May 1925.
55. See *Pioneer*, 29 May 1925 and 1 January 1925.
56. *LWR*, 2 May 1925, 5.
57. Omu, *Press and Politics*, 64–65.
58. 7 August 1925.
59. 6 July 1931.
60. *LDN*, 2 July and 6 July, 1931.
61. See July, *Modern African Thought*, 381; see also Wole Soyinka, *You Must Set Forth at Dawn: Memoirs* (Ibadan: Bookcraft, 2006), 46.
62. *West Africa*, 31 July 1931.
63. *LWR*, 19 September 1925, 29 September 1925, 3 October 1925.
64. Cole, *Modern and Traditional Elites*, 261.

65. Cole, *Modern and Traditional Elites*, 147–148.
66. *LDN*, 25, 26, 27, 28 February 1929, 1, 5 March 1929, 18 April 1929.
67. For details, see Ibhawoh's *Imperial Justice*, chapter 5.
68. Cole, *Modern and Traditional Elites*, 148.
69. *LDN*, 10 April 1931.
70. Cole, *Modern and Traditional Elites*, 264.
71. Including editions of 9, 10, 11 April 1931, 13, 16 June 1931.
72. 6 July 1931.
73. 6 July 1931.
74. 6 July 1931.
75. 6 July 1931.
76. Cooper, *Colonialism in Question*, 117.
77. 24 July 1936, emphasis added.
78. 24 July 1936, emphasis added.
79. 4 November 1932.
80. 4 November 1932.
81. 25 October 1932.
82. Cooper, *Colonialism in Question*, 122.
83. David Scott, *Refashioning Futures* (Princeton, NJ: Princeton University Press, 1999), 26, 40, 52; emphasis added.
84. Cole, *Modern and Traditional Elites*, 151.
85. 3, 4, 29 September 1931, 1, 5, 16 October 1931.
86. Peter Wagner, *Modernity: Understanding the Present* (Cambridge: Polity Press, 2012), 4.
87. Dilip M. Menon, "Religion and Colonial Modernity: Rethinking Belief and Identity," *Economic and Political Weekly* 37, no. 17 (2002): 1162.
88. Ntongela Masilela, "African Intellectual Responses to Colonial Modernity in South Africa," in *Grappling with the Beast: Indigenous Southern African Responses to Colonialism, 1840–1930*, ed. Peter Limb, Norman Etherington, and Peter Midley (Leiden: Brill, 2010), 246.
89. *LDN*, 7 December 1936.
90. *LDN*, 7 December 1936.
91. 9 May 1946.

PART II

Experiments with Genre

CHAPTER 6

Experiments with Genre in Yoruba Newspapers of the 1920s

KARIN BARBER

The 1920s were a period of intense vitality in the Lagos press. Newspapers had been an established feature of Lagos city life since the 1860s, and numerous titles had come and gone.[1] But the 1920s saw an upsurge of new activity. At the beginning of the decade there were two English-language weekly papers,[2] and none in Yoruba. By the end of the decade, nine new English-language papers—including five dailies—had been launched, and no less than five Yoruba-language weeklies. New printing presses were established, and the papers' print runs increased by leaps and bounds throughout the decade. The readership widened, not only within Lagos, but among the cities of the hinterland, where Lagosian editors assiduously cultivated subscribers, agents, and contacts to send in information and distribute copies of their papers. The Lagos papers constituted an interactive network with each other and with numerous periodicals published along the anglophone West African coast and in Britain. They existed on a linguistic interface: the Yoruba and English languages cohabited, and many of the elite were bilingual. All the "Yoruba" papers also contained English sections; some of the English papers included occasional Yoruba pieces, and generally showed awareness of the Yoruba discourses flourishing all around them.

This was the context in which the Yoruba press became the site of profuse and innovative experimentation. Several major new genres were first tried out in the newspapers' pages, and subsequently consolidated by republication as books: among them, the novel and new styles of modern written poetry.[3] These are now seen by literary scholars as the foundations of one of the Afri-

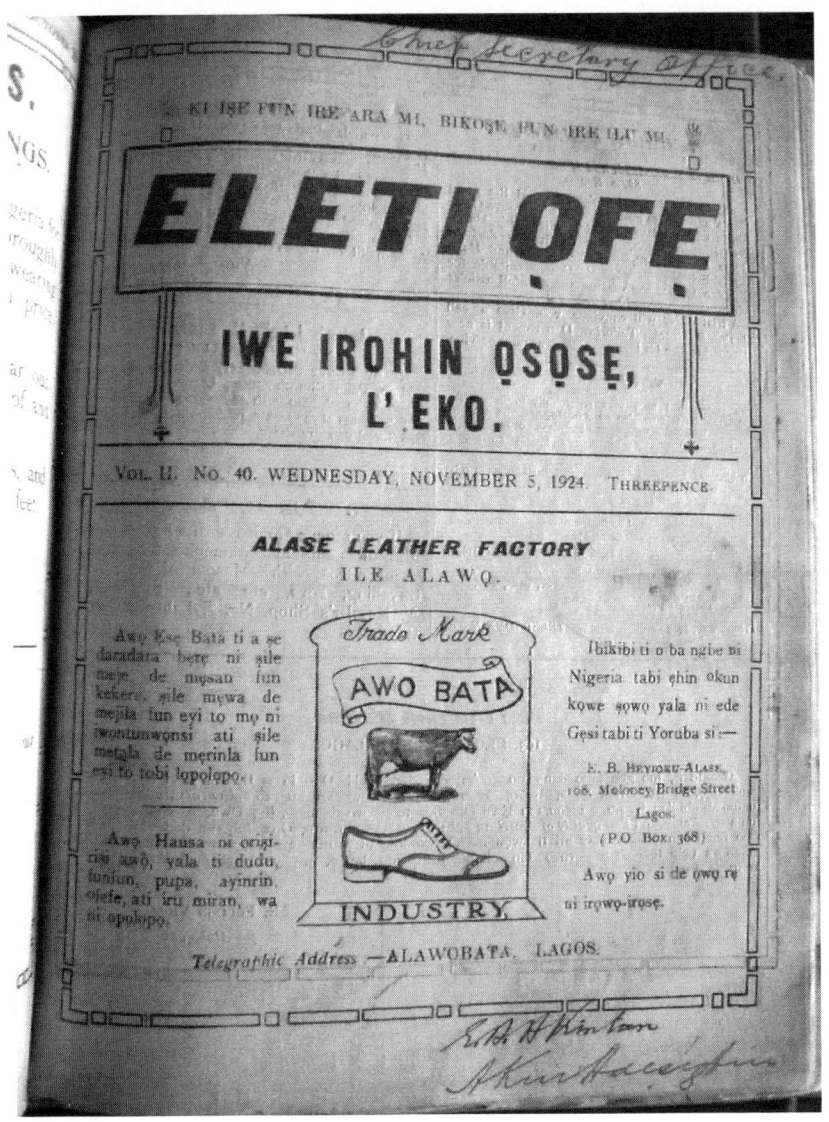

Fig. 1. Front page of *Eleti Ọfẹ*.

can continent's largest and most dazzling modern literary traditions. But these landmark innovations emerged from a sea of small experiments sponsored and hosted by the Yoruba weekly press—ways of announcing events, forms of commentary and reflection—some of which became the newspapers' stock in trade (and can be seen in the Yoruba papers of today), while others were tried out and then abandoned.

In this chapter I seek to understand the historical and social circumstances that were conducive to this efflorescence of textual innovation in the Yoruba-language papers. One of the strengths of an ethnographic approach to the past is that it can look closely at how and why new things emerge, in a specific context at a particular moment; how some innovations catch on and others don't; and thus offer an entry point to the way local forms of creativity work. Though ethnography is usually thought of as inhabiting lived experience typically accessible through present-day fieldwork, the recurrence, responsiveness, interaction, volatility, and focus on social minutiae of the Yoruba newspapers of eighty years ago do offer a field of inquiry that in some ways resembles a living ethnographic field site.

FERMENT IN 1920S LAGOS

The 1920s in Lagos has sometimes been seen as a rather staid period, dominated by a conservative Anglophile elite—well after the cultural extravagances of "Victorian Lagos," but well before the radical anticolonial activism of Zik and Awo. But when freed from a teleological nationalist narrative perspective, these years reveal themselves as characterized by intense local political ferment that found expression in litigation and above all in the press.

Lagos was the capital, administrative headquarters, and principal port of Nigeria. A British crown colony since annexation in 1861, it was subject to direct rule by the governor and his officials. The political, social, and cultural life of the city was dominated by a very small educated elite,[4] mainly Christian, many of them professionals (lawyers, doctors, clergymen, surveyors, engineers) or wealthy and successful businessmen. At the core of this small elite were the "Saro," Sierra Leoneans, so called because they were descended from recaptives, who had been intercepted by the British Naval Squadron in the first half of the nineteenth century and deposited in the Sierra Leone colony, where they became English-speakers, literates, and often Christian converts. They were culturally different from the Lagosian indigenes, and conscious of it: they called themselves "the long-trousered Creoles" as distinct from the majority illiterate pagan or Muslim *alagbada* (gown-wearers). In the nineteenth century they had invested cultural energy in preserving their distinctiveness and proximity to the British, but by the beginning of the twentieth century things were beginning to shift: disappointed with British failure to vacate positions of power for them to take over, the more radical wing of the elite began to seek alliances with the majority in order to campaign for a modification and eventual elimination of British rule.

Early colonial Lagos was characterized by a volatile economy; a reliance on commerce and waged labor (food was imported from the mainland); rapid population increase caused by in-migration from the hinterland and neighboring countries; and a rapid increase in the school-going population: according to the 1921 census, Lagos had already achieved remarkable levels of literacy, with 30 percent able to read, though only 10 percent able to write. The 1920s was also a time of intensifying political agitation. Since the early years of the twentieth century there had been mass protests against the water rate; by the 1920s, added to this were land cases, crisis in the majority Muslim community, and above all the deposition of the traditional ruler, the Eleko—who, though reduced to a figurehead since the imposition of colonial rule, retained prestige and symbolic significance to the Lagos indigenes. The incumbent Eleko, Eṣugbayi, was seen by the colonial government and its supporters as a pest, a fool, or a rascal, and after being suspended and reinstated he was finally deposed and exiled to Ọyọ in 1925. Throughout the 1920s, from his first suspension, there was an intense and vocal popular campaign for his reinstatement, conducted through the press, public events, and a relentless series of legal challenges mounted by Lagos's formidable cadre of lawyers. Eventually the colonial government gave in and recalled the Eleko from exile in 1931. Politically radical members of the elite, led by Herbert Macaulay, championed the cause of the Eleko, orchestrated popular protest, and secured for themselves a following that not only helped Macaulay's Nigerian National Democratic Party to win every election to the Nigerian Legislative Council from its inception in 1922 up to the late 1930s,[5] but also lent credibility to the Saros' claim to be the natural successors to the colonial rulers.

The Eleko affair was the most immediate trigger of new press activity. The papers campaigned incessantly. All the Yoruba papers and several of the English-language papers were pro-Eleko; some of the English-language papers such as the *Nigerian Pioneer* were pro-government. Wars of words ensued.[6] As political contestation heated up, the Lagos elite began to feel the need to extend its reach down the social scale, to draw in a constituency of potential popular supporters. This, therefore, was a formative moment when the public addressed by these small local presses was expanding and becoming diverse and multiscalar.

EXPERIMENTATION IN THE YORUBA PAPERS

The Yoruba and English newspapers that flourished in this climate, whatever their political position, had a number of structural features in common. First of all, they were not *news* papers in the modern sense. Most were one-man bands or very small businesses, and even the most successful had meagre resources; they could not afford to run a staff of investigative reporters or fact-gatherers. Much of the content of all the papers was opinion and editorializing; there was much reprinting and culling from other papers; much space was given to gossip and social news about the comings and goings of the tiny and highly visible elite. Entire sermons and political speeches could be reproduced in all of them, as well as official notices and government communications. All carried extensive advertising, including on the front page, as well as many types of material for which publication fees were charged, such as legal notices, announcements of name changes, obituaries, thanks for sympathy, and In Memoriam poems.

There was a high prevalence of serial format publications, where a slot was unfailingly filled every week by a continuation of the theme of the previous week. The *Lagos Weekly Record* published the equivalent of several whole books in this way (for example, a wide-ranging, intelligently prosecutorial examination of Governor Clifford's address to the Nigerian Council in 1921 took twelve consecutive issues, each featuring a very extensive text taking up almost the whole newspaper each week). In all the papers, there was a porosity that allowed newspaper pieces to be reprinted as pamphlets and booklets; sermons and lectures to be published as newspaper articles; books to be serialized, serials to be republished as books. The print sphere as a whole was seen as an interconnected space, so that a reader might write to *Akede Eko*, for example, to complain about a letter published in the *African Messenger* in response to a column culled from *West Africa* magazine. It was assumed that the reading public read across the whole field: and the editors certainly did, and often announced their culled material as having "just arrived" in the mail steamer.

However, there were striking differences between the English and Yoruba papers. The English-language papers gave far more space to foreign news, much of it sourced from English newspapers, from Reuters telegrams, or from contributors based in London. They also reprinted lighthearted material from British sources: the *Lagos Weekly Record* ran a whole series of romantic short stories set in the English upper middle classes, and the *Nigerian Pioneer* featured regular pages of British "humor." The local news, for these papers, included complete texts of government ordinances, speeches by government officials, and the minutes of government meetings. The Yoruba papers made much less use of this kind of material. Rather, they fomented a whole range of formats that permitted linguistic play. These included editorials, satirical and philosophical columns, narratives of travel into the interior or to neighboring countries, advice columns to designated categories of readers, open letters to prominent people, topical poems, and historical narratives usually focused on nineteenth-century Lagos politics. All these formats provided spaces in which verbal experiments took place. Adeoye Deniga, editor of the first of the new Yoruba papers, *Eko Akete*, made every headline into a proverb, praise epithet, or "deep Yoruba" idiom, often with a surprising twist.

While the English-language papers' use of replicated slots tended toward controlled predictability, the Yoruba papers more often used the format as a laboratory for trial runs. Recurrence can stagnate, but it can also offer a space for relatively inexpensive tryouts. If readers of innovations in the Yoruba papers showed signs of approval and anticipation, the series would carry on. If not, it could be quietly dropped and replaced with something else.

For example, soon after its launch in 1922, *Eko Akete* started a weekly column of moral advice for schoolchildren by someone writing under the pseudonym "Eleti Ọfẹ" (quite probably E. A. Akintan, who the following year founded his own newspaper of the same name). These homilies—work hard; be punctual; don't be disobedient—ran under the heading "Ipo ti awọn ọmọde" ("The position of children") as a numbered series, but its format was that of a letter directed to "ẹnyin ọrẹ mi kekere" ("you, my little friends"). The author asked his young readers to respond, and in the sixth week, he was overjoyed to announce that he had indeed received a letter from a young reader. This, he said, is a great encouragement: it shows that people are actually reading his advice—so he has now definitely decided to continue writing the column every week. The letter, from "a Muslim School Boy," is published on the same page, so that the reader's response is not only foregrounded as the main reason for continuing and further developing a new format, but also staged as a textual interaction within the paper: Eleti Ọfẹ solicits letters, gets one, and spends half of his next column responding to it and soliciting more. Not only this, he immediately launches a new idea—a competition for young readers with two prizes of 6d each for the best answers. Such was the success of the format that Akintan's own paper, *Eleti Ọfẹ*, continued it, with a series of advice columns aimed at young women, this time by the pseudonymous "Awọlujẹ" (quite probably I. B. Thomas, who wrote for several papers before founding his own *Akede Eko* in 1928). A reader wrote in praising the series and concluding,

> In fact, my neighbours who cannot read, used to ask me every week if 'ELETI-ỌFẸ' has come and what are AWỌLUJẸ's messages to our girls this week (*Eleti Ọfẹ*, 9 July 1924, 10).

Causing a stir, raising readers' anticipation, and even reaching beyond the literate readership—with this kind of encouragement, the series continued for a full fourteen weeks with ever more animated disquisitions on the proper behavior for young ladies. But when Awọlujẹ turned his hand to advice to young men, no response from readers appears to have been elicited, and the series was abandoned after only five episodes.

The weekly slot permitted author-editors to run up a flag and see if anyone saluted. If there was an encouraging response, they could prolong the series, embellish the format, and diversify it into several variants. If there was little response—or if the author-editors themselves simply lost interest—they could switch to something else without the loss of face, and waste of time and investment, that would be incurred by a failed book publication. Not only did the weekly serial format allow swift reader response from the inception of the series, but the response itself could be caught up and captured in the open web of textual interaction that the Yoruba newspapers (much more than the English ones) always hosted. The hospitality of the Yoruba papers to multiple and diverse contributors is signaled in the convention that all kinds of material, including regular columns by famous names, were presented in epistolary form.

ADDRESSIVITY

Voice, address, was the central element of all the Yoruba papers' experiments. And it was not only in the major literary forms such as the novel and modern print poetry that this was the case, but in a host of other genres across the whole field of newspaper publication.

This intense attention to addressivity was largely lacking in the English-language papers. The measured, polished rhetoric—whether the stuffy conservatism of Sir Kitoyi Ajasa (*Nigerian Pioneer*) or the intelligent critical analysis of Thomas Horatio Jackson (*Lagos Weekly Record*)—remained impersonal.

Here's an illustration. In 1923, a famous wealthy Saro called Michael Daniel Elliot[t] died, and a lavish funeral was held in Lagos. Chief among his claims to fame was the fact that he had purchased, years before his demise, a fancy brass coffin that he used to try out from time to time. This is how it is reported in the *Nigerian Pioneer* (27 April 1923, 7):

DEATH OF M.D. ELLIOT

The death occurred on Monday morning of Mr M.D. Elliott, well known as a money lender, at his residence at Olowogbowo, and his remains were buried at Ikoyi cemetry accompanied by a concourse of people who were eager to view the brazen coffin containing the corpse.

THE BRAZEN COFFIN AND THE FUNERAL

For some twenty years or thereabouts the deceased had bought and owned a coffin very richly ornamented with brass fittings, upholstered inside and covered with costly silk, which was expected to encase himself.

This coffin, some three feet in height, which has been noised abroad for its beauty was the object of curiosity which attracted the greater multitude to the funeral. The deceased was in the habit, during his lifetime, of setting a day apart for the commemoration of the impending day of his death, when he would bring out the coffin, rest himself in it pretending to enjoy its repose, and at the same time arranged a feast for the children of the neighbourhood; no doubt these would miss their feast. The shroud, a very rich and costly mildewy silk had been in store for some time prior to the death of Mr Elliot and the vault which was specially prepared were outstanding features of the funeral ceremony which made the procession very crowd and noisy.

This account is certainly more entertaining than much of the *Nigerian Pioneer*'s content. The writer describes the famous coffin in some detail and conveys something of the excitement that it stirred up. Nonetheless, the writ-

Fig. 2. "Brazen coffin" item in *Nigerian Pioneer*.

er's position is aloof and a touch disdainful. Elliot[t] is described only as a "money lender." There is the suggestion that of all the mourners the children would be the most bereaved, because they would "miss their feast"; and that the majority of the mourners were there only to goggle at the coffin. Even the sumptuous display is described with disparaging touches: the shroud is "mildewy." The great concourse of people at the funeral—one of the most-desired outcomes of a successful life—is merely "crowd and noisy": in other words, a nuisance.

Reporting on the same event, the headline in the Yoruba paper *Eko Akete* (28 April 1923, 6) takes the form of an intense personal address to the deceased, replete with praise epithets and blessings:

OYI-BIRI GBOJU-ỌNA-KAN-KAN KAN
ỌKỌ TẸJUMADE! AKODU MADA, ỌKỌNRIN-TA-FI-NṢEPE ỌKỌNRIN, ỌRUN A GBE Ọ! ! !

One who spins around and takes command of the whole road
Husband of Tẹjumade! "Akodu-Mada," man [so powerful] we use [his name] to curse other men, may heaven bless you! ! !

This quotation of a fragment of the deceased's *oriki* (praise poetry) opens up an intense channel of communication with him, enhancing his aura and (as in oral funeral chants and invocations at ancestors' burial places) forging a connection between the world of the living and that of the dead.

The article continues:

Ilu rọ kẹ̀kẹ́ ni *Sunday* to kọja nigbati a gbọ pe DADDY MICHAEL DANIEL ELLIOT ẹniti apele rẹ njẹ AKODU, tẹrigbasọ lalẹ ọjọ na ni ile rẹ loke Olowogbowo. Bi omi ni enia nwọ lọjọ keji nibi oku na, lati lọ wo Posi Ọgbẹni-Olowo-soke-dilẹ yi, ti a gbọ pe o ti ranṣẹ fun ni ilu Oyinbo fun £95 niwọn ọdun mẹtadilogun sẹhin (1906:) nigbati a si fi oju "ganni" rẹ, a ke "Safula" fun okuru Idẹ ti a fi ṣe e.

The city was in uproar last Sunday when we heard that Daddy Michael Daniel Elliot, whose nickname was Akodu, had kicked the bucket that evening in his house in Olowogbowo. People flooded like water to the place of the deceased on the next day, to look at the Coffin of this Gentleman, One-with-wealth-enough-to-level-mountains, which we hear he had ordered from England for £95 about seventeen years ago (1906): and when we clapped eyes on it, we were thunderstruck [we exclaimed "Safula!"] at the solid brass that it was made of.

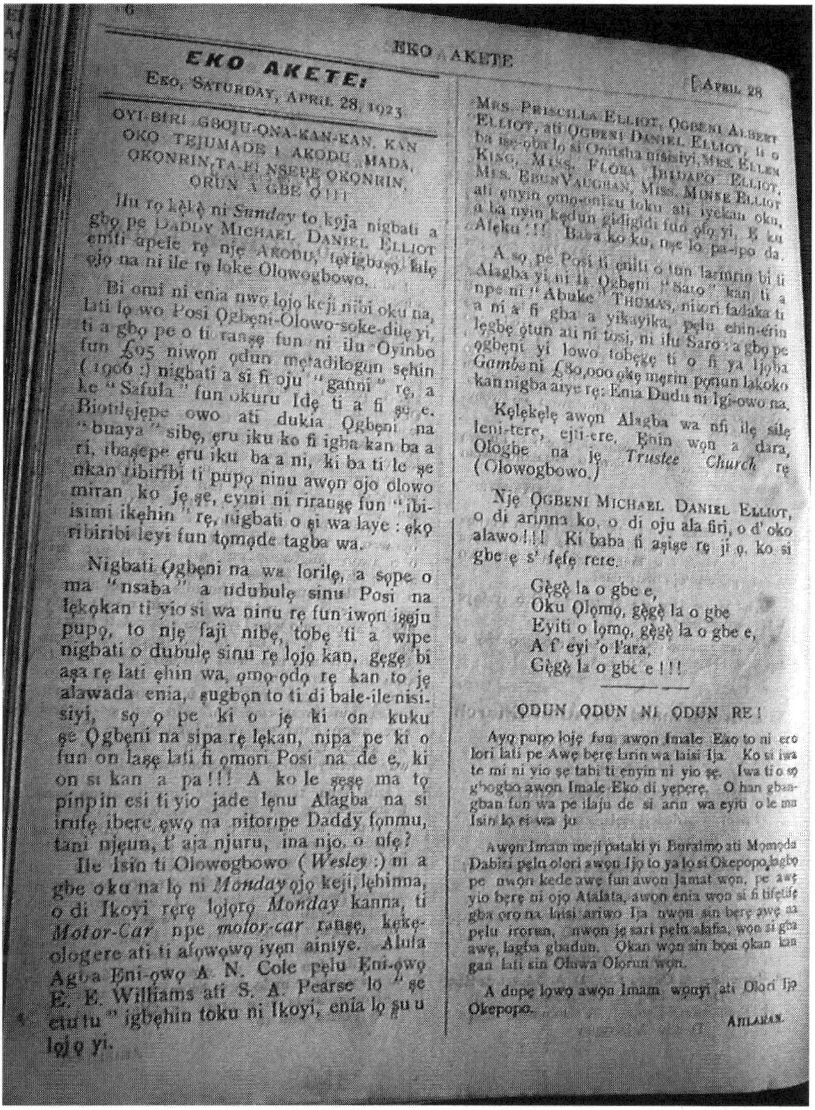

6 EKO AKETE [APRIL 28

EKO AKETE:

EKO, SATURDAY, APRIL 28, 1923

OYI-BIRI GBOJU-ỌNA-KAN-KAN. KAN OKO TEJUMADE I AKODU MADA, ỌKỌNRIN, TA-FI NSEPE OKỌNRIN, ỌRUN A GBE Ọ!!!

Ilu rọ kẹkẹ ni *Sunday* to kọja nigbati a gbọ pe DADDY MICHAEL DANIEL ELLIOT eniti apele rẹ njẹ AKODU, tẹrigbaṣọ, kilẹ ọjọ na ni ile rẹ loke Olowogbowo.

Bi omi ni enia nwọ lọjọ keji nibi oku na, lati lọ wo Posi Ọgbẹni-Olowo-soke-dilẹ yi, ti a gbọ pe o ti ranṣẹ fun ni ilu Oyinbo fun £95 niwọn ọdun mẹtadilogun sẹhin (1906 :) nigbati a si fi oju "ganni" rẹ, a ke "Safula" fun okuru Idẹ ti a fi ṣọ e. Biotilẹjẹpe owo ati dukia Ọgbẹni na "buaya" sibẹ, ẹru iku ko fi igba kan ba a ri, ibaṣepe ẹru iku ba a ni, ki ba ti le ṣe nkan ribiribi ti pupọ ninu awọn ojo olowo miran ko jẹ ṣe, eyini ni riranṣẹ fun "ibi-isimi ikẹhin" rẹ, nigbati o ṣi wa laye : ẹkọ ribiribi leyi fun tọmọde tagba wa.

Nigbati Ọgbẹni na wa lorilẹ, a sọpe o ma "nsaba" a ndubulẹ sinu Posi na lẹkọkan ti yio si wa ninu rẹ fun iwọn igeju pupọ, to njẹ faji nibẹ, tobẹ ti a wipe nigbati o dubulẹ sinu rẹ lọjọ kan, gẹgẹ bi aṣa rẹ lati ẹhin wa, ọmọ-ọdọ rẹ kan to jẹ alawada enia, ṣugbọn to ti di bale-ile nisisiyi, sọ ọ pe ki o jẹ ki on kuku ṣe Ọgbẹni na sipa rẹ lẹkan, nipa pe ki o fun on laṣẹ lati fi ọmori Posi na de e, ki on si kan a pa!!! A ko le ṣeṣe ma tọ pinpin esi ti yio jade lẹnu Alagba na si irufẹ ibere ẹwọ na nitoripe Daddy fọnmu, tani njẹun, t' aja njuru, ina njo, o nfẹ?

Ile Isin ti Olowogbowo (*Wesley* :) ni a gbe oku na lọ ni *Monday* ọjọ keji, lẹhinna, o di Ikoyi rẹrẹ lọjọrọ *Monday* kanna, ti *Motor-Car* npe *motor-car* ranṣẹ, kẹkẹ-ologere ati ti afọwọwọ iyẹn ainiye. Alufa Agba Ẹni-ọwọ A. N. Cole pẹlu Ẹni-ọwọ E. E. Williams ati S. A. Pearse lo "ṣe etutu" igbẹhin toku ni Ikoyi, enia lọ ṣu u lọjọ yi.

MRS. PRISCILLA ELLIOT, ỌGBENI ALBERT ELLIOT, ati ỌGBENI DANIEL ELLIOT, ti o ba iṣe-ọba lọ si Onitsha nisisiyi, MRS. ELLEN KING, MISS. FLORA IBIDAPO ELLIOT, MRS. EBUN VAUGHAN, MISS. MINSE ELLIOT ati ẹnyin ọmọ-omọ-oku toku ati iyekan oku, a ba nyin kẹdun gidigidi fun ọfọ yi. Ẹ ku Afẹku!!! Baba ko ku, nṣe lo pa-ipo da.

A sọ pe Posi ti ẹniti o tun larinrin bi ti Alagba yi ni ti Ọgbẹni "Saro" kan ti a npe ni "Abuke" THOMAS, nitori fadaka ti a ni a fi gba a yikayika, pẹlu ehin-erin lẹgbẹ ọtun ati ni tosi, ni ilu Saro : a gbọ pe ọgbẹni yi lowo tobẹẹ ti o fi ya Ijọba *Gambe* ni £80,000 ọkẹ mẹrin pọnun lakoko kan nigba aiye rẹ : Enia Dudu ni Igi-owo na.

Kẹlẹkẹlẹ awọn Alagba wa nfi ilẹ silẹ leni-tere, ejti-ere. Ẹnin wọn a dara, Ologbe na jẹ *Trustee Church* rẹ (Olowogbowo.)

Njẹ ỌGBENI MICHAEL DANIEL ELLIOT, o di arinna ko, o di oju ala firi, o d' oko alawo!!! Ki baba fi aṣiṣe rẹ ji ọ, ko si gbe ẹ s' fẹfẹ rere.

Gẹgẹ la o gbe e,
Oku Ọlọmọ, gẹgẹ la o gbe
Eyiti o lọmọ, gẹgẹ la o gbe e,
A f' eyi 'o l'ara,
Gẹgẹ la o gbe e!!!

ỌDUN ỌDUN NI ỌDUN RE!

Ayọ pupọ lojẹ fun awọn Imale Eko to ni ero lori lati pe Awẹ bẹrẹ larin wa laisi Ija. Ko si iwa te mi ni yio ṣe tabi ti enyin ni yio ṣe. Iwa ti o sọ gbogbo awọn Imale Eko di yẹpẹrẹ. O han gbangban fun wa pe ilaju de si arin wa eyiti o le mu Isin lọ si wa ju.

Awọn Imam meji pataki yi Buraimọ ati Mọmọdu Dabiri pẹlu olori awọn Ijọ to ya lọ si Okepopo, lagbọ pe nwọn kede awẹ fun awọn Jamat wọn, pe awẹ yio bẹrẹ ni ojọ Atalata, awọn enia wọn si fi tifẹtifẹ gba ọro na laisi ariwo Ija nwọn sin bẹrẹ awẹ na pẹlu irọrun, nwọn jẹ sari pẹlu alafia, wọn si gba awẹ, lagba gbadun. Okan wọn sin bọsi ọkan kan gan lati sin Oluwa Olọrun wọn.

A dupẹ lọwọ awọn Imam wọnyi ati Olori Ijọ Okepopo.

AHLAHAN.

Fig. 3. "Brazen coffin" item in *Eko Akete*.

Though the event and the background story in this text are the same as in the *Nigerian Pioneer* report, the point of view is quite different. The writer dramatizes the city's shock—and it is the whole city that is shaken by the news of the death. The speaker demonstrates an affectionate familiarity with the deceased by including his honorific "Daddy," his full name, and his nickname. The crowds flooding to the house of the deceased ("like water") are evoked not as a nuisance but as an indication of his status and of the attraction of the wondrous brass coffin—seen as an attribute and manifestation of the power of great wealth. The text is specific about the cost and the date of acquisition of the coffin, which is described from the point of view of one of the crowd who went to look at it. The impact of its resplendence is underlined by the writer's resorting to Hausa loan words ("Ganni" for "to see") and idiomatic exaggeration ("ke 'Safula!,'" literally "to cry out 'Safula!'"—an exclamation of respect and astonishment). The writer goes on to praise Mr. Elliot[t]'s courage: other, more cowardly rich men would not have had the nerve to prepare their last resting place in advance, and "ẹkọ ribiribi leyi fun tọmọde tagba wa": this is an important lesson for us all, old and young alike. The story about Mr. Elliot[t]'s habit of lying in his own coffin is elaborated with a detail about a servant of his ("a joker, but now the head of his own household") who asked him if he should close the lid and nail it down: "No need to investigate far to know the answer that the elder gave to this outrageous question." There follows an exultant description of the throng at the funeral, where "motorcars were sending motorcars on errands, and motorbikes and push-bikes were there without number"; the names of all of the officiating clergy; and a list of all the family members present, couched as a greeting, and concluding, "ati ẹnyin ọmọ-oniku toku ati iyekan oku, a ba nyin kẹdun gidgidi fun ọfọ yi. Ẹ ku Afẹku!!! Baba ko ku, nṣe lo pa-ipo da" ("And the rest of you members of the bereaved family on both sides, we sincerely sympathize with you on your bereavement. Greetings for your loss!!! [But] the father has not died, he's merely changed his place"). The writer goes on to compare Daddy Elliot[t] with the only other person known to have purchased such a resplendent coffin—a Sierra Leone man who was so rich that he lent the Gambian government £80,000! Finally, the writer reflects on changing times: "All our elders are leaving us one by one," and concludes with standard mourning formulas, prayers, and a song sung at funerals, inviting not only recognition but participation by the reader.

The report in the other Yoruba paper then in existence, *Eleti Ọfẹ* (25 April 1923, 3, 7), though less detailed, shares key features with that of *Eko Akete*: dramatization of the impact of Daddy Elliot[t]'s death ("the earth shook"), exclamations ("Shock, horror, the man has gone! Daddy Elliott is no more!"), recourse to standard funeral formulas, prayers and condolences, positioning of the writer as one of the astonished crowd, and the invitation to readers to join in a song (this time, a song in praise of wealth: "Money! Come and see what money has accomplished, money!").

The difference in mode of address between the *Nigerian Pioneer* piece and the two Yoruba pieces is striking. The *Nigerian Pioneer* writer maintains a fastidious distance from the people and scenes he is describing. The Yoruba papers are inclusive; the writer is one of the participants in the event, sharing the emotions of shock at Elliot[t]'s death, wonder at the coffin, pleasure in the stories about his rehearsals of interment, and admiration for the impressive turnout at the cemetery. Everything in the *Eko Akete* text is addressed to someone involved in the event: the focus of the address shifts from moment to moment, from the deceased himself, to the witnessing public, the participating crowd, the deceased's relatives, well-wishers and mourners, and the readers of the paper, who are invited to learn an important lesson from Daddy Elliot[t]'s fortitude and participate in singing his send-off song. The reader is invited to be complicit with the text by recognizing the shared coin of *oriki*, prayers, blessings, processional songs, and local slang.

THE EMERGENCE OF NEW GENRES

Bakhtin said that "addressivity, the quality of turning to someone," that is, the way the text addresses a reader or listener, is "a constitutive feature of the utterance; without it the utterance does not and cannot exist" (utterance in his terminology including written texts as well as speech; and differing from grammatical categories such as the sentence in that the utterance has completion, and at its end, awaits a response. Thus it is part of an ongoing chain of exchanges). He goes on to say, "The various typical forms this addressivity assumes and the various concepts of the addressee are constitutive, definitive features of various speech genres."[7] It would appear to be no accident, then, that at this period of intense engagement with new forms of print addressivity to a reading public, the Yoruba press fomented a whole array of new genres.

In some of the new textual forms tried out in the Yoruba press, experiments with address could lead to complex layering and levels of inclusiveness. One of the significant genres that took shape in the weekly Yoruba papers of the 1920s was the first-person travel narrative (see Jones, this volume). Reports on journeys were not new, but in *Eleti Ọfẹ* and *Akede Eko* there appeared for the first time extended, multipart, detailed, vivid, personal stories focusing on the experience of the journey itself, the means of transport, the traveler's feelings, gossip, and personal encounters along the way. As Rebecca Jones explains, these narratives were an extension and establishment of sociality through travel and through the narration of travel. E. A. Akintan's fourteen-part travel narrative of 1926–27 in *Eleti Ọfẹ*, "Irin Ajo Lati Eko lọ si Ileṣa" ("A Journey from Lagos to Ileṣa") continually describes people he encountered along the way—other editors, priests, writers, teachers, and "an elderly gentleman" selling newspapers:

> O ni gbogbo iwe irohin Eko li on nka; mo juwe ara mi fun u pe Oniwe-irohin Eleti-Ọfẹ ni mi; ẹnu ya a inu rẹ si dun lati ri mi; ọkan ninu awọn ọrọ rẹ niyi: "Are you the Editor? I have read of your tour in the paper, I am pleased to meet you." (*Eleti Ọfẹ* 9 February 1927, 4).

> He said he read all the Lagos newspapers. I explained that I was the editor of *Eleti-Ọfẹ*. He was surprised and happy to see me. One of the things he said was this: "Are you the editor? I have read of your tour in the paper, I am pleased to meet you."

By foregrounding himself and his interlocutors, quoting dialogue, and chattily sharing this with his readers, he establishes a circle of sociability inseparable from the business of disseminating the newspaper. This reader is incorporated into the narrative as a speaking interlocutor: the audience member is represented as part of the text, for other readers to model their reactions upon.

In another genre adopted by several of the Yoruba papers, the open letter to prominent people, multiple layers and scales of addressee are carefully orchestrated. The ostensible addressee is the prominent person himself, who is hailed in direct and sometimes surprisingly familiar tones. A simulacrum of rapport is established with the prominent person. But in some cases, the prominent person could not be expected to be the actual reader,[8] as for instance when the editor-authors chose to address British colonial officials whose knowledge of Yoruba was limited if not nonexistent. Rather, the appearance of an intense engagement with the addressee is put on display for a wider audience to admire. The pervasively epistolary character of the Yoruba-language press creates a warren of staged, multiplex addressivity.

THE YORUBA NOVEL

Probably the most significant new form to emerge from this scene of experimentation was the extended, realistic fictional narrative. In the 1920s papers we see the appearance in serial form of what may now be classed as the first two Yoruba novels: *Itan Emi Ọmọ Orukan* (The Story of Me, an Orphan) in *Eleti Ọfẹ*; and *Itan Igbesi Aiye Emi Sẹgilọla* (The Life Story of Me, Sẹgilọla) in *Akede Eko*.⁹ They had overlapping print histories, with E. A. Akintan's text in *Eleti Ọfẹ* starting first, in 1926, but proceeding in fits and starts and ending after I. B. Thomas, the editor of *Akede Eko*, had not only published the whole of the Sẹgilọla text in his newspaper, but had also republished it as a book in 1930, thus giving it claims to priority. Remarkably, these two early Yoruba fictional texts—now regarded as the starting point in the history of an important and flourishing genre—were both first-person narratives, told in the voice of a woman by a male author. Each traces the events in the life of the protagonist from her childhood up to the present (the putative time of writing). Interestingly enough, given their intertwined temporal emergence, the narrative arcs of these two stories are almost perfect inversions of each other: the story of the orphan is about a good girl who starts with nothing and ends up as the wife of a king, while the story of Sẹgilọla is about a girl who starts in a good family but goes to the bad, becomes a prostitute, ends up destitute, diseased, and dying, and is now writing to the paper to confess her sins and provide a valuable moral lesson—an uncompromising warning—for others to heed.¹⁰ *Sẹgilọla* was the more famous of the two stories, and the one that became folded into a retrospective literary history as a foundational text; it was also by far the more daring in its textual experiments.

I have described elsewhere the smoke-and-mirrors games that I. B. Thomas played with the persona of Sẹgilọla.¹¹ Sẹgilọla's letters were colloquial and looked real, an impression that Thomas reinforced by corroborating her story, referring to alleged personal interactions with her, and devoting editorials to discussion of her theme. Events in her narrative are plugged into real time and set in real and immediately recognizable places. Even the name of the steamship on which she eloped to the Gold Coast is real. Readers were apparently convinced of her existence. A popular poet sent in a poem about her; a woman reader calling herself "Jumọkẹ" sent ten shillings to alleviate her suffering; "D.A.N." wrote in from Ibadan to say, "I take my hat off to you, woman of the fascinating eyes." Yet all is not transparent: Thomas emphasizes—as she does— that Sẹgilọla is only a nickname, and that her true identity will not be revealed until after her (imminent) death. Ṣẹgilọla drops hints and teases the reader, veiling and half-drawing the veil. She suggests that if she wished, she could expose many prominent men still alive in Lagos for their traffic with her in her heyday—but the editor has warned her that the law forbids this.

The fascinating effects of the narrative revolve around the question of who is speaking, and to whom. Here is a voice that insists on being heard and yet shrinks from identification; a speaker who continually repeats the emphatic noun-like pronoun *èmi* (me/I) conjoined with a name that is not her real one; a narrative that purports to be a confession but which is couched almost entirely in public and generic formulas.

She has layers of imagined readers. Her first and most immediate addressee is the editor, whom she praises with fervent yet respectful warmth as a kind benefactor and true gentleman. She thanks him repeatedly for keeping his promise not to reveal her true identity: it is the keeping of this one secret, she says, that enables her to reveal others. She recalls personal interactions with him (as when he delivers Jumọkẹ's ten-shilling note) and at times changes places and becomes his reader and supporter (as when she comments on one of his editorials in which he reveals the paper's financial difficulties: if only she had the ability, as in the past, to help him out by tapping the wealth of a few of her besotted admirers!). A second layer of readers are the named individuals such as "D.A.N." and "Jumọkẹ," to whom she replies at length, postponing the next episode of the narrative in order to devote a whole letter to each of them. A third layer is a specifically Lagosian readership able to recognize her continual allusions to local knowledge, couched in sayings, songs, and fleeting references to shared urban folklore. And beyond this readership is a public conceptualized as indefinitely comprehensive and extensive, stretching out over time as well as space: "everyone, young and old, male and female, whether in this city of ours or in other parts," "all of you readers of my story all over the world," and "all of you of my generation and race and the generations that are to come."

It is in the nature of an epistolary genre to be addressed personally to someone. But in this text, Ṣẹgilọla's mode of address to her readers is the engine that drives the whole narrative. It is for their moral benefit that she has decided to tell the story in the first place; it is the tension of her hidden identity as speaker that binds her to the editor and provokes the curiosity of many readers; her colloquial, exclamatory, lachrymose address continually demands readers' participation and response. The outcome of the story (her miserable demise) is announced from the beginning: what gives the narrative its momentum and power to tantalize is not how it will end but how much of it she will tell—and whether she (and the newspaper) will survive long enough to complete it. She

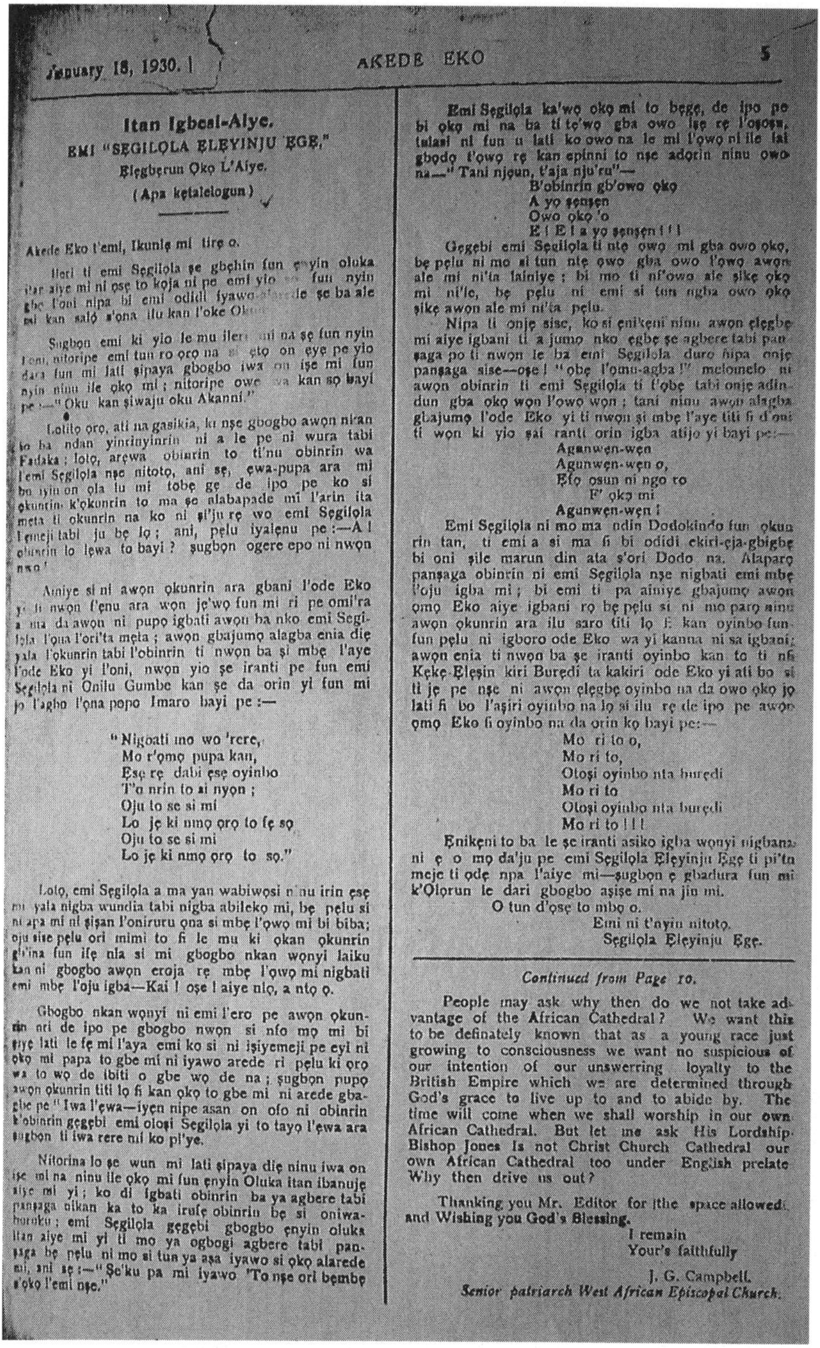

Fig. 4. Page from Ṣẹgilọla story, showing use of popular songs.

wishes her readers long life and good health, so that "all of you people who have begun to read my life story from episode one will have the opportunity to read it to the end." The narrator, newspaper, and reader are mutually dependent, and for the narrative to do its good work all three must survive.

The narrator, the editor, and the readers appeared to be unanimous about the moral lesson that this narrative teaches. And yet the fictional first-person mode allowed hesitations, contradictions, and heteroglossia that had no place in other prevailing moral discourses—the sermon, the editorial, the advice column, the open letter—on which this narrative so heavily drew for its ingredients. Sẹgilọla's letters are studded with popular songs and sayings. This urban street culture sounds a note that runs athwart the ostensibly univocal Christian moralizing of the narrative's "I/me." It is a worldly, resigned, humorous, half-cynical note recalling a more relaxed popular sexual morality in which adultery and fornication are facts of life, and a man who fathers your child is de facto your "husband." "We met it in the world / Fornication, taking lovers / It is not we who started it!" The double displacement of a nonidentifiable, veiled, and in fact fictional speaker quoting sentiments emanating from nonidentifiable popular sources ("a song we used to sing at the time") opens up space for an inclusiveness not possible in the more monologic genres that dominated in the press of the time. Contradictory moral perspectives are orchestrated but not synthesized, with haunting and unsettling effects. Popular audiences with a less stiff version of Christian morality than the one the Anglophile elite ostensibly adhered to could be made to feel at home. I suggest that the huge success of this narrative, which provoked more response than any other item in the Yoruba-language press of this period, was due not only to its sensational subject matter, but also to its bringing, through the artifice of fiction, popular voices and perspectives into play without abandoning its endorsement of the moral lesson.

It was their ebullient experiments with addressivity that gave all the new genres floated in the 1920s Yoruba press their energy and appeal. Travel narratives, advice columns, open letters, obituaries, and even apparently routine reports on events past or announcements of events to come were addressed directly to the reader, or to multiple scales and layers of readers. The editor-authors were explicit about their conception of the potentialities of print: it was public; it exposed secrets; it was immediate, specific, and detailed, tracking and dating local events as they happened; and it reached "the four corners of the world." All the newspaper genres shared this sense of inhabiting a whole new sphere that combined intimacy with extensivity; dyadic buttonholing with projection to a vast imagined public; reference to highly specific shared local knowledge with grandiose didactic generality.

YORUBA AND ENGLISH

We have seen that a number of general contextual features help to account for the upsurge of innovation of genres in the 1920s Yoruba papers: the social transformations under way in Lagos, the political ferment that found much of its expression in the press, the amenability of the weekly newspaper serial format to trying new things out with low investment and quick response. But this does not go far enough. The English-language papers participated in all these conditions and yet were not a site for textual innovation and experimentation with genre until much later. Why was there this difference between the Yoruba- and English-language papers?

The editor-proprietors of the English-language papers in early colonial Lagos, regardless of their political orientation, were, by and large, of higher levels of education and higher social status than the editor-proprietors of the Yoruba-language papers. Kitoyi Ajasa (*Nigerian Pioneer*) was a barrister-at-law who had done part of his schooling in England and then qualified as a lawyer at the Inner Temple. He was trusted by the colonial government and sat on almost every official body to which African members could be co-opted—the Legislative Council, the Nigerian Council, the Lagos Town Council, the Licensing Board, the Pilotage Board, the Committee for the Assessment of Rates and Taxes—and was eventually knighted in 1928. He was socially prominent and tightly tied into the network of marriage alliances that, according to Kristin Mann, consolidated elite privilege and distinctiveness before the First World War[12] and that maintained much of its grip up to the 1930s. His chief antagonist, Herbert Macaulay (*Lagos Daily News*), was of an even more distinguished family background, son of Bishop Crowther's daughter and the revered headmaster T. B. Macaulay. He was a qualified surveyor, a talented violinist, a leading light in innumerable elite cultural events. J. P. Jackson (*Lagos Weekly Record*), G. A. Williams (*Lagos Standard*), and barrister Adeyẹmọ Alakija, chair of the board of the *Nigerian Daily Times*, are all included in Mann's list of the top two hundred educated male members of the Lagos elite.

None of the editors of the Yoruba-language papers was included in this exclusive circle. Three of them were at various times primary school teachers. Adeoye Deniga, of *Eko Akete*, "started life in the Civil Service as Express Delivery mail-man in the local Post Office" (*Times of Nigeria*, 7 March 1921, 6), then became a schoolteacher and later a headmaster. He gave this up in 1911 in order to devote himself to writing, editing, and giving public lectures, many of which he subsequently published as pamphlets and which earned him the sobriquet "Professor." He eked out his income by working as a licensed public letter writer. He wrote in English as well as in Yoruba, but the anglophone elite tended to be disparaging about his abilities and condescending about his status. Noting that Deniga had published a pamphlet of his lectures on African leaders, the editor of the *Lagos Standard* sniffed that he was not going to review it: "The lecturer we feel would not expect it, for he certainly will agree with us that it claims no right to literary merit" (*Lagos Standard*, 3 March 1915, 4). E. A. Akintan (founder-editor of *Eleti Ọfẹ*) was a respected headmaster and author of educational books, but not a member of the Saro elite. I. B. Thomas (*Akede Eko*) was of Saro origin and claimed links of kinship and friendship with Herbert Macaulay and Adeyẹmọ Alakija, but he did not have the benefit of higher education, and he gave up primary school teaching to become first a cashier for Leventis Bros and then a precariously freelance editor and writer. His English was colorful but lacked the immaculate polish and literary allusions of Ajasa's, Jackson's, and Macaulay's writing.

For the topmost echelons of the Saro elite, often with degrees and professional qualifications acquired in England, there was an obvious investment in the English language and in maintaining and displaying their command of its loftiest registers. The English-language papers, no matter what their political orientation, were de facto addressing a small elite capable of reading elevated English prose. Their actual and imagined audience was known to them—very well known—and was strictly limited. Even for the radicals like Macaulay, who assiduously courted and won a huge popular following, writing in a populist, accessible English was not yet an attractive proposition. (One press historian speaks of Macaulay's "ponderous political essays" with "long-winded and high-sounding phraseology" and "a strong preference for long, sonorous words of Latin origin.")[13] Too much of their prestige and influence with the British depended on demonstrating their impeccable credentials as masters of the British repertoire. This mastery enabled them to speak with confidence to, and of, the British officials. Thomas Horatio Jackson, heir to his father John Payne Jackson's radical *Lagos Weekly Record*, went so far as to patronize the governor himself. He opens his twelve-part critique of Sir Hugh Clifford's address to the Nigerian Council with the statement,

Fig. 5. I.B. Thomas in later life - on an editors' delegation to the United Kingdom.

There can be no question that an impartial critic must necessarily admire His Excellency for manifesting the courage of his convictions, for his naïve frankness, his surprising command of the English language and lucidity of expression which suggest the qualities of an experienced author and accomplished writer and his profusion of ideas supported by a wealth of imagery—the products of an exhuberant [sic] imagination though based, we regret to say, in many instances upon faulty logic or hasty generalisations. (*Lagos Weekly Record*, 29 January 1921, 5)

"His surprising command of the English language"—take that, Sir Hugh! Such a magnificent putdown was only possible from a master of English prose. Small wonder that these magisterial polemicists saw nothing to be gained from forays into the unknown territory of popular, accessible writing. And this was not for lack of models. The English-language papers frequently reprinted articles from British papers and magazines that were written in a much more lively colloquial style. Nor was it due to a lack of capability. Among themselves, the elite writers could cultivate an affable, even jocular style, redolent of the clubhouse. A notable example is Walter L. Edwin, a journalist from Sierra Leone, who briefly edited the *Times of Nigeria* in 1920 after the death of its founder-editor, James Bright Davies.[14] Edwin adopted an informal and humorous style of address to his readers in a recurrent feature entitled "Five O'clock Tea with Your Editor." But his chat is directed to a limited audience: the majority of Lagosians are referred to as "the Lagos crowd," the "masses," who at one point are said to practice a "mysterious rite Native"; readers are exhorted to "teach the masses the meaning of civic government." Though one of the paper's aims is to draw the masses into responsible political involvement, the paper is not addressed to them. It was not until the old Saro dominance of politics and culture was swept away by a new generation of nationalist anticolonial activists toward the end of the 1930s that a new style of journalism was created to reflect their views, most prominently in Nnamdi Azikiwe's *West African Pilot*. In the 1920s, when the Yoruba papers were experimenting most effervescently, the English-language papers continued using a style that had been set decades earlier.

As postcolonial critical theory has long maintained, mastery of a very complex foreign communicative register, to the point where the foreigner can be challenged on his own ground, does not initially leave much room for creativity or innovation. The point is to do it perfectly, not to mess about with the rules. This was surely one reason for the elite's adherence to a lofty style. But there may have been another reason too. An elevated, impersonal style, not addressed directly to any category of readers, produces an impression of impartiality. It would seem to conform to the idea, then under active development among West African coastal elites, of disinterested civic virtue and espousal of the public good. Habermas describes participants in the bourgeois public sphere of late eighteenth-century Europe as considering themselves to be "bracketing" their personal status and interests in order to serve a wider public good.[15] There was something of this in the Lagos elite's conception of their role. With minuscule provision for elected representation—a franchise of a few hundred people electing three of their own number to seats in a consultative assembly overwhelmingly dominated by government appointees—civic concerns and public interest were believed to be represented by the press more than by the Nigerian Council or the Lagos Town Council.[16] The newspaper editors saw themselves as not only representing, but informing and shaping, public opinion; and public debate often meant one newspaper arguing with another. Indeed, the press was itself considered to *be* "public opinion," and public debates took place not between frequenters of coffeehouses or debating chambers so much as between newspapers. Editorials lamented that there was "not enough" public opinion, that it was still to develop, that it was much more advanced in the Gold Coast, and so on. The impersonal, elevated prose of the English-language papers may thus have constituted a claim to a deliberative space that was public-spirited, nonpartisan, and formal, uncontaminated by individual interest and personal taste: a space encompassing the good of the whole community. In actuality, though, their discourse was sealed off from the "general public" in whose interests they claimed to be speaking.

While the English-language papers of the 1920s were speaking only to the elite, the Yoruba-language papers were deliberately reaching out to a much larger potential audience. The 20 percent of the Lagos population who in the 1921 census were documented as being able to read but not write were almost certain to have been able to read only in Yoruba, since the first years of elementary school education were in the mother tongue. Many pupils dropped out after two or three years and entered a large constituency of clerks, artisans, apprentices, and traders who used literacy to some extent in their daily life but were not advanced in English. The Yoruba papers' mottoes made clear their intention to align themselves with this constituency of potential readers: "I will inform the powerful of the grievances of the poor / the lower classes, and I will be the spokesman for the dumb" (*Eko Akete*);[17] "For God, the King, and the poor / the lower classes" (*Eko Igbẹhin*); and in typically loquacious vein, *Akede Eko*'s mission "to proclaim our sympathy for the destitute and the lower classes and to rescue those who are suffering from the persecution of the powerful." They were going to explain things to this larger, lower-class public, draw it in, align it behind their political campaigns, especially the Eleko campaign, and demonstrate to the British colonial government that the small elite dominated by "native foreigners" was nonetheless better fitted to represent and lead the country than the old traditional chiefs, favored by Lugard's policy of indirect rule.

But though their immediate potential readers were the Lagos lower classes, the Yoruba-language editors, as we have seen, could also address a public conceived of as indefinitely extensive, greatly exceeding any known or potential stratum of Lagos or even the Yoruba-speaking millions in the hinterland. However, even when their imagined audience was a vast, anonymous public, they addressed it in the most personal, engaging way. The first and second pronouns dominate; hardly anything is in the third person. There is always a direct address—sometimes simultaneous direct addresses to layers of addressees—always sounding as if a response is expected.

Thus, to recapitulate, the English-language newspaper writers adopted an impersonal style but were read by a tiny audience personally very well known to them; the Yoruba papers adopted an intensely personal and addressive style, but were projected out to an indefinitely large and unknown audience. Or rather, a complex of shifting, expanding, and contracting audiences: for as the brass coffin piece and *Ṣẹgilọla* have shown, these writers were adept at switching addressees and layering the known, personal participants upon a larger unknown collection of readers and even nonreaders.

This reaching out—seeking to seize and bind the attention of the Yoruba readers and the nonreaders to whom the readers would pass on the papers' key messages—is, I have suggested, what fueled the continual and fertile experimentation that revolved so much around modes of address. The Yoruba-language writers were entering a vast unexplored field, bursting with a heterogeneous array of materials and models—oral and written, old and new, local and foreign—any and all of which could be incorporated and transformed. There was plenty of material in hand with which to forge these new styles of writing: including a vast oral repertoire (note that *oriki*, the oral genre they probably knew best, is entirely and intensely addressed to the praisee) and a street culture of incredible sleaze and vitality, full of songs, anecdotes, and sayings, which the English-language papers stood aloof from but which the Yoruba papers, with sometimes rueful complicity, could exploit to create new genres. In this way they could establish a common ground with their hoped-for readers.

New genres come into existence when a changing social reality demands a new lens, new means to see, comprehend, and manage it.[18] In the first instance, it was the need to connect with the increasingly vocal and turbulent Lagosian crowd that precipitated the expansion and dynamism of Yoruba print culture. Beyond that, there was an emergent awareness of Yoruba readers outside Lagos, in their southwestern Nigerian heartland or scattered by commerce or profession across Nigeria and the West African coast; and of real or imagined interconnections, made possible by the press, across the empire and to the "four corners of the world." These were among the factors that precipitated the creation of the 1920s Yoruba newspapers and fueled their creative experimentation with new formats.

BIBLIOGRAPHY

Baker, Pauline H. *Urbanization and Political Change: The Politics of Lagos, 1917–1967*. Berkeley: University of California Press, 1974.

Bakhtin, M. M. "The Problem of Speech Genres." In *Speech Genres and Other Late Essays*, edited by Caryl Emerson and Michael Holquist, translated by Vern W. McGee, 60–102. Austin: University of Texas Press, 1986.

Barber, Karin. "Time, Space and Writing in Three Colonial Yorùbá Novels." *Yearbook of English Studies* 27 (1997): 108–29.

Barber, Karin. *Print Culture and the First Yoruba Novel: I.B. Thomas's "Life Story of Me, Segilola" and Other Texts*. Leiden: Brill, 2012.

Barber, Karin. "Experiments with Text: Fagunwa and His Precursors, E.A. Akintan and I.B. Thomas." In *Celebrating D. O. Fagunwa: Aspects of African and World Literary History*, edited by Adeleke Adeẹkọ and Akin Adesọkan. Ibadan: Bookcraft, forthcoming 2016.

Coker, Increase H. E. *Landmarks of the Nigerian Press: An Outline of the Origins and Development of the Newspaper Press in Nigeria, 1859 to 1965*. N.p.: n.p., 1968.

Cole, Patrick. *Modern and Traditional Elites in the Politics of Lagos*. Cambridge: Cambridge University Press, 1975.

Falọla, Toyin. "Earliest Yoruba Writers." In *Perspectives on Nigerian Literature, 1700 to the Present*, edited by Yẹmi Ogunbiyi, 1:22–32. Lagos: Guardian Books Nigeria, 1988.

Frow, John. *Genre*. London: Routledge, 2006.

Habermas, Jürgen. *The Structural Transformation of the Public Sphere*. Translated by Thomas Burger with Frederick Lawrence. Cambridge MA: MIT Press, 1992.

Mann, Kristin. *Marrying Well: Marriage, Status and Social Change among the Educated Elite in Colonial Lagos*. Cambridge: Cambridge University Press, 1985.

Medvedev, P. N., and M. M. Bakhtin. *The Formal Method in Literary Scholarship: A Critical Introduction to Sociological Poetics*. Translated by Albert J. Wehrle. Baltimore: Johns Hopkins University Press, 1978.

Newell, Stephanie. *The Power to Name: A History of Anonymity in Colonial West Africa*. Athens: Ohio University Press, 2013.

Ọlabimtan, Afọlabi. "Language and Style in Obasa's Poetry." In *Yoruba Oral Tradition: Poetry in Music, Dance and Drama*, edited by Wande Abimbọla, 1031–69. Ifẹ: Department of African Languages and Literatures, University of Ifẹ, 1975.

Omu, Fred I. A. *Press and Politics in Nigeria, 1880–1937*. Atlantic Highlands, NJ: Humanities Press, 1978.

NOTES TO CHAPTER SIX

1. The first weekly paper in the region, dating back to 1859, was *Iwe Irohin*, a Yoruba-language newsletter published by the Church Missionary Society in Abẹokuta, a city that had close and multifarious social, political, and economic links with Lagos. In Lagos, soon afterward, privately owned, mainly English-language papers began to be established, with a civic, political, and cultural—rather than evangelical—orientation. Some quickly expired; others flourished for decades. The only Yoruba-language paper published in Lagos in the nineteenth century, *Iwe Irohin Eko* (Lagos Newspaper), survived for only four years (1888–92). But some of the English-language papers lasted well into the 1920s and beyond: the *Lagos Weekly Record*, founded in 1890, continued to be published up to 1930 and was one of the most radical of the English-language papers of the 1920s. The *Nigerian Pioneer*, a conservative progovernment paper founded in 1914, lasted until 1936. For details see Fred I. A. Omu, *Press and Politics in Nigeria, 1880–1937* (Atlantic Highlands, NJ: Humanities Press, 1978).

2. Or three, if you count the *Lagos Standard*, which just made it into the decade, closing at the end of January 1920.

3. The Lagos papers promoted a variety of styles of Yoruba poetry including poems in the style of famous popular singers, acrostic obituary poems, and Yoruba-English macaronic texts. However, the longest-lasting innovations in poetry in this period were carried by the Ibadan paper, *Iwe Irohin / Yoruba News*, which was edited by the noted poet D. A. Ọbasa. A comparison of the Ibadan and Lagos papers as sites of genre innovation must await a future study.

4. For the composition of this elite up to about 1915, see Kristin Mann, *Marrying Well: Marriage, Status and Social Change among the Educated Elite in Colonial Lagos* (Cambridge: Cambridge University Press, 1985).

5. For details of electoral politics in this period of Lagos history, see Pauline H. Baker, *Urbanization and Political Change: The Politics of Lagos, 1917–1967* (Berkeley: University of California Press, 1974).

6. For discussion of the role of the Lagos elite in the Eleko affair, see Patrick Cole, *Modern and Traditional Elites in the Politics of Lagos* (Cambridge: Cambridge University Press, 1975).

7. M. M. Bakhtin, "The Problem of Speech Genres," in *Speech Genres and Other Late Essays*, ed. Caryl Emerson and Michael Holquist, trans. Vern W. McGee (Austin: University of Texas Press 1986), 99. The mode of address, of course, is not the only defining feature of a genre. As John Frow specifies, there are other dimensions of an utterance/text that are also relevant to an audience's recognition of it as participating in a particular genre: these include formal features; thematic structure; the rhetorical function (i.e., what the speaker is doing in producing

the utterance that participates in that genre); and the physical setting, which may function as a regulative frame. See John Frow, *Genre* (London: Routledge, 2006).

8. For representational works of art, Peter Rabinowitz distinguishes between four audiences: the "actual audience" who read or watch the text; the "authorial audience" assumed by the author and expected by the author to have certain "beliefs, knowledge, and familiarity with conventions"; the "narrative audience" implied by the genre (for example, if a novel is presented as a history, then the narrative audience is one that reads the story as history, accepting that the characters really existed); and the "ideal narrative audience" that is internally posited as part of the fiction. Peter Rabinowitz, "Truth in Fiction: A Re-examination of Audiences," *Critical Inquiry* 4, no. 1 (1977): 121–41.

9. An even earlier fictional text is mentioned by Falọla: a pamphlet entitled *Dọlapọ, Aṣẹwo Ọmọ Aṣẹwo* (Dọlapọ, the Prostitute, Daughter of a Prostitute), which Falọla describes as "an obscene romantic fiction written in the 1890s." I have not been able to locate this piece, but judging by the title and Falọla's plot summary it is possible that it served as a prompt for the theme of I. B. Thomas's narrative. See "Earliest Yoruba Writers," by Toyin Falọla, in *Perspectives on Nigerian Literature*, vol. 1, ed. Yẹmi Ogunbiyi (Lagos: Guardian Books, 1988), 22–32.

10. For a fuller comparison of these two novels in their social context, see Karin Barber, "Experiments with Text: Fagunwa and His Precursors, E.A. Akintan and I.B. Thomas," in *Celebrating D. O. Fagunwa: Aspects of African and World Literary History*, ed. Adeleke Adeẹkọ and Akin Adesọkan (Ibadan: Bookcraft, forthcoming).

11. Karin Barber, *Print Culture and the First Yoruba Novel: I.B. Thomas's "Life Story of Me, Segilọla" and Other Texts* (Leiden: Brill, 2012). See also Karin Barber, "Time, Space and Writing in Three Yoruba Novels," *Yearbook of English Studies* 27 (1997): 108–29, and Stephanie Newell, *The Power to Name: A History of Anonymity in Colonial West Africa* (Athens: Ohio University Press, 2013):137–150.

12. Mann, *Marrying Well*, 92.

13. See Increase H. E. Coker, *Landmarks of the Nigerian Press: An Outline of the Origins and Development of the Newspaper Press in Nigeria 1859 to 1965* (n.p.: n.p., 1968), 18.

14. The *Times of Nigeria* was one of the most interesting of the English-language papers of the period. After the death of the founder-editor, James Bright Davies, it passed into the ownership of Sheikh Adam I. Animashaun, "the Arabic Astrologer and author of the Nigerian Arabic Almanack" (*Times of Nigeria*, 22 March 1920, 3), who ensured that Islamic issues were prominently featured.

15. The point clearly is not that these prosperous, privileged, male members of a rising European bourgeoisie were *really* speaking and acting disinterestedly

for the common good. The point is that at that historical moment, they not only espoused this as an ideal but believed themselves to be achieving it. The elites of early twentieth-century Lagos seem to have entertained similar beliefs.

16. See Newell, *Power to Name*, for an illuminating discussion of the idea of the West African colonial press as the "fourth estate."

17. A quotation from W. T. Stead, the inspiration of the "New Journalism" in Britain.

18. P. N. Medvedev and M. M. Bakhtin, *The Formal Method in Literary Scholarship: A Critical Introduction to Sociological Poetics* (1928), trans. Albert J. Wehrle (Baltimore: Johns Hopkins University Press, 1978), 131.

CHAPTER 7

Everyday Poetry from Tanzania

Microcosm of the Newspaper Genre

KELLY ASKEW

EVERYDAY POETRY

For centuries, ordinary people in East Africa have responded to events of all kinds through Swahili poetry.[1] Until the emergence of Swahili-language (Swahiliphone) newspapers in the late nineteenth century, however, the written record favored not their contributions but those of master poets, typically male, from the coastal regions of today's Kenya and Tanzania, where the art form originated. Examples include the poetry of Fumo Liyongo, the legendary warrior prince of the northern Swahili coast believed to have lived sometime between the ninth and twelfth centuries, or Muyaka bin Haji of Mombasa (1776–1840).[2] Yet one notable exception signaling the *everydayness* of Swahili poetry, proving that it did not only and always focus on battles won, praises of rulers, or devout retellings of the life of Prophet Muhammed, is the *Utendi wa Mwana Kupona* (1810–60).[3] Composed by Mwana Kupona binti Mshamu, wife of the ruler of Siyu, the poem offers advice and admonishment to her daughter, exhorting her to be a good wife and always honor her husband, but possibly allowing a subversive view on the patriarchalism of the time.[4] Mwana Kupona was not alone in her poetic endeavors as someone falling outside the definition of "powerful" (on account of her gender). Indeed, scholars tell us that though certainly embraced by elites who had the luxury of time to devote to it, poetry was in fact especially associated with nonelites and the poor.[5] They also tell us that although we have written poetic texts dating back to the fifteenth century, Swahili poetry was not typically confined to the page but performed—either sung to musical accompaniment (as *nyimbo* or *taarab*) or intoned in recitative style (*mashairi*). Poetic duels (*mashairi ya malumbano* or *kujibizana*) were a common pastime wherein poets would improvise before an audience, vying to compose poetry more complex in meaning, more formally pristine, employing more opaque metaphor, and using a higher degree of "inner" Swahili (*Kiswahili cha ndani*) than their rivals.[6]

It was during the German colonial period that Swahili poetry transitioned from being a predominantly (but not exclusively) oral art form to becoming a mainstay of contemporary East African print culture. (Let it be noted, however, that given the high percentage of Swahili historical scrolls collected by missionaries and early scholars devoted to poetry, it clearly was also a mainstay of nineteenth-century Swahili print culture.)[7] Some of the earliest published newspapers in the former Deutsch-Ostafrika sought to include the poetry of local poets within their pages both to show off local talent and to inspire German settlers to learn Swahili. By the 1910s, Swahili poetry constituted a regular feature of both government and missionary newspapers in Tanzania. The number of newspapers grew exponentially over subsequent decades and with it the demand for more poetry. In Tanganyika, there were 20 print periodicals before the start of World War I (eleven in German, six in Swahili, and three in other African languages), which grew to 50 in 1954, 119 in 1986, and with liberalization of the media to over 323 periodicals (the vast majority in Swahili) registered by 1996.[8] Tanzanian newspapers include dailies, nightlies, weeklies, biweeklies, monthlies, and specialty sports and entertainment newspapers (see Reuster-Jahn, this volume)—some published by the government or the ruling party and the majority by private entities. The decision after independence to make Swahili the national language in Tanzania—and corollary decisions that primary education, parliamentary deliberations, and judicial decisions (except at the highest courts) be in Swahili—helped nationalize the language in a way that has not happened in any other East African state. This level of commitment expunged lingering associations of Swahili with the colonial order and went a long way toward facilitating in Tanzania a popular medium of national discourse that unites all segments of society.[9] In comparison, Kenya's Swahili press has always been meager relative to Tanzania's. It saw a brief period of growth between 1945 and 1952 but was never terribly strong because "Swahili was not universally understood whereas vernacular papers could be and frequently were read to the uneducated."[10] However, poetry did appear in several Kenyan Swahili periodicals, such as *Baraza* (The Council), published by the East African Standard in Nairobi, and the popular magazine *Nyota Yetu*.[11]

Finally, Swahili poetry is a required element of the Tanzanian secondary school curriculum. Students throughout the country are taught to appreciate fine Swahili poetry by reading and interpreting the work of master poets and trying their own hand at composition. Swahili poetry traditionally adheres to a canon of compositional rules concerning rhyme (*vina*), meter (*mizani*), strophe (*mabeti*), refrain (*kipokeo* or *kibwagizo*), and the division of lines (*mishororo*) into hemistiches (*vipande*).[12] Wide variation in form can be found, as well as in topic, but common throughout is a passion for subtlety and artful deployment of language. From the 1960s to the mid-1990s when the state ran national arts competitions, one category of competition was poetry performance, and teams of school students would vie for the chance to win honors for their district, region, and zone.[13]

So to summarize, five factors have contributed to the efflorescence of Swahili newspaper poetry in Tanzania: (1) the long-standing tradition of Swahili poetry along the coast, recognized as one of the world's great poetic traditions;[14] (2) the spread of Swahili language and poetry along trade routes that popularized it throughout the region; (3) nationalization of the Swahili language, which enabled people from all corners of the country to speak, read, and write in a single medium; (4) liberalization of the media in the early 1990s that spawned a vibrant and extensive Swahili press; and (5) a national curriculum that prescribed the study of poetry for all secondary school students. As a result, one finds hundreds of Swahili poems published each week in Tanzania, with newspapers devoting entire pages or regular sections to poetry submitted by readers. Though the frequency of publication has started to decline in recent years, another domain that seems to be making up the difference is online publishing. Swahili poetry blogs, websites, and online hangouts are new venues that are attracting the talents of a new generation of everyday Swahili poets.[15]

Despite the daunting abundance of *mashairi ya magazeti* (newspaper poetry) published from the early 1900s to the present, there has been an astonishing lack of attention paid to it. Cursory mention appears in a few texts, such as Ann Biersteker's note that Sheikh Ali bin Hemedy el-Buhriy, teacher of renowned poet Shaaban Robert, published his poems in the British colonial newspaper *Mambo Leo* (Current Events), which also in 1929 published the *Utendi wa Mwana Kupona* (1996).[16] Thomas Geider (2002) and Emma Hunter (2012) acknowledge newspaper poems in their respective essays on ethnohistories and biographies from East Africa (Geider), and on global affiliations and affinities among readers of *Mambo Leo* (Hunter; see also her chapter in this volume).[17] Maria Suriano (2011) examines debates waged through *Mambo Leo* readers' letters and poems on the moral and aesthetic value of popular *dansi* music, viewed by some as a marker of modernity and by others as societal decay.[18] And James Brennan (2012, chap. 4) mines newspaper letters, articles, and poetry for evidence of nationalist and racial ideology in 1940s Tanganyika.[19] The most sustained analysis, however, is Aldin Mutembei's book (2009) on newspaper poems about HIV/AIDS.[20] In it, he collected over a hundred newspaper poems dated 1982–2006 and examined the euphemisms used to discuss the disease, interpretations about how one succumbs, and the lack of a cure. It is an impressive work, but inaccessible to many since it is written in Swahili. And in a brief essay, Swahili poet and novelist Euphrase Kezilahabi analyzes the "everydayness" of Swahili poetry, arguing against ideas of Swahili poetry as limited to classical masterpieces and archaic language use. To support his argument, he analyzes a single newspaper poem but prefaces his analysis by describing the poem as "badly written," exposing an elitist bias against newspaper poets, who are always presumed to be inferior in talent. He elaborates by claiming that "the ideas and arguments advanced by the poet are not coherently presented. The poet is not rich in vocabulary and as a result the poem is paradigmatically limping."[21]

Nevertheless Kezilahabi extracts from this poem, "Maji ya Kifuu" ("Water in a Coconut Shell"), by a poet who self-identifies by the poetic pseudonym of *The Mimi* (The Me), five characteristics denoting the "everydayness" of Swahili poetry generally: (1) its *quotidian* nature, due to its focus on the lived experience of ordinary people; (2) its *immediacy*, with poets responding to events right after they happen and responding to each other in quick reply; (3) its *dialogic* nature, inviting debate from readers and fellow poets alike; (4) its *closeness to being*, by expressing the inner feelings and experiences of those who compose it; and (5) its grounding in *ethical and moral* stances.[22] M. M. Mulokozi drew similar conclusions in an earlier article, stating, "Swahili poetry can be identified, not so much by its formal aspects, but rather by its historical determinants, the language medium, and the cultural and social values that it expresses. It is these and not the 'vina' [rhyme] and 'mizani' [meter] which differentiate Swahili Poetry from other world poetries."[23]

What follows is a brief history of Swahili newspaper poetry and analysis of the subgenres it comprises. Newspaper poetry counts as "everyday" in Kezilahabi's sense, through its content and language use, as well as by virtue of being produced and received primarily by nonelites. It is also an "everyday" phenomenon because of the sheer ubiquity of poems that pepper the pages of the Swahili press. And it is "everyday" in the sense forwarded by Karin Barber (2006) of facilitating an "everyday literary culture" via the social environs and engagements born of newspaper readerships, be they discussions beside newspaper vendors (*barabarani*), on street corners (*maskani*), in homes (*nyumbani*), or at neighborhood coffee spots (*barazani*). Here readers dynamically reconstitute texts—poetry and prose—by interpreting them, critiquing them, reacting to them, re-oralizing them by reading them aloud, and both deriving from and giving them new meanings. As for the poets, their voluminous amounts of poetry help "constitute new forms of consciousness ... new forms of self-examination ... [and] new styles of self-projection and self-dramatization."[24] Thus "everyday poetry" paradoxically produces locality by grounding poets and audience in familiar time and space, while simultaneously stretching beyond to unknown futures and hoped-for outcomes for self and society.

NEWSPAPER POETRY IN TANZANIA: COLONIAL BEGINNINGS

The earliest Swahili newspapers in the former Deutsch-Ostafrika (Tanzanian mainland) and the British Protectorate of Zanzibar were Anglican missionary publications and because the "contents often were of European origin and did not serve the needs of the indigenous population,"[25] they likely did not feature Swahili poetry. However, poetry became a regular element in the first secular Swahili newspaper, *Kiongozi* (The Leader), launched in 1904. Published by the German colonial state-run Tanga School, *Kiongozi* provided information and government agendas for literate Africans and become the most influential newspaper of the period.[26] In her 1929 doctoral thesis on Swahili periodicals in Deutsch-Ostafrika, Hilde Lemke comments, "In almost all newspapers, poetry plays a big role. The Swahili can express everything in their poetic language ... and newspaper editors always succeeded in acquiring one or more poets for their papers."[27] German editors appreciated Swahili praise poetry and would periodically commission poets to compose poems. On occasion these would be translated into German with the versions published together so readers could compare the two and try to teach themselves either Swahili or German. *Kiongozi* thus transferred into mass mediated format the Swahili passion for verse. One finds poems of praise for the kaiser on his birthday and for his might in quashing the MajiMaji "rebellion," establishing the praise poem as a regular subgenre of newspaper poetry.[28] One Swahili poet, Hamisi Auwi, who composed a poem entitled "Who Has the True Authority If Not the Kaiser?" was even rewarded with a trip to Germany to meet the kaiser, who according to Lemke "richly rewarded" him.[29]

German missionaries entered newspaper publishing two decades after their English counterparts, not producing the Swahili-language *Pwani na Bara* (Coast and Hinterland) until 1910. In this religious alternative to *Kiongozi*, poetry also quickly established itself. An example is the 1911 acrostic praise poem for Kaiser Wilhelm II by Jakobo Ngombo entitled "Shukrani za Africa" ("Thanks from Africa") (figure 1).[30]

The First World War brought an end to Deutsch-Ostafrika and a temporary cessation of the Swahili press in East Africa. None of the above publications survived into the postwar period.[31] Under British colonial rule, the Education Department launched *Mambo Leo* in 1923. A popular monthly, it included poetry,[32] and though it served as a mouthpiece for the colonial government, subtle critique protected by a sense of artistic license made its way onto the printed page via readers' poems and letters.

THE EMERGENCE OF NATIONALIST POETICS

In 1937 Tanganyika's first African independent periodical went public: *Kwetu* (Our Home), edited by Erica Fiah, a businessman formerly of Uganda. According to Scotton, Fiah promoted "arguments for equal treatment and eventually even self-government for Africans."[33] Its first issue (18 November 1937) contained

> the report of the recent meeting of the Legislative Council, news of the League of Nations debate on Italy's invasion of Ethiopia, and a brief summary of international events. Sports, *poetry*, and a few small advertisements filled out the small publication.[34]

Kwetu ceased publication in the mid-1940s but in 1948 another private newspaper appeared in Dar es Salaam, the weekly *Zuhra* (The Wanderer), owned and edited by a South Asian businessman named Ramadhan Machado Plantan, and featuring increasingly political poetry. This was now the period of preindependence political mobilization in which newspapers played import-

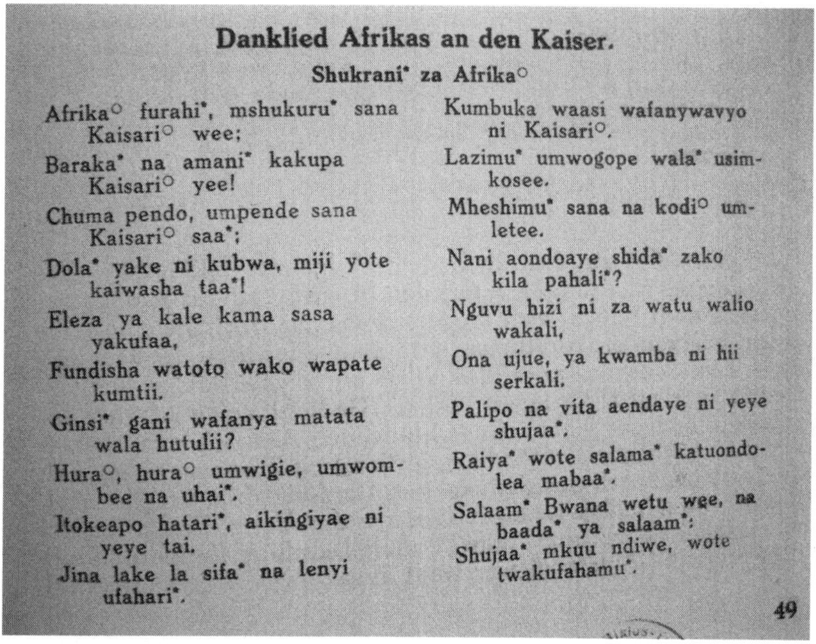

> **Danklied Afrikas an den Kaiser.**
> **Shukrani* za Afrika°**
>
> Afrika° furahi*, mshukuru* sana Kaisari° wee;
> Baraka* na amani* kakupa Kaisari° yee!
> Chuma pendo, umpende sana Kaisari° saa*;
> Dola* yake ni kubwa, miji yote kaiwasha taa*!
> Eleza ya kale kama sasa yakufaa,
> Fundisha watoto wako wapate kumtii.
> Ginsi* gani wafanya matata wala hutulii?
> Hura°, hura° umwigie, umwombee na uhai*.
> Itokeapo hatari*, aikingiyae ni yeye tai.
> Jina lake la sifa* na lenyi ufahari*.
>
> Kumbuka waasi wafanywavyo ni Kaisari°.
> Lazimu* umwogope wala* usimkosee.
> Mheshimu* sana na kodi° umletee.
> Nani aondoaye shida* zako kila pahali*?
> Nguvu hizi ni za watu walio wakali,
> Ona ujue, ya kwamba ni hii serkali.
> Palipo na vita aendaye ni yeye shujaa*.
> Raiya* wote salama* katuondolea mabaa*.
> Salaam* Bwana wetu wee, na baada* ya salaam*:
> Shujaa* mkuu ndiwe, wote twakufahamu*.
>
> 49

Fig. 1. From Hilde Lemke, *Die Suaheli-Zeitungen und –Zeitschriften in Deutsch Ost-Afrika* (1929), 49.

ant roles. Government newspapers like *Mambo Leo* sought to persuade readers to accept a slow and prolonged transition toward self-rule. However, Julius Nyerere and the Tanganyika African National Union (TANU) called for independence and a boycott of the colonial government's newspapers.[35] The boycott contributed to the demise of *Mambo Leo* and the rise of *Mwafrika* (The African), a private newspaper founded in 1957 that came to be identified with TANU's policies as much or more so than the official TANU periodical *Sauti ya TANU* (Voice of TANU). In the span of only one year, *Mwafrika*'s circulation reached twenty-five thousand, the highest of any newspaper. Poetry featured in all these publications (examples to be discussed below), and significantly the Catholic newspaper *Kiongozi*'s (not to be confused with the German-era Tanga School newspaper) conversion to the nationalist cause was signaled in April 1958 when "the lead story in *Kiongozi* was an interview with Nyerere on the future of Tanganyika, and six months later a poem in praise of the TANU leader was published."[36]

POSTINDEPENDENCE SWAHILI NEWSPAPER POETRY

From the 1960s through the 1990s, newspapers quadrupled in number, resulting in a concomitant demand for more poetry, now an established element of the medium. Hence an effusion of poetic output marks this period. Poems covered a wide range of topics from the personal and the local to the national and the international, and filled the pages of Swahiliphone newspapers.

A blurring of topical boundaries between poetry and prose is evident, an example being the following from the first African-owned independent newspaper in Zanzibar, called *Afrika Kwetu* (Our Africa). Here in the 17 January 1963 issue under an unrelated headline about Tanganyikans rejecting multiparty politics, a page features side-by-side assessments of the assassination of Togolese president Sylvanus Olympio four days earlier, an article "Askari wa Jeshi Wamehuni Togoland" ("Army Soldiers Betray Togoland"), and a poem "Mtenda Mema Haishi, Mwisho Hudhulumiwa" ("The Good One Won't Survive and Will Suffer Persecution") (figure 2).

The poet, identified only as "Mt," writes:

1. *Msiba umeingia kifo cha Olymphia*[37]
Uhuru kaupigania na Jamhuri kaitia
Kifo kimemtokea ghafla hakujijuwa
Mtenda mema haishi mwisho hudhulumiwa . . .

3. *Msiba umewafika ndugu zetu wa Togo*
Mwanaume msifika kimeanguka kigogo
Olymphia kadhulumika kama jembe na ndago
Mtenda mema haishi mwisho hudhulumiwa . . .

1. *A funeral is upon us for the death of Olympio*
He fought for freedom and founded the Republic
Death took him suddenly, he didn't expect it
The good one won't survive and will suffer persecution . . .

3. *A funeral has beset our brethren in Togo*
A praiseworthy man, a giant, has fallen
Olympio was struck as a hoe cleaves grass
The good one won't survive and will suffer persecution . . .

That same week in the Moshi-based newspaper *Kusare* a large number of international news items populated the issue alongside local and national

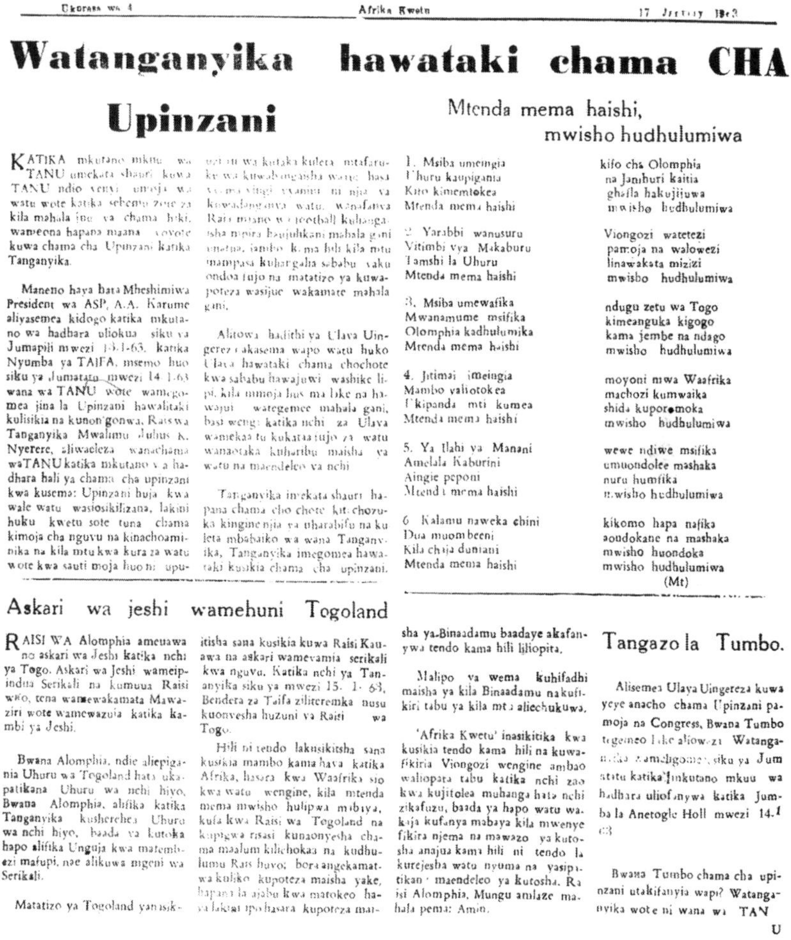

Ukurasa wa 4 Afrika Kwetu 17

Watanganyika hawataki chama CHA Upinzani

KATIKA mkutano mkuu wa TANU umekata shauri kuwa TANU ndio yenye umoja wa watu wote katika sehemu zote za kila mahala ine ya chama hiki, wameona hapana maana yoyote kuwa chama cha Upinzani katika Tanganyika.

Maneno haya bata Mheshimiwa President wa ASP, A.A. Karume aliyasemea kidogo katika mkutano wa hadbara uliokua siku ya Jumapili mwezi 13-1-63, katika Nyumba ya TAIFA, msemo huo siku ya Jumatatu mwezi 14-1-63 wana wa TANU wote wamegomea jina la Upinzani hawalitaki kulisikia na kunon'gonwa, Rais wa Tanganyika Mwalimu Julius K. Nyerere, aliwaeleza wanachama waTANU katika mkutano wa hadhara hali ya chama cha upinzani kwa kusema: Upinzani huja kwa wale watu wasiosikilizana, lakini huku kwetu sote tuna chama kimoja cha nguvu na kinachoaminika na kila mtu kwa kura za watu wote kwa sauti moja huo ni upuuzi tu wa kutaka kuleta mtafaruku wa kuwababaisha watu hasa wa mambo mengi vyanini ni njia ya kuwadanganya watu. Wanafanya Rais mpira wa football kuhangaisha mpira haujulikani mahala gani unatua, jambo kama hili kila mtu mampasa kuhangalia sababu yaku ondoa fujo na matatizo ya kuwapoteza wasijue wakamate mahala gani.

Alitowa hadithi ya Ulaya Uingereza akasema wapo watu huko Ulaya hawataki chama chochote kwa sababu hawajuwi washike lipi, kila mmoja hus ma bke na hawajui wategemee mahala gani, basi wengi katika nchi za Ulaya wamekaa tu kukataa fujo za watu wanaotaka kuharibu maisha ya watu na maendeleo ya nchi.

Tanganyika imekata shauri hapana chama cho chote kitachozuka kingine njia ya uharabifu na kuleta mbabaiko wa wana Tanganyika, Tanganyika imegomea hawataki kusikia chama cha upinzani.

Mtenda mema haishi, mwisho hudhulumiwa

1. Msiba umeingia
Uhuru kaupigania
Kifo kimemtokea
Mtenda mema haishi

kifo cha Olomphia
na Jamhuri kaitia
ghafla hakujijuwa
mwisho hudhulumiwa

2. Yarabbi wanusuru
Vitimbi vya Makaburu
Tamshi la Uhuru
Mtenda mema haishi

Viongozi watetezi
pamoja na walowezi
linawakata mizizi
mwisho hudhulumiwa

3. Msiba umewafika
Mwanamume msifika
Olomphia kadhulumika
Mtenda mema haishi

ndugu zetu wa Togo
kimeanguka kigogo
kama jembe na ndago
mwisho hudhulumiwa

4. Jitimai imeingia
Mambo yaliotokea
Ukipanda mti kumea
Mtenda mema haishi

moyoni mwa Waafrika
machozi kumwaika
shida kuporomoka
mwisho hudhulumiwa

5. Ya Ilahi ya Manani
Amelala Kaburini
Aingie peponi
Mtenda mema haishi

wewe ndiwe msifika
umuondolee mashaka
nuru humfika
mwisho hudhulumiwa

6 Kalamu naweka chini
Dua muombeeni
Kila chaja duniani
Mtenda mema haishi

kikomo hapa nafika
aondokane na mashaka
mwisho huondoka
mwisho hudhulumiwa

(Mt)

Askari wa jeshi wamehuni Togoland

RAISI WA Alomphia ameuawa na askari wa Jeshi katika nchi ya Togo. Askari wa Jeshi wameipindua Serikali na kumuua Raisi wao, tena wamewakamata Mawaziri wote wamewazuia katika kambi ya Jeshi.

Bwana Alomphia, ndie aliepigania Uhuru wa Togoland hata ukapatikana Uhuru wa nchi hiyo, Bwana Alomphia, alifika katika Tanganyika kusherehea Uhuru wa nchi hiyo, baada ya kutoka hapo alifika Unguja kwa matembezi mafupi, nae alikuwa mgeni wa Serikali.

Matatizo ya Togoland yanasikitisha sana kusikia kuwa Raisi Kauawa na askari wamevamia serikali kwa nguvu. Katika nchi ya Tanganyika siku ya mwezi 15-1-63, Bendera za Taifa ziliteremka nusu kuonyesha huzuni ya Raisi wa Togo.

Hili ni tendo lakusikitsha sana kusikia mambo kama haya katika Afrika, hasara kwa Waafrika sio kwa watu wengine, kila mtenda mema mwisho hulipwa mibaya, kufa kwa Raisi wa Togoland na kupigwa risasi kunaonyesha chama maalum kilichokaa na kudhulumu Rais huyo; bora angekamatwa kuliko kupoteza maisha yake, hapana la ajabu kwa matokeo haya lakini ipo hasara kupoteza maisha ya Binaadamu baadaye akafanywa tendo kama hili liliopita.

Malipo ya wema kuhifadhi maisha ya kila Binaadamu nakufikiri tabu ya kila mtu aliechukuwa.

'Afrika Kwetu' inasikitika kwa kusikia tendo kama hili na kuwafikiria Viongozi wengine ambao waliopata tabu katika nchi zao kwa kujitolea muhanga hata nchi zikafuzu, baada ya hapo watu wakaja kufanya mabaya kila mwenye fikira njema na mawazo ya kutosha anajua kama hili ni tendo la kurejesha watu nyuma na yasipatikane maendeleo ya kutosha. Raisi Alomphia, Mungu amlaze mahala pema: Amin.

Tangazo la Tumbo.

Alisemea Ulaya Uingereza kuwa yeye anacho chama Upinzani pamoja na Congress, Bwana Tumbo tegemeo lake aliowezi Watanganyika wamemgomea siku ya Jumatatu katika mkutano mkuu wa hadhara uliofanywa katika Jumba la Anetogle Holl mwezi 14-1-63

Bwana Tumbo chama cha upinzani utakifanyia wapi? Watanganyika wote ni wana wa TANU

Fig. 2. From the 17 January 1963 issue of *Afrika Kwetu*, published in Zanzibar.

items (figure 3). An article congratulated Dr. Martin Luther King Jr., "Kiongozi wa Wanegro" ("Leader of the Blacks"), for being named *Time* magazine's "Man of the Year," and the editor congratulated President John F. Kennedy for a speech he gave, and reported on how the U.S. ambassador to Tanganyika congratulated the new nation on its progress sinceindependence. These appeared with news about meetings to be held in Moshi by the Organization of African and Asian Unity, and the good fortune of several journalists who

Fig. 3. From the 19 January 1963 issue of Moshi-based newspaper *Kusare*.

had received support to pursue study in the United States. Opposite the page congratulating King, Kennedy, and the U.S. ambassador was a poem called "Kiti Kashika Nyerere" ("Nyerere Has Taken the Chair"), which praised Nyerere as leader of an independent Tanganyika and expressed pride in his accomplishments, just as the U.S. ambassador had done. A second poem in the same issue titled "Chunga Vyema Shamba" Lako" ("Take Good Care of Your Farm") extoled the value of agriculture, a key principle of Nyerere's government, and a theme permeating most issues of *Kusare*, Moshi being a fertile agricultural region.[38]

Yet a perusal of poetry from this same time period reveals topics not found in prose sections of the paper. Limiting ourselves to *Kusare* for the moment, these include poems that criticize unsocial behavior, such as gossiping, uncontrolled displays of anger, lack of compassion, and sheer malice:

- "Fitina" ("Intrigue"), 24 November 1962
- "Hasira Hasara" ("Anger Brings Loss") (a proverbial saying), 29 December 1962
- "Wako Wapi Wapendanao" ("Where Are The Ones Who Love Each Other?"), 29 December 1962
- "Binadamu Acha Kijicho" ("Humans, Stop Your Malice"), 12 January 1963

One poet offers personal advice:

- "Ukitaka Owa Mke" ("If You Wish, Take a Wife"), 8 December 1962

Another laments the general state of the world:

- "Dunia Raha Gani?" ("What Joy Exists in This World?"), 26 August 1967

And two more cloak their meaning in metaphor:

- "Kokomanga Tunda Tukufu Mola Katuumbia" ("The Pomegranate Is a Holy Fruit Created for Us by God"), 26 August 1967
- "Kinda Mwenye Viota Vingi" ("Baby Pigeon with Lots of Fluffy Down"), 26 August 1967

It was during this period that newspaper editors started setting aside dedicated poetry sections to accommodate the flurry of everyday artistic activity (figures 4–7).

MICROCOSM OF THE NEWSPAPER FORM

Mashairi ya magazeti (newspaper poetry) can be viewed as a microcosm of the newspaper form because, as illustrated above, one finds poems addressing topics found discussed in prose in the same papers. These span (1a) description and commentary on *national and local events/news*; (1b) description

Table 1: Newspaper Poetry Sections

NEWSPAPER	POETRY SECTION
Bahari ("Sea")	*Mashairi* ("Poetry")
Baraza ("Council")	*Mashairi Yenu Matamu* ("Your Sweet Poetry")
Baraza ("Council")	*Mashairi Matamu ya Wiki* ("Sweet Poetry of the Week") —Thursday edition
Dira ("Compass")	*Bustani ya Washairi* ("Garden of Poets")
Heko ("Hurrah!")	*Washairi Wetu* ("Our Poets")
Kusare[1]	*Mashairi* ("Poetry")
Majira ("Season")	*Tungo* ("Compositions")
Mambo Leo ("Current Events")	*Mashairi Yenu* ("Your Poetry")
Mshindi ("The Victor")	*Ukumbi wa Washairi* ("Forum for Poets")
Mwafrika ("The African")	*Mawaidha ya Washairi* ("Poets' Advice")
Mwananchi ("The Citizen")	*Wasemavyo Washairi* ("What the Poets Say")
Nipashe ("Tell Me")	*Mashairi* ("Poetry")
Uhuru ("Freedom")	*Maoni ya Washairi* ("Poets' Opinions")
Zanzibar Leo ("Zanzibar Today")	*Bustani ya Washairi* ("Garden of the Poets")

1. I could not determine the meaning of "Kusare."

and commentary on *international news*; (1c) *praise poems* for politicians and other community leaders; (1d) *obituaries*; (1e) *editorials* on social issues, for example, moral decline or corruption; (1f) "Dear Abby"-like calls for and offers of *advice*;[39] and even (1g) *personal ads* seeking a spouse. Everyday poets also, however, contribute elements *not* typically found in newspapers, including (2a) thanksgiving to God for *prayers* answered; (2b) poems asserting affiliation with a *community of poets* and/or with a particular newspaper; (2c) *love poems*; and (2d) *enigma poems*, in which a conundrum is posed and fellow poets challenged to resolve it.[40]

While the majority of newspaper poets are relatively unknown, some make a name for themselves within a particular newspaper by being regular contributors and forming a following for themselves and the paper for which they write. Poets reference each other's work in their poems and openly challenge each other to respond to their poems. Occasionally a famous poet, such as Shaaban Robert, would publish in newspapers, but that constitutes the exception that proves the rule of everydayness. Newspaper poetry pages are the domain of ordinary citizens, poetry being a national pastime and the newspaper a social equalizer of talent, as well as gender, class, and status. The following examines the aforementioned subgenres of *mashairi ya magazeti* and offers examples drawn from across multiple time periods and newspapers.

1a. National and Local Events Poems

In 1995, Tanzania held its very first national-level multiparty elections. Introducing electoral democracy was a key agenda item of the international donor community in the 1990s as an indicator of the state's commitment to good governance and rule of law. Though the transition out of socialism in other contexts typically meant the demise of the ruling socialist party, in Tanzania the 1995 elections presented a sound victory for the ruling party, Chama cha Mapinduzi (CCM, or "Party of the Revolution"), which remains in power today. The elections featured a fragmented, politically immature opposition, and with its well-honed capabilities, including greater access to media, and with popular allegiance to Julius Nyerere, who founded the party, CCM won a handy victory. Still, opposition parties got their foot in the door and have used that opening to strengthen their standing and their political agendas.

The following poem by Annet Mbwambo, an everyday poetess in Dar es Salaam, appeared in the newspaper *Nipashe* ("Tell Me") two weeks before the 1995 national elections. She urges her fellow citizens to cast their votes and choose a leader who will benefit the country, not one "causing us to investigate him" afterward. Poets typically sign their poems with both their real names *and* a self-designated poetic title, called a *lakabu*. Mbwambo's *lakabu* is *Mama Kilimo* (Mother Agriculture) and she ends her poem emphasizing the nationalist value of returning to the land to cultivate.

"Uchaguzi" ("The Election")
Bibi Annet Mbwambo (*Mama Kilimo*—"Mama Agriculture")
Nipashe, 10 October 1995, 13

1. Leo mtunzi Aneti, habari ninawapasha	1. Today poet Annet has news to tell you
Nlo Tanga na Babati, Moshi pamwe na Arusha	You in Tanga and Babati, Moshi as well as Arusha
Nia yangu madhubuti, tusikose uchaguzi	My intention is good, let's not miss the election[41]
Tuliojiandikisha, tusikose uchaguzi . . .	We who have registered, let's not miss the election . . .
6. Chagua kiongozi bora. Mbwambo nawafahamisha	6. Choose a good leader, I, Mbwambo, tell you
Tupate ile tijara, yaani mema maisha[42]	So that we may benefit and have a better life

Fig. 4. "Sweet Poetry of the Week," *Baraza*, 16 May 1968.

Tunenepe na kufura, yetu afya kuboresha	We should grow strong and healthier
Tuliojiandikisha, tusikose uchaguzi	We who have registered, let's not miss the election
7. Wala tusishawishike, mtu kuja tupotosha	7. And let's not be tempted by one who'll mislead us
Akataka tukiuke, tuache kumfatisha	Who'll step over us, causing us to investigate him
Mtu huyo sio tuke, zimeshampeperusha	Someone like that isn't sane. His sense has been blown away
Tuliojiandikisha, tusikose uchaguzi ...	We who have registered, let's not miss the election ...

Fig. 5. "Forum for Poets," *Mshindi*, no. 4, 1981

9. Tama kwayo ndugu zangu, usemi ninafupisha
Nilosema si mizungu, wakati uneni-isha
Shambani nakwenda zangu, kilimo kwenda tunisha
Tuliojiandikisha, tusikose uchaguzi

9. Finally, fellows, I shorten my remarks
What I say is not secret. Time has run out
I am going back to my field to resume farming
We who have registered, let's not miss the election

Figs. 6 & 7. "Compositions," *Majira*, 23 March 1995 and "Garden of Poets," *Dira*, 17–23 October 2003.

Circling back in time to Tanganyikan independence in 1961 and the jubilation accompanying it, a twenty-two-stanza poem by Shaaban Robert celebrating the significance of freedom from colonial rule was published in *Mambo Leo*, excerpted here.

"Istaklali ya Tanganyika" ("Tanganyika's Independence")[43]
Shaaban Robert
Mambo Leo, January 1962, 8

1. Katika vitu vizuri, hapana kama Uhuru, Ni neno lenye fahari, daraka la kuamru, Uhuru huja na ari, na uthabiti na nuru.	1. Among all that is good, there's nothing like Freedom, A term denoting pride and commanding power. Freedom comes with dignity, stability, and brilliance.
2. Huja na matumaini, uhuru kwa kila mtu, Uhuru sawa na Dini, kwa utukufu wa watu, Na furaha ya moyoni, katika maisha yetu . . .	2. It comes with the hope for freedom for everyone Freedom like Religion bestows magnificence on people And instills joy in hearts during our lifetimes . . .
17. Uwapi utumwa wetu, ni wapi ulipokuwa, Watasadikije watu, kwamba hapa ulikaa! Hubadili kila kitu, mzunguko wa dunia.	17. Where is our slavery? Where was it? How will people believe it once existed here? Everything in this world is subject to change.
18. Dunia inavyoduru, hutosha kuajabisha, Tunao sasa uhuru, wa kadiri ya kutosha, Wajibu ni kushukuru, kuona haya maisha.	18. It never ceases to amaze how the world turns Now we have our freedom, in the fullness that we desired We must give thanks that this has happened in our life.

Shairi la Kuadimika Pesa.

1. Karatasi nakutuma hima nikwenda haraka,
   Ufike kwa wasomaji pasi ijara kutaka
   Ila ni senti kumi ukisha pata ondoka,
   Pesa limeadimika lahaula wala kuwa.

2. Wala usikawilie miezi miwili kupita
   Ikiwa hapana budi September uwe hapa,
   Haya ondoka haraka wende kwa mpiga Chapa,
   Pesa limeadimika lahaula wala kuwa.

3. Na tuinue mikono tumuombe aombwaye,
   Nema na heri zake kwa hima atuletee,
   Takabali mwenye Enzi wajao tuangalie,
   Pesa limeadimika lahaula wala kuwa.

4. Lahaula wala kuwa hatuna la kufanyiza,
   Utuondolee mashaka isiwe kutwangamiza,
   Jalla man khalaka Subhana ya Aziza,
   Pesa limeadimika lahaula wala kuwa.

5. Twali hituma sadaka zamani zilizopita,
   Na kafara za mizuka kusudi kwako kutaka,
   Haja zetu kutimiza pasi moja la matata,
   Pesa limeadimika lahaula wala kuwa.

6. Leo haifai Nadhiri japo tilia ubani,
   Ukusanye na Bukhuri na kafara za jinani,
   Utazidi pata shari za Shetani na Maruhani,
   Pesa limeadimika lahaula wala kuwa.

7. Japo kuwamo kazini upate muradi wako,
   Patazuka mafitini watowe chakula chako,
   Ilahi tupe imani na huu msukosuko,
   Pesa limeadimika lahaula wala kuwa.

8. Tumekuwa kama nyama sisi kwa sisi hulana,
   Hapana imani tena japo kuwa mwenye maana,
   Utaingia ribani kwa kutaka muawana,
   Pesa limeadimika lahaula wala kuwa.

9. Utokeapo uhitaji Pesa tunapolitaka,
   Kutwa huzunguka Mji na majasho kukutoka
   Huyatamani mauti ajali haijafika,
   Pesa limeadimika lahaula wala kuwa.

10. Haufai umaarufu na Ikbala hapana,
    Ila sharti mwenye kitu chenye thamani na kima,
    Masikini wanuka Ufu maana vitu hawana,
    Pesa limeadimika lahaula wala kuwa.

11. Umetuingia ugonjwa usioingia Dawani,
    Japo fanza masadaka na kafara za Majini,
    Jala ya Khalik tuamue Subhani,
    Pesa limeadimika lahaula wala kuwa.

12. Umetuletea Tauni ni heri magonjwa pia,
    Ingawa ni mukdiri wa haya kuyaondoa,
    Na kama hii adabu toba tunakutubia,
    Pesa limeadimika lahaula wala kuwa.

13. Utujalie sitara Raia na Mawaziri,
    Mfalme na Makadhi Bawabu na Askari,
    Neema itushukilie tuafike mafakiri,
    Pesa limeadimika lahaula wala kuwa.

14. Ndi wewe mwenye hazina hapana wa kukushinda,
    Moja ni kututupia japo tutarambaramba,
    Wajao tunaumia hatuna tena pa kwenda,
    Pesa limeadimika lahaula wala kuwa.

15. Kadtama nanyamaa nisaidieni wenzangu,
    Mikono ni kuinua tumwombee wetu Mungu,
    Auni tutaletewa yatuondoke machungu,
    Pesa limeadimika lahaula wala kuwa.

UBWA BIN SALIM, Zanzibar.

Shairi la Wali.

Watu wawili walihojiana katika kula, akikaribishwa mwenye njaa, atanawa ale au atakula ndipo anawe?

(Swala) Muhibu mwenye akili, nakualiza swala,
Njaa imekukabili, nusu ya mwezi hujala,
Likaja kombe la wali, ukawekewa mahala,
Hunawa mwanzo ukala, hula ndipo ukanawa?

(Majibu) Njaa ni nusu ya adwele, na chakula ndiyo dawa,
Haifai sharti nile, nijue kuwa tapoa,
Chakula kiwekwe pale, makusudi nimepewa,
Hula ndipo nikanawa, baada ya kwisha kula.

(Swala) Kama mgeni gharibu, umefanyiwa jamala,
Kwa chakula na sharabu, ukapewa kwa jumula,
Watu wakajitanibu, ukaambiwa Bismilla,
Hunawa mwanzo ukala, hula ndipo ukanawa?

(Majibu) Njaa haina adabu, nawe hali ya kujua,
Ijapokuwa gharibu, haya utaziondoa,
Chakula kuwa zabibu, nikikifunuwa kawa,
Hula ndipo nikanawa, baada ya kwisha kula.

BUKU BIN ATHMANI.

Hakuna Wapendanao.

1. Mwinyiheri natamka kutoka kukusaidia:
   Hayo yal.yokupata wengi yamewafikia,
   Roho zimeingia shaka kwa uliyokutwambia,
   Kwa dalili zaonyesha bure twasumbukia,
   Hakuna wapendanao Mwinyiheri nakwambia.

2. Mwinyiheri nakwambia tuliza wako mtima:
   Huwapati wapendanao abadani nakwambia,
   Usaliao ubazazi kutaka liwa rupia,
   Tumekwisha valia njuga, kutaka didimizwa,
   Hakuna wapendanao Mwinyiheri nakwambia.

3. Mwinyiheri nakwambia tuliza wako mtima,
   usiyazidishe mapenzi, utazidi kwangamia,
   Nimesha kuwasaka nami sijawafikia
   Unyumba wetu wa leo ni kanga na rupia
   Hakuna wapendanao Mwinyiheri nakwambia.

4. Mwinyiheri nakwambia tuliza wako mtima,
   Jogoo alisema ya kale leo hakuna,
   Wangapi wahasirio pasi kujulikana?
   Wana mulku zao za mali, wapita wakiloloma,
   Basi wa wapi leo wapendanao, abadani hakuna.

5. Hakuna wapendanao Mwinyiheri nakwambia,
   Mambo Leo yalisema Ha mbili zimekwisha
   Zimesalia hizi mbili ndizo zinazotumika,
   Hapana wapendanao Mwinyiheri nakwambia
   Hapana wapendanao Mwinyiheri nakwambia.

6. Mwinyiheri nakwambia tuliza wako mtima,
   Ha ya kwanza ni Huruma nayo imefutika
   Hapana apendwaye isipokuwa hekima,
   Neno hili hulipati humu mwetu Tanganyika
   Hakuna wapendanao Mwinyiheri nakwambia.

7. Mwinyiheri nakwambia tuliza wako mtima
   Ha, ya pili ni Haya nazo zimeondoka
   Hazipati mtu duni ambaye azipata
   Na utakapo amani ni heri kuliwacha
   Hakuna wapendanao Mwinyiheri nakukanya.

8. Mwinyiheri hima lache mwana kwetu nakukanya,
   Bure utasumbuka na hana kukupata
   Waliopendana ni wa kale hizo zama za zama
   Wakipendana kweli kweli wala sifanye mzaha
   Hakuna leo huwapati, wawili wakipendana.

9. Mwinyiheri nakwambia tuliza wako mtima,
   Ukipata pesa zako ni heri kujitia
   Zibanie kweli kweli uzikaze wa mafundo
   Ushishie chege chege utapatwa na majuto
   Hauna wapendanao mwana wetu nakwambia.

WAZIRI MWINYIAMANEI, Kisiwani.

Fig. 8. Selection of Poems, *Mambo Leo,* August 1928.

1b. International Events Poems

As previously discussed, international news like the coup in Togo appeared in poetic form as well as prose. However, Tanzanian papers feature more poems on national and local events than international events. The Nairobi-based newspaper *Baraza* seems to have been the paper where Tanzanian poets sent their poems about international events. Sturmer writes, "A very popular Swahili paper in Tanganyika at that time was the Kenyan *Baraza* (The Council).... In fact, the weekly even had a broader circulation in Tanganyika than in its country of origin."[44]

In *Baraza* from 1968 to 1969, for example, one finds the following by Tanzanian poets. Note the immediacy of poets' responses to these events, sometimes publishing their poems within days of the original event.

Assassination of Martin Luther King Jr. on 4 April 1968 (see also figure 4)

- "Mola Irehemu Roho ya King" ("God Have Mercy on King's Soul"), by Hussein Ally Guni of Moshi, 18 April 1968
- Untitled, by Abbas S. Athumani of Tanga, 18 April 1968
- Untitled, by Paulo Luther Kyombo of Musoma, 18 April 1968

The Biafra Secession in Nigeria (1967–70)

- "Kutambua Biafra" ("To Recognize Biafra"), by Hussein Ally Guni of Moshi, 16 May 1968
- "Twatambua Biafra" ("We Recognize Biafra"), by K. S. Kamana of Dar es Salaam, 6 June 1968
- "Vita vya Nigeria" ("War in Nigeria"), by Swalehe Hamisi of Tanga, 8 August 1968

Assassination of Robert Kennedy on 6 June 1968

- "Dunia Yasikitika" ("The World Is Sad"), by Abbas S. Athumani of Tanga, 20 June 1968
- "Rambirambi Zangu" ("My Condolences"), by Bai Mohamed of Zanzibar, 4 July 1968

- "Ni Kifo Kizito" ("It's a Heavy Death"), by R. A. Mwanahewa of Dar es Salaam, 4 July 1968
- "Bobby Katutoka" ("Bobby Has Left Us"), by M. K. Machumu of Musoma, 4 July 1968

Assassination of FRELIMO leader Eduardo Mondlane by a parcel bomb in Dar es Salaam on 3 February 1969

- "Alikuwa ni Taa" ("He Was a Light"), by Mzee S. N. Mkwawa of Dar es Salaam, 20 February 1969
- "Kitendo cha Uhaini" ("An Evil Deed"), by Bi Nautaka Saidi of Dar es Salaam, 20 February 1969
- "Hasara kwa Afrika" ("Africa's Loss"), by Saidi Ndembo of Dar es Salaam, 27 February 1969
- "Maskini Mondlane" ("Poor Mondlane"), by Tatu binti Saidi Sadallah of Dar es Salaam, 6 March 1969

Landing of Apollo 11 on the Moon on 20 July 1969

- "Maajabu Duniani" ("Wonders of the World"), by D. K. Mswanyama of Tabora, 7 August 1969
- "Nawapongeza" ("I Congratulate Them"), by Hussein Ally Guni of Moshi, 7 August 1969

Internationally focused poems would also appear in Tanzanian papers, but not with this level of frequency.

1c. Praise Poems

Demonstrating the Swahili passion for wordplay, "Shukrani za Africa," mentioned earlier, appeared in 1911 in the German colonial paper *Pwani na Bara* (figure 1).[45] It is an acrostic: each line of poetry begins with a successive letter in the Roman alphabet. It features a loose poetic structure composed of rhymed couplets and triplets that do not adhere to a strict syllabic count. Heavy-handed in its praise of the kaiser, it slides into obsequiousness, urging residents to pay their taxes and pray for the kaiser's continued existence.

Excerpt from "Shukrani za Africa" ("Thanks from Africa")
Jakobo Ngombo, *Pwani na Bara*, January 1911

Afrika furahi, mshukuru sana Kaisari wee;	Rejoice, Africa, be very grateful to your Kaiser.
Baraka na amani kakupa Kaisari yee!	Blessing and peace the Kaiser has given to you.
Chuma pendo, umpende sana Kaisari saa;	Gather love that you may love dearly the Kaiser.
Dola yake ni kubwa, miji yote kaiwasha taa!	His authority is great; in all towns he has lit lamps.
Eleza ya kale kama sasa yakufaa,	Tell of the past and how it benefits you now.
Fundisha watoto wako wapate kumtii.	Teach your children to honor him.

Praise poems would change and over time adopt a more critical stance as poets shed colonial proscriptions and developed the political self-confidence and openness for which Tanzania has become known.[46] Yet praise continues to constitute common fodder for poetry as well as prose sections of newspapers—especially extolling political leaders. And many poems praise their newspapers as well as other entities such as political parties and other associations.

1d. Obituary Poems

Essentially another form of praise, obituary poems flag the "everydayness" of newspaper poetry, since people send in poems memorializing their loved ones—spouses, parents, relatives, friends, colleagues. They also, as already described, lament the passing of extraordinary figures such as Martin Luther King and Eduardo Mondlane. Lamenting the loss of his wife, a man whose *lakabu* (poetic pseudonym) is *Sikiliza* ("Listen!"), published the following with a picture of the deceased Bibiana.

"Mke Wangu Bibiana, Marehemu Mke Wangu"
("My Wife Bibiana, My Deceased Wife")
Adriano J. Mwinyi Mkuu Kwembe (*Sikiliza*—"Listen!"),
Majira, 1 October 1995

1. *Mhariri napandisha, nasema kwa kunong'ona,*	1. Editor, I take the stand, speaking in a whisper

Sauti nimekausha, siko kwa juzi na jana,	My voice has dried out these past days
Malenga nawajulisha, nimefiwa na kimwana,	Poets, I inform you: I've lost my beloved
Mke wangu Bibiana, Mungu muweke peponi.	May God bring to Heaven my wife Bibiana.
3. Wajibu aliuweza, wala hatukugombana,	3. She bore her responsibilities without complaint
Watoto aliwakuza, kwa mabibi na mabwana,	Raising children into grown women and men
Wajukuu wanawaza, Bibi bila kumuona,	The grandchildren think of her though they cannot see her
Mke wangu Bibiana, Mungu muweke peponi.	May God bring to Heaven my wife Bibiana.
5. Ndugu walimsifia, ucheshi tulilingana,	5. Relatives praised her. We matched in our cheerfulness
Tabu alivumilia, hakupenda kujiona,	She endured hardship and didn't think of herself
Nikifikiri nalia, hatutaonana tena,	I cry when I think we'll not see each other again
Mke wangu Bibiana, Mungu muweke peponi.	May God bring to Heaven my wife Bibiana.

1e. Social Commentary Poems

Whereas authors of news articles tend to present their topics from a position of assumed neutrality by sticking to "the facts" and drawing conclusions from them, poets assume the role of public conscience. Like editors, everyday poets take it upon themselves to assess the state of society and admonish when necessary. They take regular stock of social relations, economic trends, and political structures and call attention to abuses. There was a slew of poems by mostly male poets in the 1960s debating the controversial fashion trends of Afro hairstyles and wearing tight and short clothing (*taiti*):[47]

- "Vazi la Aibu!" ("Shameful Clothing!"), by C. S. M. Kavawili Kalunga of Tabora, *Baraza*, 4 April 1968

- "Acheni Taiti Fupi" ("Stop Wearing Tight and Short Clothing"), by Juma Amani Zawavai of Dar es Salaam, *Baraza*, 11 July 1968

Amid a seeming consensus of censure against tight clothing, a poem called "Taiti Ni Nzuri" ("Tight Clothing Is Good") was published by Radi Badona of Mombasa, Kenya (*Baraza*, 30 January 1969), who argued that tight clothing can be beautiful and is only despised by those who are envious.

Quite commonly, poets direct their critical verse at political abuses. The following condemns the abandonment of public service ethics among parliamentarians, who according to the poet, do nothing at all.

"Hutusaidii Kitu" ("You Do Nothing for Us")
Sammy Makilla (*Mshairi Mkazi*—"Resident Poet")
Mwananchi, 28 October 2011, 8

1. Kitu hutusaidii, tukwitaje kiongozi	1. You do nothing for us, so how can we call you a leader?
Twaona ni usanii, mbunge hauna kazi	We see you don't take us seriously. Member of Parliament, you are useless.
Jimbo bado asubuhi, twataka mchapakazi	The state is still young. We want a hard worker
Hutusaidii kitu, tukwitaje kiongozi? . . .	You do nothing for us, so how can we call you a leader? . . .
3. Maiti mtu hatufai, sawa nfu kiongozi	3. Having a corpse as a leader doesn't suit us
Ambaye kura adai, na maendeleo hawazi	Someone who demands votes but doesn't seek development
Ningeshaitoa rai, leo kumfukuza kazi	I would already have recommended he be dismissed
Hutusaidii kitu, tukwitaje kiongozi?	You do nothing for us, so how can we call you a leader?

Finally, moving from the weighty to the quotidian, a droll poem complains about the irritating habit of "beeping": calling and hanging up after only one ring as a signal for that person to call you back. An accommodation arising from meager resources and the high cost of phone vouchers, "beeping" (*kubipu* in Swahili) can create awkwardnesses and even disrupt marital relations, as poet Raphael Meshack Mwamwego tells us:

"Kwa Wanaobipu" ("For Those Who Beep")
Raphael Meshack Mwambwego
Uhuru, 12 September 2012, 15

1. Wanaudhi kama nini, sijui lengo ninini,
Unaweza kutamani, kuwatusi ya nguoni,
Ubinadamu lakini, hukwepusha matusini,
Kwa wale wanaobipu, hakika mna maudhi!

5. Unapoisha kwanini, muda wa kuwa hewani,
Wenzako wawatesani, kubipu mara tenini,
Wawakosesha amani, wamelala kulikoni,
Kwa wale wanaobipu, hakika mna maudhi!

8. Ndoa ziko mashakani, kwa wenu uhayawani,
Mkeo hakuamini, kwamba haiwezekani,
Wafanya hamjuani, iweje mara sitini,
Kwa wale wanaobipu, hakika mna maudhi!

1. You annoy us no end, I don't know your intent
Making you wish to swear profanities at them
But humanity keeps you away from invectives
For those who beep, truly you annoy us!

5. Why, when you are out of phone minutes,
Do you bother your friends, beeping them ten times?
You disturb their peace, even their sleep—why?
For those who beep, truly you annoy us!

8. Marital discord emerges due to your beastly behavior
A wife loses trust, for how can it be that
You pretend not to know someone who calls sixty times?
For those who beep, truly you annoy us!

1f. Advice Poems

Another common variety of poem, related to social commentary poems except directed at individuals, is advice poems. A recurrent title, for instance, is "Mpende Akupendae" ("Love the One Who Loves You"). These poems advise that you tame your heart and not languish with longing for someone who spurns you but instead accept the love of someone who loves you truly. Other poems offer directives in response to previously published poetic pleas for advice, like "Nitumie Mbinu Gani" ("What Strategy Should I Pursue"?) or "Wahenga Nifanye Nini?" ("Ancestors, What Shall I Do?). To these come versified responses, such as the following:

- "Tafuta Mke Uoe" ("Go Find a Woman to Marry"), by Mohamed K. Kirobo (*Al Hakir*) of Zanzibar, *Zanzibar Leo*, 27 February 2002
- "Peleka Kesi kwa Jumbe (Jibu)" ("Take Your Case to the Local Leader (Reply)"), by Nuhu S. Mbiling'i of Dar es Salaam, *Majira*, 1 October 1995
- "Ndoa Kuvumiliana" ("Marriage Means Tolerating Each Other"), by Jaha H. Jaha of Zanzibar, *Zanzibar Leo* 13 July 2002

And a poem written for one woman from another in response to a request for advice is the following:

"Tajiri Akuoe" ("Get Married to a Rich Man")
M. binti Ramadhani
Baraza, 27 June 1968, 3

1. Mariamu binti Ali, majibu yako pokea,	1. Mariam, daughter of Ali, receive your answer
Nakujibu bilkuli, usome na kutulia,	I'll answer you honestly: settle down and focus on your studies
Ya watu usikubali, hayo yangu kusikia,	Don't listen to others. Take my advice
Sikia dada sikia, uolewe na tajiri.	Listen, sister, listen: get married to a rich man.
2. Masikini ana tabu, na tena ana balaa,	2. Poverty brings hardship and troubles
Hamwishi kwenda kwa babu, kwenda kushitakiana,	You'll keep returning to the elders for mediation due to constantly blaming each other
Kwakua wapata tabu, huwezi kuvumilia,	For facing hardship that you're unable to endure
Sikia dada sikia, uolewe na tajiri.	Listen, sister, listen: get married to a rich man.
3. Mke huishi dhiki, ukweli ninakwambia,	3. A wife's life is difficult: I'm telling you the truth

Nakwambia yenye haki, siyo nakuo-gopea,	I tell you what is right, not in order to frighten you
Mwenyewe utasadiki, mengi ukifikira,	You'll believe it if you reflect on things
Sikia dada sikia, uolewe na tajiri . . .	Listen, sister, listen: get married to a rich man . . .

1g. Poetic Personal Ads

An unexpected newspaper element to appear in verse is the "personal ad." An amusing example comes from a Dar es Salaam–based poet, Ally Ndutike, published with a photo of himself (figure 6):

"Mimi Ni Ally Ndutike" ("I Am Ally Ndutike")
Ally Ndutike (*Wema Haujengeki*—"Good Cannot Be Built")
Majira, 23 March 1995, 11

1. Mimi ni Ali Ndutike, ndivyo nilivyo umbika,	1. I am Ally Ndutike, and this is how I was created
Sura ya aina yake, kaibariki Rabuka,	A face of its own style, blessed by God
Utanipenda nicheke, na kimo nimerefuka,	You'll desire my laughter and resent my tall height
Ndivyo nilivyo umbika, mimi ni Ali Ndutike.	This is how I was created, I am Ali Ndutike.
2. Mwili wangu si mnene, mwembamba nimenyooka,	2. My body is not fat, it is thin and straight
Picha yangu muione, humu nimeitundika,	You can see my photo, I have displayed it here
Zanzibari na kwingine, Moro hata Amerika,	Whether in Zanzibar, Morogoro, or even America
Ndivyo nilivyo umbika, mimi ni Ali Ndutike.	This is how I was created, I am Ali Ndutike.
5. Umri ninawambia, ni nne tatu miaka,	5. I'll tell you my age, it is forty-three years
Shuleni nimepitia, sekondari sikufika,	I finished school, but didn't reach secondary

Ila nilichojazia, Korani nimeishika,	But I thoroughly studied and know the Koran
Ndivyo nilivyo umbika, mimi ni Ali Ndutike...	This is how I was created, I am Ali Ndutike...
8. Tena mpenda ibada, mskitini nanifika,	8. And I love to pray, going to the mosque
Sala ninavyoipenda, kama wali wa kupika,	I love praying just as I love cooking rice
Ibada ina muda, sala tano nakumbuka,	Prayer has its special times, I perform the five prayers
Ndivyo nilivyo umbika, mimi ni Ali Ndutike.	This is how I was created, I am Ali Ndutike.

While the subgenres discussed thus far can be matched to other parts of the newspaper form rendered in prose, what follows are four subgenres that cannot be matched to conventional newspaper elements. They are straight from the Swahili poetic tradition and have forced their way onto newspaper pages: prayers, poems that produce poetry publics, love poems, and enigma poems. They are taken below in turn.

2a. Prayer Poems

Prayer poems span pleadings for divine assistance, praise and thanks for prayers answered, and devotional poetry admiring God's creations and might. The following 1928 poem by poetess Ubwa bin Salim describes the pains and humiliations of poverty. It evolves into a prayer, supplicating God for succor and warning others not to seek assistance from spirits lest evil jinns respond instead.

"Shairi la Kuadimika Pesa" ("Poem about Money's Scarcity")[48]
Ubwa bin Salim, Zanzibar
Mambo Leo, August 1928, 936

3. Na tuinue mikono tumuombe aombwaye,	3. Let us raise our hands in prayer to God
Nema na heri zake kwa hima atuletee,	That he should bestow grace and happiness on us
Takabali mwenye Enzi wajao tuangalie,	Accept our prayer, Almighty God, watch over us, your creatures

Pesa limeadimika lahaula wala kuwa....	Money has become scarce and is no more...
6. Leo haifai Nadhiri japo tilia ubani,	6. Today it's wrong to make a vow except with incense
Ukusanye na Bukhuri na kafara za jinani	Gather and burn incense, make offerings to the spirits
Utazidi pata shari za Shetani na Maruhani,	You'll meet with the violence of devils and jinns
Pesa limeadimika lahaula wala kuwa....	Money has become scarce and is no more...
15. Kadtama nanyamaa nisaidieni wenzangu,	15. Finally I end. Please help me, my friends
Mikono ni kuinua tumwombee wetu Mungu	Let us lift our hands to beseech our God
Auni tutaletewa yatuondoke machungu,	We'll receive aid to remove our bitterness
Pesa limeadimika lahaula wala kuwa.	Money has become scarce and is no more.

2b. Poetry Publics

Poets frequently align themselves with the newspapers for which they regularly compose, forming collective identities and loyalties akin to those of football club fans. They also generate a transnewspaper, East African collective of *washairi* (poets), as the following two poems illustrate. Worth noting is that the poets refer to each other by their *lakabu*, or poetic pseudonyms, rather than by their real names.

"Washairi Tanganyika" ("Poets of Tanganyika")
P. J. Ndabaga, *Mwafrika*, 8 February 1964
P.O. Box 109, Mbeya

1. Mchapaji Mwafrika, shairi langu pokea	1. Editor of Mwafrika, receive my poem
Salamu naleta kaka, nami nipate tokea	I greet you, brother, that I may present myself
Shairi kulipachika, gazetini kutokea	Include this poem, let it appear in the newspaper
Washairi Tanganyika, salamu nawatolea . . .	Tanganyikan poets, I greet you . . .
3. Dua ninawaombea, washairi watukuka	3. I pray for you, you noble poets
Tuzidi kuendelea, wote tukiunganika	So that we continue to be united
Kwa sasa na baadae, hapa petu Tanganyika	Now and in the future, here in our Tanganyika
Washairi Tanganyika, salamu nawatolea	Tanganyikan poets, I greet you
4. Salamu zangu pokea, Jitu Kali na Mwaruka	4. Receive my greetings, Jitu Kali and Mwaruka
Salamu kwa Chekanae, Mwanahewa kadhalika	Greetings to Chekanae and to Mwanahewa
Salama nawaombea, Mungu awape baraka	I pray for your safety and that God may bless you
Washairi Tanganyika, salamu nawatolea	Tanganyikan poets, I greet you

"Tunaitwa Washairi" ("We Poets are Being Called")
Shaaban Issa Tengeni ("Polite Boy")
Mfanyakazi, 29 December 1999

1. Tunaitwa washairi, safuni Mfanyakazi
Tulete tungo mahiri, tumuonyeshe ujuzi
Malumbano ya fahari, nafasi sasa i-wazi
Safuni Mfanyakazi, tunaitwa washairi

2. Pande zote Tanzania, leteni bila ajizi
Jamii yasubiria, kuupata utambuzi

Mengi wanajipatia, kupitia yenu kazi
Safuni Mfanyakazi, tunaitwa washairi . . .

5. Makacha wito itika, Andanenga kazi kazi
Leteni tungo haraka, na Mukki Mkurugenzi
Njooni mwahitajika, hata mlo wanafunzi
Safuni Mfanyakazi, tunaitwa washairi . . .

8. Mpo wengi washairi, kutaja wote siwezi
Sina budi kughairi, niwaachieni kazi

Myalete mashairi, kama zipo pia tenzi
Safuni Mfanyakazi, tunaitwa washairi

1. Poets, we are being called to queue up at Mfanyakazi
Let us bring our refined compositions, let us show our skill
Now there is space for meaningful debates
Queue up at Mfanyakazi, we poets are being called

2. From all corners of Tanzania, submit them without hesitation
This society is waiting to receive enlightenment
They reap great benefit from your works
Queue up at Mfanyakazi, we poets are being called . . .

5. Makacha, answer the call. Andanenga, it's time to work!
Hurry and bring your compositions, including you, Mukki the Great
Come all, you are needed, even you who are still novices
Queue up at Mfanyakazi, we poets are being called . . .

8. There are many of you poets, I cannot name you all
I have to decline and leave the work to you
Bring forth your poems, including epic ones if they are there
Queue up at Mfanyakazi, we poets are being called

However, just as with football clubs, intense rivalries emerge. The long-standing poetic tradition of dialogic poetry, referred to as *kujibizana* (to evoke a response)[49] appears in newspaper pages as well. A poem might evoke a response several weeks later from another poet. Or if the exchange had been ongoing, the editor might wait and publish the poems side by side, emphasizing the dialogic element. The following was published as a three-way exchange in *Uhuru* with even the editor entering the poetic fray:[50]

"Tunaihama Uhuru" ("We Are Leaving *Uhuru*")
Abdallah S. Matawa (Mbwenzi), Dodoma
Uhuru, 5 January 1993, 11

4. Tuaifata thamani, mwenye kututhaminia,	4. We seek the honor of being valued by an editor
Kurasa zake za shani, nadhifu zinavutia,	Whose pages are full of novelty and orderliness
Uhuru latia soni, jinsi lilivyo fifia,	Uhuru instead shames us the way that it is declining
Mwananchi twahamia, Uhuru la Morogoro.	We will move to Mwananchi, from Uhuru of Morogoro.

"Hamieni Mpendako" ("Move Wherever You Wish to Go")
Muhariri ("Editor")—8/10/1992
Uhuru, 5 January 1993, 11

1. Walisema wa zamani, wazama zilopitia,	1. They said long ago, in times since past
Mtu kuzawa bandani, kunyonya na kukulia,	That if someone born, nursed, and raised in a hut
Akikodi ghorofani, banda ulitukania,	Moved to a fancy apartment, he would disdain the hut
Sawa ya Mbenzi tabia, hamieni mpendako.	That's the behavior of a rich person (Mbenzi). So move wherever you wish to go.

"Wachafuzi Wanahama" ("The Troublemakers Are Leaving")
Shekhe Ally Sefu Mkwachu (Liwajika), Dar es Salaam
Uhuru, 5 January 1993, 11

5. Lingwele sasa eneza, habari iliyo njema,	5. Lingwele, let it be known, this wonderful news
Mwanza Rufiji Muheza, Lindi Pemba na Kigoma,	In Mwanza, Rufiji, Muheza, Lindi, Pemba and Kigoma

Wachafuzi wameoza, wamebaki wa heshima,	The troublemakers have rotted leaving only the respected ones
Wa Dodoma wakihama, Uhuru litapendeza.	When the Dodoma ones leave, Uhuru will be better off.

2c. Love Poems

Love, a preoccupation of Swahili poets from ancient times into the present, also appears with regularity in newspapers—poems about love found, love lost, love betrayed, love triumphant. One sample comes from Zanzibar, from Mussa M. Ali with a sweet *lakabu*: *Peremende ya Moyo* ("Candy for the Heart").

"Rejea Mpenzi Wangu" ("Return, My Love")
Mussa M. Ali (*Peremende ya Moyo*—"Candy for the Heart"), Zanzibar
Zanzibar Leo, 28 October 2002, 9

1. *Machungu yanisokota, Kuingia ulingoni*	1. Grief tosses and pushes me about as in a boxing ring
Natembea nikisota, Bila viatu nyayoni	I walk in deep pain without shoes on my feet
Huku nikigutaguta, Sijakutia machoni	Murmuring to myself, since I've not laid eyes on you
Rejea mpenzi wangu, Tuishi kama zamani	Return my love. Let's live like before
2. *Rejea wangu mpenzi, Nakupenda kwa yakini*	2. Return my love, I love you truly
Utowe wangu majonzi, Yalonijaa moyoni	Remove my sorrow, which fills my heart
Tuishi enzi na enzi, Kwa penzi lenye thamani	Let's live from age to age with a love of great value
Rejea mpenzi wangu, Tuishi kama zamani	Return my love. Let's live like before

2d. Enigma Poems—Dialogue Poems

Finally, newspapers also feature enigma poems, which invite dialogue among poets as they try to compose the wisest and most poetic response to a challenge or riddle. These include the global mind-teaser "Kuku na Yai" ("Chicken and Egg"), or the location of the waist of a millipede (*Jongoo*). Some pose the enigma and response within a single poem, such as the following example about which comes first for a starving person: good manners or satiating hunger.

"Shairi la Wali" ("Poem about Cooked Rice")[51]
Buku bin Athmani
Mambo Leo, August 1928, 936

(Swala) Muhibu mwenye akili, naku-uliza swala,	(Question) My intelligent sweetheart, I ask you a question
Njaa imekukabili, nusu ya mwezi hujala	If faced with hunger after half a month without eating
Likaja kombe la wali, ukawekewa mahala,	And there arrived a cup of rice laid out just for you
Hunawa mwanzo ukala, hula ndipo ukanawa?	Would you wash before eating, or eat and then wash?
(Majibu) Njaa ni nusu ya ndwele, na chakula ndiyo dawa,	(Answers) Hunger is half an ailment and food is its cure
Haifai sharti nile, nijue kuwa tapoa,	No way! I must eat. I should eat before it gets cold
Chakula kiwekwe pale, makusudi nimepewa,	If food is laid out for the purpose of being given to me
Hula ndipo nikanawa, baada ya kwisha kula.	I'd eat first then wash after finishing the meal.

In February 2002 poet Khamis M. Khamis threw out for consideration "Gunia" ("Sack"), addressing it to fellow poets of his newspaper *Zanzibar Leo*. He asked them to ease his anxieties, reduce his fever, and alleviate his insomnia by solving the riddle.

"Gunia (Swali)" ("Sack"—Question)
Khamis M. Khamis, Zanzibar
Zanzibar Leo, 28 February 2002, 9

1. Mbio Yomba ninakuja, Kimtende nisaini	1. Yomba, I come fast. Kimtende, sign me up.
Nakuja nia yangu hoja, Iliyo mwangu moyoni	I'm coming with my argument, located in my heart

Nipate zenu faraja, Kuniponza miongoni	That you may relieve me of this anxiety among others
Hili ni gunia gani, Lisiloweza kubebwa	What kind of sack is this, which cannot be carried?
2. *Uzito wake gunia, Nataka kuulewa*	2. I want to know the weight of the sack
Kilo ngapi watimia, Na nini kilichotiwa	How many kilos does it weigh? What does it contain?
Hivyo vyote Tanzania, Jibu mutalitolea	You should provide answers to all in Tanzania
Hili ni gunia gani, Lisiloweza kubebwa	What kind of sack is this, which cannot be carried? ...
7. *Bin Mussa naungama, Pamoja nanyi watunzi*	7. Bin Mussa, I confess to you and to all the poets
Kwa jibu mtaligema, Kunipunguza simanzi	You'll find the answer and lessen my sorrows
Kadhalika yangu homa, Na kupata usingizi	And reduce my fever and sleeplessness
Hili ni gunia gani, Lisiloweza kubebwa	What kind of sack is this, which cannot be carried?

One month later, the following appeared:

"Gunia (Jibu)" ("Sack"—Answer)
Saidi Salum (*Kipusa*—"Rhino's Horn"), Zanzibar
Zanzibar Leo, 20 March 2002

1. *Khamis natarajia, Angalau kwa uhaba*	1. Khamis, I hope that however lacking
Haya ninayokwambia, Yataleta matilaba	What I tell you will fulfill your wish
Gunia kulivamia, Mara mtu humkaba	If the sack is lifted in haste, it will give a person problems
Mola pekee hubeba, Na gunia ni dunia	Only God carries this sack, which is the world ...

3. *Vyote vinavyo tembea, Utulivu wa mashamba*
Kama tembo na ngamia, Na aridhi yenye shaba
Jumla vimetulia, Bila ya kufungwa kamba
Mola pekee hubeba, Na gunia ni dunia . . .

7. *Uzitowe kajalia, Vitokako kavi-umba*

Nguvu zimemuenea, Kila kitu kaki-kumba
Kaweka kwenye gunia, Hili linalo-kutimba
Mola pekee hubeba, Na gunia ni dunia

8. *Tama ana arishia, Na watumishi kwa namba*
Akitaka liachia, Kama andiko na raba
Sote tutaangamia, Ndani ya dakika saba
Mola pekee hubeba, Na gunia ni dunia

9. *Nadhani utatulia, Lala na macho kufumba*
Nimemaliza udhia, Si gunia la mtumba
Lile tulilozoea, Kwenda posea wachumba
Mola pekee hubeba, Na gunia ni dunia

3. All that moves, and the stillness of the fields
Elephants and camels, and land rich in copper
All these have settled within, not bound by a rope
Only God carries this sack, which is the world . . .

7. God has willed the weight of these things. He created them and their origins
In his omnipotence he has gathered everything
And placed them in the sack—this one that causes you anxiety
Only God carries this sack, which is the world . . .

8. Finally, he has the throne and servants in great numbers
If he wants to drop it, like eliminating writing with an eraser
All of us will be destroyed, within seven minutes
Only God carries this sack, which is the world

9. I think now you'll calm down. Sleep and close your eyes
I have removed the irritant. This is not a sack of used clothing
Those used in the engagement of a fiancée
Only God carries this sack, which is the world

Directly addressing Khamis's text via reference to his anxiety and insomnia, Saidi Salum crafts a reply intertwining his answer to the riddle with the elements of a prayer. Like the sack it describes, the poem bears a wealth of substance and beauty. It reveals the collective identity that these poets share among themselves. It praises God, the beauty of the earth and its resources, and God's indomitable power. And it offers advice to all humanity in reminding us that disaster can strike at any moment and within seven minutes (that symbolically laden number) destroy the entirety of creation. Like other poems above, it cannot so easily be relegated to a single type but melds and merges, showcasing the artistry and wordplay associated with the Swahili poetic tradition.

CONCLUSION

This chapter explores Swahili newspaper poetry (*mashairi ya magazeti*) by examining its history, the range of topics engaged, ties to other sections of the newspaper form, and poets' engagement with readers and each other as they generate newspaper publics, national publics, and poetic publics through their artistry. An abbreviated history of the rise of newspaper poetry in Tanzania identified factors that facilitated the transformation of an art previously associated with the coast into a national passion. A subgenre-by-subgenre analysis of the key types of newspaper poetry confirms the arguments Kezilahabi makes for Swahili poetry in general (this despite the dim view he takes of newspaper poetry). To recap, these are (1) its *quotidian* nature, due to its focus on the lived experience of ordinary people; (2) its *immediacy*, with poets responding to events right after they happen and responding to each other in quick reply; (3) its *dialogic* nature, inviting debate from readers and fellow poets alike; (4) its *closeness to being*, by tapping into the inner feelings and experiences of those composing it; and (5) its grounding in *ethical and moral* stances. All these have been found to hold true with ample evidence provided from thousands of poems surveyed in preparation for this essay.

What has not been previously discussed, however, is what makes Swahili newspaper poetry part of a particular print culture tied to the newspaper form. *Mashairi ya magazeti* encompass the major elements of newspapers, from news reportage (local, national, and international) to editorials, from advice columns to obituaries, and more. Poems were found celebrating football victories and constituting advertisements for specific products, but had to be passed over because of limitations of space.

The participatory and dialogic nature of Swahili poetry has been analyzed by others, as has its association with nonelites. Beyond the extraordinary master poets whose names dominate discussions of Swahili literary arts, ordinary citizens employ poetry to offer advice, thanks, praise, and critique of their children, leaders, neighbors, and society at large. Poetry creates—indeed demands—debate and engagement, recalling Marshall McLuhan's distinction between *hot* and *cool* media. *Hot* media, he argues, are formal and high definition—they fill in all detail and allow little room for audience engagement; examples are film and novels. *Cool* media by virtue of their low definition and indeterminateness require more audience participation in the production of meaning; examples here include TV and newspapers.[52] One might extend this analogy to the different subgenres found within a given media form. The newspaper has hot sections, like journalists' authoritative descriptions of events, which readers are supposed to receive and learn from, and cool sections like advice columns, obituaries, and—it is posited here—*poetry*, where their interventions are welcomed. Simply by being open to anyone, not the exclusive realm of staff writers, the poetry pages even today remain a section of the newspaper where political and social commentary from below thrives. *Mashairi ya magazeti* merit overdue recognition as Swahili poetry worthy of attention, as well as being a populist form of Swahili print culture.

REFERENCES

Abdulaziz, Mohamed. *Muyaka*. Nairobi: Kenya Literature Bureau, 1979.
Abedi, K. Amri. *Sheria za Kutunga Mashairi na Diwani ya Amri*. Nairobi: East African Literature Bureau, 1954.
Allen, J. W. T. *Tendi: Six Examples of a Classical Swahili Verse Form with Translation and Notes*. New York: Africana, 1971.
Arnold, R. "Swahili Literature and Modern History: A Necessary Remark on Literary Criticism." *Swahili* 42–43, no. 2 (1973): 68–73.
Askew, Kelly. "As Plato Duly Warned: Music, Politics and Social Change in East Africa." *Anthropological Quarterly* 76, no. 4 (2003): 609–37.
Askew, Kelly. *Performing the Nation: Swahili Music and Cultural Politics in Tanzania*. Chicago: University of Chicago Press, 2002.

Askew, Kelly. "Tanzanian Newspaper Poetry: Political Commentary in Verse." *Journal of Eastern African Studies* 8, no. 3 (2014): 515–37.

Barber, Karin, ed. *Africa's Hidden Histories: Everyday Literacy and Making the Self.* Bloomington: Indiana University Press, 2006.

Biersteker, Ann. *Kujibizana: Questions of Language and Power in Nineteenth- and Twentieth-Century Poetry in Kiswahili.* East Lansing: Michigan State University Press, 1996.

Biersteker, Ann. "Language, Poetry and Power: A Reconsideration of 'Utendi wa Mwana Kupona.'" In *Faces of Islam in African Literature*, edited by Kenneth Harrow, 59–77. Portsmouth, NH: Heinemann, 1991.

Biersteker, Ann, and Mark Plane. "Swahili Manuscripts and the Study of Swahili Literature." *Research in African Literatures* 20, no. 3 (1989): 449–72.

Biersteker, Ann, and Ibrahim Noor Shariff, eds. *Mashairi ya Vita vya Kuduhu: War Poetry in Kiswahili Exchanged at the Time of the Battle of Kuduhu.* East Lansing: Michigan State University Press, 1995.

Brennan, James R. *Taifa: Making Nation and Race in Urban Tanzania.* Athens: Ohio University Press, 2012.

Fabian, Johannes. *Language and Colonial Power: The Appropriation of Swahili in the Former Belgian Congo, 1880–1938.* Berkeley: University of California Press, 1986.

Finnegan, Ruth. *Oral Literature in Africa.* Nairobi: Oxford University Press, 1970.

Frederiksen, Bodil Folke. "Print, Newspapers and Audiences in Colonial Kenya: African and Indian Improvement, Protest and Connection." *Africa* 81, no. 1 (2011): 155–72.

Gadsen, Fay. "The African Press in Kenya, 1945–1952." *Journal of African History* 21, no. 4 (1980): 515–35.

Geider, Thomas. "The Paper Memory of East Africa: Ethnohistories and Biographies Written in Swahili." In *A Place in the World: New Local Historiographies from Africa and South Asia*, edited by Axel Harneit-Sievers, 255–88. Leiden: Brill, 2002.

Greene, Roland, et al. *The Princeton Encyclopedia of Poetry and Poetics.* Princeton, NJ: Princeton University Press, 2012.

Gunner, Liz, ed. *Politics and Performance: Theatre, Poetry, and Song in Southern Africa.* Johannesburg: Witwatersrand University Press, 1994.

Harries, Lyndon. "Cultural Verse-Forms in Swahili." *African Studies* 15, no. 4 (1956): 176–87.

Harries, Lyndon. *Swahili Poetry.* Oxford: Clarendon Press, 1962.

Hunter, Emma. "'Our Common Humanity': Print, Power, and the Colonial Press in Interwar Tanganyika and French Cameroun." *Journal of Global History* 7 (2012): 279–301.

Hunter, Emma. "Revisiting *Ujamaa*: Political Legitimacy and the Construction of Community in Post-colonial Tanzania." *Journal of Eastern African Studies* 2, no. 3 (2008): 471–85.

Inter-territorial Language Committee. *Mashairi ya Mambo Leo, Kitabu cha Kwanza* [Poems from the Swahili newspaper *Mambo Leo*, vol. 1]. Selected by the Inter-territorial Language Committee. London: Sheldon Press, 1946.

Inter-territorial Language Committee. [Poems from the Swahili newspaper *Mambo Leo*, vol. 3.] Selected by the Inter-territorial Language Committee. London: Sheldon Press, 1946.

Ivaska, Andrew. *Cultured States: Youth, Gender, and Modern Style in 1960s Dar es Salaam*. Durham, NC: Duke University Press, 2011.

Kezilahabi, Euphrase. "The Development of Swahili Poetry: 18th–20th Century," *Swahili* 42–43, nos. 1–2 (1973): 62–67.

Kezilahabi, Euphrase. "The House of Everydayness: Swahili Poetry in Tanzanian Newspapers." In *Beyond the Language Issue: The Production, Mediation and Reception of Creative Writing in African Languages*, edited by Anja Oed and Uta Reuster-Jahn, 191–97. Cologne: Rüdiger Köppe Verlag, 2008.

Komba, S. M. *Uwanja wa Mashairi*. Dar es Salaam: Longman, 1976.

Lemke, Hilde. "Die Suaheli-Zeitungen und -Zeitschriften in Deutsch-Ost-Afrika" ["The Swahili Newspapers and Magazines in German East Africa"]. PhD dissertation, University of Leipzig, 1929.

Madumulla, Joshua, Elena Bertoncini, and Jan Blommaert. "Politics, Ideology and Poetic Form: The Literary Debate in Tanzania." In *Language Ideological Debates*, edited by Jan Blommaert, 307–41. New York: Mouton de Gruyter, 1999.

Maw, Joan. *Fire and Lightning: Language, Affect and Society in 20th Century Swahili Poetry*. Vienna: Institute für Afrikanistik und Ägyptologie der Universität Wien, 1999.

McLuhan, Marshall. *Understanding Media: The Extensions of Man*. Cambridge, MA: MIT Press, 1997.

Miehe, Gudrun. *Poems Attributed to Fumo Liyongo*. Cologne: Rüdiger Köppe Verlag, 2004.

Miehe, Gudrun, et al., eds. *Kala Shairi: German East Africa in Swahili Poems*. Cologne: Rüdiger Köppe Verlag, 2002.

Mitchell, J. Clyde. *The Kalela Dance: Aspects of Social Relationships among Urban Africans in Northern Rhodesia*. Manchester: Manchester University Press, 1956.

Mulokozi, M. M. "Revolution and Reaction in Swahili Poetry." *Swahili* 45, no. 2 (1975): 46–65.

Mulokozi, M. M., and T. S. Y. Sengo. *History of Kiswahili Poetry [AD 1000–2000]*

Dar es Salaam: Institute of Kiswahili Research, University of Dar es Salaam, 1995.

Mutembei, Aldin K. *UKIMWI katika Fasihi ya Kiswahili, 1982–2006*. Dar es Salaam: Institute of Swahili Studies, University of Dar es Salaam, 2009.

Newell, Stephanie. *Literary Culture in Colonial Ghana: "How to Play the Game of Life."* Bloomington: Indiana University Press, 2002.

Njogu, Kimani. *Reading Poetry as Dialogue: An East African Literary Tradition*. Nairobi: Jomo Kenyatta Foundation, 2004.

Ogola, George. "The Political Economy of the Media in Kenya: From Kenyatta's Nation-Building Press to Kibaki's Local-Language FM Radio." *Africa Today* 57, no. 3 (2011): 77–95.

Peterson, Derek. *Creative Writing: Translation, Bookkeeping, and the Work of the Imagination in Colonial Kenya*. Portsmouth, NH: Heinemann, 2004.

Richter, Reynolds L. "Argwings-Kodhek, Chiedo More Gem (1923–1969)." In *Dictionary of African Biography* edited by Emmanuel K. Akyeampong and Henry Louis Gates, 266. Oxford: Oxford University Press, 2011.

Scott, James C. *Domination and the Arts of Resistance: Hidden Transcripts*. New Haven: Yale University Press, 1990.

Scotton, James F. "Tanganyika's African Press, 1937–1960: A Nearly Forgotten Pre-independence Forum." *African Studies Review* 21, no. 1 (1978): 1–18.

Shariff, Ibrahim Noor. *Tungo Zetu: Msingi wa Mashairi na Tungo Nyinginezo*. Trenton, NJ: Red Sea Press, 1988.

Sheldon, Kathleen E. *Historical Dictionary of Women in Sub-Saharan Africa*. Lanham, MD: Scarecrow Press, 2005.

Sturmer, Martin. *The Media History of Tanzania*. Ndanda via Mtwara, Tanzania: Ndanda Mission Press, 1998.

Suriano, Maria. "Letters to the Editors and Poems: *Mambo Leo* and Readers' Debates on *Dansi, Ustaarabu*, Respectability, and Modernity in Tanganyika, 1940–1950s." *Africa Today* 57, no. 3 (2011): 39–55.

Tracey, Hugh. *Chopi Musicians: Their Music, Poetry, and Instruments*. London: Oxford University Press, 1948.

Vail, Leroy, and Landeg White. *Power and the Praise Poem: Southern African Voices in History*. Charlottesville: University Press of Virginia, 1991.

Velten, Carl. *Prosa und Poesie der Suaheli*. Berlin: C. Velten, im Selbstverlag des Verfassers, 1907.

Zache, Hans. "Beiträge zur Suaheli-Litteratur." *Zeitschrift für afrikanische und oceanische Sprachen* 3 (1897): 131–39, 250–67.

NOTES TO CHAPTER SEVEN

1. Unless identified otherwise, all translations of poetry are by the author and master Kenyan poet Abdilatif Abdalla, to whom I am greatly indebted. Research for this essay was supported by the University of Michigan Associate Professor Support Fund and the Wissenschaftskolleg zu Berlin. Early drafts received critical feedback from the African Print Cultures network, composed of Karin Barber, Emma Hunter, Rebecca Jones, Stephanie Newell, Derek Peterson, David Pratten, and Kate Skinner, and presentations of draft versions at Humboldt University, Bayreuth University, Michigan State University and the 2012 ASAUK conference. My sincere thanks to all the above. I also thank my research assistants, who helped compile and catalog the poetry that populates this essay: Kristen Sukraw, Hannah Makowske, and Christopher Askew-Merwin. All errors and infelicities, however, are of course my own.

2. Mohamed Abdulaziz, *Muyaka* (Nairobi: Kenya Literature Bureau, 1979); Gudrun Miehe et al., *Poems Attributed to Fumo Liyongo* (Cologne: Rüdiger Köppe Verlag, 2004); M. M. Mulokozi, "Revolution and Reaction in Swahili Poetry," *Swahili* 45, no. 2 (1975): 46–65; M. M. Mulokozi and T. S. Y. Sengo, *History of Kiswahili Poetry, A.D. 1000–2000* (Dar es Salaam: Institute of Kiswahili Research, 1995).

3. J. W. T. Allen, *Tendi: Six Examples of a Swahili Classical Verse Form*, with translations and notes by J. W. T. Allen (New York: Africana, 1971); Ann Biersteker, *Kujibizana: Questions of Language and Power in Nineteenth- and Twentieth-Century Poetry in Kiswahili* (East Lansing: Michigan State University Press, 1996); Ann Biersteker, "Language, Poetry and Power: A Reconsideration of 'Utendi wa Mwana Kupona,'" in *Faces of Islam in African Literature*, ed. Kenneth Harrow (Portsmouth, NH: Heinemann, 1991), 59–77; Kathleen E. Sheldon, *Historical Dictionary of Women in Sub-Saharan Africa* (Lanham, MD: Scarecrow Press, 2005), 162.

4. Biersteker, "Language, Poetry and Power"; Biersteker, *Kujibizana*, 267–318; Mulokozi, "Revolution and Reaction."

5. Mulokozi and Sengo, *History of Kiswahili Poetry*; Euphrase Kezilahabi, "The House of Everydayness: Swahili Poetry in Tanzanian Newspapers," in *Beyond the Language Issue: The Production, Mediation and Reception of Creative Writing in African Languages*, ed. Anja Oed and Uta Reuster-Jahn (Cologne: Rüdiger Köppe Verlag, 2008), 191–97.

6. Ann Biersteker and Ibrahim Noor Shariff, eds., *Mashairi ya Vita vya Kuduhu: War Poetry in Kiswahili Exchanged at the Time of the Battle of Kuduhu* (East Lansing: Michigan State University Press, 1995); Biersteker, *Kujibizana*; Ibrahim Noor Shariff, *Tungo Zetu: Msingi wa Mashairi na Tungo Nyinginezo* (Trenton, NJ: Red Sea Press, 1988); Mulokozi and Sengo, *History of Swahili Poetry*.

7. Ann Biersteker and Mark Plane, "Swahili Manuscripts and the Study of

Swahili Literature," *Research in African Literatures* 20, no. 3 (1989): 449–72; Allen, *Tendi*; Miehe et al., *Poems Attributed to Fumo Liyongo*.

8. Martin Sturmer, *Media History of Tanzania* (Ndanda via Mtwara, Tanzania: Ndanda Mission Press, 1998), 42–45, 65, 178; also Kezilahabi, "The House of Everydayness," 191.

9. See Johannes Fabian, *Language and Colonial Power: The Appropriation of Swahili in the Former Belgian Congo, 1880–1938* (Berkeley: University of California Press, 1986), for discussion of the very different position of Swahili in the Belgian Congo.

10. Fay Gadsen, "The African Press in Kenya, 1945–1952," *Journal of African History* 21, no. 4 (1980): 519; see also Bodil Folke Frederiksen, "Print, Newspapers and Audiences in Colonial Kenya: African and Indian Improvement, Protest and Connection," *Africa* 81, no. 1 (2011): 155–72; and George Ogola, "The Political Economy of Media in Kenya: From Kenyatta's Nation-Building Press to Kibaki's Local-Language FM Radio," *Africa Today* 57, no. 3 (2011): 77–95.

11. Neither continues today, but they nevertheless confirm a broader regional attachment to Swahili poetic production. I've been unable to research whether or not the remaining Swahili periodical in Kenya today, *Taifa Leo*, includes poetry by its readers.

12. For more on the varying traditions and structures of Swahili poetry, please see K. Amri Abedi, *Sheria za Kutunga Mashairi na Diwani ya Amri* (Nairobi: East African Literature Bureau, 1954); Biersteker, *Kujibizana*; Lyndon Harries, "Cultural Verse-Forms in Swahili," *African Studies* 15, no. 4 (1956): 176–87; Lyndon Harries, *Swahili Poetry* (Oxford: Clarendon Press, 1962); S. M. Komba, *Uwanja wa Mashairi* (Dar es Salaam: Longman, 1976); Joan Maw, *Fire and Lightning: Language, Affect and Society in 20th Century Swahili Poetry* (Vienna: Institute für Afrikanistik und Ägyptologie der Universität Wien, 1999); Gudrun Miehe et al., eds., *Kala Shairi: German East Africa in Swahili Poems* (Cologne: Rüdiger Köppe Verlag, 2002); Mulokozi and Sengo, *History of Kiswahili Poetry*; Kimani Njogu, *Reading Poetry as Dialogue: An East African Literary Tradition* (Nairobi: Jomo Kenyatta Foundation, 2004); Shariff, *Tungo Zetu*. A modernist school of Swahili poetry rejecting the traditional rules of composition and advocating free verse did emerge in the 1970s, but this has not proved popular. See Joshua Madumulla et al., "Politics, Ideology and Poetic Form: The Literary Debate in Tanzania," in *Language Ideological Debates*, ed. Jan Blommaert (New York: Mouton de Gruyter, 1999), 307–41.

13. Kelly Askew, *Performing the Nation: Swahili Music and Cultural Politics in Tanzania* (Chicago: University of Chicago Press, 2002), chap. 6.

14. Roland Greene, *Princeton Encyclopedia of Poetry and Poetics* (Princeton, NJ: Princeton University Press, 2012), 1380–82.

15. Some examples include http://mashairiyamakilla.blogspot.com/ (accessed 27 May 2015); https://hamzaamohammed.wordpress.com/ (accessed 27 May 2015); http://mitaaflani.blogspot.com/ (accessed 27 May 2015); http://issamichuzi.blogspot.com/2013/06/shairi-amani-idumu.html (accessed 27 May 2015); or the Facebook group called "Malenga" established by Ignas Komba.

16. Biersteker, *Kujibizana*, 81, 281.

17. Thomas Geider, "The Paper Memory of East Africa: Ethnohistories and Biographies Written in Swahili," in *A Place in the World: New Local Historiographies from Africa and South Asia*, ed. Axel Harneit-Sievers (Leiden: Brill, 2002), 255–88; and Emma Hunter, "'Our Common Humanity': Print, Power, and the Colonial Press in Interwar Tanganyika and French Cameroun," *Journal of Global History* 7 (2012): 279–301.

18. Maria Suriano, "Letters to the Editor and Poems: *Mambo Leo* and Readers' Debates on *Dansi*, *Ustaarabu*, Respectability, and Modernity in Tanganyika, 1940–1950s," *Africa Today* 57, no. 3 (2011): 55.

19. James R. Brennan, *Taifa: Making Nation and Race in Urban Tanzania* (Athens: Ohio University Press), 118–58.

20. Aldin Mutembei, *UKIMWI katika Fasihi ya Kiswahili, 1982–2006* (Dar es Salaam: Institute of Swahili Studies, 2009). I thank Ann Biersteker for this reference.

21. Kezilahabi, "The House of Everydayness," 192.

22. Kezilahabi, "The House of Everydayness, 191–92.

23. Mulokozi, "Revolution and Reaction," 46.

24. Karin Barber, ed., *Africa's Hidden Histories: Everyday Literacy and Making the Self* (Bloomington: Indiana University Press, 2006), 8; see also Stephanie Newell, *Literary Culture in Colonial Ghana* (Bloomington: Indiana University Press, 2002) and Derek Peterson, *Creative Writing: Translation, Bookkeeping, and the Work of the Imagination in Colonial Kenya* (Portsmouth, NH: Heinemann, 2004).

25. Sturmer, *Media History of Tanzania*, 30.

26. Hilda Lemke, "Die Suaheli-Zeitungen und -Zeitschriften in Deutsch-Ost-Afrika" ["The Swahili Newspapers and Magazines in German East Africa"], PhD dissertation, University of Leipzig, 1929; Sturmer, *Media History of Tanzania*.

27. Hilde Lemke, "Die Suaheli-Zeitungen," 44. "In fast allen Zeitungen spielt die Dichtung eine große Rolle. Alles können die Suaheli in ihrer Dichtersprache ... ausdrücken, und es ist den Redakteuren der Zeitungen stets gelungen, einen oder mehrere Dichter für ihr Blatt zu gewinnen." Translated by Ben Fortson. See also Miehe et al., *Kala Shairi*.

28. Kelly Askew, "Tanzanian Newspaper Poetry: Political Commentary in Verse," *Journal of Eastern African Studies* 8, no. 3 (2014): 515–37.

29. Lemke, "Die Suaheli-Zeitungen," 44. For the text, see Carl Velten, *Prosa und Poesie der Suaheli* (Berlin: C. Velten, im Selbstverlag des Verfassers, 1907), 343–49; Miehe et al., *Kala Shairi*, 471–77.

30. For more on this poem, see Lemke, "Die Suaheli-Zeitungen," 48–51; and Askew, "Tanzanian Newspaper Poetry," 17–18.

31. However, *Pwani na Bara*, which initially ran from 1910 to 1916, was relaunched in 1978 and was still in print as of the time of Sturmer's writing in 1998. A new *Kiongozi* completely unrelated to the Tanga School newspaper was launched in 1950 as the main publication of the Catholic Church and continues today. See Sturmer, *Media History of Tanzania*.

32. As discussed by Suriano, "Letters to the Editor"; Hunter, "Our Common Humanity"; and Brennan, *Taifa*.

33. James F. Scotton, "Tanganyika's African Press, 1937–1960: A Nearly Forgotten Pre-independence Forum," *African Studies Review* 21, no. 1 (1978): 1.

34. Scotton, "Tanganyika's African Press," 3–4, emphasis added.

35. Scotton, "Tanganyika's African Press," 13.

36. Scotton, "Tanganyika's African Press," 12.

37. Olympio's name has been slightly altered by the poet to fit the rhyme scheme.

38. For example, the previous issue of 12 January featured an article called *Nendeni Mhimize Kilimo* ("Go and Speed Up Agriculture"). See Hunter, "Revisiting Ujamaa: Political Legitimacy and the Construction of Community in Postcolonial Tanzania," *Journal of Eastern African Studies* 2, no. 3 (2008): 471–85.

39. "Dear Abby" is the name of one of the most iconic and long-running advice columns in US newspapers penned by Pauline Phillips under the pseudonym Abigail Van Buren. It was launched in 1956 and continues today by Phillips's daughter Jeanne.

40. Lyndon Harries, "Cultural Verse-Forms in Swahili," *African Studies* 15, no. 4 (1956): 176–87.

41. There is a mistake here. The second caesura is apparently missing and was mistakenly filled in with the second caesura of the refrain.

42. I corrected this line, removing the "*ni*," which ruined the meter, and fixing "*meme*" to "*mema*."

43. *Istiklali* is from the Arabic *istiqlal*, meaning "independence" and is more commonly rendered in Kiswahili as *istiklali*.

44. Sturmer, *Media History of Tanzania*, 60. In an online chat room popular among Tanzanians called JamiiForums.com, a 4 March 2014 thread titled "Kenya kuna gazeti moja tu la Kiswahili" ("Kenya only has one Swahili newspaper") discussed the geographic span of Swahili language use, commenting on its stron-

ger presence in Tanzania and Kenya. Someone responded on 11 March, to say, "Back in the 1950s and 1960s there was another very famous newspaper called '*BARAZA*'. It was especially well-read here in Tanzania, especially in Moshi and Arusha." *Miaka hiyo ya 50 mpaka 60 pia walikuwa na gazeti maarufu sana liitwalo "BARAZA." Lilikuwa linasomwa sana hapa Tanzania hasa Moshi na Arusha.* http://www.jamiiforums.com/jukwaa-la-lugha/618005-kenya-kuna-gazeti-moja-tu-la-kiswahili.html (accessed 30 May 2014).

45. See Askew, "Tanzanian Newspaper Poetry" for more discussion of this example and political praise poetry representing different periods in Tanzanian history.

46. Askew, "Tanzanian Newspaper Poetry."

47. See also Andrew Ivaska, *Cultured States: Youth, Gender, and Modern Style in 1960s Dar es Salaam* (Durham, NC: Duke University Press, 2011).

48. Translated by Kelly Askew and Deo Ngonyani, May 2014. This poem also appears in a subsequent collection: Inter-territorial Language Committee, *Mashairi ya Mambo Leo*, vol. 3, 10–12.

49. See Biersteker, *Kujibizana*.

50. The fact that the stanzas are numbered indicates that each poem was much longer than what was actually published.

51. Also appears in the collection: Inter-territorial Language Committee, *Mashairi ya Mambo Leo*, vol. 1, 50.

52. Marshall McLuhan, *Understanding Media: The Extensions of Man* (1964; Cambridge, MA: MIT Press, 1997).

CHAPTER 8

Private Entertainment Magazines and Popular Literature Production in Socialist Tanzania

UTA REUSTER-JAHN

In the postindependence socialist state of Tanzania, the creation of a national culture was a central yet contentious project. However, while the views of the government and the ruling party differed in some respects, they were nevertheless united in their rejection of "decadent" forms of Western culture, such as miniskirts and bell-bottom trousers, as well as Western films and magazines.[1] Despite this rejection, there were nonetheless a surprising number of creative and ambitious young men who produced entertainment magazines in the national language, Swahili, to provide a form of localized modern urban leisure. Usually trained for completely unrelated work, these men decided to pursue the uncertain life of editors and cultural entrepreneurs in a politically and economically difficult environment. In many respects, they operated at the margins of what was allowed: they ran private businesses in a period of economic nationalization, adapted transnational templates in a time of cultural nationalization, and presented a potential threat to the information monopoly of the state by publishing magazines with high print runs.

The role of the editors within socialist Tanzania was intriguing. Imaginative, playful, ambitious, and determined, they sought to delight and educate—and to attain financial success and carve a legitimate place for themselves within the limits of the socialist state. Their actions and their lives raise a number of curious and vexing questions: How was it possible for private editors to run entertainment magazines in socialist Tanzania? How did they manage their relationship to the state? How did they survive in a steadily declining economy? How did they gain readers and keep them? And, finally, how did the magazines secure themselves a position within the broader context of Swahili literature?

In my search to answer these questions I went to Tanzania, where I collected data through a series of interviews with the former editors.[2] In addition, I analyzed the magazines of the era, which were available often only as sporadic issues, in the Tanzanian National Library in Dar es Salaam.[3] I wish to express my sincere gratitude to the writers and editors who talked to me about their hopes and visions that inspired them to venture into magazine production, and the experiences they subsequently had. I also wish to thank Matthias Krings who initially drew my attention to the Swahili photonovel and provided me with copies of the magazine *New Film Azania*.

This chapter sheds light on the private magazine culture and popular literature production that flourished, and withered, during Tanzania's socialist era. The magazines, mainly monthlies, exploited the narrow leeway that existed in the postcolonial socialist state for private entertainment media. They were affected by state politics, which not only pursued a socialist society but also had embarked on a project of forging a national identity through culture. This ambitious project aimed at restoring pride in local cultures after the colonial experience, using as a basis selected elements from the more than one hundred ethnic groups.[4] While state policies promoted nationalized forms of culture, they contrasted them with urban decadence.[5] However, even Rashidi Kawawa, Tanzania's first prime minister and a strong advocate of statism in Tanzania, conceded in 1965, "It is necessary to entertain the nation as well as to educate it."[6] With regard to the mass media, the daily newspapers, which by 1976 had all been nationalized, largely failed to entertain their readers. Even the radio, which traditionally had provided entertainment, increasingly became a vehicle for preaching politics. After the Arusha Declaration laid the basis for the socialist transformation of Tanzania in 1967 and prioritized agriculture, the mass media concentrated on promoting improved agricultural techniques, popularly known as *Kilimo bora*. But according to many Tanzanians who were young in those days, people soon got bored with those lessons and longed for entertainment and diversion. Until the early 1970s, print entertainment could only be found in imported English-language magazines that were available in a few bookshops in Dar es Salaam and some provincial towns. Their readers, who comprised only a tiny part of the population, were predominantly male urbanites as well as students of secondary schools and institutions of higher learning. The magazines were few but the curiosity great, so that a single copy would often be read by whole populations of dormitories. There was a clear if unstated demand for domestic production of more magazines, written in Swahili, that might possibly even cater to a broader clientele.

In their entertainment magazines, the editors concentrated on stories and used the magazines to convey pages of fiction to avid readers. As a result, these magazines are today inseparable from the history of popular Swahili literature. Moreover, because the editors also wrote numerous books that have become classics, they are also regarded as the founding fathers of popular Swahili fiction. In addition, they were great experimenters, using their magazines to tell stories in various forms: as photoplays, serial fiction, short stories, graphic novels, comics, and cartoons.[7]

FILM TANZANIA, THE FIRST PRIVATE ENTERTAINMENT MAGAZINE IN TANZANIA

Every movement has its pioneers, and in Tanzania a pioneer and undisputed leader in the publication of entertainment magazines was Faraji H. H. Katalambulla. His role in building up and sustaining the photonovel magazine was remarkable and places him firmly among Tanzania's most influential cultural entrepreneurs. In 1969, just two years after the Arusha Declaration, Katalambulla launched his Swahili photonovel magazine *Film Tanzania*. At this time he was already well known as the author of a successful novel.

Like most Tanzanian authors, Katalambulla, who was born in central Tanzania in 1942, started writing while in secondary school.[8] From 1959 onward, during the last years of British rule and the first years of independence, his short stories in Swahili were published in the Catholic fortnightly *Kiongozi* (The Leader), which was produced in his hometown Tabora,[9] and later even in the Kenyan Swahili weeklies *Baraza* (Public Audience) and *Taifa* (Nation) *Weekly*.[10] During the same period he wrote radio plays for the Tanganyika Broadcasting Corporation (TBC), a genre that enjoyed great popularity in Tanzania for decades. Katalambulla's passion for storytelling was to characterize the rest of his creative career.

After leaving school, he wanted to study journalism, but there was no formal training for journalists in Tanzania at that time.[11] Katalambulla found a job at an oil company in Dar es Salaam. However, when the ruling party established its Mwananchi Printing and Publishing Company, which published the dailies *Uhuru* (Independence) and *The Nationalist*,[12] he found employment as an untrained subeditor in 1964. There he acquired the skills and connections that later helped him run his own magazine.

During his last year in school in 1962, Katalambulla submitted a novel to a writing competition organized by the East African Literature Bureau (EALB) in Nairobi.[13] It was published in 1964 with the EALB under the title *Simu ya Kifo* (Trail of Death)[14] and became "one of the most popular titles in Tanzanian fiction."[15] In fact, the novel was reprinted fifteen times between 1965 and 1980 by different publishing houses in Tanzania and Kenya.[16] It was used in Swahili classes at schools and colleges, which were in urgent need of suitable reading material because Swahili was now the national and official language of Tanzania. The novel's success provided Katalambulla with the capital to start his own entertainment magazine and the renown to draw new readers. It was the enterprising author's idea to produce a Swahili equivalent of the weekly English-language photonovel magazine *African Film*, which was published by Drum Publications in South Africa.[17] The magazine featured the adventures of the smart private detective Lance Spearman and, as Matthias Krings has argued, "introduced an African visual modernity"[18] with its urban street scenes and modern interiors inhabited by fashionably dressed people. During the period of its publication from 1968 to 1972, *African Film* was popular among mainly male students and educated urbanites in Tanzania. Many identified with the magazine's African hero and became members of the first fan clubs in Tanzania, where they communally expressed and cultivated their admiration for Lance Spearman ("The Spear").[19]

Establishing *Film Tanzania*

Katalambulla was the first in Tanzania to rework the template of *African Film* into a local magazine when in 1969 he launched *Film Tanzania*.[20] Himself an enthusiastic reader of *African Film*, he saw the market potential for a similar product in Swahili and quit his salaried job to become a self-employed editor and publisher. With his experience from the editorial office at Mwananchi, he could understand the production process behind *African Film* and was confident that he could edit such a magazine himself. For printing, he soon got a good offer by Printpak, one of the two major printers in Dar es Salaam. For distribution, Katalambulla entered into a contract with the Tanzania Standard (Newspapers) Ltd., a cooperation that was crucial for reaching customers and monitoring returns from the vendors. This was a fortunate partnership for Katalambulla because it was the only distribution infrastructure available to him at the time. The first years yielded excellent results, with print runs of fifty thousand and a temporary switch from monthly to fortnightly publication. The initial success of *Film Tanzania* attracted the advertising budgets of numerous large companies, including Tanzania Breweries, National Milling Corporation, and the National Bank of Commerce, in addition to local businesses, guesthouses, and bars. The editor established long-term contracts that provided him with a secure income.

Localization of the Photonovel

With *Film Tanzania*, Katalambulla initially aimed at a Swahili version of *African Film*, closely modeled along the transnational template. Thus, in September 1969 he serialized *Maovu Kivulini* (Evil in the Shadow), a detective story similar to those of *African Film*. Instead of Lance Spearman with his assistant Sonia, *Film Tanzania* introduced Inspecta Kikaango ("Frying pan") and his task force, including the fashionable female officer Mazua, in their fight against Dar es Salaam's criminals. While both magazines showed that crime does not pay, *Film Tanzania* also showed that people living in luxury could not be a role model in socialist Tanzania.

Because urban riches with all their temptations did not exist in Tanzania of the 1970s, Katalambulla soon abandoned the stories where rich people were robbed by gangsters and helped by the police to get their money back. In the same vein, the fantastic, which constituted part of *African Film*'s escapist appeal,[21] did not work in stories set in the context of *ujamaa* politics and the socialist transformation of the Tanzanian society. *Film Tanzania*'s transition toward stories about common Tanzanians and their problems took place during the first year of publication. As Katalambulla put it, "Things from day-to-day life helped me to become accepted. The education I offered made it easy to be accepted, and it helped to sell." His comment about education refers to the traditional perception of storytellers as educators of society, who are expected to teach their audience moral lessons. Localization is also expressed in the 1970 change of the magazine's subtitle from *East African Pictorial Swahili Magazine* to *Gazeti la Kiswahili la Mapicha* (Swahili Photo Magazine).

Film Tanzania had a thoroughly local yet predominantly urban setting from its very inception. The photos showed offices and bars in the city as well as modern urban interiors in local "Swahili houses,"[22] demonstrating that a local modernity was possible (even if not to be found in the living conditions of the readers, which were generally much simpler). Katalambulla's city dwellers had well-equipped kitchens and comfortable living rooms. They drove cars and motorbikes, read newspapers—and during the early years were dressed in Western style, right down to daringly short miniskirts. The references to Western fashion touched on the controversy swirling around the length of women's skirts in Tanzania. From 1968 to 1973, miniskirts were at the center of a heated debate about nationalizing urban style, whose underlying issues of gender, generation, and materiality have been discussed by Andrew Ivaska.[23] They were rejected by predominantly male youth associations as the epitome of Western decadence, and a ban was planned and enforced by the Tanzania Youth League in campaigns called Operation Vijana.[24] Katalambulla, whose fascination with modern urbanity is clearly evident in the first two years of his magazine, remembered an instance of intervention by the party concerning this issue. He was warned to lengthen the skirts and for a while had to submit his magazine to the party's cultural department for approval before it could go to print. As a consequence, Katalambulla moved away from showcasing modern urban culture in his stories and shifted to more rural settings with more traditionally dressed protagonists. There was another reason why the emphasis on modernity in the photo-stories lessened over the years: people were increasingly preoccupied with securing their basic needs because of the deterioration of the Tanzanian economy. Miniskirts and Western-style modernity became frivolities that had no place in the Tanzanian society and little place in its entertainment magazines. Thus, after some years, *Film Tanzania* had considerably departed from the initial idea and its template. It differed from *African Film* also in another respect: Katalambulla did not establish a hero like Lance Spearman. His Inspector Frying Pan, as the name suggests, was a comic and likable officer, but not a virile and admirable heroic figure.

When Katalambulla departed from detective stories after one year, he returned to the subject matter of his early short stories and plays: family conflicts and common people struggling with their imperfections and faults while trying to improve their situation. From 15 September to 1 December 1970, he serialized the photonovel *Pendo Pevu* (Ideal Love), which warns of the peril of too much individual freedom. In *Pendo Pevu*, a young man falls madly in love with a modern city girl the day before his wedding and so cancels it. Disowned by his parents, he goes away to earn money to marry his new sweetheart. But upon his return, she is marrying another man. Unlike him, the girl had complied with her family's plans. Despite the racy developments of the story, it is in essence conservative. Many of Katalambulla's stories oscillate between the droll and the moral. Characters represent types rather than individuals. Young men fall heedlessly in love with beautiful women, while older men lust after young women or wealth. Modern girls are beautiful but unreliable; traditional and often submissive housewives find ways to cheat on their husbands. Like many Swahili popular stories, Katalambulla's are strongly didactic. They go back to orally transmitted folk stories, in which bad outcomes warn the audience that it is better to live according to the social norms.

Katalambulla's stories never commented directly on political issues. He kept politics in the background, describing instead people's living conditions, their hopes, and their aspirations. Although there was formal press freedom in Tanzania, editors knew that criticism was not appreciated by the ruling party and the government and were consequently cautious.[25] Katalambulla's concern with maintaining good relations with the party and government was expressed when, after President Nyerere was confirmed in office in the presidential elections of 1980, he congratulated him in a full-page note in his magazine.

Two Sides of the Coin: Reader Relationships and Rotating Stories

Katalambulla was both a passionate editor and a cost-conscious businessman. As fervent editor, he loved his readers and wanted to establish a close relationship to them, but as clever businessman he was equally aware that this close relationship meant customer loyalty and continued sales. Thus from the start he fostered a kind of personal relationship with his anonymous audience. He never failed to attach his photo to his editorial address, which he usually concluded with the signature phrase "the one who loves you." Thus, he wrote, "This play was invented, written, produced, and directed by the very one who loves you—Katalambulla"[26] or, even more intimately using his first name, "These words have not been said by just somebody but they have come from the mouth of the very Faraji, who loves you."[27] Personal address created customer loyalty by transforming the commercial relationship with the readers into a personal one and drawing them into an imagined community of like-minded people.[28] Essentially, it made purchasing the magazine an act of moral obligation, as toward a relative or dear friend. The editor even proudly announced his daughter's graduation from Dar es Salaam University, as if telling friends about this family affair.[29] For their part, readers responded and interacted with the editor of *Film Tanzania* by sending in comments, congratulations, stories, photos, and even applications as actors.[30] Katalambulla also addressed music bands and sports clubs in Dar es Salaam and the

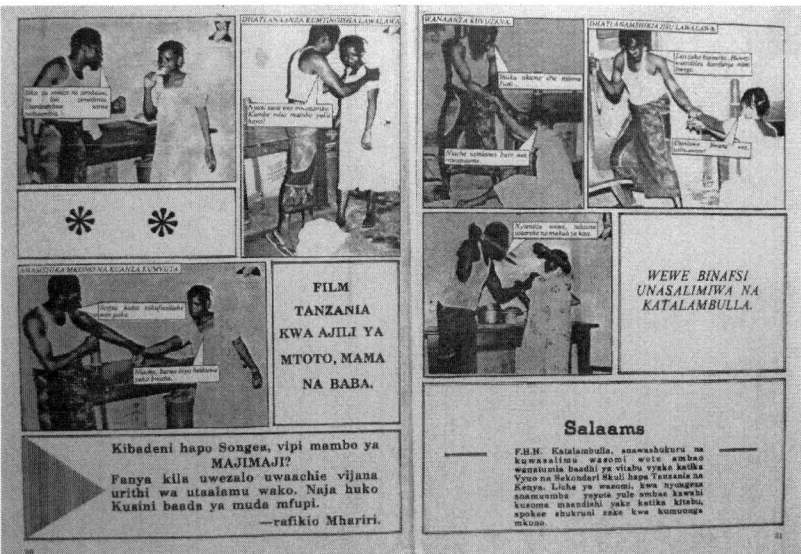

Fig. 1. Film *Tanzania* no. 118, scene from *Lawalawa*, part 4. The inserted address by Katalambulla on page 20 cheers on the leader of the Majimaji Football Club of Songea, telling him that "your friend, the editor" will soon come to Songea. On page 21 the reader is told that "you personally are greeted by Katalambulla." Below this greeting the editor thanks everybody who reads his books.

regions, thanking them for a good performance, or cheering them on. Thus, Katalambulla sent personal messages through his print medium, while simultaneously showing that he was well connected in urban cultural life. Those addresses and messages displayed the editor's "sociability in print."[31]

Another instance of the interplay between creativity and commercial concern was Katalambulla's approach of "rotating stories," where he reused his stories and adapted them to different media and narrative forms. His approach is well illustrated by *Picha ya Pacha* (Pacha's Photo), a variation of the theme of a young man sacrificing his prospects in life for a girl whom in the end he will not win. Katalambulla published it as a serial story in *Film Tanzania* in 1980, as a photo-story in the magazine in 1997, and as a play in book form in 2007. Similarly, he initially wrote the story "Pendo Pevu" as a radio play for the TBC, then adapted it as a photo-story in 1970, and eventually published it as a play in book form in 1976.[32] In fact, most of Katalambulla's works that were printed as books had previously appeared in *Film Tanzania* in the form of photo-stories.[33] As the author explained, all his activities with writing, editing, and publishing revolved around a "stock of plots" that he altered according to the "medium in question" (*chombo husika*). He told me:

> The stories are rotating. They start at the time when I began writing and sending my stories to papers such as *Kiongozi*. Later when I established that magazine I remembered them. I had a nice stock. I did not need contributors. So you see that they [the stories] rotate. Often they are built on a short story, an unusual event.

His statement shows that for him commercial considerations are inseparably connected with artistic concerns, since saving money to pay external contributors and recycling narrative material went hand in hand with his creative experimentation. No matter which form he chose, his narrative style was always characterized by his "ability to present highly dramatic situations."[34] His readers were enthralled and engaged, sending in letters and comments and eagerly awaiting next issues. Katalambulla thus successfully maximized reader pleasure and loyalty while minimizing editorial costs—an effective business model that was to last many years.

FILM TANZANIA AND ITS IMITATORS

Film Tanzania's success inspired other creative and entrepreneurial people to embark on similar projects. However, none of them was initially able to overcome two major obstacles: financing and distribution. This applied even to Eddie Ganzel, an early, famous popular writer particularly known for his serial novels in Kenyan Swahili papers and one of the first to follow in Katalambulla's footsteps.[35] Ganzel was involved in the magazine *Tamasha* (Spectacle), which had been launched in 1971.[36] In the first issue, the editor, Hamidi Saidi, announced that *Tamasha* was intended to become a hall for spectacles (*ukumbi wa tamasha*) in which films would be presented through photos. Thus this issue would be wholly dedicated to the first part of a film based on the story "Achana Naye" ("Leave Her") by Eddie Ganzel. The editor explained:

> The intention of launching the "hall for spectacles" is to give our East African writers the opportunity to turn their stories into pictures. We hope that

this measure will encourage those who are talented to write more and better stories, so that when they send them to us we can show them in pictures like films. Moreover, it is our hope that by the time our countries are able to manage the production of cinema films, our writers will already have got some experience.

This concept of photonovels as precursors of a future domestic film industry gave them a patriotic meaning in the local context. Here, indeed, photonovels were seen in a perspective of film and can be retrospectively interpreted as a "prequel to Nollywood," as Matthias Krings has shown."[37] In contrast, the Nigerian photonovel tied in with the tradition of live theater.[38] However, in the case of *Tamasha*, the attempt to build a prosperous business failed, primarily because the magazine lacked an effective distributor.

In actuality, the pioneer Katalambulla remained without serious competitors for almost ten years. It was not until 1978, as the country was experiencing an economic decline, that the situation changed. In the late 1970s, the production of Katalambulla's magazine was affected by repeated paper shortages, which resulted from Tanzania's dependency on imported paper. The government had restricted the import of goods because foreign currency had become scarce, following the country's strategy of nationalization and self-reliance laid down in the Arusha Declaration. Agriculture was given priority over industrialization, which was supposed to follow in a second step. The resulting economic decline was aggravated by the war with Uganda from 1978 to 1979, the second global oil crisis from 1979 to 1980, and terms of trade that were increasingly unfavorable for Tanzania's agricultural exports.

Hampered in his efforts to publish, Katalambulla decided in 1978 to move his magazine to Kenya. There, the editor experienced bureaucratic obstacles that delayed the registration of his magazine, which he named *Swahili Film*. When publication began a year later, Katalambulla found it very difficult to find advertisers because the audience interested in a Swahili-language magazine proved too small. With a print run of five thousand copies, he could neither attract advertisers nor make sufficient profit from the sales. Thus, after two years in Kenya he abandoned the experiment and returned to Tanzania, where his presence was needed to defend his enterprise. To his surprise he encountered not only new competitors but also a new way of doing business: Asian-Tanzanian businessmen had jumped on the Swahili print entertainment bandwagon as business partners.

Asian-Tanzanian Businessmen as Financiers and distributors

In the late 1970s, the time was right in Tanzania for cooperation between editors and businessmen. With Katalambulla in Kenya, two young men, Andrew Manjwili and G'ray Mchome from Moshi, saw the opportunity to fill the gap with a photo-story magazine of their own.[39] What they lacked in training, experience, and capital they made up for in talent, confidence, and audacity. For example, they cleverly capitalized on the popularity of Katalambulla's *Film Tanzania* by calling their photo-magazine *New Film Tanzania*. While registration of this new magazine was easy, financing and distribution were proving to be insurmountable challenges. It is at this point that the role of the Asian-Tanzanian businessmen becomes apparent. Manjwili had been unable to secure a public or private loan to print the magazine and thus turned to Murtaza Alidina, a Dar es Salaam businessman of Asian descent whose company, International Publishers Agencies Ltd., imported books. This was a fortuitous move on his part because Alidina was at that time looking for a new market. Book imports had become almost impossible because of foreign currency controls. Since 1976, booksellers had to apply at the Exchange Control Department of the Bank of Tanzania for an import license, which was increasingly rejected. As a result, the few major bookshops, including Alidina's, had to rely entirely on local publishers.[40] Alidina agreed to both finance and distribute the magazine. As former circulation manager with the Standard Newspapers, he had an excellent distribution network in the regions that consisted mainly of Asian-Tanzanian shopowners. His network even reached beyond the Tanzanian border, in particular to Uganda, where after the dictator's Idi Amin defeat in 1979, President Milton Obote invited businesspeople of Asian descent to come back and participate in the economic reconstruction of the country.[41] The contract between Alidina and the editors was made by word of mouth, and the new magazine was first produced in early 1979. In a few days it was sold out.

When Katalambulla heard about this magazine, "He came running from Nairobi," as Manjwili put it, and protested at the registrar against the hijacking of his magazine's name. Manjwili and Mchome then changed their magazine's name to the very similar sounding *New Film Azania*, which Katalambulla grudgingly had to accept. Katalambulla subsequently resumed publication of his *Film Tanzania*. While the market absorbed both magazines without problem, tension remained among the editors.

The business relationship with Alidina had far-reaching consequences

Fig. 2. Covers: *Film Tanzania* no. 29 (1970) and *New Film Azania* no. 13 (1981)

for Tanzanian print culture. Since it had become evident how hungry a considerable number of Tanzanians were for entertaining reading matter, Alidina instigated the launch of more magazines. The editors operated their magazines from under his wing while remaining the nominal owners of their enterprises. Alidina did not interfere in the production of the magazines because, as their financier and distributor, he was only interested in sales figures: when they were good, he increased the print run; when they were not, he decreased it. The average print run was fifteen thousand. Revenue from advertisements remained with the editors as their extra profit; hence each tried to acquire as much advertising as possible. As the business prospered, Alidina soon got a competitor. Akberali Nayani, also of Asian descent and owner of Nayani Bookstall in the center of Dar es Salaam's Kariakoo business district, offered a similar business model. The editors' attitude toward their financiers was ambivalent. They talked about them as "Wahindi wetu" ("our Indians") in a mixture of fondness and sarcasm, saying "walitusaidia" ("they helped us") but also "walitunyonya vizuri" ("they exploited us pretty well"). Nevertheless, they all acknowledged the crucial role of the Asian-Tanzanians in popular literature production. Alidina and Nayani even competed for editors. Manjwili remembers that they moved between the two financiers, following better offers regarding the share paid to them. Meanwhile, the private entertainment magazines flourished and attracted further creative personalities.

"We loved amusement": A New Generation of Editors and Their Magazines

Because of the informality of the sector, personal relationships were pivotal in the establishment of new magazines.[42] Thus, a number of magazines were launched because Manjwili and Mchome connected their friends interested in literature and magazines with their financiers. Moreover, editors often ran their magazines with a partner to minimize risks and share the responsibility. Manjwili's and Mchome's friends Kajubi Mukajanga and Kassim Chande, for example, jointly registered their magazine *Hamasa* (Enthusiasm) in 1980. In the first issues they serialized the photo-story *Kitanda cha Mauti* (Bed of Death), which Mukajanga later published as a book in 1982. A main role in the story was played by the librarian Salim A. M. Kitogo, another friend of Manjwili. Kitogo did the editorial work for *Hamasa* during the first year before he launched his own magazine *Johari* (Jewel) in 1981. Manjwili's younger brother Barnaba Mbungo contributed articles to various magazines and in 1982 launched the magazine *Wasaa* (Opportunity) together with his friend Shaaban Scotto. Almost all editors of the time sooner or later moved to Dar es Salaam, where the financiers, distributors, and printers were located. They formed a community in the city, meeting at the printers and also at bars and clubs. "Tulipenda starehe" ("We loved amusement"), said Manjwili with a twinkle in his eye.

While these editors may have loved amusement, they also wanted to avoid conflict with the state. Although the Tanzanian constitution guaranteed the freedom to run and publish mass media, magazines and newspapers could easily be banned and prohibited by a provision of the Newspaper Act of 1976, which gave considerable authority to the state and its organs. It was made very clear to the editors that they were not allowed to write hard news and that there were limits in their freedom concerning topics and criticism. The enthusiastic young men did not see that as a problem because they did not intend to challenge the government or the ruling party. All in all, they felt that they were treated benevolently, which they attributed to the need for Swahili reading material that their magazines provided.

Thus circumspect on the one hand, the editors sought on the other hand to give their magazines a profile that distinguished them from others. *New Film Azania*'s stories were more provocative than those of Katalambulla, but their

| NAYANI BOOKSTAL MKUNGUNI ST. KARIAKOO S.L.P. 5048, DAR ES SALAAM. MUUZAJI WA ZA NAKALA ZA JUMLA MISAKATO, FILM AZANIA, HAMASA, EQUATOR, FILM, TOHARI BUSARA, NA MALIMWENGU. | BANTU FILM KILA MWEZI WAGAWAJI RASMI KWA JUMLA TUU International Publishers Agencies Ltd., P.O. BOX 21341, Dar es Salaam. Telephone: 21930/27458 VILEVILE WANAGAWA JUMLA MAGAZETI YAFUATAYO: NEW FILM AZANIA MISAKATO FAHARI MCHESHI MSHINDI CHEKA |

Fig. 3. Left: Advertisement for the Nayani Bookstall in *New Film Azania* 13 (1980) for wholesale of *Misakato, New Film Azania, Hamasa, Equator Film, Johari, Busara, Malimwengu*. Right: Advert of International Publishers Agencies in *Bantu Film* 12 (1981) for wholesale of *New Film Azania, Misakato, Fahari, Mcheshi, Mshindi, Cheka*.

ultimate goal also was to educate and maintain social mores. The story "Pigo la Penzi" ("Stroke of Love"), serialized in 1981, shows how a young woman and her fiancé cheat on the girl's boss, whose mistress she becomes. The story shows a reversion of the usual moral, which would have the girl punished. In the logic of "Pigo la Penzi" the boss's punishment is morally justified because he had neglected his wife and six children. Thus, the story commented on the problem of useless managers of the mostly statal and parastatal companies in Tanzania, who abused their position to spend public money for private enjoyment. Even more provocative is the plot of "Tamu ya Tamaa" ("Sweetness of Desire"), serialized in 1982, which presents a family conflict. A man has been working in South African mines for years, sending money home to his wife. When their child, a girl, becomes an adolescent, she quarrels with her mother and leaves the home. After the father comes back, they meet by chance in a street and the man seduces the young woman, not knowing that she is his daughter. This story is concerned with the disruption of families caused by the money economy and the anonymity of the city and expresses this through the incestuous relationship—a recurrent trope in Swahili popular fiction. In interviews, the writers claimed that by raising issues of social relevance, they pursued didactic goals. Thus, beneath the photo showing the girl leaving home, the reader is told: "When you read *New Film Azania*, remember that while relaxing you educate yourself and the whole of society."[43]

Bantu Film, established in 1980 by Omar A. Mbega and owned by Bantu Publishers, set each story in a different town with local actors. Like most of his colleagues, Mbega concentrated on stories about common Tanzanians. He was the only editor, however, who provided a column for poems, which could be used by readers to comment in verse on a range of concerns. Poetry as a form of public discourse has a long tradition as an oral genre on the Swahili coast and as a print genre in Swahili newspapers.[44] Poetry was generally not to be found in the magazines, probably because the editors chose to experiment with modern forms. Moreover, the magazines were not meant as platforms for debate. *Equator Film*, owned and edited by Tonny Kamkanda, differed from the others as its stories were in essence propaganda for state policies. Kamkanda's first photo-story, starting in 1980, was "Tonny na Matatizo ya Mjini" ("Tonny and the Problems in Town"), which supported the campaign of the party and the government to control youth coming to town from the rural areas in search of a better life. In 1981, he presented a photo-story about the last days of the Ugandan dictator Idi Amin, who was ousted as a result of his military defeat in the Uganda-Tanzanian war in 1979.[45] The story shows the dictator surrounded by sinister advisors trying to stop the advancing Tanzanian troops. His witch doctor tells him that he must eat the heart of his child (which he does), while his security advisor pretends that everything is under control. There is also a white foreign advisor, who secretly pursues racist aims. In the speech bubbles one can read his thoughts: "The Africans will kill each other and then I will go home to Europe when things have become bad.... We will test our weapons on the Africans in order to know whether they are suitable."[46] The story reflected and reinforced the pride that Tanzanians took in the defeat of Idi Amin, along with popular stereotypes about the external enemies of the young postcolonial, socialist state.

The *Sani* Comic Magazine and the Move toward Mixed Content

While photonovel magazines were still enjoying enormous success, creative minds began looking across the Tanzanian border for innovation and ways to diversify print entertainment. In 1978, a transnational template was adopted from the Kenyan *Joe* magazine with the launch of the magazine *Sani*.[47] This magazine was a joint project of Nicco ye Mbajo[48] and Saidi Bawji. Mbajo, born in 1950, was highly talented and versatile: an artist, actor, playwright, musician, conductor and composer of choir music, writer, illustrator—and soccer player. A fan of the Kenyan *Joe* magazine, he wanted to launch a Swahili version of it.[49] As he told me, he personally sought permission from *Joe*'s editor in Nairobi. Mbajo partnered with Bawji, a bank clerk who secured a loan from the savings and credits association of bank workers to finance publication of the magazine—in addition to sharing Mbajo's love for the arts and writing stories himself.[50] The core idea of their magazine was to create a set of comic characters representing popular stereotypes, such as the crook, the city loafer, the backwoodsman, the elder, the womanizer, and the city girl, and to dedicate each issue to a certain topical issue, for example, problems during public holidays, when people drank too much and family conflicts tended to arise. The magazine was meant to hold a mirror up to Tanzanians, who could then laugh at themselves and experience a kind of catharsis. In addition to comics, the magazine featured short stories, readers' letters, and pen friendships. It did very well, but Bawji, reportedly outsmarting Mbajo, broke the partnership after only four issues and became the sole owner of the company.[51] He continued *Sani* with other cartoonists, many of whom became very well known, as did the magazine itself.[52] The impact of *Sani* on the Tanzanian magazine culture was considerable. It broke the hold of the photo-magazine and created new reader expectations through its use of humor and satire. Other editors, including Katalambulla, followed this new trend by incorporating comics and cartoons into their magazines.

The Years 1980 to 1985: From Boom to Collapse

Increased literacy in Tanzania led to an increased demand for reading matter. In only five years, an impressive number of new magazines sprang up in the country, paradoxically in a time of increasing economic depression.[53] This was only possible through the continuing financial backing by and extensive distribution network of the Asian-Tanzanian businessmen. Manjwili and Mchome, editors of *New Film Azania*, established the first Swahili sports and culture magazine, *Misakato* (Pounding Movements) in mid-1980. It featured background articles on musicians, music bands (including some from Western countries), cultural groups, athletes, and sports teams. In addition, the magazine printed readers' letters and offered a Misakato Club for pen pals. During the interview in 2014, Manjwili could only laugh at their initial naïveté. For example, he said, they had no idea of columns but used the whole page "like in a letter." Professionalism was acquired through learning by doing and from advice by the printers.

In 1982, Manjwili's younger brother Barnaba Mbungo, together with Shaaban Scotto, founded the magazine *Wasaa* (Opportunity), which tried to inform its readers about political and social affairs. Scotto stated that they had to limit their scope to local news as the National News Agency (Shihata) held the monopoly on national news. Thus, an editorial on "modern agriculture," a government slogan since the Arusha Declaration, concluded by calling for better access to implements for peasants.[54] In other cases their approach was satirical: a comic showed a doctor who tells a poor man that he has no medicine, but gives it to his next patient, a pretty girl, in exchange for a date with her.[55] Such comments on societal problems bore risks, and sometimes the editors were ordered by security personnel present at the printers to remove articles. Nicco ye Mbajo launched his own magazine in 1980, naming it *Mcheshi* (The Humorist / The One Who Laughs) to express that he bore no grudge toward his former partner from *Sani*. *Mcheshi* became affiliated with Alidina, and Mbajo even got an office at Alidina's bookshop, where he did the artwork for his magazine. *Mcheshi* was initially a combination of the *Sani* concept and photo-stories for which Mbajo relied on choir members and his family as actors. However, the editor soon abandoned photo-stories altogether. The magazine *Cheka* (Laugh!), subtitled *Gazeti la Starehe la Tanzania* (Tanzanian Leisure Magazine), launched by Kassim Mussa Kassam concentrated on entertainment, including cartoons, short graphic stories, and serial fiction. SAM Kitogo continued this approach of mixed content with his *Johari* magazine, which he published through his company G. J. Publishers and Artists from 1981 onward. Hammie Rajab, who would become one of the "big names" in Swahili popular literature, established the bilingual *Busara-Wisdom* in 1981. Alidina even took on *Fahari*, an overtly political magazine launched by the journalist Fred Jim Mdoe.[56] One of the last magazines Alidina financed and distributed was *Heko* (Hurrah) by Ben R. Mtobwa, who later became a prominent editor, publisher, and writer of fiction.

The vast majority of the editors were not oppositional; on the contrary, as they told me, they felt they were *wazalendo* (patriots) and initially most were *wajamaa* (socialists). What emerged from the interviews is that they grew critical toward the government over time and with increasing economic problems but did not want to jeopardize their magazines. There were grievances in the society that they did not want to leave uncommented, but they usually voiced their criticism indirectly. The editor of *Mcheshi*, Mbajo, recalled that he was once summoned by the security because he had published a cartoon that showed a man eating alone in his house while a crowd of hungry people was watching him through the windows—certainly a subversive depiction of social reality in the country. Mbajo was admonished, and subsequently tried to avoid another clash. The incident shows that the government kept its eye on the private magazines and that the magazines had to walk a thin line.

Magazines and Book Production

The rise in the number of magazines was accompanied by an increasing production of popular fiction books, also financed and distributed by the Asian-Tanzanian businessmen. There was a curious correlation between magazine and book production. Inspired by the success of the magazines and needing books to sell, Alidina and Nayani approached editors and asked them if they would not be interested in writing books. The editors, many of them already authors, readily agreed. The difficult political and economic situation of the late 1970s and early 1980s thus paradoxically accounts for the sudden high output of fiction books.[57] In most cases, the books were published by their writers' own publishing houses and financed by Alidina or Nayani, while sometimes the writers published their books with other publishers.[58] In both cases, the agreement was that they would be paid royalties. The writers usually advertised their books in their magazines. The Tanzanian government was ambivalent toward this burgeoning of magazines and books. On the one hand, they contributed to the project of nation-building through promoting the national language, Swahili. And through their use of Swahili and their stories about ordinary Tanzanians, the publications could not be easily rejected as foreign or elitist. On the other hand, many of the magazines cultivated a distinct urban style, which the party regarded with suspicion.[59] Also, while the entertainment satisfied people's need for diversion and distracted from dissatisfaction, it was not really controllable—a state of affairs that could not be acceptable to a socialist administration aiming for greater regulations. When the paper shortage increased, it provided the government with a reason, if not a pretense, to repress the magazines. Printers were advised to give priority to official publications, and, consequently, the magazines could no longer be published on a regular basis. Alidina imported paper from Kenya a few times to print the magazines, but this was not a sustainable solution. On the other hand, these government regulations stimulated book production because book printing was exempted from the restrictions.

The final nail in the coffin came in 1985, when the fruitful partnership with Alidina and Nayani could not continue for political reasons. The boom ended as abruptly as it had started. Although President Julius Nyerere always "advocated race-blind policies that treated all citizens equally,"[60] Asian businesspeople still were the main target of campaigns against economic saboteurs that were launched in the late 1970s.[61] The aim of these campaigns was to prevent capital flight and the holding of large amounts of foreign currency, along with smuggling and hoarding scarce goods. In early 1983, the Economic Sabotage (Special Provisions) Act was decreed, and "the government launched a nationwide search campaign to seek out hoarded goods, detaining suspects and charging them before the special tribunals."[62] In April of the same year, "the National Assembly passed an Economic Crimes Bill, which instituted more special tribunals, harsh penalties, property seizures, and party and vigilante searches of suspected economic saboteurs."[63] Although the campaign did not reveal any large hoards, it did contribute crucially to racial animosities and increased insecurity among Asian-Tanzanians. Seeing their freedom and livelihood jeopardized, both Alidina and Nayani emigrated to Canada in 1985. There was nobody left to finance and distribute the magazines and books in Tanzania. The editors responded to the demise of their publications with great emotion. Manjwili stated that "tumeanguka wote" ("we all fell down"), while Mbajo even said that he felt as if his parent had died.

Repopulation of the Private Publishing Landscape

Given the difficult economic situation, some writers and editors gave up their magazines, among them Manjwili, Mchome, Mbajo, Mbega, Rajab, and Kamkanda. Moreover, most of them did not publish a single book afterward, even in better times. Mbajo turned to the Lutheran Church as a composer and choir leader and in 1994 became the editor of the church's magazine, *Pwani na Bara* (Coast and Hinterland).[64] Mchome made a career as a politician with the ruling party, while Manjwili did informal work, sometimes in relation with writing, sometimes not. The few magazines that had not depended on Alidina or Nayani, such as *Film Tanzania* and *Sani*, were not directly affected by the departure of the Asian-Tanzanian businessmen, but they too had a difficult time and could not appear regularly. The situation became better as domestic paper production started when Southern Paper Mills went into operation in late 1985. Editors and writers were able to find other financiers for the production of their magazines and books. However, distribution remained a big problem.

The time of the collapse of magazine and popular book production was also a turning point in Tanzanian politics. Under pressure from international donors and institutions and because the country had become one of the poorest in the world, President Nyerere admitted the failure of the socialist project and stepped down. His successor, Ali Hassan Mwinyi, elected in 1985, ushered in transition toward a capitalist market economy and multiparty democracy. This led to a gradual recovery of the private print sector. Kajubi Mukajanga established a new magazine, *Wakati ni Huu*

(This is the Time) in 1985, which together with Ben Mtobwa's *Heko* actively promoted Swahili literature through book reviews and authors' portraits.[65] Mbajo sold his *Mcheshi* to another editor who reanimated it in the 1990s with a new concept as a graphic magazine featuring erotic stories, a development that reflects the tremendous cultural changes that had come with liberalization. Similarly, a number of other magazines were borrowed, sold, or relaunched after a period of dormancy, and in the process sometimes changed their character profoundly. *Film Tanzania*, the first Tanzanian private entertainment magazine, occasionally tried a comeback but could not compete against the newer publications.[66] In 1993, Katalambulla launched a mixed-content magazine, *Upeo* (Horizon), which soon folded. In the 2000s, he concentrated on reprinting his books and sold the film rights of his novel *Simu ya Kifo*.

During the ten years of President Mwinyi's office, from 1985 to 1995, Tanzanian society underwent a profound transformation. With increased individual freedom, people wanted to know more about politics and the new possibilities, particularly at the time of the first multiparty elections in 1995. This was the time when people sought information rather than entertainment, and the magazines responded to that change. They kept entertainment as a feature of their papers, but increasingly included news, reports, and opinion articles. The magazine format, which in popular perception had become associated with entertainment, was gradually replaced by the tabloid format, which was associated with hard news and political information.[67] Many of the entertainment magazines such as *Heko* and *Wasaa* became important sources of information, particularly about oppositional parties and opinions, and flourished again.[68] Others woke from their dormancy, and a great number of new ones were registered. They played an important role in the democratization process, in Swahili called *mageuzi* (transformation), even at the price of becoming targets of state control. Most of the papers that were famous during the period of change discontinued publication because of the increasing engagement of big companies in the print media sector. Some of them folded, while others from the late 1990s onward changed back into predominantly entertainment tabloids modeled along the template of the British *Sun*. *Ijumaa*, one such tabloid, published by Global Publishers, currently the biggest publisher of entertainment tabloids in Tanzania, goes back to SAM Kitogo's *Johari*. Like the early editors, the owner of Global Publishers, Eric Shigongo, is also a writer who serializes epic novels in each of his papers.[69] *Sani* also became a tabloid, but it is the only magazine that through all periods and changes has survived till today with the same publisher and owner.[70]

244 • AFRICAN PRINT CULTURES

Fig. 4. Transformation of *Sani* from A4 magazine into tabloid. Left: no. 21 (12/1986), right: no. 963 (7-12/11/2012).

CONCLUSION

The entertainment magazines that flourished in the socialist era of postcolonial Tanzania were an important source of pleasure and information for the rising number of educated and urban citizens of the time. These magazines filled the void that had developed when Tanzanian national cultural politics blocked out Western culture, which was perceived as imperialist and decadent. By adapting the content of their magazines to local conditions, the writers and editors contributed to the slowly increasing urbanity of the socialist country: now its citizens had the opportunity to participate in the modern cultural practice of magazine consumption. Moreover, by localizing specific transnational templates such as *African Film* and *Joe* magazine, the editors gave their readers the chance to connect to cultures beyond their borders.

In a relatively short period of time, the editors formed a local intelligentsia in Dar es Salaam and cultivated an urban lifestyle when they met in bars and clubs, discussing books and business. While they were all creative, self-made editors, there were admittedly only a few pioneering innovators who adapted new formats from transnational templates. Thus a steady interplay of innovation and imitation characterized the development of the entertainment magazines. The state accepted the magazines as seemingly harmless entertainment, and the magazines thus existed in a niche where they were tolerated but monitored. The state felt secure that there would never be extensive magazine production because financing was difficult and distribution could not be managed by the editors themselves. Indeed, for a long time there was only one magazine available: Katalambulla's *Film Tanzania*. However, the economic deterioration of the late 1970s rather surprisingly provided the breeding ground for cooperation between the editors and Asian-Tanzanian businessmen. Moreover, this cooperation contributed substantially to the creation of a body of popular fiction books that are now considered classics. The role of the Asian-Tanzanian businessmen in the development of Swahili popular literature, previously overlooked, must therefore be recognized.

The above realizations offer first insights into the content and production of Swahili magazines in socialist Tanzania. Further scholarly research, however, is needed to illuminate a number of issues in more detail. For example, the content and form of the magazines need to be more fully analyzed. Additionally, a closer look must be paid to the social function of these magazines and the fluid boundaries between entertainment and critical discourse. The magazines' reception by their readers, and their place among other forms of urban leisure, also need further investigation. Above all, the nexus between these magazines and Swahili popular literature calls for further research.

The entertainment magazines must be acknowledged as the sites where literary works of their editor-writers were published. Often these works were presented in a multitude of forms, thanks to the rotational approach that was initiated and popularized by Katalambulla. But whatever the form, the emphasis was always on storytelling, and the editors created a solid core of Swahili popular literature. Indeed, the legacy of their magazines and their books is palpable today in the works of contemporary Tanzanian popular writers.

REFERENCES

Aminzade, Ronald. *Race, Nation and Citizenship in Post-colonial Africa: The Case of Tanzania*. New York: Cambridge University Press, 2013.

Askew, Kelly M. *Performing the Nation: Swahili Music and Cultural Politics in Tanzania*. Chicago: University of Chicago Press, 2002.

Beez, Jigal. "Stupid Hares and Margarine: Early Swahili Comics." In *Cartooning in Africa*, edited by John A. Lent, 137–57. Cresskill, NJ: Hampton Press, 2009.

Bertoncini Zúbková, Elena. "Contemporary Prose Fiction: The Tanzanian Mainland. From the 1960s to the 1980s." In *Outline of Swahili Literature: Prose Fiction and Drama*, 2nd ed., edited by Elena Bertoncini Zúbková et al., 74–117. Boston: Brill, 2009.

Bertoncini Zúbková, Elena, et al. *Outline of Swahili Literature: Prose Fiction and Drama*. 2nd ed. Boston: Brill, 2009.

Bgoya, Walter. *Books and Reading in Tanzania*. Paris: UNESCO, n.d. [ca. 1985].

Frederiksen, Bodil Folke. "Joe, the Sweetest Reading in Africa: Documentation and Discussion of a Popular Magazine in Kenya." *African Languages and Cultures* 4, no. 2 (1991): 135–55.

Ivaska, Andrew. 2011. *Cultured States: Youth, Gender and Modern Style in Dar es Salaam*. Durham, NC: Duke University Press, 2011.

Katalambulla, Faraji H. H. *Pendo Pevu*. Dar es Salaam: East African Literature Bureau, 1976.

Katalambulla, Faraji H. H. *Picha ya Pacha*. Dar es Salaam: Film Tanzania Publications, 2007.

Katalambulla, Faraji H. H. *Simu ya Kifo*. Dar es Salaam: East African Literature Bureau, 1965.

Katalambulla, Faraji H. H., and Mark Lemki. *Pili Pilipili*. Dar es Salaam: East African Literature Bureau, 1977.

Krings, Matthias. "A Prequel to Nollywood: South African Photo Novels and Their Pan-African Consumption in the Late 1960s." *Journal of African Cultural Studies* 22, no. 1 (2010): 75–89.

Lange, Siri. "Managing Modernity: Gender, State and Nation in the Popular Drama of Dar es Salaam, Tanzania." PhD dissertation, Department of Social Anthropology, University of Bergen, Norway, 2002.

Meisler, Stanley. "Look-Reads." *Africa Report* 14, nos. 5–6 (1969): 80–83.

Mwaffisi, Maurice S. "Broadcasting in Tanzania: Case Study of a Broadcasting System." MA thesis, University of Washington, 1985.

Reuster-Jahn, Uta. "Newspaper Serials in Tanzania: The Case of Eric James Shigongo (with an Interview)." *Swahili Forum* 15 (2008): 25–50.

Reuster-Jahn, Uta. "Vom mündlichen Erzählen zum Internetroman: Transmediale Kommunikation und Interaktion von Rezipienten in Tansania." In *Medien—Erzählen—Gesellschaft: Transmediales Erzählen im Zeitalter der Medienkonvergenz*, edited by Karl N. Renner et al., 163–87. Boston: de Gruyter, 2013.

Sturmer, Martin. *The Media History of Tanzania*. Ndanda, Tanzania: Ndanda Mission Press, 1998.

NOTES TO CHAPTER EIGHT

1. See Andrew Ivaska, *Cultured States: Youth, Gender and Modern Style in Dar es Salaam* (Durham, NC: Duke University Press, 2011) and Ronald Aminzade, *Race, Nation and Citizenship in Post-colonial Africa: The Case of Tanzania* (New York: Cambridge University Press, 2013), 185–92.

2. Interviews in Swahili were conducted in Dar es Salaam with the following editors: Faraji H. H. Katalambulla (6 August 2010), Andrew Manjwili (6 March 2014), Nicco ye Mbajo (20 August 2010, 5 March 2014), SAM Kitogo (25 February 2014, 10 March 2014), Shaaban Scotto (28 February 2014). All translations not otherwise attributed are the author's.

3. There is a restricted availability of magazines, as they were not systematically archived. None of the editors interviewed had even a single copy left.

4. For a detailed analysis of cultural politics in Tanzania see Kelly Askew, *Performing the Nation: Swahili Music and Cultural Politics in Tanzania* (Chicago: University of Chicago Press, 2002).

5. See Ivaska, *Cultured States*, 5.

6. Parliament of Tanzania, *Parliamentary Debates of March 16th 1965*, Dar es Salaam. Quoted from Maurice S. Mwaffisi, "Broadcasting in Tanzania: Case Study of a Broadcasting System," MA thesis, University of Washington, 1985, 60.

7. As Karin Barber shows in this volume, a similar period of experimentation characterized the early development of Yoruba newspapers in Nigeria.

8. This information and other references in this section to Katalambulla's life and works are, if not otherwise stated, based on the interview conducted with him in 2010 in Dar es Salaam, or derived from his magazine.

9. On the early history of *Kiongozi*, see Martin Sturmer, *The Media History of Tanzania* (Ndanda, Tanzania: Ndanda Mission Press, 1998), 70, 89, 104.

10. *Baraza* was published by the East African Standard Ltd., and *Taifa Weekly* by East African Newspaper Ltd.

11. The Catholic Church of Tanzania founded its Institute of Publicity Media in Mwanza in 1963, which provided a basic course in journalism; see Sturmer, *Media History of Tanzania*, 151.

12. See Sturmer, *Media History of Tanzania*, 107.

13. The EALB was established in 1948 to promote literature production in East Africa, particularly in Swahili.

14. This English translation is Katalambulla's own, which he added to his book's title. The literal translation of *Simu ya Kifo* is "death call."

15. Elena Bertoncini Zúbková, "Contemporary Prose Fiction: The Tanzanian Mainland. From the 1960s to the 1980s," in *Outline of Swahili Literature: Prose Fiction and Drama*, 2nd ed., ed. Elena Bertoncini Zúbková et al. (Leiden: Brill, 2009), 101.

16. See the list in the revised edition of *Simu ya Kifo*, published by Katalambulla's Film Tanzania Publications, Dar es Salaam, 2004.

17. *African Film* was the name of the West and East African editions of the South African *Spear* magazine in which references to apartheid South Africa were erased. See Stanley Meisler, "Look-Reads," *Africa Report* 14, nos. 5–6 (1969): 80–81.

18. Matthias Krings, "A Prequel to Nollywood: South African Photo Novels and Their Pan-African Consumption in the Late 1960s," *Journal of African Cultural Studies* 22, no. 1 (2010): 75.

19. Krings, "Prequel to Nollywood," 84–86.

20. Krings, "Prequel to Nollywood," 87.

21. See Krings, "Prequel to Nollywood," 80, 88.

22. For details on Swahili houses see Siri Lange, "Managing Modernity: Gender, State and Nation in the Popular Drama of Dar es Salaam, Tanzania," PhD dissertation, University of Bergen, Norway, 2002, 26–29.

23. Ivaska, *Cultured States*.

24. See Ivaska, *Cultured States*, 60–66, 86–123.

25. This was expressed by all editors interviewed. See also Sturmer, *Media History of Tanzania*, 119.

26. *Film Tanzania* 106 (1979): 1.

27. *Film Tanzania* 115 (1980): 1.

28. See also Barber, this volume, on "addressivity" as a feature of Nigerian Yoruba newspapers.

29. *Film Tanzania* 137, back cover.

30. Katalambulla in interview from 6 August 2010. Writer-reader interaction is a continuous feature of Swahili magazines and serial stories, rooted in oral storytelling practices; see Uta Reuster-Jahn, "Vom mündlichen Erzählen zum Internetroman: Transmediale Kommunikation und Interaktion von Rezipienten in Tansania," in *Medien—Erzählen—Gesellschaft*, ed. Karl N. Renner et al. (Berlin: de Gruyter, 2013), 163–87.

31. See Rebecca Jones, this volume, on Nigerian editors' "sociability in print."

32. Almost all of Katalambulla's books of the 1970s were published with the EALB.

33. Except the play *Pili Pilipili*, which, according to Katalambulla, never was adapted as a photonovel, and *Simu ya Kifo*, where the book preceded the photonovel.

34. Bertoncini Zúbková, "Contemporary Prose Fiction," 102.

35. Ganzel (1946–2001) used to serialize novels in newspapers, above all in the Kenyan *Taifa Weekly*, but also published some of his thrillers as books between 1972 and 1981; see Bertoncini Zúbková et al., "Outline of Swahili Literature," 241.

36. The publisher, Tamasha Publications in Dar es Salaam, also published most of Ganzel's books, which suggests that he was its owner. No clear information is so far available.

37. Krings, "Prequel to Nollywood."

38. See Gbagedesin, this volume.

39. This section is based on interviews with Manjwili and Katalambulla (see note 2).

40. Walter Bgoya, *Books and Reading in Tanzania* (Paris: UNESCO, n.d. [ca. 1985]), 33.

41. Idi Amin expelled all Ugandans of Asian descent in 1972.

42. This section is based on interviews with Manjwili, Kitogo, Scotto, and Mbajo (see note 2).

43. *New Film Azania* 14 (1982): 10.

44. See Askew, this volume.

45. Idi Amin ordered Ugandan military to invade the northwestern Tanzanian region of Kagera in October 1978. This provoked the second Uganda-Tanzanian war.

46. See *Equator Film*, no number, ca. 1981, 22, 25.

47. This section is based on the interviews with Mbajo (see note 2).

48. A pen name derived from the editor's real name, Nicodemus Yehoswa Mbajo.

49. *Joe* magazine existed between 1973 and 1979; see Bodil F. Frederiksen, "Joe, the Sweetest Reading in Africa: Documentation and Discussion of a Popular Magazine in Kenya," *African Languages and Cultures* 4, no. 2 (1991): 135–55.

50. The name *Sani* was made up from the first two letters of the editors' first names.

51. The publisher of *Sani* is the company WAMASA (Watoaji wa Maandishi ya Sani [Publishers of the Texts of *Sani*]).

52. See Jigal Beez, "Stupid Hares and Margarine: Early Swahili Comics," in *Cartooning in Africa*, ed. John A. Lent (Cresskill, NJ: Hampton Press, 2009), 137–57.

53. This and the following two sections are based on information obtained through the interviews with all editors (see note 2).

54. *Wasaa* 5 (December 1986): 2.

55. *Wasaa* 5 (December 1986): 7.

56. According to Sturmer (*Media History of Tanzania*, 218), *Fahari* was registered in 1978 and came off the presses in 1981.

57. Between 1980 and 1985, the editors published many books. At a minimum: K. Mukajanga (four), K. Chande (three), N. Mbajo (seven), SAM Kitogo (four), G. Mchome (three), O. Mbega (one), K. Kassam (four), H. Rajab (sixteen). Eddie Ganzel had one book printed and others reprinted and distributed by Nayani.

58. A number of books were published by Press and Publicity Centre, which belonged to Mohamedali Manji, also of Asian descent.

59. Ivaska, *Cultured States*.

60. Aminzade, *Race, Nation and Citizenship*, 208.

61. Aminzade, *Race, Nation and Citizenship*, 232.

62. Aminzade, *Race, Nation and Citizenship*, 233.

63. Aminzade, *Race, Nation and Citizenship*, 233.

64. *Pwani na Bara* initially existed between 1910 and 1916, and was revived in 1978; see Sturmer, *Media History of Tanzania*, 38–40, 44. In 2012, its name was changed to *Upendo* (Love).

65. Kajubi Mukajanga and Ben Mtobwa later became prominent figures in Tanzanian journalism. Mukajanga was appointed Executive Secretary of the Media Council of Tanzania in 2008. His magazine *Wakati ni Huu* existed until the mid-1990s. *Heko* folded two years before Ben Mtobwa's death in November 2008.

66. In contrast to the information given by Sturmer (1998, 219) about fortnightly publication of *Film Tanzania* in the 1990s, only a few issues were published between 1990 and 2006. No. 141 (2006) was the last issue before Katambulla's death in 2012.

67. During the socialist period, all Swahili newspapers were in tabloid format.

68. *Wasaa* supported the oppositional party NCCR-Mageuzi.

69. See Uta Reuster-Jahn, "Newspaper Serials in Tanzania: The Case of Eric James Shigongo (with an Interview)," *Swahili Forum* 15 (2008): 25–50.

70. After Saidi Bawji's death in 1993, WAMASA, and *Sani* with it, were continued by his younger brothers.

CHAPTER 9

"True to Life"

Illuminating the Processes and
Modes of Yoruba Photoplays

OLUBUKOLA A. GBADEGESIN

Derived from established Yoruba popular theater practices that preceded them, photoplays were introduced to Nigerian audiences during a period of cultural transformation and political instability.[1] Within a decade of attaining independence from Great Britain in 1960, Nigeria had experienced the first of many coups, and civil war loomed on the horizons. Amid these political struggles, individuals and institutions alike sought participatory inclusion in modern globalized culture and world economies in myriad ways. To a certain extent, photoplays satisfied these aspirations. In form and content, photoplays were tangible symbols of modernity that delivered narratives about the challenges of that very modernity against the backdrop of existing traditional codes and practices. Much like popular theater, photoplays provided sustaining and sustained discursive environments through which audiences and performers alike could actively make sense of their lived experiences in meaningful and enduring ways. To explore this point, I approach these photoplays as "texts" that enacted, and were enacted by, the collective assumptions of their interpretive community and its power differentials.

Theoretically, this chapter is informed by Karin Barber's "generative" critical analysis of popular theater practices, which examined how lives, practices, and knowledge produced ideas and texts, thereby revealing "every moment and every level of production [as] a site of creative potentiality."[2] But rather than transpose Barber's insightful analyses onto the overlooked corpus of photoplays, I seek to examine how the "creative potentiality" that she attributes to popular theater practices was complicated and amplified in the production processes, expressive modes, and cocreative audiences convened by the photoplays. Though deeply conversant with popular theater practices, photoplays had their own unique, generative processes that mingled with, reconfigured, and rivaled those of the popular theater plays.[3] Although much of Barber's critical interventions with popular theater placed the practice in dialectical opposition to literacy (i.e., photoplays as "*written* representations" of "orally generated dramas"), this correlation drastically underestimates the sovereign value of photoplays as densely constituted, meaning-producing *texts*.[4] Photoplays manifest the "virtual literacy" to which, Barber argues, popular theater practices aspired. Moreover, I argue that by commingling multiple expressive modes, photoplays functioned beyond the limited written/oral dyad and entered into the crucial tetrad of the sonic (oral and aural), literary (written), visual (photographic), and kinetic (performative).[5] The interplay of these modes further iterates the "open and incorporative" nature of "many West African cultural forms" and situates photoplays within that legacy.[6] In large part because of their genealogical relationship to this heritage, photoplays cultivated dynamic, mutually demanding, and cocritical audiences around dominant moral themes that were articulated in layered mythical, political, and social narratives. At its core, this chapter examines how photoplays contributed to and transformed the sense-making processes and practices of their audiences.

BIRTH OF PHOTOPLAYS

While performative practices in Nigeria have been examined in depth, the published counterparts of these practices have been significantly less studied.[7] In one of the earliest scholarly essays on photonovels in Africa, Matthias Krings argued that these photonovels (also known as photocomics) had roots in cinematically inspired *fotoromanzi* and *cineromanzi* formats that emerged in postwar Italy in the early 1930s.[8] These early European formats migrated along colonial channels of cultural exchange to France, Spain, and South America in the late 1940s before they finally appeared in South African markets in the 1960s, where they were adopted by Drum Publications.[9] Although the renowned publishing house experimented with the format throughout the 1950s, it did not produce stand-alone photonovels for African audiences until the late 1960s. Drum Publications' first stride into this arena was *African Film*, an iconic crime-busters serial, illustrated with sequential and midaction photographs, arranged in graphic panels, and narrated with caption boxes, thought, and speech bubbles. Known in South Africa as "look-reads,"[10] photonovels like *African Film* enjoyed expansive distribution and enthusiastic readership across the continent from Ghana to Kenya, much like the publishers' flagship magazine, *Drum*.[11] Importantly, Saint observes that "South African photocomic producers followed European examples by both revamping Italian ones for South African consumption . . . and by producing their own series of photocomics." Indeed, *African Film* broke from the precedent of all-white actors in Italian *fotoromanzi* and instead featured a cast of majority black African actors in its photonovels. As politically impactful as this modification was to an apartheid-era readership, it did not structurally challenge the generic, Eurocentric origins of the format. The casting changes emphasized the Africanness of the characters in the photonovel and downplayed its colonial influences, presumably in an attempt to sidestep growing antiapartheid sentiments among targeted black audiences.

Even though South Africa's *African Film* was not radically different in narrative or format from Italian predecessors, its localized modern, consumerist, and cinematic overtones made it incredibly appealing to the predominantly youthful African audiences who bought and read the series. Saint contextualizes the production and consumption of the photonovel in apartheid-era South Africa while also examining how the popular subgenre of the American Western undermined the illusion of absolute racial segregation.[12] She suggests that in South Africa, photonovels "traveled more freely than humans across the racial divides cemented and policed by the apartheid state. The cover tales they [told] about race in their plots, aesthetics, and in the networks of consumption they precipitated [forged] interracial relations (at least at the imaginative level), even while their segregated format seemed to foreclose this."[13] At least in this South African context, it seemed that photonovels offered a subversive yet accessible way for audiences to engage with their sociopolitical realities through a theatrical play of ideas. To this point, photonovels and their derivatives thrived insofar as they conversed with their audience and responded to the milieu in which they existed.[14]

In a Yoruba market already experiencing a successful and widely popular theater naissance, *African Film* was popular but lacked the cultural specificity and active engagement to which Yoruba audiences were accustomed. When photonovels were reconfigured into photoplays, they paraphrased the evanescent syntax of the emergent theatrical vernacular and added much more.

Like theatrical precursors, photoplays were inspired by the convergences of modernist impulses, pan-ethnic cultural interests, and nascent national political subjectivities. These convergences were evident in the folkloric, magical, melodramatic, and comedic narratives of popular plays and photoplays alike.

POLITICAL AND PERFORMATIVE INFLUENCES OF A NASCENT REPUBLIC

The decade leading up to Nigeria's independence from Great Britain in 1960 was a watershed period when important policy initiatives and crucial dialogues on identity were under way. In particular, ethno-nationalists proposed radical education initiatives and social welfare ideas designed to promote pan-Yoruba ethnic solidarity in southwest Nigeria. Under the leadership of Ọbafẹmi Awolọwọ, Action Group championed literacy and launched a free primary school education scheme. Education was framed as the key to successful postindependence economic prosperity, participatory democracy, and ethnic solidarity. Language (as ethnic identifier) and education were two primary foci of the ethno-nationalist movement. In fact, the proliferation and popularity of Yoruba-language novels, plays, and poetry from the 1940s through the late 1960s can be traced to these political agendas. In her seminal text, Ẹbun Clark observes that during this independence period, there was an awareness of "the importance of a Nigerian theatre existing not only as a vehicle for entertainment and social comment but also as a platform for political action and education."[15] This awareness was particularly evident in the predominantly Yoruba southwestern region of Nigeria, where Hubert Ogunde innovated a contemporary popular theater practice featuring professional actors, indoor proscenium stages, and secular public patrons.[16] Deeply rooted in Yoruba performative practices, this contemporary popular theater became an important vehicle for Yoruba cultural associations and nationalist political organizations that campaigned for independence and competed to fill the voids of leadership left by British withdrawal.

These popular plays inspired several related streams—radio programs, video-films, and photoplays—that were born from the dramatic wellspring of live drama. Enduring in their own rights, these artistic tributaries nourished each other even as they made discrete interventions into the theatrical realm. Reliant on the purely sonic—a simultaneous limitation and uniqueness—radio programs were most likely to reach isolated rural audiences using captivating dialogue and narratives that could animate the story through primarily sonic mode. Like radio, video-films interfaced with audiences through technologies that engendered a sense of participatory modernity. Video-film—the juggernaut form that would overtake even popular theater—was incredibly successful at fusing "tradition" and modernity, reality and fantasy, while its material commodity status gave audiences literal "ownership" where direct interpolation was absent. Photoplays, however, interjected a discrete literary element absent in its affiliate forms, while also paraphrasing the unique mediations—written, visual, sonic, kinetic—that these other forms offered.

The first and longest-running title, *Yoruba Photoplay Series* were first published in 1967 when independence exuberance had begun to wane and postcolonial reforms and promises had started to fail.[17] By this period, the first in a long line of military coups had already occurred and set the Biafran conflict into motion. Against the backdrop of this political foment, photoplays flourished.

WHAT'S IN A NAME? TRACING THE EVOLVING TERMS OF PHOTOPLAYS

Despite the increasing upheaval in the Nigeria political landscape, a number of economic sectors, such as publishing, continued to thrive. Indeed, Drum Publication and *African Film* did not enjoy complete hegemony over anglophone popular publishing industries: local spaces where homegrown presses often thrived and had fingers on the pulse of the immediate cultural and political economy. Though it enjoyed less visibility than its South African counterpart, Lagos-based West African Book Publishers (WABP) had points in common with, as well as advantages over, Drum Publications. Like Drum, the WABP was owned by an expatriate, American businessman Richard Ian Gamble, who immediately saw the need to have a versatile local editor at helm of the venture and appraised the potential market for locally produced and focused publications.[18] Gamble hired Ṣẹgun Ṣofọwọtẹ, a media luminary based in Ibadan, whose incomparable experiences—as a member Wọle Ṣoyinka's 1960 Masks, a producer with the WMTV station, print advertiser, radio announcer with Nigerian Television Service (NTS), and copywriter—uniquely equipped him to launch the WABP's two inaugural projects; *Magnet: The Nigerian Photoplay Magazine* and the *Yoruba Photoplay Series*, which was known as *Atọka: The Yoruba Photoplay Series* by 1971.[19] The titles given to these projects provide valuable insight into how the photoplays were distinguished from the photonovel genre and made conversant with Yoruba audiences and expectations.

Under production in 1967—a full year before *African Film* was published in 1968—the *Magnet* photocomic serial seemed to be an inevitable experiment inspired by the serialized photocomics found in the *Nigeria Drum* edition. Starring Johnny "Thunderman" Nelson and based in Nigeria, *Magnet* was entirely written in English and uncannily similar to *African Film* in visual and narrative content. The full title of the photocomic read *Magnet: The Nigerian Photoplay Magazine*. Although the subtitle is often ignored or dropped in references to the publication, it provides insights into how the WABP conceived of the text.[20] While *Magnet* was not a true "photo*play*" (in that it was not derived from a theatrical/cinematic source), the descriptor was used to distinguish the WABP's early publications from the generic (and often foreign) "photonovel." Moreover, as the *Nigerian* photoplay magazine, *Magnet* made a claim to national identity and inclusive Nigerianness that emphatically set it apart from the generically named *African Film*. Conversely, the decision to make its sister publication a Yoruba-language text and title it the *Yoruba Photoplay Series* emphasized the pan-ethnic or ethno-nationalist tenor of the fortnightly magazine. Even though the thematic arcs in the magazine addressed issues intended to resonate over varied cultural or moral terrains, the title of the magazine firmly grounded it in a pan-ethnic production that linked it to an immediate Yoruba audience.[21] In spite of their distinct nationalist mandates, these two titles worked in concert to support and promote each other. To this point, before its official release, *Magnet* was promoted in the first volume of the *Yoruba Photoplay Series* along with products from advertisers whose sponsorship supported the enterprise.

The seemingly innocuous editorial decision to prefix the Yoruba word *Atọka*—translated as "the act of pointing a finger at"—to the *Yoruba Photoplay Series* tethered the publication to a Yoruba-centric project, and further distinguished it from photonovels originating from other parts of the continent. At a time when there was need for critique and so much appetite for original entertainment, *Atọka* satisfied both. With this new title, the magazine was branded as an apparatus of social commentary that scrutinized individual, institutional, or cultural shortcomings, using a disarmingly comic/satirical manner. The photoplays linguistically convened the readership with standard Yoruba; a constructed dialect that was stripped of subethnic partiality and

Fig. 1. Advertisement for "Magnet: The Nigerian Photoplay Magazine" in Yoruba Ronu, vol. 1, no. 1 (Lagos, Nigeria: West African Book Publishers, 1967; unpaginated).

quickly became the most widely known and read, largely because of the free primary school education curriculum. The language itself became a "tethering post for even more expanded cultural allegiances" that allowed the photoplays to engage a pan-Yoruba constituency—and even more, expanded the potential commercial readership base from which the WABP could draw.[22] As Barber suggests, the mere fact of being addressed in standard Yoruba was as important as the content of the communication itself. The nature and manner of linguistic encounter in the photoplays contributed to the way in which readers constituted *themselves* as a form of collectivity, brought together by the photoplays. Nnodim describes a period when poetic audience address shifted from an immediate space to a more translocal range.[23] Indeed, the success of the photoplays was predicated on their ability to reach broader, translocal readers, and the serial did so by using standard Yoruba—which was broadly appealing to multiple dialects—to capture a wider swath of potential readers in a linguistic dragnet, and reconstituting them as a reading public through the photoplays.

Even though the photoplays were modeled on *African Film* photonovels, they were reconfigured for predominantly Yoruba audiences that often referred to them as *iwe alaworan* (picture book).[24] Inherent within the term *alaworan* is a sense of active, visual engagement with pictorial material that challenges the strict understanding of *iwe* (book) as a written, passively read literary text. Moreover, the term privileges the pictorial material as the primary mechanism of narrative transmission, without abandoning the denotative or prestige value of script. With an increasingly, but not all together, literate readership, it was undoubtedly vital that the concept of "reading public" not be limited to text/script—but rather, include images that could be "read," as well.[25] Perhaps, it is unsurprising then that *iwe alaworan* is such a close cognate with *iwe aworan* (photo album). After all, photoplays are choreographed similarly as photo albums—one of several already familiar texts through which *audiences* made sense of the visual codes and conventions based on cultural and personal assumptions. Arranged like photographs in an album, the midaction frames in photoplays were read across the gutters that separated each panel. As readers' eyes moved from one panel to the next, readers reflexively animated the narratives through the interplay of sequentially arranged, yet distinct, images.[26] Though these photographs were mediated by text and other elements—which are discussed later—the fact that the comic design of photoplays was located within an already conversant visual genealogy that included photo albums and other genres) was crucial to engaging its interpretive community in the texts. Importantly the appellations that have been assigned to these photoplays are revealing of how publishers, editors, and audiences understood and situated these texts within their existing repertoires.

(RE)MAKING THE PLAYS: PARSING THE PHOTOPLAY PRODUCTION PROCESS

Photoplays were born from complex production processes that were informed by, yet rivaled, those of popular theater.[27] Like the popular plays, the photoplays were inspired by aggregate sources and reconstituted by various editors and editorial layers. As with the photoplays (which centered around the editor), the making of the popular plays hinged around the theater troupe leaders, who "began by 'getting an idea' from the sea of possibilities surrounding them in popular narrative, personal anecdotes, print fiction, traditional legend, and the plays of other theatre companies, as well as their own past experiences."[28] In this initial editorial layer, the troupe leader synthesized different source "texts" to create a unique script idea that became the "working tool" or "working text" for the production.[29] Then troupe actors were invited to collaboratively develop the idea by bringing the characters to life, fleshing out the scenes and, ultimately, producing a collective product through a process of rehearsals, rearticulations, and revisions. Unlike with the photoplays, the scripts for popular plays were rarely ever written down, and the "working text" continually evolved with each staging.[30] The photoplays intervened in this revising cycle, suspending it long enough to distill the cumulative effect of the actors' organic gestures, expressions, and speeches into densely packed, still images that could be visually grasped and reanimated by the readers. Rooted in these deeply visual performances, photoplays underscored the endurance, formal pliability, and the audience-convening potential of these texts while allowing for alternative (but just as participatory) means for readers to deploy these texts.[31]

From the onset, the production process was overseen by Ṣẹgun Ṣofọwọtẹ, the primary editor of the photoplay series, who had extensive background experience in theater, television, production, and advertising.[32] During the process, he took on the responsibilities of the troupe leader—who may have been present but was subordinate to the editor in this context.[33] In this capacity, Ṣofọwọtẹ reworked (and *wrote out*) scripts, codirected the actors, recast roles, and selected costumes and makeup.[34] The troupe staged the play, making print-friendly changes where necessary, and halting intermittently to allow photographs to be taken. In order to adapt the play to a photoplay format, Ṣofọwọtẹ made executive creative decisions that often altered the plot. However, for some changes, he conferred with troupe members—who had a performative experience—and with codirector and photographer Abimbade Oladẹjọ—who had a visual perspective. Importantly, rather than simply impose his own vision onto the actors; Ṣofọwọtẹ amplified the collective editing work that already characterized popular theater practices. This deliberative method interpenetrated three distinct spheres of artistic production: the literary, the theatrical, and the photographic.[35] In straddling these multiple realms, photoplays amplified the potential for creative interventions beyond that of popular theater alone.

INTRICACIES OF MODES

While the photoplay is typically analyzed through a visual/text dyad, I argue that this format engaged with the complex tetrad of the sonic (oral and aural), literary (written), visual (photographic) and kinetic (performative). To this point, this chapter is primarily concerned with those expressive modes of the photoplays that were circumscribed by these production processes.

Nowhere was the literary aspect of this modal tetrad more pronounced than in *Ọmuti* (vol. 3). The illustrated banner on the title introduced the photoplay as a unique, discrete work in and of itself while also crediting the cocreative parties that made it possible: "This is a play by Kọla Ogunmọla and his troupe. . . . We extracted it from the fictional story 'Palm Wine Drinkard' which Amos Tutuọla wrote in English." This inscription not only recognized Amos Tutuọla for originating the story, but also salutes the troupe leader, Kọla Ogunmọla, and his troupe of actors for their parts in reimagining the novel as *Ọmuti*. This example of shared creative collaboration supports Barber's contention that "Yoruba oral and written texts deeply interpenetrated, through mutual incorporation, quotation, emulation, and representation. The common people, not the educated elite, had command of it."[36] In this particular instance, it seemed that the blurring of the lines between the literary author (Tutuọla), the theatrical author (Ogunmọla), and the troupe allowed for an informal reinvention of the *Palm Wine Drinkard* that implicated "the common people" (audience) as well. Notably, all of these parties were equally credited.[37] The most popular and recognizable collaborators involved in the creative process got top billing for authorial credit for the photoplays. Audiences cared more about those names than they did about those of mediators (like Ṣofọwọtẹ and Ọladẹjọ) who created the photoplays, and the authorial credits knowingly reflected this awareness. Thus, photoplays acknowledged authorship in a manner similar enough to popular plays so as to orient audiences to the new format.

The literary tangle of the photoplay was further complicated when series editor Ṣegun Ṣofọwọtẹ took pen to paper to create his own original photoplay titled *Asiko Na To* (vol. 19). While the previous photoplays had been adapted from the repertoires of various popular theater troupes, *Asiko Na To* was a play originally *intended* for print. Here Ṣofọwọtẹ was not only the originator of the *idea* but also the writer/transcriber of the photoplay *script*. Perhaps his previous experience as a scriptwriter explains why this photoplay was more verbose than any other before it, such that the speech bubbles seemed barely

"True to Life" • 261

Fig. 2. Banner Inscription in "Omuti", vol. 3, no.1 (Lagos, Nigeria: West African Book Publishers, 1968), 1.

able to contain long lines of dialogue. The cover page further elaborates the authorial relationships at play: "asiko na to! ere ṣegun ṣofọwọte kan ti iṣola ogunṣola ati awọn elere rẹ ṣe" ("the time is now! a play by ṣegun ṣofọwọte performed by iṣola ogunṣola and his troupe").

As expected, primacy is given to the title of the photoplay, which is emblazoned in the largest font in this main header. Reading on, it is apparent that even though Ṣegun Ṣofọwọte's name comes first, it is printed in noticeably smaller font size than that of Iṣola Ogunṣola. The troupe members are recognized passingly as *awọn elere rẹ* (his [Ogunṣola's] actors). Presumably, Ṣofọwọte's play could not have been staged without Ogunṣola's willingness to make his troupe available for the rehearsals and the subsequent photo-shoot. Thus, even though his name is listed second, Ogunṣola's is integral to this process as troupe procurer and for his name recognition. With these subtly written cues, this header suggests how authorial credit ought to be weighted within the complicated creative matrices of the photoplays. Here, though the process remains largely collaborative, certain contributors are foregrounded in a manner that implies some hierarchy of author-ity.

The visual parameters of the photoplay are extended in drawings that poignantly illustrate the essential core of various narratives and serve as creative counterpoints to the photographs. For instance, the splash page of *Ọmuti* features a caricature-like sketch of a rotund man—his diminutive appendages dwarfed by his massive torso—slumped before an oversized calabash of palm wine from which he drinks. The drawing is a visual opening to the narrative, a reminder of the fictive project at hand and the varied modes of visuality deployed in these texts. Immediately beneath this sketch is a larger splash panel containing the photo-realistic version of the same drunken character. Here, sitting in front of another oversized calabash and laughing with his friends, he is brought to life through the positivist veracity projected by the photograph. The juxtaposition of the sketch with this photographic panel seems to suggest that the photoplays function within the liminal spaces between the real and the fictive.

Although most of the photographs in the photoplays were unadulterated, carefully staged shots, some volumes experimented with altered images. In the second issue of *Ọmuti*, several photographs were manually modified to produce a particularly magical effect demanded by the narrative. In one instance, a persistent, amorous young woman, Bisi, is lured into the woods and captured by a "family of skulls" intent on cannibalizing her. To render this visual effect, rudimentary skeletal figures were hand-drawn onto the photographs and actors' heads were closely cropped and pasted atop these illustrations. The monochromatic tones of the black-and-white photograph camouflaged the seams of these spliced images so that in a reading glance they appeared to be captures of true sight. As these supernatural hybrids interacted convincingly with the "real" actors in the scene, the lines are blurred between realism and fiction.[38] These postproduction edits show how resourcefully photoplays manipulated visual methods to mediate an imaginative intimacy and sense-making between the audience and the narrative.

Photoplays were an enlightening cultural text, but they were also a commercial endeavor that relied on advertising and sales to survive: nowhere was this consumerist nature clearer than in the advertisements within their pages.[39] Most advertisements featured photographs of urbane models hawking products like schnapps, wigs, vitamins, beer, recombined milk, and malaria meds—modestly priced imported goods that might appeal to the wide range of potential consumers that the photoplays attracted. To engage these patrons, advertisers not only used Yoruba-language text to promote their merchandise, they also adapted to the visual idiom of the

Fig. 3. "Omuti", vol. 3, no. 1(Lagos, Nigeria: West African Book Publishers, 1968), 14.

photoplays, using overlapping pictorial strategies to redirect readers toward their products.

Some advertisements used hand-drawn comic forms, several used a combination of illustrations and photographs, and one in particular used the same sequential photographic approach as the photoplay itself. In Hubert Ogunde's *Awo Mimọ* (vol. 7) the advertising campaign for the pain reliever Cafenol was strikingly aligned with the visual aesthetic of the photoplays. At first glance, the page appears like others before it—with sequential photographic panels depicting characters in midaction, speaking through speech bubbles. However, the panels to the right of the page are enclosed by a thick black border that separates them from the main narrative. Inside this delimited space, people are dressed in a contemporary style of indigenous clothing that distinguishes them from their counterparts in the main narrative. By visually echoing the form of the photoplay, this subtle but significant extradiegetic advert simultaneously reinforced and subverted the fictive spaces of the photoplay. As engrossed readers made their way across the page, they may have initially interpreted the advert as part of the narrative, but as the true intent was grasped, readers were abruptly returned to the reality of material concerns.[40] The tensions between constructed and lived realities are maintained even through the extradiegetic elements of the photoplay.

Like its advertisers, the WABP itself took advantage of its popularity by advertising its own publications in the pages of the photoplays. According to Ṣofọwọtẹ, while the *Yoruba Photoplay Series* enjoyed wide popularity largely due to its uniqueness, *Magnet* was not so lucky. The English-language serial experienced competition from the concurrently available *African Film*, which kept sales modest. Perhaps in anticipation of this challenge, the WABP promoted *Magnet* in the first published volumes of the *Yoruba Photoplay Series* well before its official release. Visuals were a major aspect of this promotional push, which used dramatically illustrative magazine covers to attract new readers. While these covers were initially interspersed within the main body of the photoplays, in later volumes they were given designated pages in the magazines' back covers. Whether or not this preemptive decision had any effect on the sales of *Magnet* (or later volumes of the *Yoruba Photoplay Series*), it reiterated the visually innovative and self-referential approach that the editors took in proliferating the photoplays.

In some cases, photoplays exploited popular culture references for their own sake; directly tying proverbs, popular songs, and lyrical sounds into the content in order to advance the point of a particular narrative. For example,

Fig. 4. Cafenol advertisement, vol.7, no.1 (Lagos, Nigeria: West African Book Publishers, 1967), 15.

Oyin Adejọbi's *Orogun Adedigba* (vol. 12) relates the story of a young man, Adegbindin, and his three wives, Tẹjumade, Kikẹlọmọ, and young Awẹle, who was selfish to the detriment of all others. The opening preamble of this photoplay refers to "owe awọn agba" ("parable/proverb of the elders"): "ṣebi owe awọn agba sọ wipe 'bi ẹiyẹ ko ba nii fi ẹiyẹ níràn, oju ọrun to ẹiyẹ fò laikọlu ra wọn'" ("is it not the proverb of the elders that says that 'if a bird is not seeking an occasion for dispute, the sky is big enough for all birds to fly without colliding with each other'").

Like most generational counsel, these kinds of proverbs were typically transmitted verbally. And even in this textual form, the proverb evokes the lyrical cadences and euphonic tones that characterize such exchanges.[41] Moreover, the coda to the second and final issue of this same volume continues this sonic allusion by quoting a popular song that embodied the moral lesson of the story:

> *Awọn olorin a maa kọrin bayi pe:*
> *"Ẹniti nsere, kò mura si 're*
> *Ẹniti nṣika kò mura si 'ka*
> *At'ore at'ika, ọkan ki i gbe . . ."*
> *Ẹ ò rii pe ododo ọrọ ni orin yi bi?*
>
> Singers sing as follows:
> "Whoever is good should keep on being good
> Whoever is evil should keep on being evil
> Neither good nor evil deed is lost——"
> Don't we see that there is a very strong truth in this song?

This excerpt marshals a popular song—which offers a warning and a judgment on individuals' behaviors—to advance the notion that a product of artistic imagination could be the vehicle for an essential "truth." Just like this song, these fantastical photoplays also carried "truths" that were transmitted in a web of expressive modes. These "truths" were not located in the plotlines of the narratives, but rather in the usable lessons that they conveyed to the public: these lessons were crucial to how the photoplays were received and valued by their readership. The dynamic, multimodal manner in which the editors translated the plays into the photoplay format helped to mediate the continued meaning-making relationship between the audience and the narratives.

The composition of the first two graphic panels in *Yoruba Ronu* (vol. 1),

Fig. 5. Panels 1 & 2 in English edition "Yoruba Ronu" vol. 1, no. 1 (Lagos, Nigeria: West African Book Publishers, 1967; unpaginated)

in particular, demonstrates how integral oral practice is to making meaning of the photoplays. The first panel opens with a dramatic announcement delivered by a royal crier pictured in the frame: "Citizens of the King's City, the day is here. Today is our festival!" The pictured crier stands on soapbox (his would-be stage) and directly addresses the readers (his would-be audience) as he summons them to hear the coming narrative. As evident in the second panel, when a royal *gbẹdu* drum booms out "Bọntọn! Bọntọn! Bọntọn!," even the objects speak. The drum responds to the crier and calls the readership/audience to attention the same way that an opening musical glee would have done in a live popular play.[42] Moreover, the character forms of the language contribute to this synesthetic moment, in which the written word gives the impression of voice and sound. That is, the necessary diacritics and particular phonetics that give meaning to Yoruba words also lend the language a natural spoken onomatopoeic effect that manifests and reinforces the entanglement of the oral and the text.[43] Therefore, the readers' experiences with these texts are largely guided by their primarily oral relationship with the language.

When the verses or stanzas would not suffice, the melodious sounds made by the objects, instruments, and characters were visually encoded by musical notes, hand-drawn into speech bubbles to denote their mellifluous qualities to the reader. In *Aropin n'Tenia* (vol. 4), another Hubert Ogunde production, the first frame welcomes readers into the story with an opening glee performed by a group of women. In this scene, musical notations—treble clef sign and paired (often distorted) eighth notes—are hand-drawn inside a common speech bubble that points to several singing characters. Though useless in any practical sense and passingly unfamiliar to many readers, the visible presence of these notations suggested a musicality that the text alone could not manage. This device is repeated throughout the volume to more visibly convey the sonic staging of the scene.

As relates to these sonic concerns and the subtle kinetic and gestural representations in photoplays, Ṣofọwọtẹ described the experience as follows: "As it was I had to rewrite a lot of the material and adapt it for that kind of medium because what they did on stage was a lot of singing and dancing, all of that which is difficult to convey in pictures. So I would have to rewrite the plays to make it all dialogue and action and so on."[44] In rewriting, he made choices. Importantly, in spite of the still photographs, Ṣofọwọtẹ still recognized a strong element of "action" in the manner that the live performances were translated into the photoplays. As editor, he deployed various devices to convey this kinetic sensibility though an otherwise inert format.

The photographic camera is clearly limited in its ability to capture the actors' expressive choreography and animated gestures; however, Ṣofọwọtẹ attempts to reanimate these kinetic moments by annotating them in the narrative boxes. In the first volume, *Yoruba Ronu*, several scenes of revelry and dancing were visually abbreviated and only somewhat elaborated through the text.[45] In one scene, after an ominous stage-setting prophecy, court musicians strike up a song to lighten the mood and the people begin to dance. The narrative boxes concisely describe the characters' actions against the backdrop of accompanying still images—"The people dance for their king. . . . They are highly exhilarated." Though this approach is limited by comparison to the live performance, the concise description of the scene and the still image provide an opening for audiences to interpolate their own imagined ideas of how each scene unfolded.

Surprisingly, even in their limited parameters, the still photographs in the photoplays seemed to urge readers to imagine a performance that transcended the fixity of the depicted moment. By capturing actors in energetic actions and demonstrative gestures that emphasized the physicality and embodied nature of the dialogue, these photographs worked in tandem with the text to activate the scene and advance the narrative. Moreover, the spirited actions captured in stills allude to the immediacy and presentness of the depicted events. Even as the gestural photographs invite viewers into the key dramatic moments of the performance, they also demand that these same readers envisage and animate the intervening actions, and thereby bridge the empty gutter spaces that separate empaneled images. That is, they demand that readers make their own sense of the images, as they see fit. To facilitate this process, some images were modified in postproduction with techniques like motion blurring to give the impression of movement captured in the fixed image as described above. This visual intervention lured readers into an interpretive engagement with the photoplays that enlivened the inherent stillness and passivity of the format.

COCREATIVE AUDIENCES AND DISCURSIVE REGISTERS

Although it took some time before enabling mechanisms were introduced into the pages of the photoplays, audiences were not intended to be passive readers. The success of the *Yoruba Photoplay Series* was due in part to the publication's ability to induce reader participation in an otherwise passive reading experience. To this point, many of the stories published had already been performed for some time by the originating troupe and enjoyed some popularity with theater audiences. These photoplays were published to capitalize on this previous success but also to access untapped audiences who may not have had occasion to see the theatrical production.

Moreover, these narratives exuded a sense of timeliness and timelessness that seemed to invite readers into currently unfolding stories. In one instance, the preface to the second issue of *Oju Eni Ma La* (vol. 13) entreats the audience to rejoin the developing story, reading: "E maa kaa lọ" ("Come along with us"). The story is reframed as an excursion, a journey of revelation and understanding undertaken by readers and narrator alike, the promises not only an entertaining story but also moral guidance. This standing invitation to the story is never rescinded—any reader may return to the photoplay even decades after the initial publication and be greeted with the same ever-present welcome. Indeed, readers responded enthusiastically to these invitations.

The topical presentness of the stories in the photoplays crucially contributed to its ability to convene audiences. Printed in 1967, *Yoruba Ronu* was the first volume in the *Yoruba Photoplay Series* and demonstrated the multiple discursive registers through which photoplays operated. As a play, *Yoruba Ronu* had made waves several years earlier as a scathing moralistic critique of the internal power struggles within Action Group, the predominantly Yoruba political party that controlled the western government of Nigeria. Nearly two years after being banned by the western government of Nigeria, Hubert Ogunde's controversial protest play was resanctioned and exploded back onto the political stage, capturing popular consciousness in photoplay form. In one case, another Ogunde play, *Ologbo Dudu* (vol. 2), takes on the issue of growing criminality in the southwestern Yoruba region. Ṣofọwọtẹ explains the rationale for choosing his play, saying, "That was the time when armed crime started in Nigeria and we always wanted to be topical." This topicality touched on the contemporary experiences of readers and organically drew them to the photoplays. Although not all photoplays were as politically critical as Ogunde's work, several made use of mythic, comedic, or melodramatic motifs to convey moral-didactic messages that were closely tied to cultural-historical events and present discourses.[46] In this manner, photoplays often operated on multiple discursive registers and across genres.

Photoplays had moralistic, didactic undercurrents that, much like the popular theater, inspired readers to see their lives and concerns mirrored and addressed within its pages.[47] Consequently, readers did not perceive photoplays solely as consumable products, but rather as useful sources of knowl-

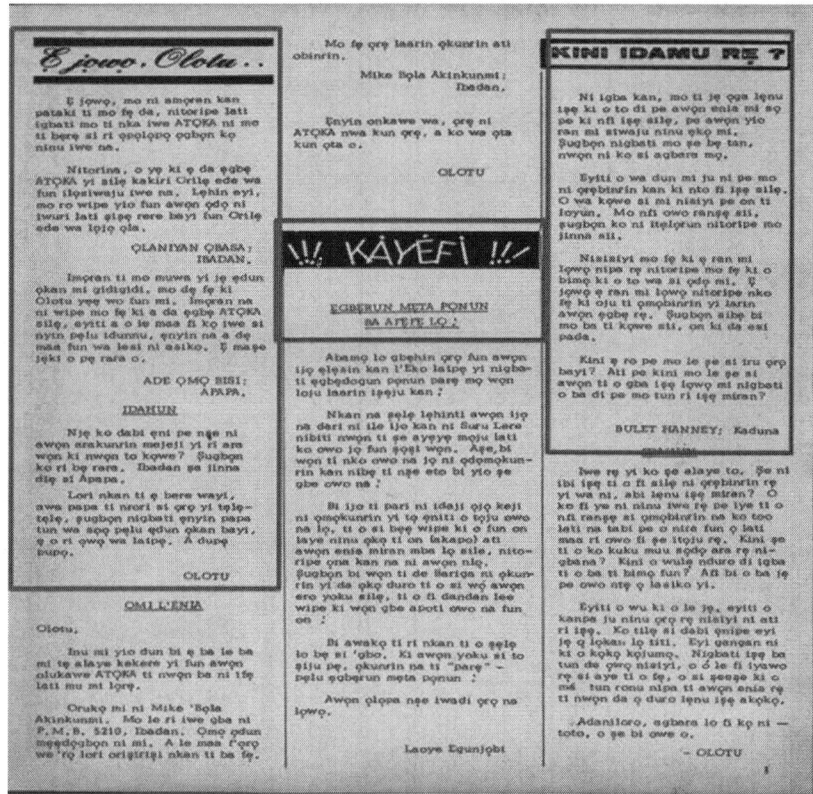

Fig. 6. Letters to the Editor in "Iyawo Alalubosa...", vol. 27, no. 4 (Lagos, Nigeria: West African Book Publishers, 1971), 1.

edge and life lessons from which they could benefit.[48] In both a metaphorical and a literal sense, readers wanted to see themselves in the pages of the photoplays, precipitating some postreading practices that brought the magazine and readers closer together.

By 1971, *Atọka* began to invite readers to write in and directly register their opinions and experiences in the magazine alongside the featured narratives. Reader write-ins quickly became a popular addition to the photoplay. Initially these letters were only printed on a single page, but their allotted space soon increased dramatically and they began to share columns with advertisements and interrupt the stream of graphic panels. In their letters, readers suggested improvement to the photoplays ("E jọwọ, Olotu"); they sought advice about their troubles ("Kini Idamu Re"); and shared disastrous regional news items ("Kayẹfi!!!"). In one instance, two readers independently wrote to the magazine with uncannily similar comments and requests. The first writer felt compelled to testify about the "wisdom" he had culled from the magazine; but both writers suggested that *Atọka* fan clubs be established all over the nation for the sake of educating the masses, facilitating communications between readers and the editor, and, importantly, transforming casual postreading experiences into organized assemblies where readers could convene as a collective. That two geographically unrelated writers arrived at such similar ideas regarding the photoplays demonstrated the success of the magazine's homogenized approach to audience address. Other writers shared their own tangled tales of woe—often as dramatic as the photoplays—and sought advice from other readers and the editor. Indeed, these writers/readers saw elements of their own struggles reflected in those of the characters in the narratives. By writing to *Atọka*, they interpolated their own lives onto the pages of the photoplays and aligned their troubles alongside those of their favorite fictional protagonists.

CONCLUSION

As a speculative, yet ultimately efficacious, artifact of the "creative potentiality" in Yoruba cultural production, photoplays were a unique, generative marriage of the crucial tetrad of sonic (oral and aural), literary (written), visual (photographic), and kinetic (performative). Even in its collective authorial process of rehearsals, rearticulations, and revisions, the format challenged the presumptive parameters of performance and literature. Photoplays occupied the interstices between genres and cultivated dynamic, mutually demanding, and cocritical audiences that animated and made sense of narrative content.

During the height of its popularity, the *Yoruba Photoplay Series* mediated a unique relationship between performativity and literature that was as timely as it was resonant with an increasingly educated and experimental, aspiring readership. It was this relationship with its readership that allowed the photoplays to continue through the late 1980s, when the rise of the videofilm industry and rising costs of production overtook the publication and forced its demise. The capacity and complexity of the audience-convening work accomplished in the photoplays are arguably unmatched by subsequent formats.

BIBLIOGRAPHY

Barber, Karin. *The Generation of Plays: Yoruba Popular Life in Theater*. Bloomington: Indiana University Press, 2000.

Barber, Karin. "Introduction" to *West African Popular Theatre*, edited by Karin Barber, John Collins, and Alain Ricard, vii–xix. Bloomington: Indiana University Press, 1997.

Barber, Karin. "Literacy, Improvisation and the Virtual Script in Yoruba Popular Theatre." In *African Drama and Performance*, edited by John Conteh-Morgan and Tẹjumọla Ọlaniyan, 176–88. Bloomington: Indiana University Press, 2004.

Barber, Karin. "Preliminary Notes on Audiences in Africa." *Africa: Journal of the International African Institute* 67, no. 3 (1997): 347–62.

Barthes, Roland. "From Work to Text." In *Image, Music, Text*, translated by Stephen Heath, 155–64. New York: Hill and Wang, 1977.

Clark, Ẹbun. *Hubert Ogunde: The Making of Nigerian Theatre*. Oxford: Oxford University Press, 1979.

Drum Publications. *African Film*, no. 2 (1967).

Flemming, Tyler, and Toyin Falọla, "Africa's Media Empire: Drum's Expansion to Nigeria." *History in Africa* 32 (2005): 133–64.

Krings, Matthias. "A Prequel to Nollywood: South African Photo Novels and Their Pan-African Consumption in the Late 1960s." *Journal of African Cultural Studies* 22, no. 1 (2010): 75–89.

Nnodim, Rita. "Configuring Audiences in Yoruba Novels, Print and Media Poetry." *Research in African Literatures* 37, no. 3 (2006): 154–75.

Saint, Lily. "Not Western: Race, Reading, and the South African Photocomic." *Journal of Southern African Studies* 36, no. 4 (2010): 939–58.

West African Book Publishers. "Iyawo Alalubọsa, Part 1." *Atọka: Yoruba Photoplay Series* 27, no. 1 (1971).

West African Book Publishers. "Ologbo Dudu, Part 1." *Yoruba Photoplay Series* 2, no. 1 (1968).

West African Book Publishers. "Ọmuti, Part 1." *Yoruba Photoplay Series* 3, no. 1 (1968).

West African Book Publishers. "Yoruba Ronu." *Yoruba Photoplay Series* 1, no. 1 (1967).

NOTES TO CHAPTER NINE

1. As this chapter will later argue, photoplays should be considered distinct from the already circulating photonovel format of publications like *African Film*.

2. Karin Barber, *The Generation of Plays: Yoruba Popular Life in Theater* (Bloomington: Indiana University Press, 2000), 7–9.

3. Popular plays are created from a collaborative process (involving multiple actors, audiences, improvisations, feedback, and restagings), which still occurs in the construction of photoplays, but overwritten by the equally collaborative, production processes of the photoplay, which will be discussed in more detail later.

4. Barber has argued convincingly that popular theater audiences were "only to a limited extent a 'reading public' but were more comprehensively, a public informed by the idea of reading." She continues: "Orally generated dramas found written representation as photoplay stories in *Atọka* and sometimes as published plays intended to be read as literature rather than acted.... 'Not many people read the newspapers,' and the strength of the theater was that it offered an allotrope of written media. It was a genre that aspired to the prestige of the literate world without actually requiring the practitioners and readers to read and without sacrificing the flexibility and living immediacy of speech." However, I contend that much of this analysis limits literacy to a written concern that omits the other modal forms that are subtly invoked in the photoplays. Karin Barber, "Literacy, Improvisation and the Virtual Script in Yoruba Popular Theatre," in *African Drama and Performance*, ed. John Conteh-Morgan and Tẹjumọla Ọlaniyan (Bloomington: Indiana University Press, 2004), 185.

5. Barber suggests that Yoruba popular theater practitioners do not necessarily see themselves as being "cut off from the prestigious sphere of written culture, but in continuity with it and potentially able to enter further into it." (Barber, *Generation of Plays*, 311). In advancing this point, I would argue that photoplays are the vehicles through which theater is able to "enter further into" written culture, as Barber has suggested. However, photoplays do not simply allow theater to enter further into the written; they reconceptualize the relationship between the sonic, literary, visual, and kinetic.

6. Barber, *Generation of Plays*, 6.

7. Yoruba photoplays were referenced by Karin Barber in *Generation of Plays*. Matthias Krings devoted some attention to photoplays in his solid essay on South African "look-reads," "A Prequel to Nollywood: South African Photo Novels and Their Pan-African Consumption in the Late 1960s," *Journal of African Cultural Studies* 22, no. 1 (2010): 75–89. However, beyond these texts, photoplays have minimal mentions in encyclopedias, websites, and sweeping surveys of West African print culture.

8. Krings, "Prequel to Nollywood," 76. Although Lily Saint, in "Not Western: Race, Reading, and the South African Photocomic," *Journal of Southern African Studies* 36, no. 4 (2010): 942, echoes Krings's widely accepted assumption about the postwar Italian origins of the photonovel, she also offers other theories about

the multigeneric origins/nature of the format, ending with its obvious debt to the comic format. In fact, myriad labels have been attached to the format as it moved from region to region over the decades, as will become apparent even in this brief discussion of its manifestations on the continent.

9. Krings, "Prequel to Nollywood," 76–77.

10. Saint, "Not Western," 942–43. Interestingly, Saint predominantly uses "photocomics" to refer these formats. However, this choice of terminology doubly emphasizes the visual elements of the format ("photo" and "comic") without the same reference to its textual components. In this chapter, l adopted the term "photonovel," which equally implicates the linguistic and the visual elements of the format. I will elaborate further on this point in later discussions of the term "photoplay."

11. Tyler Flemming and Toyin Falola, "Africa's Media Empire: Drum's Expansion to Nigeria," *History in Africa* 32 (2005): 148–49. Although it took some time for *Drum* magazine to become profitable in Nigeria and elsewhere, there was no doubt that the magazine was well received by these markets.

12. Saint, "Not Western," 944. Photonovels like *African Film* were so deeply conversant with the realities of sociocultural topographies that they "persistently remind us how difficult it was for apartheid to erase the mixture that was not only a part of everyday life in South Africa but even a part of Afrikaner heritage—and whiteness—itself" (944).

13. Saint, "Not Western," 945.

14. This is particularly demonstrated with the "photoplay" format, which was hugely inspired by the existing theatrical practices of Yoruba traveling plays.

15. Ẹbun Clark, *Hubert Ogunnde: The Making of Nigerian Theatre* (New York: Oxford University Press, 1979), xi.

16. Clark, *Hubert Ogunnde*, 4.

17. The promise of prosperous industries dissolved into economic discontent as expectant but largely unskilled rural populations flocked to the cities in search of work in the new postcolonial economy. Ever resourceful, these populations adapted to economic scarcities by cultivating existing informal practices that would sustain them during extended periods of economic stagnancy. They found little relief from the newly formed federal government, which had become engulfed in corruption and ethnic rivalries, and the growing threat of internal civil conflicts.

18. In the 29 September 1970 (vol. 71) issue of the *Princeton Alumni Weekly*, Richard Ian Gamble is quoted writing, "Published twice a month, our Yoruba photoplay series sells about 80,000 copies per issue and is the only large-scale mass market publication in the vernacular." The alumni publication also features a photograph of Gamble with Hubert Ogunde and his troupe at the photoshoot for *Yoruba Ronu* (the first volume of the series).

19. Ṣẹgun Ṣofọwọtẹ, personal communication, 15 April 2013. Interestingly, all of Ṣofọwọtẹ's previous careers intersected with the various modes through which popular plays had been projects or transmitted to its audiences. This became incredibly important to his ability to comprehend, mediate, and distill the key elements of popular theater in the photoplays.

20. Though it is unknown whether WABP editors were aware of it, the term "photoplay" was first coined in the early Hollywood film industry and used from the 1910s through the 1940s to describe primarily literary novels that were adapted from popular *films* and sold to audience as aftermarket merchandise. Rick Miller, *Photoplay Editions: A Collector's Guide* (Jefferson, NC: McFarland, 2002). Originating from different performative sources, the American and Yoruba versions of the "photoplay" sought to expand these otherwise limited viewing performances to broader audiences.

21. Barber, *Generation of Plays*, 420–21.

22. Karin Barber, "Preliminary Notes on Audiences in Africa," *Africa: Journal of the International African Institute* 67, no. 3 (1997): 355.

23. Rita Nnodim, "Configuring Audiences in Yoruba Novels, Print and Media Poetry," *Research in African Literatures* 37, no. 3 (2006): 157.

24. This term identifies the various expressive modes at work in the photoplays: *iwe* (or "book") and *alaworan* (or "pictures to look at"). This term identifies photoplays as a "book" through which one could "look at picture," similarly to a live interaction, an inference full of intertextual implications.

25. The term *iwe alaworan* implies a production beyond the conventional notion of a literary work, and more aligned with the methodological field that Barthes has identified as "texts." Roland Barthes, "From Work to Text," in *Image, Music, Text*, trans. Stephen Heath (New York: Hill and Wang, 1977), 155–64.

26. Even though the photographic panels were ordered in sequence, several appeared altogether on a single page, ready to be simultaneously and instantly seen/absorbed. In fact, this was one of the major ways that photoplays stood apart from other forms of narrative production at this time. They provided an immediacy of access that gave audiences more latitude in how they engaged with the narrative. The way in which readers reflectively animated the sequences is part of a more elaborate cocreative process that will be discussed in more depth in another paper.

27. The production processes of theater and photoplays were compatible in large part because those directly involved in producing the magazine were often familiar with a variety of media arts, though Sofọwọtẹ had the most varied proficiencies. For some time, theater companies had used posters to advertise their peripatetic performances, so they were versed with the use of visual media to advance their work. Several of these theater groups had performed their dramas

on television or on radio stations, so they were well aware of the range of performative media. Similarly, a good number of the actors were literate or semiliterate, which gave them some familiarity with written interfaces.

28. Barber, *Generation of Plays*, 135.

29. Karin Barber, "introduction" to *West African popular Theatre*, by Karin Barber, John Collins, and Alain Ricard (Bloomington: Indiana University Press, 1997), xiii.

30. Typically, this unwritten process gave troupes the latitude to rework the production at any point, based on the actors' assessment or audience reception—thus implicating viewers as yet another editorial interval in the perpetual refining process. This will be discussed in more depth later in this chapter.

31. As will be discussed later in this chapter, audiences were part of the production process: they would write to the editor suggesting which plays the press should publish; advice letters and story reflections would also published as part of the publication.

32. As a local press, the WABP was limited in its resources, as were most theater companies, therefore demanding variable skills sets from all involved. Sofọwọte wrote the scripts and directed the actors, supervised photographer Abimbade Ọladẹjọ, and interfaced with various illustrators and the printer. One staff liaison was tasked with approaching troupe leaders, negotiating the collaboration, setting schedules, and scouting the photoshoot locations. At first, Rashidi Onikoye shared this role with Ọladẹjọ, but upon Onikoye's departure from the press Ọladẹjọ took the role over entirely.

33. Ṣegun Sofọwọte, personal communication, 15 April 2013. Of the troupe leader, Sofọwọte commented, "His job was to simply provide his team, his group, to do the things they had been doing on stage." This statement makes it clear that the troupe leader did not enjoy the level of decision-making power that he normally enjoyed in the generative process of popular plays.

34. Ṣegun Sofọwọte, personal communication, 15 April 2013. Importantly, as Barber describes, theater troupes primarily worked form "virtual scripts" that did not necessarily elaborate on the specifics of actors' speech. A great deal of the performance was left to the spontaneity of the moment (Barber, "Literacy, Improvisation," 185).

35. In previous instances where popular plays were translated to television, for instance, "It was clear that television authorities exercised only intermittent and haphazard control [over the television production of plays]. They vetted synopses but accepted programs that did not conform to them; they fixed dates for filming but repeatedly broke them; they commissioned series and canceled them; they bought series that they had not commissioned. Television as a medium was so weak and hungry that the live theater companies could invade it with impu-

nity, importing blatantly populist lampoons of authority even while proclaiming themselves, in all sincerity, as the bearers of forma-sector "enlightenment" (Barber, *Generation of Plays*, 248–49). Ṣofọwọtẹ's previous experiences in theater and television undoubtedly made him sensitive to the process of each, so as to reach a manageable medium with the photoplays.

36. Barber, *Generation of Plays*, 311. Each photoplay opened with a brief written prologue that outlined the premise of the story in a third-person voice, addressed an external audience, and provided the context necessary to understand the ensuing narrative. For *Ọmuti*, this prologue was taken verbatim from the introduction of Amos Tutuọla's *The Palmwine Drinkard* and translated into Yoruba: "Lankẹ ọmu sọ nipa ara rẹ bayi pe: Lati kekere ni mo ti jẹ ẹlẹmu wa! Lati ibẹrẹ ni emi ti mmu amu-takiti!" ("Lankẹ, the alcoholic, said about himself as follows: I have been a palm wine drinker since I was young. From the beginning, I have been drinking beyond my capacity"). In this further example of the incorporative nature of the photoplays, we see how the form is able to make distinguished material accessible to a "common" audience.

37. Unsurprisingly, the complexities of these cocreative processes are often caught up in the linguistic labyrinth of language and translation. To this point, the codicil to the author credits reads; "Lati owo Kola Ọgunmọla" ("From the hand of Kola Ọgunmọla"). This interesting turn of phrase suggests that the photoplay was literally penned by Ọgunmọla, when in fact he never put *Ọmuti* into fully scripted form. Rather, the use of "hand" subtly likens Ọgunmọla's "mental blueprint" of the play with the more conventional written product of the literary author. In fact, the texts in all the photoplays were largely written by Ṣegun Ṣofọwọtẹ, the series editor who was absent from the author credits. Omitting the names of Ṣofọwọtẹ and the WABP was most likely a strategic decision whereby more primacy was given to names (such as Tutuọla and Ọgunmọla) that were more familiar and marketable to the reading audience of everyday people. This particularly savvy move reminds us that the ultimate objective was the marketing and commercial success of the photoplay, even at the risk of omitting those who were crucial to the process. Moreover, the increasingly overlapping relationship between literature and language was well represented in these examples from *Ọmuti* and even more so because *The Palmwine Drinkard* (which inspired it) was itself controversial for its use of "pidgin" English.

38. *Ọmuti* (Lagos, Nigeria: West African Book Publishers, 1968) (vol. 3, no. 1): 13–16.

39. Even though they are not the focus of this study, the role and content of advertisements is very important to the very existence of the photonovels. In the case of the Yoruba-language photoplays, the advertisements were one part of the

two-pronged promotion strategy of WABP, which also relied heavily on the widespread popularity of the original live plays to ensure the interest of the readership in the photonovel adaptations of these performances.

40. Perhaps the correlation is not so surprising considering that advertisements, like photoplays, exploit the ambivalences of certain media to fashion persuasive fantasies for receptive audiences.

41. Moreover, by characterizing this proverb as that "of the elders," this statement suggests that the narrator and readers are peers, positioned to lay claim to a youthful group identity that extends to the photoplays' readership. This mode of indirect address subtly captures a demographic and distinguishes it from others, without seeming to do so.

42. The Yoruba edition of the photoplay reads: "Ilu Ọba papa gbe l'ohun," which loosely translates into "The King's drum augments his voice" or, as the English edition reads, "The King's drum serves as royal confirmation." The verbiage in this text suggests that the drum itself acts similarly as a voice, a device that is not without precedent in Yoruba culture (i.e., the talking drum). This anticipates a later discussion in this chapter about the manner in which photoplays paraphrase the kinetic aspect of live theater performances.

43. Significantly, the diacritics implicate oral, text, and the visual because in the early volumes of the photoplays, the phonetic markings on and around the texts were added by hand, drawn onto the initial proofs before final printings were completed. Notwithstanding the practical reasons for this choice, the result was that the texts were made into illustrated phonograms of a kind, an austere kind of illuminated script.

44. Ṣẹgun Ṣofọwọtẹ, personal communication, 15 April 2013.

45. Interestingly, it is predominantly the Hubert Ogunde vehicles—which are known for their musical and aerobatic dynamism—that trigger these extratextual annotations and creative expressive devices.

46. Nnodim, "Configuring Audiences," 62–63.

47. Barber observes that "in discussions afterwards, people took the 'lessons' of the play to heart, seeking ways to expand them and apply them by relating them to anecdotes of their own experience and observation. Several of them remarked that what the play portrayed was true to life: that the events it depicted were exactly what was happening nowadays and that times were changing for the worse. The play, clearly, captured a vision of contemporary moral crisis which the audience recognized, and offered a solution which they warmly endorsed" (Barber, *Generation of Plays*, 200).

48. Barber, *Generation of Plays*, 216–25.

PART III

Newspapers and Their Publics

CHAPTER 10

Komkya *and the Convening of a Chagga Public, 1953–1961*

EMMA HUNTER

In 1953, a new newspaper was born in the town of Moshi, a thriving town on the slopes of Kilimanjaro in northeastern Tanganyika.[1] Published under the auspices of the local government body, the Chagga Council, it had its office in their new and impressive council buildings. The newspaper was called by the Chagga-language word *Komkya*, rendered into English as "Chagga Dawn." It was conceived in part as an element of the nation-building project of a newly elected paramount chief of the Chagga, Thomas Marealle. But as a district newspaper published in Swahili, the lingua franca of the Trusteeship Territory of Tanganyika, it was also inscribed in a late colonial project, part of a wider set of social development initiatives closely tied to the development efforts of the "second colonial occupation."[2]

Historians would once not have paused long over a local government newspaper like *Komkya*, and from this short description we can already begin to see why. For a long time, historians have tended to focus more on what newspapers *ought* to have done than on what they actually did. When historians first began to write the history of newspapers in Africa, they did so in search of the roots of anticolonial nationalism. Their attention was drawn to the oppositional voices in African newspapers, and particularly to the lively anticolonial press that emerged in West Africa from the late 1930s.[3] Newspapers operating within the framework of the colonial state could not and did not adopt an openly anticolonial stance, and accordingly drew less attention. At the same time, a second body of literature, concerned with the roots of civil society and driven by contemporary concerns with the development of an independent critical press, has similarly found less to say about newspapers that were run under the auspices of government, whether local or national, and that did not see themselves as existing in opposition to government.[4]

More recently, historical writing about newspapers has returned to the question of the nation, but from a different perspective. For some years, historical writing about newspapers in the colonial world has been both inspired and restricted by a framework proposed by Benedict Anderson, first in his book *Imagined Communities* and then in his later work *The Spectre of Comparisons*. For Anderson, the modern world is defined by a new form of collective consciousness, that of the nation. He asks the important question of how the nation came to be understood as normal, as not only *a* politically thinkable form of legitimate community but as the only politically thinkable form of legitimate community. This is a story that has print capitalism, the newspaper and the novel, at its heart. Of central importance is the concept, borrowed from Walter Benjamin, of "homogenous, empty time," in which readers of newspapers are brought together as a community through the shared ritual of reading a daily newspaper.[5] It is this simultaneity that "allows one to imagine a limited sovereign community beyond face-to-face relations as well as to envision other limited sovereignties besides one's own as equivalent."[6]

Anderson's thinking about the nation offers radical possibilities for rethinking the universalization of the national form in the modern world. Yet it is not clear that it ought to frame our readings of late colonial newspapers. One problem is empirical. In many parts of the world, daily newspapers were exceptional; more common were weekly or monthly newspapers, which might reach their readers' hands days or even months after their original publication. This is not the realm of homogenous empty time.

But a deeper problem is that Anderson's model relies on an understanding of the nation as the "dominant framework of collective life."[7] He wrote both *Imagined Communities* and *The Spectre of Comparisons* in the late twentieth century, at a time when it seemed that national identity had indeed come to dominate the collective consciousness. Explaining this process was the problem that Anderson sought to solve. Yet from the vantage point of the twenty-first century, at a greater critical distance from the nationalist movements whose self-serving histories were once accepted as truth, it is no longer so clear that nationalism *has* come to dominate the collective consciousness in the way that Anderson thought he identified. Older and newer forms of connection and understandings of legitimate authority, defined by religion or heredity, are powerful and tenacious. And therefore, as Karin Barber suggests, the new collective subjectivities created through print were just as likely to be smaller or larger than the nation. As Barber writes, "The role of print (and subsequently the electronic media) in the constitution of a *national* imagined community was only one strand in a history that included the simultaneous consolidation of local ethnic and other identities and the imagining of supranational communities."[8]

But print was not only a vector in the creation and consolidation of new forms of identity. As Tony Ballantyne has recently argued in another context, "Our abiding preoccupation with the story of the nation has been a key factor in encouraging cultural and intellectual historians to invest considerable energy into producing histories of identities like 'Maori,' 'settler' or 'Pakeha,' and 'New Zealander.'"[9] Historians have often explored the production of these identities through print culture. But if print served to create identity, it did much else besides. Print also created new spaces for virtual exchange in which new kinds of networks were created. The networks constituted by and through print were contingent, fragile, and unstable, but nonetheless played a critical role in forging the intellectual worlds of late colonialism.

Analytically, one way into exploring these networks is through the concept of the "public." In a 1992 article, the literary theorist Michael Warner describes a particular type of public constituted through and in relation to texts. This type of public is neither an all-encompassing, socially defined group or "social totality," such as "the state," nor a bounded group such as an audience united to watch a performance, but rather a public "that comes into being only in relation to texts and their circulation."[10]

My concern here is therefore not with the creation of new identities, but rather the creation of new publics through print. To this end, this chapter explores a newspaper, *Komkya*, whose importance lay not in its role as a tool of identity formation or as the cultural or political project of a named person, though some initially hoped it would play that role. Rather, as one of a new genre of district newspapers that became an important part of the newspaper landscape in 1950s Tanganyika, *Komkya* served to call a new public into being, one that was both bounded and unbounded, unitary and segmented.

To make this argument, I start by outlining the local history of this newspaper, *Komkya*, before setting it in a wider context of district newspapers in late colonial Tanganyika. I then offer a reading of the public it served to create, before concluding with some reflections on what this case study might suggest for our understanding of newspapers in late colonial Africa, and the wider intellectual history of late colonial Africa.

KOMKYA AS A POLITICAL PROJECT

Komkya appeared for the first time in March 1953 as a monthly newspaper.[11] The cost was twenty shillings, a typical price for such newspapers, and it was also available by post for thirty shillings.[12] Announcements and advertisements were welcome, at a cost of twenty pence per word. Letters and news items could be sent to the editor, and each issue contained at least one full page of letters from readers.

In many ways, and as we shall see in more detail later on, *Komkya* was typical of the many district and provincial newspapers established in the early 1950s in Tanganyika. It was published by the Chagga Council, just as other local newspapers were published by Native Authorities or District Commissioners. Like the other district and provincial newspapers, it was written in Swahili, and its circulation benefited from very high literacy rates in Moshi District.[13] But it was also different, because it came into being at a particularly momentous time in the local political history of Kilimanjaro, for its birth coincided with a local campaign to have a paramount chief, or *Mangi Mkuu*, of the Chagga, and the election of the first and last person to hold the position, Thomas Marealle.

In the late 1940s, two veteran politicians, Petro Njau and Joseph Merinyo, had returned to Kilimanjaro after a long absence and taken over the local branch of the African Association. They attacked recent constitutional reforms that had placed three divisional chiefs at the head of local government in Moshi, and called for the appointment of a paramount chief. The outcome of a new round of constitutional reform was the agreement that a paramount chief, or *Mangi Mkuu*, would be popularly elected and placed above the three divisional chiefs. An election was held, and Merinyo and Njau put their weight behind Thomas Marealle, a colonial civil servant and grandson of a leading chief at the turn of the century. Marealle was duly elected, defeating his rivals by a considerable margin.[14]

Marealle was installed on 17 January 1952. A few months later, in September 1952, the district commissioner for Moshi, Basil Stubbings, wrote to Marealle proposing a newspaper for Moshi District and setting out his reasons. He wrote: "With a growing and dynamic society like the Chagga, a medium of disseminating reliable information is not only advisable but essential. The written word may be misread or misinterpreted but the spoken one can be dangerously distorted and twisted to suit narrow and selfish ends. I would like to see in the new Chagga Council building, the embryo of a Chagga 'public relations office' through which the suggested 'Chagga newspaper' would be published."[15] For Stubbings and other local officials, the newspaper promised to serve a valuable political purpose. The written word would have the authority that the oral word lacked. An authoritative local newspaper would, local officials hoped, put a stop to the rumors that had animated local politics in recent years, and create a more stable political life on the mountain.

The new paramount chief shared the view that this should be "strictly a 'Newspaper' and not a 'Views-paper.'" Spelling out in more detail what he meant, Marealle made clear that "the paper will publish news in the form of reports of what actually takes place or will take place in Uchagga, and not of what should or should not take place. In other words 'criticism' is to be avoided as far as possible, unless such criticism is constructive."[16] But if part of the purpose of the newspaper as far as local colonial officials and the new paramount chief were concerned lay in snuffing out a lively local politics, the paper was nevertheless, from its foundation, intensely political.

At Marealle's installation as paramount chief, the governor, Edward Twining, announced that Marealle had been "elected by the people" in order to be "the principal mouth-piece of the Chagga people and their liaison with Government."[17] But Marealle's sense of his own role was far grander than that of an intermediary, for he saw his role as that of building a Chagga nation. In his first year in office, he instituted the new public holiday of Chagga Day, to be held annually on 10 November, a day that, Marealle explained in a brochure produced to celebrate Chagga Day, represented "the historic come-together of the whole tribe."[18] Marealle also commissioned a new history of the Chagga, to be written by Kathleen Stahl, and a Chagga flag was produced to fly above the new Chagga Council building.[19]

For Marealle, the newspaper was conceived as part of this nation-building project. But the letters exchanged between Marealle and the district commissioner, alongside the minutes of meetings held by a committee set up to establish the newspaper, indicate a certain tension between this conception and an alternative conception of the newspaper as a space of free speech in which all could engage. There were two particular areas of controversy, of which one was language and the other was ownership.

Language and Ownership

Language was an important part of Marealle's wider nation-building efforts. As he explained in a letter to the district commissioner in October 1952, he believed that "a local dialect is the very basis of tribal or national thought and there is much to be gained by preserving it."[20] Yet he was concerned that owing to the distinctions between dialects of Kichagga, the language would soon die out. He envisaged appointing "a Chagga Dialect Committee composed of people from all the three Divisions with the idea of striking a happy medium between the three dialectic groupings," which would then serve as the "basis of a Chagga English Dictionary, a vocabulary and School primers."[21]

A key question in establishing *Komkya* was therefore that of which language to use. As already mentioned, most of the district and provincial newspapers were published in Swahili, though some, like the newspaper *Lembuka* published in Tukuyu in western Tanzania, also included material in the vernacular.[22] Swahili's dominant position by 1952 led James Scotton to conclude that by this point it had "clearly become the *lingua franca* of Tanganyika."[23] But it is perhaps more accurate to say that it had become the lingua franca of print, the result of first German and then British policies privileging Swahili as a language of administration, education, and the production of literature. While there was some evidence of a demand for vernacular languages, and Horace Mason, the social development officer in the Pare district who had been responsible for the highly successful *Habari za Upare*, reported being "continually asked" why the local language, Chasu, was not used "as the language for the paper," this impetus was outweighed by the demand for Swahili. Those targeted by the government's mass literacy campaign in the Pare mountains insisted that they wanted to learn to read and write Swahili, not the Pare language, because Swahili was understood to be the language of education.[24]

In early discussions about the newspaper, Marealle, however, argued for the use of Kichagga, if not solely then at least alongside Swahili. Marealle made clear that he saw the newspaper as an opportunity to promote the Chagga language as part of his wider project of Chagga nation-building. But Marealle found himself faced with opposition from local officials, who turned to Horace Mason, the Pare social development officer, for advice. Mason agreed with officials in Moshi that the forces militating for Swahili were far stronger than arguments in favor of a local language. After all, "Presumably one of the aims of the paper will be not merely to tell the Wachagga what is happening in their country but also other people." And there was also an acknowledgment that a territory-wide Swahiliphone public sphere already existed, and that "other papers, in particular 'Mambo Leo,'" relied on having access to local news in a shared language that they could reprint "for territorial circulation."[25] Mason suggested as a compromise that they might include "a column of matter in Kichagga—poems, proverbs etc. so as to make quite clear that there is no deliberate intention to kill the local language."[26]

Faced with these arguments, Marealle retreated from his initial position on the question of language. Rather than argue for the use of Kichagga as one of the main languages of the newspaper, he now suggested simply that it "allow for some space however little of putting across the new dialect even if that space was not more than a quarter page a time," and indeed said that it had never been his intention that Kichagga should be one of the "formal languages used."[27] But if Marealle quickly changed his position on the language to be used in the newspaper, he was able to have his own way on the question of ownership against his political rivals.

A committee was set up in the autumn of 1952 to take the project forward and included the district commissioner, Basil Stubbings, and the three divisional chiefs representing the three sections of the mountain, alongside Marealle in the chair. Also on the committee was A. L. B. Bennett, European adviser to the local cooperative union, the Kilimanjaro Native Co-operative Union, or KNCU, which was responsible for marketing the coffee that was the basis of Kilimanjaro's wealth.

It was clear from the discussions in the committee around the question of financing and control that other local leaders were concerned the newspaper would become a vehicle for Marealle to build up his own power base. When Marealle proposed setting up the newspaper directly under the auspices of the Chagga Council, both Bennett and Abdiel Shangali, one of the divisional chiefs who had stood, unsuccessfully, for election to the new position of paramount chief, expressed reservations. Bennett agreed that he wanted a newspaper that would set out the truth and "not contain insults or news which would hurt a person or people's families," but said that he did not want it to be run by the Chagga Council. Rather, "It should be run by a company and helped by the Chagga Council until it could be self-supporting."[28] Bennett went on to say that in this way "readers would not think that it was the newspaper of the Chagga Council" or feel that they did not have the freedom "to say other things on top of those which were said by the Chagga Council." The committee met again two weeks later, and this time Marealle had his arguments ready. He proposed that it should start out under the auspices of the Chagga Council and be transferred to a company at a later date. He argued that if the money would in any case be coming from the Chagga Treasury, it would be dishonest to give the impression that it was owned by a company, and moreover that "because many natives do not yet know what freedom of the press means it is better that the Chagga Council supports this newspaper for the moment."[29] On this occasion, Bennett and Shangali accepted the decision, so *Komkya* became a Chagga Council newspaper and remained so for the duration of its existence.

The birth of the newspaper was therefore closely linked to Marealle's political project. Indeed, to this day the newspaper is remembered in the area as Marealle's newspaper.[30] But the newspaper in fact outlasted Marealle's fall from power. In 1960, a referendum was held to determine the future both of Marealle and of the office of paramount chief. Marealle and his supporters lost, and Marealle was replaced with a new president of the Chagga, Solomon Eliufoo, a leading member of TANU and son-in-law of Marealle's rival, Abdiel Shangali. Eliufoo also made use of the newspaper, employing its columns to offer a series of reflections on political change, the meaning and practice of democracy, and the nature of virtuous conduct in politics. The paper changed its name to *Kusare* in 1961 and, following constitutional reforms in 1962, became the newspaper of the Kilimanjaro District Council rather than the now defunct Chagga Council, and in this form continued to be published until 1967.

Not only did *Komkya* survive after Marealle had departed Kilimanjaro's political stage, but even at the time when Marealle was still in power *Komkya* had an appeal that went far beyond Marealle's political supporters. According to Helen Kitchen's 1958 study, *Komkya*'s "content and appeal" meant that its circulation extended "beyond the districts and tribes" for whom it was initially intended.[31] *Komkya*'s late colonial popularity, coupled with its longevity, suggests that it became more than a new paramount chief's means of shoring up support.

KOMKYA AS A DISTRICT NEWSPAPER

Komkya's foundation was linked to the election of Thomas Marealle, but as we have suggested, the model was that of a new genre of Swahili-language district newspapers that emerged in the 1950s in Tanganyika, produced by local councils or district offices.[32] These newspapers ranged widely in size, content, and professionalism. Some were cyclostyled, consisted of only two sides of A4, and circulated in a small local area. At the other extreme, the broadsheet *Habari za Upare*, based at Pare Council Headquarters in northeastern Tanganyika, extended to fourteen pages and was professionally printed, its pages filled by a team of local reporters.[33]

As mentioned at the beginning of this chapter, district newspapers, produced by local government organizations as part of a wider project of mass education, social development, and political education, have attracted little attention from historians.[34] In his memoir of 1950s Tanganyika, Godfrey Mwakikagile described them as an attempt by the colonial government to "undermine the nationalist cause" and to "project a good image of the government among the indigenous people."[35] While the government hoped they would develop an independent existence, they were, he suggested, encouraged "to portray the colonial rulers in a positive way" and contained "little criticism of government policies when the papers were first launched, although this changed later in a number of cases."[36] Yet we should not be so quick to pigeonhole these newspapers as of interest only as tools of colonial development policy, government propaganda, or precursors of a nationalist press, for in Tanganyika they rapidly became the major way in which most people outside the main urban centers encountered a newspaper. The reason for that lies in the history of the press in Tanzania.

In her 1958 volume documenting Africa's newspapers, Helen Kitchen suggested that the Tanganyikan case had little of interest to offer those interested in African newspapers. "The limited political development of Tanganyika's African population and the small size of the European colony," she noted, "are reflected in the country's newspapers, which are few in number and largely non-controversial in character."[37] There was, Kitchen continued, only one "independent African paper of any consequence," which was the newspaper *Bukya na Gandi*, edited by E. R. Munseri and published in English, Haya, and Swahili.[38] She might also have mentioned *Zuhra*, edited by R. M. Plantan in Dar es Salaam. Yet these were rare examples, for in contrast both to West Africa and to Tanganyika's neighbors to the north, Kenya and Uganda, all with a lively independent press, Tanganyika's public sphere was dominated by government and mission newspapers.

The colonial government was aware of this peculiarity, and in his annual report for 1952 the public relations officer, G. K. Whitlamsmith, reflected on the reasons why an independent press had not developed in Tanganyika. He suggested that "general confidence in the Government has something to do with it, as has also the fact that the Africans of Tanganyika are less politically mature than the inhabitants of many other colonies. An additional cause may be that the inhabitants of Tanganyika have other means of expressing their discontents, such as writing petitions to the Trusteeship Council and voicing their criticisms on the local government bodies in their districts, on which the non-hereditary elements have been increasingly represented in recent years."[39] In his report the following year, Whitlamsmith repeated his comments, while also suggesting that lack of "business acumen" among Tanganyikans was a possible further reason.[40]

Whitlamsmith expressed his desire to foster the development of an independent press. "The establishment of a sound independent African press is essential," he argued, "if Africans are to advance toward political maturity. Publications in which they can give vent to their feelings are a valuable safety valve and also give Government useful information on the state of public opinion."[41] But he did not discuss the significant challenges that stood in the way of such a press. When an independent press began to appear from 1952, the government of Tanganyika acted quickly to restrict it, extending an earlier requirement that a bond be paid in respect of any newspaper published at fourteen-day intervals.[42] The level of the bond was also tripled.[43] A new sedition law passed in 1955 further curtailed the freedom of the press.

Yet if Tanganyika's independent press before around 1957 was weak and stuttering, this was only true of the *independent* African press. Contained within the public relations officer's 1952 report was a hint as to another reason why an independent press had not emerged. For, it seems, some of the demand for newspapers was being met by the very particular genre of the district newspaper.

District newspapers had emerged after 1945, largely as a result of local initiative. They were mostly written in Swahili and were edited by Africans with advice and support from local officials.[44] In his report for 1952, Whitlamsmith had been unable to give circulation information on these papers, but by 1953, having undertaken a survey to see whether it might be possible to organize advertising centrally, thus improving the financial position of the district newspapers, he was able to report the scale that these newspapers had now reached. The circulation of individual titles ranged from three hundred to three thousand a month, which produced a combined figure of twenty-seven thousand. To put this in context, *Mambo Leo*, the largest-selling newspaper in East Africa, was selling approximately fifty thousand copies a month by the end of 1952.[45] By 1958, Helen Kitchen estimated that some of the most popular district newspapers were selling up to five thousand copies a month.[46]

The district papers were clearly reaching a wide audience and developing an importance beyond that initially anticipated. Their roots lay in the history of postwar development in East Africa and particularly policies that aimed to expand literacy rates. This was particularly true in the case of one of the most popular district newspapers, *Habari za Upare*, which appeared for the first time in April 1951.[47] Its origins reached back to a proposal put forward by Professor C. N. Philips in 1947 for a Mass Literacy and Community Development Scheme in the Pare mountains of northern Tanganyika. One part of his proposal for community development was that a community newspaper should be established, but it quickly became apparent that a newspaper would be important for the mass literacy program as well.[48] The social development team sent to the area found that while books were popular with children, they were less popular with adults. Their analysis was that "poor lighting in homes and a gregarious social life militated against the reading habit, which could only be found in adults with a background of more than ten years' formal schooling."[49] But if books were relatively unpopular, newspapers and magazines were in demand. A periodical produced by local people for the community thus seemed to combine community development objectives and supply much-needed follow-up literature for those who had recently learned to read.

The motivation to produce *Habari za Upare* may well have been social development, but it rapidly became a very different proposition. Initially produced by the social development officer and his team using stencils and a typewriter, the printing was soon handed over to the KNCU printing works in Moshi. In 1954 an African editor employed by the local authority took over. Reflecting on the ways in which the newspaper had changed in the first six years of its existence in 1957, Horace Mason concluded that *Habari za Upare* had evolved from being "an instrument of development" to the "organ of a local government body, combining the dissemination of accurate local news and general interest reading matter with the publicizing of local government activities," its running costs funded by commercial advertising.[50] With a circulation of three thousand copies every month, around 10 percent of which went to Pare working away from the district, the newspaper had, Mason concluded, succeeded in appealing to a significant reading public, which included both those outside the district who "want to be informed about progress at home and news of their friends" and those at home who were interested less "in the minutiae of local news, but more in the overall development picture of the district and news of the territory as a whole and of the outside world."[51]

Habari za Upare had gone far beyond the initial aims of its founders, but its rapid progress was typical of Tanganyika's district newspapers in general. In his report for 1955, the new director of public relations, K. B. A. Dobson, remarked that they were "quite a feature of this country and, when the adverse circumstances under which they work is taken into consideration, they reflect credit on their promoters and editors."[52] If the editors of district newspapers were deserving of credit, this credit was rarely publicly given, for their identities were largely concealed: and here lies one of the crucial differences between Tanganyika's district newspapers and the independent vernacular newspapers in other parts of East Africa. As Dobson explained, the excellent work done by the editors of government newspapers was performed "in the traditional cloak of editorial anonymity."[53] The editor was anonymous and also, as we shall see, at least to some extent nonpartisan.

Editorial anonymity serves to distinguish this genre of newspapers from many of the projects discussed in this volume. In many other cases explored here, the editor *was* the newspaper. Editors used their newspapers as a tool to perform political and cultural work, advocating political causes, imposing new cultural forms, even disciplining language through the regularization of orthography. But while there was an editorial line in *Komkya*, it was less closely tied to a named individual.

District newspapers were, of course, published under the watchful eye of the colonial state and were therefore subject to the discipline of that state. African editors who published material that the colonial state found too oppositional or simply too political were swiftly dismissed, as in 1959 when the Lushoto newspaper *Kinyeme* published an edition including a long speech by one of TANU's leading figures, Rashidi Kawawa.[54] Power thus continued to lie with those who produced, financed, and censored district newspapers, but in the absence of a named editorial voice, that power was more diffuse than in other newspapers, opening the newspaper up to be appropriated by different people and different groups. We can almost see agency lying with the form of the newspaper itself, with the newspaper acting as a forum through which new virtual communities could be created.

VIRTUAL COMMUNITIES AND CHAGGA PUBLICS

If newspapers could serve to call into being a virtual community, this was a particular type of community. It was unstable, porous, and characterized by tension and conflict as much as by unity. In his account of the publics created by and through texts, Michael Warner explores the tensions inherent in such publics. They are both inclusionary and exclusionary: inclusionary in that anyone can become a member simply through the act of picking up and engaging with the text, and exclusionary in that not everyone has access to the language used in the text or the codes it employs. They are also a "relation among strangers" in which membership has a hidden dimension to it: no one can ever know exactly who is a member at any one time.[55]

Warner's explanation of the hidden rules of the publics with which we are so familiar is helpful in directing us toward the workings of *Komkya*. If textual publics are simultaneously both inclusive and exclusionary, *Komkya*'s public was no different. Anyone who could read Swahili could, by virtue of picking up a newspaper or writing to the letters' page, become a member of this public. But those who engaged with the newspaper and employed its pages often addressed a group that was imagined to be bounded, and did so by explicitly addressing a Chagga public.

When correspondents to *Komkya* began their letters by expressing a desire to communicate with their "fellow Wachagga," they rhetorically called an imagined Chagga public into being, which could, in theory, encompass all Chagga. They drew on a long tradition of print culture on the slopes of Kilimanjaro, including earlier newspapers and periodicals such as the KNCU's *Uremi* that had similarly conjured a Chagga public into being.[56] Yet the publics that *Komkya* created were both larger and smaller than this suggests. They were larger because the newspaper was published in Swahili and sent by post across Tanganyika and Kenya. *Komkya*'s potential readership therefore stretched far beyond a linguistically, spatially, or politically defined Chagga community. But they were also smaller because the newspaper was a forum open only to those literate in Swahili and those able and willing to adopt the newspaper's own vernaculars. These dynamics of inclusion and exclusion meant that while on the one hand *Komkya* created an imagined community of all Chagga, this was not one unified body but a set of multiple and overlapping networks that were always in formation and never stable.

Vernaculars of Progress

As Warner reminds us, publics have their own vernaculars. *Komkya* had its own vernacular in the sense that the editorial line committed the newspaper to an overarching narrative of progress toward enlightenment. The newspaper's title, *Chagga Dawn*, was employed by correspondents as a metaphor for this transition from darkness into light, suggesting that the Chagga people were leaving a state of ignorance and entering enlightenment.[57] While readers might disagree about what exactly constituted enlightened behavior and how to get there, participating in *Komkya*'s pages meant accepting this as a goal, and this code of membership framed their contributions.

In September 1953, *Komkya*'s editor intervened in a lively debate taking place in its pages over the questions of bridewealth and female circumcision. In an editorial entitled "Customs and Traditions" ("Mila na Jadi"), the editor summarized the contributions received thus far as representing the dissatisfaction felt by a new generation at the argument made by their parents that these practices should continue to be followed simply because they had always been followed. But, the editor asked, what did the parents think? Why were they not writing to *Komkya* themselves, and did this reluctance to intervene in *Komkya*'s pages indicate that they in fact agreed with the younger generation?[58]

While this direct editorial invitation did draw a response from the older generation, in general the pages of *Komkya* were indeed dominated by the young and by the self-consciously progressive. When conservative voices appeared, the conventions of the newspaper demanded that they frame their arguments within the same overarching commitment to progress. In 1955, a controversy emerged between a neotraditionalist political party led by Petro Njau, the veteran activist who had campaigned for a paramount chief, and the Lutheran Church. Njau's party called for the reinstitution of a practice whereby land disputes were settled by swearing an oath. The Lutheran Church was fundamentally opposed to any return to what it understood to be a pagan practice. One supporter of Njau's position wrote to *Komkya* in support, but tellingly did so not in terms of a generic defense of tradition but by employing arguments drawn from global comparisons, in much the same way as the younger generation drew on examples from elsewhere to advocate the abandonment of traditions. He began his letter by saying that the Lutheran rejection of the oath should not pass without comment from those who supported the oath. "All tribes in the world," he wrote, "are governed by various traditions, and not only in Africa, but also in Asia, Europe, Australia and so on." The Chagga should therefore think carefully before throwing out their traditions.[59]

Shadow Publics

Yet within this encompassing vernacular of progress lay further lines of demarcation. The active readership, in the sense of those who participated in the letters pages and employed *Komkya* as a public forum, was overwhelmingly weighted toward the young, educated, and male. This fitted the profile of the imagined reader, suggested by the tendency for readers to specifically address "our parents" or "the elders" or "Chagga girls" when an alternative perspective was required.

Yet there were other spaces within the newspapers where alternative forms of sociality were constructed. As in other district newspapers, such as *Habari za Upare*, there was a specific "Women's page" that very quickly became a space in which matters such as women's inheritance rights, girls' education, and female circumcision were debated and argued over. Letters on these subjects were often written by women, yet not exclusively so. At times young men wrote in to support the position taken by a female correspondent; at other times they wrote to disagree.

The contrast between the main letters' page and the women's page is suggested by looking at the example of an issue from December 1954. The main letters' page included one letter from a male reader worrying about girls wearing makeup, and another, also from a male reader, expressing concerns about girls going to live in town. In both cases, the imagined readers appeared to be fellow men. In contrast, the "Women's page" was taken up in that issue by a long letter from a female reader about the need for more educational opportunities for women in the district, part of an ongoing discussion of women's education that took place on that page.[60] This domain of female sociality within *Komkya* was not oppositional, but emerged in the interstices of the newspaper. Thus if the dominant mode of sociality created in *Komkya*'s pages connected the young, male, and educated, *Komkya* also served to constitute alternative or shadow publics.

The same was true in relation to political divides. The official editorial line was one of neutrality, and ongoing political conflicts in the district were rarely discussed openly. In July 1955, the editor announced that there would be a special series on famous people, but specified that politicians would not be included because to do so would suggest that *Komkya* favored one side or the other.[61] But at times letters hinted at conflicts behind the scenes. One example emerged in the spring and summer of 1955, as criticism of the paramount chief was mounting. A letter published in the 15 August 1955 issue suggested that *Komkya* was little read in a particular administrative district associated with opposition to Marealle. While this reading was rebutted by other correspondents, another letter complained about the unequal distribution of resources between the three major administrative sections of the district.[62] The response of the editor was to reiterate the common refrain that "unity is strength," and indeed it was unity that the newspaper preferred to stress; but it could never entirely hide deep political divisions present behind the scenes.

Print, Language, and Space

Print had the power to travel across distance, and this too served both to include and to exclude. The novelty and value of print and the form of the newspaper lay in part in its ability to connect those Chagga living in Moshi and on the slopes of Kilimanjaro both with each other and with those living far away from home. If the Pare newspaper, *Habari za Upare*, sold about 10 percent of its copies by post, the number of letters with addresses in other parts of Tanganyika or in Kenya suggest that a similar if not greater proportion of *Komkya* readers were outside the district.

Yet correspondents often drew a distinction between those Chagga living in "Chaggaland" (Uchaggani) and those who were away from the district. While *Komkya*'s ability to bring both groups together was celebrated, there were also limits to the ability of *Komkya* to transcend these divides. On 15 September 1954, the paramount chief reported in the pages of *Komkya* on progress toward the development of a new Chagga national song. The song had, he wrote, been discussed in the Chagga Council, in all the chiefs' *barazas* on the mountain as well as in *Komkya*. The resulting song was set out underneath his letter, both in Kichagga and in a Swahili translation. Readers were called upon to study the words carefully, and to remember that it would forever be their national song, just as in South Africa the song "Tusekelele Afrika" was known everywhere and understood to be the song of the "whole nation."[63] The problem for readers living far away was that *Komkya* had supplied the words but not the tune. One reader, R. Y. Lyimo, wrote from Malindi on the Kenyan coast to ask how those living far away could find out the tune to accompany the words. Would it, he asked, be possible to make a gramophone recording so that they too could learn the song?[64] At other times the complaint was more practical. Each issue of *Komkya* contained a crossword puzzle, but, one reader complained, the deadline for entries did not leave enough time for readers who lived far away to receive their copies, complete the crossword, and send back their solutions.[65]

At other times, readers living in Moshi District suggested that those who had moved away had lost touch with local realities. In 1957, a correspondent named E. Solomon Z. Kaale, who gave his address as Mombasa, wrote to ask why the newspaper's title was in the Chagga language but the content was in Swahili. This was, he suggested, akin to mixing salt and sugar. Surely a Chagga newspaper should be written in the Chagga language? *Komkya*, he pointed out, was sold across East Africa, but he suspected it would not be bought if potential purchasers thought it was written in the Chagga language.[66] Responding, Theophil J. S. Anthony suggested that Kaale had been away too long and forgotten that there was no unified Chagga language.[67] Amending Kaale's metaphor, Anthony suggested it was less a case of sugar mixed with salt than a case of butter added to bread—the Chagga name sent out a signal but also allowed the Chagga to showcase their progress across East Africa.

One of the paradoxes of late colonial Tanganyika was that new ethnic patriotisms were developed in the lingua franca of Swahili.[68] As a result, Chagga reflected on their own nation, its past, present, and future, in a language shared with others in East Africa. *Komkya* was a space in which Chagga defined themselves to the outside world, and reflected publicly on how they appeared. As *Komkya*'s first editorial reminded readers, the newspaper would travel far beyond the mountain, and would "visit many places in Tanganyika and in East Africa." The words printed and the ideas exchanged in the pages of *Komkya* would be seen by other peoples, who could make judgments about the level of progress achieved by the Chagga.[69] At the same time, those Chagga who were not literate in Swahili could not read *Komkya*.

CONCLUSION

Thomas Marealle had hoped that a newspaper would shore up support behind him and create a unified Chagga people under his leadership. That it did not do so was partly a function of the format of the district newspaper and the fact that it could not be explicitly partisan. But it was also because of the nature of print. Nobody was entirely in control of this space, in which, to a certain degree, print took on a life of its own. *Komkya* provided a virtual space for debate and disagreement while also excluding those who were not literate in Swahili or did not subscribe to an ideology of "progress." As we have seen, *Komkya* created new publics, but these publics were unstable and experienced in different ways, at different times, by different members. In this way, *Komkya* perhaps had more in common with the electronic media of today than with the campaigning newspapers of the 1950s.

Exploring *Komkya* through this analytical lens, not as a tool of identity formation but as a virtual community in flux, offers a powerful example of the role that newspapers could play in creating new and distinctive modes of late colonial sociality. But reading the newspaper in this way also serves as a way into the intellectual history of late colonial Africa. Networks of print constituted one way in which ideas were formed, worked out, and argued over. It reminds us that readers and writers were members of multiple networks, which at times reinforced and at times contradicted each other. This is precisely what made life difficult for those political entrepreneurs who sought to discipline their followers, both before and after independence. But it is also what makes the close study of late colonial newspapers so important.

BIBLIOGRAPHY

Anderson, Benedict. *Imagined Communities: Reflections on the Origin and Spread of Nationalism*. Rev. ed. London: Verso, 1991.

Anderson, Benedict. The *Spectre of Comparisons: Nationalism, South East Asia and the World*. London: Verso, 1998.

Ballantyne, Tony. "Thinking Local: Knowledge, Sociability and Community in Gore's Intellectual Life, 1875–1914." *New Zealand Journal of History* 44 (2010): 138–56.

Barber, Karin. *The Anthropology of Texts, Persons and Publics: Oral and Written Culture in Africa and Beyond*. Cambridge: Cambridge University Press, 2007.

Barber, Karin. "I.B. Akinyele and Early Yoruba Print Culture." In *Recasting the Past: History Writing and Political Work in Modern Africa*, edited by Derek Peterson and Giacomo Macola, 31–49. Athens: Ohio University Press, 2009.

Cheah, Pheng, "Grounds of Comparison." In *Grounds of Comparison: Around the Work of Benedict Anderson*, edited by Jonathan Culler and Pheng Cheah, 1–20. London: Routledge, 2003.

Duara, Prasenjit. *Rescuing History from the Nation: Questioning Narratives of Modern China*. Chicago: University of Chicago Press, 1995.

Gadsden, Fay. "The African Press in Kenya, 1945–1952." *Journal of African History* 21 (1980): 515–35.

Government of Tanganyika. *Annual Report of the Public Relations Department, 1952*. Dar es Salaam: Government of Tanganyika, 1953.

Government of Tanganyika. *Annual Report of the Public Relations Department, 1953*. Dar es Salaam: Government of Tanganyika, 1954.

Government of Tanganyika. *Annual Report of the Public Relations Department, 1955*. Dar es Salaam: Government of Tanganyika, 1956.

Hunter, Emma. "'In Pursuit of the Higher Medievalism': Local History and Politics in Kilimanjaro." In *Recasting the Past: History Writing and Political Work in Modern Africa*, edited by Derek Peterson and Giacomo Macola, 149–67. Athens: Ohio University Press, 2009.

Kasoma, Francis P. "The Role of the Independent Media in Africa's Change to Democracy." *Media, Culture and Society* 17 (1995): 537–55.

Kitchen, Helen. *The Press in Africa*. Washington, DC: Ruth Sloan Associates, 1958.

Lederbogen, Utz. *Watchdog or Missionary? A Portrait of African News People and Their Work*. Frankfurt am Main: Peter Lang, 1992.

Lonsdale, John. "Anti-colonial Nationalism and Patriotism in Sub-Saharan Africa." In *Oxford Handbook of the History of Nationalism*, edited by John Breuilly, 318–40. Oxford: Oxford University Press, 2013.

Low, D. A., and J. M. Lonsdale. "Introduction: Towards the New Order 1945–1963." In *History of East Africa*, edited by D. A. Low and Alison Smith, vol. 3, 1–63. Oxford: Clarendon Press, 1976.

Mason, Horace. "Pare News and Other Publications of the Pare Mass Literacy and Community Development Scheme." *Reports and Papers on Mass Communication: Periodicals for New Literates. Seven Case Histories* 24 (1957): 19–23.

Millonzi, Joel Carl. *Citizenship in Africa: The Role of Adult Education in the Political Socialization of Tanganyikans, 1891–1961*. Syracuse, NY: Maxwell School of Citizenship and Public Affairs, 1975.

Moore, Sally Falk. *Social Facts and Fabrications: "Customary" Law on Kilimanjaro, 1880–1980*. Cambridge: Cambridge University Press, 1986.

Mwakikagale, Godfrey. *Life in Tanganyika in the Fifties: My Reflections and Narratives from the White Settler Community and Others*. Grand Rapids, MI: Continental Press, 2006.

Newell, Stephanie. *Power to Name: A History of Anonymity in Colonial West Africa*. Athens: Ohio University Press, 2013.

Ng'wanakilala, Nkwabi. *Mass Communication and Development of Socialism in Tanzania*. Dar es Salaam: Tanzania Publishing House, 1981.

Peterson, Derek. *Ethnic Patriotism and the East African Revival: A History of Dissent, c. 1935–1972*. Cambridge: Cambridge University Press, 2012.

Rogers, Susan G. "Search for Political Focus on Kilimanjaro: A History of Chagga Politics, 1916–1952, with Special Reference to the Cooperative Movement and Indirect Rule." PhD dissertation, University of Dar es Salaam, 1972.

Scotton, James F. "Growth of the Vernacular Press in Colonial East Africa: Patterns of Government Control." PhD dissertation, University of Wisconsin, 1971.

Scotton, James F. "Tanganyika's African Press, 1937–1960: A Nearly Forgotten Pre-independence Forum," *African Studies Review* 21, no. 1 (1978): 1–18.

Sturmer, Martin. *The Media History of Tanzania*. Ndanda, Tanzania: Ndanda Mission Press, 1998.

Warner, Michael. "Publics and Counterpublics." *Public Culture* 14 (2002): 49–90.

Whitlamsmith, G. K. *Recent Trends in Chagga Political Development.* Moshi: KNCU Printing Press, 1955.

NOTES TO CHAPTER 10

1. I am grateful to members of the African Print Cultures network, particularly Kelly Askew, Stephanie Newell, and Derek Peterson, to Charles West and to the anonymous readers for comments on earlier drafts of this chapter.

2. On the late colonial development initiatives referred to as the "second colonial occupation," see D. A. Low and J. M. Lonsdale, "Introduction: Towards the New Order 1945–1963," in *History of East Africa,* ed. D. A. Low and Alison Smith, vol. 3 (Oxford: Clarendon Press, 1976), 1–63.

3. For a helpful critique, see Stephanie Newell, *The Power to Name: A History of Anonymity in Colonial West Africa* (Athens: Ohio University Press, 2013), 47–49.

4. See, for example, Francis P. Kasoma, "The Role of the Independent Media in Africa's Change to Democracy," *Media, Culture and Society* 17, no. 4 (1995): 537–55.

5. Benedict Anderson, *Imagined Communities: Reflections on the Origin and Spread of Nationalism,* rev. ed. (London: Verso, 1991), 24; Benedict Anderson, *The Spectre of Comparisons: Nationalism, South East Asia and the World* (London: Verso, 1998), 29–45.

6. Pheng Cheah, "Grounds of Comparison," in *Grounds of Comparison: Around the Work of Benedict Anderson,* ed. Jonathan Culler and Pheng Cheah (London: Routledge, 2003), 6–7.

7. Cheah, "Grounds of Comparison," 6.

8. Karin Barber, *The Anthropology of Texts, Persons and Publics: Oral and Written Culture in Africa and Beyond* (Cambridge: Cambridge University Press, 2007), 145.

9. Tony Ballantyne, "Thinking Local: Knowledge, Sociability and Community in Gore's Intellectual Life, 1875–1914," *New Zealand Journal of History* 44, no. 2 (2010): 138.

10. Michael Warner, "Publics and Counterpublics," *Public Culture* 14, no. 1 (2002): 50.

11. Issues of *Komkya* from 1953, 54, 55, 59, 60, and 61, and *Kusare* from 1961, 62, 63, 65, 65, 66, and 67, can be consulted in the East Africana Collection of the University of Dar es Salaam. Issues of *Kusare* from 1962, 63, 64, and 67, are available on microfilm at the Library of Congress, Washington, DC.

12. See *Habari za Upare,* August 1952, Tanzania National Archives (hereafter TNA) 41176, f. 519.

13. Joel Millonzi cites United Nations figures suggesting that literacy rates among the Chagga people of Moshi district were "close to 100 percent" by 1958.

Joel Carl Millonzi, *Citizenship in Africa: The Role of Adult Education in the Political Socialization of Tanganyikans, 1891–1961* (Syracuse, NY: Maxwell School of Citizenship and Public Affairs, 1975), 86.

14. Susan G. Rogers, "Search for Political Focus on Kilimanjaro: A History of Chagga Politics, 1916–1952, with Special Reference to the Cooperative Movement and Indirect Rule," PhD dissertation, University of Dar es Salaam, 1972.

15. Letter from District Commissioner to Mangi Mkuu, 19 September 1952, TNA 5/10/21, f. 1.

16. "New Paper for the Wachagga: Notes," no date, TNA 5/10/21, f. 10.

17. G. K. Whitlamsmith, *Recent Trends in Chagga Political Development* (Moshi: KNCU Printing Press, 1955), n.p.

18. Whitlamsmith, *Recent Trends*, n.p.

19. "Two Tusks from Kilimanjaro," *Tanganyika Standard*, cited in Whitlamsmith, *Recent Trends*, n.p.

20. Letter from Mangi Mkuu to District Commissioner, Moshi, 20 October 1952, TNA 5/10/21, f. 6.

21. Letter from Mangi Mkuu to District Commissioner.

22. Martin Sturmer, *The Media History of Tanzania* (Ndanda, Tanzania: Ndanda Mission Press, 1998), 64.

23. James F. Scotton, "Tanganyika's African Press, 1937–1960: A Nearly Forgotten Pre-independence Forum," *African Studies Review* 21, no. 1 (1978): 8.

24. Horace Mason, "Pare News and Other Publications of the Pare Mass Literacy and Community Development Scheme," *Reports and Papers on Mass Communication: Periodicals for New Literates. Seven Case Histories* 24 (1957): 19. With the dominance of a lingua franca, Tanganyika's print culture had more in common with northern Nigeria, where similar steps had been taken to promote Hausa as a language of administration and literature, and which had a vibrant Hausa-language press, than with its East African neighbors. In Kenya, there was a lively Kikuyu- and Luo-language press, and in Buganda a Luganda press. See James F. Scotton, "Growth of the Vernacular Press in Colonial East Africa: Patterns of Government Control," PhD dissertation, University of Wisconsin, 1971; Fay Gadsden, "The African Press in Kenya, 1945–1952," *Journal of African History* 21, no. 4 (1980): 515–35.

25. Letter from Horace Mason, "Chagga Newspaper," 31 October 1952, TNA 5/10/21, f. 14.

26. Letter from Horace Mason.

27. Letter from Mangi Mkuu to District Commissioner, Moshi, 20 October 1952, TNA 5/10/21, f. 6.

28. Kumbukumbu za Mkutano wa Gazeti la Wachagga Uliofanyika Chagga Council Tarekh 3.12.52 [Minutes of a meeting concerning the Chagga Newspaper

held at the Chagga Council, 3 December 1952], TNA 5/10/21, f. 20. All translations are my own.

29. Kumbukumbu za Mkutano wa Gazeti la Wachagga Uliofanyika Chagga Council Tarekh, f. 29.

30. In a discussion on an Internet forum in June 2011 one participant recalled that Marealle's "government ran a newspaper at that time which was called 'Komkya.'" www.jamiiforums.com/habari-na-hoja-mchanganyiko/146471-ukoo-wa-marealle-waandamwa-na-dhambi-ya-kupenda-madaraka-2.html (accessed 31 December 2013).

31. Helen Kitchen, ed., *The Press in Africa* (Washington, DC: Ruth Sloan Associates, 1958), 38n.

32. Sturmer, *Media History of Tanzania*, 64. *Komkya* had its offices in the town's impressive new Chagga Council buildings. "Two Tusks from Kilimanjaro," *Tanganyika Standard*, reprinted in Whitlamsmith, *Recent Trends*, viii.

33. Scotton, "Vernacular Press," 8. Copies of *Habari za Upare* are preserved in TNA 41176.

34. Nkwabi Ng'wanakilala, *Mass Communication and Development of Socialism in Tanzania* (Dar es Salaam: Tanzania Publishing House, 1981), 17; Utz Lederbogen, *Watchdog or Missionary? A Portrait of African News People and Their Work* (Frankfurt am Main, Peter Lang, 1992), 25.

35. Godfrey Mwakikagale, *Life in Tanganyika in the Fifties: My Reflections and Narratives from the White Settler Community and Others* (Grand Rapids, MI: Continental Press, 2006), 68.

36. Mwakikagale, *Life in Tanganyika*, 69.

37. Kitchen, *Press in Africa*, 36.

38. Scotton, "Tanganyika's African Press," 8.

39. Government of Tanganyika, *Annual Report of the Public Relations Department, 1952* (Dar es Salaam: Government of Tanganyika, 1953), 4.

40. Government of Tanganyika, *Annual Report of the Public Relations Department, 1953* (Dar es Salaam: Government of Tanganyika, 1954), 4.

41. Tanganyika, *Public Relations Department, 1952*, 4.

42. Sturmer, *Media History of Tanzania*, 74.

43. Sturmer, *Media History of Tanzania*, 74.

44. Government of Tanganyika, *Annual Report of the Public Relations Department, 1955* (Dar es Salaam: Government of Tanganyika, 1956), 4.

45. Tanganyika, *Public Relations Department, 1952*, 2.

46. Kitchen, *Press in Africa*, 36.

47. Mason, "Pare News," 19.

48. Mason, "Pare News," 19.

49. Mason, "Pare News," 20.

50. Mason, "Pare News," 23.

51. Mason, "Pare News," 23.

52. Tanganyika, *Public Relations Department, 1955*, 4.

53. Tanganyika, *Public Relations Department, 1955*, 4. On pseudonymity see Newell, *Power to Name*.

54. D. C. Lushoto to Provincial Public Relations Officer, Tanga, FCO 141/17949, f. 74, 9 May 1959.

55. Warner, "Publics and Counterpublics," 55.

56. On which see Emma Hunter, "'In Pursuit of the Higher Medievalism': Local History and Politics in Kilimanjaro," in *Recasting the Past: History Writing and Political Work in Modern Africa*, edited by Derek Peterson and Giacomo Macola (Athens: Ohio University Press, 2009), 155. Cf. Karin Barber, "I.B. Akinyele and Early Yoruba Print Culture," also in *Recasting the Past*, 31–49.

57. A letter that appeared in the "Women's Page" in November 1953 employed this contrast between "darkness" or "ignorance" (*gizani*), and *komkya* to good effect to complain about people who risked their lives by failing to go to hospital until it was too late and instead relying on traditional medicine. Letter from M. Waryaurangiso Elisaa, *Komkya*, November 1953, 7.

58. Editorial, "Mila na Jadi," *Komkya*, September 1953, 2.

59. Letter from A. E. Kimambo, *Komkya*, 1 November 1955, 3.

60. The term used was "Uchagga," or Chaggaland.

61. Editorial, "Watu Mashuhuri," *Komkya*, 15 July 1955, 2.

62. Letter from Mwl. M. Sh. J. Shuma, *Komkya*, 15 October 1955, 3.

63. "Letter from the Mangi Mkuu to All Chagga," *Komkya*, 15 September 1954, 3. This was a reference to the song "Nkosi Sikilel'i Afrika."

64. Letter from R. Y. Lyimo, "Wimbo wa Kichagga," *Komkya*, 1 December 1954, 3.

65. Letter from N. A. H. Kombe, "Shindano la Komkya," *Komkya*, 1 November 1954, 3.

66. Letter from E. Solomon Z. Kaale, *Komkya*, 15 February 1957, 3.

67. Letter from Theosophil, "Lugha ya 'Komkya,'" *Komkya*, 15 March 1957, 3.

68. John Lonsdale, "Anti-colonial Nationalism and Patriotism in Sub-Saharan Africa," in *Oxford Handbook of the History of Nationalism*, edited by John Breuilly (Oxford: Oxford University Press, 2013), 318–40; Derek Peterson, *Ethnic Patriotism and the East African Revival: A History of Dissent, c. 1935–1972* (Cambridge: Cambridge University Press, 2012).

69. Editorial, *Komkya*, March 1954, 2. This was a regular theme in colonial newspapers; see, for example, Barber, *Print Culture*, 48; and Jones, this volume.

CHAPTER 11

Making Constituency in the Province

The *Osumare Egba* (1935–1937) and the Agenda of Abẹokuta Modernization

OLUWATOYIN BABATUNDE ODUNTAN

INTRODUCTION

The profundity of social and cultural change during the inter-war years, and how through it the identity and roles of the Nigerian intelligentsia were fashioned, continues to attract scholarly interest. Prior to the First World War, the Lagos intelligentsia had transitioned from a Victorian image to making indigenous cultural claims and inventions; after the war they became further invested in the expansion of the colony into the provinces. The war strengthened their sense of belonging in the empire, and its global mission of "civilization" against "tyrannical, oppressive and illiberal" colonialism. Newspapers, including those that were previously critical of colonial racialism, adopted the empire's "titanic struggle" as "our destiny" to secure "the benign influences of British imperial rule, whose watch words are liberty and progress."[1]

The induction of the African educated elite added legitimacy to colonial authority and enabled the shift from colonial conquests and pacification toward more intrusive policies of economic extraction and political control. The administrative reach of empire extended beyond colonial capitals to the provinces, carrying with it the cultural claims and infrastructures of the colonial state. Educated Africans who were previously congregated around the main centers of colonial administration and trade followed along, partly to take advantage of expanded opportunities, and as an extension of the cultural projects started before the war. They joined a small number of educated provincial residents to compose new constituencies crafting spaces of expression and influence in societies on colonial margins. The newspapers that they published in the provinces were influenced by and aspired to the prestige and effectiveness of those published in the colonial metropolis, yet they reference indigenous conversations and cultural productions peculiar to their contexts. This chapter focuses on one such newspaper, the *Osumare Egba*, to explore how newspapers as local and transnational objects generated and managed a literary public in predominantly illiterate societies. It complements the histories of the Nigerian press explored in chapters by Karin Barber, Rebecca Jones, and Wale Adebanwi in this volume, by highlighting the trajectory of literary expansion from cosmopolitan Lagos, with its Atlantic networks, to the comparatively more indigenous hinterland. Specifically, it narrates a different context of the form, strategies, and challenges of Western-educated Africans as they used newspapers to expand a constituency committed to modernization, and thereby craft spaces of expression in local politics and culture.

Historical studies of the African press tend to be dominated by its production and roles in the larger urban settings, neglecting those published outside very strong colonial conditions. This is more evidently the case for West Africa than for southern Africa. Whereas in the former, most educated Africans congregated in colonial centers like Freetown, Accra, Dakar, and Lagos, exclusion from large white settler colonies in southern Africa appears to have dispersed educated Africans more widely to smaller regional towns, where they published many impactful provincial newspapers.[2] The broad representation of the history of newspapers in West Africa narrates how influential newspapermen and political leaders used them to mobilize publics in their struggles for social recognition, political representation, and power in the colonial state. Scholars using these newspapers for commentaries on contemporary affairs tend to consider provincial ones as irrelevant to what they saw as the more cogent colonial and nationalist discourses. Among them, Fred Omu surmises, "Provincial newspapers are of little importance in the political evolution of Nigeria. They certainly contributed to inculcating the habits of reading and general enlightenment . . . but they did not make any noteworthy contributions to the advancement of political ideas or to the resolution of political controversies."[3] Similar views underscore the paucity of academic studies of provincial newspapers, as scholars have tended to focus on grander narratives of African history. As Jennifer Hasty demonstrates, news on the Gold Coast was dominated by a narrow anglophile intelligentsia, for whom "local (Accra) politics [was] synonymous with national politics and newsworthy stories from the regions were sporadic and generally less sensational."[4] Assumptions that they were inconsequential to what really mattered underlie the comparative neglect of newspapers and literary culture in regions outside of the major colonial capitals.

However, many newspapers were published outside of the colonial capitals and need to be seen as more than mere appendages to the dominant perspectives on newspaper history. In Nigeria, newspapers were published in Calabar, Aba, Onitsha, Port Harcourt, Ibadan, Abẹokuta, Ijebu-Ode, and Oṣogbo between 1920 and 1960.[5] Apart from filling gaps in historical knowledge, these newspapers offer an unexplored dimension of what the press meant for many Africans beyond the broad narrative of African newspaper history. Where the historiography narrates the West African press in terms of the evolution of Western-educated elites who were closely connected to Atlantic circuits, the literati of provincial newspapers more likely evolved indigenously as products of mission schools run by native pastorates. Educated Africans in the provinces had limited access to the wide Atlantic connections and were excluded from the privileges and exclusive social unions of the metropolitan elite, which Kristin Mann describes in *Marrying Well*.[6] Their social aspiration was similar to but also transcended that of the "non-elite" "intermediary" class, who aspired to the social and material status of the "lawyer-merchant intelligentsia" and assumed that (British) language, literacy, and notions of success were the required qualities for social elevation.[7] Yet, while young men in Accra and other colonial African metropolises operated where structures already existed for their aspirations, the native intelligentsia in the provinces existed within indigenous societies that did not value these qualities as highly. Being at the margins of direct colonial control, the provincial literati was not availed the colonial and Atlantic resources that the metropolitan intelligentsia rode upon to acquire wealth and power. Thus, while they shared in the self-conceptions and aspirations of the metropolitan elite as modernizing agents and adopted similar strategies (including publishing newspapers), the Western-educated Africans in the provinces had much more limited means of pushing their agendas. Building newspaper-reading publics, crafting spaces of expression and influence, and expanding political platforms, and so on, was apparently more challenging for the native educated elite. The *Osumare Egba* shares in the broad trajectory of the African press in how it brought writers and artists together with an audience, created literatures and a culture for textual news, poetry, arts, and intellectual ideas, and promoted an ideology of modernization. Yet its path to occupy and claim the culture-space and politics of Abẹokuta marks it apart from many accounts of the roles and influence of newspapers in Africa.

INTERWAR ABẸOKUTA: THE NATIVE LITERATI'S MODERNITY

Abẹokuta, where the *Osumare Egba* operated, offers a valuable example of a society on the margins of colonial power. Founded around 1830 by refugees fleeing from regional wars, its early history was of intense competition among its component parts to define its politics, identity, history, and culture. From the 1840s, liberated slaves, returnee creoles from Sierra Leone, and European missionaries entered into preexisting discourses and contestations. Neither the indigenous groups nor the Saro creoles and European immigrants constituted unambiguously coherent identities; rather, competing national, doctrinal, commercial, and imperial rivalries formed fluid alliances with different competing segments of Abẹokuta society. From 1865, a section of Western-educated Africans joined with a section of chiefs to modernize the government in a bid to mitigate British missionary and colonial attempts to influence the creation of a centralized monarchy suited to colonial control. Their success secured sovereignty for Abẹokuta during the European Scrambles and made it survive colonial conquest until 1914, and afterward the town retained significant internal autonomy under British rule.[8] By its relative newness, its competing discourses, and its complex relations with Europeans, Abẹokuta escapes assumptions of the immutability of African cultures against which a Western form can be distinctively contrasted. Its modernization evolved from multiple sources, not just European ones, which individuals and groups drew upon in competition with one another. Therefore, it evinces a trajectory in which an African society evolved in a process of struggles and interactions, domestically forged its process of social transformation, and was not singularly determined by colonial power and control.

Newspapers emerged within this intensely contested politics, of elites mapping ethnic identities, crafting histories, constructing traditions, and appropriating the modern to claim and establish precedence over one another. The first newspaper, *Iwe Irohin* (1859–67) started as an experiment of the Church Missionary Society to sustain creole converts "lest they revert to heathenism."[9] Henry Townsend, the resident missionary, conceived of the bilingual newspaper as a means of instruction and enlightenment.[10] However, the *Iwe Irohin* was soon mired in Abẹokuta's struggles and set against a segment of the chiefly elite with which some creole returnees had allied to form a republican government, the Egba United Board of Management (EUBM). The newspaper ceased publishing following the *Ifọle* (lit. house-breaking) that broke out on account of these political struggles and led to the expulsion of Europeans from the city in 1867.[11] Other experiments at news publishing followed the demise of the *Iwe Irohin*, with the EUBM attempting to continue the literary tradition by publishing a *EUBM Gazette* until 1874. Upon the collapse of the EUBM, its successor administration, the Egba United Government, published the EUG *Gazette* from 1904 until 1920, when now under British colonization, the Egba Native Administration (ENA) published a *Bulletin*.[12] The *Gazette* and *Bulletin* published government edicts, official correspondences, as well as commentaries and letters from readers.

These early experiments were powerful interjections into the cultural space of Abẹokuta. Whereas most of the earliest print materials were theological ones, the *Iwe Irohin* set a precedent as a public media for secular news by drawing natives, literate and nonliterates alike, as reporters, carriers of news, and news-subjects, from whom the editors drew local information they could not otherwise obtain. The newspaper's detailed reports of the Egba-Dahomey battles, the Ijaye wars, movement of slaves, slave markets, chiefly politics, comparative commodity prices, local perceptions of the British and French, and so on, do not just offer valuable insights into political developments in the region: they reveal literary texts as mediums around which news, opinions, propaganda, and discourse converged. *Iwe Irohin* attracted a significant number of youths as apprentices, printers, distributors, vendors, and writers. Apparently one of them became its editor in 1865 when Henry Townsend returned back to England.[13] By constituting a growing public around its bimonthly publications, it became a powerful tool for building a political constituency—the Christian Party—which by the 1880s had become powerful enough to challenge chiefly authority.[14] Its value as a powerful tool of mobilization endeared it to chiefly elites, who, as J. D. Y. Peel correctly observes, were already losing many women and slaves to Christian conversion, and now had to deal with indigenous youths captured by the attractions of the new literary media.[15] Such chiefs quickly invested in the evolving literary culture by employing clerks to read, translate, and write their letters, treaties, and petitions. Merchants like the renowned Madam Tinubu employed creoles to organize trade accounts and as letter writers.[16] That the *Gazettes* were published despite the expulsion of British missionaries in 1867 by Abẹokuta's (chiefly led) governments underscores how quickly this society adopted and adapted literary texts.

These publications bequeathed a heritage of cultural innovation in writing and other literary forms from which a vibrant intellectual community developed. That community grew at pace as educational facilities expanded, widening the reading public. In regard to Western education, Abẹokuta compared favorably with the colonial metropolises. In 1851, the Wesley Methodist Missionary Society reported 80 day-scholars attended two schools in Abẹokuta.[17] Starting with an elementary school in 1850, the CMS grew a chain of schools that graduated many for which an advanced technical institution was created to train missionaries, teachers, and medical doctors.[18] To underscore the enthusiasm with which young people took to education in Abẹokuta, Frederick Bühler, who managed the training institute, wrote: "I myself saw how necessary it was to instruct the young men who were waiting almost two years for regular instruction. We want more agents; there is no want of young men, they only want to be instructed."[19]

By 1907, Abẹokuta's government had an inspectorate devoted to supervising schools and conducting examinations, and the government also organized school essay-writing competitions.[20] Furthermore, printing also became established as a fully engaging vocation organized around apprenticeship at the mission printing presses and those of the governments. Therefore, by the time the *Osumare Egba* began to publish in 1935, Abẹokuta already had a sustained tradition in print culture and a considerable reading public. This public was also closely connected to Lagos and the modern Atlantic because it supplied the colony with some of the leading journalists, editors, and writers of Lagos newspapers. Lagos newspapers regularly reported on Abẹokuta, celebrating its independence (up till 1914) and its modern government and "civilized king" from 1920. Indeed, the *Lagos Standard* (1894–1920) and *Nigerian Pioneer* (1914–36) devoted special sections to Abeokuta news. On the other hand, Lagos became the benchmark by which educated elites in Abẹokuta and its diaspora measured the "slow" progress of their nation. They lamented the "glorious old days when the Egba led in everything," and viewed the contemporary condition of their country as retrogression. They could not accept that Ibadan, which they saw as backward, could sustain a newspaper. Local intellectuals publicly wondered why all the wealthy chiefs, powerful Ẹgba sons, and professionals were incapable of civilizing Abẹokuta, the first step of which would be publishing a newspaper. The *Osumare Egba* newspaper declared itself as fulfilling that mission. In its inaugural edition, it recalled that for many years, "all Egbas have been waiting for who will bell the cat."[21]

Despite its early experience with literacy, Abẹokuta's literati was always a narrow minority struggling to craft a space in a political system organized around chiefly power. Colonial conquest in 1914 did not significantly alter the political system enough to expand opportunities for educated elites; rather, colonialism remained practically nonintrusive, because the British retained the existing political structure and indeed strengthened the *Alake*'s (king) power as sole native authority.[22] Chiefs in Abẹokuta continued to act as though their country was sovereign, and only in friendly relations with the British. They interpreted and reshaped the colonial native administration system to be the continuation of an older experiment in political modernization since the mid-nineteenth century. The ENA issued bulletins in a mode similar to the EUBM and the EUG *Gazettes* before it, and continued to define itself as a modern sovereign government. In the same vein, colonialism did not quench the sharp divisions and struggles of Abẹokuta's politics. It remained organized around four main principalities, the kings of which claimed internal independence and manipulated colonial and other resources in their struggle for dominance. The Alake held the advantage because it was erroneously determined to be king of all Abẹokuta by the British and was made sole native administrator. However, British power did not douse the persistent claims and opposition of other sections and their chiefs, but rather reinforced them.[23] In this predominantly chiefly structure, therefore, Western education and literacy did not confer much immediate recognition or privilege on literate citizens. The prevailing system offered limited life options, employment opportunities, access to land, role in politics, and so on, to the Western educated. On the contrary, it made many chiefs wealthy from their control of land and labor in the vibrant cash crop economy, and powerful as a consequence of the British indirect rule system.

Furthermore, Abẹokuta's literary public evolved within these struggles between sectional identities, religious and doctrinal divergences, and competing political ideologies. Its literati were not a single agency with a coherent ideology, but were widely divided along Abẹokuta's many contesting pulls. Writers differed over the meanings of Ẹgba nationhood, over citizenship and its responsibilities; they lined up on either sides of monarchical centralization and chiefly federalism, claimed membership of different subethnic groups, and struggled over the meanings and implications of customs and traditions, the extent and legitimacy of chiefly power, the place of women, the roles of the educated, and so on. Yet they could converge around a loose definition of modernity, using newspapers to debate its particulars, and to craft a constituency for the pursuit of their goal of pushing Abẹokuta toward their imagined society.

This is well demonstrated in debates among the town's leading intellectuals during Abẹokuta's centenary celebration in 1930. A. K. Ajisafẹ, Adebẹshin Fọlarin, and Ladipo Solankẹ were without a doubt Abẹokuta's leading intellectuals and most prodigious writers. Ajisafẹ, born Emmanuel Moore, was of creole (Saro) heritage and thus connected to families in Sierra Leone and Lagos. He had worked with the EUG until 1911, when he was convicted of fraud and incarcerated, which subsequently limited the publishing outlets for his prodigious intellectual productions.[24] In some contrast, Ladipo Solankẹ was related to several Ẹgba chiefs but spent most of his life studying and practicing law in the UK, where he founded the West African Students Union (WASU) and was very active in the colonial and Atlantic intellectual circuits. Fọlarin left his profitable law practice in Lagos to accept the lower wage of president of Abẹokuta's "Grade A" court in 1928, going on to publish four books, including *The Laws and Customs of Egbaland*. At the Centenary Lecture in 1930, Solankẹ called for the proper definition and codification of Ẹgba citizenship, and by inference challenged Ajisafẹ's locus for writing the *History of Abeokuta*. In a reaction titled *The Errors and Defeat of Ladipo Solanke, M.A., B.C.L., L.L.B.* (1930), Ajisafẹ accused Solankẹ of having lost "the Purely Native Mind" necessary to interpret realities in Abẹokuta, on account of his long sojourns and absence. He further termed Solakẹ's proposal for citizenship law as an "Unrighteous and Iniquitous Decree," a direct reference to the Bible, which underscores the contemporary influence of Christianity in framing ideas of the civilized society.[25] In 1931, Solakẹ referred to Ajisafẹ as a "layman in the science of the law,"[26] and therefore incompetent, and fraudulent for writing *The Laws and Customs of the Yoruba People* (1924). Fọlarin entered the fray with his *A Short Review of the Life of the Egbas* (1931). He had previously been accused of being unpatriotic for demanding "such heavy wage to serve his fatherland" as court president.[27]

These encounters demonstrate the rich exchange of ideas among the educated elite in Abẹokuta. They reference a world of cultural multiplicity, confused identities, and contested imaginations of the future. Yet the intelligentsia converged around the idea of an "Egba nation, taking its place among the nations of the world."[28] By documenting histories, codifying laws, reformulating traditions, and so on, they were also placing signification on their place in it and their roles as modernizing agents and culture brokers. This tradition and imagination of Abẹokuta's sovereignty continued well into the late 1940s, when educated elites constituted a national conference in a bid to draft a constitution and flag in anticipation of Abẹokuta's statehood. The written text as a medium of discourse was a critical part of the educated elite's identity, and their strategy to establish their place in the society and to claim the lead voice in the making of its future. Their strategy included widening the reading public by which they could create and expand a constituency invested in their vision of Abẹokuta and thereby secure their claims to its leadership.

Therefore, Ẹgba discourses were fully engaging and dynamic because in their intense competition, various sections and chiefs were indiscriminate in their adoption and adaptation of new ideas. During the nineteenth century, they successfully *domesticated* and divided European Christian missions among them—with the Ake, Oke-Ọna, Owu, and Gbagura sections claiming British CMS, Wesleyan Methodist, Baptist, and French Catholicism respectively.[29] As they tried under colonial rule to imprint their ideas and influence on Abẹokuta, the literati were also exposed to the attractions of chiefly power and resources offered by diverse competing forces of Ẹgba politics. They were directly invested in sectional identity as subjects of sectional chiefs, and they necessarily depended on wealthy chiefs for access to land, labor, capital, employment, and other chiefly privileges.

It can be erroneous to separate educated and chiefly elites of Abẹokuta on either side of "modern" or "traditional" considering the multiple appropriations and crisscrossing alliances that saw chiefs appropriating modern ideas and Western-educated elites trying to secure chiefly power. It is for these reasons that the newspapers they published were shades different from more metropolitan ventures. The literati in Abẹokuta were small in number, marginal, comparatively poor, and divided, and were very reliant on the extant social and political structures. The society in which they evolved and on which they tried to impose their ideas of modernization was dynamic rather than traditional; it was one open to appropriating and capable of domestication *foreign* ideas. Furthermore, because the British indirect rule system was predicated on the idea of minimal intervention in native government, it enabled chiefs and educated elites to imagine and craft modernization on local terms. In the light of the distance of colonial power from Abẹokuta, the metadiscourses of colonialism, Africanism, and Westernization that more metropolitan colonial elites engaged were secondary to the lived experiences of Abẹokuta's politics and society. In publishing newspapers to craft a constituency, Abẹokuta's intellectuals had to focus on local issues much more than colonial ones. Whereas Lagos newspapers published many accounts of the British Empire, of Atlantic and Africanist discourses, only limited mentions of these can be found in Abẹokuta newspapers. For instance, the death of King George V, which was widely announced and mourned by Lagos newspapers from 21 January 1936, was mentioned only once in the *Osumare Egba*; and only then as a public announcement paid for by the Alake in his capacity as colonial sole native authority.[30] In the same vein, the ferment of 1920s Lagos, which revitalized, radicalized, and popularized the colony's newspapers, revolved mainly around colonial issues. As Karin Barber demonstrates in this volume, politically radical members of the Lagos elite used the deposition and exile of the Eleko (1925), mass protests against the water rate, and other political agitations to build a mass following by which they established credibility as leaders.[31] In Abẹokuta, the cumulativeness of British indirect rule policy, chiefly claims to sovereignty, and continuities in social and political structure meant that disaffections were not targeted at colonial rule. That crucial medial space that the Lagos elite could locate itself in to claim and expand a constituency[32] was critically lacking for Abẹokuta's educated elite.

OSUMARE AND THE AGENDA OF POLITICAL MODERNIZATION

Published weekly in eight pages of 19" × 11.5" paper, the *Osumare Egba* hit the newsstands on 7 December 1935. It had been long in the making, from 1925 when the editor first unsuccessfully applied for a newspaper license, and because he had not found anyone wealthy enough to sponsor the venture. This is significant because it shows that unlike Lagos, where the colonial economy enabled the likes of Victor Babamuboni, a former vendor, to become publisher of the *Lagos Daily News*, the educated elite here could not muster enough funds to fulfill the conditions for registering and publishing without support from chiefly patrons.[33] Sponsorship was eventually secured in 1935 from an "educated" chief and owner of the Nigerian Blessed Press. D. Bamgbọṣe owned a printing press stationed at Ibara and, if we go by reports of his regular travels, may have also owned another in Lagos. As one of many "educated chiefs," he symbolizes Roger Gocking's thesis of the conflation of African elite identity, and the discursive limitation of sharply separating a modern elite from a traditional one.³⁴ As publisher of the *Osumare Egba*, Bamgboṣe depicts the tensional inclusiveness of tradition and modernity, and highlights how these were ideological resources that elites deployed and struggled over.

The printing press was located at Ibara on the road to Lagos, which had grown from being a slave factory, to Europeans merchants' shops during the nineteenth century, to become the commercial hub of Abẹokuta. It was at a short distance from the government offices where the Native Administration Press published the *ENA Bulletin*, and was also close to the railway line linking Lagos to the Nigerian interior. With Abeokuta Grammar School nearby, from where the renowned Reverend Ransome Kuti founded and chaired the Nigerian Union of Teachers, and the books market midway between the government printing press and the bookstore, the *Osumare* was well located amid Abẹokuta's literary infrastructure. It could access an existing intellectual community, an active vocational industry, and a commercial market and entrepôt of the city. These factors were promising for its profitability with the editor assured that at the copy sale price of 1d, it was sustainable, "if only Egbas would fulfill their patriotic duties of patronizing it."³⁵ The fear that the people of Abẹokuta might not patronize the newspaper or accept it as their own was well borne because this location was at the very margin of a large city. Local perceptions of Ibara as being *outside* Abẹokuta (slave market and European shops) also underscore the challenge of the newspaper's anticipated acceptance as an indigenous project. While it might be suggested that newspapers were *foreign* to Africa anyway, it is valuable to recall that the *Iwe Irohin* (1859–67) was published in the Church Missionary Society mission at Ake, right in heart of the city, close to the Ake palace and with the Ita Ogboni (where the council of elders) met, within reach. Accordingly, whereas the *Iwe Irohin* could interact very closely with the citizens and become enmeshed in local identity and politics, the *Osumare Egba* struggled to find an inroad in Abẹokuta society.

Furthermore, the newspaper also had to contend with literary materials and influences from Lagos, where newspaper production was much more advanced, boosted by the related processes of Nigerian nationalist gestation and Yoruba ethno-construction. The project of a pan-Yoruba identity, well illustrated by J. D. Y. Peel,³⁶ went alongside the expansion of nationalist consciousness as the Lagos-based elite expanded their claim of representation beyond Lagos. Both of these processes adopted print culture, especially newspapers, to craft reading publics and cultural and political constituencies. According to Karin Barber, the discourses they generated enhanced the proliferation of Yoruba-language newspapers as part of the discursive and territorial widening of the literary public to include less-literate natives in Lagos and beyond.[37] However, these were mainly Lagos colonial discourses, and they drew limited traction in the provinces. Yoruba cultural revivalism was mainly a response to colonial racialist exclusions, while Nigerian nationalism grew as opposition to government policies and to take advantage of political opportunities, most of which were centered in the city. In these struggles, Lagos elites responded to new legislative political opportunities opened up by the Clifford Constitution of 1922 to form political parties. As those opportunities widened in line with further bureaucratic incorporation of regions outside the colony, educated elites refashioned associations like the Lagos Youth Movement into the Nigerian Youth Movement in 1936. Newspapers were important media by which Lagos elites mobilized colonial subjects in Lagos to challenge adverse colonial policies and push electioneering politics, but these issues were hardly cogent in the provinces. Regardless, provincial newspapers like the *Osumare Egba* had to contend with the forays of these powerful movements as well as compete with their intellectual and cultural productions as they claimed brokerage of Nigeria, including the provinces.

The main challenge for the *Osumare Egba*, therefore, was to keep the influence of Lagos at bay and constitute, manage, and retain a readership committed to the local newspaper and its agenda of change. To achieve this, the editors tried to locate the paper as well as possible within Abẹokuta's collective nationhood by claiming to be its national symbol. The choice of the motto "Do your duty come what may" was clearly aimed at driving a patriotic zeal for Ẹgba nationalism and, flowing from that, support for *Osumare*, its national symbol. The title, translated "Rainbow of the Ẹgba," recognized the many different tones and textures of the city's cultures and politics. Its inaugural edition had the king's goodwill message and pleas for national unity and progress on the front page. The editorial narrated the making of the Ẹgba nation from an original homestead to the present state of progress under a modern and progressive king. There were congratulatory messages from Ẹgba nationals in Lagos, celebrating it as the revival of "civilization"[38]

The agenda of change was explicit. The *Osumare* anticipated rolling away of the current order and explained its inevitability as the law of nature and the godly designed way:

> The old order changeth yielding place to the new and God fulfils Himself in many ways lest one good custom should corrupt the world. . . . When the

time comes, the old order, old friends must pass away from us leaving in their place the new.[39]

To achieve the change to prosperity and peace required unity, which according to the paper, the Ęgbas were lacking in. It advocated unity and cooperation under the leadership of the Alake, "the first education ruler in Nigeria" (*Osumare Egba*, 4 January, 11).

Being national required a careful navigation of Abęokuta's many contradictory pulls, not only in its intense sectional politics, but also in the society's class and social structure. On one hand, celebrating the Alake as the "only civilized king in all of Africa," and the Ęgba nation for having the most influential educated elements, somewhat contradicted the paper's promise to be the "the voice of the masses,"[40] to promote democracy and good government, especially because these aspirations may rightly be construed as opposition to the monarch. Abęokuta during the 1930s was in a ferment of popular uprisings, including the 1933 protests by market women against the government's ban on caustic soda.[41] Market women protested against the imposition of market leaders on them in 1934, just as there were public agitations against increased taxation, and the activities of the *wole-wole* (lit. house searchers) sanitary inspectors.[42]

The fallout of the conflicts during the 1920s, such as the Adubi revolt, in which peasants resisted taxation, as well as crises arising from the Alake's attempt to suspend or depose sectional chiefs, remained unresolved well past the period of *Osumare Egba*'s publication.[43] In all these cases, public discontents were targeted at the Alake and the NA (native authority) rather than against British colonialism. To have sided with an unpopular ruler made sense with respect to the newspaper's claim to represent the nation, but did not confirm its capacity to equally defend the masses. Furthermore, "masses" in Abęokuta's context necessarily invoked subethnic connotations because of the sectional configuration of its politics. Indeed, the Ake section, the king of which the British privileged, constituted a numerical minority to the three other sections, and most of their masses were conceivably dissatisfied with the central monarchy. The *Osumare* had to determine which of the masses it sought to protect. From its early edition the newspaper's predilection toward a section was apparent, writing, "We are now anxious to enter into journalistic career with a view to promote the literary activity in Gbagura section as far as we are concerned; the day is gone-by when education in Gbagura section is being considered as 'Rara Avis.'"⁴⁴ Despite proclaiming an Egba national agenda under the king's sovereignty, the paper contradictorily committed to a subethnic agenda.

This posture is meaningful in the light of contemporary developments in Abẹokuta's politics. Being sole native administrator empowered the Alake to reduce the sectional monarchs to his vassals, requiring them to attend the Native Council as advisers, appointing them to executive positions as his lieutenants, and so on, sometimes suspending them for insubordination and interfering in the traditional processes of appointments in their sections. Confrontations with the sectional ọbas (kings) often resulted in violence, as was the case in the Adubi War (1917), Agura Stool crisis (1936), Owu succession crisis (1936–37), and so on.⁴⁵ They also divided the educated elite, which organized around subnational associations such as the Lisabi Club, Owu National Association, and Gbagura Union, among others. These groups saw the Alake and council as drawing power and resources away from their sections. "Akeism," as the *Osumare* labeled it, concentrated too much power in the Alake to the detriment of progress elsewhere.

Promoting sectional agendas was a valuable way by which the native educated elite could find inroads into chiefly politics. The *Osumare Egba* held "uneducated and uncivilized" chiefs responsible for Gbagura's comparative "backwardness" and its disadvantaged position in Abẹokuta's political structure. It depicted Ake's dominance as the cunning of an educated ọba using modern resources against those stuck in the past.⁴⁶ Following the death of the Agura (king of Gbagura) in January 1936, the paper launched a campaign for the democratization or openness of the selection process of electing a new one. It particularly insisted that an educated element be chosen as successor. This was unprecedented in many ways. First, the traditional system for succession was well defined—leading Ogboni chiefs of the section met to ratify the candidate of the next royal house in succession and presented that choice to the public. Usually, the prince-designate was already well known, and in this case was already being prepared. Apparently aware of this, the newspaper argued that the overriding consideration must change in favor of modernization and civilization.

> As a rule, the chiefs are supposed to give their opinion to the authorities . . . and their opinion is expected to be Dogmatic [sic] under collective security in order to avoid strife. [Yet] Nigeria at present is advancing in civilization and the cry for civilized rulers is absolutely due for consideration.⁴⁷

OSUMARE EGBA

A WEEKLY NEWS-PAPER

MOTTO:—"DO YOUR DUTY COME WHAT MAY."

VOL: 1 No. 12   ABẸOKUTA   SATURDAY FEBRUARY 29, 1936.   Price 1d only

Who will be the New Agura
By F. O. Deigh.

In the Yoruba Countries it has been usual to be suggesting a new ruler when a stool is vacant since it was, and it is, according to Native Customs as the man to be are not generally known. And as a rule the chiefs are supposed to give their opinion to the authorities in favour of their selection and their opinion is expected to be Dogmatic under collective security in order to avoid political strife. Nigeria at present is advancing in civilization and the cry for civilized rulers is absolutely due for consideration. The former Agura, was an illiterate and it is said that he was able to govern his people Satisfactorily for 22 years. But it should be borne in mind that after the death of an illiterate ruler an enlightened ruler is the requirement of the people now-a-days. As there is a Community already familiar with usages of modern civilization and their co-operation with the primitive tribes should be invaluable. Hence an educated ruler with modern civilization who will be able to face the atmospheric condition of the political affairs of the country will be valuable to His Highness and the country. Majority of the citizens of Gbagura are supposed to be men of education and the selection of an illiterate ruler may be invaluable. Education and modern civilization is taking a seat, almost in every countries in the Southern provinces. It is advantageous to replace civilized rulers on vacant stools in the country now-a-days.

In view of this the public who had retrospect of the condition of some countries in the protectorate could verify the improvements since the proclamation and occupation of civilized rulers. Although an illiterate ruler could carry on since he is rampaged by the educated elements, but as a ruler, he may display his loyalty according to the merit and dignity of his position which may not suit or irregular with modern civilization. In comparison, the recent improvement in Abeokuta since the occupation of a civilized ruler is on the "push" thereby it is explicit that the four civilized rulers in the protectorate are bowed of examples.

"Choose a wise Selection"

As a regular reader of this valuable journal I would observe that there are two candidates on the pole, Lasisi Bakare and Laloko in true sense of it majority of the people of Gbagura are in favour of a civilized ruler and even the resolution passed by the Gbagura Youngmen Improvement Association on the 15th instant including the letter from Lisabi Society from Lagos expressing the advisability of filling the post of Agura with educated candidate the two leading Journals in Lagos of the 6th & 7th instant respectively has given comments which are worthy and deserves keen consideration, and His Highness advice for the Gbagura people to place an educated man on the vacant stool which will be of good use to them. It is said that chief Amodu Lalekan is strongly in favour of Laloko. Although we are not to oppose the chief with the strongest possible adjectives neither be is using domineering attitude on the selection of Laloko as he is known to be the "Big Gun" in the community. In order to scrape off, some doubts, it would have been possible for a state discussion on the matter that if the weight of the Mohamedans elections are above the Christian elections on each of the two candidates now in the public eye. If the census of religionist in the Southern provinces is being taken, one could clearly understand that each country individually in Nigeria is in her religion Mohamedanism to the extent of nearly two thirds of her people and the Christian religion to the extent of rather not more than one third. A regular reader of this Journal could testify that the selection of Laloko is probably due that he is being a man who lives a country life and has made himself conversant with the people and since an illiterate ruler was able to satisfy them, Laloko is therefore their immediate choice. It would not have been an impossibility within the educated elements either Mohamedans or Christians in religion to have been keen after the education of the sons of the illiterate chiefs or Obas, the weak point is if Laloko had been an educated man, or if the chiefs are going amiss in their choice? "Per contra" the two candidates in question as I see it, are Mohamedan in religion, Lasisi Bakare is an educated man and Laloko has none thereby, since they are both members of the same religion the matter deserves a careful consideration. It appears that almost two thirds of the people are

Continue on page 3.

Fig. 1. Osumare Egba 1 (12) (1936).

nigbati (Driver) Dẹrẹba ti o ọna Ilọrin bọ ri pe (Driver) Dẹrẹla ti o nti ọna Inulende bọ ko ni ya fun on, nje ki on ya fun ni o yi ayida sinu koto lo ṣubu. Nkan ti o mâ ṣeoi kogbo, ninu gbogbo awọn towa ninu mọto na a fi ọkurin kan lo fi ara pa die. Bo ba ku ki Oluwa ko ṣoni o.

IROHIN EDẸ

Ni ọjọ alẹ Jimọh 10/1/36 ti ọkọ Oshogbo ni lati de Station (Ibuduro ọkọ ilẹ) eyi ti on lọ ni o; bi ọkọ na ti gunlẹ tan, nibẹ ni a ri awọn Egbẹ Alalikali ti nwọn njo wa si idi-ọkọ, ati ọmọdẹ wọn a ti agbalagba inu nwọn, apapọ gbogbo nwọn jẹ 30 [ogbọn] enia Ọga awọn Alalikali to nṣe itọju wọn ni ọjọ na oruko rẹ nje Solomon, ọpọlọpọ ni o yọju ni idi ọkọ ki tosi, nigbati ọkọ si tan, nwọn dori kọ ọna ấrin ilu, ni ọjọ kanna ni wọn sin pada. Ki Ọlọrun jẹ ki a ṣe amọdun.

ỌLADAPỌ AKANMU

Ọtọ ni ṣegede da igba tirẹ

Nigbati o ku ọla ti afẹ fi Ọlarewaju Akanmu jẹ Balogun Ibadin, ni Ọladapọ Akanmu bẹrẹ si ṣe jijẹ ati mimu fun gbogbo awọn enia ti o nwa ki wọn, ti awọn onibẹnbẹ Akanmu fi ṣere mẹju ọjọ na, o da aṣọ fun Atanda gẹgẹ bi ọga awọn alalikali ni alẹ ọjọ na. Lẹninia Ogunmọla Balogun awọn Alaṣbẹdẹ Adodo ko ere ogun wa si ibi oye na, titi ilẹ fi ṣu nijọ oye na ni awọn ṣanmọri elẹṣin awọn egbẹ rẹ ti Ibadan ti Suarawu jẹ Manija wọn, ti Ọladapọ si jẹ Baba egbẹ fun wọn nṣere.

Gbogbo awọn egbẹ wọnyi loṣe gẹgẹ bi awọn egbẹ Kila ti ma ṣe fun ọmọ Ajibodu ni Abeokuta, ki ade ko pẹ lori, ki bata pẹ lẹṣẹ, iṣẹ ti Akanmu ṣe ni ọjọ na o fi ain jo iṣe ti Aminu Egbeyemi ti Ago-Owu ma nṣe. Die ninu awọn egbẹ na niyi:— Adedekun alao, Salami Ladipo, Karimu Muṣkuyọmi, Oyelẹkẹ t B a l o g u n, Akanmu aṣaju, Suarawu ati Salimọnu, Badiru, ki Ọlọrun jẹ ki ọmọ to Baba, Amin.

A ṣe idanwo fun awọn to fẹ gba Iṣ Akọda Ibadan ni 4/1/36, esi awọn to ṣe dada ninu idanwo na si jade ni 13/1/36. Iye ti a fi ṣe maki (mark) idanwo na je 190. Gbogbo awọn to ṣe dada ninu Idanwo na ni a to oruko wọn wọnyi:— J. A. Adeniji 145, J. L. Kolapọ 139, E. L. Ogunjinmi 128, F. Oyediran 121, E. Adetunji 120, Y. B. Ayilara Arẹ 119, M. O. Akande 118, J. Abegunde, 115, J. Agboọla 112, Y. Akinọla 111, J. Ọmoboyeji 110', F. Luitan 109, E. Ajao Giwa 108, J. B. Ajao 107, S. Adeniji 105, Jimo 104, J. P. Binuyo 103, E. A. Oyesola 100, E. Dawodu 99, J. Onawale 98, J. A. Ajiwon 97, P. O. Sinyẹnbọla 96, S. Afọlabi 95, S. Akanuu 95, Onaọlapọ 95, J. Adejare 95, J. Olabiyi 95 J. O. Akintunde 95, D. O. Akindiya 95, S. Ajani 95, Mr. S. Vincent Latunde ni Secretary wọn

AWỌN OYE MẸTA TI AJẸ NI ILU IBADAN NIYI NI ỌJỌ JIMOH 10th JANUARY 1936

Oruko awọn gbajumọ mẹta ti a fi joye ni ilu Ibadan na nwọnyi. Oruko ekinni amaje Ọlanrewaju Akanmu ara ile Ogunmọla leti (court) Aiapo; Ekeji Fashile, ẹkẹta amaje Fagbinrin ọmọ Akere, Ọlanrewaju Akanmu ti afifi jẹ Osi Balogun a wa yi oye rẹ si Otun Balogun, beni arakunrin wa kẹta ti otijẹ Ashipa-ri, awa fi jẹ Osi Balogun o.

Gẹgẹ bi atiṣe eto, ati iyẹsi oye na ni wọnyi:— Nigbati odi ọjọ Jimoh na ni dede agogo mẹju to fi di agogo mẹwa owuro, ita Balẹ ko gba enia fun ẹṣẹ lọkunrin, lobinrin tọmọde tagba, ati gbogbo awọn oloye pataki-pataki to wa ni ilu Ibadan, gẹgẹ bi ọgbeni wa Acting Resident Captain E. J. G. Kelley, Adebisi Asipa of Ibadan, Ọtun Balẹ Gbadamọsi Otiti; Gbadamọsi Afunieyin, I. B. Akinyẹle Ibadan Conncillor, oloye akọwe Igbimọ Ibadan, olori awọn Gambari ni Sabo ti oruko rẹ nje Abudu ati awọn ẹmẹwa rẹ pẹlu ni ọjọ na, nwọn gun ẹsin ati awọn oloye pataki-pataki ti nwọn wa pẹlu gẹgẹ bi Iyalode Ibadan ti a npe Ruka.

Madam Moradewan eyi ti iṣe Ọtun Iyalode Ibadan wa pẹin ati awọn ẹmẹwa rẹ pẹlu sin wa ni ọjọ na, Iyalode yi jẹ obinrin kan ti oruko fẹ han pupọ ni ilu Ibadan ti ofi jẹ pe ile rẹ ni a gbo wipe nwọn ngun ogi ti nwọn fi nṣe ẹkọ fun awọn ọlẹwọn.

Nigbati oye awọn oloye mẹtẹta yi pe si ile Balẹ Ibadan tan, ni nwọn tẹ jẹ oye na, a pẹ pupọ, ohun ti oṣi jẹ ki ọpẹ ni pe ọpẹgun ti wọn nreti, Balẹ rànṣẹ lọ gte ọpagun na, o wa gbe fun Ọlanrewaju Akanmu ẹniti nwọn fi jẹ Balogun na.

Lẹhin ti wọn jẹ oye yi tan, ni awọn oni ilu pẹlu oni ṣekẹrẹ, Bẹmbẹ, agogo ifa ati awọn ọdẹ, oni Band bẹrẹ si ṣe ere fun ariya yi ni ile Balẹ, awọn oni Ibọn nyin Ibọn awọn ni nwọn niwaju Balẹ, nigbati nwọn kuro ni ti Balẹ ni nwọn tun bẹrẹ si ṣe ere titi de ile Balogun, Balogun na wa ni ori ẹṣin ati awọn Oloye miran pẹlu, Osi nikan ni a ri ninu mọto rẹ 60 1509.

Lẹhinna ni arakunrin wa kan ti oruko rẹ nje Jimoh Arowolo ọmọ Arẹ Ibadan odindi Mọte kan lo gba, Lẹhinnu ni a ri arakunrin wa kan ti oruko rẹ njẹ Lasisi Ọlanipekun ni ori ẹṣin pẹlu awọn Dongari ni egbẹ Kinni mẹjọ ni egbe keji ni ọjọ na, okiki oye na yi gbogbo ilu Ibadan ka ni ọjọ na, lẹhinna ni ari awọn arakunrin wa nwọnyi ti ...wa lati idalẹ fun ti oye yi, Ajimi Alowo E 1., Iwo, F. Ajani Iwo, Samuel ọmọ Idawu Olu...tun Iwo, Salami Olukosi Iwo, ati awọn ara Edẹ I a vọni Ajala, Bello Fajọhi ati awọn ẹmẹwa wọn pẹlu awọn Ọlọpa Balẹ ti afi tọju awọn enia wọn yi ni nwọnyi, Busari jẹ onitọju kan ati awọn ara rẹ yoku, apapọ awọn ọlọpa na je 40 (ogoji) lẹhinna ni ọmọ rẹ obinrin ko awọn egbẹ rẹ si ẹhin pẹlu awọn ṣoni ṣekẹrẹ ti nwọn jo kiri ilu oruko ọmọ rẹ obinrin na ni Ọlanrewaju ọmọ na ṣe eyẹ oye na fun ọpọlọpọ igba ti o fi jẹ wipe okiki ọmọ na kan de Kano. Adura ti a ṣe fun awọn Oloye na ni wipe, Ki Ọlọrun Olodumare ko jọ Oye na ko mọ wọn lori amin, kọ ṣe o.

Ki Ọlọrun fi Ọkan wọn balẹ si ori Oye gegebi apata inu ominamin.

Koi ti pari.

Published by Dr. A. S. BAMGBOYE, O Sokori Oje P. O. Box No. 3 Abeokuta Printed by the Nigerian Blessed Press, Ib Abeokuta.

In response to those who contended that the former ruler was an illiterate and yet had ruled satisfactorily for twenty-two years, the paper wrote: "It should be borne in mind that after the death of an illiterate ruler, an enlightened ruler is the requirement of the people now-a-days."[48] In emboldened letters the paper appealed to the British resident to intervene and ensure that the position was filled with the "best" candidate. It invited all who were qualified to send their genealogies to be published in the paper so that all Gbagura communities could solve the problem. The paper challenged the secrecy of the chiefly process, queried why educated chiefs like "Chief Okunkenu, the leading educated chief," were not members of the selection committee, which, according to the editorial, comprised illiterate chiefs with "domineering attitude," and why they could not conduct a mass meeting to elect the people's choice.[49]

Similar campaigns were mounted for other chiefly vacancies in Owu and Oke-Ona sections. Whenever an educated person was made chief, the paper wrote glowing editorials in celebration. Such was the case when Akin Oshin and Adelani Gbogboade were made chiefs in Owu. Akin Oshin was then the editor of the *Times* (Lagos) and leader of the sectionalist Owu National Society, and with Gbogboade, who later became king of Owu, he led stringent opposition against the Alake (July 1936). The *Osumare* opposed those who argued that by their antecedents the "Lagos Owu" chiefs were divisive and were threats to peace and stability, and advised "turn coats [to] remain mute."[50]

The *Osumare*'s campaign for modernization gave voice to Abęokuta's literate community, many of whom were excluded from the city's political system. Unlike the metropolis, where educated persons could seek employment in the colonial public service or at least find space in the fast-growing economy, Abęokuta had a smaller government centered on the Alake as sole administrator. The Egba native authority employed only a handful of educated Africans; most of its employees, including the *Oga Olopa*, head of the native police, were unlettered. Its greater needs were engineers and medical doctors for its modernization projects, and since not many natives were qualified, it relied on European personnel and nonnative Africans. Furthermore, its judicial system was organized around native courts under chiefs, and provided limited opportunities for lawyers or even clerks. In August 1936, the *Osumare Egba* celebrated Abęokuta's employment of Adebęshin as the head of the Grade "A" court, the only qualified lawyer to be so engaged. With a vibrant economy dominated by production and trade of traditional commodities like textiles, foodstuffs, and produce, there were limited life options for the literate citizens. By campaigning for the replacement of traditional chiefs with educated ones, the paper was pushing the literati's case for better opportunities.

Aside from pushing its political agenda, the newspaper energized its constituency in other ways. It was a valuable medium for the literati to express their frustrations at Abẹokuta's politics and economic system. Contributors wrote about limited opportunities for employment in Abẹokuta, lack of access to capital to engage in trade, and how the guild system excluded educated persons from the textile and produce trades. Some of its contributors appear to be high school students and young graduates, such as "Neat Boy," pseudonym of a regular contributor. Neat Boy narrated his experience of being unemployed five years after graduating from Abeokuta Grammar School, and observed that many more educated youths were "kicking dust about the town."[51] In "An Appeal to the Authorities Concerned on Behalf of Educated Youths in Abeokuta," he lamented that all he had ever earned from his beloved nation was 17/–6d despite his investment in education.[52] In his words, the elders and chiefs of Abẹokuta were doing grave disservice to its youths by employing expatriates because those foreigners will not sacrifice for the nation. He further argued that when "Queen Victoria said, 'I put my reliance on the wisdom of the Parliament and upon the loyalty and devotion of my people,' who were the people she spoke of? They were the educated elements of her time."[53] A similar self-conception of their critical importance to the state and their frustrations at the limited opportunities were reflected by other contributors, with one reader writing that although the *Osumare* had become his daily bread, he could not afford to buy it.

The transformation of Abẹokuta's chiefly government and its economy were pertinent interests around which educated persons in Abẹokuta could converge. The centralization of the government under the Alake as sole native authority precluded an expansion of the civil service and, accordingly, employment opportunities for educated persons. Besides, conscious of British influence, the Alake's council had to consider colonial recommendations for critical positions in the public service. Engineers and medical doctors were employed based on the recommendations of the colonial government. By fighting the cause of the sectional *ọbas*, educated elites stood to gain from the expansion of employment opportunities as those governments could then create bureaucratic positions of their own. The *Osumare Egba* denounced the injustices and disrespect meted out to sectional kings and pushed the council to "build palaces befitting of their royalty . . . [hadn't] the Ake palace been built by the common pool of Egba money collected from all sections?"⁵⁴ The paper also demanded the employment and payment of qualified secretaries for all ọbas, and the expansion of electricity and water to all sectional ọbas.

Clearly, Abẹokuta's economy was much less directly supervised by the colonial administration than Lagos's. A long tradition of economic management had been established since the 1860s when the Egba United Board of Management tried to regulate and document customs and excise.⁵⁵ In spite of this, Abẹokuta was as exposed to the global depression of the interwar years. Unlike Lagos, where economic difficulties intensified anticolonial opposition, youth restiveness, and nationalism, the colonial government was never mentioned or targeted as being responsible for economic difficulties. The *Osumare* accounted for the economic difficulties in many ways, including that Abẹokuta's slow pace of progress and lack of civilization was responsible for the economic crises of the interwar years. The editorial of 2 May 1936 interpreted economic difficulties as the "sign of the times" and prescribed more hard work and patience. In contrast to the literati, many other constituencies of the city blamed the king. Market women protested these difficult conditions, ascribing their losses to the king's taxes, *Jẹja* (extortions) by government-appointed market agents, and the administration's policies, which drove up the cost of textile inputs. Commentators in the *Osumare* ascribed the difficulties to the slow pace of modernization, to the employment of illiterate and incompetent policemen, to corrupt government officials, and to the unwillingness of people to work hard.

It may not be possible to clearly establish the contributions of the *Osumare Egba* toward reshaping Abẹokuta's political structure. The expansion of the Native Council to provide space for more educated elites was not achieved until the 1940s, long after the demise of the newspaper. Even then, Abẹokuta's politics continued to be dominated by chiefs, which further encouraged the educated elites to seek chiefly offices. We can only speculate that the newspaper continued the process of sensitization by which the educated elite crafted spaces. Indeed, by 1948, the titles of chieftaincies and the processes of their selection were codified; they subsequently provided space for educated persons to intervene in the process.⁵⁶ What cannot be denied are *Osumare Egba*'s contributions to creating a constituency invested in modernization. Of its eight pages, at least two were regularly devoted to readers' comments and letters. Letters from as far away as Kano in the northern provinces, and Enugu in the east, reveal the wideness of its readership. Most of the letters were by people who identified themselves as Ẹgba and with its nationhood.

Contributors wrote on a broad range of topics, many of them comparing Abẹokuta with other places, the past with the present, and the comparative values of traditional and modern ways. Apparently there was a consensus that Abẹokuta was lagging behind other places. One writer, F. O. Deigh, attracted many comments by serializing his views of Abẹokuta, comparing the city with Lagos, Ibadan, Freetown, Abyssinia, London, and Rome. It was a masterstroke, if we go by the debate it generated. Many responders lamented that their city could never be like Lagos or Rome or Freetown, and that Ibadan and Ijebu were fast catching up and surpassing it. Most identified the factor responsible as "the lack of unity," and uneducated chiefs running the country in the old ways. Some lamented that educated Ẹgbas were doing well outside of Abẹokuta, but could not return home to contribute their quota because of "lack of unity."[57]

Osumare Egba's constituency was not an uncritical one. Its members were vigilant that the paper conform to the standard of the best journalistic practices. Readers wrote about the quality of the newspaper and to highlight its language and typographic errors. Just as the *Osumare* served as medium for the expression of the literati's disappointments and frustrations at their nation, it was also often challenged not to bring shame upon Abẹokuta. Facility in the English language was a major elite attribute, and many writers critically evaluated the quality of written grammar and expressions. In several editions writers wondered at the quality of the editorial staff of the paper and debated over whose responsibility it was to ensure editorial quality between the editor and printers. In its edition of 6 October 1936, the paper published a list of errata claiming that noticed errors were committed by "incompetent printers of now-a-days," promising to employ "printers who understand the rudiments of printing work," and assuring that the editor did "not need more editorial training under Times or Telegraph (Lagos) . . . having been taking a course in Europe on journalism . . . [that] shall never fail him in English vocabulary."[58]

Abẹokuta was not lacking in scandals, and the *Osumare* did a particularly good job of following up on them in successive editions. For instance, from October through December 1936, the *Osumare* reported the case of a money-doubling fraud in which a leading chief, Raimi Ẹgbẹyemi, was implicated. Commentaries on the case did not just focus on the scandal: writers debated if and why it was a crime to double money. In this case, the accused claimed to have in his house pots that yielded money and thereby defrauded his victims. Writers were divided over whether it was possible to have angels or demons deliver money spiritually, and if victims did not deserve their experience for being foolish. Going by reader's letters and comments, many of which encouraged the newspaper in its investigative journalism, we may conclude that such stories energized the newspaper public. Scandals involving chiefs granted the educated elite the opportunity to foray into chiefly realms and to debate the relevance of customs.

In particular, the Alake's scandal-filled reign subjected the monarchy to explorations bordering on ridicule. In one of many scandals, in which an *Olori* (one of the *ọba*'s wives) got pregnant for another man, the *Osumare Egba* blamed the culprit entirely for trespassing his bounds. The paper reported that the man was lucky that Ọba Ademọla was educated and civilized; otherwise, he would have experienced the appropriate traditional judgment. The paper was curiously silent on what Lagos newspapers revealed—that the *Olori* was in fact the accused's wife previously "seized" by the Alake. This was at a period when the Lagos newspapers were filled with accounts of the misdemeanors of the Alake, including the finding of several escaped married women among his harem. In one such case, a young girl who had been declared missing in Ibadan in 1935 had become one of the wives of the Alake. The *Daily Times* (Lagos) report titled the "Missing Girl in Ibadan" ran for weeks, with many readers writing to express their opprobrium at the abduction. The *Osumare Egba* pleaded for understanding the Alake's defense.[59] The *Osumare* definitely contributed to the sensitization of the public, including women, to a critical evaluation of the authority of the monarch. The *Dipomu* system (harem holdings) was one of the factors around which women began organizing, leading to the women's revolt led by Funmilayo Ransome-Kuti in the 1940s.[60]

The *Osumare* also kept hold of its constituency by serializing stories over many editions. The influence of Lagos press appears evident on the stories serialized in the *Osumare*.[61] For instance, the story of Comfort Efunyinka, which appeared in the 4 January 1936 edition of the paper, is quite similar to that of Segilola, which was serialized by the *Akede Eko* in the 1920s. Similarly written in Yoruba language and well dramatized with periodic songs, it narrates Comfort Efunyinka's resurrection from death by drowning in the Atlantic, surmising that miracles still happen like in the days of Jonah. Unlike the Segilola story, Comfort Efunyinka's was only published in two issues and stopped without any explanation from the publisher. In response to a reader who demanded to know why the story of the "wonderful Jonah" stopped appearing in the paper, the editor responded that it was due to the lack of space in the paper.[62]

DEMISE OF *OSUMARE EGBA*: IMPACTS AND CONTRIBUTIONS

An assessment of the contributions of the *Osumare Egba* to life and society in Abẹokuta must factor in its provinciality. In contrast to the celebrated contributions of newspapers in the colonial metropolis to public literacy, expansion of global capitalism, anticolonialism, cultural revival, and innovations, newspapers in the provinces operated under different conditions. Compared to more metropolitan newspapers, the influence of the paper might appear insignificant. The *Osumare* certainly expanded literacy, enlarged and gave voice to the provincial literati, and made it possible for this constituency to explore innovations in arts and culture and to advocate change. Seen in the context of its provinciality, the newspaper contributed to Abẹokuta's society by expanding the space of social discourse, bringing into the public space voices that otherwise would have been silenced. It inhabited a world much more complicated in its diversity and contestations than a colonial binary can sufficiently explain. Yet its roles and impact should not be overstretched in the larger scope of social change in the province. First, neither its agenda nor its public could be unambiguously distinctive. Unlike in the colonial metropolis, where the educated elite identity and its discourse were distinctively mapped apart from the colonial government, and where newspapers could claim to represent blacks against the colonized, Abẹokuta was much more widely diffused in its politics and culture. While the literati converged around the need for change toward the modern, their conception of modernity was never coherent except around Western education. Yet even while advocating for educated public officials and chiefs, the educated elite was divided over sectional interests. Furthermore, the political system already anticipated the dichotomy of modernity and traditions in having an educated ọba (king), and in the tradition of dynamic modulations and domestication of new ideas. The *Osumare Egba* could not pose itself in any sharp difference as foreign or new because of Abẹokuta's antecedence in modernization and its local reading public, which was intricately linked to and totally invested in Ẹgba (rather than Westernized) identity. The literati could not celebrate such a heritage, promote its nationality, its civilized ọba and at the same time denigrate its traditions.

By December 1936, the *Osumare Egba* was in huge debt, and it soon quit publishing, in March 1937. For sure, the paper did not have a strong financial base. The one-pound-per-copy price did not yield enough to cover the expenses incurred, and many of those who made financial and material promises at the launching in 1935 did not fulfill them. The Alake on his part was reluctant to be financially identified with the paper and contributed little more than an annual one pound as a New Year present. When the paper could not meet its financial commitments promptly, the printers began to decline credit. In December, the paper changed its printers from Nigeria Blessed Printers to Abẹokuta Printing and Publishing Works.

Aside from financial difficulties, the *Osumare Egba* may have compromised itself by its ambivalence. In trying to be everything, it failed to secure faithful commitment from its constituency. The paper made enemies of the influential illiterate chiefs and accordingly could not get necessary support from this class. This is particularly instructive because in the colonial period literacy did not constitute a measure of wealth. As Ruth Watson shows in her study of Ibadan, the moneyed class actually had few educated people, and many educated people served in the employ of wealthy illiterates.[63] Also, being critical of the Egba Native Authority and castigating it as unprogressive while at the same time exonerating the Alake who was the head of that government is a contradiction and partly accounts for why the Alake was reticent to support the paper. It compromised the goodwill that the paper could have secured from the administration. The ideological divide also affected relations among the staff and management of the paper, with regular conflicts between the publisher and the editorial. Chief Bamgboye, a traditional chief, wanted a more cautious posture in the reportage of the Egba Native Council. On the other hand, the younger Ṣowande as editor insisted on his creed to "speak the truth . . . I will not be quiet."[64] The *Egbaland Echo*, which emerged in 1940, accounted for the demise of the *Osumare Egba* in the following words:

> The Osumare Egba died a natural death when the proprietor tendered apology on a series of reports, which appeared in his newspaper without the knowledge, and consent of the editor.[65]

In its twilight years, the *Osumare Egba* reviewed its policies. Its 1937 editions were less radical. In its first "Weekly Digest of the New Year," the paper wrote: "It is not within the scope of our journalistic principle . . . to interrogate the historical references and institutions."[66] The paper no longer accused the Egba council of injustice and negligence, as it did prior to 1937. Rather, the writers used such careful wordings as "the body politic appears to be very busy engaged in managing the administration in such a way to satisfy all classes of people,"[67] when prior to this period it would have accused the government of favoritism and incompetence. By 1937, such pliant editorials came too late.

BIBLIOGRAPHY

Ajayi, J. F. Ade. *Christian Missions in Nigeria, 1841–1891: The Making of a New Elite*. London: Longman, 1965.

Ajisafẹ, A. K. *Abeokuta Centenary and Its Celebrations*. Lagos: Ife-Olu Printing Works, 1931.

Ayandele, E. A. *Iwe Irohin and the Representation of the Universal in Nineteenth Century Egbaland*. London: Longman, 1966.

Barber, Karin, ed. *Africa's Hidden Histories: Everyday Literacy and Making the Self*. Bloomington: Indiana University Press, 2006.

Barber, Karin. *Print Culture and the First Yoruba Novel: I.B. Thomas's "Life Story of Me, Segilola" and Other Texts*. Boston: Brill, 2012.

Barber, Karin. "Translation, Publics and the Vernacular Press in 1920s Lagos." In *Christianity and Social Change in Africa: Essays in Honor of J. D. Y. Peel*, edited by Toyin Falola, 187–208. Durham, NC: Carolina Academic Press, 2005.

Berry, Sara. *Chiefs Know Their Boundaries: Essays on Property, Power and the Past in Asante, 1896–1996*. Oxford: James Curry, 2001.

Byfield, Judith. *The Bluest Hands: A Social and Economic History of Women Dyers in Abeokuta*. Portsmouth, NH: Heinemann, 2002.

Doortmont, Michael R. "Recapturing the Past: Samuel Johnson and the Construction of the History of the Yoruba." Ph.D. dissertation, Erasmus University, 1994.

Fox, William, ed. *A Brief History of Wesleyan Missions in the Coast of West Africa*. London: Aylott and Jones, 1851.

Gailey, Harry. *Lugard and the Abẹokuta Uprising: The Demise of Ẹgba Independence*. London: F. Cass, 1982.

Gocking, Roger. "Indirect Rule in the Gold Coast: Competition for Office and the Invention of Tradition." *Journal of African Studies* 28, no. 4 (1994): 421–46.

Hasty, Jennifer. *The Press and Political Culture in Ghana*. Bloomington: Indiana University Press, 2005.

Ibhawoh, Bonny. *Imperialism and Human Rights: Colonial Discourses of Rights and Liberties in African History*. New York: University of New York Press, 2007.

Johnson-Odim, Cheryl, and Nina Mba. *For Women and the Nation: Funmilayo Ransome-Kuti of Nigeria*. Urbana: University of Illinois Press, 1997.

Mann, Kristin. *Marrying Well: Marriage, Status, and Social Change among the Educated Elite in Colonial Lagos*. Cambridge: Cambridge University Press, 1985.

Newell, Stephanie. "Newspapers, New Spaces, New Writers: The First World War and Print Culture in Colonial Ghana." *Research in African Literatures* 40, no. 2 (2009): 1–15.

Newell, Stephanie. "Paracolonial Networks: Some Speculations on Local Readership in Colonial West Africa." *Interventions: International Journal of Postcolonial Studies* 3, no. 3 (2001): 336–54.

Oduntan, Oluwatoyin. "Iwe Irohin and the Representation of the Universal in Nineteenth Century Egbaland." *History in Africa* 32 (2005): 295–305.

Omu, Fred. *Press and Politics in Nigeria, 1880–1930*. London: Longman, 1978.

Osuntokun, Jide. *Nigeria in the First World War*. Atlantic Highlands, NJ: Humanities Press, 1979.

Pallinder-Law, Agneta. "Aborted Modernization in West Africa? The Case of Abeokuta." *Journal of African Studies* 15, no. 1 (1974): 65–82.

Peel, J. D. Y. "The Cultural Work of Yoruba Ethnogenesis." In *History and Ethnicity*, edited by Elizabeth Tonkin, Maryon MacDonald, and Malcolm Chapman, 189–215. London: Routledge, 1989.

Zachernuk, Philip S. *Colonial Subjects: An African Intelligentsia and Atlantic Ideas*. Charlottesville: University Press of Virginia, 2000.

NOTES TO CHAPTER 11

1. *Lagos Standard*, 10 August 1916; *Lagos Weekly Record*, 10 October 1914. On Lagos elites' participation in the First World War see Bonny Ibhawoh, *Imperialism and Human Rights: Colonial Discourses of Rights and Liberties in African History* (New York: University of New York Press, 2007), 145; on the expansion of colonial administration following the war see Jide Osuntokun, *Nigeria in the First World War* (Atlantic Highlands, NJ: Humanities Press, 1979); also James Coleman, *Nigeria: Background to Nationalism* (Berkeley: University of California Press, 1971), traces the claims of Lagos nationalists to represent all "natives" of Nigeria.

2. Newspapers were published in many small regional towns in South Africa. Les Switzer, "The Beginnings of African Protest Journalism at the Cape," in *South Africa's Alternative Press: Voices of Protest and Resistance, 1880s–1960s* (Cambridge: Cambridge University Press, 1997), 67–76.

3. Fred Omu, *Press and Politics in Nigeria, 1880–1930* (London: Longman, 1978), 27.

4. Jennifer Hasty, *The Press and Political Culture in Ghana* (Bloomington:

Indiana University Press, 2005), 97. Recently, authors examine texts (books, diaries, letters, etc.) by persons outside colonial capitals. Karin Barber, ed., *Africa's Hidden Histories: Everyday Literacy and Making the Self* (Bloomington: Indiana University Press, 2006); Derek Peterson and Giacomo Macola, eds., *History Writing and Political Work in Modern Africa* (Athens: Ohio University Press, 2009).

5. Omu, *Press and Politics*, 29; see Pratten, this volume.

6. Kristin Mann, *Marrying Well: Marriage, Status, and Social Change among the Educated Elite in Colonial Lagos* (Cambridge: Cambridge University Press, 1985). For the Atlantic connections of African intellectuals see also Philip S. Zachernuk, *Colonial Subjects: An African Intelligentsia and Atlantic Ideas* (Charlottesville: University of Virginia Press, 2000).

7. Stephanie Newell, "Newspapers, New Spaces, New Writers: The First World War and Print Culture in Colonial Ghana," *Research in African Literatures* 40, no. 2 (2009): 4; also Stephanie Newell, "Paracolonial Networks: Some Speculations on Local Readerships in Colonial West Africa," *Interventions: International Journal of Post-colonial Studies* 3, no. 3 (2001): 341.

8. On nineteenth-century Abẹokuta see Harry Gailey, *Lugard and the Abẹokuta Uprising: The Demise of Ẹgba Independence* (London: F. Cass, 1982); Agneta Pallinder-Law, "Aborted Modernization in West Africa? The Case of Abeokuta," *Journal of African History* 15, no. 1 (1974): 65–82.

9. J. F. Ade Ajayi, *Christian Missions in Nigeria* (London: Longman, 1965), 198.

10. CMS archive CA2/085 Papers Townsend to Venn, 28 February 1860; Eugene Stock, *History of the Church Missionary Society* (London; CMS, 1899); CA2/085, Townsend to Venn, 2 June 1859.

11. Gailey, *Lugard*, 28.

12. See sample copy of *ENA Bulletin*.

13. Oluwatoyin Oduntan, "*Iwe Irohin* and the Representation of the Universal in Nineteenth Century Egbaland," *History in Africa* 32 (2005): 295–305.

14. E. A. Ayandele, *The Missionary Impact on Modern Nigeria, 1842–1914* (London: Longmans, 1966), 11, 47.

15. J. D. Y. Peel, *Religious Encounter and the Making of the Yoruba* (Bloomington: Indiana University Press, 2003), 103.

16. *Lagos Weekly Record*, 24 December 1892, reports on educated persons who served as clerks to chiefs. For Ibadan, see Ruth Watson, "*Civil Disorder Is the Disease of Ibadan*": *Chieftaincy and Civic Culture in a Yoruba City* (Ibadan: Heinemann, 2003).

17. William Fox, comp., *A Brief History of Wesleyan Missions on the West Coast of Africa* (London: Aylott and Jones, 1851).

18. G. Bühler, Report of Training Institution, 30 September 1858, CMS C/

A2/O24/42. On medical training at the Training Institute see Adebola Adeloye, "Some Nigerian Doctors and Their Contribution to Modern Medicine in West Africa," *Medical History* 18 (1974): 275–93.

19. *Dictionary of African Christian Biography*, www.dacb.org/stories/nigeria/buhler_gottlieb.html (accessed: 26 May 2015].

20. "Result of Teachers for Certificate, Class II," *Egba Government Gazette*, 31 August 1912.

21. "Message to the Public from the Proprietor and Publisher," *Osumare Egba*, 7 December 1935.

22. Gailey, *Lugard*, 74.

23. On how indirect rule privileged chiefly accumulation and stimulated opposition against chiefs leading to the invention of traditions, see Sara Berry, *Chiefs Know Their Boundaries: Essays on Property, Power and the Past in Asante, 1896–1996* (Oxford: James Currey, 2001); Roger Gocking, "Indirect Rule in the Gold Coast: Competition for Office and the Invention of Tradition," *Journal of African Studies* 28, no. 4 (1994): 421–46.

24. The CMS refused his manuscripts because of "the man's past history." Michel R. Doortmont, "Recapturing the Past: Samuel Johnson and the Construction of the History of the Yoruba," Ph.D. dissertation, Erasmus University, Rotterdam, 1994, 47. Ajisafẹ claimed to be resisting dictatorship and personal animosity in his critiques of the government. Ajisafẹ, *The Errors* (Lagos: Hope Rising Press, 1930). In 1935, Ladipo Solanke advised him to be less critical: NAA, LSP/46, Egba Affairs Letter Book, 1.1, Solanke to Ademola, 14 May 1935. Falola suggests that Ajisafẹ produced over fifty books. Toyin Falola, *Yoruba Gurus: Indigenous Production of Knowledge in Africa* (Trenton, NJ: Africa World Press, 1999), 13.

25. A. K. Ajisafẹ, *Errors and Defeat of Ladipo Solanke* (Lagos, 1931), 2. "Woe to those who decree iniquitous decrees, and the writers who keep writing oppression." Isaiah 10.1.

26. Solanke, "A Special Lecture Addressed to A. K. Ajisafe on Egba Constitutional Law and Its Historical Development" (Lagos, 1931), 7.

27. On debates among Abẹokuta's intellectuals, see Oluwatoyin Oduntan, "Elite Identity and Power," PhD dissertation, Dalhousie University, 2010, 288–93.

28. A. K. Ajisafẹ, *Abeokuta Centenary and Its Celebrations* (Lagos: Ife-Olu Printing Works, 1931).

29. CA2/02/1–13, Missionary Conference held at Ake, Abẹokuta, 28 April to 2 May 1859; *cf.* "Extract of Letter from the Rev. Matthew Grimmer, Lagos, November 4, 1867," *Wesleyan Missionary Notices* 3, no. 16 (1868).

30. "Death of His Majesty King George V, by Alake's Command," *Osumare*, 25 January 1936. For Lagos newspapers' treatment of British monarchy see Nozomi

Sawada, "The Educated Elite and Associational Life in the Lagos Press," PhD dissertation, University of Birmingham, 2011, 280–81.

31. Barber, this volume.
32. Zachernuk, *Colonial Subjects*, 14.
33. Sawada, "The Educated Elite," 3.
34. Gocking, "Indirect Rule."
35. *Osumare Egba*, 7 December 1935.
36. J. D. Y. Peel, "The Cultural Work of Yoruba Ethnogenesis," in *History and Ethnicity*, ed. Elizabeth Tonkin, Maryon MacDonald, and Malcolm Chapman (London: Routledge, 1989), 187–215.
37. Karin Barber, "Translation, Publics and the Vernacular Press in 1920s Lagos," in *Christianity and Social Change in Africa: Essays in Honor of J. D. Y. Peel*, ed. Toyin Falola (Durham, NC: Carolina Academic Press, 2005), 187–208.
38. *Osumare Egba*, 7 December 1935.
39. *Osumare Egba*, 4 January 1936.
40. *Osumare Egba*, 14 November 1925.
41. Judith Byfield, *The Bluest Hands: A Social and Economic History of Women Dyers in Abeokuta* (Portsmouth, NH: Heinemann, 2002).
42. "That Ignominious Jeja," *Osumare Egba*, 25 January 1936; "Bombata Ni Egbe Alaro Aladire Abeokuta," 9 September 1936.
43. National Archives Ibadan (NAI), Abeprof 2/52, "Decision Extract from the Minutes of Council Meeting held on Thursday, the 25th of November, 1929."
44. *Osumare Egba*, 11 January 1936.
45. "Who Will Be the New Agura," *Osumare Egba*, 29 February 1936.
46. *Osumare Egba*, 18 January 1936.
47. *Osumare Egba*, 18 January 1936, 2.
48. *Osumare Egba*, 18 January 1936, 2.
49. *Osumare Egba*, 18 January 1936, 4.
50. "Grand Installation Ceremony: Turn Coat Chiefs Remain Mute," *Osumare Egba*, 21 November 1936.
51. "Gbagura Shall Rise by Neat-Boy," *Osumare Egba*, 14 December 1935.
52. *Osumare Egba*, 17 May 1936, 6.
53. *Osumare Egba*, 17 May 1936, 6.
54. CSO 26/2, 14605, Letter: Adedamola, the Osile to Resident Abẹokuta, 11 March 1925.
55. Pallinder-Law, "Aborted Modernization," 65–82.
56. NAA 52/2/16, "Introduction," "Declaration made under Section 4 (3) of the Chiefs Law, 1952, Setting out the Customary Law Regulating the Selection to the Seriki Egba Chieftaincy Title."

57. F. O. Deigh, "Looking at Abeokuta," *Osumare Egba*, 8, 15, 22, 29 February 1936.

58. *Osumare Egba*, 8 February 1936.

59. *Osumare Egba*, 16 May 1936.

60. Cheryl Johnson-Odim and Nina Mba, *For Women and the Nation: Funmilayo Ransome-Kuti of Nigeria* (Urbana: University of Illinois Press, 1997).

61. Karin Barber, *Print Culture and the First Yoruba Novel: I.B. Thomas's "Life Story of Me, Segilola" and Other Texts* (Boston: Brill, 2012).

62. *Osumare Egba*, 4, 7 March 1936.

63. Ruth Watson, *"Civil Disorder Is the Disease of Ibadan": Chieftaincy and Civic Culture in a Yoruba City* (Ibadan: Heinemann, 2003); also Olufemi Vaughan, *Nigerian Chiefs: Traditional Power in Modern Politics, 1890s–1990s* (Rochester, NY: University of Rochester Press, 2000).

64. *Osumare Egba*, 5 December 1936.

65. *Egbaland Echo*, 17 January 1941.

66. *Osumare Egba*, 5 January 1937.

67. *Osumare Egba*, 5 January 1937.

CHAPTER 12

"I will decide who will speak"

Street Parliaments and the Newspaper Ecology in Eldoret's *Kamukunji*

DUNCAN OMANGA

Always forming around the newspaper vendor's "premises" is Eldoret's *kamukunji*, sometimes referred to as people's parliament, a near-permanent feature of busy Elijah Cheruiyot Street in Eldoret, a bustling city to the west of Kenya's capital, Nairobi.[1] While the dynamics of the *kamukunji*'s form and how its adherents use it to imagine change from below has been documented,[2] the role of the newspaper as a central organizing agent in constituting the *kamukunji* has not been explored. In actual fact, without the newspaper it is difficult and cumbersome for the *kamukunji* to convene. Although the *kamukunji* traces origins to Kenya's historical, cultural, and political culture, the use here of the term *kamukunji* specifically refers to the street assemblies constituted around newspaper reading culture in Kenya's urban centers. In Eldoret, for instance, the newspaper remains the focal point of the *kamukunji*. This chapter shows how at the height of an election year the newspaper and the *kamukunji* evinced a unique relationship that involved news reading, debates, and the discursive construction of collective imaginaries. Additionally, this chapter shows how the newspaper ecology produced in the *kamukunji* structured discursive possibilities and internal power dynamics, and how the constituted public used the newspaper to resist, select, and negotiate specific social-political realities.

INTRODUCTION

If a survey were to be done on the most effective newspaper vendors in Eldoret town[3] based on the sale of newspapers, Francis Kegode would most likely appear near the bottom. Despite this, he remains one of the most recognizable and well-known newspaper vendors in Eldoret. A veteran of Eldoret town, he remembers migrating to the town in the late 1980s, when Eldoret's residents were barely 50,000, from his native Nyanza region in order to secure work in the then fledgling textile industries. His entry into the newspaper-selling business was not by choice, but was a necessity brought about by the collapse of nearly all the textile industries in Eldoret following the liberalizing of the market in line with the controversial International Monetary Fund–driven structural adjustments programs launched in the 1980s and early 1990s. Finding himself out of work and with a family to feed, Kegode resorted to selling newspapers along Elijah Cheruiyot Street, one of the busiest in Eldoret town. However, what marks him out among all other vendors is the routine gathering around his "premises" conveniently located under a tree, on a busy junction at the heart of the city. These gatherings, commonly referred to as the *kamukunji*, a Swahili word with heavy political connotations, have meant that Kegode pays a hefty price in hosting the *kamukunji*. As the de facto "speaker" of these spaces of urban political orality, he has to balance between earning a living through newspaper sales and moderating/hosting the *kamukunji*, two nearly incompatible alternatives. The *kamukunji* normally registers between ten and a hundred members on a daily basis and is purely constituted around political discourse. The numbers are largely dependent on the degree of political "heat" in the country, and while this should naturally mean more newspaper sales for Kegode, the large gatherings on these occasions discourage potential customers who might view the *kamukunji*, almost always dominated by men, suspiciously as a space teeming with unemployed idlers and potential urban opportunists.

Kegode and the *kamukunji* represent an interesting aspect of a postcolonial newspaper culture in Kenya that conflates street political deliberation with modern mass-media forms such as the newspaper. With varying degrees of sophistication, the *kamukunji* is a near-permanent feature of how the urban spaces are used in most towns in Kenya. However, while studies have been done on the nature of deliberative spaces "from below" in Kenya and across Africa,[4] insights into how the African newspaper has transformed and refashioned street parliaments such as the *kamukunji* in Eldoret have not been fully explored. In this volume, Hunter[5] looks backward into how a colonial era newspaper, *Komkya*, among the Chagga in Tanganyika was both a tool of identity formation and a powerful example of the role played by newspapers in creating new and distinctive modes of late colonial sociality. More specifically, through an empirically grounded study of the relevant phenomena, the paper reveals the ecological manifestations occasioned by the nexus between the newspaper and deliberative practice in the *kamukunji*.

The idea of studying any media and its (urban) ecology can be traced to the work of Marshall McLuhan and his focus on how media technologies create restraints and possibilities. Postman[6] was the first to explicitly call for an effort to study media as environments, arguing that environments structure what we can see, say, and do. They also assign roles and pressure us to play them. In like manner, media environments specify what we can do and what we cannot do.[7] In African studies, several scholars have already made tentative investigations into the communicative ecology of media.[8] In these studies, there is a recurring pattern of taking a "holistic" view of the interactions between media and their users. Generally, the media ecology envisaged in this study explores the kind of roles particular media force, or position individuals to play, and how the media structure ways of seeing and thinking, and even prompting particular actions.

This chapter draws inspiration from the work of Karin Barber, who has studied audiences in Africa. Barber[9] argues that the "public" constituted in a performance, or fora such as the *kamukunji*, can only be understood if the forms of address, the staging, and the use of space as well as the interactions between performers and spectators are empirically established in detail. I adopt the term "audience" from Barber, who refers to audiences as the body of people who grant the speaker the space and time to verbally communicate his or her competence, and it emphasizes the creativity and activity of the group in coproducing this competence by bending the normal patterns of communicative turn-taking.[10] It is worth noting that the roles of audience and particular speakers in the *kamukunji* are not rigid, but are fluid and seem to interchange depending on several factors explained in later sections of this chapter.

Accordingly, this chapter seeks to explicitly describe the environment created as a result of the interface between the newspaper and street parliaments in the Kenyan urban space. In other words, the role of the newspaper as a key component of the *Kamukunji* is fully explored. Without ignoring other factors that have shaped urban deliberative political culture, this chapter seeks to empirically detail the ecology of the newspaper vis-à-vis the *kamukunji*, in other words the transformations, possibilities, and restraints that the Kenyan newspaper has made on the current complexion of the *kamukunji*. At the same time, the chapter seeks to empirically detail the use of space, the interaction between individual speakers, the constituted audience, and the audience convened around the newspaper that forms the *kamukunji*.

In answering the questions raised, it is important to keep in mind that a medium's environment is potentially boundless and, accordingly, there is a need to determine the scope and context of this environment before launching into the discussion. Second, media environments are not homogeneous, but are a factor of time, space, and place. Accordingly, I nominate a specific context of time and place in order to understand how the interface of the newspaper in Kenya and urban deliberative practices merged. In this sense, I argue that the media ecology envisaged in similar efforts, especially those that attempt to account for Africa's media environment, must also be specific, and avoid the temptations to extrapolate findings across place, time, and context. For this particular study, the period coming shortly before the 2007 general elections, and a few months after, were used to account for the media environment created by the newspaper. These polls were bitterly contested and led to unprecedented violence in the country that left hundreds dead and hundreds of thousands displaced from their homes. This study was carried out two months before the polls and two months after the controversial polls were declared. More importantly, Eldoret was the epicenter of this violence and the scene of frequent confrontations between the police and members of the public. Former United Nations secretary general Kofi Annan was later invited into the country in early 2008 to broker a political deal between opposition leader Raila Odinga (Orange Democratic Party—ODM) and then incumbent president Mwai Kibaki (Party of National Unity—PNU). All opinion polls prior to the 2007 general elections had indicated that Kibaki would lose the elections.

While deliberative practices similar to those seen in the *kamukunji* were present in other Kenyan cities, the Eldoret *kamukunji* was unique in the sense that it allowed the researcher to see how the unfolding crisis was articulated and integrated into urban deliberative spaces. More germane to this study, since the newspaper supply to Eldoret was irregular as a result of the violence, the researcher was able to observe the ambiguous roles played by the newspaper within the *kamukunji*'s political debates. It is also normally the case that at a time of high-stakes political competition, when demand for news is high, the *kamukunji* is more vibrant.

Participatory methods were used to do the research with a gradual progression from a passive participant to a more active participant in the *kamukunji*. As will be shown, although the *kamukunji* is largely informal, it obtains an unstated "formality" understood and practiced as rules and norms, which must be learned and internalized in order to understand how the gatherings function. This chapter is structured in three sections; the first section provides a background account of the *kamukunji*, the second section probes how the newspaper ecology structures the *kamukunji*, while the last section provides a detailed account of deliberative practice within the *kamukunji* and how newspaper headlines function as nodal points of political deliberative practice in street parliaments.

STREET PARLIAMENTS, URBAN SOCIABILITIES, AND KENYA'S DELIBERATIVE PRACTICES

The origins of the present-day political street assemblies in Kenya reflect aspects of precolonial and postcolonial life that were part of the social and political routine of most communities in Kenya. Among the Abagusii, the *egesarate*, a particularly gendered space where the family head invited his friends, provided a congenial space and forum for harnessing and coalescing opinion on issues of communal concern.[11] And among the Luo community, a similar deliberative sphere, the *duol*, formed a nascent outgrowth of political consciousness and opinion formation in post-colonial Luo societies.[12] Closer to the *kamukunji* in form and function is the *baraza*. For centuries the *baraza* was a space of masculine sociabilities among the coastal communities of Kenya, Tanzania, and Zanzibar. Loimeier's[13] description of the *Swahili baraza* reveals a striking similarity with the precolonial *egesarate* among the Abagusii and the Luo *duol*. As seen, traces of organized deliberative action as a precedent to the modern form of the *kamukunji* were an important facet of the social and political makeup of precolonial communities in Kenya. Organized deliberative action was an important facet of the social and political makeup of precolonial communities in Kenya, and traces of these appear from my sustained observations over four months to have influenced the modern form of the *kamukunji*.

In the colonial period, the *baraza* as a term referred to a more formal public gathering specifically for the purpose of interaction between the governed and the governors. Haugerud[14] observes that the *baraza* in the postcolonial period in Kenya gained extensive use as a quasi-compulsory public meeting addressed by politicians and civil servants. Politically, the postcolonial Kenyan *baraza* revealed undercurrents of inclusion and exclusionary politics, a feature that would characterize the *kamukunji* in the late 1990s and into the new millennium. This was evident through discursive behavior within the *baraza* on who is invited to speak and for how long, and also seen through the deliberate choice of issues given prominence.

As an urban phenomenon, these political street assemblies draw their origin from several social political dynamics in postcolonial Kenya. During the rapid urbanization that characterized Kenya from the late 1950s and onward, the emerging urban centers became bases for cultural syncretism, labor, and political protests. The rural migrants came to the emerging cities with overlays of strong rural tribal tradition and established ways of doing things, of loyalty, and of obligation patterns.[15] A considerable number of so-called welfare associations, all tribal based, were formed. The most prominent were the Luo Union, which had active branches in ninety urban centers in the 1950s. Other communities like the Mijikenda, the Kikuyu, and the Abagusii also formed their own welfare bodies. These welfare associations greatly influenced individual choices of location of residence that created ethnic enclaves in urban centers in Kenya that are still present to this day.[16]

Broadly speaking the discursive spheres previously rooted in the rural areas not only found their way into the urban but incorporated prevailing social and political realities of the urban life. Consequently, staid traditions of gatherings such as the *barazas*,[17] the *duols*, and the *egesarates*[18] formed templates for new forms of deliberative action in the migrant ethnic enclaves within Kenyan urban centers. For instance, in Eldoret town the Luo inhabited mostly the areas around Langas, while the Abaluhyia preferred the neighborhoods of Mwanzo and Kidiwa estates. In these estates, it was common for the community to gather as a unit every Sunday afternoon for open-air deliberations on the welfare of the community. At the onset, the groups' agenda was concerned mostly with issues such as funerals, disputes, and the general welfare of members. Bound by a common language and culture, membership was informal and open to anyone from the community; however, attendance at these meetings was equally highly gendered.

The transformation of these ethnic-based discursive communities into the present street-based deliberative spaces was a result of two broad factors: the urban space itself as a congenial site for politics and a sociopolitical context that constructed particular communities as antiestablishment (opposition). In Kenya, urban centers have always been hotbeds of political activity and dissent. Similarly, the urban mass in the country constitutes a particularly highly politicized category of the populace, and thus provided the context and structures through which state legitimacy was debated and interrogated.[19] Around 1992, a growing disillusionment with the one-party regime produced an intense agitation for political pluralism.[20] In this period, reformist politicians organized large political gatherings, which they called *kamukunjis*. At the height of the struggle for multiparty democracy, these gatherings often ended up in running battles with police, and the *kamukunjis* became spaces of resistance and mobilization against the state.[21] The present meaning of the term *kamukunji* can be traced to the *kamukunji* grounds, an open field between Pumwani and Shauri Moyo—two poor neighborhoods on Nairobi's Eastlands—which were the site of the 1990 "saba saba"[22] demonstrations for multiparty democracy, and also the site of earlier urban forms of anticolonial struggle.[23] Through reference to these historical events the term *kamukunji* became mainstreamed in the Kenyan discourse as a term with connotations of prodemocratic struggles.[24] As political pluralism set in after 1992, political competition became synonymous with political violence, often manifested as ethnic conflicts. More importantly, elections were seen as opportunities for particular ethnic communities to enjoy state largesse at the expense of others; political discourse at campaigns would urge the electorate to vote so as to be "in the government."[25] This binary discourse, coupled with politicization of ethnicity in which ethnic communities were exploited as vehicles for political office, produced a siege mentality for those ethnic groups perceived to be "outside the government" (as a result of voting for a losing candidate). Soon, the communal gatherings in estates such as Langas in Eldoret broadened their focus beyond mere welfare and began to evince a peculiar kind of oppositional politics. Soon, the previously ethnic-based discursive spheres in working-class neighborhoods spread to the streets as the *kamukunji*, or street assemblies, whose primary focus was now politics. Beyond the then prevailing political context, the spread of the *kamukunjis* from the neighborhoods to the streets was significantly driven by the newspaper and the ecology produced by the newspaper. Indeed, in most major cities in Kenya today there exist specific *vikao* (sittings) that obtain a symbiotic relationship between newspapers and political deliberative practices. In the city of Kisumu there is the decades-old *Kondele* "base."[26] *Ngumo* in the Kibera slums, *Kikao*[27] in the Mathare slums, and Jeevanjee gardens in Nairobi.[28] As such, deliberative practices around newspaper-selling urban spaces are not specific to Eldoret but are a feature of everyday urban life in Kenya.

THE NEWSPAPER ECOLOGY AND THE *KAMUKUNJIS*

While the *kamukunji* was among many other forms of political conversation or political action among a much wider citizenry, it was the pivotal role of the newspaper[29] that made the *kamukunji* unique. In actual sense, the newspaper assured the *kamukunji* a prime urban space in the city center. While authorities occasionally frowned at the *kamukunji*, it was not possible for them to scatter the gatherings as they were a fusion of legitimate business, freedom of expression, and political deliberative practice. Without the newspaper, the *kamukunjis* would be difficult to convene and acquire a "structure." As the reemergence of the neighborhood gatherings to Eldoret streets mutated into more formal and regular spaces of political talk, the role of the newspaper in transforming the *kamukunji* became more apparent. For instance, the newspaper had a significant role to play in *de-ethnicizing* the newly forming *kamukunji* that had hitherto been domiciled and patronized along ethnic categories. Although these structures of ethnic exclusivity are residual of the *kamukunji*'s own history in the neighborhoods, the centrality of the newspaper as both a commodity and a site of energizing and shaping political talk enfeebled blatant ethnic-based affinities.

Additionally, since the newspapers are mostly in English and the profit imperative implied that vendors like Kegode must be welcoming to everyone, the *kamukunji*'s environment gradually began to change to reflect the diversity of the assembled audience. In addition, the newspaper projected and sought to construct new identities that were for the most part political, meaning that political opinion and political identity formed the unstated password for gaining admission into the *kamukunji*. Consequently, the language within the *kamukunji* is for the most part Kiswahili,[30] which is understood by everyone. In the few instances when deliberations veered to one the local languages and Kegode failed to intervene, the *kamukunji* faced the grim possibility of splintering into varied ethnic enclaves.

The newspaper structured a disciplined and predictable ritual of deliberative practice within the *kamukunji*. While the neighborhood gatherings were a once-a-week, Sunday afternoon communal affairs, the newspaper ritualized a daily gathering in line with its daily issue. As the most central organizing feature of the *kamukunji*, the newspaper structured the lives of its members to its own; essentially positioning members to meet each day, as each issue of the paper hit the newsstands. For audience members to balance both work and their other commitments, the *kamukunji* is at its full throttle everyday between 1:00 and 2:00 p.m. during the lunch breaks. At these times, when the attendance of the *kamukunji* swells, the role of the newspapers shifts slightly from commodities for sale to unique nodal points of deliberative action and spatial configuration of the *kamukunji*. More than once, Kegode articulated his continuously ambiguous roles within the *kamukunji*:

> Mimi hapa ndiye Koffi Annan. Mimi ndiye nitaamua nani atasema. Wacha huyu ndugu atueleze kisha wewe utafuata. Kama mtu analeta fujo basi lazima ajue hapa tuko Kazi.

> I am the Kofi Annan of this forum, and I will decide who will speak and who will not. We will let this brother speak first, and you will respond. If anyone becomes unruly, they must understand we are here for serious business.

Kegode, seated behind the pile of newspapers, equates his status to that of Kofi Annan, who at the time was leading mediation talks to bring to an end the political stalemate in Kenya after the disputed presidential polls. The newspaper's location relative to Kegode's physical position forms an invisible marker of the deployment of this informal power. When seated behind the newspapers, Kegode assumes a dominant and assertive role both in selling newspapers and in moderating the *kamukunji*. In the ensuing "ecology" occasioned by the centrality of the newspaper were constructed hierarchies and possibilities of self-realization that were hitherto not possible. Kegode, the de facto speaker of the *kamukunji*, experimented with newfound responsibilities that evinced an ambiguous display of informal power. This social capital was also anchored by the fact that he owned the "premises" and managed turn-taking, thus enabling him to play out the role of a small-scale businessperson and a "street parliament" speaker all at the same time. More importantly, for the majority of *kamukunji* members who could not pay for a newspaper, he reserved the power to grant newspaper access beyond the headlines. But for the likes of Omondi, a well-known regular and much-liked *kamukunji* debater, some preferential treatment was evident.

On this bright sunlit afternoon, Omondi crosses the road linking Kenyatta Street to Elijah Cheruiyot Street, glancing sideways to avoid speeding vehicles as he darts toward the *kamukunji*. He wastes little time. He makes his way to the heart of the gathering, shoving aside the growing mass of less active members, the majority of whom are workers in the informal sector taking their "lunch break." Others in this category are drawn from the night shift in the textile factories in the town, which are beginning to pick up, or the dozens of commercial colleges in town, or job seekers. Others see the *kamukunji* as one way of packing the day with something "worthwhile." This category, always young men between the ages of twenty to thirty-five, comprises about 90 percent of the participants of the *kamukunji*. As the loudspeakers blare out a "praise and worship" session from the numerous "lunch hour" Christian services in one of the unfinished buildings, Omondi ignores the din around him, and the uncoordinated debate in the *kamukunji*, and finds himself a sitting space next to Kegode, who acknowledges his presence with a smile. As Kegode rises to evict a drunken member whose unruly shouts threaten to derail debate, Omondi grabs one of the newspapers and flips through the first five pages. These are the pages that contain the latest political news. He glosses through the opinion articles, and then neatly folds back the paper to the floor. As an active member, he is "allowed" to read the paper without paying.

Kegode's generosity was possibly born out of a realization of the parasitic relationship that exists between the ritual of reading the newspaper and deliberation in the *kamukunji*. Aware of this, Kegode allowed the more active members to read newspapers without paying. In return, however, an unspoken rule bound them to enrich the debate after the reading. While the obvious consequence of this action apart from diminished sales is the construction of hierarchies based on active/passive audience categories, it also produced a disciplined form of deliberative pattern in terms of the scope and the general conduct of the *kamukunji*. Precisely, the consumption of the newspaper meant that mostly political debate or issues of political consequences were discussed. It also meant that frivolity and other issues outside the domain of the prevailing political discourse could not be a subject of the debate. Accordingly, the *kamukunji*, though vibrant, animated, and sometimes feisty, was largely impersonal. The perceived social connections were directly linked to the substantive content of the newspaper and political talk accruing form the nexus of the newspaper and its social context. However, some, like Omondi and Bernand, another regular *kamukunji* member whom he interrupts in midspeech, have known each other for several years. Omondi marks his entry with a blunt interjection:

> Lakini inafaa tujue tofauti kati ya Head of State na Head of Government. Hii mambo ya coordinator of government sio sawa na waziri mkuu kuwa head of government.

> We need to know the difference between a head of state and a head of government; this thing of being a coordinator of government is not the same as being the head of government.

Apparently, a political deal had been announced the previous day by the lead mediator, Kofi Annan, which proposed an end to the political stalemate. Raila Odinga, the opposition leader who many in the *kamukunji* believed had won the presidency, was to become prime minister and Mwai Kibaki to continue as president. While some, like Bernard, an insurance agent, believed the deal made the prime minister the head of government and the president the head of state, a few like Omondi call attention to the fact that the deal suggested "coordinator" of government. According to Omondi, this was a raw deal to the opposition. As active and well-known participants of the *kamukunji*, both Bernard and Omondi commanded respect both from the audience and from Kegode. Kegode watches as the two spar on the merits of the agreement. Kiptoo, a passive member who makes it a habit to pass by the *kamukunji* when he has some free time, lingers cautiously along the margins of the *kamukunji*, close enough to follow proceedings without attracting too much attention. Since he graduated from a local college, the *kamukunji* provided Kiptoo a refreshing break from the agonizing routine of job searching. He hoped to voice his political opinion someday but always held back, especially after noticing a palpable yet peculiar concurrence, a kind of groupthink that ruled and directed discursive behavior in the *kamukunji*.[31]

Like Kiptoo, most passers-by and the ordinary newspaper buyers were potential participants. For unclear reasons, males were more likely than females to become either active or passive participants. A passive listener joined the *kamukunji* at the peripheral point. His behavior was characterized by a fleeting participation, mostly listening briefly and then walking off and on rare occasions mumbling a few words (either in support of a point or a feeble objection that scarcely disrupted debate in the *kamukunji*). Such transient opinion was often aimed at a fellow passive participant or no one in particular. At other times active participants passed off as passive participants. These are active members who appeared at the periphery of the group and studied the group's composition and the prevailing level of debate. If they were not impressed, they moved on and later reappeared when things changed, either when there was an increase in active participants or a juicier debate. Also, a passive participant could "graduate" into an active participant based on his frequency of attendance, or his personality, education level, and knowledge of politics.

At some point Kiptoo decides to leave, but Kegode's next question prompts him to stay on.

Sasa, tofauti kati ya state na government ni ipi?

Now, what is the distinction between state and government?

He had also been wrestling with the same dilemma since the political deal was announced a few days back. There is no meaningful response forthcoming until Wamalwa, a local lawyer who has just arrived, proffers a distinction of the two. Wamalwa is part of the elite segment of the *kamukunji*. He dutifully buys his papers from Kegode every morning, and when his lunch schedule allows he savors the *kamukunji*, which, coincidentally, convenes right across from his high-rise office block. This elite segment of the *kamukunji* in my estimation comprises only about 2 percent of the entire group and can be rightly described as the real opinion movers of the *kamukunji*. They command recognizable respect and are spared the usual interruptions or contentions and would always seem to overshadow Kegode. Their presence enhanced group discipline and gave the *kamukunji* an unusual aura of formality. While their influence undermined democracy and the logic of equivalence, it allowed them to speak even against the dominant grain within the *kamukunji*.

As earlier hinted, debate largely reflected a one-sided political persuasion, as the *kamukunji* seemed structured to affirm rather than challenge dominant thoughts. Not surprising, a Manichaean interpretation of political events covered as news reports produced a curious othering, an "us against them" dichotomy that inevitably became a source of exclusion to those who did not share the dominant political mind-set. Reflective of prevailing national politics and Kenya's political history, these exclusionary patterns manifested themselves in the *kamukunji* along ethnic lines.[32] Accordingly, a pattern akin

"I will decide who will speak" • 347

Fig.1. Eldoret town. The *Kamukunji* starts to convene with few members before peak hours. Kegode is often seated under the tree, at the background. On the foreground are passersby. Photo courtesy of Simwa Obayi, August 2012.

to groupthink was noticeable, as well as a concurrence of perspectives and debate among participants. While heated debates and differences of opinion did exist, there was always an imperceptible overarching convergence of ideas. However, for "opinion formers" such as Wamalwa, there were no consequences in displaying less overt conformity to the *kamukunji*'s discursive patterns. Participants occasionally absorbed hard and blunt analysis of political events from an "expert" whom they considered as one of their own. Still, even with the elite members, after internalizing the *kamukunji*'s patterns of political thought and deeply entrenched proclivities, there was always the need to deliberately suppress utterances that might create disunity, controversy, or a heightened anxiety.

NEWSPAPER HEADLINES AND THE *KAMUKUNJI*

Kenya's newspaper readership is dominated by two English papers, namely the *Nation* and the *Standard*, which together command a market share of nearly 90 percent. During electoral politics, the two papers are sometimes perceived to be on the opposite ends of the unfolding political events. As a result, while the *Nation* commands almost 70 percent of Kenya's newspaper readership, sales of the papers in different parts of Kenya reflect the varied regional political inclinations. The Eldoret *kamukunji* and the newspaper interface thus reproduce an environment that is sensitive to how the leading newspapers seek to report and interpret political events as they unfold. At the time of the research, *kamukunji* participants felt that the *Standard* was sympathetic to the opposition (ODM, Orange Democratic Party), while the *Nation* was sympathetic to the then ruling Party of National Unity (PNU). Interviews with journalists[33] from the two leading newspapers revealed skewed sales in line with existing political proclivities. The *Standard*'s superior sales in Eldoret were reflected in the *kamukunji* as well. At Kegode's "shop," piles of the *Nation* would still linger long after the morning sales. In this section I present analysis of newspaper headlines from the two newspapers during the election week of 2007–8. I argue that newspaper headlines played a pivotal role in the *kamukunji* and, acting with other factors, legitimized and made possible deliberative action in the *kamukunji*.

For those who could not afford to buy the newspapers and who lacked the necessary social capital to access the whole paper, the front pages was the furthest point they could get to reading the news. However, this did not necessarily imply that they wanted to read the paper. In actual fact, the discourse, debates, and interpretations around an issue were valued more than the reading of the entire newspaper. Indeed, in times of a specific issue of political anxiety, the *kamukunji* members preferred something close to a communal uptake of news, where orally analyzed news complete with its subjectivities was consumed alongside news in print. Largely because of its accessibility, the front pages (headlines) almost always form the subject of debate. Apart from their ease in terms of access, the headlines and the front page mark the entry point into the deliberative space of the *kamukunji*. In signature fashion, headlines will guide *kamukunji* participants on the most immediate issue of debate. At the same time, headlines provided an opportunity for the researcher to observe the vagaries of discourse, and how collective imaginaries and affiliation were enacted, appropriated and at times resisted. In this section an attempt is made to reveal how headlines served a crucial role of anchoring discourse on an issue, of indicting, fact checking, and at the same time revealing the interests and the discursive biases inherent in the *kamukunji*. Notably, this section highlights how newspaper headlines were appropriated as sites of resistance, fixation, and affirmation.

Resistance was particularly explicit when headlines, mostly accompanied with pictures, appeared to dismantle and challenge entrenched positions. As the poll day approached, the publication of opinion polls and the coverage of the progress of the candidates were all interpreted in light of the extent to which they affirmed or confuted the *kamukunji*'s dominant narrative. For instance, on 23 December 2007, one of the fringe candidates, Kalonzo Musyoka, held his final presidential rally in Nairobi, which surprisingly, according to published media reports, drew a mammoth crowd. Both the leading papers gave extensive coverage to the rally, as it was the only major political event. In the *Daily Nation* of 24 December, a full-page image of Kalonzo riding in an open car under the headline "Last Minute Pledges" was published. The picture is taken to capture both the candidate and the huge gathering in the background draped in uniform yellow and green campaign colors. That morning, the *kamukunji* was unusually full for a morning session. In the ensuing deliberations the *kamukunji* participants, the majority of whom openly identified with the leading opposition candidate, Raila Odinga, seemed more to seek concurrence and affirmation on the anxiety created by the foregoing than to debate the ramifications of Kalonzo's candidacy.

> Kegode: Mambo gani hii? Eti wanasema Kalonzo alijaza Uhuru Park na watu karibu millioni, mnasemaje? Kwani huyu jamaa ni tishio hivi?
>
> What is this? They say that Kalonzo attracted a million people at Uhuru park, what do you think? So this man can be a threat?
>
> Speaker A: Hapana, hawa watu Karibu wote walibebwa na basi. Ebu niambie kama Nairobi Kalonzo anaweza kupata Kura. Tunajua hii mambo, alikomboa umati (laughter).
>
> No, most of these people were bused to the venue. Tell me—is it possible for Kalonzo to get votes in Nairobi? We know these things, he hired the crowd.
>
> Speaker B: *Hata opinion polls kila siku zinaonyesha huyu Kalonzo atapata 8percent pekee yake. Mtu wa 8 percent hawezi pata watu kama hao Nairobi. Hii umati ni ile ya kununuliwa. Wanawekwa kwa basi, na fifty bob ya lunch alafu wanarudishwa nyumbani baadaye. Mara ngapi hii inafanyika hata hapa Eldoret?*

Even daily opinion polls show that Kalonzo will only garner 8 percent, so he cannot possibly attract such a crowd in Nairobi. This crowd is the kind that is bought. You pack people into buses, pay them fifty shillings for lunch, then you drive them back home after the rally. How many times have we seen such things even here in Eldoret?

The manifest concurrence does not necessarily mean that dissenting opinion is absent, or that voices sympathetic to other candidates do not exist within the *kamukunji*. However, a process akin to a gradual muting of divergent and dissident opinion seems to be present. Similar to what media theorist Noelle-Neumann[34] observed in her study of public opinion, the dominating opinion compels compliance of attitude and behavior in that it threatens the dissenting individual with isolation. It is possible, following Noelle-Neumann, that after observing the social environment and assessing the distribution of opinion circulating within the *kamukunji* for or against one's own opinions, many fear the possible group "isolation," or doubt their own judgments, and instead opt to suppress these opinions. Since it was believed that a good showing by Kalonzo would jeopardize the chances of ODM winning the election, the elaborate coverage the rally received in the papers was systematically disparaged, the effect of which was the continued affirmation of the dominant opinion.

Since the *kamukunji* has a "mind," a particular provincial partisan view that equally structured newspaper consumption, the reading of the newspaper and the subsequent debate served a political imperative of linking those with similar political outlooks. Despite the content and the valence of the political views of the news reports expressed in the newspaper, debates and interpretations were largely aimed at consonance and validation, and were for the most part lacking a critical edge. As a result, members used the interpretations emerging from the *kamukunji* to manage both pleasant and unpleasant feelings brought about by highlighted newspaper content. On the polling day, 27 December 2007, the *kamukunji* was virtually deserted, but on 28 and 29 December visibly excited participants thronged Kegode's shop throughout the day as news of Odinga's lead in the count dominated coverage. While both the *Nation* and the *Standard* headlines on 28 December largely dwelled on the voter turnout, the *Standard* gave indications that things looked good for the opposition. "Results Trickle in after Record Voter Turn Out" screamed the *Nation*, adding that both candidates had a good showing in their strongholds. On the twenty-ninth, however, the debates in the *kamukunji* were more animated and audibly expectant; both leading papers indicated that a gap of close to a million votes separated the two. "Giants Kicked Out," *The Nation* headline roared, as a subheadline added that the vice president and sixteen other ministers had lost their seats in an ODM wave across the country. Below it, the latest figures from the vote count indicated that incumbent president Kibaki was trailing Odinga by about a million votes. Similarly on this day, the *Standard* was more specific, with the headlines "Raila Takes Early Lead," and a subheadline expounding on Kalonzo's poor showing, alongside the fact that a host of ministers had been vanquished at constituency levels. Unlike other days, the *kamukunji* was almost imploding in an excited debate. In the fusion of both the flippant and the more serious deliberations, a palpable connection between the contents of the headline and the prevailing mood was evident. If the *kamukunji* can be argued to be reflective of how change from below is imagined, then the newspapers displayed for sale were reflective of the realization of these aspirations. At this particular moment, the newspapers (especially the headlines) conflated a profit imperative while at the same time acting as artifacts that allowed urban spaces to actualize civic participation and political affiliation.

The political reality changed drastically after 29 December as Kibaki closed the gap. On 30 December Kibaki was pronounced winner and hurriedly sworn in as dusk fell in Kenya. The controversy and violence that followed these events are well documented. As the government moved in to ban live broadcasts in an attempt to manage the crisis, the *kamukunji*'s role went beyond that of deliberative practice and became a site of seeking and sharing information and also of managing and coping with the political uncertainty that followed. During these times, the *kamukunji* hosted attendees from virtually all spheres with numbers that were over one hundred and fifty in a single sitting. Notably, with the absence of news updates and no newspapers coming in from Nairobi, the *kamukunji* still held sittings, evidence of a subtle institutionalization, or metamorphosis to a less informal setting that transcends the newspaper itself. In the context of a possible systemic strain in Kenya, Eldoret residents used the *kamukunji* as a space where participants actively sought each other's support and perspective concerning what was happening. The *kamukunji* also became a deliberative space that participants used as a reference point in gaining "meaning." In a sense, the affinity and sense of political collectivity meant that as the crisis unfolded, individual participants used the *kamukunji* as a reference point to construct and establish a concrete, acceptable shared conception on which to develop new collective imaginaries and, where possible, to coordinate collective action such as street protests. Since fresh dailies had difficulty reaching Eldoret because of the violence, Kegode's use of old papers played a crucial function in this time. In this moment of uncertainty, the display of past issues served not only the practical function of anchoring space and symbolic purpose of inviting members but also the crucial function of fact checking, of indictment and of anchoring debate on the electoral fraud. In some cases, the display of past issues of newspapers was done alongside the latest issues for purposes of prompting debate along a desired issue. Having understood and internalized the logic running the *kamukunji,* Kegode displayed particular past issues with a view of inviting feedback and debate on an issue that might not be the subject of the headlines. This was the case when newspapers ran headline stories that were of no immediate interest to participants. In most cases, Kegode used newspaper headlines, either consciously or unconsciously, as a means of resisting unpleasant political realities that were incompatible with the "mind" of the *kamukunji.* For close to three weeks after the poll outcome, Kegode had both the *Standard* and the *Nation* newspapers of 29 December (which indicated a possible Raila win) displayed alongside issues of that day. In this time, members of the *kamukunji*, though aware that so much was unfolding daily, found solace in freezing a pleasant "political" moment, and the headlines served the evidentiary purpose that their collective aspirations were at one time almost realized. More important, in the context of what was believed to be an outright electoral fraud, the newspaper acted as evidence, as fact (printed on paper), that was used in order to indict and contrast fact with the fiction of an "electoral win" for the incumbent. Indeed, the past issues of the paper achieved a kind of fact-effect, and that in turn gave Kegode the leverage with which to show Kibaki's victory to be a fraud. More generally, Kenyans in 2008 were avidly looking at preelection opinion polls and early election results in order to show how far, exactly, Kibaki had stolen the election. In this case, the newspapers indicating a Raila win, standing in contrast to a political reality of the incumbent's win, were displayed as a harsh indictment of the blatant social injustice committed by the political elite. At the deliberative level, discussions were thus limited and directed at how the political realities could be undone, and justice served.

More generally, the use of these headlines reflected the lack of closure that the controversial elections had for most Kenyans after the disputed 2007 presidential polls. After a political deal was announced between Raila Odinga and Mwai Kibaki to form a grand collation government in late February, it was not surprising when participants in the *kamukunji* greeted each other with "Happy new year." For most, time froze on 30 December 2007, when Kibaki was sworn in for a second term.

CONCLUSION

In summing up, the question is likely to be asked if there is, in the strictest sense, a debate within the *kamukunji*, or is it a space of affirmation of already staked-out positions. Since, to a large degree, members tend to be cautious about disrupting "hegemonic" ideas, it might be difficult to refer to the *kamukunji* as a space of open democratic deliberative practice. However, even if there was some homogeneity of political affiliation, this does not mean that there was absence of debate within these homogeneous positions. At the same time, it is important to clarify that although some opinion appeared mainstreamed, there were several instances where the dominant opinion was contested and interrogated. While the wider impact of the *kamukunji* on the rest of the town's population is unlikely to be significant, in the sense that debates generated momentum beyond the *kamukunji*, the near permanence of the *kamukunji* in the town over the years is not something that can be ignored. Every time a significant political contest emerges, Kegode marshals his forces in a performance that is becoming more and more predictable. I close this chapter by musing on the future relationship between the newspaper and the *kamukunji* and what we are likely to see. First, for all the time that I did the research, the *kamukunji* was a purely male affair. This is not surprising but is reflective of its history, the hard-core political content and also the masculinized urban spaces that legitimize the *kamukunji* as a platform of masculine sociabilities. The evolution of the *kamukunji* can largely follow the more established street parliament in Nairobi, appropriately named *Bunge la Wananchi* (people's parliament). The *Bunge*, as it is commonly called, was a similar outfit that has grown to become one of the most active civil societies in Kenya today. The Nairobi-based *Bunge* has a formal membership, elections, and a constitution that guides its operations. It remains to be seen if the Eldoret *kamukunji* follows a similar path.

REFERENCES

Aseka, Erick Masinde. "Industrialization." In *Themes in Kenyan History*, edited by William Ochieng, 44–47. Nairobi: Heinemann Kenya, 1990.

Banegas, Richard, Florence Brisset-Foucault, and Armando Cutolo. "Espaces publics de la parole et pratiques de la citoyennete en Afrique." *Politique Africaine* 127 (2012): 5–20.

Barber, Karin. "Preliminary Notes on Audiences in Africa." *Africa* 67, no. 3 (1997): 347–61.

Brisset-Foucault, Florence. "A Citizenship of Distinction in the Open Radio Debates of Kampala." *Africa* 83, no. 2 (2013): 251–69.

Dugrand, Camille. "'Combattants de la parole': Parlementaires-debout et mobilisation partisane a Kinshasa." *Politique Africaine* 127 (2012): 49–70.

Guitard, Emilie. "Le Chef et le tas d'ordures: La gestion des dechets comme arene politique et attribut du pouvoir au Cameroun." *Politique Africaine* 127 (2012): 155–78.

Haugerud, Angelique. *The Culture of Politics in Modern Kenya*. Cambridge: Cambridge University Press, 1995.

Loimeier, Roman. "Sit Local, Think Global: The Baraza in Zanzibar." *Journal of Islamic Studies* 27 (2007): 16–38.

Maupeu, Hervé. "Political Activism in Nairobi: Violence and Resilience of Kenya Authoritarianism." In *Nairobi Today: The Paradox of a Fragmented City*, edited by Hélène Charton-Bigot and Deyssi Rodriguez-Torres, 381–404. Nairobi: Institute for French Research in Africa, 2010.

Muigai, Githu. "Kenya's Opposition and the Crises of Governance." *Journal of Opinion* 21, nos. 1–2 (1993): 26–34.

Murunga, Godwin. "Urban Violence in Kenya's Transition to Pluralist Politics, 1982–1992." *African Development* 24, nos. 1–2 (1999): 165–98.

Mutunga, Willy. *Constitution-Making from the Middle: Civil Society and Transition Politics in Kenya, 1992–1997*. Nairobi: Sareat and Mwengo, 1999.

Noelle-Neumann, Elisabeth. "The Spiral of Silence: A Theory of Public Opinion." *Journal of Communication* 24, no. 2 (1974): 43–51.

Ochieng, William. *A Pre-colonial History of the Gusii of Western Kenya C. A. 1500–1914*. Nairobi: East African Literature Bureau, 1974.

Price, Monroe, and Nicole Stremlau. "Media and Transitional Justice: Towards a Systematic Approach." *International Journal of Communication* 2 (2012): 1077–99.

Rasmussen, Jacob, and Duncan Omanga. "Les Parlements du peuple au Kenya: Debat public et participation politique a Eldoret et Nairobi." *Politique Africaine* 127 (2012): 71–90.

Scolari, Carlos A. "Media Ecology: Exploring the Metaphor to Expand the Theory." *Communication Theory* 22, no. 2 (2012): 204–25.

Tacchi, Jo, Don Slater, and Greg Hearn. *Ethnographic Action Research: UNESCO Users Handbook*. Paris: UNESCO, 2003.

Throup, David. *Economic and Social Origins of Mau Mau, 1945–53*. Nairobi: Heinemann Kenya, 1988.

NOTES

1. *Kamukunji* is a Swahili word for a political assembly with mostly subversive connotations. In this instance it refers to a particular street assembly, sometimes known as the people's parliament, which gathers around newspaper selling points.

2. See Jacob Rasmussen and Duncan Omanga, "Les parlements du peuple au Kenya: Debat public et participation politique a Eldoret et Nairobi," *Politique Africaine* 127 (2012): 71.

3. The city of Eldoret is in western Kenya and the headquarters of Uasin Gishu County, in the Rift Valley Province. In the 1980s and early 1990s the town was one of the fastest-growing towns in the country because of its textile industries, educational institutions, major hospitals, and highly developed agriculture. This has made Eldoret attract skilled and unskilled labor to service its major industries. It is a mostly cosmopolitan town, with the ethnic Nandis forming the majority of the town's 300,000 people, according to current estimates.

4. Richard Banegas, Florence Brisset-Foucault, and Armando Cutolo, "Espaces publics de la parole et pratiques de la citoyennete en Afrique," *Politique Africaine* 127 (2012): 5. See also Camille Dugrand, "'Combattants de la parole': Parlementaires-debout et mobilisation partisane a Kinshasa," *Politique Africaine* 127 (2012): 49; Emilie Guitard, "Le chef et le tas d'ordures: La gestion des dechets comme arene politique et attribut du pouvoir au Cameroun," *Politique Africaine* 127 (2012): 155.

5. Hunter, this volume.

6. Neil Postman, "The Reformed English Curriculum," in *High School 1980: The Shape of the Future in American Secondary Education*, ed. Alvin C. Eurich (New York: Pitman, 1970), 160.

7. Carlos A. Scolari, "Media Ecology: Exploring the Metaphor to Expand the Theory," *Communication Theory* 22, no. 2 (2012): 205.

8. See also Jo Tacchi, Don Slater, and Greg Hearn, *Ethnographic Action Research: UNESCO Users Handbook* (Paris: UNESCO, 2003). For a more academic approach see the work of Monroe Price and Nicole Stremlau, "Media and Transitional Justice: Towards a Systematic Approach," *International Journal of Communication* 2 (2012): 1077.

9. Karin Baber. "Preliminary Notes on Audiences in Africa," *Africa* 67, no. 3 (1997): 347. This is one of the most authoritative texts on how audiences in Africa are cajoled through a communicative act of performance.

10. Barber, "Preliminary Notes," 347.

11. William Ochieng, *A Pre-colonial History of the Gusii of Western Kenya C. A. D. 1500–1914*. (Nairobi: East African Literature Bureau, 1974).

12. Ochieng, *Pre-colonial History*, 205.

13. Roman Loimeier, "Sit Local, Think Global: The Baraza in Zanzibar," *Journal of Islamic Studies* 27 (2007): 16.

14. Angelique Haugerud, *The Culture of Politics in Modern Kenya* (Cambridge: Cambridge University Press, 1995), 2–4.

15. Erick Masinde Aseka, "Industrialization," in *Themes in Kenyan History*, ed. William Ochieng (Kenya: Heinemann, 1990), 45.

16. Aseka, "Industrialization," 60.

17. I refer here to the precolonial *baraza* and not the colonial and postcolonial formations under a similar name.

18. I use these three as broad terms to subsume similar patterns and deliberative action in other communities. Accordingly, the three are merely representative of what actually existed in virtually all other communities in Kenya.

19. Godwin Murunga, "Urban Violence in Kenya's Transition to Pluralist Politics, 1982–1992," *African Development* 25, nos. 1–2 (1999): 165.

20. Murunga, "Urban Violence," 167.

21. For more details see Hervé Maupeu, "Political Activism in Nairobi: Violence and Resilience of Kenyan Authoritarianism," in *Nairobi Today: The Paradox of a Fragmented City*, ed. Hélène Charton-Bigot and Deyssi Rodriguez-Torres (Nairobi: Institute for French Research in Africa, 2009), 382.

22. *Saba saba* means "7/7" in Swahili and refers to the date, 7 July, that has been etched in Kenya's recent history as a date synonymous with prodemocracy agitations. On 7 July 1990, this date secured its place in Kenya's history when prodemocracy groups convened at *kamukunji* grounds in Nairobi in a rare face-off with Moi's government. Tens of people died and hundreds more were injured in the ensuing standoff, which also saw the arrest of the leading opposition leaders and the detention without trial of several others. Since then, *saba saba* has always carried connotations of the start of the so-called second liberation.

23. Since 1969 *kamukunji* has also been the name of the electoral constituency covering the area around the Kamukunji Ground in Nairobi's Eastlands.

24. Willy Mutunga, *Constitution-Making from the Middle: Civil Society and Transition Politics in Kenya, 1992–1997* (Nairobi: Sareat and Mwengo, 1999), 170.

25. Githu Muigai, "Kenya's Opposition and the Crises of Governance," *A Journal of Opinion* 21, nos. 1–2 (1993): 28.

26. Interview with historian Eliud Biegon as part of an earlier but related research on 3 August 2007.

27. From conversations with anthropologist Jacob Rasmussen, January 2012, Nairobi.

28. Rasmussen and Omanga, "Les Parlements du Peuple," 81.

29. Kenya's newspaper landscape is a near duopoly of two English papers, namely the *Daily Nation*, simply and often referred to as the *Nation*, and the *Standard*. Between them they command a market share of nearly 90 percent. Others are the *Star* and the *People Daily*, a free paper.

30. This might appear like a contradiction since the newspapers are themselves written in English. English is the language of instruction in schools, so most Kenyans who have attended school read English well. However, Kiswahili is the language of everyday use.

31. Interviews with Kiptoo (not his real name), done two weeks before the 27 December 2007 presidential elections.

32. At the time of doing the research, the political union involving mostly Kalenjin and Luo political elite at the national level "reproduced" a similar pattern within the *kamukunji*, seen in the degree of participation in the group.

33. Interview with *Standard* bureau chief, Western Kenya, Stephen Makapila, January 2008 and *Daily Nation* staff in Eldoret, March 2008.

34. Elisabeth Noelle-Neumann, "The Spiral of Silence: A Theory of Public Opinion," *Journal of Communication* 24, no. 2 (1974): 44.

PART IV

Afterlives

CHAPTER 13

The Afterlife of Words
Magema Fuze, Bilingual Print Journalism, and the Making of a Self-Archive

HLONIPHA MOKOENA

INTRODUCTION

The historiography on the black press in South Africa owes much of its vibrancy to the seminal bibliography published by Les and Donna Switzer titled *The Black Press in South Africa and Lesotho: A Descriptive Bibliographic Guide to African, Coloured and Indian Newspapers, Newsletters and Magazines, 1836–1976*.[1] The specificity of the concept of the "black press" not only reflects the contemporary paucity of literature on this publishing history but also encapsulates the Switzers' attempt to cover an enormous historical period that would have otherwise been ignored or subsumed under a general history of newspapers in South Africa. As evidenced in recent publications, this historiography that was inaugurated by *The Black Press in South Africa* has grown enormously and matured through nuanced and detailed focus on individual newspapers, editors, writers, and publishers; and, the "glamour" quality of magazines such as *Drum* has also indirectly contributed to an expanding interest in the history of the "black press" in South Africa. In her recent book, *Gandhi's Printing Press: Experiments in Slow Reading*, Isabel Hofmeyr captures one of the main defining characteristics of the printed and circulated texts that comprise the "black press." She writes that Gandhi's *Indian Opinion* (established in 1903) and the printing press that produced it, "on a daily basis enacted a novel order of community, drawing in different castes, religions, languages, races, and genders."[2] Later on she describes the

361

context of imperial and colonial South Africa, and specifically the port city of Durban, as having engendered "zones of enforced cosmopolitanism."[3] These characteristics were not unique to Gandhi's experiments with publishing but can be generalized and applied to the entire "black press." As with the image of "India" that defined much of Gandhi's writing and publishing, Africans—especially those who had grown up on mission stations—published and wrote not as "Xhosas," "Zulus," or "Sothos" but as "New Africans"[4] who were attempting to come to terms with their subjugation as imperial subjects while constructing new notions of nationhood that were capacious enough to accommodate ethnic nationalism while also not contradicting the promise of Victorian imperialism.

Magema Magwaza Fuze (c. 1840–1922) was such an imperial subject. Writing and publishing in mission newspapers from the 1890s onward, his life and career as a printer are emblematic of the convolutions and imbrications of empire and nation and localized and globalized self-identities. Elsewhere I have written about his fuller biography, but the basic critical events and moments in his life are worth repeating. Magema Magwaza Fuze[5] was born in the colony of Natal, and his father, Magwaza, sent him to be educated at *Ekukhanyeni* (The Place of Light) as part of a larger group of young boys who were sent to the newly arrived bishop of Natal, John William Colenso. From the moment he left his home in 1856, Magema Fuze experienced the meaning of being a colonial subject: his separation from his mother at the age of about twelve; his enrollment at Colenso's *Ekukhanyeni* school; his 1859 baptism, which made him the first in his family to be baptized as a convert to Christianity; his learning to write; and his service as an assistant and printer for the bishop of Natal all placed him in the forefront of the major events and crises that shaped the relationship between colonial Natal and the independent Zulu kingdom that was still in existence across the Thukela River. As with many of his contemporaries, his chosen vocation as a writer was a consequence of his education at a mission school and his residence at a mission station. Importantly, his inculcation[6] into the culture of letters[7] began when he was the scribe of the controversial and notorious John W. Colenso, whose views on the contribution of Africans to biblical exegesis earned him the accusation of being a heretic.[8]

The extent to which the *amakholwa* (African converts) represent a unique class of individuals in colonial society has been debated in the literature for decades. Most recently, Paul la Hausse's *Restless Identities*[9] foregrounded the literary careers of the two protagonists who are the center of his historical explication. In defining their historical role as intermediaries and translators of Zulu culture, he noted their

> operating in the no man's land between the powerful and the dispossessed; between the respectable and the disreputable. They lived—and died—at the broken boundaries between nominally distinct worlds and came into their own as mediators between chiefly and other forms of authority, brokers between written and oral forms of knowledge, interpreters of modernism in a world of traditionalism, translators of the religious in secular terms and redeemers of the past for the present.[10]

It is the last function of the redeeming of the past for the present that may be said to define Fuze's singular contribution to the Zulu language canon. To understand the specificities of what these authors contributed to the historical memory and commemoration of the past, we have to turn to an early twentieth-century scholar of the Zulu language, Clement Doke, who in the 1930s and 1940s published articles in the journal *Bantu Studies* on the contemporary state of Zulu literature. Doke was also in the years 1932 to 1933 the convener of a committee that investigated the state of African literatures in southern Africa. The committee's report made special mention of newspapers as a medium through which "vernacular" writers were expressing their literary creativity. The authors of the report stated,

> The part played by the "Native Press" constitutes a special subject fit for investigation.... Much of the writing in newspapers is admittedly poor, but some is of a much higher standard. Often gems of literature, praise songs, history, folk-lore, etc., find their way into the Bantu papers. The best-known names are the following: Umteteli wa Bantu, Abantu-Batho (now defunct), Ilanga lase Natal, Imvo Zabantsundu.[11]

Although Doke would not have used the term "memory" to describe the "gems of literature" that he enumerates, Fuze and his contemporaries imagined themselves as preservers of the collective memory of the Zulu people and Africans in general. Expressing the point differently, La Hausse argues that the Zulu intelligentsia of the early twentieth century "confronted the challenge of rendering literate forms of knowledge in popularly accessible form."[12] Consequently, as populists they "had to create languages appropriate to different audiences."[13] This same predicament and challenge is present even in the efforts of the earlier generation of Zulu intellectuals to which Fuze belongs. As in the 1910s and 1920s, the intellectual output of the writers who were Fuze's contemporaries was imbricated in the politics of Zulu ethnic nationalism and the contingencies of a Zulu kingdom threatened with implosion and external invasion. Thus, memory does not just play the role of accounting for the present, but is also a chronicle of the growth of this intellectual class. Selecting a single writer as a representative of this social and cultural milieu has the effect of occluding the fact that Fuze was not a lone voice but a participant in a dialogue that found the newspaper an amenable medium. Thus, medium and memory become one, since Fuze and his contemporaries even debated whether copies of the newspaper should be collected and kept by readers. Importantly, as La Hausse notes, at the turn of the twentieth century, the bilingual newspaper *Ilanga lase Natal* began publishing "turn-of-the-century reflections on ethnic history and identity [that] were not only the result of a deepening sense of pessimism about the future but also reflected a sagacious grasp of the politics of the history."[14]

The newspaper *Ilanga lase Natal* is central to understanding who Fuze was as a writer because it is here that he was given a platform to be both a popular historian and a prolific letter writer and commentator. This body of work also corresponds with Fuze's twilight years and his explicit meditations on death and the afterlife. His relationship with the newspaper was, however, also personal since he was related to John Dube, the founder and editor of the newspaper.[15] In the prologue to *The Black People and Whence They Came*, Fuze describes his relationship to Dube by referencing the newspaper itself:

> For today we are fortunate in the mutual acquaintance we receive through the services of the newspaper [*Ilanga lase Natal*] produced by the son of a chief of the Ngcobo people, the Rev. J.L. Dube, son of James, also son of a chief, which makes observations for us throughout this country of ours in Africa.[16]

Contained in this introduction of *Ilanga* and Dube is the dual role of the editor as the creator of "mutual acquaintances" and the newspaper itself as playing the same role. When André Odendaal published his history of black protest politics, he underscored Dube's poll position in early twentieth-century Natal African politics and how he had achieved this status partly through his editorship of *Ilanga*. As with its predecessor *Ipepa lo Hlanga*, which was founded in 1900, *Ilanga* was regarded as suspicious by the Natal authorities, and his proof for this suspicious surveillance is that "regular translations of the newspaper's Zulu columns in the Native Affairs Department files testify to this."[17] Importantly, Dube's *Ilanga* was also a founding example of the "black press" because of its geographical proximity and, for a brief period, shared printing press with Gandhi's *Indian Opinion*.[18] Both men were involved in imagining nations through the medium of the newspaper, and although they were independent of each other, their proximity hints at the lost opportunity of dialogue between "India" and "Africa." Moreover, in her recent biography of Dube, Heather Hughes warns against a quick reading of this proximity and shared infrastructure as a symbolic expression of common goals and ideologies. Rather, she paints a picture of two leaders who although aware of the existence of the other's struggles were nonetheless separated by politics and prejudice. The fact of interdependence, especially in advertising, between Indian merchants and African newspapers, she argues, may have served to intensify the communal animosities rather than quell them.[19] Thus, if as La Hausse asserts, Dube often wrote in *Ilanga* to express "his own sense of history as the discourse of identity,"[20] he probably shared these sentiments with and encouraged Fuze's experimentation with different modes of writing history. This is especially evident in the fact that although Fuze published articles in *Ilanga* in the mid-decade in the 1920s, he was never explicitly introduced to the readers by an editorial written by Dube. It is as if both Dube and Fuze assumed that Fuze, perhaps through his previous writing and work with missionary presses, was familiar to the readers and therefore needed no introduction. Such tacit agreements with the reading public seemed to have relied on a shared "discourse of identity" that went beyond the obvious ethnic and cultural affinity but was also about Fuze's identity as a writer. By extension, the invisible personal signature that identified Fuze as a writer also undersigned what would become his "self-archive"—that is, since his authorial voice was distinct and identifiable to the readers, it also meant that Fuze was potentially aware that the newspaper itself was the site of his archiving.

Thus, it is not surprising that when Fuze announced that he was writing a book, he did so on the pages of *Ilanga* and continued to use the pages of the newspaper to appeal for financial support. On 25 February 1921 he published a letter titled "Ngebhuku laBantu" ("On the Black People's Book")[21] in which he not only named some of his sponsors but castigated his readers for expecting the book to write itself. In several statements in this letter Fuze makes it apparent that the work of writing a book is handiwork and cannot be accomplished without the "hands" of the creative person who is the author. This extended disquisition on the role of the author as a creator is among Fuze's most articulate testimonies about the vocation of writing. Although it is not possible to accurately date when Fuze actually began writing *Abantu Abamnyama Lapa Bavela Ngakona*,[22] since his translator, Harry Lugg, states that he met Fuze in 1902 and that "he had then written or partially written his book, and was a frequent visitor to our Native Affairs Department seeking financial aid for its publication."[23] It is clear that by the time he published the book, Fuze was adept at negotiating the volatile politics and economics of publishing in a colonial society. His own struggles to find patrons to subvent his book symbolize the predicaments of being a black and vernacular-language writer in South Africa. His life as a writer therefore consists of the simultaneous pressures of being given recognition by the publishing world while also creating or satisfying an audience that may or may not be receptive to your ideas. In this chapter, I will present Magema Fuze as an author who was acutely aware of the fact that his audience was not just his contemporaries but that writing was an implicit engagement with one's posterity and also with the posterity of one's words. This double consciousness erupted on the pages of *Ilanga lase Natal* as Fuze and his readers debated the immortality of the soul while also speculating on the future of *isiZulu* (Zulu) words and literature.

Although he was a singular voice, it is important to note that Fuze was not entirely unique in his preoccupations. In real terms his life spans the period that marked the destruction of the Zulu kingdom, and therefore the end of Zulu self-determination, while the end of his life coincided with the emergence of explicitly nationalist and Africanist political organizations. These two historical polarities allow him to be compared to other "mission-educated" writers in the region while also allowing for his own emergent nationalist awakening. When compared to other mission converts, Fuze could be said to represent the "accelerated development"[24] that Mgadla and Volz note in the Batswana converts who read and contributed to the newspaper *Mahoko a Becwana* (published from 1883 until 1896). In the same way that these Setswana writers were juggling competing identities of being "Tswana," "Christian," and "South African," Fuze was likewise contending with equivalent identities and also the inevitable pressure to conform to and confirm the "assumed existence of a cultural unity among the newspaper's readers" even while newspapers were becoming the repositories of "standard, official written language."[25] By contrast, the end of his life in 1922 also terminated his potential as an explicitly nationalist writer. In his study of the weekly *Abantu-Batho* (The People) which was published from 1912 until 1931, Peter Limb notes that the establishment of the African National Congress (ANC) and this allied newspaper was the beginning of the era of the "subaltern press," which was more radical and independent than the mission-based newspapers that preceded it. Thus, from a geographical and national purview Fuze was a hybridized writer who embodied both the dilemmas of Christian and mission-based writing as well as the later nationalist discourses that would dominate the "protest press" of the early twentieth century.

EPISTOLARY ASSEMBLIES

Although he seems to have written for *Ilanga lase Natal* from its inception in 1903, Fuze's writing career began elsewhere. As might be expected of an *ikholwa*, Fuze's writing began on the mission station of Bishopstowe / Ekukhanyeni with John William Colenso his mentor. However, contrary to the biographies of other *kholwa* writers, Fuze did not begin by writing religious texts or working for the mission press. Instead, Fuze's literary career began with travel writing. When Colenso visited the aging Zulu king, Mpande, in 1859, he gave his young charges notebooks, and he instructed them to keep diaries. He then published these accounts as *Three Native Accounts of the Visit of the Bishop of Natal in September and October, 1859, to Umpande, King of the Zulus*,[26] and the text became an early "classic" of Zulu literature.[27] The genre of travel writing would appear again in 1877 when Fuze made his own journey to Zululand and published this account as "A Visit to King Ketshwayo."[28] The first exercise in printing by Fuze, as a young and trained printer, is an idiosyncratic versified transcription of everyday conversations, which Colenso titled "Amazwi Abantu"[29] ("The People's Words [Voices]") and then sent to Wilhelm Bleek in Cape Town. The two texts, *Three Native Accounts* and "Amazwi Abantu," represent the "mission" period in Fuze's development as a writer since they were the product of his tutelage by Colenso. However, this is not to suggest that they are devoid of an imaginative and singular authorial voice. On the contrary, even as a young man, Fuze was able to appreciate the unique social milieu of the mission station since many of the residents often received news and rumors coming southward from the "Zulu country," that is, the independent Zulu kingdom. Also included were the names and sometimes descriptions of human and veterinary diseases and cures. Such a medley is therefore not easy to categorize, but it could be described as a vox populi and a barometer of the social norms, values, and vocal styles of the inhabitants of Ekukhanyeni and its surrounds. When considered as part of Fuze's body of work, these mission life narratives presage Fuze's later engagement with the more substantive question of Colenso's role and impact as a missionary. Thus, by the time he published his biographical series "Ukutunywa kukaSobantu" ("Sobantu's Mission") in *Ilanga* in 1920, Fuze had had some experience in writing within the liminal space between biography and autobiography since he was writing about his own experiences as a Christian convert and resident of Ekukhanyeni and also taking stock of the legacy of his guardian, John William Colenso. Thus, competing genres and modes of self-expression were part of Fuze's training and aspirations as a writer; he continued to mix and match these genres and was never writing from within only one type. In thinking about what connects his newspaper writing, his epistolary dialogues, and his seminal book, it is therefore paramount not to assume that these were markers of a teleological maturation in his writing. Rather, it is more useful to think of Fuze as the consummate bricoleur, that is, he deployed whatever genre and style of writing was useful to his purpose. Importantly, even his final statement, the book *Abantu Abamnyama*, has the character of a stitched text since portions of it correspond almost exactly to a series he published in *Ilanga lase Natal* in 1921 under the title "UDinuzulu: Ukuzalwa Nokuba-ko Kwake"[30] ("Dinizulu: His Birth and Existence"). Thus, although it is true that as with other African literates and devotees of the written word, Fuze was part of the institutionalization of the printing press that "made it possible to realign a diverse heterocosm of cultural identities into the makings of a more singular cultural order,"[31] it is also equally true that his writing practice and self-conception as a writer were always heterodox.

In practical terms, the relationship between newspaper writing and other types of texts can be explained as a consequence of Fuze's participation in various epistolary networks. These networks, writes Khumalo, consisted of a variety of writers who, having "mastered the technology of letter-writing ... sought to conquer space through ink and were able to establish connections that did not rely on physical face-to-face proximity."[32] Although Khumalo is mainly writing about letters that were exchanged via the colonial postal service, this concept is not limited to these instruments of interpersonal and direct communication, since, as he notes, "the network shaped what I call here a *sphere*; that is, an imaginary environment where these letter-writers felt free to converse among themselves about issues that affected their lives. Such an environment was akin to what the writers called an *ibandla*."[33] It is this constituent assembly of letter writers and readers[34] that was transferred to the emerging newspaper culture of the late nineteenth century. As I observed in an "Assembly of Readers," the term *ibandla* derives its power and significance from the fact that it has both mundane and profound meanings:

> This broad sphere of readers and writers was dubbed an "ibandla," a term with both traditional and modern connotations, including a gathering or assembly, a denomination or congregation, and a meeting rhetorically addressed. This ambiguity enabled the term in both its traditional and religious senses to "summon" an audience. My reference to an "assembly of readers" recognises that the term "ibandla" encompassed both "traditionalists" and "the converted." The Ekukhanyeni "Class of 1856,"[35] in popularising Zulu-language publications, were instrumental in creating this assembly of readers and in thereby founding a Zulu literary culture that borrowed its idiom of readership from the traditional vocabulary of public assembly.[36]

When readers were assembled around a letter or a newspaper, it became an object for public discussion. As Khumalo writes, it was assumed that letters were written to be read in public, and privacy had to be explicitly specified: "Most letters were read in public. If a writer wanted a letter to be private, he or she needed to insist that a particular letter was directed specifically to one person. For if that was not specified, everybody could gain access to people's 'private matters.'"[37] This lack of a boundary between the private and the public was also essential to the published letters that readers sent to newspapers. In the late 1890s, when Fuze wrote for two newspapers, *Inkanyiso Yase Natal* (The Enlightener of Natal, established in 1889) and *Ipepa Lo Hlanga* (The National Newspaper, established in 1894), he transferred to these new media not only the culture of the Ekukhanyeni epistolary network, but also to some extent the conventions of public address that had governed his letter-writing activities. The novelty of *Inkanyiso*, for example, is that although it began as an Anglican mission newspaper, printed at St. Alban's College in Pietermaritzburg, editorial control was quickly given to the Africans who wrote and contributed to it. As the "first native journal in Natal,"[38] *Inkanyiso* exhibited the "protest" language that would be present in Dube's *Ilanga*. Although the full extent of Fuze's contribution to *Inkanyiso* and *Ipepa Lo Hlanga* cannot be spelled out here, it is sufficient to point out that the readership of both newspapers was impressive: by 1891 *Inkanyiso* claimed to have 2,500 subscribers,[39] while *Ipepa* was not only the earliest known African-owned newspaper in Natal, it was also independent of missionary influence, and many of its contributors were members of the Natal Native Congress.[40] To provide a sense of the coalescing and overlapping conventions of letter writing and protest, it may be useful to read a letter that Fuze wrote and published in *Inkanyiso* in 1892 concerning the issue of Natal's agitation for responsible government. It was one of several letters he wrote about the condition of being a colonial subject, but it also stands out because it articulates a controversial subject, which many readers were often afraid to write about lest they be accused of radicalism. A year earlier, Fuze had published a letter warning the readers to be vigilant and read government notices. The letter[41] that Fuze published in *Inkanyiso* on 28 January 1892 pointed to two aspects of colonial politics that he wanted the readers to write and think about: first was the political implications of the colony of Natal being granted responsible government;[42] second was the absence of a person to represent the black people's point of view. Although the letter is putatively addressed to the "Editor," it is clear from his language that he is also simultaneously addressing the readership of the newspaper:

> MNGANE,–Epepeni lako lika Jan. 21, 1892, ngifumana amazwi ako okululeka uhlanga lwakiti, ngokuti uba "abamnyama babe nendoda yokubamela, ibe amehlo, ibe umlomo wabo, nxa kukulunywa umteto we *Responsible Government*."
>
> Lawamazwi okusiluleka kwako ngiyawabonga, Mhleli, kodwa ngicela abafundi bepepa lako uba nabo bake bapendule ukuba batini ngalaw'amazwi, njengoba seloku waqala ukuluma ngalol'udaba kako noyedwa obuzisisayo kwabakiti uba yini yona leyo, sekuze kungeloku le'ndaba siyayazi, kubelapo singazi luto; kupela silibele zindaba zokupikisana okulize okungayikusisiza ngaluto nabantwana betu emva kwetu.[43]

> FRIEND,—In your paper of Jan. 21, 1892, I found your words of advice to our kinfolk, saying, what if "the black people had a man to represent them, to be their eyes, their mouth, when the law of *Responsible Government* is discussed."
>
> I thank those words of advice, Editor, but I am asking the readers of your paper to at least reply and say something about these words. Ever since you began talking about this matter there hasn't been one who has asked from our kin about what it is. It is as if we know about this matter, when in fact we know nothing, since we are busy with quarrelsome matters that amount to naught and will not at all help us and our children who come after us.

In his previous letters about the nature of colonial governance, Fuze had resorted to metaphorical language and euphemism, but in this statement he is explicit about what it meant to live as a subject without political representation. As a committed newspaper writer, he, however, did not just end at being critical of the lack of representation. Instead, he offered the newspaper as a substitute for the absent representative. As with his other letters on the issue, the general tone and import of the argument is that he is requesting the readers participate in the political debates on the pages of *Inkanyiso*. As is clear in this letter, the readers weren't enthusiastic about criticizing the colonial government. His own summation was that they were distracted by petty quarrels and couldn't see that their neglect of politics affected not just their future but that of their children. Fuze was therefore writing to accuse his readers of being inert and passive and by implication, highlighting his own activism and political vigilance. The fact of their observed silence may be yet more proof that they didn't want to be identified with the "rebellious" ideas that Fuze was asking them to contemplate and write about. This sense of the newspaper as a sentinel also informed Dube's editorship of *Ilanga*:

> *Ilanga* pledged to open the eyes of the people to their own best interests, and it took a strong position on what these were. Throughout its pages, but especially in editorials, was an exhortation to an "improving Christianity": to gain education, start a business (and advertise it in *Ilanga*...), buy land, play an active role in social welfare, petition for the rights of citizenship—all in a measured and responsible, yet purposeful, manner.... In calling for the defence of the *uhlanga*, the African nation, by opposing injustice and the regrettable defects of colonial rule, it spoke for the literature and illiterate alike.[44]

Fuze would not have faulted the above summary not only of the career of John Dube as the founder and editor of *Ilanga* but of his own transition from the political activism that defined the mission station of Ekukhanyeni to the activism of the printed and political epistle. It is this transition that also created the possibilities and limits of a self-created archive: by being both a letter writer and a political commentator Fuze ensured that even if he was not remembered by those who read his personal letters, he would be remembered by the readers of *Inkanyiso*, *Ipepa*, and *Ilanga*.

PERFORMING WRITING

If Fuze's earliest writing was characterized by heterodoxy and bricolage that was partly a consequence of the mission context from within which he wrote, then we could date his emergence as an independent writer to the death of Colenso in 1883. By the time he died, Colenso was no longer just a missionary bishop and Zulu linguist,[45] he was also an *uSuthu* advocate; that is, he was Cetshwayo's supporter and defender. The death of Colenso also coincided rather tragically with the beginning of the civil war in Zululand that eventually led to the deposition of Cetshwayo, the partition of his kingdom, and his eventual death in self-imposed exile in 1884. Fuze was Colenso's amanuensis in cataloging the atrocities committed by the British, often working in alliance with Cetshwayo's enemies. The letter-writing activities noted above were in part in the service of this growing traffic in news and reports that traversed the ill-defined geography of "kingdom" versus "colony." Africans such as Fuze who were living on mission stations were the embodiment of this binary: although on paper they were "British subjects," in reality they were often called upon to speak to or on behalf of the denizens of the Zulu kingdom to whom they were often tied by threads of kinship, imagined and real. The death of Colenso, and other unanticipated events such as the fire that gutted Bishopstowe and his printing press in 1884, pushed Fuze toward a more precarious existence as a typesetter. He was, however, never too far away from the legacy of Colenso, which was carried forward after his death by his daughter, Harriette Colenso. In an unexpected turn to the publication of *Magema Fuze: The Making of a* Kholwa *Intellectual*, an antiquarian bookseller[46] contacted me about a curious document he had found between the pages of a book in his stock. The document is headed with the handwritten inscription "With Miss Colenso's compliments," and the typewritten heading reads, "Abantu Abamnyama, Lapa Bavela Ngakona: Table of Contents." There is no date on the document, but unexpectedly it is written in English rather than Zulu, which is unusual for Fuze. The fact that the handwritten inscription refers to "Miss Colenso," presumably Harriette Colenso,[47] suggests that if it was written by Fuze, it was meant to function as a prospectus for interested publishers and patrons. The directness and halting quality of the prose gives away Fuze's discomfort at using the English language to promote a text that was in Zulu. It is therefore surprising to read one of the opening articles of the prospectus:

> IX.—Been striving long time for this performance, till at last N.J.N. Masuku seconds me, and I believe that soon very many will want their children taught in schools from it, whence we come.

All the paragraphs in the prospectus are numbered with Roman numerals, which suggests that Fuze was excerpting the main points of his argument and attempting to put this in a précis of some kind. But the real revelation of article IX is that Fuze used the word "performance" to define his task of writing and soliciting funds for the publication of his book. This use of the notion of performance has a literal quality to it because he was translating from his *isiZulu* text and providing the English reader with a concise summation of his struggles as a writer. Yet when this is compared to the final published text, a different meaning of "performing" becomes apparent.

In a letter published in the bilingual Zulu-English newspaper *Ilanga lase Natal*,[48] Fuze wrote a lengthy update addressed to his readers about the funding he had received but also asking for more support. The letter articulates what Fuze understood to be the vocation of a printer, and importantly, he also uses the letter to share his work ethic and aspirations as a writer. Some of his main sponsors included Nicholas Masuku, N. J. N. Masuku, R. M. Siboto, and his own son Solomon. Fuze then chastised his other readers by telling them:

> Inningi leli litule liqintile, libheke ukuba inncwadi lena izicindezele yona ngokwayo, ukuze liti libona ibe sei yisideku esipeleleyo, esizenzileyo.
>
> Kanti, bakiti, awuko nowodwa umsebenzi ozenzayo. Konke kwenziwa ng'abantu ngezandhla nangekanda. Seloku kwakunjalo nasendulo njengoba kuse njalo nanamuhla, abantu bayasebenza ngezandhla nangamatupana abo, basebenza imisebenzi eyakugcina ngokubukwa ng'abanye; bati bonke labo abayibukayo balinganise osongati ayenziwanga ngezandhla.[49]

> The majority of you are silent and idly standing by, expecting that the book will print itself, so that you will suddenly find that it is a substantial and complete thing that has made itself.
>
> On the contrary, folks, there is no work that completes itself. Everything is done by people with hands and mind. It's been like that since time immemorial and it's still like that today. People work with their hands and fingers; they do work that others will marvel at, and those who see the work will pass judgment [compare] as if it wasn't done by hands.

Fuze was essentially telling his readers that they did not understand the labor and sacrifice involved in being a printer and writer. There is a clear tone of irritation in his castigating statements, but there is also a lesson in the work ethic, which he thinks has existed since time immemorial.

In the translated book, *The Black People and Whence They Came*, Fuze's voice of an irritated and frustrated writer turns to resignation as he commends his patron Masuku while also reminding the readers that he has been requesting their support for some time. He wryly states:

> For a very long time I have been urging our people to come together and produce a book about the black people and whence they came, but my entreaties have been to no avail. Had they complied, the book would have been produced many years ago.[50]

It is at this point that he mentions the patronage of "Mr. N.J.N. Masuku," without whom the book would not have been published. The above English translation, however, lacks the nuance of the original *isiZulu* text, in which Fuze distinguished between the published book ("le'nncwadi") and his envisioned book ("l'ibhuku"). In the original Zulu text the last sentence reads: "Sekweqe iminyaka nezikati engakube le'nncwadi seyaba l'*ibhuku* ukuba bavumile ukukwenza loko."[51] Superficially, it could be said that Fuze is merely using *incwadi* (book/letter) and *ibhuku* (the transliteration of the word "book") as synonyms; this is the opinion and choice of the translator. However, another interpretation is also possible. If we follow the logic of Fuze's use of the word "performance," then the alternating use of "letter" and "book" refers to the fact that he sees his own effort as minor compared to his intended "performance," namely, the production of a cultural encyclopedia and historical text. In other words, Fuze probably thought of *Abantu Abamnyama* as a monologic treatise that fell short of the dialogic compendium that he had envisioned. For him, therefore, "performance" would have consisted of collective labor whose outcome would have been a book with many authors rather than a "letter" authored by a single voice. This is not to suggest that Fuze was reverting to some precolonial "communal" value. Rather, it is to suggest that his conception of a book on the history of "the black people" implied multiple authors since it was such an enormous task. The fact that his contemporaries did not respond to his entreaties is the reason why he has become the sole author of the text. In this too, the notion of a "self-archive" becomes important since the failure of the collective to support Fuze necessarily ends with him being a sole author and therefore also the author of his own archive.

In comparing the publication of Fuze's *Abantu Abamnyama* to that of his near contemporary and popular historian Petros Lamula's *UZulukaMalandela*[52] (published in 1924), La Hausse offers several explanations for why Fuze's book was not the success he hoped it would be. First, he points to the fact that the book received very little publicity in the black press and, second, that Fuze died in 1922, the same year the book was published. Importantly, the lack of capital and the low buying power of literate Africans meant that "for a black writer to publish a book in Zulu during the 1920s was an historic act of courage bordering on the reckless."[53] Thus, what La Hausse calls the "vagaries of the 1920s book market" must have affected the availability and sale of Fuze's book. This makes it near impossible to estimate the costs of publication, since Fuze never revealed the amount of money he had received from his main sponsor, N. J. N. Masuku. However, there is yet another possible explanation. The presence of the prospectus written in English also underscores a second aspect of Magema Fuze's life as a writer, and that is that regardless of his commitment to the publication of books written in *isiZulu*, the English-speaking world of newspapers and book publishing was hovering in the background, influencing the "standards" expected of a publication but also competing for the limited numbers of patrons of "Zulu books." Thus, when Fuze published his book in 1922 in the original *isiZulu*, he was taking sides in a cultural tussle that had no clear rules of engagement. While missionaries and colonial administrators such as Henry Callaway, author of *The Religious System of the Amazulu*; A. T. Bryant, who wrote *Olden Times in Zululand and Natal*; and Harry Lugg, Fuze's translator and former magistrate, and others were compiling books and dictionaries on Zulu culture and language, Fuze and his contemporaries contested some of these publications on the pages of newspapers. A bilingual dialogue was therefore an inevitable consequence of the large presence of English-speaking readers who were interested in Zulu culture and who were also publishing in newspapers and in book form their own versions of this culture. Secondarily, the publication of *The Black People and Whence They Came* in English in 1979 converted *Abantu Abamnyama* from being a collector's item into an accessible text that could be annotated and used in the many debates on Zulu history that were raging in the 1970s and 1980s.[54] As a writer Fuze is therefore available as both a vernacular and a translated author. He is thus a "translated man."[55] When he is considered as a translated man, Fuze's authorship of *Abantu Abamnyama* fits into the general predicament of defining the task of translation. As Walter Benjamin expressed it:

> A translation issues from the original—not so much from its life as from its afterlife. For a translation comes later than the original, and since the important works of world literature never find their chosen translators at the time of their origin, their translation marks their stage of continued life.[56]

The notion of an "afterlife" of a written text implies that there will always be a disjuncture and incommensurability between reading a translated text and comparing it with the original thought and ideas that inspired the untranslated text.

The accidental resurfacing of Fuze's *Abantu Abamnyama* prospectus adds new meaning to the notion of an "afterlife" while also revealing the type of audience and readership he was anticipating while writing the book. The fact that the prospectus was written in English for a book that was to be published in the Zulu language means that the act of compiling the prospectus was already an act of translation or even an anticipation of translation. By giving the English-speaking reader a pointed summary of his Zulu book, Fuze was both approximating and distancing himself from the missionary and amateur scholarship that had defined the literature on Zulu culture. He was expressing his awareness that his work could only be published if it had the support and maybe even imprimatur of the extant experts on Zulu culture. These readers were also linked to networks of patronage, so it was equally important to address them as potential funders. The confluence between readership and power asserts itself most forcefully in Fuze's colonial setting, since Fuze had to also be aware that he was addressing readers who played dual roles in the colony.

Thus, "performing" writing was for Fuze about linking his newspaper readers to a future and envisioned book-reading public. It was about extending the temporalities of reading by expecting readers to contribute to the debates in the weeklies while also projecting into the future and producing *amabhuku* (books). In Fuze's idealization of the practice of writing, the individuality of the author did not preclude the collective action of compiling an anthology of texts for the benefit of future generations. This explicit engagement with the future is in itself a performance because it implies that as an author Fuze had to assume that his particular obsession with the origins of "the black people" would have longevity and be able to vivify future debates about history and Zulu culture. This assumption is especially important considering that Fuze was a colonial subject and was aware of how much the power of the colonial state and its administrators influenced the kinds of texts available to African-language readers. His book was meant to address this specific paucity, but it was also meant to contest the terrain that was being charted by the bureaucrat-authors who were civil servants within the British Empire and also dilettanti of Zulu culture and history. His being a colonized subject thus meant that the domain of reading and writing was for Fuze also circumscribed by the contingencies of colonial overrule. Whether it was on the pages of newspapers or in his book *Abantu Abamnyama*, Fuze was aware that publishing was about timeliness, and his own lifetime's worth of colonial experiences meant that he wanted to produce a record of his own politicization but also express a grander theory about what "the black people" were before the arrival of European colonialism. The performing of writing is thus a contemporary response to colonial subjecthood that he hoped would resonate with future generations who may or may not be caught in the same predicament.

Lost Lives / Lost Generations

One of the ways in which Fuze uses writing to ensure his posterity is by writing about the death (and lives) of others. As a former student of *Ekukhanyeni* and Colenso's printer, he writes about the personalities who inhabited his life on the mission station with vivacity touched by a nostalgia for the bygone era of the "noble" missionary. His coming-of-age story as a young man and student at Colenso's school is part of the obituary he wrote for another former student and friend, Bubi [Mubi] Nondenisa.[57] However, the fullest expression of Fuze's awareness that his life was enmeshed with the legacy of his missionary mentor, John William Colenso, is the series of articles he published in *Ilanga* in 1920 with the title *Ukutunywa kukaSobantu* (Sobantu's Mission).[58] The latter was not just an obituary of Colenso, who had been dead since 1883, but a retrospective on the meaning of conversion, mission life, education, conquest, and Christian ethics. The fact that it took Fuze thirty-seven years to write his mentor's memoirs is not a reflection of neglect or forgetfulness. Rather, the publication of the series of articles on *Sobantu* ("Father of the People," Colenso's Zulu name) was only a recent example of Fuze's version of Colenso's biography. In 1901, he and Bubi had written another series of articles on Colenso and his mission station and school, and published it in the newspaper *Ipepa lo Hlanga*. Thus, it is possible to state that Fuze's role as a biographer was an evolving one rather than a one-off instance of memorialization. This implies that, despite or because of the ravages of time, Fuze was constantly revising and retelling the story of his own conversion and maturation. He perceived even his autobiography to be a narrative that could be retold and reedited as the years went by. These meditations on loss and death culminated, and may even have been the product of, Fuze's most radical reinterpretation of his biblical and religious education, namely, that in the last years of his life he published a series of articles in *Ilanga* titled *Umuntu Kafi*

Apele (When a Person Dies That Is Not the End of Him).[59] Although it would be simplistic to equate Fuze's grief at being the sole survivor and inheritor of the Colenso legacy with his articulation of eschatological ideas that differed from his Christian faith, there is nonetheless a parallelism that exists between his meditations on death, as the end of life or not, and his exhortations for his work to be carried forth by future generations. It could be argued that while contemplating his own mortality, Fuze also thought about the destiny of the "race" or nation.

In his preoccupation with end-of-life narratives and obituaries, Fuze was typical of a newspaper writer and reader of his generation. As part of the staple of local and international news, death was routinely written about in the bilingual black press. The obituaries of both ordinary and notable personalities were regularly published. The *kholwa* community was especially concerned to commemorate the lives of those Africans who had served as missionaries or clerics. Peculiarly however, the vocabulary for writing about death could vary markedly. An advert printed in *Ipepa Lo Hlanga* in 1901 represents the instability and irregularity in the writing of advertising copy. since the owner, presumably "J. Coney," describes himself as a "maker of sleeping boxes" ("Umenzi Wama Bhokisi Okulala"). It is not until one reads the entire advert that one realizes that "J. Coney" is a coffin maker rather than a cot or bedstead maker. By contrast, the death of Booker T. Washington in 1915 was written about in both *isiZulu* and English, and the language in both was very precise. In the Zulu version published in *Ilanga lase Natal* on 19 November 1915, the author of the notice writes that Booker T. Washington was the formidable principal of Tuskegee ("iPrincipal etusekayo yase Tuskegee"). However, what is notable is that even in this very brief notice, the emphasis is on Washington's character. The writer notes, "Kufe indoda yamadoda eyabe ihlonitshwa na amakosi abelungu" ("A man amongst men has died; he was respected even by white leaders"). The last sentence of the death notice leaves the reader in anticipation since it states that the full account of his life and work will be written about in the forthcoming edition. This full account is, however, not published until 14 January 1916, and it is in English and clearly copied verbatim from an American newspaper. The switch between the two languages clearly assumes bilingualism on the part of the readers. Only the reader who had read the first notice on his death published four days after the event would have waited to read the obituary published nearly two months after Washington's death. The obituary, moreover, is notable because it preserves the "timeliness" of the original obituary. Even though *Ilanga* published the obituary on 14 January, the text still reads, "died early to-day Nov. 14." Although this exemplifies the cut-and-paste modus operandi of these bilingual newspapers, it also reinforces their dependency on a network of other publications, since African newspapers were not part of the Associated Press and other wire services to which the English-speaking newspapers had access. Yet, despite these limitations, these newspapers still treated their readers as if the news of Booker T. Washington's death was "hot off the wires." This deliberate anachronism is at disturbing, since it attempts to create the false impression of urgency, and yet, even despite this, it cannot be argued that Washington's obituary had somehow lost its urgency two months after his passing. Regardless of the reasons for the failure to edit the obituary, its inclusion represents a much broader question of the relationship between *kholwa* ideals of the self and the content of the newspaper. Each edition of *Ilanga* could contain news about sporting events, weddings, divorces, and of course obituaries, and there wasn't a distinction between "news" and "lifestyle" columns and items. The layout of the newspaper suggests a continuity between *kholwa* self-awareness and notions of progress espoused in editorials and articles. To understand this self-awareness, Tim Couzens cites the seminal importance of the publication in 1930 of T. D. Mweli Skota's *The African Yearly Register: Being an Illustrated National Biography Dictionary (Who's Who) of Black Folks in Africa*. What was distinctive about Skota's register was not only that it included the biographies of the living as well as the dead, but that there were recurring phrases and patterns. One example that Couzens writes about is the recurrent presence of the word "progressive":

> The word "progressive" appears fourteen times in eighty-five portraits; this must have some significance. In fact, the word is clearly the ideological touchstone or keyword of the whole book.[60]

In her biography of John Dube, Heather Hughes identifies Dube's publication in 1928 of a Zulu book titled *Ukuziphatha Kahle* (Good Manners) as an expression of the "insistent effort among the African intelligentsia through the 1920s to demonstrate progress, respectability and capacity for civilisation."[61] More importantly, she defines this genre as "conduct of life literature" and notes,

> *Ukuziphatha* belongs to that genre that became known as conduct of life literature, after Ralph Waldo Emerson's volume of the same name, with its central

question, "How shall I live?" Such works explored the relationship between fate and character, interior self and public persona. . . . The conduct of life idea featured strongly in the works of thinkers as widely divergent as Booker Washington and Marcus Garvey. While it had been a theme in Dube's earlier work, this was his more sustained attempt to lay down a series of guidelines that might yield results in South African conditions, where alignment of old and new was an added concern.[62]

Such, then, were the literary culture and conventions on writing about loss and death that Magema Fuze was contributing to when he wrote his belated obituaries of his contemporaries and missionary mentor. The fact that Magema Fuze waited for over three decades to write and publish an appraisal of his mentor's career as a missionary and bishop shows that he was following the conventions of the newspapers he routinely published in: death and loss could be written about days, months, and years after they had actually taken place. This explains why when Fuze published *Ukutunywa kukaSobantu*, he still elicited passionate responses from readers. The latter still remembered the controversies surrounding Colenso, but they were also perhaps now ready to deliberate on the metaphoric meaning of Fuze's biography. That is, after three decades had passed, these *kholwa* literates could distance themselves from the history of nineteenth-century missionary work and think about the twentieth-century decline in the idealistic aspirations that Fuze's generation had imbibed from mission schools and radically thinking mentors such as Colenso.

At least one of these idealistic aspirations was the notion of nationalist revival. In order to understand why Fuze writes so volubly about the political necessity of "unity" and cultural resurgence, one has to be willing to accept the congruence that he draws between the organic life span of a person and the organic life span of a nation. In a telling metaphor, Fuze calls for unity in the following terms:

> You will attain nothing by your present state of disorganization. Unite in friendliness like the enlightened nations. Do not merely look on heedlessly when others are being exploited. So long as you desire evil to one another, you will never be a people of any consequence; but you will become the manure for fertilizing the crops of the enlightened nations, disorderly, useless, and without responsibility.[63]

By equating the creation of a nation with the organic processes of agriculture and cultivation Fuze was explicitly making a nationalist argument that also appealed to his *kholwa* readers who aspired to emulate the progress of "enlightened nations." By cautioning them to first solidify into a united body before pursuing their individual desires, Fuze was also making it clear that his book was a political tract and should be read thus.

CONCLUSION

The uniqueness of Magema Fuze as a biographical subject rests on many pillars: he was the first Zulu speaker to publish a book in the Zulu language; he was trained as a printer for the infamous bishop of Natal, Colenso; he was a witness to the many events and conspiracies that led to the destruction of the Zulu kingdom begun in 1879; and he was a compelling writer whose literary career only becomes visible once we go beyond the publication in 1922 of *Abantu Abamnyama Lapa Bavela Ngakona*. Although important and certainly the source of Fuze's literary longevity, the 1922 book only makes sense when understood as the final stage in a continuum of writerly interventions and expositions that had engaged Fuze for much of his adult life. That he was consciously pursuing the posterity conferred by a published oeuvre is clearly evident in the numerous letters he wrote to his readers explaining his encyclopedic project of writing the history of the "black people and whence they came." Whether one regards the publication of *Abantu Abamnyama* as a successful outcome of this objective is immaterial to the fact that Fuze succeeded in getting his name associated with a historical endeavor that was not realized in his lifetime but which now reveals to us the innumerable losses suffered by black intellectuals in nineteenth-century South Africa. Although his work could now simply be dismissed as "self-archiving" in an autobiographical sense, this chapter has attempted to show that even during his lifetime Fuze understood the "self-archive" to be a communal enterprise as much as an individualist confession. His continuous addressing of an audience, contemporary and future, shows that he was aware that even as he was expressing his own disappointment at the lack of financial support for his book, future generations would want to read about their history, culture, and the immediate events surrounding his life, about which he was such a vocal and gifted historian.

BIBLIOGRAPHY

Attwell, David. *Rewriting Modernity: Studies in Black South African Literary History*. Pietermaritzburg: University of KwaZulu-Natal Press, 2005.

Benjamin, Walter. *Illuminations*. Edited by Arendt, Hannah. Translated by Harry Zohn. New York: Schocken, 1968.

Bryant, Alfred T. *Olden Times in Zululand and Natal Containing Earlier Political History of the Eastern-Nguni Clans*. London: Longmans, Green, 1929.

Callaway, Rev. Canon [Henry]. *The Religious System of the Amazulu. Izinyanga Zokubula. Or, Divination as Existing among the Amazulu in Their Own Words with a Translation into English and Notes*. Springvale: John A. Blair; Pietermaritzburg: Davis and Sons; Durban: Adams & Co, 1870.

Casanova, Pascale. *The World Republic of Letters*. Translated by M. B. DeBevoise. Cambridge, MA: Harvard University Press, 2004.

Coetzee, John M. *White Writing: On the Culture of Letters in South Africa*. New Haven: Yale University Press, 1988.

Colenso, John W. *Three Native Accounts of the Visit of the Bishop of Natal in September and October, 1859, to Umpande, King of the Zulus; With Explanatory Notes and a Literal Translation, and a Glossary of All the Zulu Words Employed in the Same: Designed for the Use of Students of the Zulu Language*. 3rd ed. Pietermaritzburg: Vause, Slatter, 1901.

Couzens, Tim. *The New African: A Study of the Life and Work of H. I. E. Dhlomo*. Johannesburg: Ravan Press, 1985.

Davis, R. Hunt, Jr. "'Qude maniki!': John L. Dube, Pioneer Editor of *Ilanga lase Natal*." In *South Africa's Alternative Press: Voices of Protest and Resistance 1880s–1960s*, edited by Les Switzer, 83–98. Cambridge: Cambridge University Press, 1997.

De Kock, Leon. "Metonymies of Lead: Bullets, Type and Print Culture in South African Missionary Colonialism." In *Print, Text and Book Cultures In South Africa*, edited by Andrew Edward Van der Vlies, 50–73. Johannesburg: Witwatersrand University Press, 2012.

Doke, Clement M. "Bantu Language Pioneers of the Nineteenth Century." *Bantu Studies* 14 (1940): 207–46.

Doke, Clement M. "A Preliminary Investigation into the State of the Native Languages of South Africa with Suggestions as to Research and Development of Literature." *Bantu Studies* 7 (1933): 1–99.

Fuze, M. M. *Abantu Abamnyama Lapa Bavela Ngakona*. Pietermaritzburg: City Printing Works, 1922.

Fuze, Magema. "Abantu Abamnyama Lapa Bavela Ngakona: Prospectus." N.d.

Fuze, Magema. "Amazwi Abantu." In *Grey Manuscript Collection [G10 C31]*. Cape Town: National Library of South Africa, 1859.

Fuze, Magema M. *The Black People and Whence They Came: A Zulu View*. Pietermaritzburg: University of Natal Press; Durban: Killie Campbell Africana Library, 1979.

Fuze (Magwaza), Magema. "Ku Mhleli we Nkanyiso." *Inkanyiso*, 28 January 1892.

Fuze, M. M. "Ngebhuku laBantu." *Ilanga lase Natal*, 25 February 1921.

Fuze, M. M. "UDinuzulu: Ukuzalwa Nokuba-ko Kwake." *Ilanga lase Natal*, 18 February 1921.

Fuze (Magwaza), Magema. "A Visit to King Ketshwayo." *Macmillan's Magazine* 37 (1878): 421–32.

Guest, Bill. "Towards Responsible Government, 1879–1893." In *Natal and Zululand from Earliest Times to 1910: A New History*, edited by Andrew Duminy and Bill Guest, 233–48. Pietermaritzburg: University of Natal Press and Shuter & Shooter, 1989.

Guy, Jeff. *The Heretic: A Study of the Life of John William Colenso, 1814–1883*. Johannesburg: Ravan Press; Pietermaritzburg: University of Natal Press, 1983.

Guy, Jeff. *The View across the River: Harriette Colenso and the Zulu Struggle against Imperialism*. Cape Town: David Philip, 2001.

Hamilton, Carolyn. *The Mfecane Aftermath: Reconstructive Debates in Southern African History*. Johannesburg: Witwatersrand University Press; Pietermaritzburg: University of Natal Press, 1995.

Hofmeyr, Isabel. *Gandhi's Printing Press: Experiments in Slow Reading*. Cambridge, MA: Harvard University Press, 2013.

Hughes, Heather. *First President: A Life of John Dube, Founding President of the ANC*. Auckland Park, South Africa: Jacana Media, 2011.

Khumalo, Vukile. "The Class of 1856 and the Politics of Cultural Production(s) in the Emergence of Ekukhanyeni, 1855–1910." In *The Eye of the Storm: Bishop John William Colenso and the Crisis of Biblical Inspiration*, edited by Jonathan A. Draper, 207–40. Pietermaritzburg: Cluster Publications, 2003.

Khumalo, Vukile. "Ekukhanyeni Letter-Writers: A Historical Inquiry into Epistolary Network(s) and Political Imagination in KwaZulu-Natal, South Africa." In *Africa's Hidden Histories: Everyday Literacy and Making the Self*, edited by Karin Barber, 113–42. Bloomington: Indiana University Press, 2006.

la Hausse de Lalouviére, Paul. *Restless Identities: Signatures of Nationalism, Zulu Ethnicity and History in the Lives of Petros Lamula (c. 1881–1948) and Lymon Maling (1889–c. 1936)*. Pietermaritzburg: University of Natal Press, 2000.

Lamula, Petros. *UZulukaMalandela: A Most Practical and Concise Compendium* of *African History Combined with Genealogy, Chronology, Geography and Biography*. Durban: Star Printing Works, 1924. Reprint, Durban: Josiah Jones, 1931; Marianhill: Marianhill Mission Press, 1939.

Limb, Peter. *The People's Paper: A Centenary History and Anthology of Abantu-Batho*. Johannesburg: Wits University Press, 2012.

Lugg, Harry C. "Translator's Preface." In *The Black People and Whence They Came: A Zulu View*, xvii–xviii. Pietermaritzburg: University of Natal Press; Durban: Killie Campbell African Library, 1979.

Mgadla, Part T., and Stephen C. Volz. *Words of Batswana: Letters to Mahoko a Becwana, 1883–1896*. Cape Town: Van Riebeeck Society, 2006.

Mokoena, Hlonipha. "An Assembly of Readers: Magema Fuze and His *Ilanga lase Natal* Readers." *Journal of Southern African Studies* 35, no. 3 (2009): 595–607.

Mokoena, Hlonipha. *Magema Fuze: The Making of a* Kholwa *Intellectual*. Scottsville, South Africa: University of KwaZulu-Natal Press, 2011.

Mokoena, Hlonipha. "The Queen's Bishop: A Convert's Memoir of John W. Colenso." *Journal of Religion in Africa* 38, no. 3 (2008): 312–42.

Ngcobo, Sol M. "Umbiko: M. M. Fuze." *Ilanga lase Natal*, 17 November 1922.

Odendaal, André. *Black Protest Politics in South Africa to 1912*. Totowa, NJ: Barnes & Noble, 1984.

Ricard, Alain. *The Languages and Literatures of Africa: The Sands of Babel*. Translated by Naomi Morgan. Oxford: James Currey; Trenton, NJ: Africa World Press; Cape Town: David Philip, 2004.

Switzer, Les, and Donna Switzer. *The Black Press in South Africa and Lesotho: A Descriptive Bibliographic Guide to African, Coloured and Indian Newspapers, Newsletters and Magazines, 1836–1976*. Boston: G. K. Hall, 1979.

NOTES TO CHAPTER 13

1. Les Switzer and Donna Switzer, *The Black Press in South Africa and Lesotho: A Descriptive Bibliographic Guide to African, Coloured and Indian Newspapers, Newsletters and Magazines, 1836–1976* (Boston: G. K. Hall, 1979).

2. Isabel Hofmeyr, *Gandhi's Printing Press: Experiments in Slow Reading* (Cambridge, MA: Harvard University Press, 2013), 3.

3. Hofmeyr, *Gandhi's Printing Press*, 8.

4. On defining "New Africans" see David Attwell, *Rewriting Modernity: Studies in Black South African Literary History* (Pietermaritzburg: University of KwaZulu-Natal Press, 2005), 8, 55. For a book-length exposition on the term see Tim Couzens's *The New African: A Study of the Life and Work of H. I. E. Dhlomo, the New African: A Study of the Life and Work of H. I. E. Dhlomo* (Johannesburg: Ravan Press, 1985).

5. At different times in his life Magema Fuze used different surnames and signed his name differently: he sometimes wrote as "Magema Magwaza" at other times as "Magema M. Fuze," and when he wrote for *Ilanga lase Natal* he signed his articles as "M. M. Fuze." In the notice about his death, published in *Ilanga*, his son Sol M. Ngcobo called him "u Magema ka Magwaza ubaba wakwa Ngcobo" ("Magema Magwaza the father of the Ngcobo family") while also mentioning that "Owaziwa kakulu ngokuti uFuze" ("He is well-known as Fuze"). Ngcobo, "Umbiko: M. M. Fuze, *Ilanga lase Natal*, 17 November 1922, 5. This suggests that Magema Fuze could have at other times used the surname "Ngcobo"; his own account of his genealogy suggests that the clan names "Fuze" and "Ngcobo" could be used interchangeably. Fuze, *Abantu Abamnyama Lapa Bavela Ngakona* (Pietermaritzburg: City Printing Works, 1922), iii. In compiling the bibliography I have used the surname "Fuze," but have indicated in brackets when the surname Magwaza was used. I have also used the initials "M. M." when he used them and "Magema M." when he signed himself in this way. I have also been unable to establish whether an original manuscript of *Abantu Abamnyama Lapa Bavela Ngakona* exists. Citations of the book therefore refer to the book published by City Printing Works in 1922.

6. In his essay "Metonymies of Lead," Leon De Kock uses the concept of "inculcation" in a more precise meaning by referring to the instances in which British soldiers, fighting on the "frontier" in the 1840s, resorted to melting the lead type from the printing press at Lovedale (a mission school). This interchangeability between "type" and "bullets" is summarized in the observation that "print culture, the technological base item of which was 'hot metal' or 'type'— individual letters and words fashioned in metal and arranged into the template of rectangular folios by human hand—was historically implicated in a singularly brutal metonymy of lead." Leon De Kock, "Metonymies of Lead: Bullets, Type and Print Culture in South African Missionary Colonialism," in *Print, Text and Book Cultures in South Africa*, ed. Van der Vlies and Andrew Edward (Johannesburg: Witwatersrand University Press, 2012), 52.

7. This phrase is borrowed from John M. Coetzee's book *White Writing: On the Culture of Letters in South Africa* (New Haven: Yale University Press, 1988).

8. See Jeff Guy's *The Heretic: A Study of the Life of John William Colenso, 1814–1883* (Johannesburg: Ravan Press; Pietermaritzburg: University of Natal Press, 1983).

9. Paul la Hausse de Lalouviére, *Restless Identities: Signatures of Nationalism, Zulu Ethnicity and History in the Lives of Petros Lamula (c. 1881–1948) and Lymon Maling (1889–c. 1936)* (Pietermaritzburg: University of Natal Press, 2000).

10. La Hausse de Lalouviére, *Restless Identities*, 2.

11. Clement M. Doke, "A Preliminary Investigation into the State of the Na-

tive Languages of South Africa with Suggestions as to Research and Development of Literature," *Bantu Studies* 7 (1933): 28.

12. La Hausse de Lalouviére, *Restless Identities*, 265.
13. La Hausse de Lalouviére, *Restless Identities*, 265.
14. La Hausse de Lalouviére, *Restless Identities*, 12.
15. See Heather Hughes, *First President: A Life of John Dube, Founding President of the ANC* (Auckland Park, South Africa: Jacana Media, 2011), 61.
16. Magema Fuze, *The Black People and Whence They Came: A Zulu View* (Pietermaritzburg: University of Natal Press; Durban: Killie Campbell Africana Library, 1979), i.
17. André Odendaal, *Black Protest Politics in South Africa to 1912* (Totowa, NJ: Barnes & Noble, 1984), 62.
18. Odendaal, *Black Protest Politics*, 62.
19. Hughes, *First President*, 111; Hofmeyr, *Gandhi's Printing Press*, 10.
20. la Hausse de Lalouviére, *Restless Identities*, 12.
21. Fuze, "Ngebhuku laBantu," *Ilanga lase Natal*, 25 February 1921, 2.
22. Fuze, *Abantu Abamnyama*.
23. Harry C. Lugg, "Translator's Preface," in Fuze, *Black People*, xviii.
24. Part T. Mgadla and Stephen C. Volz, *Words of Batswana: Letters to Mahoko a Becwana, 1883–1896* (Cape Town: Van Riebeeck Society, 2006), xvii.
25. Mgadla and Volz, *Words of Batswana*, xix.
26. John William Colenso, *Three Native Accounts of the Visit of the Bishop of Natal in September and October, 1859, to Umpande, King of the Zulus; With Explanatory Notes and a Literal Translation, and a Glossary of All the Zulu Words Employed in the Same: Designed for the Use of Students of the Zulu Language* (Pietermaritzburg: Vause, Slatter, 1901).
27. Alain Ricard, *The Languages and Literatures of Africa: The Sands of Babel* (Oxford: James Currey; Trenton, NJ: Africa World Press; Cape Town: David Philip, 2004), 111–12; Clement M. Doke, "Bantu Language Pioneers of the Nineteenth Century," *Bantu Studies* 14 (1940): 234–35.
28. Magema Fuze (Magwaza), "A Visit to King Ketshwayo," *Macmillan's Magazine* 37 (1878): 421–32.
29. Fuze, *Amazwi Abantu*.
30. Magema Fuze, UDinuzulu: Ukuzalwa Nokuba-ko Kwake," *Ilanga lase Natal*, 18 February 1921.
31. De Kock, "Metonymies of Lead," 53.
32. Vukile Khumalo, "Ekukhanyeni Letter-Writers: A Historical Inquiry into Epistolary Network(s) and Political Imagination in KwaZulu-Natal, South Africa," in *Africa's Hidden Histories: Everyday Literacy and Making the Self*, ed. Karin Barber (Bloomington: Indiana University Press, 2006), 115.

33. Khumalo, "Ekukhanyeni Letter-Writers," 115.

34. Hlonipha Mokoena, "An Assembly of Readers: Magema Fuze and His *Ilanga lase Natal* Readers," *Journal of Southern African Studies* 35, no. 3 (2009): 595–607.

35. Khumalo, "The Class of 1856 and the Politics of Cultural Production(s) in the Emergence of Ekukhanyeni, 1855–1910," in *The Eye of the Storm: Bishop John William Colenso and the Crisis of Biblical Inspiration*, ed. Jonathan A. Draper (Pietermaritzburg: Cluster Publications, 2003).

36. Mokoena, "Assembly of Readers," 603.

37. Khumalo, "Ekukhanyeni Letter-Writers," 125.

38. Switzer and Switzer, *Black Press*, 249.

39. Switzer and Switzer, *Black Press*, 249.

40. Switzer and Switzer, *Black Press*, 45.

41. The quality of the microfilm was very poor, so only the first two paragraphs of this letter are legible.

42. The colony was granted responsible government in 1893. For a thorough account on the history of Natal's bid for representative government, and some descriptions of how it affected the lives and civil rights of Africans see Bill Guest, "Towards Responsible Government, 1879–1893," in *Natal and Zululand from Earliest Times to 1910: A New History*, ed. Andrew Duminy and Bill Guest, 233–48 (Pietermaritzburg: University of Natal Press and Shuter & Shooter, 1989).

43. Fuze (Magwaza), "Ku Mhleli we Nkanyiso," *Inkanyiso*, 28 January 1892.

44. Hughes, *First President*, 104–5.

45. For a concise summary of Colenso's contribution to Zulu linguistics and lexicography, see Doke, "Bantu Language Pioneers," 234–35.

46. Thank you to Ian Snelling from SA Book Connection in Hillcrest, KwaZulu-Natal, for contacting me about this document and sending me scanned copies.

47. See Jeff Guy's *The View across the River: Harriette Colenso and the Zulu Struggle against Imperialism* (Cape Town: David Philip, 2001).

48. On *Ilanga lase Natal*, especially on the founder and editor, John Langalibalele Dube, see R. Hunt Davis Jr., "Qude maniki! John L. Dube, Pioneer Editor of *Ilanga lase Natal*," in *South Africa's Alternative Press: Voices of Protest and Resistance, 1880s–1960s*, ed. Les Switzer, 83–98 (Cambridge: Cambridge University Press, 1997).

49. Fuze, "Ngebhuku laBantu," 2; Fuze, *Abantu Abamnyama*, 211.

50. Fuze, *Black People*, v.

51. Fuze, *Abantu Abamnyama*, ix.

52. Petros Lamula, *UZulukaMalandela: A Most Practical and Concise Com-*

pendium of African History Combined with Genealogy, Chronology, Geography and Biography (Durban: Star Printing Works, 1924).

53. La Hausse de Lalouviére, *Restless Identities*, 103.

54. One such debate is the "Mfecane" debate—namely, the question of whether the emergence and rulership of Shaka Zulu precipitated the dispersal of populations living in close proximity to the Zulu kingdom. Although there were many installments in the development of the "Mfecane" debate, the best anthology on the historiography is Carolyn Hamilton, *The Mfecane Aftermath: Reconstructive Debates in Southern African History* (Johannesburg: Witwatersrand University Press; Pietermaritzburg: University of Natal Press, 1995).

55. For a fuller discussion of "The Tragedy of Translated Men," see Pascale Casanova, *The World Republic of Letters* (Cambridge, MA: Harvard University Press, 2004), 257.

56. Walter Benjamin, *Illuminations*, ed. Hannah Arendt, trans. Harry Zohn (New York: Schocken, 1968), 71.

57. For a discussion of the relationship between Fuze and Nondenisa, see Mokoena, *Magema Fuze: The Making of a* Kholwa *Intellectual* (Scottsville, South Africa: University of KwaZulu-Natal Press, 2011), 67, 257–260.

58. Fuze's biography of his mentor, Colenso, receives extensive close reading in Mokoena, "The Queen's Bishop: A Convert's Memoir of John W. Colenso," *Journal of Religion in Africa* 38, no. 3 (2008): 312–42.

59. In the book *Magema Fuze: The Making of a* Kholwa *Intellectual*, I write about the complicated and inadequate translation of Fuze's enigmatic phrase and title. I also dedicated a whole chapter to his ideas about death, reincarnation, burial customs, etc. See Mokoena, *Magema Fuze*, 253ff.

60. Couzens, *The New African*, 7.

61. Hughes, *First President*, 238.

62. Hughes, *First President*, 239.

63. Fuze, *Black People*, viii.

CHAPTER 14

From Corpse to Corpus

The Printing of Death in Colonial West Africa

STEPHANIE NEWELL

THE SUBJECT OF DEATH

African funeral rites,[1] bereavement customs, burial practices, and local understandings of death and dying have been a source of fascination for social anthropologists of Africa for more than a century.[2] In the last three decades, however, paralleling the rapid spread of HIV/AIDS on the continent and a resurgence of interest in death studies in the West, increasing numbers of social histories of death in Africa have brought historical and cultural complexity to the field. One particular cluster includes Kwame Arhin's, T. C. McCaskie's, Suzanne Gott's, Sjaak van der Geest's, and Marleen de Witte's detailed studies of Akan obituaries and funeral practices in Ghana.[3] Another rich set of themes for the social history of death is offered by historians of central and southern Africa.[4] In *Death, Belief and Politics in Central African History*, for example, Walima Kalusa and Megan Vaughan use death as the vector for understanding changing class, gender, sexual, urban, religious, and ethnic identities in Malawi and Zambia.[5] In so doing, they attempt to break away from the HIV/AIDS-focused "research industry" that caused one Malawian scholar to comment ascerbically to Vaughan, "What are you people going to do when we stop dying?"[6] Together, these recent studies bring a multiplicity of African death practices into focus to demonstrate how local understandings of dead and dying bodies can be produced in diverse, contradictory ways, providing no clear-cut trajectories for historians to illuminate.[7]

Inspired by this recent body of work, this chapter asks about the ways in which the subject of death—in both senses of subject—can be used to facilitate a scholarly understanding of particular moments of self-representation and transformation in West African print cultures between the 1880s and the late 1930s. As Kalusa and Vaughan demonstrate, death is anything but static or singular: "it" has a cultural history in colonial Africa that merits detailed examination, helping to illuminate transformations to, and the consolidation of, local power relations in different locales and periods.[8] Approaching the subject of death through the medium of print helps to make visible a variety of strategies of mediation that might otherwise be overlooked by scholars. Rather than treating the corpse as a material object, a focus on printed representations of dead people helps to highlight the ways in which bodies can be produced through genre, narrative perspective, language, and style.

In order to fully appreciate printed material about the dead, and the specificity of printed subjectivities compared with other types of agency in the colonial public sphere, it is of course important to situate newspaper discourses of death in the context of the vast array of oral genres for the articulation of death in West Africa, including laments, dirges, eulogies, and other types of funeral oration. As James Gibbs points out in his study of Ghanaian funeral brochures, the authors of printed tributes in West Africa participate in a long, inherited oral tradition: the inclusion of sayings such as "a great tree that has fallen in the forest," or "X has gone to the village" is an example of a kind of cut-and-paste technique whereby oral mourning genres are transcribed into print, adding rhetorical weight to printed material about the deceased.[9] Similarly, in her doctoral thesis on the press in colonial Lagos, Nozomi Sawada borrows from Peter Burke's study of history as social memory to argue that printed obituaries, memorials, and other "materialized forms of memory" in colonial Nigeria, including monuments and souvenirs, all functioned as "mediums of social memory" that borrowed heavily from oral traditions and sought to preserve unwritten local performance genres such as praise poems and proverbs in print.[10]

Perhaps more than any granite inscription, the production of one's reputation by others for posterity "sets in stone" how one's biography is retold to subsequent generations. Numerous scholars of West Africa have observed that funerals are major occasions for social and economic display, and for the memorialization of the dead through live performance.[11] In narrative terms, a funeral represents a critical chapter in a person's life story. At funerals in eastern Nigeria, for example, the good name one has built up since birth can be reinforced or shattered by the oral performances of different groups of mourners (see Newell 2006). Core participants in the ceremonies—such as age-grades, women's groups, and lineage groups—can bring shame on the deceased by boycotting the activities required of them in protest at his or her poor behavior. How one is named at death is therefore crucial to one's life story, and an understanding of biography as a genre in West Africa can be filtered through the proliferation of printed materials about death since the late nineteenth century.

Focusing on newspapers and posters, this chapter will situate printed obituaries and memorial poems in relation to colonial rule and the "great lives" tradition of biographical writing promoted by missionaries and educationists in Britain and the colonies from the mid-nineteenth century onward.[12] In the second half of the chapter, a case study of the Sierra Leonean political activist and prolific journalist I. T. A. Wallace-Johnson (1894–1965) will show how printed funeral genres had become such an established form by the late 1930s that they provided material for political appropriation and satirical remobilization in the public sphere.[13]

The first newspapers in West Africa date back to the early nineteenth century when Christian-educated, liberated slaves from diverse parts of the world returned to Sierra Leone and the Republic of Liberia, and set up their own printing presses, partly in a bid to use print to Christianize and "civilize" local populations, and partly in order to establish their own—in their view, God-given—right to political leadership in the region.[14] From this moment of inception, the region's newspapers were inextricable from the intertwined cultural histories of African diasporas, African elites, the spread of mission Christianity, and the consolidation of the colonial state.[15]

Dead people form a vital constituency represented by the press. From the outset, newspapers were deployed by editors and contributors to reflect on the lives—and to commemorate the deaths—of prominent Africans. Through biographies of long-dead men,[16] and through obituaries of the newly dead, literate West Africans in colonial settings generated an archive of African heroes to inspire local populations as reference points for personal achievement.[17] In the political context of increasing racial discrimination against Africans and the consolidation of British colonial rule from the 1890s onward, these locally printed "halls of fame" can be regarded as contributing to a countercolonial, if not an overtly anticolonial, historical archive of black role models for readers to emulate.

In Africa as elsewhere, dead bodies contain just as much potential for entextualization as live ones, and are equally subject to social and historical currents, including the transformations that occur over time to print, information, and communications technologies. In British West Africa, for example, printed materials relating to death were often used to assert—to intervene in and attempt to transform—local power relations in the colonial public sphere.[18] "Entextualization" is a useful concept for the analysis of these processes. The polar opposite of entombment, entextualization signifies the transformation of a practice or process into a cultural object that can be interpreted in the manner of a text.[19] Widely used in social anthropology and sociolinguistics, and deployed in its complexity in the work of Karin Barber on African oral praise poetry,[20] entextualization allows one to appreciate the cultural processes through which a material corpse passes en route to becoming part of a printed corpus of materials about death.

In the view of Nigerian literary scholar Kevin Anenechukwu Amoke, death, dying, and dead bodies in Africa, both on and off the printed page, offer numerous rich "spaces for reading," not least with respect to "gender, subjectivity, power, class struggle, hegemony and dominance."[21] As the remainder of this chapter will suggest, such power-inflected spaces for entextualization can be located not only through the oral performance of dirges and other live bereavement genres, but also through reproducible media such as newspapers, funeral posters, photographs, cards, and booklets.

BRINGING OUT THE DEAD

In his study of the production of funeral brochures in Ghana, James Gibbs finds that printing costs have come to be regarded by the families of deceased people as a legitimate and necessary part of funeral expenditure.[22] Gibbs focuses on the evolution of a new publication form that emerged between the 1970s and the 1990s in Ghana, a period in which funeral pamphlets moved away from the "old-style cyclostyled Order of Service," a product of the cheapest mass-production technology of the 1970s, and became "an elegantly printed Order of Service [that is often] garish, competing in a reckless display of conspicuous consumption" to display the best color images, elaborate fonts, and glossy pages.[23] Packed with biographical content and reflecting the development of local publishing in West Africa from cyclostyled duplication to desktop publishing, funeral brochures should, in Gibbs's view, be regarded as an important "part of the Story of the Book in Ghana."[24]

Printed obituaries and creative modes of memorialization such as poems,

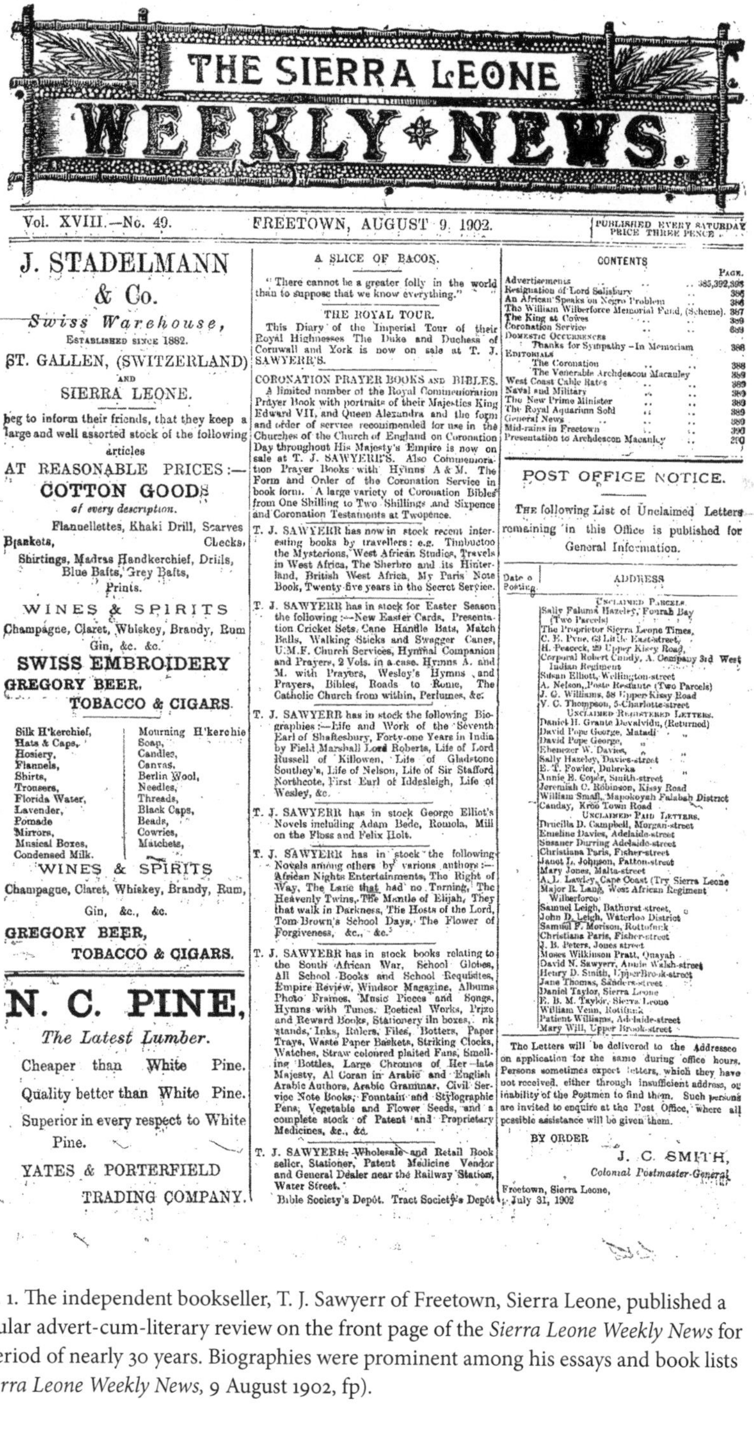

THE SIERRA LEONE WEEKLY NEWS.

Vol. XVIII.—No. 49. FREETOWN, AUGUST 9. 1902. PUBLISHED EVERY SATURDAY PRICE THREE PENCE.

J. STADELMANN & Co.

Swiss Warehouse,

ESTABLISHED SINCE 1882.

ST. GALLEN, (SWITZERLAND) AND SIERRA LEONE.

beg to inform their friends, that they keep a large and well assorted stock of the following articles

AT REASONABLE PRICES:—

COTTON GOODS

of every description.

Flannelettes, Khaki Drill, Scarves Blankets, Checks, Shirtings, Madras Handkerchief, Drills, Blue Bafts, Grey Bafts, Prints.

WINES & SPIRITS

Champagne, Claret, Whiskey, Brandy, Rum Gin, &c. &c.

SWISS EMBROIDERY

GREGORY BEER,

TOBACCO & CIGARS.

Silk H'kerchief, Hats & Caps, Hosiery, Flannels, Shirts, Trousers, Florida Water, Lavender, Pomade Mirrors, Musical Boxes, Condensed Milk.

Mourning H'kerchie Soap, Candles, Canvas, Berlin Wool, Needles, Threads, Black Caps, Beads, Cowries, Matchets,

WINES & SPIRITS

Champagne, Claret, Whiskey, Brandy, Rum, Gin, &c., &c.

GREGORY BEER,

TOBACCO & CIGARS.

N. C. PINE,

The Latest Lumber.

Cheaper than White Pine.

Quality better than White Pine.

Superior in every respect to White Pine.

YATES & PORTERFIELD TRADING COMPANY.

A SLICE OF BACON.

"There cannot be a greater folly in the world than to suppose that we know everything."

THE ROYAL TOUR.

This Diary of the Imperial Tour of their Royal Highnesses The Duke and Duchess of Cornwall and York is now on sale at T. J. SAWYERR'S.

CORONATION PRAYER BOOKS AND BIBLES.

A limited number of the Royal Commemoration Prayer Book with portraits of their Majesties King Edward VII, and Queen Alexandra and the form and order of service recommended for use in the Churches of the Church of England on Coronation Day throughout His Majesty's Empire is now on sale at T. J. SAWYERR'S. Also Commemoration Prayer Books with Hymns A & M. The Form and Order of the Coronation Service in book form. A large variety of Coronation Bibles from One Shilling to Two Shillings and Sixpence and Coronation Testaments at Twopence.

T. J. SAWYERR has now in stock recent interesting books by travellers: e.g. Timbuctoo the Mysterious, West African Studies, Travels in West Africa, The Sherbro and its Hinterland, British West Africa, My Paris Note Book, Twenty-five years in the Secret Service.

T. J. SAWYERR has in stock for Easter Season the following:—New Easter Cards, Presentation Cricket Sets, Cane Handle Bats, Match Balls, Walking Sticks and Swagger Canes, U.M.F. Church Services, Hymnal Companion and Prayers, 2 Vols. in a case. Hymns A. and M. with Prayers, Wesley's Hymns and Prayers, Bibles, Roads to Rome, The Catholic Church from within, Perfumes, &c.

T. J. SAWYERR has in stock the following Biographies:—Life and Work of the Seventh Earl of Shaftesbury, Forty-one Years in India by Field Marshall Lord Roberts, Life of Lord Russell of Killowen, Life of Gladstone Southey's, Life of Nelson, Life of Sir Stafford Northcote, First Earl of Iddesleigh, Life of Wesley, &c.

T. J. SAWYERR has in stock George Elliot's Novels including Adam Bede, Romola, Mill on the Floss and Felix Holt.

T. J. SAWYERR has in stock the following Novels among others by various authors:—African Nights Entertainments, The Right of Way, The Lane that had no Turning, The Heavenly Twins, The Mantle of Elijah, They that walk in Darkness, The Hosts of the Lord, Tom Brown's School Days, The Flower of Forgiveness, &c., &c.

T. J. SAWYERR has in stock books relating to the South African War, School Globes, All School Books and School Requisites, Empire Review, Windsor Magazine, Albums Photo Frames, Music Pieces and Songs, Hymns with Tunes. Poetical Works, Prize and Reward Books, Stationery in boxes, Ink stands, Inks, Rulers, Files, Blotters, Paper Trays, Waste Paper Baskets, Striking Clocks, Watches, Straw coloured plaited Fans, Smelling Bottles, Large Chromos of Her late Majesty, Al Coran in Arabic and English Arabic Authors, Arabic Grammar, Civil Service Note Books, Fountain and Stylographic Pens, Vegetable and Flower Seeds, and a complete stock of Patent and Proprietary Medicines, &c., &c.

T. J. SAWYERR, Wholesale and Retail Book seller, Stationer, Patent Medicine Vendor and General Dealer near the Railway Station, Water Street.

Bible Society's Depôt. Tract Society's Depôt

CONTENTS

	PAGE.
Advertisements	385,392,393
Resignation of Lord Salisbury	386
An African Speaks on Negro Problem	386
The William Wilberforce Memorial Fund, (Scheme).	387
The King at Cowes	389
Coronation Service	389
DOMESTIC OCCURRENCES	
Thanks for Sympathy—In Memoriam	388
EDITORIALS	
The Coronation	388
The Venerable Archdeacon Macauley	389
West Coast Cable Rates	389
Naval and Military	389
The New Prime Minister	389
The Royal Aquarium Sold	389
General News	389
Mid-rains in Freetown	390
Presentation to Archdeacon Macauley	390

POST OFFICE NOTICE.

THE following List of Unclaimed Letters remaining in this Office is published for General Information.

Date of Posting. | ADDRESS

UNCLAIMED PARCELS.

Sally Faluma Hazeley, Fourah Bay (Two Parcels)
The Proprietor Sierra Leone Times,
C. E. Pyne, 63 Little East-street,
H. Peacock, 29 Upper Kissy Road,
Corporal Robert Candy, A. Company 3rd West Indian Regiment
Susan Elliott, Wellington-street
A. Nelson, Poste Restante (Two Parcels)
J. G. Williams, 58 Upper Kissy Road
V. C. Thompson, 5 Charlotte-street

UNCLAIMED REGISTERED LETTERS.

Daniel H. Grante Devalvidu, (Returned)
David Pope George, Matadi ,,
David Pope George, ,,
Ebenezer W. Davies, ,,
Sally Hazeley, Davies-street ,,
E. T. Fowler, Dubreka ,,
Annie E. Coper, Smith-street
Jeremiah C. Robinson, Kissy Road
William Small, Mapokoyah Falabah District
Canday, Kroo Town Road

UNCLAIMED PAID LETTERS.

Drucilla D. Campbell, Morgan-street
Emeline Davies, Adelaide-street
Susaner Durring Adelaide-street
Christiana Paris, Fisher-street
Janet L. Johnson, Patton-street
Mary Jones, Malta-street
A. L. Lawley, Cape Coast (Try Sierra Leone
Major R. Lang, West African Regiment Wilberforce
Samuel Leigh, Bathurst street,
John D. Leigh, Waterloo District
Samuel F. Morison, Rottofunk
Christiana Paris, Fisher-street
J. B. Peters, Jones street
Moses Wilkinson Pratt, Quayah
David N. Sawyerr, Annie Walsh-street
Henry D. Smith, UpperBrook-street
Jane Thomas, Sanders-street
Daniel Taylor, Sierra Leone
E. B. M. Taylor, Sierra Leone
William Venn, Rotifunk
Patient Williams, Adelaide-street
Mary Will, Upper Brook-street

The Letters will be delivered to the Addressee on application for the same during office hours. Persons sometimes expect letters, which they have not received, either through insufficient address, or inability of the Postmen to find them. Such persons are invited to enquire at the Post Office, where all possible assistance will be given them.

BY ORDER

J. C. SMITH,

Colonial Postmaster-General

Freetown, Sierra Leone, July 31, 1902

Fig. 1. The independent bookseller, T. J. Sawyerr of Freetown, Sierra Leone, published a regular advert-cum-literary review on the front page of the *Sierra Leone Weekly News* for a period of nearly 30 years. Biographies were prominent among his essays and book lists (*Sierra Leone Weekly News*, 9 August 1902, fp).

"pen-pictures,"[25] and pamphlets have a long history in West Africa, dating back at least a century before the material analyzed by Gibbs. Precursors to contemporary funeral brochures proliferated in late nineteenth-century West Africa and played an important role in the content of local newspapers. Newspaper portraits of "great men of affairs" burgeoned after the 1880s, modeled on a tradition inherited from missionaries in the previous half-century through which Christian teachers instilled Africans with morally uplifting leadership models. Among the missionary "book depots" in major British West African towns by the early twentieth century were the Wesleyan Book Depot, the Basel Mission Book Depot, the Methodist Book Depot, and the CMS Bookshop. So-called book stewards at these depots published regular adverts in local African-owned newspapers with lists of "good" reading.[26] With a view to the moral improvement of African readers, these bookshops advertised "unlimited supplies of good literature, social and religious, in English and the vernacular."[27]

Individual morality was respected and promoted in this English post-Victorian "lives and letters" tradition. African schoolchildren and literate locals were provided with numerous textbooks and pamphlets containing celebrations of exemplary people, all of whom, with the exception of Touissant-Louverture, were European and white, and most of whom were men (figure 1). Even the influential Pan-Africanist leader E. W. Blyden (1832–1912)—who was hailed in one biographically challenging article as simultaneously "the Negro Napoleon, the African Cicero and the Ethiopian Gladstone"[28]—was an especially vocal promoter of the study of biography in the face of European assertions of racial superiority over Africans. Of particular relevance to Blyden's Pan-Africanism is a debate that erupted in the *Sierra Leone Weekly News* after his lecture to the Young Men's Literary Association of Sierra Leone on 19 May 1892, "Study and Race," in which he refused to discriminate between the value of studying African, as opposed to European, biographical role models.[29] Blyden controversially advised members of the Association to

> endeavour to think the thoughts and live the lives of the great and good of past and contemporary times, so far as you have access to information about them . . . take, say for one evening, William Wilberforce; for another, Sir Thomas Fowell Buxton, or Macaulay, Livingstone, Gladstone, Beaconsfield, Touissant, Bishop Crowther, &c., &c., for Biography.[30]

Lives such as these were offered, postmortem, by Victorian educationists, missionaries, and African cultural nationalists for reflection and emulation.

(Of the few female role models to be found in the extensive lists of biographical texts recommended for African schools and churches in the early twentieth century were Florence Nightingale and Hester Ann Rogers.)

Adapted as a vehicle for the memorialization of Africans after the 1880s, the hagiographic "lives and letters" genre proved enormously popular and influential in the newspaper columns, books, and speeches of African cultural nationalists and Pan-Africanists. Against Blyden's universalist stance, from the turn of the century onward,[31] increasing numbers of books started to appear with titles such as *Memoirs of West African Celebrities* and *Gold Coast Men of Affairs: Past and Present*.[32] Alongside Allister Macmillan's *The Red Book of West Africa* (1920), with its racially undiscriminating profiles of locally based entrepreneurs, one of the most popular examples of this genre was Charles Francis Hutchison's *The Pen-Pictures of Modern Africans and African Celebrities*, published in 1930 with 162 biographical sketches and photographs of prominent Gold Coasters (Ghanaians) stretching from the early nineteenth century to the 1920s.[33] Each entry in Hutchison's book was written in blank verse, and, at the end, the author included a long list of "famous deceased people" as a roll call of influential Africans.[34] These genres were precursors to the current tradition of hagiographical writing whereby celebrities and political heavyweights offer lucrative commissions to local authors, often drawn from the poorly paid academic community, particularly in Nigeria, to write eulogistic biographies for publication on private presses, which are then distributed to bookshops.

Newspapers also carried numerous written and, from the mid-1930s, photographic portraits of heroic past Africans, explicitly offering them to readers as role models for emulation. In the "stormy 1930s" of anticolonial protest, the nationalist leader and later first president of Nigeria, Nnamdi Azikiwe (1904–1996)—himself a prominent newspaperman, public speaker, and obituarist—was a particularly enthusiastic producer of black role models for young West Africans. In November 1934, at a speech in the Glover Memorial Hall in Lagos, Azikiwe "told the story of the African in world history" to emphasize "the capacity of the black peoples."[35] Inspired by the "race pride" of W. E. B. DuBois (1868–1963)—himself an African hero who promoted the centrality of African heroes to world history—Azikiwe also made use of his own newspapers, the *African Morning Post* and the *West African Pilot*, to produce biographies illustrating Africans' capacities for self-rule.

In recognizing the need for past heroes, Azikiwe, like DuBois before him, illustrated the necessity for anticolonial nationalist movements to construct their own separate cultural histories in reaction against European cultural influences.³⁶ As part of this cultural nationalist tradition of memorialization, a particular mode of naming, or history-making, emerged through the obituary columns of West African newspapers. The deaths of prominent local men, such as the celebrated educationist James E. K. Aggrey (1875–1927), popularly known as "Aggrey of Africa," or the Ghanaian newspaperman and church minister Reverend S. R. B. Attoh-Ahuma (1863–1921), plus countless other African "men of affairs," are presented in a thoroughly print-mediated manner. The obituary of Attoh-Ahuma reproduced in figure 2, for example, opens with a textual rather than a biographical set of references: "There lies before us a booklet, entitled 'The Gold Coast Nation and National Consciousness,' which will repay careful reading from cover to cover by thoughtful British West Africans," the obituary begins.³⁷ This booklet, the editorial continues, is "from the pen of the late Rev. Attoh-Ahuma, M.A., whose lamentable death this present number of the 'Leader' further commemorates."³⁸ Circling around the *Leader*'s own pivotal position in giving a platform to Attoh-Ahuma, the column cites a list of additional publications and literary achievements before disclosing that the deceased's seminal publication, *The Gold Coast Nation and National Consciousness*, comprised nothing less than reprints of articles first published in the *Leader* itself.³⁹

Such newspaper memorializations contributed to the emergence of a form of biography in which the newspaper adopted a position superior to living subjects as the vehicle for memory, offering itself to readers for posterity, sitting in between remembered individuals and their survivors. Not only do such memorializations establish their authority through a prose-conscious literary style, but in a more fundamental way the corpse *becomes* the corpus in these publications: as in the case of Attoh-Ahuma, in numerous newspaper columns dedicated to prominent men's deaths, correspondents cite previously published books, pamphlets, and newspaper articles in which the dead subjects' political speeches or sayings are preserved. Rarely, if ever, do they turn to oral histories or quote from oral bereavement genres to represent their subjects. Rather, editors reprint decades-old articles and extracts from columns and speeches published in previous newspapers in order to draw comparisons and establish continuities with Africans' political demands or social progress in the present.

Writing and death were inextricable in other ways in the colonial period. Many shifts in West African cultures of death were made possible by literacy and print. In the late nineteenth and early twentieth centuries, memorial associations started to spring up in Lagos and other West African cities

4 THE GOLD COAST LEADER JANUARY 28 1922.

REV. SAMUEL RICHARD BREW ATTOH-AHUMA, M.A.

Born December 22, 1863. Died December 14, 1921.

MEMOIR AND APPRECIATIONS.

EDITORIAL NOTES.

THERE lies before us a booklet, entitled, "The Gold Coast Nation and National Consciousness," which will repay careful reading from cover to cover by thoughtful British West Africans. It is from the pen of the late Rev. Attoh-Ahuma, M.A., whose lamentable death this present number of the "Leader" further commemorates. The author is described on the title page as "Principal of Zion College:" Editor of the "Gold Coast Leader," Secretary of the "Gold Coast Aborigines' Rights Protection Society," Official Lecturer for the "Fanti National Education Trust;" etc: Also as author of "Memoirs of West African Celebrities;" All's Well; "Cruel as the Grave;" His Quest and Conquest; "Colony or Protectorate—Which?" etc, etc. That catalogue is fairly full; and it shows a life of varied activities in the intellectual sphere. He must have been an intellectual giant to have combined teaching with journalism and authorship at the same time.

But it is as the Editor of this paper with which we are for the moment concerned. For, as we are told in the foreword, the pamphlet we are considering is a reprint of articles contributed by him to the "Gold Coast Leader," and is full of matter. Therein, we are told, that the author indulges the hope that the principles therein set forth......may *influence* for good, not his contemporaries only, but also—and especially—the members of the rising generation. And presently we come upon an extraordinary paradox. For he holds as the "birthright, privilege, duty and honour of the youths of West Africa to usher in an era of Backward Movement, which to all cultured West Africans is synonymous with the highest conception of progress and advancement." This is a startling thought, and few will find it easy to accept, or even comprehend. But when we realise that all that this signifies is that we should return to the Simple Life and to nature and mother earth, much that was obscure begins to clear up. And he forces the thought a step further by impressing that it is to the simple life of our progenitors that he makes the appeal. This presupposes that such simple life is not in conflict with real advance, with our progress as a people. He holds a desire on our part to rid ourselves of foreign accretions and excrescences as an indispensable condition of National Resurrection and National Prosperity. And this is the sum total of the lesson which his message is intended to teach.

Unfortunately, our sense of the essential conditions of progress is so warped that at times it becomes bewilderingly difficult to discriminate between what is false and what is true. The standards that are set before us, the goal we are bidden to reach, the course necessary to the end, have not received from us that calm scrutiny which would enable us to give a reason for the faith that is in us. We do certain things because we follow aimlessly the dictates of a civilisation which is yet on its trial. We refrain from others because of a desire to be in keeping with a fashion which may be a mere pose. Such are the contradictions of our existence, which have attracted the thinking minds of our race. Though a Nation, with national standards and a national *rightness* of our own, we have allowed our vision to be so blurred as to be unable to discriminate between the things which matter and those that don't.

Take one or two instances at random. Our national standard of values has considerably altered for the worse. When we tossed overboard the simple life, we freighted the national argosy with the idle cares and worries of an effete civilisation. Our forebears, of course, understood how to make money. But the making of money was not the be-all and end-all of life with them. They made a little go a long way, because they cared little for the luxuries to which we have become accustomed, and which fill our lives with toil and anxiety when we might be at peace and contentment as with our progenitors.

To-day it is heart-rending the havoc that has been wrought among our men of enterprise by this wrong sense of values. Scores have made their thousands and are at present consumed by the debris of lost hopes and vanished fortunes. Some mourn in silent places; others have taken to drink to drown their sorrows. But few will learn the lesson that to the African the true object of life is not the amassing of wealth for its own sake, but only as a means to national ends. And if you observe carefully even the older generations of our own day, you will find that their sense of values is healthier than that of the younger generation. The unspoilt African, when he makes money, does not at all change his way of life and suddenly become Europeanised but remains and continues as he was. But you will find that gradually he will work himself into prominence and usefulness in his own state, thereby contributing to the general progress. The moral, therefore, is simply this, that, in the present world conditions, we must acquire all the knowledge necessary for successful competition in the acquisition of a competence; but, for heaven's sake, let us all the while learn to discriminate sharply between the course that makes for our happiness and peace as contradistinguished from that which brings us perplexities, difficulties, and doubts.

In other respects, our outlook upon life is getting warped. We have set a different standard of *rightness* from that which was so considered in the wisdom of our progenitors. The normal life, which was considered right before, is now considered abnormal; and if you pressed for a cause, it would be found that there is no ground or justification save that such and such is the practice of the white man. We drink as he drinks; we eat as he eats; we marry as he marries, and so through a long string of trivialities, and all the time we think that we have evolved a superior measure of life by which we condemn or applaud. Of course this leads to all sorts of inconsistencies, and the result is a Pharisaism which is smothering our national life out of all recognition. Hence the value of the great message of him whom we mourn. It will bear repetition. Says he: "Intelligent Retrogression is the only Progression that will save our beloved country." We say: aim high, work hard, keep heart, but BACK TO THE SIMPLE LIFE.

Attoh-Ahuma was keen upon Gold Coast nationhood, and sought in his day to promote national consciousness. Dwelling upon this matter, he argues that since we own a political constitution, a concentric system of government, of one race, born and bred upon our own soil, nationhood cannot be denied us. And he concludes; "In spite therefore of the dogmas and ipse dixits of those wiseacres who would fain deny to us, as a people, the inalienable heritage of nationality, we dare affirm, with the sanctity of reason and with the emphasis of conviction, that—WE ARE A NATION." This is stimulating after the onslaught of Sir Hugh Clifford, charging the promoters of the Congress movement with folly for the assumption of nationhood. This booklet was published in 1911. If we were a nation then, much more so must we be in 1922 with unmistakable tokens wherever we turn.

In the particular article upon which we have just dwelt he holds that "in matters of the soul our rulers are inaccessible, unapproachable." This is a dictum that will not go down with superficial observers—certainly not with the Administration of which his Excellency Sir Frederick Guggisberg is the head. Our Governor, judging from his public utterances, has fathomed the soul of the black man. He knows more about his psychology than the keener African observer, and would probably resent a suggestion of his utter incapacity to understand him first-hand. And yet, the most scientific observers have always held that the only one who can truly interpret the African to the outside world is the African himself. At least such was the view of Attoh-Ahuma. Says he: "We need intermediaries—Buffers between the people and the Government. The materials are ready to hand, and it is for the powers that be to utilize them in his Majesty's Service. There are well-tried and experienced Native Africans whose undoubted qualifications might be usefully employed for executive and administrative purposes. It is their duty to serve their country, and it is the duty of the Government to acknowledge the fact and give practical effect to it. The sooner the better, for no foreign administration that ignores or sets aside the people—such a people as those inhabiting this country—can achieve any success in the long run. For their own sakes, and for the sake of the people whose ancestors voluntarily placed themselves under the guidance and protection of VICTORIA THE GOOD we pray the authorities to afford the educated Native of probity and worth such facilities as shall enable him to discharge his national obligations, in spite of the preposterous attitude taken by those whose chief end is to glorify themselves at the expense of People, Country, and Race."

These views are sound. They are statesmanlike. If in 1911 there existed such material, in the opinion of a competent judge, for Executive and Administrative purposes, much more must the quality have improved in 1922. And so we might go on, column after column, discussing the thoughts in which this booklet abounds. But we have said enough to reveal the inner workings of a great mind. He dealt with our national problems first-hand and with authority at a time not so propitious as the present. And it is no wonder that when the fitting moment came in the Congress movement, though then retired from active public life, he should have thrown himself into it heart and soul, dying, as it were, in harness. Such was the man—such the temper of his mind and the type of his patriotism. Take him for all in all he was a man every inch of him. And, somehow, we prefer not to think of him as the embodiment of wisdom, or as a saint. We like to think of him as one of us, with the same trials and struggles and failures, ever striving to perfect his warfare, and at last overcoming from a sheer sense of duty and of service to his day and generation—to his country and people. And that is the meaning of the scores of telegrams of sincere regret, which have poured in upon his poor widow and step-son, Mr. W. E. Esuman-Gwira Sekyi, M.A. (Lond.) some of which we take the liberty of reproducing below:

"To Mrs Attoh-Ahuma, Cape Coast:

"Am deeply grieved accept my sincerest sympathy personal and on behalf of our Methodist Church."—Chairman.

"Accept deepest sympathies from Master, Officers, members Saint George's Lodge for loss of a good husband and sincere brother deputation attending funeral—Vardon, Secretary"

"Unexpected death husband has been great shock to us your great loss is the common concern of Church and country accept our deepest sympathy"—Mr and Mrs Bannerman Martin.

"Winnebah Zion Church mourns deeply for loss of Rev Ahuma"—Ntedu Kyirous.

"My profound sympathy with you on sad death my dearest Master and Friend Rev Ahuma—Sam Wood."

"Warm sympathy from Winnebah Church and community expect me—Ekuban."

"Deeply regret death of your husband sympathy from the family—Ababio"

"Officers members Macarthy Lodge of Freemasons tender their sincerest sympathies for irreparable loss sustained—Secretary."

"Attusbu Society leaders myself send you heartfelt sympathy—Markin."

"Gold Coast community Kano sends deepest sympathy—Ewusie"

"Accept heartfelt sympathy for irreparable loss sustained—Korsah."

"To Barrister Sekyi, Cape Coast: Please convey to Mrs Ahuma and the family profoundest regret and deepest sympathy death my kinsman comrade and friend Ahuma stop in him country has lost a great man and Congress cause a staunch fearless and sincere champion—Casely Hayford."

"Coomassie Endeavour Society extends deepest sympathy to you and family for irreparable loss sustained—Cole."

"Profoundest sympathy for self mother and family death our revered Rev Attoh-Ahuma—Sampson."

"Sad news just received accept our deepest sympathy—Bannerman."

"Deeply regret news of Rev Attoh-Ahuma's death stop defending murder case Assizes but will proceed first opportunity—Williams."

"Sad demise accept my sympathy and convey to Ewuraba and family my condolence—Nana Acquah III."

"Accept our heartfelt sympathy and convey same mother—Kojo Thompson."

"Wife family desire convey sincere sympathy brother and self sad loss—Nicol."

"Profound sympathy my grief and tears—Orgle."

"Regret sad news deepest sympathy to all—Archie Casely Hayford."

"Accept self and mother heartfelt condolence Rev Ahuma's death—Degraft Johnson."

"Convey to family our condolence hope you are well—Kwatei-Papafio."

These are faint memorials, but the permanent one is the character he has left behind him of noble service and self-sacrificing zeal.

TO CORRESPONDENTS

Intelligent correspondence on matters of interest touching the welfare of the Country is invited.

Anonymous letters will not be attended to, or returned.

A *nom-de-plume* or initials should be given if it is desired that the real name shall not appear in the paper.

Name and address must accompany all communications as a guarantee of good faith.

Communications must reach the Office not later than Wednesday.

Rejected communications cannot be returned.

Communications to which replies may be expected must be accompanied with stamps.

Correspondents will please write legibly and on one side of the paper only.

The Gold Coast Leader.

CAPE COAST, JAN. 28, 1922.

OUR CATHOLIC FRIENDS AND SECONDARY EDUCATION.

WE have been following with great interest, amounting to enthusiasm, the effort of our Catholic brethren to promote secondary education in the country. It is a right move

Fig. 2. "Obituary: Rev. S. R. B. Attoh-Ahuma," *Gold Coast Leader*, 28 January 1922, 4.

to honor and campaign for the public remembrance of "worthy" local individuals. Such associations represented the interests of the living as much as the dead. Members engaged in campaigns to promote the memories of "big men and big women," with petitions for portraits, public statues, and public buildings, and through these activities the campaign leaders would themselves become named, "fixed," and publicly recognized through the medium of newsprint.[40]

West African newspapers also carried numerous advertisements for commodities or souvenirs relating to the newly dead, and in this way helped to materialize the obituary as an object with aesthetic qualities for circulation and preservation. In December 1885, for example, the Sierra Leonean newspaper *Sawyerr's Bookselling, Printing and Stationery Trade Circular* advertised "The Penny Packet of Mourning Stationery," containing three sheets of black-bordered notepaper and three matching envelopes.[41] Similarly, from the 1880s onward, the printing of death became increasingly commercialized as hard-pressed newspaper editors, struggling to secure regular subscriptions from readers, advertised the services of their presses for funeral and death announcements, as well as for private print jobs, including the production of mourning cards, booklets, and funeral posters. As demonstrated by the booklet advertised in figure 3, in which the late James Johnson is memorialized (and commodified for a shilling plus postage), printed obituaries and death notices can be seen as a popular form of life-writing through which lives are produced as material objects for preservation in readers' personal libraries.

The sheer quantities of memorializations in the African-owned press tell a story of their own about the uses of print in the colonial period. A cursory word-count of the West African newspapers on the Readex World Newspaper Archive reveals 718 appearances of the word "obituary" between 1881 and 1922 and, in the same period, 3,184 counts of the word "funeral," 1,085 counts of "in memoriam," 3,830 of the phrase "in memory of," and 701 of "in loving memory," making a total of nearly ten thousand death-related words over a forty-year period.

Memorial poems should be added to these other printed genres for the remembrance of dead people. Contrasting the masked, pseudonymous personae to be found in the majority of articles and correspondence in early twentieth-century newspapers, the authors and subjects of memorial poems are often named many times over, literally re-membered, put together through acrostics and tributes that gave thickness and textual form to the name of the deceased (see figures 4 and 5).[42]

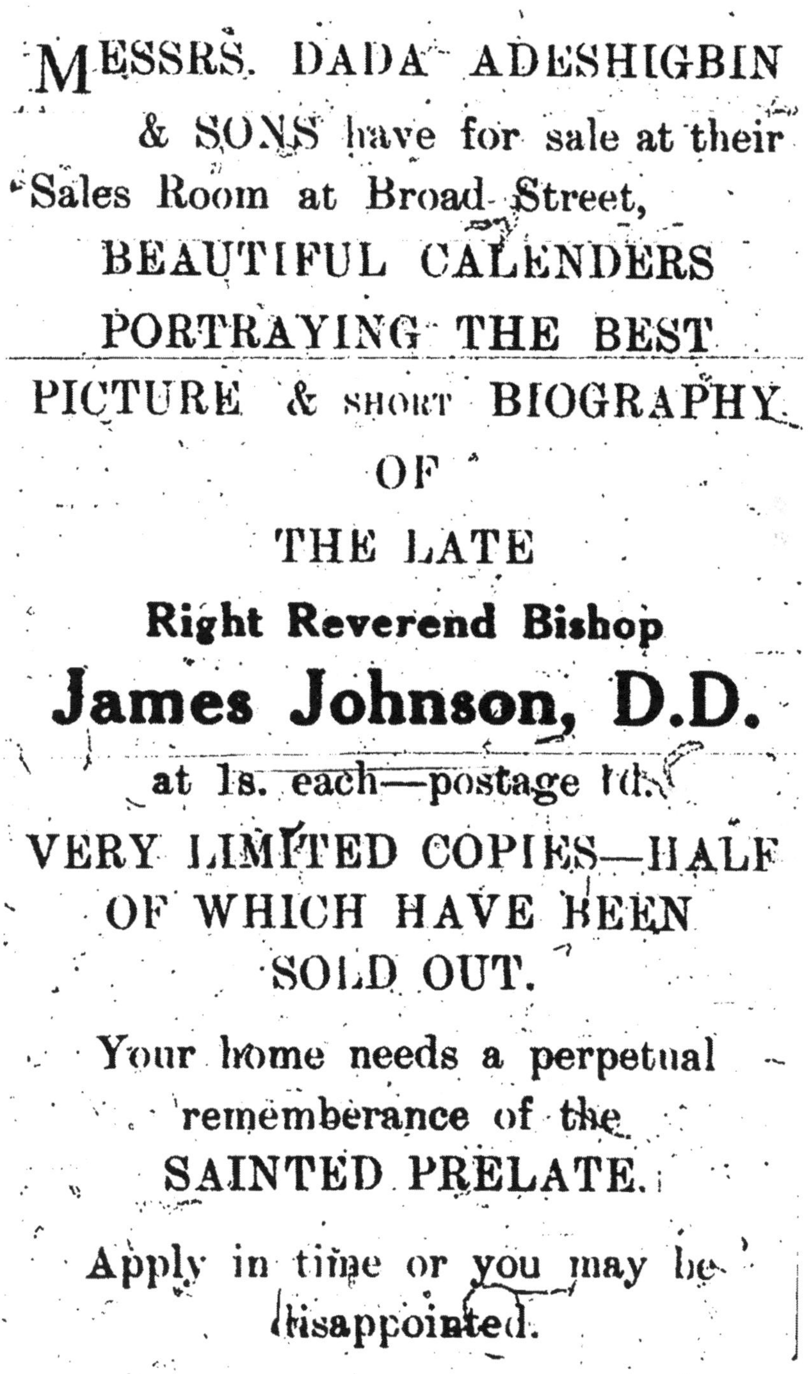

MESSRS. DADA ADESHIGBIN & SONS have for sale at their Sales Room at Broad Street, BEAUTIFUL CALENDERS PORTRAYING THE BEST PICTURE & SHORT BIOGRAPHY OF THE LATE Right Reverend Bishop **James Johnson, D.D.** at 1s. each—postage 1d. VERY LIMITED COPIES—HALF OF WHICH HAVE BEEN SOLD OUT.

Your home needs a perpetual rememberance of the SAINTED PRELATE.

Apply in time or you may be disappointed.

Fig. 3. Advertisement in *Nigerian Pioneer*, 22 February 1918, 4.

IN MEMORIAM.

In loving memory of the two brothers who died respectively on the 16th June 1914, and on the 10th July 1914.

C hildren's father Charlie is gathered to his fathers.
H ow beneficent and benevolent was he!
A las the day! since Job's news unexpectedly
R eached his brother Joe, Joe never smiled again.
L ast time that they bade Good-bye to each other, only
E arth forboded that they would meet again only in her bosom.
S uddenly and silently did he shuffle off the mortal coil.

A t my house that he last visited and conversed with me,
N o man could make me believe that it was valedictory.
D eath, to be the last enemy that shall destroy, is God's truth,

J uly, O hone! brought Job's news to the House-of-mourning.
P oor brother Joe was summoned to follow his brother Charlie.

B arrister well-experienced, popular, and munificent was he.
R emember, O earth, how he held his advocacy to excellence!
O h! who could fathom the weird that they respectively dread,
W hen shall I behold their loving faces once more?
N ot on earth but in heaven at last I know.

P atiently am I biding my time to meet them there where they are biding tryst.

O , may the Creator and Redeemer accept the souls of the two
B rothers, and let them have an eternal joy, and
E verlasting bliss, and peace, to sound His praises; and, in the
E nd, let me meet them Home, when I cross over Jordan!

SAMUEL ASAAM QUAORAINIE.

Appam, July 1915.

Fig. 4. "In Memoriam," *Gold Coast Leader* 17 July 1915, 2.

The two brothers named in the acrostic in figure 4, J. P. Brown-Pobee and Charles Pobee, were well-connected members of the Gold Coast elite, both being barristers-at-law trained at Lincoln's Inn in London and active members of local societies including the "African Society" and the Freemasons in Cape Coast.[43] As a headmaster and ordained minister, Reverend J. S. Fanimokun (figure 5) was of similar status to the Brown-Pobee brothers, with a key leadership role in the local community. Each of these dead subjects thus occupies a social interface in colonial society, and their memorialization in newsprint contributes to the insertion of their social class into the dynamic power relations of the colonial public sphere.

Many less prominent images were also named for posterity in these

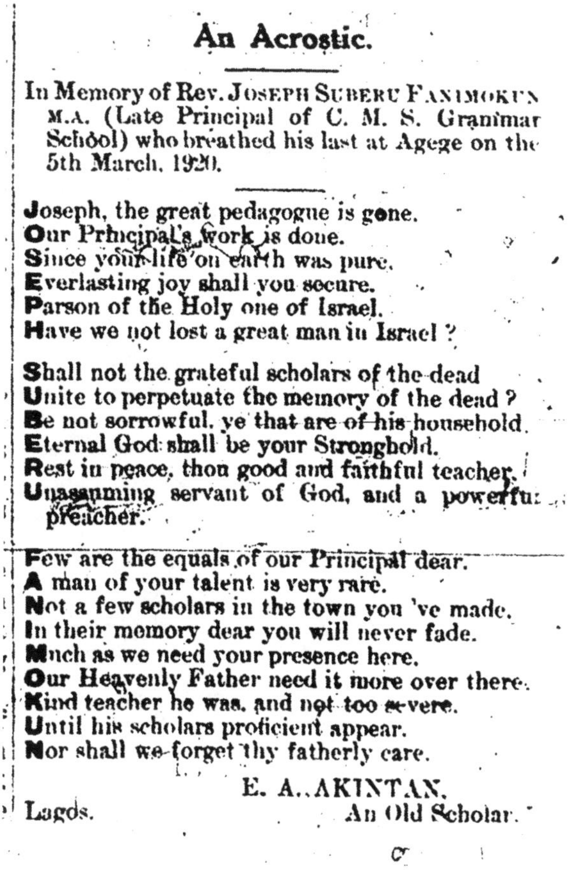

An Acrostic.

In Memory of Rev. JOSEPH SUBERU FANIMOKUN M.A. (Late Principal of C. M. S. Grammar School) who breathed his last at Agege on the 5th March, 1920.

Joseph, the great pedagogue is gone.
Our Principal's work is done.
Since your life on earth was pure,
Everlasting joy shall you secure.
Parson of the Holy one of Israel.
Have we not lost a great man in Israel?

Shall not the grateful scholars of the dead
Unite to perpetuate the memory of the dead?
Be not sorrowful, ye that are of his household.
Eternal God shall be your Stronghold.
Rest in peace, thou good and faithful teacher,
Unassuming servant of God, and a powerful preacher.

Few are the equals of our Principal dear.
A man of your talent is very rare.
Not a few scholars in the town you 've made.
In their memory dear you will never fade.
Much as we need your presence here,
Our Heavenly Father need it more over there.
Kind teacher he was, and not too severe.
Until his scholars proficient appear.
Nor shall we forget thy fatherly care.

E. A. AKINTAN,
Lagos. An Old Scholar.

Fig. 5. "An Acrostic," *Lagos Weekly Record* 20 March 1920, 6.

acrostics and poems. The price of inserting memorials and notices of death decreased substantially between the 1880s and 1920s: in Lagos by 1920 the cost had decreased from up to fifteen shillings to five shillings for twelve lines.[44] In the Gold Coast by 1917, the cost was two shillings for four lines, and sixpence for every additional line.[45] Rates stabilized at four shillings per insertion in most newspapers by the early 1920s, with charges for "Death" and "Thanks for Sympathy" notices listed alongside the rates for other types of advertisement (see figure 6).

Unlike the lengthy obituaries and roll calls in the "great man" tradition, the short "In Memoriam" columns that proliferated in the 1910s and 1920s provided one of the few public arenas through which those Africans who

> For Advertising Rates apply to:—
>
> **MESSRS. MATHER & CROWTHER, Ltd.**
> New Bridge Street,
> LONDON.
>
> ## NOTICE TO ADVERTISERS
>
> There is but one way of obtaining Business—Publicity: But one way of gaining Publicity—advertising:—*Blackwood.*
>
> Our terms are:—
> Situations wanted, three lines... 1/-
> Every additional line... ... -/3
> Servants, clerks, or assistants wanted, three lines 2/-.
> All other Advertisements may be inserted at the rate of *Sixpence per line* or part of a line, or under special contracts for long periods.
>
> JOBBING AND FANCY PRINTING.
>
> Visiting Cards, Trade Cards, Circulars, Invitations, Notices, Programmes and other kinds of work undertaken at most reasonable terms.
>
> The charge for announcements of Births, Marriages, Deaths, and In Memoriam notices (which must be authenticated by the name and address of the sender) 2/- for four lines and every additional line of about 9 words or less -/6.

Fig. 6. "Notice to Advertisers," *Gold Coast Nation* 3 November 1917, fp.

were not necessarily educated to the standard of the professional elites who owned the region's newspapers could remember their loved ones to the reading public through the citation of lines from poetry about death and loss, and, less often, through the composition of original verse. Popular citations included verses and lines from hymns including "Brief Life Is Here Our Portion," "The Saints of God, Their Wanderings Done," and "For the Soul[s] Thou Holdest Dearest, Let Prayers Arise" (see figures 7–9).[46]

Memorial columns of this type flourished in the 1920s as a vehicle for the expression of grief in the newspapers. According to Sawada, out of the tradition of paying homage to "great men" arose this "other custom of memorialis-

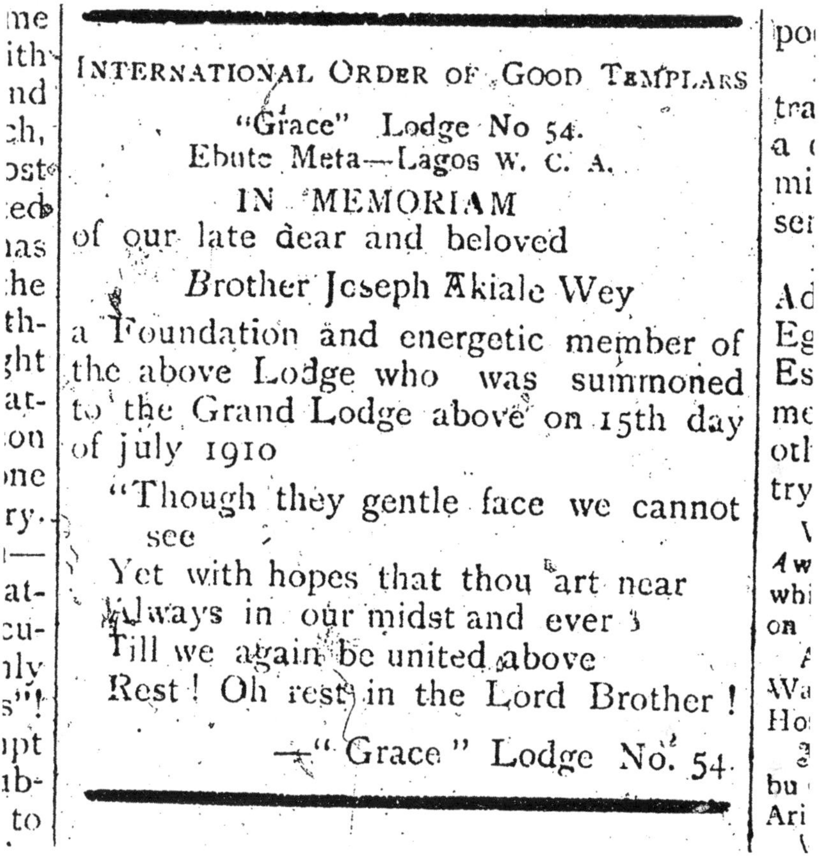

> INTERNATIONAL ORDER OF GOOD TEMPLARS
> "Grace" Lodge No 54.
> Ebute Meta—Lagos W. C. A.
> IN MEMORIAM
> of our late dear and beloved
> Brother Joseph Akiale Wey
> a Foundation and energetic member of the above Lodge who was summoned to the Grand Lodge above on 15th day of July 1910
>
> "Though they gentle face we cannot see
> Yet with hopes that thou art near
> Always in our midst and ever
> Till we again be united above
> Rest! Oh rest in the Lord Brother!
> —"Grace" Lodge No. 54.

Fig. 7. "In Memoriam: Joseph Akiale Wey," *Lagos Standard* 17 July 1912, 3.

ing family and friends."[47] As Sawada argues, these small spaces made possible the inscription of ordinary West Africans into the public sphere, including readers' beloved mothers, spouses, and family members.[48] "In ever affectionate and fragrant memory of my dear wife ... who was translated on the 1st July, 1921," one poignant announcement reads in the *Sierra Leone Weekly News*: "Her memory is still potent, Though her presence is now absent" (figure 10).[49] Often comprising ditties, short rhymes lifted from books of popular verse, hymnals or prayers, memorial poems furnished a space for local sub-elites to represent the "absent presence" of loved ones, including family members who were not in any way public images. Whether or not one regards

IN MEMORIAM.

In ever loving remembrance of my dear wife Emma Jane Abraham who suddenly but peacefully departed this life on the 4th March, 1916.

MAY SHE REST IN PEACE.

Had He asked us well we know
We would cry oh spare this blow
Yea, with streaming tears would pray
Lord, we loved her, let her stay

NOT DEAD—JUST AWAY.

"I cannot say, and I will not say
That she is dead. She is just away.
With a cheery smile and a wave of the hand,
She has wandered into an unknown land,
And left us dreaming how very fair
It needs must be, since she lingers there.
Think her of still as the same, I say,
She is not dead.. she is just away."

J. D. Abraham.

In ever loving memory of my beloved husband Barrister, Joseph Peter Brown-Pobee who departed this life on the 10th July, 1914.

Lord when Thou calledst us to resign
Those whom we prize the most.
O teach us from our heart to say
Thy will be done.

Lottie.

Catherine Cato, née Johnston.

Safely, safely gathered in,
Free from sorrow, free from sin,
Passed beyond all grief and pain,
Death for thee is truest gain:
For our loss we must not weep,
Nor our loved one long to keep
From the home of rest and peace,
Where all sin and sorrow cease.

W. S. Johnston.

Cape Coast,
30th June, 1916.

Fig. 8. "In Memoriam," *Gold Coast Nation*, 13 July 1916, 1412.

W. TAYLOR & SONS,
6, MASON'S AVENUE, COLEMAN STREET, LONDON, E.C.2.

WE SPECIALISE IN EVERYTHING SUITABLE FOR THE WEST AFRICAN MARKET.

EXPORT. Beads, Cotton, Silk and Woollen Goods, Provisions, Tobacco, Perfumes, Drugs and Chemicals.

IMPORT. Excellent Facilities for dealing with this business in regard to Shipments and Finance.

BRANCHES AND AGENCIES ALL OVER THE WORLD.

Cable: "Eximrolyat, London." Codes: A.B.C. 5th Edition and Bentleys.

Professional Announcement.

DR. A. J. FOSTER, A qualified American Graduate, in DENTISTRY, HAS OPENED CONSULTING ROOMS at No. 8, Tinubu Street, opposite Jones' Hotel, where he will be pleased to place his professional knowledge at the disposal of the public. Fees Moderate.

E. A. T. A. J. Alakija,
Auctioneer,
Appraiser, Valuer, Commission and Estate Agent,

IS prepared to undertake the Sale of all kinds of Wholesale Goods, and Properties of every description. Sales are held at the Mart, No. 119, Victoria Street, Lagos, every Monday and Thursday, commencing at 10 a.m. also at No. 106, Denton Street, Ebute Metta, every Saturday, commencing at 4 p.m. to which all are invited. Special or Private Sales effected on the best of terms. Special arrangements can be made at short notice for journeys to any part of Nigeria, for the purpose of business. Mr. Alakija is prepared to act as Agent for Owners of Properties at Ebute Metta, to give out on to collect rents, etc., on reasonable terms. Telegraphic Address: Gbajumo, Ebute Metta, Lagos Nigeria.

Solicitors,
Messrs. ALAKIJA and ALAKIJA, B.L. 6, Labinjoh Lane, Lagos.

Surveyor
ISAAC T. WEY, Esq. 24, Dosumu Street, Lagos.

VEGETABLES. VEGETABLES.
EUROPEAN AND NATIVE.
CUCUMBERS A SPECIALITY.

TERESA GARDEN will supply even at your door on receiving an order accompanied by remittance unless where special arrangements are made for monthly accounts to be kept. The above is the oldest garden in Nigeria and won the First Prize at the first Agricultural Show in Nigeria. Orders to be sent between 5 to 9 a.m. and 4 to 6 p.m.; Sundays, 5 to 8 a.m. only. Gbajumo House, I, Abibu Street, West, Ebute Metta, Lagos, Nigeria, West Africa.

AN APOLOGY:
The proprietor of above Garden regrets that owing to the conspicuousness by the absence of labour he has not been able to satisfy his customers.

THOMAS & EDGE,
Constructional Engineers,
BUILDERS and COLONIAL CONTRACTORS.

CABINET-MAKING in all its Branches.

SIERRA LEONE, LAGOS, ACCRA, SECONDEE. GRAND BASSAM WEST AFRICA.
Head Office and Works for Nigeria:—LAGOS
Head Offices and Works:—WOOLWICH, LONDON, ENGLAND.

NOTE THIS.

L. A. CARDOSO,
Licensed Auctioneer, Appraiser, Valuer, Commission Agent, etc., etc.,
22, Bamgbose Street, Lagos, undertake the Sale of all kinds of Goods, Cargoes, Consignments, and Personal and Real Properties at very moderate charges.
Accounts and payments promptly.
Sales every Monday and Thursday at 5 a.m.
A trial is respectfully solicited.

T. A. ERINOSHO,
Forwarding and Commission Agent and Estate Agent.
Apply to 43, MARINA, LAGOS, NIGERIA

Church Services.

THE BROTHERHOOD CHRISTIAN CHURCH, or The African Unitarian Church, Lagos. Service on Sundays at 7 a.m. and at 6.30 p.m. at ILUPESI HALL. Seats Free. All are welcome.
For further particulars please call on, or apply to Adedeji Isola, Esq., The Superintendent, 56, Great Bridge Street, Lagos.

ESCAPE THE HEAT!
GET A
Lake Breeze Motor Fan
and Keep Cool Everywhere.

Ventilation is essential to efficiency and in these days in which everyone should be working at his best this fan is a necessity.

Ventilation is life and it will surprise you how much better your work will be, and how greatly your comfort with a

Lake Breeze Motor Fan.
A BLESSING TO THE SICK

Too much cannot be said of the Lake Breeze Motor Fan for use with the sick, in fevers, heart involvements or labored respiration it is of the utmost benefit and bring relief and comfort to the sufferer.

Burns ordinary Kerosine.
Consumption at the rate of one penny per night. Easy to operate.
Fans and Spare Parts obtainable at the Store of

H. A. Johnson & Company,
2, GREAT BRIDGE STREET,
P.O. Box 504. IDUMAGBO.

WE ARE THE MOST UP-TO-DATE
Manufacturers & Tailors
In the Trade for
SUITS and SUITINGS
OF ALL DESCRIPTIONS FOR
TROPICAL CLIMATES.
ALL BRITISH MADE
SERGES, FLANNELS, TWEEDS, ALPACAS, ITALIANS, &c.
Write direct for Free Patterns and Catalogue to—
G. BATTYE & CO.,
10, Upper Fountaine St., LEEDS, England.

CHEAP WANTED ADVERTISEMENTS
IN THE
Lagos Weekly Record.

Words	One Insertion	Two Insertions	Three Insertions
	s. d.	s. d.	s. d.
20 words	1 0	1 9	2 6
25	1 3	2 3	3 3
30	1 6	2 9	3 9
40	2 0	3 6	5 0
50	2 6	4 6	6 0

SITUATIONS VACANT.

COOK, male or female, must be decent and know what is cleanliness all round. If female she should be able to look after grown up children in for schooling if she knows music it is all the better in her interest. Apply by letter to "CLEANLINESS" of this paper. One who knows upper about French or Portuguese cuisine is preferred.

WANTED, an energetic and active CLERK. No one need apply unless he is conscientiously satisfied as to his honesty and good manners. All applications to be accompanied with genuine credentials, and addressed to HONESTY, c/o this Paper.

SITUATIONS WANTED.

AS A CLERK or DISTRICT AGENT for European or Native Firm. The applicant has experience of produce business and cotton goods and is prepared to go any where provided inducement offers. For reference, etc., apply to E.M.A. c/o this Paper.

WANTED.

WANTED-URGENTLY, A HOUSE in a locality suitable for European residence.—Communicate RECORD, Box 68.

ONE SECOND-HAND MAGIC LANTERN with second slides, as well as scene interesting scenes about the recent great War. Forward particulars to AJAYI KOLAWOLE AJIRAPE, Eungu Ngwo. Via Port Harcourt, Nigeria.

LAND FOR LEASING.

LAND (available) TO-BE LEASED, situate at a very good place on the foreshore, Marina, Ebute Metta, for business purposes.—For particulars apply to J. ALAKIJA, Auctioneer, at 119, Victoria Street, or Gbajumo House, Ebute Metta.

FOR SALE.

MOTOR BICYCLE, 1918; American make; 3-10 h.p.; all chain drive; hand and foot clutch; kick start; three speeds; condition perfect. Price £70 lowest. Leaving Nigeria, cause of selling.—Apply, TELEGRAPH WORKSHOP, Jebba Street, Ebute Metta.

ONE COMPLETE CINEMATOGRAPH, with one lime-light generator and burner or jet, and 10 subject-pictures with 6 reels to fold the pictures, and one rewinder to rewind the pictures after using; complete with upper and lower fire proof boxes to prevent pictures from accident of fire; all is in good condition, nothing out of order; ready for use. Immense quantity of War Pictures are also included in the lot. This can be seen at Mr. JIBERU ALAKIJA'S Mart, 119, Victoria Street, Lagos.

PUBLICATIONS.

NATIVE RACES AND THEIR RULERS, by C. L. TEMPLE, C.M.G. Late Lieut. Governor, Northern Provinces, Nigeria. With over 20 Illustrations by the Author. 6/6 Nett. Copies can be obtained at the Office of this Paper, I, Forre Road, Lagos.

A RUDE AWAKENING!

PEOPLE are getting silly to their interests when they decide, and insist that their REAL and PERSONAL PROPERTIES must BE SOLD by the PUBLIC AUCTION FEE, at the VENDUE, VICTORIA STREET. Highest prices obtained. Quick payments made, and Sales effected by Public Auction or Private Contract. Valuations for Mortgagees or Probate made. Charges reasonable. NOTE THE ADDRESS:—

E. SOVEMI ALDER,
Auctioneer, Valuer, etc.,
The Vendue, Victoria Street, Lagos.

WHOLESALE ONLY.

Every Description of Goods Supplied.

STAVELEY & CO., Ltd.
REGISTERED IN ENGLAND. Office and Warehouse: Tinubu Square, LAGOS.

ALSO AT LIVERPOOL, MANCHESTER, NEW YORK, SEKONDI, COOMASSI, ACCRA, CAMEROONS.

Head Office: 60, Wilson Street, London, E.C.

IKORODU TRANSPORT SERVICE.

RELIABLE TRANSPORT SERVICE between LAGOS and IKORODU is now established for General Transport purposes. Contracts are accepted at a few hours' notice. Our GENERAL PASSENGER CANOES leave IBEBUTE ERO and IDUMOYINBO WHARVES for IKORODU at 2 p.m. prompt and leave IKORODU WHARF for Lagos at 9 p.m. every day. Fare Sixpence (6d.) per head to or from either place. No War Profiteering.
For further particulars apply to
MR. M. O. DELO DOSUMU,
Lagos, Nigeria. Manager, P. O. Box 291.
4th November, 1919.

BIRTHS, MARRIAGES, DEATHS.

IN MEMORIAM.

TEN YEARS' MISSING!
How fast time flies!!
In loving and affectionate Memory of my dearly-beloved Mother, LYDIA FAMOLUKE, who departed this life hi her residence, 33, Taiwo Street, Lagos, on Monday, 7th February, 1910.—R.I.P.
She is not dead, whose glorious mind
Lifts thine on high.
To live in the hearts of we leave behind.
Is not to die.
By her fond son; ADEOYE DENIGA.
The Literary Bureau,
24, Williams Street, Lagos.

THANKS FOR SYMPATHY.

The Reverend Apostle and Superintendent A. O. & Mrs. LIAOYE, on behalf of themselves and relatives, hereby tender their sincerest thanks to all those who had sympathised with them, by their personal calls, letters, or telegrams, for their recent affliction, and irreparable loss, sustained by the death of their beloved daughter, HANNAH MOGBEBO OLA, which occurred on the 3rd of last month.

REUTER'S TELEGRAMS.

February 5.

It is reported that, on 24th January, Czecho to the number of about 15,000 were spread out along the railway at Irkutsk and in a most precarious position. The Bolshevik headquarters at Tomsk offered them repatriation across Russia on condition that they surrendered Kolchak with his gold treasure and military supplies. The Czechs handed over Kolchak, but retained the gold. Five thousand Poles have been murdered and their officers have gone over to the Bolshevist. Semhoff's force has been reduced, owing to desertion two thousand Cossacks—Large numbers of Austrian and German soldiers have also joined the Bolshevists, who are everywhere getting the upper hand. Practically the whole population of Siberia is ready to accept Bolshevism.

Paris—Negotiations were opened at a recent meeting between King Albert and President Poincare with reference to a defensive alliance between France and Belgium. The matter has made great progress and similar conversations are pending between Belgium and Great Britain.

Fig. 9. "In Memoriam" and other advertisements, *Lagos Weekly Record*, 7 February 1920, 4.

> **IN MEMORIAM.**
>
> In ever affectionate and fragrant memory of my dear wife, Mrs. MATILDA ADJAI HANCILES (alias Teetee AGAIN) of Hamilton, who was translated on the 1st July, 1921.
>
>   Her memory is still potent
>   Though her presence is now absent
>
>   JAMES E. HANCILES.
>
> In loving memory of our late dear and beloved, mother, JULIANA LOUISA BYRON, who died July 1, 1891 and left us bewailing our loss.
>
>   "Thou father in whose hands we are left
>   Protect us day by day
>   That we too may go where she has gone
>   And never to part again."
>
>   By her beloved children,
> BABINGTON, JOHNNY, BOYZIE, JANE, JULIE, WALTER, DAVID, and GUSTA.

Fig. 10. "In Memoriam," *Sierra Leone Weekly News*, 1 July 1922, 5.

these hymns and rhymes as trivial or lowbrow, the sense of loss they convey is palpable within the four-shilling space allowed for this type of advertisement.

In among advertising spaces for Lea and Perrins and other consumer goods, lay writers could use the medium of the newspaper to insert loved ones into the supposed permanence of print—into the historical narrative—promoted by the newspapers themselves. Accordingly, the dead gained a certain consequence in relation to the living world of news. Newspaper editors promoted precisely this association: "It would be a hopeless task calling in person or writing letters to discharge this social obligation," wrote the editor of the *Times of Nigeria* of the social calls required after a death: "Well, the *Times* comes to your aid right here. All you need to do is to get up a nice little paragraph thanking sympathizers and it is soon read in every home in Lagos under the heading 'Thanks for Sympathy.' In these and many other ways, the *Times* proposes to be of service to its readers."⁵⁰

LIBELING THE DEAD

The diverse printed expressions of respect for the life stories of dead subjects in colonial West Africa make all the more scandalous the appearance, in November 1938, of two obituary notices posted overnight at various strategic locations around Freetown in Sierra Leone (see figures 11 and 12). The first notice declared: "It is with the most excellent delight that we announce the welcomed and timely demise of a Demoniacal Maniac" named "Banky," who has suffered "Death due to political diarrhoea."⁵¹ "It is our painless duty to announce," stated the second obituary, that the internment of the "Demoniacal Maniac" has already taken place, "*sans ceremonie*," at 5:00 p.m. on 1 November 1938.⁵²

The deceased, Dr. Herbert C. Bankole Bright (commonly known as "Banky," or "Bankie") was a prominent politician in Freetown and an African Unofficial Member of the Legislative Council⁵³ who had contested and lost the Freetown municipal election on the date of his alleged "internment," 1 November 1938. Bankole-Bright was renowned for his "arrogant, bullying manner" and "notoriously disreputable" private life involving not only sexual scandals but also a failed attempt to disinherit his stepmother of his father's estate.⁵⁴ The surprise winners of the election—the West African Youth League—were led by Isaac Theophilus Akunna Wallace-Johnson (1894–1965), an arch-enemy of the loser, and a perpetual thorn in the side of the British colonial administration.⁵⁵ To add insult to injury, the Central Ward seat was won from Bankole-Bright by the first, and youngest, woman to stand for political office in West Africa: Constance Agatha Cummings-John (1918–2000), who was only twenty years old at the time of her victory.⁵⁶

With the possible exception of Nnamdi Azikiwe (1904–1996) in Nigeria, there was no more inflammatory individual in 1930s West Africa than Wallace-Johnson. Born in 1894 in Sierra Leone, he became a trade union activist in Nigeria, a journalist in Ghana, Nigeria, and Sierra Leone, a friend of the Pan-Africanist George Padmore, a writer for Azikiwe's newspapers in Ghana and Nigeria, a contributor to the banned journal the *Negro Worker*, and a zealous convert to communism. He came to colonial Ghana in November 1933 via Hamburg, Moscow, and Nigeria, to continue his career in politi-

OBITUARY.

IT is with the most excellent delight that we announce the welcomed and timely demise of the Societies of City Fathers and Uncle Toms as represented in the fall of BRAHISM and the triumph of YOUTH at the Polling Stations of the City Council on Tuesday the 1st day of November, 1938, when representatives of the Ratepayers, and Liberatedites crouched on all-fours before YOUTH.

Death due to POLITICAL DIARRHOEA and the collapse of the White House Demoniacal Maniac whilst diligently oscillating the Political Pendulum of the Macroscopic Cocus suspected in the Big Cigars and the Body Politic.

Interment took place "sans ceremonie" at the Wilberforce Memorial Hall at 5 p.m., when the Registrar of Political Suicides made the following announcements:—

YOUTH CANDIDATES.

CONSTANCE AGATHA CUMMINGS-JOHN	(Central Ward)	281 Votes
EDMUND ADOLPHUS COLLINGWOODE DAVIES	do	217 do
ERNEST DUNSTAN MORGAN	(West Ward)	110 do
OLUWOLE JAMES VON BRUMM TUBOKU-METZGER	(East Ward)	Unopposed

REACTIONARIES

BRAH DUNSTAN	(Central Ward)	74 Votes — Central Ratepayers Association
BRAH NEWTON	do	63 Votes do
BRAH BOISY	(West Ward)	100 do (West Ward Ratepayers Association)

FUNERAL ODE.

Dunstan could not stand.
Newton's an old tin.
Boisy's merely noisy.
So! Banky's heart is broke!

May They Rest In Pieces !!!

Fig. 11. "Obituary," PRO CO 267/671/8. Permission: The National Archives, Kew, London.

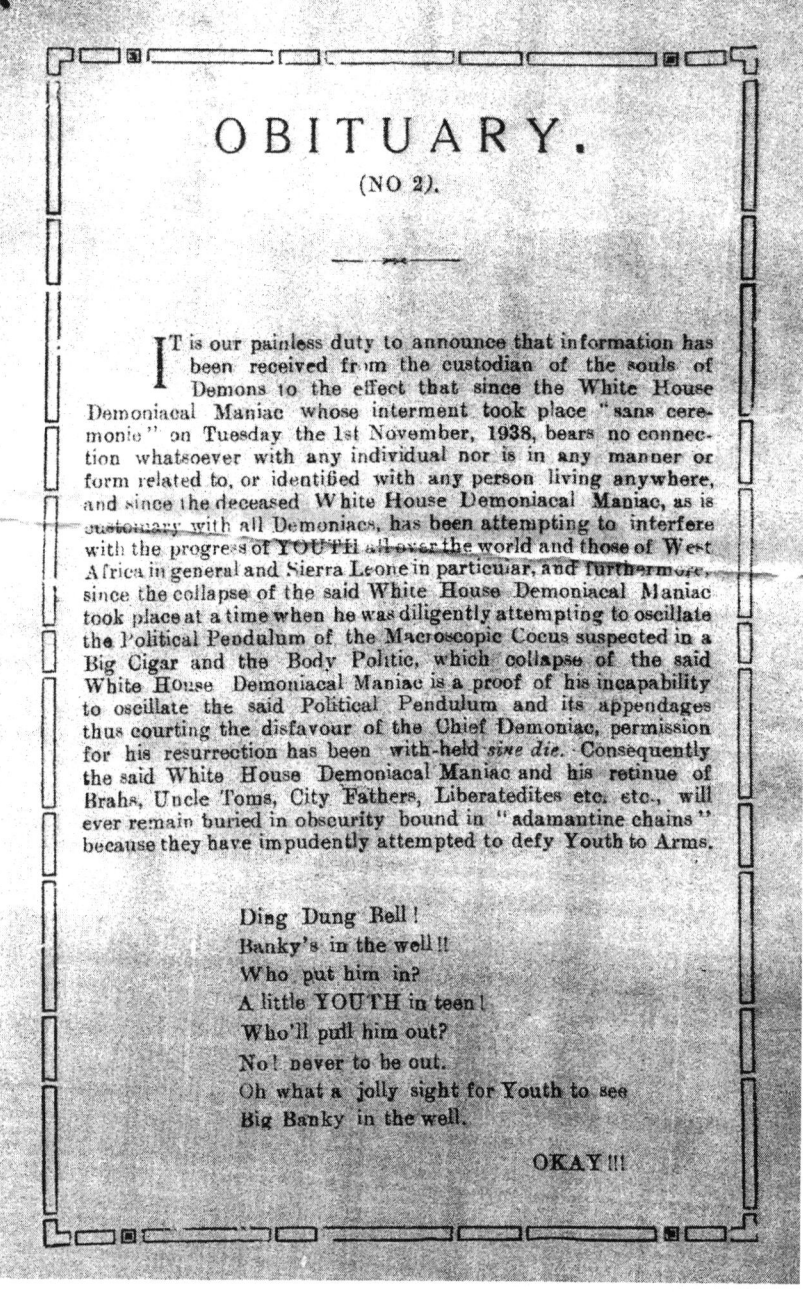

Fig. 12. "Obituary No. 2," PRO CO 267/671/8. Permission: The National Archives, Kew, London.

cal journalism and labor activism, using his own name alongside a wide variety of pseudonyms.[57] Here was an individual who had, in the words of the Gold Coast attorney general in the mid-1930s, "graduated at Moscow in the art of subversive propaganda," and "returned to West Africa as a professional agitator."[58] Anything but acquiescent with colonial rule, and always aware of the regime's surveillance, this ardent critic of colonialism used the printing press to play cat and mouse with the British, blatantly signing his name on some documents, and stamping others provocatively with the logo of the West African Youth League.

Wallace-Johnson was a notorious presence in the close-knit community of Freetown, where the once conservative creole majority, while by no means politically unified, was by the late 1930s regarded by British colonial officials as "an exceptionally difficult lot of people to handle."[59] He was no stranger to the colonial court system, and was known to the authorities throughout the British Empire as a Soviet-trained agent provocateur.[60] Even as the obituary notices were posted around Freetown, Wallace-Johnson had two court cases under way: an appeal to the Privy Council in London against the guilty verdict for his supposedly seditious article, "Has the African a God?," written under the pseudonym "Effective," and published in Azikiwe's *African Morning Post* in May 1936;[61] and a charge of contempt of court for his refusal to give his name to a colonial Commission of Enquiry into the leakage and publication of top-secret Colonial Office documents, which Wallace-Johnson had obtained in 1938.[62] While he often struggled to stay afloat as editor of the *African Standard* in the 1930s, repeatedly appealing for funds from subscribers to enable him to obtain up-to-date "printing equipment . . . to meet the demands of the public," Wallace-Johnson continuously thrived on the process whereby his outspoken sentiments became entextualized, passing into people's hands and homes in the form of incendiary textual objects—pamphlets, newspapers, and handbills.[63]

In an effort to halt the dissemination of openly subversive propaganda by the West African Youth League in the late 1930s, and the wave of unrest that spread in its wake through Sierra Leone, including the barracks, the governor, Sir Douglas Jardine, introduced a variety of measures, including a sedition ordinance, a deportation ordinance for British citizens, and an ordinance to catalog and prohibit the circulation of "undesirable publications."[64] These draconian ordinances illustrate Governor Jardine's efforts to limit Wallace-Johnson's fearless, vociferous form of anticolonialism on the eve of the Second World War. While on leave in Britain, Sir Douglas visited the Colonial

Office and "represented strongly that it was becoming necessary to put a brake upon the utterances and other activities of Mr Wallace-Johnson and the 'Youth League.'"[65] Wallace-Johnson had allegedly incited mutiny among African gunmen in the barracks at Freetown, and Youth League propaganda was also allegedly distributed to African police officers.[66] Among other punishments, the governor's new ordinances introduced a two-year prison term for "any person who imports, publishes, sells, offers for sale, distributes, or reproduces any publication the importation of which has been prohibited," with three years for subsequent offenses, and a prison term of up to one year for a person in possession of prohibited publications "without lawful excuse."[67] Steamrolled through in the face of international opposition, the legislation enabled Sir Douglas and his successor, Sir Hugh Craddock Stevenson, to remove Wallace-Johnson from the Sierra Leonean public sphere for a large portion of the Second World War.[68]

Wallace-Johnson's two obituary notices appeared in this volatile public space strewn with printed debates about African readers, and about "good" and "bad" reading materials, seditious literature, and the freedom of the press. At first sight, the two posters resonate with authenticity because they closely resemble the typical single-page obituary that would be stuck to walls and doors to announce a death, a familiar sight to urban Sierra Leoneans by the 1930s and to people in other West African towns.[69] To achieve his goals, Wallace-Johnson would have depended upon a particular set of local perceptions about the relationship between print and death because, as Linda Hutcheon observes, in order to successfully satirize a genre, the satirist needs to be confident that the public will recognize the violated target.[70] Thus, by embedding his political satire parasitically in the visuality of printed obituaries, Wallace-Johnson gleefully acknowledged the normative status of printed announcements of death in the region by the late 1930s.

On approaching the obituaries, local readers would have anticipated an announcement of loss. On seeing the content, however, their emotions would have turned into laughter or shock throughout the public urban spaces in which the posters were displayed. Wallace-Johnson specialized in disrespectful writing, deploying satire and other genres of abuse in the manner of Jonathan Swift to attack and to play with his political enemies. At all times, he attacked the system by deliberately confounding fact with fiction, and in response, again and again his targets resorted to the British colonial court system in their efforts to clear their lives of Wallace-Johnson's distortions.[71] One can only imagine the response of readers in Freetown to the vivid descriptions of the manner of Banky's demise and the statements that "permission for his resurrection has been with-held *sine die*," and that Banky "will ever remain buried in obscurity bound in 'adamantine chains.'"⁷²

As Wallace-Johnson knew full well, you cannot libel the dead. The chief problem with the two obituary notices was that Dr. Herbert Bankole-Bright (1883–1958) was very much alive and kicking in Freetown when the posters appeared, and he immediately issued an action for criminal libel against their author "for bringing him into hatred, ridicule and contempt."⁷³ A printed genre designed for public consumption in a spirit of solemnity had been appropriated and transformed, perhaps for the first time in Freetown, used to name and shame a living person rather than to commemorate or memorialize the deceased.

In the mock obituaries of 1938, one can see a similar creative process to that on display in the memorial poems published in West African newspapers during the previous three decades. The key difference, of course, is that Wallace-Johnson makes a mockery of the role of the creative imagination in the social construction of death in West Africa. Unlike the amateur poets, with their high seriousness, rhyming couplets, hymns, quotations, and acrostics, Wallace-Johnson's literary style takes the form of gibberish and offense-saturated parody, including the provocative ditty:

> *Ding Dung Bell!*
> *Banky's in the well!!*
> *Who put him in?*
> *A little youth in teen!*
> *Who'll pull him out?*
> *No! never to be out.*
> *Oh what a jolly sight for Youth to see*
> *Big Banky in the well*
> *okay!!!*⁷⁴

Wallace-Johnson seems to relish the ways in which print—particularly the anonymous, mass-produced poster—could act as a magnet for readerships in urban public spaces, drawing them into the text but frustrating them as well. A typical sentence from the second obituary reads:

> The collapse of the said White House Demoniacal Maniac took place at a time when he was diligently attempting to oscillate the Political Pendulum of the Macroscopic Cocus suspected in a Big Cigar and the Body Politic, which col-

lapse of the said White House Demoniacal Maniac is a proof of his incapability to oscillate the said Political Pendulum and its appendages thus courting the disfavour of the Chief Demoniac.[75]

Reading this, one might wonder how Bankole-Bright managed to extract sufficient sense from the poster to make any kind of a case for criminal libel.

Wallace-Johnson's ebullient nonsense should be regarded as confronting and ridiculing the seriousness of all those printed mediations of death in West African newspapers since the 1880s. His intervention represents a vital break from memorialization and hagiography. Such a break parallels Lytton Strachey's controversial publication *Eminent Victorians*, which revolutionized English biography when it appeared in 1918, containing irreverent portraits of four iconic cultural figures, including Florence Nightingale and General Gordon.[76] The extremity of Wallace-Johnson's violation of readers' expectations of an actual local death would have generated a devastating comic effect, adding public laughter to the recent political humiliation suffered by Bankole-Bright at the hands of the West African Youth League in the polls, and further damaging the future of his reputation.[77]

Not being dead, "Banky" won his case against Wallace-Johnson's intention to bring him into ridicule and contempt. If, however, as Kalusa and Vaughan argue for central and southern Africa, "Dead bodies carry, and are made to carry, a range of political messages," Wallace-Johnson's obituary notices bring the semiotics of death to bear on a live subject, an act of desecration that, in itself, highlights the political messages that are possible to articulate through funeral and obituary genres. Clearly, Wallace-Johnson relished the different types of "mediated visibility" made possible by print.[78] Trickster-like, he used printed texts to play with his proximity to readers, and he is literally "bound up" with British colonial responses to the perceived infiltration of local print cultures by anticolonial agitators. In combination with the raft of measures introduced by colonial officials in an effort to censor his press activities during the war, Wallace-Johnson's satirical printed outputs throughout his lifetime reaffirm the power of print to attach to, and corrode, the names of live subjects in a period of anticolonial agitation and political critique in West Africa.[79]

THE END

Death is not "the end" in West Africa. In many West African cultures, death is a mediating rather than a terminal event, providing a ripe opportunity for processes of entextualization and creative production. Death in Africa, as elsewhere, is both an empirical event and a dynamic social practice, and it carries a complex set of representations in its wake.[80] A focus on printed discourses of death in West African newspapers complements life-orientated research in helping one to comprehend how people's lives were given historicity and meaning by others in the colonial period. The various forms of printed memorialization analyzed in this chapter helped to produce a person's life story, and thus actively contributed to the genre of biography. In other words, the life of a person possessed an ongoing temporality that resisted the concepts of loss, ending, and "passing away" that are often identified as characteristic of death in Western cultures.[81] For this reason, no matter how brief a loved one's life, the cause of death and scene of death are rarely described in West African obituaries and memorial poems. No last words are breathed by West African subjects along the lines of the Western deathbed tradition. This is a genre in which lost lives feature more than last moments.

As with life-history research involving living subjects, the genres through which death is narrated reveal a great deal of information about changing ideas of self and the public in different cultures internationally, and colonial African newspaper cultures—the entire field of correspondents, editors, readers, printing presses, texts, genres, and technologies—can be fruitfully be evaluated in relation to such genres.

BIBLIOGRAPHY

Adjah, Olive Akpebu. "Ghanaian Funeral Brochures: An Unexplored Rich Source of Biographical Information." *African Research and Documentation* 103 (2007): 33–44.

Arhin, Kwame. "The Economic Implications of Transformations in Akan Funeral Rites." *Africa* 64, no. 3 (1994): 307–22.

Attoh-Ahuma, S. R. B. *Memoirs of West African Celebrities*. Liverpool: D. Marples, 1905.

Azikiwe, Nnamdi. *My Odyssey.* London: Hurst, 1970.

Barber, Karin. "Text and Performance in Africa," *Oral Tradition* 20, no. 2 (2005): 264–77.

Burke, Peter. "History as Social Memory." In *Memory: History, Culture and the Mind*, edited by Thomas Butler, 97–113. Oxford: Basil Blackwell, 1989.

Burrowes, Carl Patrick. *Power and Press Freedom in Liberia, 1830–1970*. Trenton, NJ: Africa World Press, 2004.

Darnton, Robert. "Literary Surveillance in the British Raj: The Contradictions of British Imperialism." *Book History* 4 (2001): 133–76.

DeBoeck, Filip. "Beyond the Grave: History, Memory, and Death in Postcolonial Congo/Zaire." In *Memory in the Postcolony: African Anthropology and the Critique of Power*, edited by Richard Werbner, 21–57. London: Zed Books, 1998.

Denzer, LeRay. "Women in Freetown Politics, 1914–61: A Preliminary Study." In *Sierra-Leone, 1787–1987: Two Centuries of Intellectual Life*, edited by Murray Last, Paul Richards, and Christopher Fyfe, 439–56. London: International African Institute; Manchester: Manchester University Press, 1987.

de Witte, Marleen. *Long Live the Dead! Changing Funeral Celebrations in Asante, Ghana*. Amsterdam: Aksant Academic Publishers, 2001.

de Witte, Marleen. "Money and Death: Funeral Business in Asante, Ghana." *Africa* 73, no. 4 (2003): 531–59.

Dollimore, Jonathan. *Death, Desire and Loss in Western Culture*. New York: Routledge, 1998.

Doortmont, Michel, ed. *The Pen-Pictures of Modern Africans and African Celebrities by Charles Francis Hutchison: A Collective Biography of Elite Society in the Gold Coast Colony*. Leiden: Brill, 2005.

Eng, David L., and David Kazanjian, eds. *Loss: The Politics of Mourning*. Berkeley: University of California Press, 2002.

Fanon, Frantz. *The Wretched of the Earth*. 1961. Translated by Richard Philcox. New York: Grove Press, 2004.

Ffoulkes, Arthur. "Funeral Customs of the Gold Coast Colony." *Journal of the Royal African Society* 8, no. 30 (1909): 154–64.

Fowler, Brigit. *The Obituary as Collective Memory*. New York: Routledge, 2007.

Fraser, Robert. "Biography and the Morality of Style." Inaugural lecture, Open University, 24 January 2012.

Fyfe, Christoper. "Bright, Herbert Christian Bankole- (1883–1958)." In *Oxford Dictionary of National Biography*, edited by H. C. G. Matthew and Brian Harrison. Oxford: Oxford University Press, 2004. Online ed. edited by Lawrence Goldman, January 2008. http://www.oxforddnb.com/view/article/76287 (accessed 28 February 2014).

Fyfe, Christopher. *A History of Sierra Leone*. Oxford: Oxford University Press, 1962.

Fyfe, Christopher. "Johnson, Isaac Theophilus Akuna Wallace- (1894–1965)." In *Oxford Dictionary of National Biography*, edited by H. C. G. Matthew and Brian Harrison. Oxford: Oxford University Press, 2004. Online ed. edited by Lawrence Goldman, January 2008. http://www.oxforddnb.com/view/article/75249 (accessed 28 February 2014).

Gadzekpo, Audrey. "Public but Private: A Transformational Reading of the Memoirs and Newspaper Writings of Mercy Ffoulkes-Crabbe." In *Africa's Hidden Histories: Everyday Literacy and Making the Self*, edited by Karin Barber, 314–37. Bloomington: Indiana University Press, 2006.

Gibbs, James. "'Give Sorrow Words': An Examination of Ghanaian Funeral Brochures and Their Place in Contemporary Local Publishing." Paper presented at the "Postcolonial Lives of the Book" conference, University of London, Institute of English Studies, 3–5 November 2005.

Gott, Suzanne. "'Onetouch' Quality and 'Marriage Silver Cup': Performative Display, Cosmopolitanism, and Marital Poatwa in Kumasi Funerals." *Africa Today* 54, no. 2 (2007): 79–106.

Harrison, Robert Pogue. *The Dominion of the Dead*. Chicago: University of Chicago Press, 2003.

Hooker, James R. *Black Revolutionary: George Padmore's Path from Communism to Pan-Africanism*. New York: Praeger, 1967.

Hutcheon, Linda. *A Theory of Parody: The Teachings of Twentieth-Century Art Forms*. London: Methuen, 1985.

Hutchison, Charles Francis. *The Pen-Pictures of Modern Africans and African Celebrities*. London: African Library Press, 1930.

Jindra, Michael, and Joël Noret, eds. *Funerals In Africa: Explorations of a Social Phenomenon*. New York: Berghahn, 2011.

Kalusa, Walima T., and Megan Vaughan. *Death, Belief and Politics in Central African History*. Lusaka: Lembani Trust, 2013.

Lee, Rebekah, and Megan Vaughan. "Death and Dying in the History of Africa since 1800." *Journal of African History* 49, no. 3 (2008): 341–59.

Macmillan, Allister. *The Red Book of West Africa*. London: Collingridge, 1920.

Mbembe, Achille. "Africa and the Night of Language: An Interview with Achille Mbembe by Annalisa Oboe." *Salon* 2 (2008). http://jwtc.org.za/the_salon/volume_2/annalisa_oboe_africa_the_night_of_language.htm (accessed: 15 September 2013.

Mbembe, Achille. "Necropolitics." *Public Culture* 15, no. 1 (2003): 11–40.

McCaskie, T. C. "Writing, Reading, and Printing Death: Obituaries and Commemoration in Asante." In *Africa's Hidden Histories: Everyday Literacy and Making the Self*, edited by Karin Barber, 341–84. Bloomington: Indiana University Press, 2006.

Newell, Stephanie. *The Forger's Tale: The Search for "Odeziaku"*. Athens: Ohio University Press, 2006.

Newell, Stephanie. *Literary Culture in Colonial Ghana*. Manchester: Manchester University Press; Bloomington: Indiana University Press, 2002.

Newell, Stephanie. *The Power to Name: A History of Anonymity in Colonial West Africa*. Athens: Ohio University Press, 2013.

Ranger, Terence. "Dignifying Death: The Politics of Burial in Bulawayo." *Journal of Religion in Africa* 34, nos. 1–2 (2004): 110–44.

Rumann, W. B. "Funeral Ceremonies for the Late Ex-Oba of Benin." *Journal of the Royal African Society* 14, no. 53 (1914): 35–39.

Sampson, Magnus J. *Gold Coast Men of Affairs: Past and Present*. London: A. H. Stockwell, 1937.

Sawada, Nozomi. "The Educated Elite and Associational Life in Early Lagos Newspapers: In Search of Unity for the Progress of Society." PhD dissertation, Centre of West African Studies, University of Birmingham, 2011.

Shaloff, Stanley. "Press Controls and Sedition Proceedings in the Gold Coast, 1933–39." *African Affairs* 71, no. 284 (1972): 241–63.

Solove, Daniel J. *The Future of Reputation: Gossip, Rumor, and Privacy on the Internet*. New Haven: Yale University Press, 2008.

Spitzer, Leo, and LaRay Denzer. "I. T. A. Wallace-Johnson and the West African Youth League." *International Journal of African Historical Studies* 6, no. 3 (1973): 413–52.

Spitzer, Leo, and LaRay Denzer. "I. T. A. Wallace-Johnson and the West African Youth League. Part II: The Sierra Leone Period, 1938–1945." *International Journal of African Historical Studies* 6, no. 4 (1973): 565–601.

Thomas, N. W. "Some Ibo Burial Customs." *Journal of the Royal Anthropological Institute of Great Britain and Ireland* 47 (1917): 160–213.

Thomas, N. W. "Notes on Edo Burial Customs." *Journal of the Royal Anthropological Institute of Great Britain and Ireland* 50 (1920): 377–411.

Thompson, John B. "The New Visibility." *Theory, Culture and Society* 22, no. 6 (2005): 31–51.

van der Geest, Sjaak. "Funerals for the Living: Conversations with Elderly People in Kwahu, Ghana." *African Studies Review* 43, no. 3 (2000): 103–29.

Widlok, Thomas. "Unearthing Culture: Khoisan Funerals and Social Change." *Anthropos* 93, no. 1 (1998): 115–26.

Wyse, Akintola. *The Krio of Sierra Leone: An Interpretive History*. London: C. Hurst, 1989.

Young, Richard F. "The Entextualization of Talk." Presented at the symposium "Defining and Assessing Speaking Ability," American Association for Applied Linguistics and the Language Testing Research Colloquium, St. Louis, Missouri, 24 February 2001. http://www.english.wisc.edu/rfyoung/Entextualization.Paper.PDF (accessed 5 December 2013).

ARCHIVAL DOCUMENTS

British Library (London, UK)

J/X/0705/1 (45). SALNEB Publication No.1 [etc]: A Series of Writings by Isaac T. A. Wallace-Johnson, SALNEB publication No. 45, 16 December 1963.

J/X/0705/1 (95), *SALNEB Publication Series 2*, No. 95, 11 May 1965.

____ *SALNEB Publication Series 2*, "Special Forty-Day Edition," 17 June 1965.

Public Record Office (London, UK)

CO 267/671/8, *Leakage of Official Information, 1938* [Sierra Leone: I. T. A. Wallace-Johnson files], Kew.

CO 267/671/ 8, *Leakage of Official Information, 1938*, "Enclosure II: Report on the Case of Rex versus I. T. A. Wallace-Johnson on the prosecution of the Hon Dr H. C. Bankole-Bright," n.d.

CO 267/672/9, *Deputation from Sierra Leone against the Recent Ordinances*, "Copy of memo," 26 July 1939.

CO 267/672/7, *Deportation, Sedition, Undesirable Literature, Trade Union and Trade Disputes Legislation—Miscellaneous Representations 1939*, "Memorandum," 26 June 1939.

CO 267/672/7, "Extract from article in the Manchester *Guardian* entitled 'Sierra Leone: The Undesirable Literature Ordinance,'" 14 June 1939.

CO 96/749/5, *Wallace-Johnson. Privy Council Appeal. I. T. A. Wallace-Johnson v. The King*, "Law Officers' Dept, Accra: Observations," 13 November 1938.

School of Oriental and African Studies (London, UK)

MMS.257 (box) 1939: 56, Methodist Missionary Society archives, SOAS.

NOTES TO CHAPTER 14

1. This chapter was completed as part of an European Research Council–funded research project, "The Cultural Politics of Dirt in Africa, 1880–Present," Identification Number: 323343. It reflects only the author's views, and the European Union is not liable for any use that may be made of the information contained therein. The author is indebted to Nico Carpentier, Leen van Brussel, Derek Peterson, and Emma Hunter for their feedback.

Abbreviations

GCL *Gold Coast Leader* (Cape Coast)

MMS Methodist Missionary Society Archives (SOAS)

SLWN *Sierra Leone Weekly News* (Freetown).

2. E.g., N. W. Thomas, "Some Ibo Burial Customs," *Journal of the Royal Anthropological Institute of Great Britain and Ireland* 47 (1917): 160–213, and "Notes on Edo Burial Customs," *Journal of the Royal Anthropological Institute of Great Britain and Ireland* 50 (1920): 377–411; Arthur Ffoulkes, "Funeral Customs of the Gold Coast Colony," *Journal of the Royal African Society* 8, no. 30 (1909): 154–64; W. B. Rumann, "Funeral Ceremonies for the Late Ex-Oba of Benin," *Journal of the Royal African Society* 14, no. 53 (1914): 35–39.

3. Kwame Arhin, "The Economic Implications of Transformations in Akan

Funeral Rites," *Africa* 64, no. 3 (1994): 307–22; T. C. McCaskie, "Writing, Reading, and Printing Death: Obituaries and Commemoration in Asante," in *Africa's Hidden Histories: Everyday Literacy and Making the Self*, ed. Karin Barber (Bloomington: Indiana University Press, 2006), 341–84; Suzanne Gott, "'Onetouch' Quality and 'Marriage Silver Cup': Performative Display, Cosmopolitanism, and Marital Poatwa in Kumasi Funerals," *Africa Today* 54, no. 2 (2007): 79–106; Sjaak van der Geest, "Funerals for the Living: Conversations with Elderly People in Kwahu, Ghana," *African Studies Review* 43, no. 3 (2000): 103–29; Marleen de Witte, *Long Live the Dead! Changing Funeral Celebrations in Asante, Ghana* (Amsterdam: Aksant Academic Publishers, 2001), and de Witte, "Money and Death: Funeral Business in Asante, Ghana," *Africa* 73, no. 4 (2003): 531–59.

4. Esp. Thomas Widlok, "Unearthing Culture: Khoisan Funerals and Social Change," *Anthropos* 93, no. 1 (1998): 115–26; Terence Ranger, "Dignifying Death: The Politics of Burial in Bulawayo," *Journal of Religion in Africa* 34, nos. 1–2 (2004): 110–44; Rebekah Lee and Megan Vaughan, "Death and Dying in the History of Africa since 1800," *Journal of African History* 49, no. 3 (2008): 341–59; Filip DeBoeck, "Beyond the Grave: History, Memory, and Death in Postcolonial Congo/Zaire," in *Memory in the Postcolony: African Anthropology and the Critique of Power*, ed. Richard Werbner (London: Zed Books, 1998), 21–57.

5. Walima T. Kalusa and Megan Vaughan, *Death, Belief and Politics in Central African History* (Lusaka: Lembani Trust, 2013).

6. Kalusa and Vaughan, *Death, Belief and Politics*, xi.

7. Kalusa and Vaughan, *Death, Belief and Politics*, xiii.

8. Kalusa and Vaughan, *Death, Belief and Politics*, xiii.

9. James Gibbs, "'Give Sorrow Words': An Examination of Ghanaian Funeral Brochures and Their Place in Contemporary Local Publishing," paper presented at the "Postcolonial Lives of the Book" conference, University of London, Institute of English Studies, 3–5 November 2005, 5; see also Olive Akpebu Adjah, "Ghanaian Funeral Brochures: An Unexplored Rich Source of Biographical Information," *African Research and Documentation* 103 (2007): 33–44.

10. Nozomi Sawada, "The Educated Elite and Associational Life in Early Lagos Newspapers: In Search of Unity for the Progress of Society," PhD dissertation, Centre of West African Studies, University of Birmingham, 2011, 128, 131–32; Peter Burke, "History as Social Memory," in *Memory: History, Culture and the Mind*, ed. Thomas Butler (Oxford: Basil Blackwell, 1989), 97–113. As later sections of this chapter will indicate, however, I could not find any evidence of this "heavy borrowing" in the newspapers selected for this study.

11. McCaskie, "Writing, Reading"; Gibbs, "Give Sorrow Words"; de Witte, *Long Live the Dead!*

12. For a historical sociology of obituaries in British newspapers, see Brigit

Fowler, *The Obituary as Collective Memory* (New York: Routledge, 2007). For a study of the significance of burial grounds in the work of major European philosophers and creative writers, see Robert Pogue Harrison, *The Dominion of the Dead* (Chicago: University of Chicago Press, 2003). For a cultural study of death in Europe, see Jonathan Dollimore, *Death, Desire and Loss in Western Culture* (New York: Routledge, 1998), and David L. Eng and David Kazanjian, eds., *Loss: The Politics of Mourning* (Berkeley: University of California Press, 2002).

13. An additional area for study is the role of fantasy, desire, and the imagination in West African representations of death. See Achille Mbembe, "Africa and the Night of Language: An Interview with Achille Mbembe by Annalisa Oboe," *Salon* 2 (2008), http://jwtc.org.za/the_salon/volume_2/annalisa_oboe_africa_the_night_of_language.htm (accessed 15 September 2013). An exhibition, "Fabulous Coffins from the UK and Ghana," at the Southbank Centre in London (January 2012) brought international media attention to Ghana's designer coffins, which have, since at least the 1940s, come in diverse creative shapes.

14. See Carl Patrick Burrowes, *Power and Press Freedom in Liberia, 1830–1970* (Trenton, NJ: Africa World Press, 2004).

15. See Stephanie Newell, *The Power to Name: A History of Anonymity in Colonial West Africa* (Athens: Ohio University Press, 2013).

16. Gender-neutral language is inappropriate because obituaries were dominated by the profiles of men in the colonial period, demonstrating which lives were "chosen for enduring memory," and which were not deemed publicly relevant (Fowler, *Obituary as Collective Memory*, 3).

17. Touissant-Louverture (c. 1743–1803), leader of the Haitian Revolution, was especially popular with West African newspapermen as an early exemplar of black nationalist self-assertion.

18. The ways in which colonial rule militated against the emergence of Habermas's ideal for a "public sphere" are debated in Newell, *Power to Name*, 29–43.

19. Richard F. Young, "The Entextualization of Talk," presented at the symposium "Defining and Assessing Speaking Ability," American Association for Applied Linguistics and the Language Testing Research Colloquium, St. Louis, Missouri, 24 February 2001, http://www.english.wisc.edu/rfyoung/Entextualization.Paper.PDF (accessed 5 December 2013); Karin Barber, "Text and Performance in Africa," *Oral Tradition* 20, no. 2 (2005): 264–77.

20. Barber, "Text and Performance."

21. http://www.asauk.net/downloads/conf/asa14_panels.pdf (accessed 10 December 2013).

22. Gibbs, "Give Sorrow Words," 2.

23. Gibbs, "Give Sorrow Words," 9.

24. Gibbs, "Give Sorrow Words," 1.

25. Charles F. Hutchison, *The Pen-Pictures of Modern Africans and African Celebrities* (London: African Library Press, 1930).

26. See Stephanie Newell, *Literary Culture in Ghana* (Manchester: Manchester University Press; Bloomington: Indiana University Press, 2002), 5, 10.

27. SOAS, MMS.257 (box) 1939, 56.

28. *SLWN*, 8 June 1907, 4.

29. *SLWN*, 27 May 1893, 2.

30. *SLWN*, 27 May 1893, 2.

31. This was a period in which the realization dawned on African educated elites that, while they might have exceptional skills and professional qualifications, the "new imperialism" excluded them from positions of political power and influence.

32. S. R. B. Attoh-Ahuma, *Memoirs of West African Celebrities* (Liverpool: D. Marples, 1905); Magnus J. Sampson, *Gold Coast Men of Affairs: Past and Present* (London: A. H. Stockwell, 1937).

33. Allister Macmillan, *The Red Book of West Africa* (London: Collingridge, 1920); Hutchison, *Pen-Pictures*.

34. Michel Doortmont, ed., *The Pen-Pictures of Modern Africans and African Celebrities by Charles Francis Hutchison: A Collective Biography of Elite Society in the Gold Coast Colony* (Leiden: Brill, 2005), 23.

35. Nnamdi Azikiwe, *My Odyssey* (London: Hurst, 1970), 226–29. Glover Memorial Hall was an architectural monument to John Hawley Glover (1829–1885), governor of Lagos Colony from 1863 to 1866.

36. See Frantz Fanon, *The Wretched of the Earth* (1961; New York: Grove Press, 2004).

37. *GCL*, 28 January 1922, 4.

38. *GCL*, 28 January 1922, 4.

39. *GCL*, 28 January 1922, 4.

40. Sawada, "The Educated Elite," 135.

41. *Sawyerr's Bookselling, Printing and Stationery Trade Circular*, 19 December 1885, n.p. In one unconventional example of their use, Dr. William MacGregor, governor of Lagos Colony from 1899 to 1904, regularly wrote letters to Dr. (later Sir) Ronald Ross on black-bordered paper about topics that were anything but somber. In July 1901, for example, he used mourning stationary to congratulate Ross on his election as a Fellow of the Royal Society (London School of Hygiene and Tropical Medicine, Ross/79/38).

42. For a detailed study of pseudonymity and anonymity in colonial West African newspapers, see Newell, *Power to Name*.

43. J. P. Brown-Pobee, who is also remembered in figure 15, is not to be confused with E. J. P. Brown of Cape Coast, onetime president of the Aborigines Rights Protection Society and Elected Member of the Gold Coast Legislative Council.

44. Sawada, "The Educated Elite," 169.

45. *Gold Coast Nation*, 3 November 1917, front page.

46. *Times of Nigeria*, 26 September 1916, 5; *SLWN*, 9 December 1922, 72; *SLWN*, 11 November 1922, 5.

47. Sawada, "The Educated Elite," 169.

48. Sawada, "The Educated Elite," 167–8.

49. *SLWN*, 1 July 1922, 16.

50. *Times of Nigeria*, 23 February 1920, 5.

51. CO 267/671/8.

52. CO 267/671/8.

53. At this time, an African "unofficial" member was an elected member of the Legislative Council who had received a majority in the municipal elections, voters being male African householders with more than a specified annual income. Previously, "unofficial" members were nominated by the colonial regime. Bankole Bright had served in the Legislative Council since 1925: as a member, he fought against racial discrimination in government and politics. Christopher Fyfe, "Bright, Herbert Christian Bankole- (1883–1958)," in *Oxford Dictionary of National Biography*, ed. H. C. G. Matthew and Brian Harris (Oxford: Oxford University Press, 2004), online ed., ed. Lawrence Goldman, http://www.oxforddnb.com/view/article/76287 (accessed 28 February 2014).

54. Fyfe, "Bright, Herbert Christian Bankole."

55. See Leo Spitzer and LaRay Denzer, "I. T. A. Wallace-Johnson and the West African Youth League. Part II: The Sierra Leone Period, 1938–1945," *International Journal of African Historical Studies* 6, no. 4 (1973): 565–601; Newell, *Power to Name*.

56. See Fyfe, "Bright, Herbert Christian Bankole"; LaRay Denzer, "Women in Freetown Politics, 1914–61: A Preliminary Study," in *Sierra-Leone, 1787–1987: Two Centuries of Intellectual Life*, ed. Murray Last, Paul Richards, and Christopher Fyfe (London: International African Institute; Manchester: Manchester University Press, 1987), 439–56.

57. See Christopher Fyfe, "Johnson, Isaac Theophilus Akuna Wallace- (1894–1965)," in Goldman, *Oxford Dictionary of National Biography*, http://www.oxforddnb.com/view/article/75249 (accessed 28 February 2014); Newell, *Power to Name*, 74–97.

58. Cited in Stanley Shaloff, "Press Controls and Sedition Proceedings in the Gold Coast, 1933–39," *African Affairs* 71, no. 284 (1972): 245.

59. CO 267/672/7, 26 June 1939. For major studies of the creoles of Sierra Leone, see Last, Richards, and Fyfe, *Sierra Leone, 1787–1987*. Each of these authors in his own right is a significant authority on Sierra Leonean history; e.g., Christopher Fyfe's *A History of Sierra Leone* (Oxford: Oxford University Press, 1962). See also Akintola Wyse, *The Krio of Sierra Leone: An Interpretive History* (London: C. Hurst, 1989).

60. CO 96/749/5, 13 November 1938.

61. See Newell, *Power to Name*, 74–97.

62. Newell, *Power to Name*, 74–97. Wallace-Johnson was so threatening to the British that legislation was created (Emergency Act of 1 September 1939) to muzzle him under wartime codes.

63. *African Standard*, 13 January 1939, 4. The concept of "incendiary texts" was first formulated by Robert Darnton, "Literary Surveillance in the British Raj: The Contradictions of British Imperialism," *Book History* 4 (2001): 133–76.

64. CO 267/672/7, Memo, 26 June 1939.

65. CO 267/672/9, *Deputation from Sierra Leone against the Recent Ordinances*, "Copy of memo," 26 July 1939.

66. "Copy of memo," 26 July 1939.

67. CO 267/672/7, 14 June 1939.

68. Spitzer and Denzer, "Wallace-Johnson . . . Part II."

69. McCaskie, "Writing, Reading."

70. Linda Hutcheon, *A Theory of Parody: The Teachings of Twentieth-Century Art Forms* (London: Methuen, 1985).

71. See Spitzer and Denzer, "Wallace-Johnson," and "Wallace-Johnson . . . Part II."

72. The phrase "adamantine chains" is lifted from John Milton's *Paradise Lost*, and refers to how Satan was "Hurled headlong flaming from th' ethereal sky / With hideous ruin and combustion, down / To bottomless perdition, there to dwell / In adamantine chains and penal firecast into hell" (Book I, lines 45–48). To associate "Banky" with Milton's vision of Satan adds further insult to the "obituary."

73. CO 267/671/ 8, n.d.

74. CO 267/671/ 8. This verse parodies the nursery rhyme "Ding dong bell / Pussy's in the well / Who put her in? / Little Johnny Flynn / Who pulled her out? / Little Tommy Stout / What a naughty boy was that / Try to drown poor Pussycat / Who ne'er did any harm / But killed all the mice / In the Farmer's barn," though

it should perhaps be noted that in earlier versions of this song the cat is left—as Banky—to drown unceremoniously in the well.

75. CO 267/671/ 8.

76. Robert Fraser, "Biography and the Morality of Style," inaugural lecture, Open University, Milton Keynes, 24 January 2012.

77. "The future of reputation" borrows from the title of a book by Daniel J. Solove, *The Future of Reputation: Gossip, Rumor, and Privacy on the Internet* (New Haven: Yale University Press, 2008).

78. See John B. Thompson, "The New Visibility," *Theory, Culture and Society* 22, no. 6 (2005): 31–51.

79. By 1963, Wallace-Johnson's one- and two-page publications were written under his new alias, "Professor W. Daniels." These Swiftean political satires—typed and photocopied rather than professionally printed—contained poetry and gossip about the corruption of unnamed local personalities. By July 1963, they had expanded to two pages (four sides), hand-stapled together, often carrying pseudocorrespondence pointing out Wallace-Johnson's political marginalization by ruling African elites (e.g., J/X/0705/1 [45], 16 December 1963). Printed by the Sierra Leone National Service Bureau (SALNEB), of which Wallace-Johnson was proprietor, editor. and chairman, these "kitchen-press" type publications were initially marked for sale at 3d per sheet, and changed to 15 cents at independence. The British Library holding of the "SALNEB Publications" runs from 25 June 1963 to 29 July 1965, including an issue on 11 May 1965 announcing Wallace-Johnson's death in a car accident in Accra, followed by a special obituary edition (J/X/0705/1, "SALNEB Publication Series 2: 11 May 1965; 17 June 1965).

80. See Michael Jindra and Joël Noret, eds., *Funerals in Africa: Explorations of a Social Phenomenon* (New York: Berghahn, 2011).

81. Dollimore, *Death, Desire and Loss.*

Afterword
STEPHANIE NEWELL

Any history of African print cultures will also be, to some extent, part of a broader history of elites and intelligentsias on the continent. The extent to which this can be mapped directly onto class in Africa is open to further investigation, but the essays in this collection clearly suggest that a history of print in Africa is part of a social, economic, and political story about the emergence and power struggles of what Karin Barber calls "local intellectuals" in relation to regional and international pressures.[1]

Alongside established elites, the assertiveness of educated subelites as writers, readers, literary activists, and discussants has featured prominently in this volume. As Duncan Omanga vividly demonstrates in his study of one "people's parliament" in Eldoret, western Kenya, the newspaper makes possible a particular type of interpretative community, bringing together urban residents in a noisily discursive public space.

Given the recent proliferation of postcolonial book history projects, and given the regrettable lack of attention to African (or, for that matter, any other non-European) languages in many of these studies, the chapters by Karin Barber, Hlonipha Mokoena, Kelly Askew, Oluwatoyin Oduntan, Emma Hunter, Uta Reuster-Jahn, Olubukola Gbadegesin, and Rebecca Jones become all the more significant as contributions to the study of print cultures. Each of these chapters demonstrates that African-language material cannot simply be passed through the dominant framework for interpreting postcolonial literary agency, whereby local authors are seen to assert their subjectivity in the face of a global or hegemonic (neo)colonial gaze, either by resisting the efforts of international publishers to exoticize them, or, according to a similar earlier model, by reacting against the imperial "center."[2]

These contributors seek to understand African print cultures through linguistically rooted concepts, and they show how the use of African languages can affect the content and form of printed texts. Local epistemological and aesthetic categories are perhaps more visible within African-language material than in European-language texts, such as the Yoruba distinction between types of knowledge as "firsthand" and "secondhand" (Jones) or Swahili ideals of linguistic beauty (Askew). As Olubukola Gbadegesin shows in her study of the multinational genealogy of Yoruba photonovels from the late 1960s, print enables technologically mediated, contemporary versions of established art forms and genres to be reiterated in print.

In charting this lineage, contributors such as Askew and Jones ask about the extent to which oral and printed literary genres engage differently from one another with the past, and preserve different types of historical narrative (or historical bias) for posterity. Imperial margins and centers dissolve into the background of many of the print cultures studied in this volume. Stark accounts of colonial and postcolonial conflicts are replaced by sensitivity to alternative, transnational print networks that, if they engage with colonialism at all, are not caught up in its priorities or spaces (see James, this volume).

Perhaps most significantly in terms of analytical frameworks, a sense of the ordinariness and everydayness of textual production is highlighted by numerous contributors. As Rebecca Jones demonstrates in her study of Yoruba travel writing in the 1920s and 1930s, a matter as apparently mundane as the affordability and accessibility of public transport can give rise to a proliferation of new, experimental literary genres in the newspapers. Jones finds that the practicalities of travel contributed to experiments with print, as an expansion of the Nigerian transport infrastructure in the 1920s enabled Lagosian journalists to move easily around the country, writing about what they saw, publishing it for consumption back home in Lagos, and, in the process, changing the very notion of "home" for Lagosians.

In spite of the complexities and crossovers between oral and printed genres, a focus on printed literatures is historically revealing in several significant ways. First, as mentioned above, a history of print in Africa is also, to some extent, a history of literate elites on the continent. The first indigenous printing presses were set up by established professional elites and remained in their hands long after decolonization. Second—and directly related to the concept of "modern African history"—the rise of the printing press in Africa brought with it particular types of historical narration that are inextricable from print.

In West Africa at least, a change of attitude toward orality occurred among literate African elites during the colonial period. Faced with colonial regimes that were obsessed with the production, dissemination, and preservation of reports, legal rulings, court transcripts, and government ordinances, between the 1880s and the 1920s African newspaper editors and members of local intelligentsias expressed ever-increasing anxieties that their communities would "forget" local histories and lose touch with long-established, but unwritten, customs and legal paradigms. In the absence of printed versions, the argument ran, African precedents would disappear beneath the distorting weight of colonial documents. "Those who possess information that will be useful to the student of the history and customs of our forefathers are often illiterate," wrote the editor of the *Gold Coast Nation* in 1915, and as a result, "in 20 years' time much interesting and useful knowledge will have been lost to the nation if immediate efforts are not made to gather it now."[3] In response to this relabeling of orality as illiteracy, numerous works of legal and cultural history were printed by educated professional elites in West Africa, the majority of whom were also founding members of political organizations. With titles such as *The Truth about the West African Land Question* (Casely Hayford [first published 1898], 1971) and *The Akan Doctrine of God* (Danquah, 1944), elite historians made a bid to capture African legal and cultural practices for posterity, and to create a literature to support their assertions of African identity.

Colonial legislation such as the marriage ordinances of the 1880s, and the contentious land bills between the 1890s and the 1910s, gave rise to a body of historical writing by local intellectuals on topics such as customary law and "native" jurisprudence. Meticulously researched, their weighty tomes were published in London from the 1890s onward. This printed material served not only to explain but also to reify customary law, and on occasion, colonial administrators found themselves turning to these books for case studies and legal precedents when deciding on land tenure legislation.

The political elites who produced these volumes also wrote works of fiction: it is as if they wished to vitalize their retrieved, freshly preserved historical worlds with speaking subjects, and to insert Africans into the histories they produced. Perhaps the most famous example of this is Sol Plaatje's *Mhudi* (1930), a historical novel set during the *mfecane* (the period of intense warfare and displacement in South Africa between the 1810s and 1840s). One of Plaatje's declared objectives in *Mhudi* was, "with the readers' money, to collect and print (for Bantu Schools) Sechuana folk-tales, which, with the spread of European ideas, are fast being forgotten. It is thus hoped to arrest this process by cultivating a love for art and literature in the Vernacular."[4] Other novels and plays by prominent African historians and political figures include *Ethiopia Unbound* (1911) by J. E. Casely Hayford, *The Blinkards* (1915) and T*he Anglo-Fanti* (1918) by Kobina Sekyi, and *The Third Woman* by J. B. Danquah (1943), not to mention the literary activities of later political leaders, such as Julius K. Nyerere (1922–99), who translated scripture and at least two Shakespeare plays into Swahili.[5]

Later African authors inherited this bias. "Some historical data was given to me by the old men of the tribe," wrote Bessie Head in a footnote to her southern African short story, "The Deep River: A Story of Ancient Tribal Migration":

> But it was unreliable as their memories had tended to fail them. A reconstruction was made therefore in my own imagination; I am also partly indebted to the London Missionary Society's "Livingstone Tswana Readers," *Padiso III*, school textbook, for those graphic paragraphs on the harvest thanksgiving ceremony which appear in the story.[6]

For more than a century, African literate elites used the medium of print to intervene in and "save" what they perceived to be vulnerable oral archives, or disappearing histories. This literature provided the cultural material that accompanied the same Africans' political struggles for self-rule.[7] Printed literature therefore generated new ways of representing and regarding the past, and the history of creative writing is intricately bound up with the history of African print cultures.

In his classic text *Imagined Communities*, Benedict Anderson offers a powerful description of the capacity of printed materials—specifically newspapers—to conjure up and convene reading communities that are invisible physically to one another, but in close proximity as members of national or regional spaces. Newspaper readers, he observes, consume the same daily or weekly text in the disembodied public space of the imagined community.[8] Anderson's conceptualizations of the relationship between newspapers and nationalism, and the dispersed presence of readers, are confirmed and extended in significant ways by Emma Hunter in her chapter on late colonial newspapers in Tanzania, by David Pratten in his examination of J. V. Clinton's political ambitions as a newspaper editor, and by Karin Barber in her examination of the reasons for the remarkable flowering of experimental Yoruba-language writing in Lagosian newspapers in the 1920s.

In more than a century of printing and publishing activity in Africa, an enormous diversity of textual practices can be categorized as "print cultures." One common theme to emerge from the many perspectives in this volume, however, is that material that might easily be labeled "ephemeral"—newspapers, leaflets, pamphlets, magazines, posters, and brochures—may, in certain circumstances, be treasured and preserved by consumers, transformed into art, artifact, or archive, given status and endowed with visible places in people's homes. What readers *do* with texts is an essential element of the history of print, in Africa as anywhere else. For this reason, it is necessary for us, as cultural historians, to displace the conjectural figure of "the reader," and to shift our focus onto historically situated readers of texts. Such a shift is not designed to reinstate an essentialist category of "real readers" over and against the implied or ideal readers suggested within texts. Nor is it designed to fetishize print in opposition to orality. The point is that readers are elusive and mobile: they respond in multiple ways to printed material; they participate in public cultures as interpreters of texts; and, on occasion, they produce their own texts. We must therefore look not simply for what people are reading, but also for what their textual interpretations reveal about local attitudes toward the *value* of literacy, in an economic, aesthetic, and moral sense.

Print cultures and technologies (including contemporary social media) offer opportunities and outlets for writers and readers that are different from oral or manuscript forms of dissemination. For scholars of African print cultures, printed literatures have relatively traceable pasts, leaving us with limited but accessible residues in the form of archives, libraries, and private collections. Printed texts also possess historical currency—or historicity—as texts that have not been updated or revised for recent audiences. This apparent permanence of accessibility can give rise to problematic assumptions, however, including the idea expressed above by literate elites in the colonial period, that printed texts are more authentic than the partial and provisional nature of oral genres. As the book historian and theorist Henri Lefebvre notes, however, print itself is partial because spaces of reception are produced differently in each society.[9]

PRINTING LIVES

From Uta Reuster-Jahn's exemplary Swahili author, Faraji H. H. Katalambulla, to Wale Adebanwi's study of Herbert Macaulay's contributions to the Nigerian press, and David Pratten's compelling "story of the life and career of a provincial creole printman," biography has surfaced in this volume as a prominent genre for the analysis of African print cultures. What are the implications of writing African cultural history through the framework of biography? The genre of life-writing generally focuses upon an individual or set of individuals in relation to contexts: are we, in other words, reproducing an individualistic approach to the study of culture through our emphasis on an individual's contributions, innovations, and emergence into public spaces?

Hlonipha Mokoena exposes and problematizes such an approach in her examination of Magema Fuze's practice of "self-archiving" in the 1890s and early twentieth century. Biographers have, she points out, produced a particular version of Fuze that is disrupted by hitherto neglected material by Fuze. In bringing this material to our attention, Mokoena shows how Fuze was a "unique biographical subject" who consciously and deliberately attempted to produce himself for posterity. The story of Fuze presents us, as scholars, with methodological challenges to our desire to impose singularity or coherence on a subject's life. African print cultures through the decades display numerous examples of playfulness with singular notions of naming and subjectivity. Indeed, the very nature of print, with its offer of typefaces rather than recognizable faces, invites an antibiographical mode of analysis. When approaching the *subject* of print, therefore, we need to exercise methodological caution in order to prevent an assumption that named and traceable individuals produce named and traceable texts.

THE VECTOR OF GENDER

Literacy and newspaper production were male dominated until at least the mid-1960s throughout Africa, as were the fields of publishing and creative writing. With few exceptions, elite men controlled the majority of African printing presses on the continent.[10] Political power as well as opposition to, and participation in, the colonial state were also largely mediated by men.

Men did not exercise hegemony over all modes of representation in the public sphere, however: some genres remained, and remain, under the ownership of women. These genres vary greatly according to region and social factors such as the seniority and the kinship status of narrators, but "feminine" genres might include funeral odes, songs of abuse, lullabies, and moral folktales.[11] The point is that particular types of discourse, and particular language registers, were often regarded by their intended audiences as having legitimacy only if presented by recognized physical agents for those genres.

Debates about gender roles and interrelationships are inextricable from the rise of print cultures in Africa. The businesses and outlets described in this book are mostly by owned and managed by men. As Hunter points out in her chapter, this must affect our understanding of any "unity"—national or otherwise—generated by newspapers and print cultures, especially in the context of the prevalent debates about marriage, polygyny, and gendered behavior in the printed materials themselves. African print cultures have been heavily gendered: in colonial Tanzania in the 1950s, Hunter finds, the topic of femininity was inextricable from printed debates about the pros and cons of customary versus modern types of marriage, about bride-wealth, and about female circumcision. As a consequence of these factors, women's contributions to print have been rather different from men's, occupying different positions in the story of print in Africa.

Colonial (and, in South Africa, apartheid) legislative interventions in the intricacies and intimacies of ordinary people's lives led to the emergence of new forms of social recognition as the state acknowledged the legitimacy of some domestic models above others. Women's rights, obligations, behavior, morality, sexuality, and roles within marriage were dominant and resilient topics in locally owned newspapers between the mid-1880s and the 1930s. Contemporary African popular literature and film continue this engagement with gender. If it was not politicized before the 1880s, gender became politicized as a consequence of these legal interventions, literally "bound up" with African elites' printed assertions of cultural identity and political authority in relation to the colonial state.

The essays in this volume reveal the unique historicity of printed materials as vectors both for the study of modern African cultures and also for the study of how those cultures came to produce and represent themselves. From the literary experiments of Yoruba newspaper contributors in the 1920s and 1930s to the poetic activities of Swahili authors in the 1990s, this book has demonstrated how attention to print in different parts of the continent provides a great deal of information about local aesthetic preferences and changing patterns of taste and consumption among ordinary Africans.

BIBLIOGRAPHY

Anderson, Benedict. *Imagined Communities: Reflections on the Origins and Spread of Nationalism*. Rev. ed. London: Verso, 1991.

Ashcroft, Bill, Gareth Griffiths, and Helen Tiffin. *The Empire Writes Back: Theory and Practice in Post-colonial Literatures*. London: Routledge, 1989.

Barber, Karin. "Editorial." *Africa* 78, no. 3 (2008): 327–32.
Casely Hayford, J. E. *Ethiopia Unbound: Studies in Race Emancipation.* 2nd ed. London: Frank Cass, 1966.
Danquah, J. B. *The Third Woman: A Play in Five Acts.* London: Lutterworth Press, 1943.
Denzer, LaRay. "Yoruba Women: A Historiographical Study." *International Journal of African Historical Studies* 27, no. 1 (1994): 1–39.
Furniss, Graham, and Liz Gunner, eds. *Power, Marginality and African Oral Literature.* Cambridge: Cambridge University Press, 1995.
Gilman, Lisa. *The Dance of Politics: Gender, Performance and Democratization in Malawi.* Philadelphia: Temple University Press, 2009.
Head, Bessie. *The Collector of Treasures and Other Botswana Village Tales.* London: Heinemann, 1977.
Huggan, Graham. *The Postcolonial Exotic: Marketing the Margins.* New York: Routledge, 2001.
Lefebvre, Henri. *The Production of Space.* Translated by Donald Nicholson-Smith. Oxford: Blackwell, 1991.
Plaatje, Sol T. *Mhudi: An Epic of South African Native Life a Hundred Years Ago.* 1930. Edited by Stephen Gray. Oxford: Heinemann Educational Books, 1978.
Sekyi, Kobina. "The Anglo-Fanti." *West Africa,* 25 May 1918—28 September 1918.
Sekyi, Kobina. *The Blinkards: A Comedy.* 1915. Ibadan: Heinemann, 1974.
Senkoro, F. E. M. K. "Understanding Gender through Genre: Oral Literature as a Vehicle for Gender Studies in East Africa." http://www.codesria.org/IMG/pdf/SENKORO-1.pdf (accessed: 14 August 2014).

NOTES TO AFTERWORD

1. Karin Barber, "Editorial," *Africa* 78, no. 3 (2008): 330–22.

2. Graham Huggan, *The Postcolonial Exotic: Marketing the Margins* (New York: Routledge, 2001); Bill Ashcroft, Gareth Griffiths, and Helen Tiffin, *The Empire Writes Back: Theory and Practice in Post-colonial Literatures* (London: Routledge, 1989).

3. Editorial, "National and Historical Research," *Gold Coast Nation,* 13 May 1915, 933.

4. Sol T. Plaatje, *Mhudi: An Epic of South African Native Life a Hundred Years Ago,* ed. Stephen Gray (1930; Oxford: Heinemann Educational Books, 1978), 3.

5. Stephen Arnold, "Tanzania," in *European-Language Writing in Sub-Saharan Africa: A Comparative History of Literatures in European Languages,* ed. Albert S. Gérard (Amsterdam: John Benjamins, 1986), 951.

6. Bessie Head, "The Deep River: A Story of Ancient Tribal Migration," in *The Collector of Treasures and Other Botswana Village Tales* (London: Heinemann, 1977), 6.

7. Following in their wake, the writers of the 1950s and 1960s often focused on cultural retrievals of precolonial traditions, or criticized the white "boss," the European missionary, and the destruction of local cultures and institutions under the legal and political impact of colonial rule.

8. Benedict Anderson, *Imagined Communities: Reflections on the Origins and Spread of Nationalism*, rev. ed. (London: Verso, 1991), 37–46.

9. Henri Lefebvre, *The Production of Space*, trans. Donald Nicholson-Smith (Oxford: Blackwell, 1991), 46.

10. See LaRay Denzer, "Yoruba Women: A Historiographical Study," *International Journal of African Historical Studies* 27, no. 1 (1994): 1–39.

11. For a sample of the many publications in this area, see F. E. M. K. Senkoro, "Understanding Gender through Genre: Oral Literature as a Vehicle for Gender Studies in East Africa," http://www.codesria.org/IMG/pdf/SENKORO-1.pdf (accessed 14 Aug 2014); Graham Furniss and Liz Gunner, eds., *Power, Marginality and African Oral Literature* (Cambridge: Cambridge University Press, 1995); Lisa Gilman, *The Dance of Politics: Gender, Performance and Democratization in Malawi* (Philadelphia: Temple University Press, 2009).

CONTRIBUTORS

Wale Adebanwi is an associate professor in African American and African Studies, University of California, Davis. He received a PhD in political science at the University of Ibadan, Nigeria, and another in social anthropology from the University of Cambridge. He is presently a Visiting Professor at Rhodes University, Grahamstown, South Africa. He is the author of *Yoruba Elites and Ethnic Politics in Nigeria: Obafemi Awolowo and Corporate Agency* (2014) and *Authority Stealing: Anti-corruption War and Democratic Politics in Post-military Nigeria* (2012). In addition, he has edited or coedited five books on democracy, democratization, politics, the state, and public intellectuals. His essays on the media have appeared in peer-reviewed journals such as *Media, Culture and Society*, *African Studies Review* and *Nationalism and Ethnic Politics*.

Kelly Askew is Director of the African Studies Center and Professor of Anthropology and African-American and African Studies at the University of Michigan. She has worked for over two decades in Tanzania and Kenya. Her writings and documentary film projects span two primary research areas: poetic arts as vehicles for populist engagement with politics, and the formalization of property rights. Recent films include *Poetry in Motion: 100 Years of Zanzibar's Nadi Ikhwan Safaa* (Buda Musique, 2016) on Zanzibar's oldest *taarab* orchestra; and *The Chairman and the Lions* (Documentary Educational Resources, 2013), which won first place at the ETNOFilm Festival (Croatia, 2013) and a Special Jury Award at the Zanzibar International Film Festival (Tanzania, 2013). She is currently in postproduction on a new film entitled *Maasai Remix* about indigenous creativity in addressing challenges to Maasai pastoralist livelihoods.

Karin Barber is Professor of African Cultural Anthropology at the University of Birmingham, United Kingdom. Her research focuses on Yoruba oral literature, popular theater, and print culture in Nigeria. She has also done comparative work on popular culture and textual production across Africa. Her recent books include *The Anthropology of Texts, Persons and Publics* (2007) and *Print Culture and the First Yoruba Novel* (2012).

Olubukola A. Gbadegesin received her PhD in art history from Emory University. Her research interests center on photography, portraiture, the politics of representation, and print culture in Africa and the diaspora. She is currently working on a book manuscript titled "Picturing Modern Selves in Colonized Places: Photography as a Strategy of Power in Lagos, Nigeria."

Emma Hunter is a Lecturer in African history at the University of Edinburgh. Her research focuses on the intellectual and political history of twentieth-century East Africa, particularly the history of political thought and the history of print culture, including newspapers and periodicals. She is the author of *Political Thought and the Public Sphere in Tanzania: Freedom, Democracy and Citizenship in the Era of Decolonization* (2015). Other major publications include "'Our Common Humanity': Print, Power and the Colonial Press in Interwar Tanganyika and French Cameroun," *Journal of Global History* 7, no. 2 (2012) and "Dutiful Subjects, Patriotic Citizens and the Concept of 'Good Citizenship' in Twentieth-Century Tanzania," *Historical Journal* 56, no. 1 (2013).

Leslie James is Leverhulme Early Career Fellow in the Department of African Studies and Anthropology, University of Birmingham. Her work focuses on the political and intellectual history of anti-imperialism in Britain and its empire, and of decolonization in Africa and the Caribbean. Her publications include *George Padmore and Decolonization from Below* (2015); *Decolonization and the Cold War: Negotiating Independence* (coedited with E. Leake, 2015), and an article in *Journal of Imperial and Commonwealth History*.

Rebecca Jones was awarded her PhD from the University of Birmingham in 2014, for a thesis on the cultural history of Nigerian travel writing in Yoruba and English. Prior to this, she received a BA in English from the University of Cambridge and an MA in African studies from the School of Oriental and African Studies, where she first studied Yoruba. She currently holds a postdoctoral research fellowship as part of the European Research Council–funded "Knowing Each Other" project, based at the University of Birmingham, which researches interreligious encounters in southwestern Nigeria.

Hlonipha Mokoena received her PhD from the University of Cape Town in 2005. She is currently an Associate Professor at the Wits Institute for Social and Economic Research at the University of the Witwatersrand, Johannesburg. She recently published *Magema Fuze: The Making of a Kholwa Intellectual* (2011), which is about Magema Magwaza Fuze, the first Zulu-speaker to publish a book in the language.

Stephanie Newell is Professor of English at Yale University. Her research focuses on the history of the public sphere in colonial West Africa and issues of gender, sexuality, and power as articulated through popular print cultures, including newspapers and pamphlets. She has published widely on the cultural histories of printing and reading in West Africa, and the spaces for local creativity and subversive resistance in colonial-era newspapers. Her most recent book is *The Power to Name: A History of Anonymity in Colonial West Africa* (2013).

Oluwatoyin Babatunde Oduntan holds a PhD from Dalhousie University, Canada, and currently teaches African history at Towson University, Maryland, United States. He focuses his research on elite formation and the intellectual ideas behind cultural identities in Africa. His publications include "Power Politics among Abeokuta Elites during the 19th Century," *African Nebula* 1 (2010): 12–25; "Samuel Johnson 1846–1901," in *Encyclopedia of African Thought*, edited by Abiola Irele and Biodun Jeyifo (2010); and "Iwe Irohin and the Representation of the Universal in 19th Century Abeokuta," *History in Africa* 32, no. 2 (2005): 295–305.

Duncan Omanga is the Head of Department, Publishing and Media Studies, Moi University, and cofounder of the Hillary Ngweno Centre for East African Media Research. His research interests are in print cultures, media ecologies, and digital media in Africa.

Derek R. Peterson is Professor of African History at the University of Michigan. He is the editor or co-editor of six books, most recently (with Kodzo Gavua and Ciraj Rassool) *The Politics of Heritage in Africa* (2015). His monograph, *Ethnic Patriotism and the East African Revival: A History of Dissent* (2012), won the Herskovits Prize of the African Studies Association and the Martin Klein Prize of the American Historical Association.

David Pratten is Associate Professor at the African Studies Centre and Institute of Social and Cultural Anthropology, Oxford University. He is author of *The Man-Leopard Murders: History and Society in Colonial Nigeria* (2007) and coedits *Africa: The Journal of the International African Institute*. His research focuses on youth, vigilantism, and masking.

Uta Reuster-Jahn, PhD, is a Lecturer of Swahili at the Asien-Afrika-Institut of Hamburg University, Germany. She is the coeditor, with Matthias Krings, of *Bongo Media Worlds: Producing and Consuming Popular Culture in Dar es Salaam* (2014) and, with Anja Oed, of *Beyond the Language Issue: The Production, Reception and Mediation of Creative Writing in African Languages* (2008). Her articles on Swahili popular literature and culture, youth language, Bongo Flava music, and storytelling practices have appeared in a number of edited volumes and journals. She is currently working on a book on Swahili popular literature and magazines in Tanzania.

INDEX

"A Banker" (editorialist), 5, 9
Abantu Abamnyama Lapa Bavela Ngakona (book), 366, 368, 377, 381
Abantu Batho (newspaper), 18, 366–67
Abęokuta, 29, 309
　politics of, 310–12, 317–19, 322–28
abolitionism, 9–10, 40
Abrahams, Peter, 57
Action Group, 254, 270
addressivity, 157–74
Adubi War, 319
African-American and Afro-Caribbean newspapers, 20–21, 25, 51–55, 58–65, 88–90, 91–93
African Film (magazine), 227, 228, 252–53, 255, 264
African Messenger (newspaper), 155
African Morning Post (newspaper), 51, 54, 55, 57, 90, 395, 410
African Orthodox Church, 20
African Standard (newspaper), 410
African Worker (newspaper), 63
Afrika Kwetu (newspaper), 186
Afro-American (newspaper), 88
Aggrey, James E.K., 396
Ajasa, Kitoyi, 135, 169
Ajiṣafę, A.K., 105–6, 111, 313
Akede Eko (newspaper), 26, 102, 113–17, 155, 163, 165, 170, 173, 326
Akintan, E.A., 105, 109, 111, 156, 164, 170
Alakija, Adeyemo, 169
Alidina, Murtaza, 234, 240, 241, 242
amakholwa, 362–63
Amin, Idi, 31, 238
Amsterdam News (newspaper), 56, 86
Anderson, Benedict, 51, 75, 76, 284, 428

Annan, Kofi, 14, 338, 343, 345
Ashanti Pioneer (newspaper), 20, 31, 49–50, 51, 57, 60–61
Ashton, Edith O., 12
Associated Press, 379
Atīrīrī (newspaper), 21–22, 32
Atọka: The Yoruba Photoplay Series (magazine), 256, 271–72
Attoh-Ahuma, Rev. S.R.B., 396
audiences, 9–11, 13–15, 32, 114–16, 157–74, 177, 269–72, 335, 365–67
authorship, 9–10, 22–25, 30, 108–9, 116, 117, 156–74, 364–67, 374–81
autobiography, 110, 368, 377, 381
Awolowo, Ọbafẹmi, 3
Azikiwe, Nnamdi, 3, 9, 54, 55, 63, 90–93, 95, 172, 395, 410

Baddeley, F.M., 135
Bakhtin, Mikael, 163
Ballantyne, Tony, 7, 285
Baltimore Afro-American (newspaper), 56
Bamgbọṣe, D., 315
Bankole-Bright, Herbert, 412–13
Bantu Film (magazine), 237–38
Baralong (people), 2
Baraza (newspaper), 197, 203–4, 226
Barbados Advocate (newspaper), 56
Barber, Karin, 251, 257, 285, 316, 337, 392
Barghash b. Saïd, 7
Bawji, Saidi, 238
Beacon (newspaper), 53
Benjamin, Walter, 375
Bermuda Recorder (newspaper), 56
Biafra, 197, 255
Biersteker, Anne, 181

439

biography, 4, 12, 80, 109, 368, 377, 379–81, 390–96, 413–14, 430
booksellers, 225, 234, 240, 394–95
Blyden, Edward Wilmot, 76, 394–95
Brennan, James, 182
Bryant, A.T., 375
Buganda (kingdom)
  boycott of Indian traders in, 18
  government of, 13
  Kabaka's deportation (1953–55) and, 15–16
  newspapers in, 15–16
  populism in, 10
Bukya na Gandi (newspaper), 2
Burton, Antoinette, 5
Bustamenta, Alexander, 64
Butler, Tubal Uriah, 53, 64

Calabar Youth League Movement, 82, 91
Callaway, Henry, 375
Cameron, Sir Donald, 139
Casely Hayford, J.E., 76, 79, 427
censorship, 18–22, 30–32, 54–55, 230, 236, 240
Chagga, 28–29, 283, 286–300
Cheka (magazine), 240
Chicago Defender (newspaper), 53, 55, 57, 86, 88, 89
chiefs, 16–18, 312, 322–28
cinema, 19–20, 233
Clarion (newspaper), 56
Clark, Ebun, 254
Clifford, Governor Hugh, 126, 133, 136–37, 155
  competence in English of, 171
Clinton, James Vivian, 13, 15, 25–26, 75, 78–96
Colclough, Stephen, 116
Cole, Patrick, 133
Coleman, James Smoot, 3
Colenso, Bishop John W., 4–5, 23, 362, 367–68, 372, 377
Colonial Office (London), 55
Convention People's Party, 50
Cooper, Frederick, 140

copyright, 5–6
Couzens, Tim, 379
Crisis (magazine), 20, 86
Crowther, Samuel Ajayi, 106, 125
culling, 5–6, 62–65, 85–86, 368
Cummings-John, Constance Agatha, 407

Daily Herald (newspaper), 62, 89
Daily Mail (newspaper), 126, 132, 133
Danquah, J.B., 427, 428
Ddobozi lya Buganda (newspaper), 15
democracy, 4, 191, 242, 290, 318, 341
Deniga, Adeoye, 156, 170
DhoLuo (language), 11, 12
Doke, Clement, 363
Domingo, Wilfrid A., 53, 54
Donnellan, Kay, 54
Douglass, Frederick, 52
Drum (magazine), 27–28, 227, 251, 255, 361
Dube, John, 30, 364, 371
DuBois, W.E.B., 20, 52, 395

East African Standard (newspaper), 8, 21, 181
Ebifa mu Buganda (newspaper), 5
Economic Crimes Bill (1983), 242
editors
  alliances of, 19–20
  and anti-colonialism, 127, 141–44
  and modernity, 128–30
  anonymity of, 294
  as moral reformers, 13, 229–30
  of photoplays, 258–59, 262, 269
  and public sphere, 172–74
  and readers, 2, 14, 104–5, 110–17, 230–31, 269–72
  in socialist Tanzania, 224–25
  training of, 8, 369–70
  as voice of the people, 15–16, 81–84
  and work, 1–2, 373–74
  writing strategies of, 26–27, 155–74
Edwin, Walter, I., 172
Egbaland Echo (newspaper), 328
Eko Akete (newspaper), 105, 156, 160, 170, 173

Eldoret, 335–53
"Eleko question", 18, 26, 27, 125–27, 130, 132–44, 154–55
Eleti-Ọfẹ (newspaper), 103, 163, 165, 170
English (language)
  contrasted with Yoruba, 156–74
  in East African newspapers, 8–9
  status and, 169–74
  and Zulu, 375–77
Equator Film (magazine), 238
von Eschen, Penny, 51, 86, 87
ethnography, 108–9
Evening Standard (newspaper), 61

Fahari (magazine), 240
Fallers, Lloyd, 17
Fiah, Erica, 184
fiction, 22–25, 163–74, 227, 241–42, 243
Film Tanzania (magazine), 227–36, 242, 243
Fọlarin, Adebẹshin, 313
Freetown, 78–79, 325, 407, 410–12
Frelimo, 198,
French (language)
  in newspapers, 8–9, 11
Fuze, Magema, 4, 362–81

Gamble, Richard Ian, 255
Gandhi, Mahatma, 3, 361–62, 365
Ganzel, Eddie, 232
Garvey, Marcus, 20, 52
La Gazette du Cameroun (newspaper), 7
Gikuyu (Kikuyu)
  language, 10, 11, 13, 21, 32
  people, 10–11, 21
Gocking, Roger, 315
Gold Coast Independent (newspaper), 62
Gold Coast Leader (newspaper), 5–6, 8, 108–9, 140, 396
Gold Coast Nation (newspaper), 396, 427
Gold Coast Spectator (newspaper), 62
government
  and anti-colonialism, 76, 127, 141–44, 410
  newspapers of, 7–8, 226–27, 290–94

  in post-colonial Africa, 30–32, 225–26, 228–29
  press controls and, 18–22, 30–32, 54–55, 230, 236, 240, 413

Habari (newspaper), 20
Habari za Upare (newspaper), 288, 290, 293, 287–88
Haggard, H. Rider, 107
Hamasa (magazine), 236
Harlem Renaissance, 52
Harrison, Hubert H., 49
Haugerud, Angelique, 340
Head, Bessie, 428
Heko (magazine), 240, 243
Hofmeyr, Isabel, 3, 5, 11, 361
Hughes, Heather, 365, 379
Hughes, Langston, 89
Hutchison, Charles Francis, 395

Ibadan, 102, 325
Ibhawoh, Bonny, 126
Ibibio Union, 82
Igbo (language), 104
Ilanga lase Natal (newspaper), 30, 364–66, 371, 373
Imvo Zabantsundu (newspaper), 8
India, 362, 365
Indian Opinion (newspaper), 361–62, 365
indirect rule, 16–18, 130, 173, 312, 314–15
Inkanyiso Yase Natal (newspaper), 7, 369, 370
International Phonetic Alphabet, 12
International Press Institute, 31
Ipepo lo Hlanga (newspaper), 23, 364, 369, 378
Italo-Abyssinian Crisis, 53, 85, 87
Ìtàn Èmi Ọmọ-Orùkàn (novel), 109, 165
Ìtàn Ìgbésí-Aiyé Èmi Ṣegilọlá (novel), 22, 109, 117, 165–69, 326
Ito, Eyo, 81
Iwe Irohin (newspaper), 7, 176, 309–10

Jabavu, John Tengo, 8
Jackson, J.P., 169

Jardine, Sir Douglas, 410–11
Joe (magazine), 238
Johari (magazine), 240
July, Robert, 3

Kadalie, Clements, 53
Kamkanda, Tonny, 238
Kasoma, Francis, 4
Kassim Mussa Kassam, 240
Katalambulla, Faraji, 2, 22, 31, 226–36, 245
Kegode, Francis, 14, 336, 342–53
Kenya, 10–11
  deliberative cultures of, 339–42
  Mau Mau detention camps in, 21–22
  newspapers of, 347–48
  politics of, 338, 341–42, 345, 347–53
  "street parliaments" in, 335–53
Kenyatta, Jomo, 3, 8, 30
Kennedy, John F., 187
Kennedy, Robert, 197
Kezilahabi, Euphrase, 182
Khumalo, Vukile, 368
Kibaki, Mwai, 338, 345, 351, 352
Kikuyu *see* Gikuyu
King, Dr. Martin Luther, 187, 197
Kiongozi (newspaper), 183, 226
Kipling, Rudyard, 49
Kiwanuka, Joseph, 15–16, 31
Komkya (newspaper), 28–29, 283–300, 337
Krings, Matthias, 252
Kusare (newspaper), 188, 290
Kwetu (newspaper), 184

Lagos, 10, 18, 26, 27, 77, 92, 102, 107–8
  and Abẹokuta, 311, 317
  and the "Eleko Question", 125–27, 132–44, 154–55
  elite in, 169–70, 306–7
  government of, 131–44, 153–54
  literacy levels in, 154
  lower classes in, 173–74
  newspapers in, 10–11, 18, 26, 27, 103, 105, 107–8, 116, 131, 141–42, 151–53, 173–74, 176

Lagos Daily News (newspaper), 17, 26, 127, 129, 131, 135–44, 169, 315
Lagos Standard (newspaper), 8, 169, 170, 311
Lagos Weekly News (newspaper), 140
Lagos Weekly Record (newspaper), 125, 136, 155, 156, 169, 170, 176
La Hausse, Paul, 362–65, 374–75
Lamula, Petros, 374
Lango (language), 12
language
  in East and West Africa, 10–11
  English and Yoruba contrasted, 156–74
  English and Zulu, 375–77
  standardization of, 11–12, 14, 31–32, 257
  Swahili in Tanzania, 180–81, 283, 287–89, 295, 298–99
  Zulu epistolary networks, 362–71
Lefebvre, Henri, 429
Le Moniteur du Sénégal et Dépendances (newspaper), 7
Leselinyana la Lesotho (newspaper), 22
Limb, Peter, 366–67
literacy levels, 53, 154, 173, 239, 286, 288, 293, 310–12, 327–28
Liyongo, Fumo, 179
Luganda (language), 11, 12
Lugard, Frederick, 85, 87–88
Lugg, Henry, 375
Luhya (people), 340
Luo (people), 12–13, 339
Luo Union, 12, 340
Luo Thrift and Trading Corporation, 9

Macaulay, Herbert, 3, 15, 17, 26, 32, 63, 76, 125–44, 154, 169, 170
  and the "Eleko Question", 125–27, 132–44
MacDonald, Malcolm, 60
Macmillan, Allister, 395
magazines, 28, 53, 95, 225–45, 293
Magnet: The Nigerian Photoplay Magazine, 255, 264
Mahoko a Becwana (newspaper), 366
Mais, Ralph, 54

Mambo Leo (newspaper), 14, 181, 185, 205–6, 211, 288, 292
Manjwili, Andrew, 234, 236
Marealle, Thomas, 283, 287–90, 299
Marita: Or the Folly of Love (novel), 22
Masuku, N.J.N., 373, 375
Mau Mau detention camps, 21–22
Mayanja, Abubakar, 5
Mbega, Omar, 237
Mbungo, Barnaba, 239
Mchesi (magazine), 240
Mchome, Gray, 234, 236
McLuhan, Marshall, 215, 337
Menon, Dilip, 143
Mhudi (novel), 24, 427
Mia Hôlô (newspaper), 7
missionaries (Christian), 7, 11–12, 183–84, 309–10, 316, 367–68, 369–70, 391, 394
  education and, 80, 127, 311–12, 362
Malakite (church), 10
Mentor, Ralph, 53
modernity, 126–44, 182, 227–30, 251, 255, 309, 313–19, 324, 327
Moeti oa Bochabela (novel), 22
Mofolo, Thomas, 22
Mondlane, Eduardo, 198
Msimulizi (newspaper), 7
Mtobwa, Ben R., 240, 243
Mulira, Eridadi, 2, 12, 13, 16
Mullen, J.G., 108–10
Munyonyozi (newspaper), 10, 16
Mutembei, Aldin, 182
Muyaka bin Haji, 179
Mwafrika (newspaper), 185
Mwananchi Printing and Publishing Company, 226
Mwigwithania (newspaper), 8, 10, 14
Mwinyi, President Ali Hassan, 242, 243

Nairobi, 9, 10–11, 197, 227, 238, 335, 341
National Congress of British West Africa, 79
National Council of Nigeria and the Cameroons, 93
Nation (newspaper), 347

nationalism, 3–4, 16–18, 75–77, 81, 90–91, 95, 144, 286–87, 362, 364, 380–81
Native Land Act (1913), 23–25
Native Life in South Africa (book), 24
Negro Worker (newspaper), 407
Negro World (newspaper), 20, 52
New Film Azania (magazine), 236–37
Newell, Stephanie, 8, 23, 30, 54, 59, 76, 89, 109, 117
newspapers
  advisory role of, 15, 81–84
  African-American and Afro-Caribbean, 20–21, 25, 51–55, 58–65, 88–90, 91–93
  and advertisements, 27, 85, 91, 155, 215, 228, 233, 235, 256, 262, 264–65, 271, 286, 292, 378, 394, 398, 401, 406
  and anti-colonialism, 57–58, 127, 141–44
  audiences of, 10, 13–15, 32, 114–16, 127–28, 157–74, 177, 269–72, 335, 365–67, 374–75
  authorship in, 9–10, 22–25, 30, 108–9, 116, 117, 156–74, 364–67
  in Caribbean, 52–55
  and campaigns, 15–18, 135–44, 317–18
  censorship of, 18–22, 30–32, 54–55, 230, 236
  and chiefs, 16–18, 322–28
  circulation of, 9–11, 27–28, 90–91, 113–17, 151, 153, 173–74, 186, 233, 235, 239, 369–70
  as collectors' items, 29–30
  colonial governments' production of, 7–8, 226–27, 290–94
  contents of, 4–6, 155–57, 197–98
  and culling, 5–6, 50–51, 62–65, 85–86, 231–32, 368
  and democracy, 4
  discourse around, 342–53, 367–71
  in East Africa, 6, 9–11, 181–82
  editors of, 8, 373–74
  experimentation in, 155–64
  and ethnic identity, 28–29, 294–99, 365–67
  fiction in, 22–25, 27, 163–74

and gender, 13, 19, 29, 58, 92, 95, 115, 122, 157, 165–66, 179, 190, 200–205, 229–30, 296–97, 312, 318, 324, 326, 430–31
headlines of, 348–53
juxtaposition in, 58–62
language of, 8–11, 156–74, 287–89
language standardization in, 11–12, 31–32
and libel, 111, 126, 412–13
in Mau Mau detention camps, 21–22
and missions, 7–8, 183–84, 309–10, 367–68, 369–70
and moral reform, 12–13, 229–30, 270–71
and nationalism, 3–4, 15–18, 284, 287, 380–81
networks of, 20–21, 25, 50–51, 110–17, 244–45, 379
obituaries in, 4–5, 199–200, 377–81, 389–92, 396, 398, 401, 407, 410–12
and objectivity, 1–2, 16–18
origins in Africa of, 7–8
and Pan-Africanism, 5, 20–21, 25, 62–65
partisanship of, 1–2, 16–18
and patriotism, 18, 380–81
and poetry, 179–215
in post-colonial Africa, 11, 30–32, 224–26
provincial, 307–9
and pseudonyms, 26, 32, 95, 105, 109, 117, 156, 157, 182, 206, 323, 398, 410
and the public sphere, 9–11, 26, 28, 131, 172–74, 368–71
and race, 5, 20–21, 25, 62–65, 87–90
scholarly appraisals of, 1, 3–4, 181–82, 336–38, 361–62
and sedition, 54, 57, 65, 90, 93, 292, 410–11
and sociability, 14, 104–5, 110–17, 230–31, 364–65
travel writing in, 105–17, 163–64, 367–68
in West Africa, 6, 9–11, 53–54

Ngugi wa Thiong'o, 22
Ngurumo (newspaper), 31
Nicco ye Mbajo, 238
Nigeria, 6, 9, 26, 76, 77, 80, 90–91, 106, 110, 112–14, 126–27, 130, 131, 139, 141, 175, 233
independence of, 254
nationalism in, 17–18, 92–93
Nigerian Daily Times (newspaper), 169
Nigerian Eastern Guardian (newspaper), 95
Nigerian Eastern Mail (newspaper), 13, 15, 25–26, 75, 78, 81–96
Nigerian National Democratic Party, 17, 154
Nigerian Pioneer (newspaper), 135, 136, 137, 154, 156, 158, 169, 176, 311
Nigerian Union of Teachers, 316
Nigerian Youth Movement, 81–82, 317
Nkrumah, Kwame, 3, 11, 30, 50
Nyerere, Julius, 185, 188, 191, 241, 428

obituaries, 4–5, 199–200, 377–81, 396–98, 407, 410–14
Obote, Milton, 31
Odendaal, André, 364
Odinga, Raila, 338, 345, 349, 352
Ogunde, Hubert, 254, 268, 270
Ogunmọla, Kọla, 260
Ohanga, Benaiah, 12, 13
Olden Times in Zululand and Natal, 375
Olympio, Sylvanus, 186
Omu, Fred, 77, 307
"Operation Vijana", 229
Orange Democratic Party, 348
Organization of African and Asian Unity, 187
oríkì, 116, 160, 174
Osumare Egba (newspaper), 15, 29, 307, 315–28

Padmore, George, 5, 20–21, 25, 31, 32, 50, 55–66, 407
Palm Wine Drinkard (novel), 260
Pan-Africanism, 5, 20–21, 25, 62–65, 80, 84, 394–95, 407

Party of National Unity, 348
patriotism, 18, 240
Peel, J.D.Y., 107, 310, 316
Penda Pevu (photonovel), 229
photographs, 258, 262, 269
photonovels, 22, 229, 232–38, 252–54, 426
photoplays, 252–72
Picha ya Pacha (play), 22, 231
Pilgrim's Progress (book), 107
Pittsburgh Courier (newspaper), 53, 55, 57, 86
Plaatje, Solomon, 1, 2, 12, 23–25, 53, 427
Plantan, Ramadhan Machado, 184
poetry, 179–215
    acrostic, 23, 198–99, 398, 400–401
popular theater, 251, 254–55
Privy Council, 125, 126, 128, 139
Public Opinion (newspaper), 51, 53, 56, 59, 63
public sphere, 9–11, 26, 28, 131, 172–74, 288, 291, 368–71, 390–92, 400, 403, 430
Pwani na Bara (newspaper), 198, 242

race, 5, 20–21, 25, 62–65, 87–90
radio, 19, 226, 255
Ramogi (newspaper), 13
readers, 10, 13–15, 32, 114–16, 127–28, 225, 227, 269–72, 296–97, 374–76, 380, 411, 413, 428–29
    and gender, 225, 227, 296–97
Readex World Newspaper Archive, 398
Rees-Williams, David, 64
Renascent Africa (book), 90
Reuters, 53, 54, 63, 156
Robert, Shabaan, 190, 195–96

Saidi, Hamid, 232
Sani (magazine), 13, 238, 242
"Saro", 108, 122, 153–54, 169–74, 309, 313
Sawyerr's Bookselling, Printing and Stationery Trade Circular (newspaper), 398
schoolteachers, 12, 111, 170, 311
Scotto, Shaaban, 239

Sechuana Proverbs with Literal Translations and Their European Equivalents, 24
Sekanyolya (newspaper), 8, 11
Sekyi, Kobina, 428
Seme, Pixley ka Isaka, 18
Sentongo, Z.K., 20
Sentongo, Sefanio, 8
Sesotho (language)
    literature in, 22
Sierra Leone Weekly News (newspaper), 80, 140, 394, 403
Simu ya Kifo (novel), 227, 243
Sklar, Richard, 126
Skota, T.D. Mweli, 379
slavery, 310, 316
    emancipation, 8, 9, 76, 106, 309, 391
sociability, 14, 104–5, 110–17, 230–31, 296–99, 364–65
socialism, 28, 225–26, 228–29
Şofọwọtẹ, Şẹgun, 255, 259, 260, 264, 268
Solankẹ, Ladipo, 313
Sorenson, Reginald, 93
South Africa
    land politics in, 23–25
    newspaper history of, 53, 361–62
South African Native National Congress, 23–24
Soyinka, Wole, 255
Spartas, Reuben, 20
Standard (newspaper), 347
Suriano, Maria, 182
Swahili (language), 11, 13–14, 342, 426
    entertainment magazines in, 28, 224–45
    newspaper poetry in, 23, 179–213
    standardization of, 31–32
Swahili Film (magazine), 233
Switzer, Donna, 361
Switzer, Les, 4, 361

Taifa (newspaper), 226
Tamasha (magazine), 232
Tanganyika *see* Tanzania
Tanganyika African National Union, 185, 290, 294

Tanzania
  economy of, 233
  elections in, 191
  liberalization in, 242–43
  national culture in, 224, 244–45
  newspapers in, 180, 236, 240, 244–45
  opposition politics in, 240
  socialism in, 28, 225–26, 228–29
Tanzania Youth League, 229
The African Yearly Register (book), 379
The Life and Struggles of Negro Toilers (book), 5, 58
The Nationalist (newspaper), 227
The People (newspaper), 51, 52, 56, 57, 63
The Religious System of the Amazulu (book), 375
The Rescue of Charlie Kalu (book), 95
Thomas, Isaac Babalọla, 2, 13, 22, 26, 32, 170
  as novelist, 22, 109, 117, 165–69
  travel writing of, 102–5, 110–17
Thompson, Graeme, 137
Three Native Accounts of the Visit of the Bishop of Natal to Umpande, King of the Zulus (book), 367
Thuku, Harry, 20
Time (magazine), 187
Times of Nigeria (newspaper), 136, 172
tradition, 129–30, 132, 143–44, 296
Transition (magazine), 31
travel writing, 105–17, 163–64, 367–68
Tsala ea Batho (newspaper), 1, 2
Tutuola, Amos, 260

Uganda, 19, 238. See Buganda.
Uganda Argus (newspaper), 9
Uganda Empya (newspaper), 2, 18
Uganda National Congress, 17
Uganda Post (newspaper), 15–16
Uhuru (newspaper), 202, 209, 227
Ukutunywa kukaSobantu (book), 377
Ukuziphatha Kahle (book), 379
Umshumayeli Wendaba (newspaper), 7
Utendi wa Mwana Kupona, 179, 181
UZulukaMalandela (book), 374

Vanguard (newspaper), 54, 57, 58
video-films, 254–55, 272

Wallace-Johnson, Isaac Theophilus Akunna, 15, 19, 30, 32, 57, 58, 76, 90, 117, 391, 407–13
Wakati ni Huu (magazine), 242–43
wa Wanjau, Gakaara, 21–22, 31–32
Warner, Michael, 285, 294–95
Wasaa (magazine), 239
Washington, Booker T., 88, 378–79
West Africa (magazine), 155
West African Book Publishers, 255
West African Pilot (newspaper), 9, 20, 51, 54–55, 58, 59, 63, 90–93, 172, 395
West African Students Union, 83, 93, 313
West African Youth League, 407, 410–13
Williams, G.A., 169
Wireless Telegraphy Ordinance, 55
When Africa Awakes (book), 49
World War I, 89, 108, 169, 184, 306
World War II, 19, 51, 52, 58–59, 75, 77, 86–87, 94, 410, 411

Yoruba
  contrasted with English, 156–74, 426
  cultural nationalism of, 254, 316–17
  experiments in, 156–74, 426
  language standardization of, 257
  novelistic literature of, 22, 109, 117, 165–69, 326
  newspapers in, 102–17, 151, 153, 155–74, 315–28
  photoplays in, 28, 252–72
  Pilgrim's Progress in, 107
  popular theater in, 251, 254–55
  populism in, 27
  proverbs, 266
  style in, 162–63
  traditio in, 129–30
  travel writing in, 26, 102–17, 163–64
  writers of, 169–72
Yoruba Photoplay Series (magazine), 255, 264, 269–72
Yoruba Ronu (magazine), 266–68

Zachernuk, Philip, 80, 84
Zanzibar Leo (newspaper), 211–23
Zuhra (newspaper), 184
Zulu
   amakholwa (converts) in, 362–63
   Colenso, Bishop John W. and, 372
   and English, 375–77
   epistolary networks in, 362–71
   historical writing in, 30, 374–81
   identity, 365–67, 380–81
   kingdom of, 362, 372
   literature of, 363–64, 367–68